J. D. Masterson

JESUS AND HIS TIMES

JESUS

AND HIS TIMES

BY

DANIEL-ROPS

Translated from the French

by

RUBY MILLAR

1954

E. P. DUTTON & CO., INC.

NEW YORK

FIRST EDITION

Library of Congress Catalog Card Number: 53-6095

AMERICAN BOOK–STRATFORD PRESS, INC., NEW YORK

CONTENTS

JESUS AND HIS TIMES

INTRODUCTION

HOW DO WE KNOW ABOUT JESUS?

The Mystery of Jesus

THERE WAS ONCE a man who lived during a precisely defined period in the reigns of Augustus and Tiberius Caesar. His existence is an incontestable fact. He was known as a manual worker, a carpenter using the hammer and the plane, with shavings curling round his ears.[1] He could be seen walking along a road which is still pointed out to us; in the evening he would be stretched out upon a bed of rushes or a string hammock, tired out and sleeping like any other man, just like one of us.

Yet he said the most surprising things that have ever been heard. He said that he was the Messiah, the heaven-sent witness through whom the chosen people were to fulfill their glorious destiny. More astounding still, he said he was the Son of God. And he was believed. He found men to accompany him along the roads of Palestine, as he traveled across the country. He performed miracles with disconcerting ease. There were many who believed that he would bring about the political independence of Israel.

But then, any mystic can collect devoted fanatics. The culmination of this scandal was that the man was suddenly wiped

[1] The sign, in ancient Jewry, of the carpenter's trade. *Tr.*

out, without putting up the slightest resistance. So far from being discouraged by this failure, several of his disciples went out into the world to bear witness to his divinity, even with their blood, and ever since mankind, seeing in this defeat the sign of victory, has prostrated itself before a common gibbet, just as if tomorrow a church should raise the scaffold for the veneration of the crowd.

The mystery of Jesus is neither more nor less than the mystery of the Incarnation. The multitude of minor puzzles on which so many glosses have been written is unimportant. What does it matter if we do not know the exact year of his birth or the particular village he came from, or whether he had any brothers or cousins? Seen in the proper perspective, all this is of very little importance; what matters is that this man like us, whose words and actions have unleashed such immeasurable forces, reveals through his agonized countenance the visage of God.

Jesus is at once of history and beyond it. Considering the number and the agreement of the witnesses concerning him and the abundance of the written testimony through which his Gospel has been transmitted, one is inclined to say that there is no individual of his time about whom we are so well informed. Yet as he himself foretold he has become the center of a thousand years of dispute, which each generation renews in contemporary terms. That this man of poor and uncultivated stock should remake the basis of philosophy and open out to the world of the future an unknown territory of thought; that this simple son of a declining people, born in an obscure district in a small Roman province, this nameless Jew like all those others despised by the Procurators of Caesar, should speak with a voice that was to sound above those of the Emperors themselves, these are the most surprising facts of history.

But his whole life, as it is recounted to us, is a tissue of miracles, shining with the light of supernatural provenance. The surprising facts cannot be detached from the stuff of his existence, except by rending the whole fabric, denying this existence, casting doubt on all those who have testified to him.

The most astonishing fact of all is that this life which culminated in agony did not end: it reappeared in a stupefying new perspective. This dead man came to life, he spoke and moved, he showed himself to those who had known him alive, and in defiance of logic, his disciples were to say that this was for them the supreme and incontestable testimony. "And if Christ be not risen, then is our preaching vain, and your faith is also vain." (I Cor. xv. 14) History must either reject Christianity or accept the Resurrection.

Yet these particular difficulties do not account for the violence and bitterness of the discussions concerning Jesus. It is hardly possible to speak of him without calling up passions in which the interests of knowledge play little or no part. In another sense also he is a "sign which shall be spoken against." He sees into the most secret places of our hearts, he judges us, we must be either with him or against him. To him every man worthy of the name says once more, "Who art Thou?" There has been a total change of morality since, on the hillside above Lake Tiberias, he pronounced the Beatitudes. Henceforward he is the measure of everything that happens. The life of Christ is contained in history and contains it. It is not merely the vindication of some nameless tragic humility, it is the supreme explanation and the final standard by which everything is measured, from which history itself takes meaning and justification.

Contemporary Witnesses

Though the prime motive of the study of the life of Christ is the enigma of our human nature transfigured by the divine, it is also possible to study it as if it were the life of any other historical personage, because the mere historical fact of this existence is the chief prime witness of the Revelation. But the historian immediately encounters at the beginning of his study the question, "How do we know about Jesus?" The difficulties of our documentation have been immensely increased by the multitude of diverse sources; and far too many Christians today, bewildered by what has been called "higher criticism," do not properly realize the solidity of the basis of their faith.

The life of Christ is set definitely in historical time, not in some remote legendary period as are the traditions concerning Orpheus, Osiris or Mithra. The Roman empire of the first century is known to us in remarkable detail. Great men like Livy or Seneca, whose work has come down to us, were writing when Jesus was alive. Virgil, had he not died at the early age of fifty-one, might have been living in his childhood; Plutarch and Tacitus were of the generation that followed him. Furthermore, very many of the personages who appear in the narratives concerning Jesus appear also in other historical documents—for example, those whom St. Luke mentions in the third chapter of his Gospel, Tiberius Caesar, Pontius Pilate, Herod, the priests Annas and Caiaphas, and John the Baptist, whose life and apostolate is recounted by Josephus.[2]

And that is not all: the ideas and the behavior, the whole setting which precisely dates a human existence, are, for those who take the trouble to compare, exactly those depicted for us by contemporary Palestinian sources.

The man therefore is fixed in a social and political milieu which has been exhaustively studied. No mythical existence could be related so precisely to its setting, unless the Evangelists and the Apostles were such specialists in historical fiction that they could compose severally a figure which throughout their works always maintains a perfect unity.

There is one apparent stumbling block. The powerful and great among the contemporaries of Jesus do not mention him. There is nothing surprising about this if we replace in its immediate perspective an event which to us is stupendous by reason of its consequences. It is difficult for us to realize that the life and teaching of Christ did not have a world-shaking effect at the time. In actual fact the affair would have seemed no more important to the average citizen of Rome under Tiberius

[2] Only one person mentioned by St. Luke in this chapter, Lysanias, tetrarch of Abilene, remains obscure, though two recently discovered local inscriptions confirm the fact of his existence.

than the appearance of a prophet in some obscure corner of Africa would seem to us.

The official records of the Roman administration show no trace of his existence. The Romans kept two sorts of archives: an official record of the senatorial meetings, the *Acta senatus*, and a record of the official correspondence addressed to the ruler, the *Commentarii principis*. There is no record of a discussion on Christianity in the Senate. Was there ever a report from Pontius Pilate to Tiberius concerning Christ? Possibly, even probably, there was, but unhappily we have not got it. Saint Justin Martyr in his *Apology* addressed to Antoninus Pius and his son Marcus Aurelius, about the year 150, refers to these "Records of Pilate" without making it clear whether he knew of them or simply guessed at them. The latter seems more probable; Tacitus has told us that the Imperial Archives were secret and that no one was allowed to consult them. Tertullian, fifty years later, read Justin's statement as affirmation and stated positively that the condemnation and the death of Christ were reported by Pilate to Tiberius. Pious falsifiers, of which there were many, actually produced such a document in the fourth century but mistakenly substituted the name of Claudius for Tiberius.

The official silence is not quite absolute. In the autumn of the year 111 there arrived as Imperial Legate in the Provinces of Bithynia and Pontus, situated on the Black Sea, a figure of considerable literary importance, Pliny the Younger. A great part of his writing took the form of correspondence; he kept a careful copy of his reports to his emperor, Trajan, so that at least a part of the Imperial Archives has been made available to posterity. He was a serious-minded and intelligent man, a weighty, rather flowery writer, perhaps occasionally a little precious, and a most meticulous administrator.

Sometime during the year 112, Pliny sent Trajan a detailed report on the subject of the Christians, a number of whom he had had arrested following denunciations of their sect. The inquiry had been pushed to the point of torture, particularly in the case of two "deaconesses," but nothing menacing to the

State had been revealed. It seemed that these Christians met together, sang their hymns to Christ and pledged themselves to avoid lying, stealing and adultery. There seemed nothing wrong in this but the priests of the gods complained that their temples were being deserted and traders complained that there was no sale for the sacrificial animals. What should the Roman magistrate do? This letter, and Trajan's reply, establishes the fact that at this period Christianity was already solidly established in Asia Minor, that the Christians at that time called themselves followers of Christ and accepted him as God.[3]

A little later, a bull from the Emperor Hadrian addressed in the year 125 to Minucius Fundamus, a proconsul in Asia, confirms Pliny's testimony. A predecessor of Minucius had called attention to abuses in connection with denunciations of the Christians, accusations to provoke civil mischief and from motives of self interest. The wise emperor ruled that accusers must appear publicly in person, and that if their accusations were found to be groundless they were to be punished.

But the years 112 and 125 are already comparatively late in the Christian era, eighty or ninety years after the death of Jesus himself. Is there no earlier testimony? The nearest approach to this is to be found in Tacitus, who was undoubtedly the most considerable of the Latin historians, whose sensibility and imagination were allied to a critical judgment rare in those times and who was given to the most scrupulous examination of his material. Tacitus, writing in his *Annals* about the year 116, refers to the Christians in connection with an outbreak of fire in Rome in the year 64. "A persistent rumor associated Nero with the starting of this fire. To combat this he decided to provide culprits and inflicted the most atrocious tortures upon that sect, popularly detested for their practices, who are known as Christians. This name comes to them from one Christ, who

---

[3] It may be asked why Pliny, who had been praetor, that is chief magistrate at Rome, should have needed to make so many inquiries about the Christians in Asia Minor when there were already plenty of them in Rome. The letter seems to suggest that, having better opportunities to study them in Asia, he had come to disassociate himself from the hostile views held in Rome about the Christian sect.

was condemned to be crucified by the procurator Pontius Pilate in the reign of Tiberius. This pernicious sect, formerly proscribed, has established itself not only throughout Judea where it originated, but in the very City itself."

Tacitus then recounts the horrible tortures inflicted on the Christians and he is humane enough to be shocked; but just the same his references reveal the fact that he knew the Christians only by hearsay and shared the common opinion of them. This hostility, however, gives additional weight to the two lines where he mentions Christ. Where did he get his information concerning him? Among his sources, Tacitus drew on the elder Pliny, the naturalist and philosopher who died in the year 79 as the result of his wish to observe the eruption of Vesuvius which buried Pompeii. Pliny the Elder was on the staff of Titus in his war against the Jews in the year 70. From him to Tacitus runs a direct tradition which has come down to us.

Another historian, Suetonius, contemporary with Tacitus and equally skillful in his use of earlier material, mentions these reprisals against the Christians in his *Lives of the Caesars.* In one passage he confirms the Neronian persecutions; in another, he tells us that Claudius "expelled the Jews from Rome because under the influence of Christ they had become a permanent source of disorder." This persecution is mentioned by St. Paul in the *Acts of the Apostles,* where he tells of meeting in Corinth a Jewish family who had been expelled from Rome. It is most unfortunate that Suetonius has said nothing about Christ in his life of Tiberius, but what he does say is sufficient to prove that about the year 50, that is to say less than twenty years after the death of Christ, there were in Rome Christians making converts among the local Jewry.

If we were to depend on the Roman testimony alone, it perhaps does not strictly establish that Christ existed or that he was condemned and crucified under Pilate, but this is made to appear highly probable and as accepted by a number of people a very short time after his death.

Further and not irrelevant testimony may be found among the adversaries of Christianity. The term Christian was originally a sobriquet, but from whom could it have been derived if it were not accepted that Christ had existed? Celsus—one of the anti-Christian polemicists of the second century whose attacks were so violent that a great Christian apologist like Origen entered the lists to refute him—does not for one moment throw doubt upon the story of Jesus as we know it. It would have been so easy to say: your Christ never existed. Yet this he never said.

The Silence of Flavius Josephus

When we turn to consider the compatriots of Jesus, those among whom his human life was spent, we do not get much further and we come up at once against a new problem. The Jews at the time of Christ included numerous literary men. In Alexandria there was Philo, the neo-platonic philosopher, who has left us some fifty treatises. He was born twenty years before Christ and died about twenty years after; he was in fact an exact contemporary. Yet nowhere does Philo mention Christ's name. Probably this rarefied intellectual, whose philosophical orientation was almost entirely Greek and Latin, felt very little curiosity about the life and teaching of yet another of those popular agitators who abounded during the last years of Israel.

But Justus of Tiberias, a Galilean like Jesus, born at the very time of Christ's death, how is it that his chronicle, which covers the period from Moses down to Herod Agrippa, does not mention him whose teaching had just stirred his people? The explanation of this silence is probably that which Photius, the ninth century Byzantine historian, who had read Justus's chronicle (which is now lost) has given us: "Jewish by race and steeped in Jewish prejudices, Justus would not make any reference to the coming of Christ, to the events of his life or to his miracles."

There are deliberate and revelatory silences. Perhaps that of Flavius Josephus was among them.

Josephus is a considerable historian and his *Hebrew An-*

tiquities is, with certain reservations, infinitely valuable in supplementing the history of the Old Testament. His *Jewish Wars,* which appeared about the year 77, that is to say very shortly after the catastrophe which annihilated the chosen people as an entity, is a document of inestimable importance. The personality of the man is not attractive. He was a member of that aristocratic priestly caste who found excellent opportunities under the Roman yoke; he was vain, self-satisfied and obsequious. He has left us some edifying details about himself: how at thirteen he was so learned in theology that the rabbis of Jerusalem used to consult him, how at sixteen he was seized with ascetic fervor and mortified himself in the desert.

In actual fact, he quickly migrated to Rome where he engaged in some useful intrigues. When the final war against the Jews broke out in the year 66 he took a command but after a fashion which foreshadowed the attitude of Bazaine at Metz in 1870. There is one particularly odd story of a certain besieged position where the defenders decided to kill themselves rather than fall into the hands of the legionaries. By a singular chance it was Josephus who survived, and capitulated, which seems a little suspect. Moreover this Jewish general finished up as a personal friend of his conqueror, Vespasian, whose accession as emperor he appears to have foretold. He added the name of his master, Flavius, to his own, like any freed slave, and sounding the abject depths of toadyism, he did not hesitate to announce that the true Messiah awaited by Israel was unquestionably Vespasian.

These traits of character must not be overlooked when considering this famous "silence of Josephus" on which there have been so many commentaries. His *Antiquities* appeared in the year 93. That he must have known of Christianity seems evident. Twenty odd years before, about the year 57, the Church had already taken an important place in Jerusalem. When St. Paul arrived in the Holy City at this date his appearance caused an uproar and he was arrested (Acts xxi. through xxvi.), yet the future historian does not seem to have noted this episode. Josephus was in Rome in the year 64, at the start of Nero's persecutions. In the affluent circles to which his friend the Jewish actor, Alityrus, introduced him, perhaps he heard nothing at all about this Christ who was agitating Roman Jewry.

Two personages contemporary with Jesus are mentioned by Josephus: John the Baptist, whose preaching and martyrdom he describes in exact detail, and James, the first bishop of Jerusalem, whose stoning to death he narrates and whom he designates with a note of disdain, "the brother of Jesus, called Christ." But to stick to the indisputable text, there is in the work of Josephus no other allusion to Christ.

The problem is complicated by the fact that in Book 18 of one version of the *Antiquities* occurs this singular passage: "At this time appeared Jesus, a wise man, *if he can be called a man.* For he performed marvelous things, and became the master of those who joyfully received the truth and many of the Jews and also the Greeks followed him. *This was the Christ.* Being denounced by the priests of our nation to Pilate, he was condemned to die on the cross, but his followers did not renounce him *for on the third day he appeared to them alive again as had been foretold by the divine prophets as well as other wonders in regard to him.* There still exists today the sect which has received from him the name of Christians."

It is sufficient to say that if Josephus really wrote this passage, and in particular the parts italicized here, he proclaims by this his adherence to Christianity. For three centuries these lines have provoked raging discussions. Some say that they are interpolated, since they break the thread of the discourse; others retort that the style is exactly that of Josephus. Eusebius, who knew and accepted the text at the beginning of the fourth century, is cited in evidence for it. Others retort that the early Fathers of the Church, Origen among others, did not know of it and even stated that Josephus did not believe that Jesus was the Messiah. Catholic scholars like Mgr. Batiffol and Père Lagrange agree with Guignebert that the passage is interpolated, while "higher critics" and Protestants like Burkett and Harnack uphold its authenticity. It may be, and Mgr. Ricciorti inclines to this view, which is also upheld by Th. Reinach, that the passage is genuine but was touched up or "strengthened" in the second century by some Christian copyist whose zeal outran his scruples.

If these lines are rejected, the silence of Flavius Josephus is impressive. It was unquestionably deliberate. Without going so far as Pascal, who said that Josephus sought to hide the shame of his people (*Pensées,* 629), or taking the paradoxical view that the silence confirms the existence of Jesus because one does not hate what did not exist, we can, because we know a good deal about the man, guess why he was silent. As a Jew, writing for a Roman public books which were meant to explain and defend his people, he would say as little as he could help about the Messianic idea since it would naturally be suspect to the Roman conquerors. He who was accustomed to paint the essential qualities of Judaism in colors appealing to the pagans would hardly be likely to report anecdotes about a fanatic who had duped a number of poor people, upset the established order and had finally finished up as he deserved. Josephus knew far too well what was due to his career and his reputation.

The Living and Perdurable Word

Putting the pagans and the Jews aside, let us turn to those who, from the beginning, were anxious to spread the news about Christ, those who came to be called Christians. Naturally it is through them that we know most about him and the weight of their evidence is so substantial that centuries of criticism have not been able to demolish it. Nevertheless, at the outset of any examination of their records, we come up against a difficulty which the modern mind cannot regard as negligible. Accustomed all our lives to learn everything by the medium of print, we all tend to think of the testimony concerning Christ as contained in a series of books. It is absolutely certain, however, that the earliest Christian teaching was not written down at all, it was given only by word of mouth.

It must not be forgotten that Jesus lived among humble people, working artisans and the fishermen of Lake Tiberias. Among his twelve disciples probably only one or two could write: Levi, afterward called Matthew, the publican and tax collector; Judas, who looked after their communal purse. Even had they all been able to write it is unlikely that they would have preferred the written to the spoken word. The whole Semitic tradition, as far back as their history goes, was to the contrary. It is barely thirty years since the "advanced" critic, Salomon Reinach, whose errors and tendentious assertions are innumerable, declared summarily that he declined "to consider writings founded upon the memory of a collection of illiterates as historical evidence for Jesus."

Renan, however, understood the background better and since his time a number of works, and particularly that of Fr. Jousse, have shown that although the disciples of Jesus might be unlettered, their testimony is none the less worthy of acceptance.

The old bishop of Phrygia, Papius, who, about the year 130, invoked the authority of "the living and perdurable word," was entirely right. The memory of the ancient Jews, like that of the Arabs, was not as shrunken and impoverished as is ours today. The disciples of a teacher were accustomed to listen and learn his words by heart, thanks to a special training which was imposed upon children from the beginning of their studies. The prophecies of Jeremiah were written down after twenty-two years of oral recitation. The *Mishna*, the most essential part of the *Talmud*, is that part which was written down later from verbal recapitulation. The *Koran* was put together entirely by this method. "A good disciple," said the Jewish rabbis, "is a cistern which retains every drop of water." So the Gospel before it was written down was stored in memories without a break which conserved it better than we can possibly imagine.

This gift of learning and retaining is allied to an art of speech, founded on rhythm and mnemotechnics, in which the whole body takes part, in mimicry, swaying and gestures almost like a dance. When St. Luke tells us of the children (vii. 31, 32) sitting in the market place, calling one to another,

"We have piped unto you and ye have not danced; we have mourned to you and ye have not wept," we get a glimpse of the method of aiding memory by means of answering refrains. A whole professional technique of such devices aided the mind to remember with precision, such as the use of regular cadences in strophe and antistrophe, the use of certain incantatory words to mark the discourse and further its development, the recourse to parallels and antitheses which themselves are almost automatic aids to memory. "Ask and ye shall be given, seek and ye shall find, knock and it shall be opened unto you"; "Judge not that ye be not judged"; these are examples of such parallels and the whole Sermon on the Mount as recorded by St. Luke (vi. 20, 29) with its succession of beatitudes and maledictions is a perfect example of this method of antithesis.

This methodical training of speech and memory enabled a man of the people, even if illiterate, to improvise a discourse and it goes a long way toward explaining the references to earlier writings and prophecies in the Gospel texts. Jesus cited the prophetic writings frequently and when the Virgin Mary uttered her sublime hymn of joy, the *Magnificat,* Biblical allusions surged up naturally from that well-spring of memory which is for us all a part of the inner being.

The teaching of Christ was thus conserved after the usual manner of the Jews. However they may have been assembled, the Gospels arrest us by the power of their beauty and the exactness of their style. They have, as Renan has well said, "a kind of brilliance at once gentle and terrible, a divine majesty which takes them out of their context and makes them easily recognizable." One can never doubt for a moment, as one reads, that these are the words that came out of Christ's mouth. In this oral tradition, which was being constructed while Jesus was alive, these striking phrases would be stored up more carefully than anything. When, after their contacts with the Greeks and the Romans, the disciples evinced the desire to set down their teaching in writing, these sayings and teachings of Jesus naturally composed the first books. They wished to give a final form to the words which he had uttered.

Probably not all the sayings of Christ have found their way into our traditional scriptures. There are in fact similar sayings which do not appear in the Gospels but which nevertheless have the force of the words of Christ. When St. Paul, in Acts xx, 35, quotes Jesus as saying, "It is better to give than to receive," one does not doubt its authenticity. Other similar sayings can be found among the works of the early Fathers of the Church and the apologists of the first centuries. "Who is near me is by the hearth and far from me is far from the Kingdom." "If you have seen your brother you have seen God." The first is from Origen, the second quoted by Clement of Alexandria and Tertullian; they are authentic jewels. Others can be found in very old sacred manuscripts such as that which Theodore of Beza found in the Convent of St. Ireneus at Lyons and sent to the University of Cambridge with this prudent note, "Better hide this and not publish it." This contains a startling remark about the Sabbath. Some are in the papyri which have come out of the sands of Egypt; of these the most famous are those of Oxyrhynque (discovered at the end of the last century) containing such pearls as, "Where there are two, they are not without God,"—recalling St. Matthew xviii, 20—and, "Raise the stone and there thou wilt find me, cleave the wood and there am I." They are only fragments, but everything concerning Jesus is precious and the reading of these *Logia*, or sayings not included in the scriptural canon, gives an excellent idea of the material of which the earliest Christian testimonies was composed.

To these sayings and teachings have been added narratives of acts of Jesus to show us what manner of man he was in his life. St. Augustine has said that, Christ being the Word of God, his actions are for us words and teaching. Certainly they would be a complete canvas of memories which these propagandists of the faith—who "from the beginning were eyewitnesses and ministers of the word," as St. Luke says in his Gospel—would bear with them. We have some idea of these records, these originals of our Gospels, from the dialogue between Peter and the centurion Cornelius recorded in Acts x.37, 41, fifteen plain and simple lines with no conscious style but setting out the essentials of Christian doctrine and indicating already the quadripartite division of Christ's life which we find in the Gospels: the mission of John the Baptist and the birth of Christ; Christ's ministry in Galilee; his coming to Jerusalem; his passion and resurrection. The foundations of the Gospel of St. Mark are there.

Certain of these records took a form more detailed than others without losing their original preaching content and, by reason of the personalities of their authors or sponsors, came to acquire an indisputable authority. Thus was formed the prime document for all study of Jesus, the Gospel.

The Canon and the Apocrypha

Many of the characteristics of the Biblical narratives upon which our knowledge of Jesus depends are explained by a consideration of the circumstances in which they were put together. When we are trying to penetrate the meaning of the Gospel we have to forget that large and heavy volume, with its heraldic binding and brass corners, from which a few fragments, hardly heard and less understood, are read to the multitudes who gather in our vast churches, adorned with marble and hung with velvet.

We have to transport ourselves to those small primitive communities where the early Christians, meeting secretly in humble rooms or in caves, received the word as if it were bread and wine for their souls, seeking always to recover, living and close to them, the immortal presence of the Friend. What the early Christians sought to bring to life was the Jesus who had talked, walked, loved and suffered on the slopes of the Palestinian hills; and this waiting for his return, at their fraternal meetings, swelled their breasts with indescribable longing. How avidly they would listen to those who had seen him with their bodily eyes. When this generation died out, there would be those who remembered them and thus was spun that direct thread of testimony. In each formulation of a traditional doctrine all would participate as collective guardians of the treasure.

Although we cannot say exactly how the oral teaching came to be set down in writing, since the actual "mementos" of the original disciples are unknown, it is possible for us to understand what are the guarantees for the fixation of the texts. No one nowadays holds the belief, fashionable in the nineteenth century, that the New Testament is a kind of "collective creation," a spontaneous communal effort by the early Christians, any more than we now believe in the multiple authorship of the *Odyssey*. In the realm of literary accomplishment communal efforts are short, unformed and puerile; only the individual genius creates. The fundamental role of these communities was to conserve the living tradition with passionate urgency and to set a seal on the testimony of Mark, Matthew, Luke and John. That seal is, in the last resort, the guarantee of the Church.

It is quite wrong to imagine that the origins of Christianity are submerged in legend. The events set down in the Gospel record were never embroidered by fables; it was later, when the events had become common knowledge, that people sought to interpret them one way or another. For instance, when about the year 170 Christianity was introduced into the kingdom of Edessa, nobody brought forward any special reason for propagating it there any more than in the neighboring territory or the whole Empire. But a century later, a tradition grew up ascribing this conversion to Jesus himself. It was said that a King of Edessa, named Abgar, being smitten with an incurable disease, had written to Jesus and had received an answer. They even produced the letter, and the reply. And Jesus had sent Thaddeus, one of his seventy original followers, to bring the glad tidings to Edessa.

In actual fact, if we study the critical standards of the Early Church, we discover that they took great pains to chase and expel legend. Tertullian, the great apologist of the third century, states that thirty years earlier a legend was current in an Asiatic province that St. Paul had converted a pagan girl named Thekla who had subsequently become a missionary of the Gospel. This legend appeared suspect and its author was found to be a simple and imaginative priest who had acted with the best intentions, but who was none the less reprimanded and degraded.

This strictness can be detected in what ultimately became Christian canon. Before anything could be accepted as the teaching of Christ it had to be known who was proffering it. A text was accepted only if it was in general use, if its doctrine was unimpeachably orthodox, and—this was the essential criterion—if it could adduce the authority of an Apostle. The Apostles were the true witnesses of Christ, hence the revealing formula, "The Gospel of Jesus Christ *according to . . .*"

It is by them and through them that the Messiah is explained. And what they say makes no sense except by reason of him. Two of the Gospels are directly guaranteed by two of the twelve, St. Matthew and St. John. The other two have the authority of St. Peter and St. Paul. As far back as we can go in our knowledge of these texts, this authority is always invoked; one could say truthfully that few ancient historical documents have had the benefit of such careful scrutiny.

We can even, in some cases, follow the critical process of the early Christians. It is known that the famous episode of the woman taken in adultery which appears in Saint John (viii) was not at first included in the Gospel text. There was considerable hesitation in accepting it; whether, as has been said, because husbands feared that their wives might regard it as encouraging, or whether it was considered out of keeping with the principles of him who had said that he came not to destroy the law but to fulfill it, we do not know. But the very differences between the Gospels constitute the most formidable evidence for the historical character of the New Testament. It would have been so easy, at the time when the texts were set down, to have produced a single narrative or at least to have omitted those portions which seem to disagree. Yet it was never done. As Renan so truly has said, "Nothing shows the complete honesty of the Church better than this."

We can obtain a very good idea of the way in which those

texts which were later to form the New Testament were collected. The oral tradition was gradually put into writing; and the Christian community, the Church, whose role in those matters was already considerable, picked out certain of these testimonies which had a guarantee of authenticity and from that time guarded them closely against later accretions. In this way a solid block of written testimony was acquired, which, although many times assaulted by waves of fable and legend, remained intact, the rock of truth.

The storms which besieged it were, heaven knows, both powerful and numerous. The Gospels and the Apostolic texts were surrounded by a mounting tide of legends, gossip, fake documents and misquoted authorities. These Apocryphal texts [4] seem to some extent to have been recognized by St. John when he says at the end of his Gospel, "And there are also many other things which Jesus did, the which, if they should be written every one, I suppose that even the world itself could not contain the books that should be written." Those who put forward these Apocrypha could thus claim to bring forward valuable testimony which the Gospels did not mention. But on reading them we are conscious of the immense gulf which separates them from the recognized Gospels. They all contain manifest exaggerations and errors of taste which betray the inventions of inferior minds. St. Jerome called them "morbid dreams" and Renan characterized most of them as "flat and feeble amplifications." The taste of those who labor to find among them secrets of wisdom not included in the New Testament can only be regarded as morbid itself.

Nevertheless it is proper to discriminate among this mass. Some of these Apocryphal texts appear to have been originally admitted by some parties in the Church but to have been later rejected either because they were incomplete or because they seemed to deviate in a direction regarded as suspect. One of these is that *Gospel According to the Hebrews*, quoted by Clement, Origen, Eusebius and Epiphanus, and known in the

---

[4] These Apocrypha have often been published.

fourth century to St. Jerome, who declared that it closely resembled the Gospel of St. Matthew. It was certainly in use among those Jewish Christian communities which knew no Greek. Only three fragments of it have come down to us. It was originally written in Aramaic, the proof of this being that it calls the Holy Spirit "mother," since the word for spirit, *rouâh,* is feminine in Aramaic. It contains some admirable things, such as a saying of Jesus, "Only be joyful when you look on your brother with love," but also some bizarre fantasies such as the transportation of Christ to the top of a mountain by the Holy Ghost holding him by a single hair!

Others of these Apocrypha reflect much less pure intentions. Plenty of them, known to us by fragments from other sources, were obviously elaborated during the earlier centuries by various heretical groups, to bring forward words and actions of Christ's which could be interpreted in the sense which these sects desired. *The Gospel of St. Peter,* which is placed under the authority of the chief of the Apostles, is certainly of great antiquity. Serapion, Bishop of Antioch about the year 200, discouraged his flock from reading it. Historically the text seems full of errors; for instance, it has Jesus condemned by Herod and, further, it is suspect of *docetism,* that is the heresy that Christ was not man incarnate but took on the appearance of man. Another text, the *Gospel of the Ebionites* was in use among that curious sect of Judaizing Christians, vegetarian and ascetic, who practiced a number of curious rites. And, finally, we may close this enumeration by mentioning the mass of gnostic speculation which came out of Alexandrian Jewry, full of strange metaphysics, introducing legions of supernatural powers, "eons," allegories, and what not, proving that Christ was simply another name for the Platonic *Logos,* the form of a superior "eon." Out of these speculations came Gospels credited to Thomas, to Philip, and even one to Eve, but from the few fragments which survive there is nothing to detain us.

A third and infinitely more curious group of Apocryphal texts has an entirely different motive. Ever since Jesus lived, the piety of the faithful has nourished a desire to know the smallest details of his life on earth. It is a natural and touching tendency and even in recent times the reception given to the revelations of St. Bridget, Maria d'Agréda and the astonishing recital of Catherine Emmerich, proves that this desire has not ceased to grow in Christian hearts. This tender curiosity gave rise to such fantastic compilations as the Gospel of the Holy Childhood, the Gospel of Pilate or the Gospel of Nicodemus and the Protogospel of St. James. The worthy compilers of these fables did not worry about verisimilitude nor did they always display the best of taste, but their lively and incontestable faith made them very popular during the Middle Ages, which were naïve and ardent themselves.

By virtue of medieval art they have passed into history. The *Golden Legend* of Jacques de Voragine and the *Miroir historique* of Vincent de Beauvais recounted many such and since the craftsmen of the time fed upon these works, we can find many traces of them in our churches. When, among the mosaics of the great arch of St. Maria Maggiore at Rome or in a stained glass window at Mans we see the curious scene where the Infant Jesus by his very presence causes the idols of an Egyptian temple to fall prostrate, we owe it to an episode in the Gospel of the Holy Childhood, and to this is also due the motif of the Star of Bethlehem supported by an angel in the choir screen of Notre Dame de Paris. We are so accustomed to seeing the ox and the ass warming the Infant Christ in the manger that we quite overlook the fact that this tradition has no canonical support and that only the Apocrypha give it. Even more striking is the fact that the Presentation of Our Lady in the Temple, a feast of the Catholic Church, is not mentioned in the Scriptures and when we admire that magnificent rendering of the scene by Titian in Venice, it is to the Protogospel of St. James that we owe it. Not everything in these Apocrypha is necessarily false but a great deal is manifestly childish.

It can easily be understood how, in the face of so many attacks, the Early Church sought to build an impregnable rampart around its authentic texts. A reading of the early Fathers of the Church shows clearly how carefully the Church sought to discriminate among all these traditions those which were incontestable and those which were not. A curious manuscript called the "Canon of Muratori" from the name of the collector who discovered it in Milan in 1740 gives a copy of the list of texts which the Church of Rome held as sacred about the years 180 to 190. With a great deal of detail, it explains that it has been found necessary to reject texts like the "Shepherd of Hermes" ("too late and not apostolic") and the pseudo epistles to the Laodiceans and the Alexandrians "attributed to St. Paul to support the Marcion heresy." It can be seen from this document that the list of the accepted and the discredited was, at that time, roughly what it is today: the two fundamental groups, first the four Gospels and the Acts and secondly, the thirteen Pauline epistles are included. It can be said without the slightest doubt that one hundred and fifty years after the death of Jesus, the essential writings by which he is known to us had already been fixed by a critical tradition.

It is not easy to say how this critical tradition had been established. With regard to the actual Gospels, it is probable that each began by recognition as authoritative in a particular community—St. Matthew in Syria, St. Luke in Greece, St. Mark in Rome. At the same time each church was amassing a collection of Apostolic epistles, from St. Paul in particular, which, although originally addressed to one community, contained teachings valuable to all. There was not for some long time an official collection accepted by the entire Church and doubtless the list of texts differed slightly from one community to another. But as opinion came unanimously to approve certain texts as possessing an indisputable authority, an official list began to establish itself. It would be silly to imagine that there was any kind of solemn ballot or scrutiny in conference; rather a spontaneous acceptance by generations of Christians going back directly to those who had known Jesus.

By the fourth century the list of texts is defined for us. Catalogues have been found in Africa (dating from 359), in Phrygia (dating from 363), in Egypt (published by St. Athanasius in 367) and one from the Roman Council of Pope Damasus. When in 397 the Council at Carthage, dominated by the figure of St. Augustine, published the most famous of these catalogues, it was merely confirming the ancient tradition and the list which it gives is exactly the same as that which the Council of Trent (1546-1563) affirmed in the face of the Protestants, who have never challenged it.[5]

The New Testament

The words "Canon" and "Testament" as we use them today manifest fidelity to an ancient tradition. They are used for the older body of the sacred writings as well as for the more recent, for those who preceded Jesus as for those which bear witness to him, a striking affirmation of that logical succession so forcibly insisted upon by Christ himself. It is not by accident that the Old and New Testaments appear in one volume, it is an organic relationship, the one leading certainly to the other which fulfills it.

The word "Canon" is derived from a Greek word signifying, as far back as the fourth century, order, standard or model. The word "Testament" is a Latin translation, due possibly to Tertullian, of the Greek word *diathèkè,* used in the Septuagint to render the Hebrew term *berith* signifying alliance or union. To fix the Canon of the New Testament is to establish the measure of the alliance with man which Christ has signed by his blood. The early Fathers of the Church, about the year 120, were already citing the words of Christ as reported by the Gospels with the same respect and the same formulae as had been traditionally used for the sacred books of Israel. The martyr Ignatius, who suffered under Trajan (98-117), explicitly ranks the Gospel with the ancient Jewish writings. The authority of the text for whatever is regarded as sacred goes back certainly to within a hundred years of the death of Christ.

[5] The only difference is that the *Epistle to the Hebrews* which the Council of Trent attributes to St. Paul was given as anonymous by the Council of Carthage and is so listed today in the Protestant Bible.

The Council of Trent fixed the number of the Sacred Books of the New Testament at twenty-seven: the Four Gospels, the Acts of the Apostles, Fourteen Epistles of St. Paul, one of St. James, two of St. Peter, three of St. John, one of St. Jude and the Apocalypse of St. John. Of these, seven are called by some authorities "deuterocanonical" because they were admitted later to the Canon. The Church did not hesitate over their merit, their orthodoxy or their truth but solely over their attribution to the authors whose names they now bear. (These books are the Epistles to the Hebrews, James, the Second Epistle of Peter, the Second and Third of John, Jude and the Apocalypse.) These twenty-seven books, making about four hundred pages of a modern printed book, form the essential basis of our knowledge of Jesus; these twenty-seven books have been guaranteed by the Church, pledging her full responsibility and the immense weight of accumulated Christian tradition.

But anyone who has ventured, however superficially, on the problems of textual criticism must ask by what means we have gained our knowledge of these writings. The textual problem of any modern book, say a novel by Balzac or Stendhal, is very easily established. We have only to refer to the first edition, made in the author's lifetime or else to the one which the writer himself regarded as most authentic. In many cases we can even refer to the manuscript. Nothing of this kind is available for ancient texts. We cannot read the Gospels in copies made when their authors were alive any more than we can read Plato or Thucydides.

It is certain that the New Testament books were originally written, either by their authors or by scribes working at their dictation, on scrolls of papyrus. The epistle of St. Paul to the Romans alone would have required a scroll about four yards long. None of these is known to us, but as these papyri were sent from one community to another, one could hardly expect this fragile material to have come down to us. But we do possess a number of fragments of such papyri, mostly found in Egyptian tombs; over fifty have actually come to light and new ones are not infrequently discovered. A comparison of these venerable fragments, some dating from the second century, with the later manuscripts enables us to establish a common relationship which is highly important as evidence of the solidity of the Christian texts as we have them.

About the third century it probably became customary to transfer these writings on to parchment to preserve them from destruction. Bound into volumes these parchments took on an appearance something like our present books. Thanks to the use of "the precious sheepskin of Pergamos" a great deal has been preserved to us. These codices, in particular the Codex Vaticanus and the Codex Sinaiticus, written in a magnificent uncial script of the fourth century, are the most important bases of our knowledge of the New Testament.

The Codex Vaticanus would seem to be one of the copies which the Emperor Constantine received about the year 340 from Athanasius. The Sinaiticus would be one of the fifty copies which Eusebius, Bishop of Caesarea, had made about 331 to the order of the Emperor Constantine who gave them to the principal churches. The copy which has come down to us takes its name from the place where it was discovered, on Mt. Sinai. Some idea of the importance of these codices may be gathered from the dimensions of the Sinaiticus, which consists of 346 and a half leaves of a very fine parchment, possibly the skin of a gazelle.

Each leaf measures fifteen inches by thirteen and a half inches, so that the manuscript must have used up a whole flock. There are "four narrow columns to each page . . . and the eight columns thus presented to the reader when the volume is opened have much of the appearance of the succession of columns in a papyrus roll; it is not at all impossible that it was actually copied from such rolls. . . . The date of the manuscript is the fourth century, probably about the middle of it." [6] The Codex Sinaiticus was discovered in the monastery of St. Catherine on Mt. Sinai in the year 1844 and presented to the Czar

---

[6] *Our Bible and the Ancient Manuscripts.* F. M. Kenyon. 1939. *Tr.*

of Russia. It was sold by the Soviet government in 1933 to the Trustees of the British Museum for 100,000 pounds, of which half was paid by the British government.

It should be noted that these codices date from the fourth century. In the main, the books of the New Testament may be dated during the years 50 and 100, but three centuries elapsed between the setting down of these texts and the first complete manuscripts in our possession. This seems an enormous stretch of time but it may be pointed out that it is nothing by comparison with the interval between the unknown originals of the classics of antiquity and the oldest copies known to us today. This is as much as fourteen hundred years in the case of the tragedies of Sophocles and for the works of Aeschylus, Aristophanes and Thucydides; sixteen hundred years for Euripides and Catullus, thirteen hundred for Plato, twelve hundred for Demosthenes. Terence and Virgil may be counted fortunate in that the gap in their cases is only seven and four centuries respectively. In the light of these comparisons the interval between the originals of the books of the New Testament and the first known copies is not very remarkable.

It is even less so when we consider the number of manuscripts involved. If we possess only one copy of a book by an author there is nothing to tell us whether the book is imperfect or incorrect. Only by comparison with others can light be cast. All the ancient writers are known to us through a small number of imperfect manuscripts; of Tacitus, for instance, we have nothing but fragments, sometimes only a single fragment. In the case of the New Testament, however, we have an almost unimaginable number of manuscripts. Of the Gospels alone there exist about 2,500 manuscripts in Greek, about forty of which date back more than a thousand years. In addition, there are about 1,500 "lectionaries" which contain the greater part of the Gospels arranged in daily lessons for the year. From the earliest times, the text has been translated into countless dialects, Syriac, Greek, Coptic, Gothic, Armenian, Georgian, Ethiopian and, of course, into Latin. Sometimes these translations are themselves older than the earliest Greek texts in our possession (for instance, there is a Theban version in Coptic dating from the third century). The only ancient Latin version we have has come down to us in some fifty manuscripts. Of the Vulgate of St. Jerome, dating from the fourth century, we have nearly 8,000 copies.

A comparison of these copies is extremely instructive. It goes without saying that being made by so many different hands a number of faults have crept in, sometimes even intentional ones. Frequently a copyist has modified the spelling, misplaced a word or added an explanation of his own or forgotten a phrase. If these "variants" are added to the number of the manuscripts we have a veritable swarm of them; the figure has been put as high as 250,000. Yet, and this is the essential fact, they do not amount to an eighth part of the total, and the "substantial variants" [7] are barely a thousandth part.

The task of the critic in establishing a definitive text was to choose among the variants those which were the oldest and the most consistent. It can be confidently stated that no other work has come down to us from antiquity in such exemplary condition.

Thus we have these twenty-seven pieces of writing from which to discover Jesus. Their historical value is of the highest order. But it must not be forgotten that the guiding instinct of those who recopied them was not scientific curiosity but an ardent faith, the desire to find in them a response to the eternal questions. Therefore, from the most ancient times, these copies were presented with the most extraordinary splendor. The very mention of them conjures up those legions of unknown copyists who for so many centuries devoted their lives to the delicate art by which they have been preserved for us. The library of the Emperor Constantine already included Gospels embellished with painted miniatures.

---

[7] A "substantial variant" is one which modifies the sense of a phrase, though often the modification is insignificant. For instance we read in Luke, vi, 10, "And looking round about upon them all, he said unto the man 'Stretch forth thy hand.'" A variant adds after "looking round"—the two words "with anger," taken from a parallel text in St. Mark. It can be seen that even these "substantial variants" do not amount to much.

From the sixth century the art developed enormously and there was hardly a library of consequence which did not possess illuminated manuscripts glittering with gold and silver, with the elaborate twisting and curving lettering to which the monks devoted years of work. In the Bibliotheque Nationale we can see the Gospel of Charlemagne, written in letters of gold on a background of purple, adorned with the fine Carolingian initials and heavy interlacing with intricate penstrokes and trellis ornament. Or that of St. Medard de Soissons, or that of *Evangeliaire de la Saint Chapelle* which Charles V loved so much that he had to buy it for his private collection. All these are noble witnesses to the art and the devotion of their makers. Right down to the eve of the invention of printing, the copyists maintained the traditions of their craft. It seemed to our forefathers that nothing but the finest work of men's hands was fit to render the beauties of the sacred text.

The Witness of St. Paul

Among the twenty-seven books of the New Testament, though all expound the doctrine of Jesus, there are some which add nothing to our historical knowledge of him. St. Peter, St. John and St. James barely allude to the daily life of their master, possibly because they were so close to it, both they themselves and their hearers. They probably considered it sufficiently well known in its essentials. Outside the Four Gospels—the bases of every study of Jesus—only in the Acts of the Apostles and the Epistles of St. Paul do we find any historical information about him and this is all the more important since these texts are of extreme antiquity.

The Acts of the Apostles is the work of St. Luke the Evangelist, who must have completed them about the year 63 since he refers to the first captivity of St. Paul which is definitely dated to that year. The object of this book is not to tell the story of the life of Christ, though we find numerous allusions to things we already know from elsewhere, such as that Christ's mother was called Mary, that he was called "Him of

Nazareth," that he was baptized by John the Baptist, that he was surrounded by twelve disciples, that he performed a number of miracles, was betrayed by Judas, that the Jews preferred the release of a robber, that he suffered under Pontius Pilate, was crucified and rose again, when, after having appeared to several persons, he ascended into heaven. We have in fact the whole Gospel in skeleton form.[8]

A similar outline of the life of Christ could be constructed from the Epistles of St. Paul and particularly from those to the Galatians, Corinthians, Hebrews, and Romans. St. Paul was a witness very near to Jesus in point of time. He would have been about twenty years of age at the Crucifixion and he was of pure Jewish stock, though born at Tarsus, that Graeco-Roman town in Cilicia where the trade routes and cultural influences of so many countries met. He was orthodox, he studied under the Pharisees and when he heard that Jesus had been condemned he considered the execution justified. Later on he even assisted, with satisfaction, at the stoning of the first martyr, Stephen. But we know how he came to see the light, through the astounding revelation on the road to Damascus, and he entered about the year 35 into the Christian community, to which he brought his superb intelligence and the ardor of his indomitable spirit. He lived for seven years in retirement, first at Damascus, then at Tarsus. In the year 42 the apostle Barnabas took him on his mission to Antioch. From that time he became a constant missionary, bearing the word throughout long voyages until the year 66 or 67 when he died in Rome by the hands of the executioners.

It was in the course of his journeys and in order to strengthen the effect of his words that St. Paul sent to the various churches letters embodying his teaching. The most stringent of modern critics do not dispute more than two of the Epistles

[8] The great difference of style between the Gospels and the Acts has frequently been noted. The living and luminous words of the Master seem to lose something of force and color in the mouths of his disciples. The eloquence of Stephen, Peter and Philip is undoubted but their words do not have the unique and striking quality which distinguishes the directly recorded teaching of Christ.

attributed to him (II Thessalonians and Ephesians); the others are undoubtedly the work of the Apostle of the Gentiles. These "Epistles" are nearly all quite literally "letters," that is to say, pastoral messages such as the bishops send out to this day. Each one is called into being by a particular circumstance, meets a definite need or links up with a definite incident. A good many show signs of hasty composition, all are evidently designed for practical rather than literary use. Their object was not to give an account of the life of Jesus; St. Paul's audience knew all the essentials of this. In his discourses he had told them about it; he himself alludes to his oral catechism on the subject in I. Cor., II, 2, and Gal. III, 1. But in his letters he is concerned with transcendentals, with morals and theology. The Christ whom he preaches lives in the souls of the saints—"It is not I who live but Christ who lives in me." The Union with the Master is by interior knowledge, which he expressly declares is by mystical experience beyond human understanding.

It is therefore the more significant that his testimony should tally so exactly with that of the Evangelists. As we go through St. Paul we find Jesus "true man born of woman," descended from Abraham through the tribe of Judah and the house of David, having "brothers" of whom one was called James, living poor and humble in the midst of his disciples, among whom Peter and John are named, appearing transfigured to some of his people, instituting the Eucharist, praying in agony on the eve of his death, suffering at the hands of Herod and Pilate, being crucified outside the gates of the city, rising again the third day and finally ascending into heaven. Even more striking than the exact schedule of the facts is the truth of the portrait of the man given in the Epistles; it is exactly that of the man portrayed in the Gospels. But how could it have been otherwise since Paul was speaking to audiences including people who had known Jesus and who had heard the immediate testimony of the Apostles? All the same he himself had not, as he tells us, seen him "according to the flesh"; at the time of the Passion he was not in Jerusalem. Probably he had at hand several of those "mementos" used by the earliest missionaries. He had certainly heard about Jesus in Jerusalem from those who had witnessed both his triumphs and his death. And later, at Antioch, he met Barnabas, one of the Apostles, with whom he became associated and whose cousin, Mark, became his closest collaborator.

One thing is certain, the Jesus of the Epistles, written less than thirty years after the Crucifixion, is the same as the Jesus of the Gospels. The sources of information may have been different, but the personality of Christ is so true and so powerful that it is unmistakably recognizable everywhere.

The Gospels: Unity in Four Recitals

We have said that the essential witness by which we are permitted to know Christ is that of the Gospels. These four small books are the bases of our Western civilization much more than all the literature of Greece and the law of Rome. They are so welded into the marrow of our being that we end by forgetting that we are what they have made us. But wherever their influence is ignored or shaken off, a mortal deficiency manifests itself and the civilization of the West is betrayed. As a moral system, the Gospel is indissociable from a certain conception of man which is itself a sign of true civilization. As a work of literature it has reached down the centuries and shed its light upon the whole world without abating any of its strange power to speak individually to every single man, of whatever race or time, in the very language he can best understand. As an historical work whose aim was not historical it has so solidly established the image of Jesus that successive generations of hostile critics have not been able to succeed in their constant attempt to demolish it.

There is in the Louvre a picture of the Four Evangelists by Jordaens; the first three, Matthew, Mark and Luke, seem, in spite of their age, to be gathered, with profound humility, round the youthful St. John, whose face is lit with mystical rapture as he reads from the Holy Book. Our medieval forefathers, who found symbols for everything, represented them by the four fantastic creatures who, in the celebrated vision of Ezekiel, accompanied the man sent from God. The angel represents St. Matthew, because his Gospel commences with the appearance of an angel to St. Joseph; the lion for St. Mark, who begins with John the Baptist in the desert; the bull for St. Luke, as he opens with the sacrifice offered by Zachariah, father of the Baptist; and the eagle for St. John, symbolizing the Apocalypse where he appears as an eagle from the sky. These different images complete each other. The Evangelists were *men* by all that we know of them from close up, in their own recitals, and at the same time they were bearers of a sublime message which transcended the material world. This double character has made their work unique, something that no other book in the world can venture to equal.

The Gospel is news, *good news.* The Jewish custom, still preserved in pontifical diplomacy, for example in the Encyclicals, was to designate a text by its opening words. The oldest Gospel, that of St. Mark, opens with the word "Evangelion" which was originally used in Greek to denote both favorable news and the gratuity which was given to the bringer of it. Later on, the term became restricted to the former sense as for example in an inscription of the first century B.C. which records the birth of Augustus. In the Greek Septuagint the word is used for the messianic promise (Isaiah xl, 9; lii, 7; xli, 27). In the New Testament the word is even more definite; the Gospel is at once the good news which Jesus himself embodied and the promise of salvation that he brought. In the words of Father Grandmaison, "The divine gift which is himself and the divine gifts he brought are indivisible."

The Gospel is thus a religious witness and a profession of faith. It issued in a sense, as we have seen, from those early Christian communities which transmitted the living tradition, but at the same time, it is obvious to all who have eyes to see that it is an individual composition, bearing the hallmark of personality. It is a work of literature which has a definite authorship, four authors, each one of whom follows a plan, has a personal style and a precise purpose. They are the inspired books of the Christian religion, that is to say their authors responded to a supernatural impulse and were assisted while they wrote so that they could plan exactly, report accurately and expound with infallible truth that which God had decreed, and only that which he had decreed, that they should write. But they are books made by the hands of men, proceeding, like all books, from authors who had their own sources of information, whether personal or acquired, and who set them down in different ways and according to their various talents.

It is possible to reconstruct pretty accurately how the Gospel arose from the oral teaching. In the midst of these fervent communities someone, either an apostle or an immediate disciple of one of the apostles, would speak about the Master. The intimacy of these early communities favored reminiscences of this kind; they could never have enough personal detail or apostolic teaching. Perhaps the speaker would have recourse to one of those "apostolic mementos" we have mentioned earlier; he might on the other hand have his own sources of information, either first hand, if he had himself known Jesus, or from the word of one of the Apostles. He would have tried to find out, by personal inquiry, as much as he could. All the time that the Christian community was collecting, sifting and accepting his testimony the author would be working, and as soon as his text was established it would, since its aim was religious rather than historical, be read with solemnity in the assembly. This explains the triple character of the Gospels, which are at once personal narratives, popular expositions and liturgical documents.

The oldest manuscripts of the Gospels which we can trace were written in Greek. Whether they were originally written in another language of which we have only very ancient translations we cannot say with certainty, though in the case of St. Mark it is probable and in the case of St. Matthew almost certain. The original language was not, as our actual text mentions in the case of St. John and St. Paul, the Hebrew which had been since the fourth century B.C. the official liturgical and literary language as was Latin in our own Middle Ages, but a Semitic dialect, imported by the nomadic bands from the northeast, which had come in the course of centuries to be in general use throughout the Fertile Crescent. This was Aramaic, the tongue which Jesus spoke. Even if the original Gospels were not actually written in this language, they show its influence to a marked degree. There are several instances where the Evangelists quote a direct phrase of Christ's in Aramaic, such as the *Talitha cumi* with which he raised the daughter of Jairus to life (Mark v, 41), in the word *Ephphatha* with which the ears of the deaf and dumb man were opened (Mark vii, 34).

Persisting through the Greek even into our modern European tongues we can trace the peculiar rhythm of Semitic poetry; which was very apparent where the text retained the old division into verses of thirty-four to thirty-eight syllables instead of the arbitrary truncation into verses of varying lengths which Robert Estienne adopted for the fourth edition of the Geneva New Testament in 1551.

It does not really matter, in the last resort, whether what we have is the original itself or a Greek version written or supervised by the author. Josephus himself wrote his *Jewish Wars* in Aramaic before translating it into Greek for publication. What is important is that from the most remote times, certainly before the end of the second century, the Church had accorded these four little books the central place in its teaching, that they were regarded as enshrining the most direct and complete testimony concerning Our Lord. Papius, the old Bishop of Phrygia, bears witness to this about the year 130; and fifty years later Ireneus, Bishop of Lyons in succession to the martyr St. Pothin—whose testimony is all the more valuable since he came from Smyrna and thus brought with him the traditions of the very first eastern Christian communities—compares the Four Gospels to the four winds of heaven and explains in minute detail how they had been collected. His evidence confirms the traditional order in which the Gospels appear, Matthew, Mark, Luke and John; this order must have been established at the time he wrote or there would have been a greater disparity in the manuscript versions.

The early Christians recognized the unity of the four Gospels' recitals as firmly as they acknowledged their truth. Ireneus speaks of the Fourfold Gospel; Origen, a century later, says that "throughout the four the Gospel is one," and in the fourth century St. Augustine writes of "the four books of the one Gospel." The formal title, "The Gospel according to . . ." affirms this indissoluble unity. There is truly only one Gospel, the one glad tidings before which those who were at once its heralds and its witnesses humbly effaced themselves. The documents and the versions may change; the message remains for ever, unique and indisputable as the very word of God.

The Synoptic Gospels

This unity is most striking when we consider the first three Gospels, those of Matthew, Mark and Luke. The most superficial reading of these shows a noticeable resemblance. Since the publication of Griesbach's *Synopsis Evangelorum* in 1774, these have generally been referred to as the Synoptic Gospels from the Greek word meaning "a parallel." In actual fact all three contain many analogous passages; there are numerous editions giving the three texts in parallel columns underlining these; and even in the year 350 Eusebius, Bishop of Caesarea, compiled a curious schedule showing that if the Gospels are divided into sections according to an idea or an incident, a surprising number will be found to be in common. St. Matthew for instance has only 62 sections of individual matter out of 355 and St. Mark only 19 in 233.

The first problem we come up against is the question of their dates. It must be admitted that for every date suggested there is a strong element of conjecture in the evidence and one argument frequently cancels out another. The prophecy of Jesus announcing the fall of the Temple is evidently, say the rationalist critics, a prophecy after the event. This would make the earliest narratives later than 70 A.D. But the historians of the Church have pointed out that all the general evidence we have regarding the state of society at the time shows that it was unstable and apprehensive of the future but not, as it was after the catastrophe of the years 66–70, in complete ruin and upheaval.

This question of date has been debated endlessly for centuries, and it turns upon only a few score years. If we admit that the text was preserved and controlled by the early Church in the way which has been described, these few decades are not of primary importance. This is what Augustine certainly meant when he said, "I would not believe in the Gospel if the authority of the Catholic Church had not brought it to me."

It may be remarked, however, that more recent criticism has tended to decrease the gap between the lifetime of Christ and the setting down of the Gospels. Whereas in 1835 David Strauss put the latter at the year 150 "at the earliest," Renan in 1877 thought that St. Matthew was probably written in the year 84, St. Mark about 76 and St. Luke about 94. In 1911 the great Protestant theologian Harnack ascribed St. Matthew to about 70 A.D., St. Mark about 65 and St. Luke about 67, and added that the common source, one of those "apostolic mementos" which have been discussed, was probably in existence about 50 A.D. or even earlier. Mgr. Ricciotti in his recent work makes the following suggestions, that the original Aramaic of St. Matthew was dated about 50–55, the Greek text coming much later; St. Mark's Gospel dates from the years between 55 and 72 when the Evangelist was in Rome with St. Peter, while that of St. Luke, which by constant tradition has been considered the latest, is ascribed by this historian to about the year 63. If we oppose to these dates those of Guignebert, who gives 75 for St. Mark, 89–90 for St. Matthew and 100–110 for St. Luke, we have the outside and inside limits of the period debated. It can be said with certainty that less than fifty years after the death of Christ, a skeleton of the Gospel as we know it existed and that the three synoptic Gospels were set down, at the latest, not more than eighty years after. There are a great many events in ancient history of which we have only much later testimony.

The first Gospel is that of St. Matthew, by reason of its position in the New Testament, by reason of its probable date of composition, but primarily because of the importance which the early Christians attached to it. This is hardly surprising. The text of St. Luke, written, as we shall see, expressly for a pagan convert, would naturally not appeal so much to the early Church as the testimony of St. Matthew who was not only a Jew by race but who, and this probably explains the choice, ended his gospel with the appeal to "go forth and teach all nations" and would thus seem, as Renan says, to be the Evangelist of the Church. Justin Martyr in the second century cites St. Matthew no less than one hundred and seventy times and we know from Ireneus that the very early heretical sect of the Ebionites recognized only the Gospel according to Matthew.

The writer was, we have said, a Jew, one of those Hellenized Jews [9] of which there had been many in Palestine for two centuries. They were influenced by the contemporary international culture but were deeply rooted in the soil of Palestine. Tradition has always identified him with that Levi called Matthew, one of the Twelve, the publican who followed Jesus (Mark, ii, 14, and Luke, v, 27). Matthew or Matthias is the Greek form of Mattayah, which in Hebrew signifies the Gift of God, of Yahweh. A publican, as an official tax collector, would be required to know how to write. This identification, affirmed about the year 130 by Papius, later by Ireneus, Tertullian and Clement of Alexandria, unquestionably dates from the earliest days of the Christian Church.

"Matthew," says Ireneus, "wrote his Gospel in a Hebrew language in the midst of the Jews." Papius says the same: "Matthew set down in order the words of the Lord in a Hebrew dialect." It is generally agreed today that the earliest

---

[9] That is, on the hypothesis that the author and the translator were one and the same person.

version of St. Matthew's Gospel was written in Aramaic and in a less connected form. This earliest Gospel, this "setting down in order the words of the Lord," as the old bishop put it, was circulated zealously among the Christian communities and each one, as Papius adds, "translated it to the best of their ability." The time came when the Church wished to codify these translations and thus we have the official Greek version, made very probably by the author himself. This version would be enlarged and completed since by this time two other Gospels, Mark and Luke, had appeared.

That the origin of the book was Jewish, that it was written for Christians of the chosen race, can be proved by the most cursory examination. St. Matthew, who describes himself as "a scribe perfectly instructed . . ." (xiii, 52), was steeped in the history and traditions of his race. Writing for his own people, he has no need to explain his allusions to the manners and customs of Palestine. He alone uses (thirty-two times) the expression, "the Kingdom of Heaven" because "Heaven" was one of the permitted substitutions for the awful name of the Most High in general use in Israel. The other Evangelists always say "the Kingdom of God." It is he who alludes to the smallest letter of the Hebrew alphabet (v, 18) in denouncing the jots and the tittles used to deflect the law of Moses (xxiii). It is he who seeks to prove throughout that Jesus is the authentic Messiah, the son of David foretold by the prophets who comes to "fulfill and not to destroy the law," who is sent to the lost sheep of the house of Israel. All through his Gospel the underlying theme is, "He came to His own and His own received him not." And, as a reply to this rejection by Israel, his Gospel concludes with the missionary injunction, the promise of the word to all nations.

From a literary standpoint the chief merit of the book, which is written in correct but undistinguished Greek, lies in the solidity of its construction and its evident fidelity to the plan laid down. It is truly, as Papius says, "the words of the Lord" which Matthew has set down, and the teaching of Christ occupies more than half of the Gospel. But it is set down soberly in its context by a scrupulous and honest writer. He does not have St. Luke's power to move us, nor yet the passion and eloquence of St. John but none of the other Evangelists gives us so forcibly the impression of being a witness who puts down what he has heard.

The second Evangelist, St. Mark, by contrast, is less interested in the words of Jesus than in his acts, and particularly in his supernatural acts, the miracles. This slender little book, the shortest of the four, a bare fifty pages, is full of the prodigious acts by which Jesus showed himself to be the Son of God. But nothing is further removed than this Gospel from that "life of Christ" which we would so love to have, a chronological sequence with precise details of time and place. Episodes follow without apparent connection, the order could be changed without essential damage. Certainly this Gospel is in form very close to those "apostolic mementos" of the earliest Christian communities; one can easily imagine these humble and unlettered folk fervently reading St. Mark's picturesque narrative with, it must be admitted, more faith than scientific scrutiny. But because it is direct, vivid and concrete, we are inclined to attach more importance to it than did the early Christian fathers, who probably found it insufficiently dogmatic.

For whom did Mark write? Certainly not for the Jews, or he would not have found it necessary to point out that Jordan is a river (i, 5) or to explain such Jewish rites as the washing of hands before meals, the bath after walking and the ritual washing of vessels. From the way he translates Aramaic expressions and converts sums of money into Roman currency, it has been thought that he wrote for the Romans. When he tells how Simon of Cyrene bore the cross he adds: "the father of Alexander and Rufus" (xv, 21). St. Paul, in his Epistle to the Romans, mentions Rufus as a person of distinction in the Roman Christian community and the more we consider what is known of Mark the more probable does it seem that it was this community whom he was addressing.

There is every probability that Mark was he who, as we have

seen, is mentioned by St. Peter, by St. Paul and in the Acts of the Apostles. He would seem to have been called John in Hebrew and Mark in Latin; he belonged to one of the oldest Christian families in Jerusalem, was a cousin of Barnabas and a son of that Mary whose substantial house was a general meeting place for the Christians and who, in the year 44, sheltered St. Peter after his miraculous deliverance from prison. Thus mingling with the original disciples, Mark must have heard their testimony at first hand. Had he himself known Christ? It is significant that when he tells the story of the arrest of Christ by the soldiers he adds a detail which is not included in any of the other Gospel narratives, the story of the young man who tried to follow the party but faced with arrest himself, fled leaving his cloak in the hands of the guards (xiv, 51). Since all the disciples had fled, none of them could have told him this story, and it has therefore been conjectured that the young man was Mark himself. He may be deemed to have signed his name by this detail as the medieval carvers would hide theirs in a rebus.

In any case, we can reconstruct him from his narrative. He was certainly not a scribe, a professional man of letters, but rather a man of the people with a certain degree of education. His Greek is colorless and poor but he retains the frank realism and original vision of the unsophisticated. If we compare him with corresponding passages in St. Luke and St. Matthew, for example when they recount how a great multitude of people surged about Jesus so that he had to get into a boat to avoid being crushed by them (iii, 7-12), the difference is startling. The two others seem flat compared with Mark's vigorous description, his style has something of the popular roughness [10] and in it we catch an echo of the actual speech of these Galilean fishermen who surrounded Christ.

All this makes highly probable Papius's statement that "Mark was the interpreter of Peter," that he repeated the

[10] The six last chapters are in a markedly different style and it has been advanced that these were written from notes or other documents some time after the rest.

testimonies of that apostle from whom he did not receive them consecutively but rather "as they were needed," taking care neither "to miss out or to distort anything which he had heard." This thesis, which was confirmed by Justin Martyr, Ireneus and Clement of Alexandria, is easily acceptable today, for it is noticeable how large a part St. Peter plays in St. Mark's Gospel, and how incidents involving St. Peter are all told from his viewpoint. For instance in the account of the Passion (xiv), St. Peter is mentioned in twenty-two of the seventy-two verses, and no one could have recounted Peter's denial of his Master but himself. Similarly, when Christ chides Peter for not believing the news of the Passion (viii) or the Transfiguration, we have the impression of direct testimony. It is probable that, sometime about the year 61, St. Mark rejoined his friend and spiritual father, St. Peter, in Rome, where the Christian community listened fervently to the witness of the chief of the Apostles, and that Mark was invited to place it on record. This explanation of the origin of this Gospel, first set forth by Clement of Alexandria, now commands general acceptance.

While St. Mark records the witness of St. Peter, St. Luke, the third evangelist, sets down St. Paul's knowledge of Christ. This is the tradition of the Church from at least as far back as the third century. Ireneus tells us formally that St. Luke, the companion of St. Paul, recorded "the Gospel as preached by him," and this is also stated in the Canon of Muratori, that fragment of unknown authorship which gives us a list of the texts accepted by the Christian community about the years 180–200. A tradition no less constant attributes to St. Luke the authorship of the Acts of the Apostles and it has frequently been observed that those passages of the latter where the author says "we" are identical in style with the third Gospel. There is good reason to believe that St. Luke the Evangelist was the man who can be traced in the wake of the Apostle to the Gentiles, accompanying him on his travels and arriving in Rome with him about the year 61, and thus doubtless, as a complement to the Gospel of St. Mark, and destined for a different public, his Gospel came to be written.

Luke came from Antioch and was probably Greek by race and certainly by education. He is the most literary of the four Evangelists and his Gospel, says Renan, "is the most beautiful book in existence." The opening of his Gospel, with its magnificent cadences, is a model of Greek prose worthy of the classics. Everything about his work points to a man of education, culture and ability; a persistent symbolical tradition has it that he was a painter. In setting down his record, he made, he tells us so, a regular plan according to the precepts of literary composition, and if he seems to depart from it here and there, inserting a parable or a discourse, without apparent sequence, because he could not find a place for it elsewhere, his recital has nevertheless more form than the others. As a storyteller he is superb, his people are solid and their psychology displayed with insight. Harnack was not far wrong in placing his story "among the finest jewels of narrative art." It should be added, however, that St. Luke was not seduced by the literary demon; he does not embroider or embellish, as the parallel records of St. Mark and St. Matthew testify.

Although he was an artist, St. Luke was also a man of science, a doctor, according to a tradition which goes back to St. Paul himself. Scholarly criticism has pointed out that his writing bears internal evidence of a knowledge of medicine based on Hippocrates, Dioscorides and others. It can be observed with some amusement how, when recounting the episode of the woman who suffered from a hemorrhage, which is also told by St. Mark, St. Luke shows us a glimpse of the doctor. While St. Mark says flatly (v, 26): "And had suffered many things of many physicians and had spent all that she had, and was nothing bettered, but rather grew worse," the Greek of St. Luke [11] says modestly (viii, 43): "which had spent all her living upon physicians neither could be healed of any."

This doctor at any rate had a sense of precision and of docu-

[11] The Vulgate text repeats more or less the words of St. Mark.

mentation as is shown by his frequent use of proper names and his relation of the Gospel story to historical events (ii, 1 and, particularly iii, 1-2). Before he began to write he endeavored to supplement the information he had from St. Paul from other sources and there is little doubt that he had read the account which St. Mark had recently compiled. It is also probable that he had other more personal sources of information; his stories of the childhood of Jesus may even come from the Virgin Mary herself of whom he says, "She pondered all these things in her heart" (ii, 19). The story of Herod Antipas may very likely have come from that woman whom he alone mentions, Joanna the wife of Chusa, the tetrarch's steward.

Whom was Luke addressing? Again, not the Jews, or he would not have explained that "the feast of unleavened bread drew nigh, which is called the Passover" (xxii, 1). Also he stresses that although the Jews were the first to be called they were not the only ones and that God has more regard for the one sheep that has strayed than for the ninety-nine others safely in the fold. His Gospel, dedicated to the "most excellent Theophilus"—doubtless an important official of the Empire—is addressed to the Gentiles, to the mass of the converted heathen. He is very careful not to offend them and the hostile references to the pagans to be found in St. Matthew are never met with in St. Luke. He refers to the Lake of Gennesaret where the others call it the Sea of Galilee, a difference of phraseology natural to a man who knew a wider world than these untraveled Jewish peasants and fishermen. We have thus the picture of St. Luke, a writer with a wide outlook, well furnished with evidence and gifted with a superb style. To all this he added the power to move the heart. Dante called him the witness of Christ's gentleness, and no others of the Gospel pages are so rich in examples of the ineffable tenderness of Christ. It is he who tells us about the Good Samaritan, of the woman taken in adultery, of the Prodigal Son so tenderly received by his father. His is the Gospel of the poor, wherein the Savior is shown bending untiringly over human suffering and misery. He is also the woman's Evangelist for he has drawn for us the faces of so many of those sinners on whom Jesus gazed with his redeeming purity and infinite pity. More than any other he saw through the God to the man, to that living heart of flesh that beat even as our own.

We have considered the three synoptic Gospels each in turn; it remains to consider them as a whole. The profound resemblance among them, transcending the differences of style, has always astonished all readers. The striking fact is that from the prophecies of John the Baptist to the Resurrection the substance of their stories is the same although, as we have seen, none of them set out to write an historical biography. It is even more striking that, in these narratives which are so largely indifferent to chronology, the events grouped together are repeated from one to another so exactly. The most superficial reader can see how many passages are almost identically worded in the three texts, and this is not confined to the actual sayings of Jesus, which natural piety would render verbally sacrosanct, but can be noted even when the Evangelists are merely recounting facts.

Yet more remarkable than the similarities are the differences, for these are many and not all are to be explained by the differing temperaments and literary skill of the writers. Some of them are in fact inexplicable, as for instance why St. Luke, the Evangelist of the Gentiles, omits the touching story of the Canaanite woman, told by St. Mark (vii, 24), which would prove the tenderness of Jesus toward the heathen who sought him. Similarly certain promises to the Gentiles given in St. Matthew do not appear in St. Luke. Other passages, although the profound meaning is not affected, show discrepancy of detail as when in St. Matthew and St. Luke, for instance, Jesus forbids the disciples to take anything with them when they set out to teach, "neither stones nor script, neither bread nor money, neither have two coats apiece"—whereas in St. Mark he advises them to take nothing at all "save a staff only."

These differences, however, are not very formidable. In fact they support rather than tell against the credibility of the Gospels, for whereas in essentials the three accounts conform with each other, the small differences that we are dealing with are three separate testimonies given by men who were not slavishly copying each other. Those resolutely secular historians, Langlois and Seignobos, have observed that "true and conclusive concordance does not reside in an exact resemblance between two accounts but rather in the interrelation of two different accounts which only resemble each other at certain points. It is natural to suppose that concordance is more telling the more the accounts agree but the truth is, paradoxically, that concordance proves more striking when it is limited to a very few points. It is precisely these few points which tally in different accounts which make the scientific establishment of historical facts." Partial and tacit agreement is more impressive than duplication.

It remains for us to account for these differences and agreements. It is generally admitted today by all students, whether Christian or not, that on the one hand the Evangelist may have worked on the testimony of one of his predecessors, on the other they might have had a common pool of information on which they all drew more or less. It has been noted that St. Matthew and St. Luke include almost the whole content of St. Mark and that they also have in common much that Mark omits. For nearly half a century, the secular critics deduced from this that Sts. Matthew and Luke had access to a source which these critics call "Q" (from the German word, *Quelle*, meaning "source") and this simple and simplifying explanation proved so seductive to the historians of the late nineteenth and even the early twentieth century that they concentrated their textual criticism on references to a document which no one has been able to find. We all know what becomes of literary criticism conducted in this fashion, even by professors of the Sorbonne.

Today such an hypothesis is not regarded as very sound. It has been observed that the Aramaic text of St. Matthew is undoubtedly older than St. Mark; and it is supposed that the Gospels drew on the oral catechisms which the Evangelists certainly had to aid in their work, and on those "missionaries' notebooks" whose existence may be presumed and on those "protogospels" to which St. Luke refers at the opening of his text.

The present state of the synoptic controversy may be summarized thus: from the apostolic catechisms proceeded first the Aramaic text of St. Matthew. St. Mark, who wrote later, followed the same oral sources, particularly the tradition of St. Peter, but he had the Aramaic text of St. Matthew already to hand. St. Luke, the latest and best documented, collected all the documents and testimonies from St. Paul and had in addition the account of St. Mark, which contained the essential part of St. Matthew's Aramaic version. Finally, when St. Matthew translated his Gospel into Greek, he strengthened and added details from St. Mark, and possibly even, although to a lesser degree, from St. Luke. This complex of influences can be traced in other literary circles where authors have known each other and have read and drawn on each other's books, and it explains both the general agreement and the particular discrepancies.

St. John

The fourth Gospel is on every count outside this group and this tradition. Neither in design, in general tone nor in its urgent intention does it resemble the synoptic Gospels. Eusebius has already noted that more than half its text—106 out of 232 sections—is original in subject matter, owing nothing to the others. Anyone who reads the famous, eloquent opening, "In the beginning was the Word, and the Word was with God and the Word was God," can appreciate immediately the gulf which separates the mystical genius who wrote it from such simple storytellers as Matthew, Mark and Luke.

So there is a double difference between the synoptic Gospels and the Fourth. The latter includes a certain number of facts which the others do not mention. It concentrates on Christ's ministry in Judea. Whereas the other three Gospels mention only one visit to Jerusalem, St. John mentions five. While the subject matter of the three synoptic Gospels could have taken place in a single year, that of St. John would require at least two or three. It seems as though the author of the Fourth Gospel was perfectly conversant with the other three texts and sought to supplement them by reference to another and different testimony whose truth he had the best of reasons to accept.

With this difference of matter goes the most striking difference of tone. It is obvious that the writer was a mystic, concerned not merely with faith but with metaphysical speculation. What interests him is the discourse between Jesus and Nicodemus, in which Christ stresses the necessity of being born again, and the raising of Lazarus affirming the victory over death. He recounts only seven miracles but five of these are not given elsewhere and all five may be interpreted as witnesses to the great truth which the whole Gospel is written to glorify, that Jesus is the Son of God, the Light of the World, the Word Incarnate. John is the Evangelist of the Word, he alone uses the term, *Logos,* which was then very much current in those eastern Mediterranean lands which were steeped in Greek philosophy, one of those consecrated words which has been enlarged in sense and meaning until its definitions have become almost contradictory. The term *Logos* is not used by St. John in the sense accepted by Philo of Alexandria, or even in that Jewish tradition which equated the Word of God with the Ineffable Name. He recreated it, gave it a new meaning, expressing for the first time one of the essential ideas of Christianity: "In Him was Life and the Life was the Light of men."

This has been held, by many non-Christian critics like Loisy, to prove that the Fourth Gospel is a piece of purely symbolic writing, a "mystical compilation," "a theological meditation on the mystery of salvation." Renan had previously countered this by saying: "Considered in itself the account of the material circumstances of the life of Jesus given by the Fourth Gospel is superior in verisimilitude to the accounts of the synoptic Gospels." St. John, for instance, gives far more precise topographical references than all the others; they can be checked on the actual soil of Palestine. He tells us precisely how much the urns used at the Cana wedding feast held, the speed of the boats fighting against the tempest. He is no less exact psychologically as in that curious passage about the family of Christ where he says that his "brethren" arranged for him to leave Galilee because they were beginning to find him something of a nuisance (John vii, 1-6). "For neither did his brethren believe in him."

To whom was his Gospel addressed? Undoubtedly to professing Christians who would not require a recital of facts which they already knew or instruction in the fundamentals of the Christian tradition. There is no essential contradiction, as critics like Guignebert advanced, between the personality of Christ as shown by St. John and that presented by the other Evangelists. But there is a subtle difference, of accent or of lighting; the Christ of the synoptic Gospels is Christ seen in his humanity, that of the Fourth Gospel is Christ shown in his divinity. The writer says in more than one place that he and his companions did not always understand the words and actions of the Master at the time and that it was only long after that they perceived the profound significance of much that he said and did. He gives the impression of a man who has long pondered the story and the teaching and has drawn out all that he can find in it.

A study of the literary style also tells us something about the author of the Fourth Gospel. It is written in indifferent Greek, not actually ungrammatical but poor and dull, nothing like the lovely fluent cadences of St. Luke. This is certainly a Jew writing in a foreign language. Antitheses and parallels are used frequently (xiii, 16 *et seq.;* xvi, 21), even the rhythm of the prologue betrays the oral tradition of Israel. The Jew, too, is betrayed by his determination to bind himself to the chosen people for "salvation comes from the Jews," the people who "would love him if they knew him." He draws his spiritual strength from "the law which cannot be broken," from the prophets whose utterances he continually cites. We can identify him as a Jew also by those passages where he indicts the rebellious people, doomed to perish because they would not recognize in Jesus the Word, the Son of God. A Jew who had turned from Judaism, speaking to a non-Jewish community, such was the writer of the Fourth Gospel whom the Church calls St. John.

All the characteristics set forth above coincide exactly with the traditional teaching that St. John, the writer of the Fourth Gospel, was a young disciple of Jesus, that he set down his Gospel at the end of his life, when he was living in the midst of the Christian community at Ephesus. It is easily understood that while he did not ignore the works of his predecessors, he would naturally draw upon his own recollections and that, having spent sixty years in meditating on the life and teachings of his Master, he would be able to draw more out of it than the others. This attribution also makes his attitude to the Jews comprehensible and the evidence of the text alone is sufficient to justify it.

There are, however, other grounds in support of this attribution. At the end of the Gospel (xxi, 24) there is a reference to "the disciple which testifieth of these things and wrote these things. And we know that his testimony is true." Who is this disciple? The answer is given in a verse which appears just before this. He is "the disciple whom Jesus loved." (xxi, 20) This cryptic designation which is repeated no less than five times throughout the Gospel certainly points to St. John, the youngest of the apostles, he who could lean his head against the breast of his Master. Reading the synoptic Gospels, it is evident that the disciples most favored by Jesus were Peter, the elder James and his younger brother John. "The disciple whom Jesus loved" could not have been Peter who is shown in the Fourth Gospel in a very different role. James could certainly not have written the book for he was put to death by Herod Agrippa in the year 44 (Acts xii, 2). It must therefore have been St. John.

A very old tradition of the Church also confirms it. Polycarp, Bishop of Smyrna about 110–120, quotes the First Epistle of

St. John, which is directly linked to the Fourth Gospel. Thirty years later, Justin cites the actual Gospel. During the controversies of the second century with the Gnostics, both sides freely quoted the Johannine text. Theophilus of Antioch about 180, Polycrates of Ephesus about 190, Ireneus of Lyons (173–185) and the Canon of Muratori about 200, all declare that the Fourth Gospel is St. John's. Typical references are those of Clement of Alexandria, quoted by Eusebius, and the famous passage of Ireneus. "St. John, the last disciple to write," says Clement, "seeing that the other Gospels had given a clear account of the external and temporal attributes of Christ, urged by his disciples and inspired by the Holy Spirit, set down in his Gospel the spiritual teaching." "John, the disciple of the Lord," says Ireneus, "who had rested his head on His bosom, also wrote his Gospel while he was living at Ephesus." When it is remembered that Ireneus had heard the teaching of Polycarp, who was martyred in 155, and that the latter had, according to Ireneus himself, followed Christ for eighty-six years, that is he would have been born about A.D. 70, it can be seen that there is an almost unbroken tradition stretching back from Ireneus to John himself.

It can be regarded as certain that the Fourth Gospel faithfully recounts the testimony of St. John. It is corroborated by the fact that neither John, his brother James, his father Zebedee nor his mother Salome is ever mentioned in the Fourth Gospel though in the other three they are directly mentioned as having been present at Calvary, on Good Friday and on Easter morning. The omission is a sign of the author's humility. It is probable that he assembled his recollections and set them down at the time when, returning from Patmos after the Domitian persecutions, he settled in Ephesus where he lived to a very great age, dying in the reign of Trajan, probably about the year 104. The Gospel may be dated between 96 and 104. A passage from Papius cited by Eusebius has led to some support for the hypothesis that the Gospel was not actually written by him but by one of his disciples, John the Presbyter or the Elder, under his direction. This theory, however, is not actually relevant though possibly dictation to a secretary might account for the difference in style between the Fourth Gospel and the Apocalypse. We do not here propose to discuss the authorship of the Apocalypse for that work throws no direct light on our knowledge of the life of Jesus. It is known that this magnificent fantasy was composed by the Saint during his exile in Patmos, c. 95-6. There is an immense difference between the styles of the Apocalypse and the Fourth Gospel, so great that it is difficult to believe that they issued from the same author. It cannot be attributed to progress in authorship, hardly possible in any case between the ages of seventy-five and ninety, for the Apocalypse is written with far greater sweep and vivacity. Yet a natural diminution of power in old age does not explain it either, for the clarity of argument and the precision of detail in the Fourth Gospel is remarkable. The possible employment of a secretary is certainly one explanation.

The only vital fact in this controversy is that we can, with certainty, invoke the authority of St. John for the Fourth Gospel. The objection that St. John, the Galilean fisherman, could not have acquired the learning displayed can be easily answered. To begin with there is evidence that Zebedee and his sons were owners of fishing boats rather than plain fishermen and further there was a solid Jewish tradition that a Rabbi should have also a manual occupation, should be a shoemaker, a joiner or something of that kind. The Rabbis Akiba, Meir and Johannan, all worked with their hands; the rabbinical learning was widely disseminated throughout Israel and the Fourth Gospel shows evident traces of it. Although John was certainly not a Rabbi, he was only twenty when he followed Jesus and between those days and the time when he wrote his book, is a full and varied seventy years, rich in experiences and personal contacts of many kinds. Probably John the fisherman could not have written the Fourth Gospel but John the sage of Ephesus could have done so.

The Fourth Gospel is an historical source of the first importance, completing the narratives of the synoptics. It is also that of which we possess the oldest attested copy, now in the Rylands Library of Manchester, a mere eight-inch fragment of Egyptian papyrus, found in 1935, on which is inscribed the dialogue between Christ and Pilate (xviii). Authorities of all schools of thought have agreed in dating this fragment to about the year 130, that is a mere thirty years after the estimated date for the actual setting down of the gospel.

If this Gospel had not come down to us, there is a great deal that we should not know about the human life of Christ. Still less should we know about that mysterious relation of Christ's humanity and his divinity in his indissociable person, that bedrock of the Christian faith. It is remarkable that those who deny the divinity of Christ always challenge the authenticity of St. John's Gospel yet many have been forced after prolonged examination to recognize the solidity of its testimony. Fr. Grandmaison has pointed out how Renan, in the earliest editions of his *Life of Jesus,* strongly attacks the Gospel of St. John, but in an appendix to the thirteenth edition, he concedes it a great deal of historical accuracy. Loisy who in 1903 referred to the Fourth Gospel as "a theorem almost devoid of historical character" had by 1921 considerably modified his opinion and had conceded it a substantial element of historicity.

There is one argument which ends all discussion. The Fourth Gospel is so different from the others. Would the early Church —whose scrupulous care in examining texts, rejecting dubious versions and eliminating errors, has been previously described —have admitted to its canon a book like this, had it not been sure that it represented an unchallengeable testimony, based on what the Church has always demanded, the apostolic guarantee? How easy it would have been to harmonize it, to unify it with the others.

The Gospels as History

Such are the four key documents for the study of Jesus. But it should be remembered that they are only documents and that it is necessary to know how to use them. Anyone writing the history of a period or a country or a man, basing it on the work of a contemporary writer, needs to check the veracity of his statements. Once this was established it would be safe to follow him as far as his method and materials allowed. But, in the vast majority of cases, history today is not written around the evidence of a Tacitus, a Thucydides or a Josephus. The reconstruction of the civilization of Egypt during the Middle Dynasty or of the Hittite Empire has to be made from a multitude of sources, archaeological and literary, which are not primarily historical in character. It frequently happens that a document without historical intention, the Song of Roland for instance, can be immensely valuable to the historian of early feudalism, while the Iliad and the Odyssey give us unique insight into the Achaean civilization and the sea-borne traffic of the Mediterranean in the twelfth century B.C.

The Gospels are certainly not romances, but neither are they historical documents. "The Evangelists," as Fr. Huby has said, "did not envisage writing a biography in the modern sense of the term, with its regard for exact chronological and topographical details; they were primarily occupied in throwing light on the religious values of the life of Christ by a choice of episodes which conveyed His teaching in themselves."

A consideration of the conditions in which the Gospels must have been written, in the midst of fervent communities who looked to their teaching for the nourishment of their own faith, makes it evident that the ends sought by the Evangelists would be very different from those pursued by Carlyle or Michelet, let alone Lavisse or Seignobos. This does not mean, however, that the Gospels are merely partisan books, a kind of pamphlet or propaganda tract. They are, as we have seen, and in the words of Justin Martyr, "the Memoirs of the Apostles," and they retain their original character, a marvelous purity of intention. Nothing in the subsequent two thousand years of Christian apologetic has ever recaptured that freshness, that transparent simplicity.

For all that, the reader who approaches them with the intellectual predispositions of the twentieth century is often disconcerted. He will find details which plunge him straight into history as in the opening of the third chapter of St. Luke, already referred to, where it is stated that John the Baptist received the Word of God "in the fifteenth year of the reign of Tiberius Caesar, Pontius Pilate being Governor of Judea, and Herod being tetrarch of Galilee, and his brother Philip tetrarch of Iturea and of the region of Trachonitis, and Lysanias, the tetrarch of Abilene." But elsewhere the picture is vague in the extreme. Between the brief passage referring to Jesus at the age of twelve with the doctors in the Temple and the beginning of his apostolate, eighteen years have passed of which we know nothing. At the end of his ninth chapter St. Luke says that Christ "set his face to go to Jerusalem." Almost immediately after he recounts an incident in a place which is certainly Bethany, after which on two occasions he appears to announce Christ's departure for the town which, all things being considered, he could not have reached till much later. Yet St. Luke is the most precise and best documented of the four evangelists.

Both chronology and geography, said to be the props of history, are equally inexplicit in the Gospels and the student is obliged to supplement them. But it is unreasonable to expect exactitude in matters which did not bother any writer of that time. Compare, for instance, the descriptions of the derisory title which Pilate affixed to the Cross; no two are alike. "This is Jesus, the King of the Jews" (Matt. xxvii, 37). "The King of the Jews" (Mark xv, 26). "This is the King of the Jews" (Luke xxiii, 38). And in St. John it becomes, "Jesus of Nazareth, King of the Jews" (xix, 19). Such details are quite unimportant, but they do prove that neither in intention nor in technique were the writers professional historians.

But this is no reason whatever for suspecting the *historical validity* of the Gospel narratives. On the contrary, the confrontation of those testimonies bears witness that we are getting history very nearly at first hand. By the very fact that they proceed from different traditions we can be quite sure that where they agree the probability of accuracy is very high indeed. It has often been advanced that their texts must have been modified and glossed during the years but no evidence of this has been forthcoming and it is practically certain that, having regard to the wide diffusion of the Gospels and the number of ancient copies which we still possess, any doctoring of this kind would have come to light.

A weightier argument against the Gospels is that the prophecies of the Old Testament, which are so freely cited throughout the Gospels, *suggested* the narratives which they serve to fortify; that is, that the writers believed that what was prophesied did in fact happen. This argument however is not so strong as it seems. It is true that the Old Testament is often invoked in reference, but the reference is usually too inexact to support the idea that it gave rise to the incident. For instance, in the story of the Passion where it is mentioned that Christ was given "wine mingled with myrrh" (St. Mark) or "vinegar to drink mixed with gall" (St. Matthew), the difference between the two denotes St. Matthew's recollection of Psalm LXIX where the righteous man said "In my thirst they gave me vinegar to drink." The bitter herb in Greek is kholè, which the Vulgate translated as "gall." "There is no episode of any Gospel narrative," writes Mgr. Battifol, "which can be established as a mythical projection of an ancient prophecy. The argument in favor of this proceeds by a minute carving up of the text into fragments which really serve only to complement each other." It is difficult not to despise critics who are so exigent when it is a matter of proving the historical accuracy of the Gospels but who fall immediately for any wild argument which seems to tell against the sacred texts.

But, in the last resort, the historical validity of the Gospels does not rest only upon external reinforcement, but upon interior knowledge. No one can dispassionately read the Four Gospels without the conviction that Jesus was a living person; he "holds" you, in the critical sense, so that beneath the apparent contradictions you feel the striking reality of a being of flesh and blood. Even Alfred Loisy said of him, "Jesus is a living being dealing with living men. The world which we see around him is the real world and its people are described with a solidity and an individuality which bears everywhere the impress of life and with it the mark of historical authenticity."

The authenticity of Jesus is even more marked when it is considered that the Jewish world of the time thought of him as very different from the figure we know in the Gospels. The compatriots of Jesus were waiting for the glorious Messiah who would recover the power of Israel; the suffering Messiah in agony in Gethsemane and dying a shameful death was a figure quite contrary to the accepted tradition, to which, as we can see in several instances, even his own disciples were attached.

One other proof may be cited, the fact that the words of Jesus, his parables and the tone of his teaching, are quite inimitable. We have already seen that the Apostles themselves cannot command this quality elsewhere, which indicates that the "words of Christ" have certainly been faithfully transmitted. Sayings such as, "Consider the lilies of the field," and "Render unto Caesar . . ." have the authentic hallmark; they could not have been invented after the event. They all have the same tone, the same style, that striking force which Renan described as at once sweet and terrible. Jesus, as he appears in the Gospels, is truly whole and entire.

What is no less important is that so also is his teaching. We have often been told that what we know as Christianity is the sum of the patient work and teaching of so many disciples, Paul in particular. But the great events, the Transfiguration, the Resurrection and the Miracles, are to be found in the most ancient testimonies. It was not Paul who invented the doctrine of the Incarnation and the Redemption. It is to be found in the Gospels and only that can explain the great phenomenon which no one can refuse to admit, the birth of the Church, the visible projection into society of the faith of the early Christians. Christianity without Christ is unthinkable, as an historical fact and as a testimony. The Church itself is a guarantee.

The "Fifth" Gospel

If there is an element of conjecture in any Life of Jesus which seeks to conform to modern usage—that is, to follow an exact chronology—the passage of Christ can nevertheless be traced with much greater accuracy than that of many other historical personages, not merely such figures as Socrates, Buddha or Mohammed but even men like Alexander or Clovis. The historian conscious of the requirements of his task can study the geographical environment and the social milieu and derive what information he can from either to illuminate the life of Jesus.

The reconstruction of the Palestine of Christ's time does not merely entail an easy and picturesque excursion into the past after the fashion of those artists like Bida and Tissot who sought to "orientalize" the settings of their Bible pictures. This kind of realism may be easy but it is not necessarily useless or inadequate. Pious usage and the historic sense alike agree that we should represent Jesus in the surroundings which were familiar to him, that we should see him baptizing on the banks of that river whose brown waters, edged by the tamarisk and the oleander, we recognize as Jordan; preaching to the multitude from his fishing boat in the soft Galilean evening, with the snowy head of Mt. Hermon reflected in the blue mirror of Lake Gennesaret; crucified in the outskirts of the town near those walls fashioned of great stones, in one of those abandoned and rubbish-strewn places which are to be found outside the gates of oriental cities. The air as he breathed it, the sun as he saw it, the rise and fall of heat or cold, the golden sheen on the barley and the early wheat, the sharp green of the sycamore and the shimmering silver gray of the olive trees, all this and the rest we have to recreate if we are to seek to give a true picture. There is value in every detail of the visible world which surrounded the corporeal being of the familiar presence which is, in so many aspects, indissolubly woven into the most secret places of our being.

So many of the concrete details of the Gospels—and they are full of concrete details—mean nothing to our Western world and need to be explained. What, for instance, was that "aneth" which Christ reproached the Pharisees for paying as tithe while they neglected much greater obligations. It was simply fennel, not the kind which the Italians use in cookery and as a garnish, but a bitter medicinal plant, used in diuretics, and of very little value. When Mary Magdalene anoints the feet of Jesus with a vessel full of nard, it is interesting to know that this precious unguent is the essence of the soft brown moss which one sees growing like fur in the hollows of the Palestinian rocks and of which it requires more than two hundred pounds to yield a single liter of perfume.

Information of this kind does not merely serve as "local color" for a "life of Jesus," it serves also to confirm the authenticity of the record. When, for instance, Christ indicates as a sign "there shall meet you a man bearing a pitcher of water" (Mark xiv, 13), this means nothing to us. But the detail in fact confirms the Jewish origin of the anecdote because in Palestine it was, and still is, the business of the women to fetch water. The words of Christ were full of pictures; they drew for images on the daily life of those who listened. Just as Paul preaching to the Greeks at Corinth drew a comparison from the races in the stadium (I Co., ix, 24:25), so Jesus, whose audience were husbandmen and fishermen, talked to them in terms of their harvests and their vines, their boats and their nets, of sheep and crows and wolves and foxes. As we read the Gospels we see the framework from which we could reconstruct the face of Palestine from these four little books alone, the wheat, the barley, the grapes, the figs and the acanthus.

The geography of the country is equally traceable in the Gospel narratives. Christ, who was to change the face and heart of the world, lived out his human life in a very small country. The traveler to Palestine, accustomed subconsciously to magnify everything connected with Jesus, is astonished to find how short are the distances and how insignificant the towns. Capernaum and Nazareth are not more than a day's journey apart, the distance from Jericho to Jerusalem is barely thirty miles. A motor car can easily cross Palestine from north to south in a day's journey, an airplane can fly from east to west in a quarter of an hour. This small compartment of the world, whose renown eclipses the magnitude of continents, is barely the size of the province of Brittany in France.

Its configuration also can be discovered from the Gospels. One is always going up or coming down a mountain, there is little plain and that only by the coast, far from the true center of the Holy Land. Christ's country was the region of broken hills, suddenly rising in brown and yellow ridges, suddenly falling in steep descent to the deep gorge where the paradoxical river Jordon burrows below the level of the Mediterranean to the metallic waters of the Dead Sea.

As for the climate, it permeates the Gospel record. Had rain been less scarce and water less precious should we have had those sublime metaphors of the water of life, or the story of Jesus and the woman of Samaria? If the Khamsin—that hot wind from the Sahara—had not reached the same terrible violence then as we know now, we might not have had those passages in St. Luke and St. Matthew where the righteous man is compared to the house founded on the rock, against which the winds may rage in vain.

There are numerous details in the Gospels which can be understood only if we know the geography. In the passage to which reference has just been made (Matt. vii, 27) we read, "And the rain descended and the floods came and the wind blew"—which makes no sense in countries like our own where the rivulets and water courses, although they are swollen by rain, do not depend upon torrents for their existence. But in Palestine, where the rivers run over pebbly beds, they owe their birth to the rains, and the winds always accompany them. There is a more striking example which, while it cannot pretend to *explain* the miraculous haul of fish, can make us envisage it in its natural setting. In the bay of Lake Gennesaret, between Ain-Tabyah and Magdala, there is today a great quantity of fish, due to the mingling of the cold water which

Jordan brings down from the snows of Hermon and the warm waters which are discharged from several mouths from the spring at Capernaum. The contrasting temperatures of the waters seem to attract large shoals of fish.

It almost seems as if, throughout the Gospel, there is a symbolical link between the geographical locations and the scenes of the life of Christ. Everything that takes place in Galilee is marked with tenderness and charity; the sermon on the mount, the call to the disciples, the marriage feast of Cana—all these happened in the smiling countryside of Galilee, with its green slopes and friendly villages where Jesus spent his childhood and knew the happiness of being loved and understood. By contrast the divine wrath, the harsh prophecies and the horror of the Passion, the other side of the Gospel diptych, reflect the savagery of the harsh land of Judea with its bare rocks and burning skies which seem to bear witness in all its pride to the unloving righteousness of the Law. Eleven of the disciples were Galileans, the one Judean was Judas.

It may be asked how closely does the geographical aspect of Palestine today resemble the country as it was at the time of Christ. In its general aspect, its color, its physical features and its climate, and even probably in its inhabitants, it cannot have changed much. We should remember however that a good deal of the vegetation which is now characteristic (and is consequently much used by painters seeking "local color") was introduced into the Holy Land at a later date. Among these plants may be mentioned the Barbary fig, the aloe and even corn, the most common grain in Palestine today. But it is reasonably certain that two thousand years ago, before the negligence of the Turks and the excessive deforestation impoverished the land, Palestine was a much greener and richer country than it appears today, when only the plain of Esdrelon and the slopes of Capernaum recall the fertility of apostolic times. With this reserve, it may be safely said that the Palestine of today can teach us much about the land that Christ knew. Without going as far as Renan, who said that the Holy Land itself formed a "fifth Gospel," we should know how to use the testimony which it provides.

The Human Setting

More interesting even than the geographical background of the life of Christ is its human setting. Once we have placed it historically in a given time and scene, we are able to draw upon that for a better knowledge of the man and the institutions with which he was contemporary. The inability or the refusal to replace the words of Christ in their setting has often led to the worst kind of confusion, as for instance when people speak of "the communism of the Gospel," associating thereby two habits of life and thought so far removed that no relationship between them can be anything but fantastic.

The study of history has familiarized us with the type of evidence which throws light upon the human setting. Judea at the time of Christ was a province of the Roman Empire and we can refer to all the Latin writers, whether historians or not, to get a picture of that society and of the Roman state. Virgil, who died nineteen years before the Christian era, would seem unlikely to be preoccupied with the coming of Christ, yet how else can we explain his famous Fourth Eclogue? If we would assess the deep spiritual need which the Gospel was to fill, we might consider the *Metamorphoses* of Ovid, the *Astronomica* of Manilius and Seneca's *Consolation to Marcia,* all of them roughly contemporary with the life of Christ. And although, as has been mentioned, the Hellenized Jewish philosopher Philo of Alexandria does not mention Christ, his judgment of Pilate is worth recording. "He was cruel by nature and shrank from nothing, his rule was marked by pride, and arrogance, and also by corruption."

We do not rely exclusively on written testimony for archaeological discovery has often most strikingly confirmed and elucidated the Gospel text. How much has been written about that "pool with five porches" (John v, 2) where Jesus cured the paralytic. All sorts of symbolical interpretations were advanced until research discovered that it referred to a rectangular pool with galleries round all four sides and with a fifth division across the center, dividing the pool into two basins and providing five porches. The recent discovery, under the foundations of the Convent of Our Lady of Sion of the very flagstones of that Pavement (John xix, 13) where Jesus was brought before Pilate, identifies for us the very scene of Christ's trial. One can even see, inscribed upon the stones, the design for a game like hopscotch (apparently played with knucklebones), which perhaps gave the soldiers the cruel idea of the crown of thorns.

More relevant to our study than these sidelights upon the Roman world of the time, however, is research into the manners and customs of the Jewish society in which Jesus grew up, lived and taught. The human life of Christ is indissolubly bound up with the life of Palestine Jewry, whose crown and achievement, in a sense, he was. It is not the least remarkable thing about him that, attached as firmly as his life was to its particular setting by so many roots, it could nevertheless transcend those limits and appeal to an ever increasing field of human experience.

The two chief sources of our knowledge of Palestine Jewry at the time of Christ are the later books of the Old Testament and the collection of rabbinical writings in the Talmud. Under the latter title is collected a somewhat heterogeneous miscellany of texts, history and commentaries. Toward the end of the second century A.D., a number of eminent rabbis, including R. Akiba, R. Meir and particularly the rabbi known as Judah the Holy or the Prince, undertook to set down in writing the teaching of their ancient predecessors and thus was formed the *Mishna.* A later, supplementary collection was called *Tosephta,* and later on, under the pretext of "completing" the work, a somewhat disorderly collection of disputations, elucidations of doubtful points of doctrine, stories, apologias and other fragments was assembled in the *Gemara.* Later on, from the fifth to the tenth centuries, were added those hortatory stories which form the *Midraschion.* The Talmud consists of the *Mishna* and the *Gemara* but as the *Gemara* was compiled by two different Jewish communities, that of Jerusalem in the fifth century and of Babylon in the seventh century, there are two distinct Talmuds known by the names of the two towns where they were produced. The Jerusalem Talmud alone comprises eleven enormous volumes.

The Talmuds are unquestionably most precious sources of our knowledge of Jewish life and, granting the fidelity of the oral tradition, which we have examined in its bearing on the ancient Christian texts, we can be certain that the *Mishna* is a faithful reflection of the Jewish mind at the time of the Christian era. The only reservation we should make, in seeking to establish a connection between the rabbinical tradition and the teaching of Christ, is in the matter of date. It is quite possible that an unavowed Christian influence might have affected the rabbis who came after the apostolate of Jesus.

We certainly cannot look to the Talmuds for any direct historical information regarding Jesus. All that the rabbis let us know about him is hostile, insulting and malevolent. Sometimes he is referred to under the name of Balaam the son of Behor, "the false prophet" who led Israel astray; sometimes under his real name of Jesus of Nazareth, but always with some insulting qualification, such as the liar, the impostor or the bastard. These fables even crystallized in the rabbinical tradition to form a blasphemous pseudo-biography, the *Toledoth Jeshua* which circulated among the Jews around the seventh or the ninth century, and which the Hohenstauffen Emperor Frederic II, that bizarre excommunicated crusader of the thirteenth century, had in his library. Voltaire, naturally, accepted it quite literally and it is current still in the ghettos of eastern Europe.

According to this compilation, Jesus was the illegitimate son of Mary, the wife of a perfumer, and of a Roman soldier, called Pandara or Panthera. He was taken by his stepfather to Egypt where he studied sorcery and was thus enabled to seduce Israel. He was arrested as an agitator and a sorcerer and turned over to the Sanhedrin, spending forty days in the pillory before he was stoned and hanged at the Feast of the Passover. It is stated with precision that in hell he suffers the torture of boiling mud. This repellent fable is so full of absurdities that it is idle to combat it; the stepfather of Jesus is called Josue ben Parania, although the personage of that name died seventy-eight years before the Christian era: the reference to Mary as the wife of a perfumer comes obviously from confusion with Mary Magdalene because "Magdala" can mean a hairdresser, while the name Panthera is probably due to an imperfect understanding of Greek since "Parthenon" means Virgin and the Christians have always referred to Christ as the Son of the Virgin. The rest is of a piece with this, so we can leave it.

What we can obtain from the Talmuds is reliable evidence about the concrete realities of the world in which Jesus worked. Upon the rabbinical methods of teaching, which in one sense Christ followed though in another sense he departed widely from them; upon the technique of oral transmission, so closely analogous with that of the early Christians, these recondite compilations can give us essential information.

Thanks to them we are well acquainted with the contemporary Jewish society. The Pharisees, who almost always figure in the Gospels as irreconcilable enemies of Jesus, can be found, with exactly the same characteristics, in the Talmud. The rabbinical tradition indeed refers to them as "dyed," i.e. hypocritical, Pharisees given over to external observances, just as Jesus called them "whited sepulchres." From the Talmudic definition of various ritual observances we can see how well justified were the sarcasms of Jesus, for instance it was forbidden to eat on the Sabbath day an egg of which the greater part had been laid by the hen before a second star was visible in the sky. On the sacred day it was as much a crime to crush a flea as to kill a camel although Rabbi Abba Saul conceded that one might gently squeeze the flea and R. Zamuel very broadmindedly allowed one to cut off its feet. To the Talmud also we owe this description of the Sadducees, the haughty aristocratic faction who held all the offices of the Temple. "They were the priests, their sons were the treasurers, and their sons-in-law were the inspectors, while their servants beat the people away with clubs." We can also see, in these rabbinical texts, their immeasurable contempt for the common people, the peasants, the *am-ha-rez,* who did not enjoy the privilege of knowing the Law. And we can understand how the Gospel, sown among these untouchables, yielded such an immediate and mighty harvest.

Drawing the Portrait of Christ

He who would be bold enough to write another life of Christ, following so many, cannot but feel scruples and a lack of confidence in himself, as he reviews the material he has at his disposal. The attempt to define the historical setting, to reconstruct as faithfully as one can whatever we know of the actions and the words of the Master, is perhaps after all a deceptive task to which the writer is impelled solely by a historian's curiosity. Those "Lives of Jesus" which pretend to be dispassionate, even if they are as well founded as Guignebert's, have something dusty and incomplete about them. Renan, writing outside the Christian obedience, could not withstand the appeal of that compelling personality and betrays the affection which he felt. So many of those writing, refusing the love of Christ, are bursting with sly rancor and can hardly conceal their antipathy. Couchard assures us that Jesus was only a myth, but with what violence in his tone!

It is absolutely impossible to write a life of Christ in the same attitude of mind that one would write of Caesar or Napoleon. If every biography tempts the writer to take sides, either for or against, how much greater the temptation when the subject is He whose example and teaching have invaded all arguments concerning the nature and destiny of mankind. "I come to the Gospel as to the very flesh of Christ," said one of the early Christian martyrs, Ignatius of Antioch. Even David Strauss, not himself a believer, has said that anyone who pretends to write of Christ with the same "scientific detachment" which one would apply to any other historical personage must be "smitten with stupidity."

This unique figure can be painted only by keeping constantly in mind that tremendous tradition which has come out of Jesus himself and which is enshrined in the Church. The Church, as we have seen, is one of the guarantors of our knowledge concerning him, because if tradition is regarded as valid from the time that it is expounded and inscribed in the Gospels, why should it cease to be valid afterward? The chain is established without a break from the hills of Palestine to the Chair of St. Peter. If it is an untenable proposition to pretend to study Christianity as a "social phenomenon" excluding Christ, it is almost as risky to try to understand him outside the perspective in which he has been placed by those for whom he is the essential of life.

But the witness of the Church includes, beyond its doctrinal teaching, the continuing experience of all those souls who are able to participate with their inmost being in the existence of Christ. There is a very special knowledge of Jesus which belongs only to the saints and the mystics, those privileged souls who have achieved a kind of unity with their Master, submitting their words and actions to conformity with his so that they have come to know instinctively how and why Jesus himself thought and acted as he did. Few of these testimonies have been made into a formal life of Christ but we need only read a phrase, from St. Bernard, St. Francis or St. John of the Cross, to strike the lightning flash which can illuminate the most obscure and difficult pages of the Gospel.

It is not only the saints who can surprise in themselves, even if only dimly and almost by stealth, this secret knowledge. Our civilization is moulded by Christianity. Everything that pertains to it, its institutions and its morality, its art and its habit of thought, its whole tradition is contained in the light of the Gospel, without which we can understand nothing about that Western world, of which we are a part. It is a world with the sign of the Cross on its heart and so there is always something in each one of us which permits us to approach Jesus. "Christianity," said Unamuno, "is a universal value of the spirit with its roots in the most profound depths of human individuality," "*Noverim me, noverim te,*" in the magnificent words of St. Augustine. "Since I know myself, I know thee."

It is far from the intention of the present work to plead for the subjective approach which has ruined so many pious "Lives of Our Savior Jesus Christ," wherein good intentions take the place of documentation. The greater the subject the more scrupulous must be the historical method. Yet an historian who cannot forget that he is also a novelist may claim the right to illuminate whatever emerges from the Gospel regarding the eternal conflict of man grappling with his condition of mortality and sin by whatever light he has been able to capture, even if it burns his fingers.

The most profound truth about Christ is not of the historical order; the true Christ is that "God in wait" lurking in us all, to use Mauriac's phrase. It is not by research or by analysis, through the higher criticism or the sociological approach, that we shall come to a complete knowledge of the Son of Man but by that mysterious force which is not a force of sentiment as this is ordinarily understood, but rather a faculty of knowledge. More indeed, it is the sum of instinctive knowledge, that mysterious cohesive force which Pascal refers to as "the heart."

It is here that our anxieties begin. For if the true Christ is the Christ within us all, the God from whom we fly or to whom we are drawn, according to our exigencies, what trepidation seizes the unworthy writer who ventures to describe him? "Whoever would paint Christ must live with Christ," said the fortunate Fra Angelico. Alas!

CHAPTER ONE

THE VOICE CRYING IN THE WILDERNESS

Bethabara

THERE IS, a little below the mouth of the Jordan where it flows into the Dead Sea, an easy fording place which has been used from the earliest times by the caravans coming down from Moab. Bethabara, "the house of the crossing," is an unpretentious place on the edge of the desert, still retaining memories of the generations of travelers who, for thousands of years, have crossed the trickle of water over the gleaming stones. Here doubtless Joshua crossed the frontier which the Lord had appointed him to attack and twelve hundred years later, another man, also ordained by God, stayed here pondering another conquest. This time the divine promise was not concerned with invasion by the force of arms but with the conquest of that interior region of which love is the master.

The river here gives an impression of power. Its fast flowing waters have eroded the clay and have opened up a gorge which cuts across the hard face of the plateau. The muddy waters spume with a noise like rustling silk, and along the banks a thick undergrowth of bushes, reeds and ferns defines with its green border the grayish-yellow desert, just as, in Central Africa, tiers of forest escort the great tropical rivers.

This valley of the lower Jordan, the only place in the world which is nearly four hundred feet below sea level, betrays its curious situation by some indefinable torpid quality in the atmosphere. It is a place fitted by nature for solitary meditation. Seen from the abrupt descent of the river banks, the surrounding landscape is one of great majesty. The circle of hills, reddish in color, is not so large that one cannot perceive, in a sort of chasm, the formation of that geological ridge which cleaves the continent from the Black Sea to Central Africa as if it were a split fruit. Toward the north, snow covered Hermon, called by the Arabs "the ancient of days," raises his head, closing the horizon so firmly by its mass that the entire world seems bounded by these harsh slopes, these forests and that dazzling whiteness skirting the place which is the abode of the Most High. Toward the south, along the purple hills of Moab, shines the Dead Sea, sometimes like a sapphire, sometimes like pewter, always immobile and with something maleficent in its beauty. The strong sun can never entirely dissipate the mist which hovers over its heavy waters and far down in the valley the smell of sulphur and bitumen persists, an odor reminiscent of Sodom and Gomorrah, of despair and sin.

In the summer, a place like this seems to reject mankind. The heat of the air burns inexorably; 100° F. and over is common. But in winter the north wind comes down with the river, it blows in the evenings bringing peace to the nights so that, for about two months, this hostile place becomes a paradise, the burning heat forgotten. Yet for all that, it remains a sad Eden, uneasiness seizes the lingering traveler. No town has ever sprung up in the heart of this valley, though to one side Jericho the proud raises her white pediments among the palms of her oases, and Jerusalem is ahead, perched on her mountains, half a day's journey on foot.

Although it can hardly be called a boundary, since the land of the Twelve Tribes of Israel extended along both banks, the river Jordan provides in its lower reaches only about four or five of these fording places. A few undistinguished buildings, inns and rest houses for travelers, mark such sites and this is all there was at Bethabara; a ford and a bridge where people foregathered and exchanged gossip. It would be a good place for a man seeking to attract followers. From the thorny undergrowth a clearing opens out to the edge of the river and here, in the gentle winter, a little grass can grow. Here one might stay awhile before rejoining the caravans, some going on toward Sion, others down to Perea and the desert.

In those days, there would be many to linger here. Among those crossing the river at this place would be not only Hebrews but Arabs from the Transjordan, Babylonians with rings through their noses, copper colored Abyssinians and black Sudanese. Some of these men might not rejoin their caravans and thus might be formed a kernel of followers of the kind which in Oriental countries gathers so easily around men with the gift of words.

So the audience formed and it grew quickly. But the ford was not the only thing which brought that audience thither. For weeks the word had been running round Palestine as a bird flies, and that word was enough to draw out of their houses and away from their business all those loyal to the ancient memories. "A Prophet!" It was five hundred years since that word, which once had meant so much for Israel, had last been heard; five hundred years since Zechariah in his eight gigantic visions contrasted the destiny of ruin for the great empires with the glorious future promised to the Tribes. The complaint of the Psalmist was repeated in Zion. "Lord, where are thy former loving kindnesses, which thou swearest unto David in thy truth. Remember, Lord, the reproach of thy servants; how I do bear in my bosom the reproach of all the mighty people." (Psalm 89.) "We see not our signs, there is no more any prophet, neither is there any among us that knoweth how long." (Ps. 74.)

No more prophets. Was God silent now? There had been plenty of persons without authority who had announced themselves inspired but they had been false prophets, deceivers of the people, base flatterers rather than lawgivers. There had been so many of these that a phrase had passed into Scripture, "neither shall they wear a rough garment to deceive." (Zech.

xiii, 3-4.) When anyone declared himself filled by the spirit, his father cursed him.

Yet there remained a hope. For Malachi, the last of the Prophets, whose text ended the Holy Scripture, had said in the name of the Lord, "Behold, I will send my messenger and he shall prepare the way before me; and the Lord, whom ye seek, shall suddenly come to his temple, even the messenger of the covenant, whom he delights in; behold, he shall come, saith the Lord of Hosts. . . . For behold the day cometh, that shall burn as an oven, and all the proud, yea and all that do wickedly, shall be stubble; and the day that cometh shall burn them up." (Malachi, iii and iv.)

The depression caused by this silence of heaven was not quite without hope. It had been foretold as a time of waiting, full of torment and anxiety. So, when the rumor spread that a true prophet was teaching on the banks of the ancestral river, all Israel was stirred. That winter was a season of unusual activity since it followed on the sabbatical year, when the law forbade all labor, but in spite of the need for redoubled effort, many left everything to hear the prophet. "Then went out to him Jerusalem and all Judea and all the region round about Jordan." (Matthew iii, 5.) So, drawn away from their legitimate interests, they came, and joined with the others, a great many others, all bearing to the same place their hope that the day of God was at hand—the time and place where, by his words alone, a man would disturb their souls.

The Prophet

This man was called John. The Hebrew form Johannan, signifying the "gift of Jehovah," was common throughout Judea. He was surnamed "the Baptist" because of the rite which he had initiated and the name had become as much a part of him as his own.

Certainly he had been, in a very special sense, the gift of God. His birth had been marked by one of those rare signs by which Jehovah had of old distinguished those who were called by him, the same sign which Abraham had been given when Sarah at the age of ninety bore him a son, the same sign which had also marked the birth of the Jewish hero Samson. The parents of John, Zacharias and Elizabeth, were growing old in that humiliation and opprobrium attaching to childless marriages in Israel, when the favor of God was granted to them.

Both were of the tribe of Levi, the priestly caste. The priests descended from Aaron were divided into twenty-four classes, each containing two or three hundred members. Each class in turn, for a period of a week, performed the Temple offices, burning the incense, sacrificing the animals, tending the sacred lamps, renewing the shewbread, accomplishing the sacred rites ordained in the twenty-third chapter of Leviticus. Zacharias belonged to the eighth class, the class of Abia.

When it came to the turn of the priests of the eighth class to see that the Temple rites were performed, the lot, by which the tasks were always chosen, fell to Zacharias to offer the incense. This was surely the hand of God, for twice a day, on the altar of Perfumes, in the solitude of the Holy place hidden by a veil from the faithful who prayed outside, Zacharias caused the sacred cloud of smoke which accompanied their prayers to ascend toward the ineffable Presence.

While he performed the appointed rite an angel appeared to him suddenly, on the right hand of the altar. Zacharias, seeing him, was seized with fear and greatly troubled. But the angel said: "Fear not, Zacharias, for thy prayer is heard; and thy wife Elizabeth shall bear thee a son and thou shalt call his name John. And thou shalt have joy and gladness and many shall rejoice at his birth. For he shall be great in the sight of the Lord." (Luke i, 12-15.)

The angel then gave certain commands. The child consecrated to God must obey certain vows similar to those of the "Nazarites"; he must not drink wine or any other strong drink. Filled with the Holy Ghost from his mother's womb, he must go forth "in the spirit and power of Elias, to make ready a people prepared for the Lord." For a Jew moulded by familiarity with the Scriptures the words used by the angel had a sense even more prodigious than their immediate content. "He will turn the hearts of the fathers to the children"; Zacharias would certainly recognize these words in which the prophet Malachi announced the herald of the Messiah, the new Elias whose life was to precede "the great and dreadful day of the Lord."

Overwhelmed by the promise of a happiness in which he could hardly believe, Zacharias asked for a sign. "How should I know this? For I am an old man and my wife is well stricken in years." The unknown replied, "I am Gabriel, that stand in the presence of God and am sent to speak unto thee, and to show thee these glad tidings. And, behold, thou shalt be dumb, and not able to speak, until the day that these things shall be performed." Abraham (Genesis xv, 8), Gideon (Judges vi, 36) and Hezekiah (2 Kings xx, 8) had requested a sign from the All Highest and had not been punished but doubtless in this case it was preferable that complete silence should envelop the mystery which was being prepared.

Zacharias returned to his village, which tradition has identified with Ain-Karim, some seven miles southwest of Jerusalem, to wait in dumb silence. A little later his wife conceived. Five months later she still remained in privacy, then when the grace that she had received became apparent, she came out publicly, praising God. When her time was accomplished, she brought a son into the world. Relatives and friends, recognizing the Divine Favor of which the child was a proof, came to rejoice with her. On the eighth day he was to be circumcised and given a name. Would it be Zacharias, after his father? No, said his mother, he will be called John. "No one in the family bears that name," objected her relatives. In the corner sat the father, deaf and dumb; but they brought him a writing tablet and he wrote, "His name is John." At that moment his speech returned and filled with the Holy Ghost he began to prophesy: "Blessed be the Lord God of Israel, for he hath visited and redeemed his people. And hath raised up a horn of salvation for us. . . . As he spake by the mouth of his holy prophets, which have been since the world began . . . And thou, child, shalt be called the prophet of the Highest, for thou shalt go before the face of the Lord, to prepare his ways; to give knowledge of salvation unto his people by the remission of their sins . . . To give light to them that sit in darkness and in the shadow of death." (Luke i, 57-80.)

The man around whom the crowd gathered at Bethabara was this predestined child. He would then have been about thirty years of age. Since adolescence he had retired into the desert as was the custom of the hermits of Israel; now he had come forth and had broken his long silence to preach the word of the Lord. He found a ready audience; the Jewish people longed to hear once more the old forgotten phrases.

We have a clear enough picture of this herald of the divine justice, this messenger calling on men to repent, even if he is almost absorbed by the light of the divinity of Christ. Although he is a mere episode in the Gospel, he displays a personality of singular power and truth. His existence and his mission are confirmed not only by the Four Gospels but by the testimony of Josephus. He has an irrefutable historical existence and only modern mytho-maniacs could contend that he is a sort of mythological hero, a later manifestation of the Babylonian Gilgamesh, or a variant of the Mesopotamian fish-god Oannes.[1]

He is certainly not an appealing character; reformers seldom are. There is nothing gracious about this harsh vehement creature announcing the wrath of God. But he was a man, a creature of unbreakable will, absorbed by this solitary, self-transcending passion. Nothing could quench the fire that burnt in him; he could be silenced only by cutting off his head and even when dead he left behind so vivid a memory of his words that his murderer lived out the rest of his days in remorse. This was no "reed shaken by the wind," and Jesus himself paid tribute to him: "Among those that are born of woman there is not a greater prophet than John the Baptist."

It is a pious buffoonery to represent this holy fanatic after

[1] See Jensen, *Das Gilgamesh-Epos in der Welt literatur*, Strasbourg, 1906, and Drews, *The Myth of Christ.*

the style of Correggio as a rosy-cheeked youth caressing a lamb or playing with the infant Christ. Even Donatello's touching young Nazarite, with his hollow cheeks and braided pigtail does not approach actuality so closely as the hairy vigorous creature who, in Matthew Grunewald's altar piece, points an accusing finger at the sinful world, or Rodin's powerful figure which combines an inexorable serenity with the suggestion of a superhuman strength.

He went on his way, his bones sticking out through a skin yellowed by fasting and exposure to the sun, preaching continually, driven by the spirit. His message was one that the world least wishes to hear: "Repent ye, repent!" He foretold the most frightful disasters, he respected neither place nor custom, he cried out to his listeners, "O generation of vipers, who hath warned you to flee from the wrath to come? . . . Every tree therefore which bringeth not forth good fruit is hewn down, and cast into the fire." (Luke iii, 7-9.) In harsh, unqualified terms he accused the tetrarch Herod Antipas, the petty king of the realm through which he traveled, of adultery with his sister-in-law. So had Isaiah and Jeremiah in their day predicted catastrophe. Even so had Nathan risen up to denounce King David and Elijah, Ahab and the terrible Jezebel.

The Evangelists Mark and Luke tell us that he wore "a robe of camel's hair and a leathern girdle about his loins and his food was locusts and wild honey." This physical description completes the portrait but it is much less remarkable than at first it appears to be. Honey produced by wild bees from the sap of certain trees is common in the Jordan valley; it is mentioned several times in the Old Testament. Locusts are no more exotic as food than those frogs and snails which delight the French and disgust the English. Leviticus admits four edible species of locust (xi, 22) and the Syrian Arabs to this day make use of certain particularly fat varieties, yellow-mauve in color, which they dry like grapes in the sun, sometimes crushing them to powder for a condiment. In other countries of the Near East they are pickled in vinegar.

As for the clothes, they reveal the nature of the wearer; Elijah also was "a hairy man and girt with a girdle of leather about his loins." (2 Kings, i, 8.)

This, then, was a prophet, they said; this man John preaching on the banks of the Jordan. He belongs in that long tradition of inspired men who during five hundred years had kept Israel alive in zeal and the love of God. Since Abraham had received the divine promise from Him whom no tongue could name, since Moses had drawn his procession of slaves from exile in Egypt, welding them by the strength of the Law into a nation, the prophets had assumed in Israel the triple task of fighting against those forces of decadence which threaten every human society, of voicing the sorrows of Zion, of preserving hope in the midst of utter national distress. In times of great trouble, when the Kingdom, divided against itself, was veering toward complete disaster, it was the prophets Elijah, Amos, Hosea, Jeremiah and the greatest of all, Isaiah, who foretold the punishment at hand. And when, at last, the blow fell, in the days of Babylonian exile, it was still the prophets, Isaiah, Ezekiel and Daniel, who maintained the sacred flame in mourning Israel. Later, again, after the return, in the midst of great difficulties, it was always the prophets, Haggai, Zechariah and Malachi, who reaffirmed the ancient loyalties and repeated once more the consoling promise of the Most High. And at this fourth and final stage, a prophetic voice was needed; and it thundered once more at Bethabara.

It was a voice to which the Jewish community was prepared to listen, a voice at once familiar and new. Whether they accepted it was another matter. So many of God's witnesses had ended their days at the hand of the executioner and by his agony also John was in the authentic succession. Christ made this plain when, placing John in the traditional teaching, he said, "The law and the prophets were unto John." (Luke xvi, 16.) It was truly a prophet who preached on the banks of Jordan, a member of the august line of divine witnesses, the last member.

It is possible to fix the exact historical date when John began preaching. It is indeed the only precise date given in the New Testament and its exactness has been questioned but little. It has been observed that, owing to the climatic conditions of the region, any concourse of people could foregather only in the winter and a logical tracing of the chronology of the ministry of Christ (his retreat into the wilderness, his sojourn in Galilee, his going to Jerusalem for the Passover), postulates for the beginning of John's mission the months of November or December.

As for the year, St. Luke gives six indications in the opening of his third chapter. "Now in the fifteenth year of the reign of Tiberius Caesar, Pontius Pilate being governor of Judea and Herod being tetrarch of Galilee and his brother Philip tetrarch of Iturea and of the region of Trachonitis, and Lysanias the tetrarch of Abilene, Annas and Caiaphas being the high priests, the word of God came unto John the son of Zacharias in the wilderness." This abundance of information shows the importance which the early Christian communities attached to this particular date, for it marked, as is said in the Acts (i, 22), the beginning of the salvation of the world, the starting point of Christ's public ministry.

Of all these references, the easiest to follow is the reference to Tiberius, whose reign is well provided with official documents which can be consulted. The Emperor Augustus died on the nineteenth of August in the year 14 of our era, the year 767 of the foundation of Rome. The fifteenth year of the reign of Tiberius brings us therefore to the nineteenth of August, of the year 29, assuming that Tiberius succeeded immediately upon the death of the previous emperor. In actual fact, Tiberius had been associated with the Imperium two years earlier; in the official sense of the term he had reigned since the year 12. Thus the fifteenth year of his reign brings us to the year 26 or 27.

This date is usually accepted today since it was the Roman usage to consider the associate Emperor as in full sovereignty. In addition it accords better with that passage where St. Luke says that Jesus at the time of his baptism was about thirty years old. We still have to settle when that "fifteenth year" began but it seems most probable that St. Luke would follow the calendar of the province of Syria, of which Palestine was a part. According to this the year begins on the first of October.

We can therefore calculate with a very good measure of accuracy that John's mission began in the month of November or December in the year 27 of the Christian era and this gives a date of about January twenty-eighth of the following year for the baptism of Christ.

A Humiliated, Pious People

If we are to comprehend the attraction that a figure such as John would have for the Jews of that time we must try to feel, as they themselves felt, the weight of sentiment, at once painful and exalting, which swelled in every Jewish heart during the long time of waiting for the wonderful events which had been foretold. No idea persisted more ardently in them than their conviction of the supernatural mission with which, for two thousand years, their race had been charged by Almighty God. To be the chosen people, the race by which the world received the testimony that there was but one God had, in the darkest hours of their history, sufficed to give them the force to retain, in spite of everything, their hope and their faith. The more the facts of history seemed to deny it, the more firmly they held to their belief that their days of glory would return, that their hostile destiny would be reversed.

For centuries it had been the incontestable glory of Israel to be essentially a religious people, the only one whose great decisions had been taken for supernatural reasons, the only one which had placed itself expressly, throughout its history, in the perspective of the divine intention. When, at the dawn of the second millennium, Abraham had left Ur and had set out with his kindred toward the hills of Haran and then to the Promised Land, his driving force had been his resistance to the idolatries of Mesopotamia and his desire to affirm the religion of the one God. Five centuries later when Moses of the shining forehead had torn the Jewish tribes from their slavery in Egypt, it was this same belief, strengthened by his genius, which served to weld the tribes into a people. Israel definitely achieved the status of a nation on the day when the tables of the Law came down from Sinai. Everything that had happened subsequently revealed the purpose of the Lord, whether he rewarded or punished his people, whether he permitted the glory of Solomon or the destruction of Zion under the blows of Nebuchadnezzar. It was the Lord and He alone who guided Israel and blessed be the name of the Lord.

The religion of Israel had, in the course of the years, drawn further and further away from the primitive conceptions and had ended up as a religion corresponding to the needs of the day, a means of spiritual development. Its history was one of progressive enlargement, or perhaps one should say progressive illumination in which the revelation begun by God's pact with Abraham seemed to grow more and more evident.

Whereas in the beginning fidelity to the national creed and the denial of idols seemed sufficient to guarantee salvation—a salvation, moreover, which was very ill-defined—little by little moral ideals became grafted on to the religion until the two had become synonymous. Faith became an interior conviction as the prophets had demonstrated in unforgettable terms. Beyond all the sacrifice of beasts and the prolonged ritual fasts, it was moral perfection and the practice of virtue which praised the Most High. Whereas in the beginning the individual had no responsibility save as a unit of the collective entity, and justice could punish each one for the sins of all, a higher moral conception gradually arose in which divine justice required that a man should be responsible for his own sins.

Thus from the faith of Abraham to the doctrine of Job and the precepts of wisdom, a moral transformation had made Israel the greatest spiritual race in the world. But, although it had become more concerned with interior faith and virtue, the religion of Israel had lost nothing of its exclusively national character. There had always been an absolute identification of the God of Israel and the God of righteousness from the time of the Patriarchs. Because the Twelve Tribes had been charged by God with the task of witnessing to the glory of his name, it was right that they should receive rewards and favors from him. If these were temporarily in abeyance, it was because the weight of individual sin was so great as to drag the whole nation toward destruction. To save oneself was to save the people, it was the same thing. This union of personal and national religion had become the spiritual basis of the Jewish community ever since their great political disasters had made their religion the sole buttress by which national consciousness could be maintained.

It was in 586 B.C. that, following on a long series of catastrophic events, the supreme misfortune had befallen the chosen people. Nebuchadnezzar's terrible armies, which had mastered the whole of western Asia, had taken the Holy City, destroyed the Temple and sent the flower of the Jews into exile. This was the logical consequence of three and a half centuries of political disorder, moral and religious backsliding. The scores of nations are always paid exactly. For fifty long years "by the waters of Babylon" the deported Jews knew the sadness of remembering a lost country, the bitterness of dwelling in a strange land. Yet never once did these exiles lose the hope of return. Faith alone enabled them to retain their national identity and they implored God, their God, to take pity on their lot.

He had had pity. In 539 B.C. Babylon, that great impregnable city, fell before Cyrus, as Daniel the prophet of God, had foretold. One year later, with great magnanimity the Persian monarch allowed the exiles to return to the Holy Land and rebuild the Temple. Thus a kind of residual nation was formed, a state, as Fr. Lagrange has put it, "whose constitution was a strict alliance of race and religion, with civil and religious legislation united in the one code and administered by one authority in the hands of the High Priest." Faith underlay everything, it was the framework of the national edifice and it was inconceivable that this regime could be considered as anything but the express will of God.

Naturally the most jealous care was taken to study the workings of this will and to preserve its utterances. About a century after the return from exile, Ezra devoted his long life to the verification of the texts of the Holy Books through which the voice of God had spoken. It was a significant moment of history; at the time when the Athenian Republic was giving the world its masterpieces of art and literature, the Parthenon and the tragedies of Sophocles, Aeschylus and Euripides, the Jewish community was enshrining in what we now know as the Old Testament, the records of its history and its beliefs, the one inseparable from the other. From that time on, the establishment of these sacred texts had continually employed the zeal of pious scholars and thus instructed in law and morals by the Holy Books, the Jews had become truly "the people of the Bible."

The bone structure of the Jewish community, for the four centuries preceding the coming of Christ, was the Law, the *Torah.* It was more than a legal code, more than a book of devotion; it was the actual testimony to the mission with which God had invested Israel. It was the proof that the hopes of the people were not vain. It was a light for the spirit and a rule of daily life; it inspired and permeated every act of a lifetime and no pious Jew could pronounce the syllables of the name without a tremor. In it were included the mosaic precepts of the Pentateuch and all that collection of mystical texts, the Psalms, Canticles and others, by which the soul is lifted up to God. Ceaselessly studied, annotated and dissected by the scribes, it fulfilled all requirements and satisfied all hearts.

It must never be forgotten that the people who came to listen to John, and would come to listen to Jesus, were completely impregnated by this tradition. Their lives were bound by observances many of which seem to us unnecessary and absurd. The yoke of the law was very heavy but the people of Israel loved it because they realized that it was the justification of their existence and its safeguard. The Pharisees, who were known for their preposterous refinements upon the exigencies of the law, may seem to us to drag religion down to the level of fetichism but it is none the less true that these rigorous observances obeyed a vital instinct. Israel was a people for whom the religious factor was the primary factor: they knew that their future rested upon their faithfulness.

It is also quite wrong to think that the Jewish religion was completely engulfed in a narrow legalism. A reading of those spiritual masterpieces, Job, Ecclesiastes and Proverbs, enables us to measure the level of Jewish thought. All those fundamental problems which have from the beginning troubled the heart of man, the meaning of life, survival after death, punishment for sin, and the problem of good and evil are reviewed and analyzed with the most acute intelligence.

Even among the common people, a deep piety animated every day life. The humblest Jew recited, with all the fervor of his heart, the famous *Schema,* "Hear, O Israel . . ." every morning and night, and praised God with the formula of the Eighteen Benedictions, eighteen being the number of prostrations customary during the recital of the prayer. On the great feasts—such as Tabernacles when families lived in huts made of branches, and when the four silver trumpets sounded on the day of Atonement, and the priest chased into the wilderness the goat charged with the sins of the people, above all at the Passover when every family slaughtered a lamb and ate unleavened bread—the hearts of the believers swelled with the liveliest faith, convinced that participation in these ceremonials was the supreme end of man.

Outside the official priesthood there were souls so obsessed by God that they devoted themselves to him entirely. In solitary places, hermits lost in contemplation were frequently encountered; John was certainly not the first of his kind to retire into the wilderness. There even existed, and not far from Bethabara, notably at Engadi by the Dead Sea, communities of monks who lived in a fashion analogous to our own Carthusians and Trappists and to the Buddhist monks of Tibet. These were known as *Essenes;* after a novitiate of one or two years, the postulant agreed to possess no personal property and to give all his belongings to the community, to renounce women (one sect permitted marriage for the sake of the continuation of the race) and to partake of communal meals of great sobriety. Ritual baths and washing formed part of the daily rule and the Essenes dressed themselves in white linen for their scanty repasts.

Side by side with these ritual minutiae, even more scrupulous than the requirements of the law (all refuse, for instance, was buried) went a great deal of serious spiritual research which sometimes took them a long way from the official Jewish standpoint toward a neo-Pythagorean system which again bore witness in its own fashion to the importance which Israel attached to the consideration of eternal things.

It was this very fervor, scattered throughout the Jewish people, which made the silence in which for centuries God had seemed to enshroud himself additionally painful. Since the Lord no longer manifested himself, did it mean that his old tenderness to his chosen peopole was no more and the sacred alliance dissolved? It was a fear that shook the heart of every pious Jew and that is also to say every patriotic Jew, for the faith and the people were one.

The abandonment, moreover, was not deserved. Since the return from captivity, Israel had shown infrangible opposition to those insidious idolatries that the older Israelites had known only too well. Entrenched in their faith, the Jews had repelled even the suspicion of pagan influence and after the passing of the Persian hegemony, the danger of infiltration had not been great. When, after the tempestuous passage of the Macedonian Alexander, who overthrew the Persian King of Kings (334–323 B.C.) his generals divided his empire, Palestine became a Greek province under Seleucus (306) and various Hellenistic and Egyptian cults might have been expected to influence Israel. They did not. Neither the cult of Serapis, that hybrid of Osiris and Dionysius, nor any other suspect deity crept into the Jewish consciousness. If some rich Jews—and there are always people ready to ingratiate themselves with a conqueror—neglected circumcision and the holy observances and showed themselves at the spectacles and games, the true reaction of the nation was expressed by the revolt of the Maccabees, axe in hand. When the extravagant Antiochus Epiphanus (175–163 B.C.) sought to install in the Temple that "abomination of desolation" prophesied by Daniel, a statue of Olympian Zeus, Judas Maccabeus and his brothers carried on a guerrilla war so ruthlessly that in the end the Greeks had to bow before the heroes. From that time the Jews, led by their High Priests, had enjoyed a century of total religious liberty.

When later the Greeks were in turn conquered by Rome and the legions swept through the Orient, Pompey, in 63 B.C., seized the Holy City. But the Jews displayed the same inflexible resistance to Latin pagan ideas as to Hellenistic mystery cults. In vain the conqueror bestowed roads, aqueducts, baths and theaters, the Jewish spirit rejected them. Later when Rome installed Herod the Idumean on the throne of David, the contempt broke out in active hostility to the half-barbarian tyrant. The touchy Jewish piety set itself against even the most superficial pagan symbols, refusing to circulate coins bearing the human figure, forbidding the eagles on the courts of justice. Israel was conquered but had not submitted, still less had she become absorbed. Far above her political liberty she valued her right to believe in the eternal verities, and she understood how to safeguard it. Such was the state of the country when John began to preach.

The history of this political and religious resistance was as fresh in the mind of Palestine Jewry at the time as is that of the German occupation and the national opposition to it in the minds of Frenchmen today. Everything that happened recalled it. The promised land was no longer the free patrimony of the tribes of Israel, the legionnaires and the tax collectors by their presence alone bore witness to that. Every Jew felt threatened and humiliated that he, the heir of a long and magnificent history, should be forced to accept the domination of this glorified township which had hardly emerged from the swamps of the Tiber when Solomon was in his glory.

To the bitter pride of a murdered nationalism was added a more personal feeling; there was hardly a Jewish family whose blood had not flowed, either in the wars of resistance and spasmodic guerrillas or in the Herodian massacres. In the last five hundred years the Jews had probably lost more than two hundred thousand men, a terrible figure for a small people, especially when it is remembered that the victims were of their bravest and best.

Waiting for the Messiah

Out of this tapestry of conviction, memory and sentiment had grown up little by little during the course of centuries that belief which, like a life-bringing breeze, restored hope to Hebrew hearts. Since Israel was the chosen people and since she had done nothing to forfeit this place, then God would see that her turn should come. Even the silence in which the Eternal seemed to shroud himself had a meaning which would be made plain in the course of time. The role of divine witness, assumed by the people of God's Promise since the time of Abraham, could not be abandoned. The day would come when Israel would shine forth before the eyes of all nations, purged forever of her guilt.

The idea was never very clearly defined and in attempting to explain it one can very easily give it a precision which would be quite wrong. It was a vague but tremendous presentiment nurtured by the succession of prophets whose mission it had been to fortify and succor the mind and soul of the people and from whom one would naturally not expect logical definition. The most powerful and dynamic myths are vague; the destinies of peoples are not swayed by precisely defined conceptions.

We do not even know when this "redemption of Israel" was expected to happen. Some envisaged a rising against the alien rule, after the fashion of the Maccabees, but this time it would be decisive and final. Others thought that the triumph would not take place till the Lord in his wrath came to smite the world with the heavenly host.

The transcendent phenomenon gradually became more and more associated with the idea of the coming of a marvelous being, the Lord's anointed (in Aramaic, *Meschiah,* in Greek, *Christos*). Nothing much was known about this longed-for personage; his title was vague and permitted quite contradictory interpretations. It is used thirty times in the Old Testament, signifying variously a king, a priest, and a patriarch, once even Cyrus the Great. Only the prophet Daniel used it in the sense in which we think of it today. Would he come as a devouring fire or the bearer of the bread of life?

This was not known either; all that was certain was that his appearance would mark the end of the sufferings of Israel. He was the repository of the love of a whole people, the being in whom was vested the fulfillment of the divine promise, the holy one of God. Pious Jews lived in the hope of his coming and even the least pious did not dare, at least in public, to cast any doubt upon it.[2]

We have only to open the Gospels to find numerous proofs of this unanimous conviction. Apostles and Pharisees, priests and common people all speak of the coming of the Messiah as of an indubitable fact. It was the first question asked of John the Baptist: "Art thou the Messiah, yes or no?" And even in pagan Samaria the woman with whom Christ spoke at the well stated her belief in the Messiah as something unquestioned.

Yet this current of belief which was often so noble in its expression and which fortified the hearts of the people of Israel was to engulf them in a position from which they were never to extricate themselves.

The pious Jews, picturing the Messiah in the light of the sacred text, would most naturally think of him in terms of a warrior chief leading Israel to victory or of a great king associating Israel with his glory. Here is a characteristic passage from the *Targams,* the rabbinical commentaries on the Law: "How beautiful he is, the Messiah king who shall arise from

---

[2] Nevertheless the Messiah's tardiness provoked a certain amount of ironical comment.

the house of Judah. He will gird up his loins and advance to do battle with his enemies and many kings shall be slain."

Sometimes his reign is described in terms of peace and plenty as in that passage from the Apocryphal psalms of Solomon, which dates from the century before the Christian era: "He will call the holy people together in justice, he will govern the sanctified tribes: no iniquity shall be allowed in them and no wicked man shall remain in their midst. For God has made him strong in the spirit of holiness and rich in the shining gift of wisdom. How happy are they who shall live in those days, to see Israel rejoicing in the assembly of her people."

But these paradisial visions were less popular than those in which the rancor, the bitterness and the fury of the humiliated people could find expression, and the Messiah came to be represented as a kind of Attila who would "break them with a rod of iron" and "dash them in pieces like a potter's vase," pile up corpses in hecatombs and pierce the hearts of his enemies with arrows.

It must be admitted that only the light of the Holy Spirit could have enabled anyone to reconcile Christ as he was with the prophetic descriptions. Yet there are also to be found in the scriptures references to the humiliated and tortured, the expiatory victim, and in the range of the prophetic testimony there can be found the vision of a lowly Messiah who should come "riding upon an ass and upon a colt the foal of an ass." (Zech. ix, 9.) Closer still there is the foreshadowing of a redeemer who was to offer his sufferings and death for the sins of the world, as in the famous passages of Isaiah (liii), which contains a true prefiguration of Calvary:

"He is despised and rejected of men; a man of sorrows, and acquainted with grief: and we hid as it were our faces from him; he was despised and we esteemed him not.

"Surely he hath borne our griefs, and carried our sorrows; yet we did esteem him stricken, smitten of God, and afflicted.

"But he was wounded for our transgressions, he was bruised for our iniquities: the chastisement of our peace was upon him; and with his stripes we are healed. . . .

"He was oppressed and he was afflicted, yet he opened not his mouth: he is brought as a lamb to the slaughter, and as a sheep before her shearers. . . . He was taken from prison and from judgment. . . ."

A nation which had always borne within itself a secret pride in its supernatural destiny and which had been driven by misfortune to a desire for vengeance would be unlikely to hesitate between these two conceptions, the sacrificed lamb and the victorious king. One would need to know little of human nature to be surprised at the choice which the majority of Jews had made. The prophecy of Isaiah, sunk in oblivion, did not assume significance until after Calvary.

Stultified by pious observances but exalted by a prodigious expectation, such was the spiritual condition of Jewry at the time when John the Baptist was preaching.

As time passed the expectation became inevitably more and more anxious. The prophecy of Daniel was re-read, foretelling that at the end of seventy "weeks of years" the troubles of Israel would end, that the Holy City would make an end of sins and iniquity and bring in everlasting righteousness (ix, 24). The calculation of those "weeks of years" had occupied generations of rabbis and wise men and it had now been decided that the time was at hand.

The Baptist's Message

To this state of mind, there was nothing surprising in the appearance of John on the banks of the Jordan and nothing disconcerting in his teaching; it seemed indeed to be divinely inspired. The silence of heaven was broken at last; once more the Chosen People were to hear one of those magnificent and familiar spokesmen of God and perhaps even now the Messiah was at hand. Naturally, when the rumor of the strange prophet reached Jerusalem, the religious leaders of the nation, the "chief priests," decided to send an official mission of enquiry, composed of priests, Levites and other competent persons. To the first question put to him: "Art thou the Messiah?"—John replied with his customary frankness, "I am not the Christ." But since every instructed Jew knew that "the Lord God will do nothing but he revealeth his secret unto his servants the prophets" (Amos iii, 7), and since Malachi had foretold that the Messiah would have a forerunner, was John then the new Elias? No. He had within him the power and the strength of Elias but he was not the prophet returned to earth. "Then said they unto him, Who art thou?"

"I am the voice of one crying in the wilderness, Make straight the way of the Lord, as said the prophet Esaias." (John i, 23.) "One mightier than I cometh, the latchet of whose shoes I am not worthy to unloose. . . . Whose fan is in his hand and he will thoroughly purge his floor and will gather the wheat into his garner; but the chaff he will burn with fire unquenchable." (Luke iii, 10-17.)

In large measure, the teaching of John was comprehensible to the Jewish people. When he cried out for repentance, and imposed fasts and prayers, he was speaking in the true prophetic tradition; so had Isaiah, Jeremiah, Amos and Hosea exhorted them.

People can only be kept upon the straight and narrow path by repeated admonitions and these allusions to an indefinable but pressing menace, to a catastrophe ready to fall upon Israel, were well within the Jewish spiritual orbit, for ever since the Exile they had experienced so much suffering that they were prepared for it by instinct; all their apocalyptic literature crackled with images of fear. John's teaching therefore fitted in with both their national and personal moral preoccupations.

He preached charity, justice and mercy. To those who asked, "What shall we do then?"—he said: "He that hath two coats let him impart to him that hath none; and he that hath meat, let him do likewise." To the collectors of taxes he said: "Exact no more than that which is appointed you." To the soldiers: "Do violence to no man, neither accuse any falsely and be content with your wages." These precepts also were in the Jewish tradition; the Mosaic laws made it a duty to allow the poor to glean the fields after the harvest, to leave the debtor with a coat against the cold and to help even one's enemy's ass if it fell on the road. Rabbi Joshua ben Gorha had indeed declared that a sin against charity was as grave as idolatry.

But in other respects the new prophet was most disappointing. Not once had he declared that this Messiah whose herald he claimed to be would re-establish Israel in power and glory. More seriously still, he did not address his teaching solely to good Jews of pure race and pious persons acquainted with the law. He gathered round him crowds including publicans, who were practically synonymous with sinners, soldiers, possibly even pagans. He even dared to say to the chosen people: "Begin not to say within yourselves, We have Abraham to our father (that is to say, we are sure of salvation because we belong to the people of the Promise). For I say unto you that God is able of these stones to raise up children unto Abraham." (Luke iii, 8.) These words, which foreshadowed the universality of Christ, could only be heard with a sense of outrage by pious Jews.

And then, he baptized people. This was his own personal rite, the invention peculiar to him. Those who wished to pledge themselves to follow the way he pointed out to them must go into the water. Perhaps it was this curious ritual which drew the crowds to the fording place by Jordan and later on, when the weather became hotter, into the Beth-shan country where there were springs known as "the wells of peace."

Such a rite was not altogether outside ancient tradition, especially Jewish tradition, but it was of such antiquity that learned rabbis could not agree whether a kind of baptism admitting pagan proselytes to the Jewish community existed before or since the Exile. There were many instances of ritual baths especially for Temple functionaries laid down by the Lord, as can be seen in Leviticus and Numbers, and on the day of Atonement it was ordained that the High Priest should take ten, with the most solemn accompaniments, on behalf of the whole Jewish people. The sect known as Essenes, whom we have already referred to, took a daily bath and even today, on the banks of the Jordan, one can come across devotees of ancient cults who still practice a daily immersion in the waters.

Until the coming of John, however, it had been a rite, nothing more. A similar rite accompanied the worship of the Egyptian goddess Isis, and Juvenal makes fun of the votaries of that goddess whose sins were so tenacious that they had to be dowsed three times in mid-winter in the icy waters of the Tiber. It was natural that the washing of the body should come to be taken as a symbol of the cleansing of sin from the soul and in the Old Testament there are frequent references. "Wash you, make you clean. Put away the evil of your doings from before my eyes; cease to do evil." (Isaiah i, 16.) "Then will I sprinkle clean water upon you," said Jehovah through the mouth of Ezekiel (xxxvi, 25). "And ye shall be clean, from all your filthiness and from all your idols, will I cleanse you."

But the baptism of John was different. For the "Baptist" himself officiated and administered the rite. We do not know how he administered it, but most probably the neophyte was immersed in the water, for it is only since the fourteenth century that religious painting has represented the baptismal rite by John's sprinkling water out of a vase or shell on the forehead of Jesus, and doubtless the older tradition goes back to the known fact. Whether the role of the Baptist himself was to pronounce a prayer, an exorcism or an invocation we do not know, but what is certain is that the intention was quite different from that of the pious Jew in his ablutions.

John's baptism was a sign of penitence. It was the sign, the outward and visible sign, of a declared intention to change the way of life. The Mosaic ablution had been merely a preliminary to a rite; later on, the ablution itself became the rite and unquestionably of spiritual significance. But in John's teaching baptism signified a complete moral transformation. It would also appear that the baptism was performed only once upon the person, who was thus, as it were, initiated into a completely new existence.

Research into the origins of John's baptismal rite has not been conclusive; the rite, as he gave it, remains particular to him. It has been advanced that he was himself of the sect of the Essenes and that he derived the rite from them. Apart from the fact that there is nothing to link John with this monastic community, there is no evidence that the bath had, for them, anything more than symbolic significance. Even if the Baptist took the idea of the rite from them, in transporting it to the banks of the Jordan and in investing it with such great significance, he may be said, in fact, to have originated it.

Those critics to whom the notion of any spontaneous creation by genius is unpalatable have been fortunate in the discovery, during the seventeenth century, of a small sect known as the Mandaeans, on the banks of the Tigris not far from Bassorah. This church comprises about fifteen hundred adherents, and they call themselves "Christians according to St. John." They hold water to be sacred, the divine element, possessing a virtue so great that it can even cleanse the soul from fleshly sins. The sacred book of this little community, called the *Ginza Rba,* has, since its discovery, caused a great deal of ink to flow. John the Baptist, under the name of Yahya-Yohanné, figures in it a great deal, and from this the critics have proceeded to deduce that John was a member of this sect (which of course was declared very ancient) and that he had set out to reform it, in the same way that Zoroaster reformed the old Iranian Mazdaism. More recent research, however, has established the fact that the doctrines of the sect are of much later, and probably debased Christian, origin. Moreover, there is the fact that the portrait of John the Baptist given by Josephus is not that of an heretical or fantastic sectary, but of an authentic Jew, a faithful and austere observer of the Law.

The truth is that here, as elsewhere, John was the Forerunner. He pointed out the way but did not trace it entirely. The baptism which he performed was not Christian baptism, in which the use of water is more than a symbol, more even than the pledge of transformation, being in itself a sacrament. In the new rite, whoever renounced his sins and accepted baptism received at once the holy spirit of God. Later on, when the Apostle Paul encountered at Ephesus "certain disciples" he said to them, "Unto what were ye baptized? And they said Unto John's baptism." (Acts xix, 3.) And he thereupon administered the baptism of Christ as a more efficacious rite, a consummation. The Prophet, who in his great humility abased himself before the Messiah, foretold this when he said, "I indeed baptize you with water, but one mightier than I cometh. . . . He shall baptize you with the Holy Ghost and with fire." (Luke iii, 16.)

The whole destiny of the Baptist, that glorious but humble messenger of the Most High, has been summed up by St. John the Evangelist in his four brief verses:

"There was a man sent from God whose name was John."

"The same came for a witness, to bear witness of the Light, that all men through him might believe."

"He was not that Light, but was sent to bear witness of that Light."

"That was the true Light which lighteth every man that cometh into the world." (John i, 6-9.)

John Baptizes Jesus

The Four Evangelists who unite in making his baptism by John the beginning of Christ's public ministry have given us a converging picture of the event. Among the crowd pressing round to hear the prophet is a man to whom nobody pays any attention. There is indeed nothing to distinguish him. His figure and face are nothing out of the ordinary; he is neither a priest, nor an aristocrat of the Sanhedrin, not even a Levite, but just a plain Jew, not one of the learned or the powerful ones. He wears, in accordance with the law, a linen tunic with long sleeves and a woollen cloak with tassels. On his head would be the "couffieh" with flaps, such as is still worn among the people of Palestine. He was just one, among a crowd.

His very name was commonplace, Jeshuah; one of those old vocables derived from the sacred synonym for the name of God, and much in favor among Jews since the return from exile. There were any number of Jeshuahs about at the time:

Josephus mentions a dozen or more. They included priests, leading citizens, simple peasants and outlaws. Perhaps there was, around the ear of this man, the symbolic shaving which denoted a carpenter and joiner, just as the dyers wore a colored rag and the scribes a pen. His tongue would proclaim him a Galilean. He would not, however, be the only carpenter among those listening to the Baptist, for there were a great many of them in Judea, and he would certainly not be among the first arrivals for it was a good four or five days journey on foot from distant Galilee to the ford of Bethabara.

Yet when Jesus approached him, the Baptist seemed to know instinctively that this purifying rite which he had imposed upon so many men was not applicable to this one. So he drew back and challenged him. "I have need to be baptized of thee, and comest thou to me?" Jesus replied: "Suffer it to be so now, for thus it becometh us to fulfill all righteousness." (Matt. iii, 14-15.) Thus, from the very first moment when he appears before us, Christ is, as always throughout his life, indifferent to worldly fame and to everything that would bring it to him, following in divine certitude the pattern known to him alone.

John will tell the story of the event later on. He carried out the baptism of Jesus. And then he saw the Holy Ghost descending from heaven in the form of a dove which came to rest upon the man who had just come out of the water. He knew that this was a sign that what God had once told him was now come to pass: he who baptized with water realized that he who was to baptize with the Holy Ghost had now appeared. It was a glorious and miraculous moment. The heavens opened and a voice from on high was heard to say, "This is my beloved son, in whom I am well pleased."

This great scene has always been commemorated by the Christian church, and religious art has given us many versions of it. Paintings in the catacombs, primitive statuary, liturgical books, stained glass and mosaics have all contributed to the theophany of Bethabara, that pledge of the eternal promise of pardon. It is a striking fact that ancient tradition has always represented this event in the plainest and most realistic fashion without decoration and embroidery. The great scenes of the Christian story are told with extreme simplicity and the revelation of the Messiah to the Baptist is one which needs no adornment. In the celebrated thirteenth century Psalter of Ingeborg of Denmark, which is marvelously embellished with gold and jewel-like colors, the artist has refrained from the use of these in depicting this particular scene and has thus made it one of the most moving of all evocations of the mystery of Bethabara. Jesus is meditating in the water which laps him up to the middle of his body; John officiates with a solemn gesture. Angels lean downward from heaven, while, symbolical of all creation stupefied by this wonder, the genius of the river, concealed by the waves, is shown in manifest astonishment. The scene demands this purity and transparency in its representation. It is recaptured again in the stained glass at Chartres and even Jean Colombe, the artist of the elaborate miniature, in the *Très Riches Heures du duc de Berry,* for all his delicate fluency, knew how to recover this contemplative strength.

Nothing however could be farther from reality than the huge conventional picture which Corot painted for the church of St. Nicolas du Chardonnet and which has had so many imitators. It is merely an occasion for the display of graceful nudities.

The Baptism of Christ is the occasion when the Divine was made manifest in a human form, like any other human form. All the rest is fancy work. The pious imagination of many of the ancient communities produced various unimportant accretions; we read, for instance, in the Apocryphal gospel of the Ebionites, how at the sound of the divine voice a great light appeared and the whole landscape was illuminated by it. Justin speaks of fire spurting up from the water, and another Apocryphal recital, the Acts of Thomas, transcribes an entire hymn which the angelic choir is said to have sung as Jesus went into the water: "O, Holy Ghost, descend. O, holy dove, descend. Descend, divine Mother." (Mother, because in Aramaic, *rouah,* spirit, is feminine.) These details in fact add nothing.

There are however certain questions raised by the accounts of the Baptism which are not without interest. Did John and Jesus know each other before they met on the banks of the Jordan? Could the scene have been concocted between them, in order to fire the imagination of the crowd? The Gospel of St. John, which states that John did not know Jesus (i, 33) is at variance with that of St. Matthew (iii, 13). If the families of the two men were connected, as would seem from the account of Mary's visit to her cousin Elizabeth, an earlier meeting between them would not seem unlikely, although one had grown up in Judea and the other in Galilee. It has sometimes been supposed that John and Jesus belonged to the same sect and that the baptism took place by a premeditated understanding, but this is only one of the gratuitous assumptions in which matters of this kind abound. If we keep to the text there are exactly two alternatives: either John did not know Jesus and it was the prophetic gift which enabled him to recognize at first sight the Messiah in the man before him; or he did know Jesus but had not recognized his supernatural quality until that instant of revelation when they met by the river. The theory of some sort of publicity campaign by which the older prophet was to launch the younger is a completely unwarranted suggestion.

More substantial is the question which the great heretic Mani, who founded the sect known as Manichaeism, raised in the third century A.D. "Could Christ sin since he accepted John's baptism?" This question in some measure arises from the astonishment of John the Baptist and his hesitation at baptizing the representative of God. The Apocryphal Gospel of the Hebrews puts this question plainly in the very mouth of Jesus. "The mother and brothers of the Lord said to him: 'John baptizes for the remission of sins. Let us also go and receive his baptism.' But he said to them, 'What sin have I committed that I should go to be baptized by him? At least for aught I know.' " If the baptism of John was a baptism of penitence, the very fact of receiving it was an admission of sin. But this is an unsupportable contention regarding one who could legitimately say: "Which of you convinceth me of sin?" (John viii, 46.) St. Ignatius the Martyr explains this by stating that Jesus desired to sanctify the water of baptism, to give it its sacramental quality. St. Thomas Aquinas also supported this view. But in truth this submission by the God who was made man to the rite instituted for sinners has a deep significance: it exemplifies sharply that trait in his personality which was to be manifest throughout his life on earth. As a man and the example to all men, he would suffer humiliation, however great it might be, in order to give a lesson; he would take upon himself the burden of the Law, so entirely inapplicable to him. He was to accept in its entirety the human condition and nothing in the whole body of Christian teaching is more fundamental than this.

One rather more subtle question arises from this. The Ebionite heretics held that, up till the time of his baptism, Christ had been a sinner as all men are, but, from the moment the dove descended, God entered into him for ever. The Ebionites considered therefore that the baptismal rite marked some profound transformation in the very being of Jesus. In their Apocryphal Gospel the voice from on high does not say, "This is my beloved son in whom I am well pleased," but: "Thou art my beloved son, this day I have begotten thee." This is the usual basis of the Gnostic theories; the "adoptionists" affirmed that "Jesus was a man like all other men but at the time of his baptism the Christ in the form of a dove descended and was implanted in him." The baptism is therefore very much more than a rite accomplished for exemplary reasons; it is the occasion when God invested the man Jesus with his Messianic mission and when he himself became conscious of his vocation. The least one can say is that these heretical theories contradict many passages of the Gospel story, in particular St. Luke's account of the birth of Christ.

In the act of baptizing Jesus, however, John had not altogether accomplished everything that he was charged to do. The day after, we are told in the fourth Gospel, the prophet, seeing Jesus approach, cried out, "Behold the lamb of God which taketh away the sins of the world." (i, 29.) The word "lamb" would immediately evoke, in the mind of every Jew, the image of the expiatory victim, the humble creature who, from the time of Moses and the exile in Egypt, had redeemed Israel by its blood.

Doubtless, too, many of the listeners, hearing those words, would recall the prophecy of Isaiah (liii, 7): "He was oppressed and he was afflicted, yet he opened not his mouth: he is brought as a lamb to the slaughter and as a sheep before her shearers is dumb, so he openeth not his mouth"—the words in which the great visionary foretold the Messiah of sorrows, he who was to redeem the world by the sacrifice of himself.

So, even while he predicted the glory of God descending upon a man, John the Forerunner had in his mind that other image of the Messiah, which Israel mostly preferred to forget. The two themes begin to be woven together by the unfathomable mystery of the ford of Bethabara; from this time on there can be no disassociation between the son of God, shewn forth by his father, and the victim destined for the redemption by blood.

CHAPTER TWO

THE VIRGIN MOTHER AND THE DIVINE CHILD

The Birth of God the Son

A HOST OF MEMORIES crowds in upon our consciousness when we recall the Gospel story about the earthly origins of Jesus. The humble parents taking shelter on their journey in a cave where the animals were tethered; the young mother who herself wrapped her child in swaddling clothes and put it down to sleep; the Divine Child lying in the straw of the manger, warmed by the breath of the ox and the ass: there is no man in the Western world who does not bear these pictures in that deep secret zone of memory wherein a whole realm of tender and enchanted images persists in spite of all the inroads of skepticism. Every one of us has dreamed sometime of that luminous star-studded night when the angel choir sang the glory of God and promised peace to all men of goodwill; the shepherds and the kings are among our most familiar memories; the poorest little Christian Crèche revives the heart of our childhood.

Of all the great liturgical feasts, none is so popular as Christmas, which is unique in its power of bringing together in its gaiety those for whom it commemorates the birth of Christ and those to whom it signifies nothing at all. The most hardened unbeliever celebrates it with turkey and plum pudding; the most frivolous all-night dancers bear witness in their fashion.

No single subject has inspired more of the great masterpieces of art than that of the young mother holding her child up before the world because he is God, holding him in her arms because he is her little one, protecting him with all the strength of her human love. Italian, Flemish, German, Spanish, every school of painting abounds in Annunciations, Nativities, Adorations and Flights into Egypt; the variations played on these unchanging themes are astonishing. From the Master of Moulins to Luini, the representation of the manger has borrowed every kind of landscape and setting. The simplicity of the primitive artists, knowing nothing of local color or historical accuracy, has led us to envisage the scene in the surroundings most familiar to ourselves, thus weaving it into the very blood and marrow of our being. Sometimes the artist's creative power has been strong enough to impose its own setting upon us, so that it is hard to visualize the cruel truth of the flight into Egypt across one of the most frightful deserts in the world, because Fra Angelico set it in Tuscany, in a landscape of soft golden-yellow, full of light and tall cypress trees.

The documents on which we depend for our knowledge of the birth do not in fact tell us very much. Neither St. Mark nor St. John mentions the Nativity in their Gospels, neither does St. Paul in his epistles. Only St. Matthew and St. Luke include it in their preliminary chapters, rather by way of an introduction to the book. Even they do not report the essential episodes in exactly the same way, and it is generally agreed nowadays that these parts of the two Gospels did not form part of the originally assembled teaching but were added afterward by the two editors according to their individual information, rather as a personal guarantee.

Fr. Lagrange has observed that in the case of many oriental sovereigns who were subsequently deified and regarded as saviors it was found necessary to ascribe miraculous circumstances to their births. In the year 238 B.C., the anniversary of

Ptolemy was declared a great feast day and as foretelling great happiness to mankind. About the first century B.C., the feast of Antiochus of Commagene was similarly observed in Asia Minor and in the year 9 of our own era, one of the Asiatic proconsuls suggested that the birthday of the "divine" Caesar Augustus should begin the official year, since it had ushered in an era of achievements for the regeneration of humanity. The Evangelists, in claiming the title of savior for a child so humble and of so little account that he was born in a stable, flouted the false glories of the materialistic world. The earliest Christians were able to go straight to the essential truth, to the apostles' witness of Christ as it is enshrined in the main Gospel texts; but as the veneration of Jesus increased, the circumstances surrounding his birth would necessarily excite more curiosity and it might have struck the Evangelists as advisable to set down these circumstances, so remarkable in their own way in contrast to the legends of the pseudo-saviors, the deified potentates of Egypt and the East.

However this may be the most ancient manuscripts of the Gospels of St. Matthew and St. Luke include these chapters, with much the same content as we have them today. In the second and third centuries, they were referred to equally by Fathers of the Church, like Justin and Ireneus, heretical disputants like Cerinthius and Carpocrates, and also the pagan apologist Celsus. They are in the same idiom as the rest of the Gospels, forming a homogeneous whole. They are clearly written in conviction of their truth. While Livy gives us to understand that he hardly takes the story of Romulus and Remus seriously and Herodotus cuts out from the story of the origins of Cyrus the bitch which was supposed to have suckled him, St. Matthew and St. Mark are obviously writing of things in which they believe.

Where did they get their information? Surely from the people among whom Jesus lived. In two places St. Luke says that Mary "kept all these things and pondered them in her heart" (Luke ii, 19:51) as if he were indicating thus one of the best of all sources. Possibly the two Evangelists made separate enquiries among the family and friends of Jesus, which would explain the slight difference in their accounts. In any case a comparison of the Gospel stories with the Apocryphal accounts is sufficient to establish that the former could not be derived from the collective imaginations of the credulous, that popular folk lore which so easily declines into the absurd. On the one hand we have, even when dealing with the miraculous, restraint and moderation; on the other, ridiculous exaggerations sometimes verging on indecency. We need not shut our eyes to the possibility that an element of poetry and conscious didacticism may have crept into these accounts of the Divine childhood—rather as they have in old French epics, such as those of the childhood of Tristan—but substantially they may be regarded as historical and in any case far removed from the pious anecdotes with which later hagiographers have embellished the origins of the saints whose lives they were writing.

The Road to Bethlehem

About thirty years before John the Baptist appeared on the banks of the Jordan, there had been an official census in Palestine. The Jews disliked these statistical formalities in which man, that unique reality, was numbered by hundreds and thousands like cattle. Moses himself had difficulty in numbering the tribes but Rome insisted throughout her provinces that every inhabitant should be inscribed on the official register with his name, rank and profession. This was to facilitate the collection of taxes and the drafting of available manpower in times of war. It is probable that this obligation was imposed on the little Jewish kingdom within the Roman orbit, or at least that Herod, always zealous to please his protectors, had taken it upon himself to extend it to his country.

There was a particular complication involved in the census of Palestine; the inhabitants were not registered in the places where they happened to live but in the places from where the families to which they belonged originally came. These family traditions had always been strong in Israel and had become more so since the teaching of Ezra about the necessity of retaining the purity of the Jewish race and against intermarriage with foreigners. Even today the humblest Oriental prides himself upon knowing his ancestors: it is possible to meet in New York descendants of Maronite emigrants who after three or four generations can still tell you which village they came from and the Arab is as conscious of the origin of his ancestral clan as was Mohammed of his forefathers.

There was nothing exceptional in taking a census by the place of origin: in 103 A.D. the prefect of Egypt, Gaius Vibias Maximus, ordered all those who were not living in the country whence their families originated to go back there for registration; the papyrus recording this order may be seen in London. Probably these migrations, this coming and going over long distances, would seem less onerous to a people of nomadic orgin like the Hebrews than they would to the Egyptians, a stay-at-home people like the French today.

And so: "There went out a decree from Caesar Augustus that all the world should be taxed. . . . And all went to be taxed, every man to his own city. And Joseph also went up from Galilee, out of the city of Nazareth into Judea, unto the city of David which is called Bethlehem; (because he was of the house and lineage of David) to be taxed with Mary his espoused wife, being great with child." (Luke ii, 1-5)

What do we know of this couple who set out on the road to obey the order of Caesar? That they were united by the sacred tie of marriage and, moreover, by affection, for it was not essential that the young wife in her condition should have accompanied her husband since only males were required to present themselves for registration. They were poor people of the working class, richer in courage than in money and docile and resigned as the humble generally are toward the powers that be. When their child was born they could afford only a pair of turtle doves for the customary offering to the Temple; the price of a lamb was beyond their means.

He was an artisan, presumably a carpenter from the references in Matthew (xiii, 55) and Luke (iv, 22), one of those craftsmen and husbandmen who formed the bulk of the population of Palestine, and whose piety, industry and discipline had permitted the Jewish community on its return from exile to establish themselves once more in the land of their forefathers. He was called Joseph, that ancient Jewish name which was borne by the famous son of Jacob whose glory in Egypt was written in the Book. The Gospels leave him in silence and obscurity; we guess him, rather than see him, as a man of mature age whom the experience of life has taught wisdom and tolerance.

She, his wife, would certainly be much younger than he, for it was customary to marry girls very early, though men rarely married before twenty-five, frequently later. A little Jewess of fourteen would be as well developed as a mature woman. She was called Mary, a name as common in Palestine then as in any of our parishes today. The name may have originated during the exile in Egypt; it was borne by the sister of Moses (Mirya, Miriam or Mariam) and its significance was something like "the beloved of the Lord" or more simply "good lady." As she walks on the road to Bethlehem we see a good little wife, modest, well trained and virtuous, obedient to her husband and looking like those young mothers whom we can still see today in the Holy Land with a baby astride shoulder or hip.

Though they were both so humble, it need not surprise us that they belonged to the royal family of Israel. There were innumerable descendants of the populous harems of David and Solomon and not all of them were rich or in high places. At the time of the Maccabees the too numerous descendants of the house of David had prevented the heroic brothers from seizing the crown. Very much later, in A.D. 81-96, the Emperor Domitian, hearing the prophecy that one descended from David would overthrow kingdoms and powers, caused a search to be made for the last representatives of the royal lines of Israel; but the two poor countrymen (grandsons of Jude the Apostle) who were brought to him seemed so humble and inoffensive that the Emperor spared their lives and sent them back to their fields.

It would seem that both Joseph and Mary were of the line of David. In the case of Joseph it is expressly stated in the Gospels, by St. Matthew (i, 1-17) at the beginning of his book, by St. Luke, when he comes to the account of the public ministry of Jesus (iii, 23-28) where it was important, because it was known that the Messiah would be born of the race of the great King, a branch of the tree of Jesse, as Isaiah had said. There are unimportant discrepancies between the two Gospel pedigrees, obvious simplifications induced by the desire to accommodate all the generations in groups of fourteen names—fourteen being the figure which corresponded to the letters of the name David.

For two hundred years Christians have been propounding ingenious explanations of these divergences but without going into complex detail we may doubt whether either of the Evangelists went into the genealogy with that precision which modern historical methods require. Their aim was not to establish but to expound, and it is quite simple to point out the errors and the gaps. It goes without saying that when St. Matthew groups the list of the forebears of Christ in three series of fourteen names he omits a good many links in the chain.

Between Joram and Ozias, for instance, three kings are omitted, and the same between Josias and Jechonias. Joachim is omitted altogether and between Phares, born in Canaan before the sons of Jacob went to Egypt, and Naason, chief of the tribes of Judah at the time of the Exodus, we are given only three generations to span three hundred years. From Zorobabel to Jacob, the father of Joseph, St. Matthew gives eight descendants while St. Luke gives seventeen.

The two genealogies follow two distinct plans: the one traces the descent from Abraham to Jesus, the other traces the line from Jesus to Adam "which was the son of God." St. Matthew sought to prove to the Jews that Jesus fulfilled the promises made to Abraham and to David. St. Luke, writing for converted pagans, was concerned to show that Christ came to save the whole posterity of Adam.

From Abraham to David the two lists are identical, but from David to St. Joseph the only names common to both are those of Salathiel and Zorobabel. Various attempts have been made to identify these personages and to account for the divergences. Here are the three principal lines of argument.

1. Among the Jews women did not figure in genealogies and transmitted no rights of blood descent. It will be remembered that a famous Jewish custom (Deuteronomy xxv, 5) laid down that if a married man died without issue, his brother should take the widow to wife and raise up children to his brother. The children thus had two fathers, one legal and one natural. A third-century writer, Julius the African, declared that the two tables referred to the legal and natural descent of Joseph.

2. Another theory is that St. Matthew gave the descent through the official heirs to the throne of David, in order to show the royal descent of Christ, while St. Luke gave the immediate direct ancestors.

This is as if, say, in trying to prove the claim of the Comte de Chambord to the French throne in 1873, two genealogists had traced his descent, the one through the series of reigning monarchs, going through the Valois (extinct after Henri III) and then the Bourbons from Henri IV, and the other following the actual father to son chain of the branch of the Bourbon family which began with Robert de Clermont, sixth son of St. Louis.

3. The simplest assumption is that St. Matthew gave the descent through Joseph and St. Luke that through Mary. The words of St. Luke (iii, 23), "Jesus being (as was supposed) the son of Joseph who was the son of Heli," could be held to mean that Jesus passed as the son of Joseph but in fact was not. The Christian tradition has always given Joachim as the name of Mary's father, and not Heli, but the Talmud gives the name of Heli to Mary's father. On the other hand, Heli is a diminutive of Eliacin which seems to have been another form of

Joachim as is proved by the book of Judith where the High Priest is called indifferently by both names.[1]

The relation of Mary to the royal house of David is traditional. St. Paul seems to confirm it (Romans i, 3). The Fathers of the Church since the second century have confirmed it and it certainly has the authority of Jewish custom behind it, for marriages within the same family group, often for legal reasons, were common. It is not, however, possible to establish the chain of descent between the mother of Jesus and David.

And so the two, Joseph and Mary, set out for Bethlehem, the town which the Sacred Writings had designated as the birthplace of the great King. The Book of Samuel mentions it directly (I Samuel xx, 6 and 28). A thousand years earlier Ruth the Moabite, seeking sustenance in a strange land, had won the heart of Boaz, in whose field she was gleaning, and from Obed, the son of that union, had sprung the "Tree of Jesse," that mighty trunk that the medieval scuptors loved to illustrate, the tree whose finest flower was David (Ruth iv, 18-22).

It was a long way from Nazareth to Bethlehem—about ninety miles. The roads, which the Romans had not had time to remake, were indifferent, and at the pace of an ass, which would be all that poor people could afford, the journey would take four full days. Traveling across the plain of Esdraelon, still associated with the warlike renown of Deborah the prophetess, they would turn toward the south where place after place would recall some personage in the long history of Israel; Shunem, where Elisha performed miracles; Jezreel, where idolatrous queen Jezebel wrought her abomination; Gilboa, where Saul and Jonathan died in battle. Then they would cross the land of Samaria, not without sadness, for what had been the Holy Land of Gerizim containing Joseph's tomb and Jacob's well was now given over to infidelity and schism. Now at last they were in the harsh and bitter land of Judah, Shiloh and Bethel. The earliest holy places of the patriarchs were nothing

[1] A full and close account of this vexed question of the genealogies can be found in Canon Auzet's annotated edition of the Gospels, published by Desclée. The present writer has drawn upon this for his summary.

now but names, but as the gorge opened out and the city of Jerusalem appeared, a white profile on the long gray mass which supported it, hedged around with walls and towers, every Jewish heart would swell with emotion, and, raising his eyes to seek out the Temple, the Temple which Herod had managed to rebuild, every son of Israel would murmur the age-old thanksgiving of his fathers.

It was a wonderful journey for a pious pilgrim but a very rough one for a pregnant woman, jogging up and down for four or five days on the back of a donkey. It is quite understandable that Apocryphal legends should declare that Mary was miraculously spared the discomforts ordinarily associated with her state. After two hours journey from the Holy City, passing the tomb of Rachel the desolate, they would reach Bethlehem.

After so many barren and desolate places, where only a few clumps of purple anemones or cyclamen showed life and color among the scrub, it must have been comforting to see the little white town perched on its twin hills. Beyond it, the land descended, a pitted gray expanse like boiling lead suddenly frozen in the bubbling state, plunging down toward the Dead Sea. But surrounding the town were orchards, blooming fields and olive groves. Beth-Lehem "the house of bread," also called *Ephratah*, "rich in fruit," well merited its names. Today it is a city of nine thousand souls, its round roofs clustering as close as grapes in a bunch, its tortuous crowded streets typical of any oriental city, unique only in that it is almost entirely Christian. The women wear a curious headgear, dating perhaps from the Frankish conquests, and pure white silk shawls. It was doubtless a much smaller place in the time of Christ but it was not insignificant and it would be very much alive to the glories of its past. For it was of Bethlehem that the prophet Micah had said, "But thou, Beth-lehem Ephratah, though thou be little among the thousands of Judah, yet out of thee shall he come forth unto me that is to be ruler in Israel, whose goings forth have been from of old, from everlasting" (Micah v, 2). Joseph and Mary, descended from David, would remember this prophecy for they knew that the child which Mary bore was the pledge of a miracle. So great would be the hope in their hearts that it might well seem that it was for this that Caesar all unknowing had signed his decree, and mobilized his army of functionaries, for the ways of God are obscure to men and the mightiest are but instruments in his hands.

The Virgin Mother

It had happened the previous year in the village of Nazareth, hidden among the hills of far-off Galilee, from which the travelers had set out. At the time Mary was only betrothed to Joseph. An angel had appeared to her and had said, "Hail, thou that are highly favored, the Lord is with thee. Blessed art thou among women." When she saw him she had been troubled; what could such a salutation mean? "Fear not, Mary," said the angel, "for thou hast found grace with God. And behold, thou shalt conceive in thy womb and bring forth a son and shalt call his name Jesus. He shall be great and shall be called the Son of the Highest: and the Lord God shall give unto him the throne of his father David. And he shall reign over the house of Jacob for ever." "How shall this be," asked Mary, "seeing I know not a man?" The angel replied, "The Holy Ghost shall come upon thee, and the power of the Highest shall overshadow thee; therefore also that holy thing which shall be born of thee shall be called the Son of God." (Luke i, 29-35.)

This famous scene has inspired so much great art that whoever seeks to visualize it is at the mercy of the thousands of pictures which rise up before the eye of the mind. It may be that beautiful Florentine garden where the angel kneels between the ordered cypresses and the bright flowers, a lily in his hands, or one of those interiors of homely simplicity but substantial comfort which the Rhenish masters drew, with the angel in a beautiful crimson mantle and the Virgin in a bright blue Sunday gown. The painters have embroidered the scene to their fancy.

But archaeology indicates nothing so sumptuous. The houses of Nazareth of that day would be hovels not too far removed from cave-dweller style—one room divided into two, half for the family and half for the cattle, or else the little wattle and daub huts, low and square, straggling among the olive trees, such as one can see today anywhere in the Galilean country.

The Church of the Annunciation, which is modern but is believed to occupy the site of the church which Saint Macarius erected at the order of Constantine, includes a tiny crypt beneath its high altar; tradition has it that this is the chamber where the Archangel Gabriel appeared to Mary, and an Apocryphal account of the Nativity adds that she was spinning wool for the use of the Temple. The Greek Church, relying on other noncanonical texts, has placed the scene by that inexhaustible well which lies at the edge of the road to Tiberias, where the women of Nazareth can still be seen today, balancing upon their heads those jars of black clay tinged with blue, on the side when they are empty, upright when they are full. The place is called to this day, "The well of Mary"—*Ain Sitti Mariam.*

The words of the angel must have overwhelmed the humble maiden to whom they were addressed but not because she could not understand them. Although a girl of barely fifteen, she would share in the hope for the Messiah common to the whole of the Jewish community, and as a descendant of the house of David she could realize the possibility that through her the sacred Tree of Jesse might propagate its supreme branch. Moreover the angelic promise was couched in exactly the terms that she would recognize; it did not refer to the suffering Messiah, the holy victim. That prophecy was to come later when the child was presented in the Temple. The angel said only that God would give her son the throne of David and eternal dominion over the house of Jacob. She asked only one simple, natural question, which perhaps revealed her secret desire to remain a virgin. Then she accepted her destiny, putting herself body and soul, her honor and her worldly prospects, into the hands of God.

But although the mystery announced by the angel was of the supernatural order, upon the very humble human plane it was going to raise a problem. Mary was affianced to Joseph and that was sufficient to establish a contract between them which our own betrothal custom does not approach. Among us, according to both canon and civil law, only the ceremony of marriage is absolute and binding; a broken engagement is not considered damaging unless the circumstances are scandalous. But among the Jews a betrothal was almost as irrevocable as marriage and conferred most of the privileges of marriage except that of actual cohabitation. For the period of a year, in the case of a virgin, or a month, in the case of a widow, the fiancée was placed under the jurisdiction of her betrothed husband, and although conjugal relations were in theory forbidden, the Talmud makes it quite clear that they were fairly frequent. The man could take possession of his future wife while she was still in her father's house and children born in those circumstances were legitimate. It follows that fidelity was a strict obligation during their pre-nuptial period, unfaithfulness was equivalent to adultery and if denounced by the betrothed husband, it carried for the woman the penalty laid down by Deuteronomy (xxii, 23): death.

When Mary had conceived "before they came together," "Joseph, her husband, being a just man and not willing to make her a publick example, was minded to put her away privily. But while he thought on these things, behold, the angel of the Lord appeared unto him in a dream saying, Joseph, thou son of David, fear not to take unto thee Mary thy wife, for that which is conceived in her is of the Holy Ghost." (Matthew I, 18-20.) Just as Mary accepted the words of the angel, Joseph accepted the revelation of the dream. They reverted at once to that supernatural world of the Old Testament in which contact with the divine power was common and its revelations came naturally to men who were humble and obedient. The character of this man who, out of the goodness of his heart, could not denounce his little betrothed in spite of the overwhelming weight of appearances, who humbly accepted the difficult part which God laid upon him, has a dignity which rises above the easy jokes of which he is so often the subject. "The noble figure of St. Joseph," says Claudel, "whose very name brings a smile to the lips of superior persons."

A little while afterward another sign confirmed the miracle which the young virgin was to bring forth. The angel spoke again, as a pledge of what had been promised. "Behold thy cousin Elizabeth, she hath also conceived a son in her old age: and this is the sixth month with her, that was called barren." In order to ascertain for herself a fact which concerned her so closely, Mary made the long journey to Judea and came to the house of Zacharias, to congratulate Elizabeth. "And it came to pass that when Elizabeth heard the salutation of Mary, the babe leaped in her womb and Elizabeth was filled with the Holy Ghost. And she spake out with a loud voice and said Blessed art thou among women and blessed is the fruit of thy womb. And whence is this to me, that the mother of my Lord should come to me. For, lo, as soon as the voice of thy salutation sounded in mine ear, the babe leaped in my womb for joy. And blessed is she that believed: for there shall be a performance of those things which were told her from the Lord." (Luke i, 40-45.)

Immediately the spirit of prophecy descended upon the young visitor also and she burst forth into a great hymn of praise to glorify God. Hymns like this were in the true tradition of Jewish prophecy; they followed a set rhythm of contrasting images and abounded with quotations from the sacred texts. Such was the hymn improvised by Hannah, the mother of Samuel. But the crown of them all is the Magnificat, that great hymn which expresses, from the depths of a profound humility, Mary's pride in the divine election.

"My soul doth magnify the Lord, and my spirit hath rejoiced in God my Savior.

For he hath regarded the low estate of his handmaiden: for, behold, from henceforth all generations shall call me blessed.

For he that is mighty hath done to me great things; and holy is his name.

And his mercy is on them that fear him from generation to generation.

He hath shewed strength with his arm; he hath scattered the proud in the imagination of their hearts.

He hath put down the mighty from their seats, and exalted them of low degree.

He hath filled the hungry with good things; and the rich he hath sent empty away.

He hath holpen his servant Israel, in remembrance of his mercy.

As he spake to our fathers, to Abraham, and to his seed for ever."

So, on the threshold of the Gospel, we encounter the moving figure of Mary, in whom Christians reverence the double ideal of that supernatural purity for which even the most depraved retain a secret longing, and of that illimitable, all-embracing tenderness which motherhood according to the flesh reserves for the children born of its flesh. The image of the Virgin Mary is at the heart of Western society, a presence so familiar that it would be impossible to measure how many things would be different, were that presence effaced. So many names, of women, girls and flowers, days in the calendar, places dedicated to her; customs, landscape, language and literature, all bear her sign. The art of the Western world has for centuries made itself her witness. St. Bernard of Clairvaux, physically so frail, drew from his love for her the strength required for his astonishing achievement. The soldiers of Godfrey of Bouillon relieved Jerusalem to the chant of the *Salve Regina.* Father de Foucauld, who brought peace to the Hoggar in Algeria, thousands of missionaries devoting their lives to the relief of suffering and the salvation of souls, have carried as their only consolation her image in their hearts. Her witnesses also are the great cathedrals, Amiens, Chartres, Rheims, Florence and Cologne, as well as the crowds that throng on pilgrimage to Lourdes or Fatima. The most tender of Christian traditions is this love for the humble young maiden who was the instrument of the will of the Most High. By it each one of us seeks to find our way back, through the most intense of our sufferings, to that secret, unattainable but never abandoned desire, the pure heart of our childhood.

It is natural that legend should proliferate around such a figure. As far back as the most ancient Apocryphal texts, pious fables were already embellishing a story whose nobility needed no elaboration. These legends, however, have a certain historical interest since so much art and literature has drawn upon them. The names of her parents, Joachim and Anne, are barely historical. Anne is said to have been married three times, her three daughters being the three Marys whom one finds near to Jesus, the daughter of Joachim, the daughter of Cleophas, and Mary Salome. The birth of the Virgin must also be made miraculous; some said that she was conceived as her mother smelt the perfume of a rose: others say that when Joachim met Anne by the Golden Gate of the Temple, God whispered that he should embrace her and from this kiss, Mary was born. An exquisite fresco in the church of St. Maria Novella in Florence illustrates this legend. When we come to the marriage of Mary and Joseph, the legends exceed themselves in the miraculous. The High Priest called all the men of the tribe of Judah together in the Temple, each man to bring a small stick. These sticks, after being deposited in the Holy of Holies, were to be returned to their bearers, a dove would fly out from the staff belonging to the man appointed by God. But the dove did not appear. Then an angel came to inform the High Priest that he had forgotten one of the sticks. It was the one brought by Joseph and as soon as it was handed back to him, the dove flew out.

Some of the other details given by the legend-mongers are less poetic. The virginity of the Mother of Jesus seemed such a prodigious miracle that it had to be abundantly demonstrated. Mary was submitted to the ordeal of the bitter water; she had to perambulate seven times around the altar; midwives were called in to testify to this miraculous anomaly. They can be seen in the stained glass windows at Laon, Le Mans and elsewhere. We are even told in the Protogospel of St. James that a certain midwife called Salome asked for a sign—as did Thomas later on in entirely different circumstances—and saw her hand wither in front of her eyes. Considering the doubtful taste of many of these anecdotes, we can say, with St. Jerome, *Deliramenta Apocryphorum.*

Secular criticism of our own time, rejecting the story of the Virgin Birth, has proposed a number of explanations. It is pointed out that miraculous births are common in oriental and hellenistic legend. The mother of the God Attis became pregnant through eating a pomegranate. Miraculous births were attributed to Pythagoras, Plato and Augustus Caesar. There is the well known legend of the birth of Perseus from the virgin Danae, who was visited by Zeus in the form of a shower of gold. It has also been put forward that the story arose among the primitive Christian communities to show that the prophecy of Isaiah, "Behold, a virgin shall conceive and bear a son," (vii, 14) had been fulfilled, a prophecy which is in fact referred to by St. Matthew (i, 21). In this connection it has been pointed out that the Greek of the Septuagint uses the word *parthenos,* a virgin, where the corresponding Hebrew text uses *almah,* which has a much wider application signifying merely a "female creature."

The Catholic critic replies to all this that similar analogies with other histories or religions could be applied with equal logic to the life of almost any historical personage. It would be possible with this method to demonstrate that the life of Napoleon was a type of solar myth. Only wishful thinking can in fact unite the stories of the metamorphosis of Zeus into a bull, a swan or a shower of gold with the unvarnished recital of St. Luke. The idea of the incarnation of a pre-existing God is not found in the whole mythology of antiquity. In any case it is most unlikely that the Judeo-Christian communities, so bitterly hostile to the penetration of foreign ideas, would have copied idolatrous fables. The argument concerning the interpretation of Isaiah is no less specious. To begin with, the exact significance of the Hebrew word *almah* is disputable, and although it is a fact that the narrators of the Gospels loved to cite ancient prophecies to support their accounts it does not follow that the accounts themselves were fabricated to show that the prophecies had been fulfilled. The discussion could go on indefinitely without proving anything. The subject is by its nature refractory to the methods of controversy. St. Thomas Aquinas, speaking of the miraculous birth of Christ and similar things has said that miracles were not *signs* of faith but *objects* of faith. (Summa Theologica, III, p. 9, 29. Art. 1 and 2.)

The promised birth must have been an object of faith to Mary also, since she accepted the message of the angel with such perfect simplicity. "Behold the handmaid of the Lord! be it done unto me according to thy word." (Luke i, 37.) "Here is the solid foundation of the devotion which the Church has always had to the Holy Virgin," wrote Bossuet. The incarnation of God required human acceptance. If man was to be saved something more than external intervention—even the intervention of God—was necessary. The effort and the consent of man was also required. Yet nothing can happen that is not the will of the Most High. This is the meaning of the prophecy that the name of the Virgin's son shall be Immanuel (Isaiah vii, 14) and of the Angel's instruction to Mary to call her child Jesus (Matthew i, 21). For *Immanuel* signifies "El (Elohim) is with us," and *Jeshouah* "Jehovah is our aid." One read with the other had an obvious significance: the miraculous birth was the promise to the world of its Savior.

The Nativity

At the entrance of the town of Bethlehem there was, for the reception of visitors, a large building which St. Luke has called an inn. Perhaps it was that same "khan of Canaan" which the Gileadite, the son of a friend of David, had built for his flocks some ten centuries before. This type of caravanserai, which is still to be found in oriental countries, is very far from comfortable: there is a square enclosure, open to the sky, for the cattle, and a wooden porch which offers indifferent shelter for human beings, together with a very few rooms to rent, extremely small and excessively dear for their quality. Even this "hotel," most of it exposed to the four winds of heaven, would have been welcome to the weary pair of travelers if there had been room among the crowd for them. But it was packed full of those nomads who came regularly to Bethlehem to buy their grain and to sell their woven cloth and their cheeses, as they still do today, and there would be, in addition, all those who had to come to Bethlehem for the census. It is easy to visualize the picturesque confusion, wagons piled up, the noisy and smelly crowd of tethered camels straining at each other, braying donkeys, women disputing possession of a corner sheltered from the drafts. Over all this varied assemblage would float that enveloping smell of hot grease which, from Greece to Egypt and from Algiers to Teheran, is invariably exhaled by an oriental crowd. We can well understand that Joseph sought to take Mary away from all this.

There was very little time, for "the days were accomplished that she should be delivered." The most ancient tradition says that Joseph installed his wife in a cave such as was used, and still is used, to shelter sheep and cattle. The hills around Bethlehem are full of them. Justin Martyr, writing at the beginning of the second century and perfectly familiar with the location, definitely makes this statement. There, at least, the young wife would find peace and quiet.

One short verse in the gospel of St. Luke (ii, 7) tells us all that we know definitely about this stupendous, yet simple, event. "And she brought forth her first born son, and wrapped him in swaddling clothes, and laid him in a manger because there was no room for them in the inn."

It is futile to attempt to embroider this plain statement. The words convey the impression that Mary was alone, that no other woman was there to give her any assistance; yet theologians have drawn from them all sorts of conclusions about the miraculous birth and the virginity of Mary in travail. The manger must have been like one of those which can still be seen today; hollows scooped out of the earth to hold the grain for the cattle. That complete humility which was to be the mark of Him who was meek and humble of heart is already manifest from the beginning. The ox and the ass, which we traditionally place on either side of the crèche, came down to us from the Apocryphal Gospel of the Nativity, by a writer who perhaps remembered certain passages of Scripture. "The ox knoweth his owner and the ass his master's crib." (Isaiah i, 3) The tradition which makes the entire created world, symbolized by the two humble beasts of burden, participate in the birth of the Savior has such essential spiritual truth that it has become incorporated in the liturgy.

It could not be said that the Church of the Nativity today has retained that touching simplicity so characteristic of the Gospel scene. It is approached as if it were a fortress. A gigantic encircling wall is breached by a massive tower, pierced only by loopholes and by a low entrance door. A narthex containing some fine mosaics admits to the basilica, one of those fourth or fifth century Byzantine buildings which convey such a powerful impression of majesty. There are five aisles, the piers of red marble with white capitals.

This magnificent edifice, which covers the spot where the divine mercy was made manifest, is the battleground of warring sects. It was even, in 1873, the scene of a physical assault by the supporters of the Orthodox Church on the Catholics. The deep subterranean crypt below the church is long and narrow but it does not in the least resemble one's conception of a manger; it does not communicate with the exterior and can be reached only by a steep stairway. The alcove which is designated as the crèche is studded with gold and precious stones: it is lined with rare marbles, jasper and porphyry, and lit by the radiance of half a hundred lamps. "It was not among gold and silver that Our Savior came into the world," said the harsh old hermit St. Jerome, who lived in a cell near by. In the middle of a slab of porphyry a bright vermilion star purports to mark the exact spot where Jesus was born. Those who do not feel that instinctive piety which from age to age has prompted pilgrims of all races to press their lips to this miserable symbol will experience the rising anger which too many of the Holy Places tend to provoke.

However, the event which took place in the poor grotto was not destined to remain private. Near by were some shepherds spending the night in the fields with their sheep, possibly some of the village herdsmen, who having driven their flocks into the caves, were taking it in turns to see that they came to no harm from wild beasts or robbers. This routine of watching the flocks by night is still followed in Palestine, the cries of the watchers piercing the darkness and the silence, sometimes alternating with the thin melody of a flute. Or perhaps they were genuine nomads who never call in their sheep but restrain them at night by attaching a foot to the long heavy tail characteristic of the Levantine breed.

"And, lo, the angel of the Lord came upon them and the glory of the Lord shone round about them and they were sore afraid. And the angel said unto them, 'Fear not! for, behold, I bring you tidings of great joy, which shall be to all people. For unto you is born this day in the city of David a Savior, which is Christ the Lord. And this shall be a sign unto you; ye shall find the babe wrapped in swaddling clothes, lying in a manger.' And suddenly there was with the angel a multitude of the heavenly host praising God and saying, Glory to God in the highest and on earth peace, goodwill towards men.

"And so it came to pass as the angels were gone away from them into heaven, the shepherds said one to another, 'Let us now go even unto Bethlehem and see this thing which has come to pass, which the Lord hath made known unto us.' And they came with haste and found Mary and Joseph and the babe lying in a manger. And when they had seen it, they made known abroad the saying which was told them concerning this child . . . and the shepherds returned, glorifying and praising God." (Luke, ii, 8-20.)

And so, to the humble guardians of the flocks, heaven revealed what the world as yet did not know, the coming of him who was to be called the Good Shepherd.

The Birthdate of Jesus

Is it possible to assign a precise date in historical time to this supreme event? We may as well admit the fact that this date, from which the whole course of Occidental history is reckoned, is merely a surmise.

We owe the establishment of the date of the birth of Christ as the starting point of our era to a Scythian monk, Dionysius Exigus, who lived in Rome during the sixth century. Studying the famous passage of St. Luke (iii, 1-2) which dates the mission of St. John the Baptist by six contemporary events, Dionysius worked it out as follows. "John began to preach in the fifteenth year of the reign of Tiberius; the ministry of Jesus began a year later. According to St. Luke (iii, 23) Jesus at the time of his baptism was aged about thirty. A simple calculation from these dates brings us to the year 754 of the Roman era, dating from the legendary founding of the city." This figure was adopted. The worthy monk, having no means of calculating the date of the death of Herod or of the census, concluded that these events were earlier than 754 and left it at that.

It is, however, by no means as simple. We have already said that the fifteenth year of the reign of Tiberius should not be dated from the death of Augustus but from the association of Tiberius with the Imperium. Nor can the statement that he was about thirty years of age be held to inform us precisely as to the birthday of Christ, for thirty was the age at which Jews customarily entered public life, and the evangelist may simply have meant by this statement that Jesus had reached legal majority and was no longer a youth. If we reckon that the baptism took place in the year 28, Jesus, if he was "about thirty years of age," must have been born at least two or three years before the year one of the Christian era.

But that is not all, for there are other chronological indications in the Gospels. According to St. Matthew (ii, 1) Jesus was born "in the days of Herod the King," which confirms St. Luke's statement about John the Baptist (i, 5) and the Annunciation (i, 26) and St. Matthew's later accounts of the visit of the Magi (ii, 3) and the Flight into Egypt (ii, 19-22). We know from Josephus that Herod died four years before the beginning of the Christian era; the historian's date is confirmed for us by his story of an eclipse of the moon which occurred just before the death of the tetrarch and which modern astronomers have reckoned as taking place about March twelfth in the year 4 B.C. Since it is known that Herod passed the last months of his life at the baths of Callirhoe, and at Jericho, and that at the time of the visit of the Magi he was still in Jerusalem, their arrival must be placed before 5 B.C., which makes the actual date of Christ's birth probably about six years before the present reckoning of the Christian era.

Another chronological indication is the census which, according to St. Luke (ii, 1-2) made it necessary for Joseph and Mary to go to Bethlehem. This census which the Gospel records as taking place "when Cyrenius was governor of Syria" has provoked a great deal of argument. History knows this "Cyrenius" as Publius Sulpicius Quirinius, a member of the Senate, formerly a Consul, who had served with the African armies and was in fact the Imperial Legate in Syria. He it was who, being deputed to keep an eye on Tiberius, then in more or less voluntary exile in Rhodes, got on so well with the future emperor that they became firm friends. It is this same Quirinius or Cyrenius who caused a scandal by his action against his divorced wife, Emilia Lepida, according to Tacitus. But unfortunately no pagan author mentions the decree "by which the whole world was to be taxed." This, however, is not surprising, for Dion Cassius, the only historian who wrote a detailed life of the Emperor Augustus, is known to us only by a few fragments. Tacitus did not begin his *Annals* until later and neither Suetonius nor Josephus has come down to us complete. The famous inscription of Augustus at Ancyrus (Ankara) mentions three censuses made by the emperor: one in the year 726 (28 B.C.), another in 746 (8 B.C.) and the last in 767 (14 A.D.). It is not known whether these returns were of all the inhabitants of the Roman Empire or only of Roman citizens or whether Quirinius was the governor at the time of the second census (8 B.C.). Only two things about his official career are definitely established: that he was twice Legate in Syria (an inscription in the Lateran Museum proves this) and that one of his terms of office was about the year 6 A.D. We do not know whether this was his first or second term because there is a break in the roll of Imperial Legates in Syria as it has come down to us between the years 4 B.C. and 1 A.D. But 4 B.C. is not 8 B.C., the date given on the Ancyrus tablet, so we must assume some other census which is not recorded, some local enumeration by Quirinius in his own provinces. This sort of thing was common enough in Roman administration which was addicted to detailed records and piled up masses of documents. The Evangelist would naturally describe this census as "the first" to distinguish it from that taken later, ten years after the death of Herod, which is mentioned both in the Acts of the Apostles and in Josephus.

It must be concluded, therefore, that Jesus was born between the years 8 and 4—most probably in the year 6—before the Christian era as now dated. As for the actual date of his birth, universally now celebrated on December twenty-fifth, it can be said at once that this is purely a tradition. In the third century A.D. Clement of Alexandria chose April nineteenth; other suggestions were May twenty-ninth and March twenty-eighth. The Eastern Church for a long time celebrated January sixth. It was only about the year 350 that our own traditional date gained general acceptance. Some have associated it with the feast of Mithra which the Roman calendar fixed at the beginning of the winter solstice and there are certainly plenty of known instances where the Christian calendar has taken over pagan feasts. Gregory the Great himself advised his missionaries to "baptize the customs and the holy places of the heathen" and our All Saints Day and feast of St. John the Baptist (Midsummer Day) undoubtedly originated that way. For us December twenty-fifth is sanctified for ever: it does not commemorate the Persian god or the sacrificial bull, nor even the sun regaining his power over the darkness of the night, but that other star of which Malachi wrote: "But unto you that fear my name shall the sun of righteousness arise." (Malachi iv, 2.)

Portents of Pain and Glory

When the child Jesus was eight days old he was duly circumcised according to the custom, which, ever since Abraham, the Jews had preserved as a sign of their pact with God. The circumcision of John the Baptist had been a family ceremonial, in the course of which his father Zacharias had testified to the glory of God. But for Jesus, born on a journey, it was brief and simple; he received the name which the angel had designated for him and the operation was performed according to the Law.

This was only one of the obligations which the Mosaic Law laid upon the parents of a son, and particularly of a first born son. "Sanctify unto me all the first born," said the Lord (Exodus xiii, 2-13) in commemoration of that night when the first born of Egypt had been smitten and the first born of Israel had been spared. The first born son was redeemed by an offering of five shekels and although the scripture did not formally require it, it was customary to present the boy to the Lord.

The Mosaic ritual also required that women after childbirth should attend the Temple for purification. For forty days after the birth of a boy and for eighty after the birth of a girl, the mother was considered unclean and at her purification she offered a sacrifice, according to her means, either a year old lamb, a pair of pigeons or turtle doves (Leviticus xii).

To fulfill these two obligations Mary and Joseph had to go to Jerusalem where they received another sign of singular importance. An old man named Simeon, just and God fearing, came into the Temple just as the poor couple from Nazareth, hemmed in among the crowd, brought their child. God had revealed to Simeon that he should not die until he had beheld the long hoped for Messiah with the eyes of the flesh. Suddenly as Mary approached, the spirit of prophecy descended upon him, he took the child from her arms and burst into that triumphant hymn of joy, that Nunc Dimittis which the Christian Church repeats at nightfall and at the hour of death as the supreme expression of our trust in God.

"Lord, now lettest thou thy servant depart in peace, according to thy word. For mine eyes have seen thy salvation, which thou hast prepared before the face of all people; a light to lighten the Gentiles and the glory of thy people Israel." (Luke ii, 29-32)

Then, turning to the child's mother he said: "Behold, this child is set for the fall and rising again of many in Israel and for a sign which shall be spoken against; (Yea, a sword shall pierce through thine own soul also,) that the thoughts of many hearts may be revealed." (Luke ii, 34-35.) Those were strange words to address to a young mother filled with joy of her child and her faith in the divine message. Yet these words, even more strikingly than the angelic salutation, foretold the true destiny of the Messiah, the universal response that would come to Jesus, along with the refusal of Israel, the conflict and the strife, the Cross, with Mary weeping at the foot.

As if to confirm the words of Simeon, an old woman named Anna, the daughter of Phanuel, also recognized in the child the future redeemer. The figures of Simeon and Anna express the best in the tradition of the ancient Jewish piety; plain and simple people cherishing God in their hearts, indifferent to the hair-splitting of the Pharisees and the political combinations of the Sadducees.

In the two Gospel narratives of the childhood of Jesus, St. Luke alone gives us the story of the Presentation in the Temple with its foreshadowing of the sufferings of Christ, while St. Matthew tells the story which above all others typifies His future glory.

"Now when Jesus was born in Bethlehem of Judea in the days of Herod the King, behold, there came wise men from the east to Jerusalem, Saying, where is he that is born King of the Jews? for we have seen his star in the east, and are come to worship him." Having learnt that according to the prophecy, he was to be born in Bethlehem, they set out thence, "And lo, the star, which they saw in the east, went before them, till it came and stood over where the young child was." Mary and Joseph, now back from Jerusalem, were no longer lodged in a manger but in a house in the neighborhood. "They saw the young child with Mary his mother and fell down and worshipped him: and when they had opened their treasures, they presented unto him gifts; gold and frankincense and myrrh." (Matt. ii, 1-12.)

The scene of the three wealthy travelers from the east bowing down before the humble cradle of the new born child is one of those which has always excited the imagination. It has been interpreted symbolically, the prostration of the princes of the earth before the Holy Child. The gifts have their meaning too: gold for a King, frankincense for a god, myrrh for the bitterness of the man foreordained to death. Most of the great masters have painted the Magi: some in garments of glowing canonical red and others running riot with gold and bejeweled embroideries in vibrant contrast to the gray and brown tones of the setting where the child lies.

Most of the artistic trappings of these pictures owe little to the Gospel narrative, nor even to the recognized Apocrypha which upon this incident are surprisingly discreet, but are from unknown sources, mostly of oriental origin. The legends which have gathered round the story of the Magi in certain places amount to an entire folk lore. The Magi were descendants of the great soothsayer Balaam. The pieces of gold which they brought to Jesus were struck by Terah, the father of Abraham, and had been given to the people of Saba by Joseph in payment for spices to embalm the body of his fathers. The number of the Magi has always been given as three, representing either the three stages of life or three branches of the human race, one, Semitic, two, all the other white races, and the third, the Negro. They have been provided with names, Caspar, Melchior and Balthasar: their names were inscribed upon ribbons as a charm against epilepsy. In the north tympanum at Chartres, they are shown lying asleep under one coverlet, doubtless an item of a legend which has been lost to us. At the Château des Baux there can still be seen a coat of arms quartering the star which testifies to the connection of this illustrious house with the glorious visitors. St. Thomas is stated to have baptized them formally into the Christian faith during his travels in the East, and the Cathedral of Cologne has received their relics.

How much historical probability is there in all these charming fables? Who were these Wise Men of the East? From the beginning of the third century, when the tradition appears to have been established by Tertullian, they are often called the Magi, or the Three Kings, doubtless in reference to Psalm 72 which says, "The Kings of Tarshish and of the isles shall bring presents, the Kings of Sheba and Seba shall offer gifts." The Magi were originally a priestly caste of the Medes and the Persians. According to Herodotus they formed a rigid caste, almost a distinct tribe, and were reputed to lead ascetic lives tending the sacred fires in the High Places, studying astrology and the divination of dreams. They were certainly powerful: one of them attempted to seize the imperial power in Persia while Cambysis was at war in Egypt, stating that he was Smerdis, the dead brother of the Emperor come back to life. But there is nothing to indicate that the Magi enjoyed any particular power under the Parthian dominion at the time of the birth of Christ. It is probable that the term was in common use for all those oriental sages, astrologers and soothsayers of whom there have always been plenty, including both genuine philosophers and charlatans. From the evidence available it would seem that the Magi of scripture belonged to the most reputable of their kind.

It is easy to understand how these men whose lives were devoted to occult studies came to be acquainted with the prophecy of a Messiah; the Jews were dispersed throughout the countries of the Orient and the adventures of Tobias and the story of Esther were actually located in far-off Persia. They would probably be acquainted with the prophecy of Balaam, "There shall come a star out of Jacob and a sceptre shall arise out of Israel" (Numbers xxiv, 17), for even Tacitus, the contemptuous Roman, wrote in his history, "It was generally believed, on the strength of ancient prophecies, that the East would arise and that in a short time men would see coming out of Judea those who would govern the universe."

The identification of the Star is more thorny. It will be asked how the "Magi," working with only the naked eye or the most rudimentary scientific instruments, could have made astronomical observations of any precision. Granting this, what are the possible hypotheses? The "star" could have been a "nova," a genuine new star such as that which appeared in the Constellation Aquila in 1918 or that which was noticed in 1572 after the massacre of St. Bartholomew's Day. Against this is the fact that none of the writers of the time have recorded such an appearance. It could have been a comet, for when on January tenth, 1910, Halley's comet was visible in Jerusalem, its light was observed to pass rapidly from east to west, becoming diffused in the east and reappearing in full visibility in the west, as indicated in the Gospel story. But Halley's comet could only have passed over the sky of the countries in question during the year 12 B.C. and not in the year 6; other comets recorded by Chinese astronomers in the years 4 and 3 B.C. would not have been visible in Western Asia. Moreover, a comet, being subject to the diurnal orbit like other stars, could not indicate a precise location, much less a particular house in a particular town. Kepler thought that this celestial phenomenon might be a conjunction of the planets Jupiter and Saturn in the zodiacal sign of Pisces and, what is remarkable, his calculations showed that this phenomenon would have occurred about the year 6 B.C., although this date was not then considered the most probable date for the birth of Christ. In any case the word "star" as used in scripture does not mean the stars ordinarily visible but indicates some astronomical phenomenon. On this borderland of science and legend we may mention Merezhkovsky's theory that the "star" of the Gospel was a rare celestial phenomenon, the equinoctial passage of Aries through Pisces, which would signify to the Babylonian Magi, haunted by the idea of a recurring deluge, an announcement of the end of the world and a new stage in the history of the human race.

Herod's Anger

There was someone else in Judea who was interested in the visit of the Magi, as much as Joseph and Mary but in a different fashion. The tetrarch Herod, the old despot rotted by disease and haunted by a fear of horrible death which was gaining upon him daily, nevertheless continued to fight as passionately as ever for the prerogatives of his petty Kingship. When the visitors from the east reached his city and the purpose of their journey was made known to him, he could not fail to be gravely concerned. After taking competent advice, he recommended that the Magi should go to Bethlehem and advise him when they had found the child, since he also would wish to pay homage. But the Magi returned by another route, without going back to Herod's palace, in accordance with a warning given them in a dream.

It was a wise precaution for Herod would stop at nothing to bar the way of anyone likely to cast a shadow over his throne. The half-breed Bedouin was an artist in cruelty. He had strangled with his own hands his brother-in-law Aristobulus, the charming seventeen-year-old priest, because he was too popular, and also, successively, his other brother-in-law Joseph, the octogenarian King Hyrcan II, his fiery and once beloved wife Mariamne; even his own sons Aristobulus and Alexander had been murdered by his orders. With one foot in the grave, he took another victim, his third son Antipater, whose head he had cut off the day before his own death. His long reign, from 40 to 4 B.C., had been deluged in blood, and wholesale massacre daunted him no more than individual executions. When the Golden Eagle with which he had desecrated the façade of the Temple was thrown down he had forty young men burned alive as living torches. In his death agony he ordered a massacre of the chief notabilities of the Jewish community "to ensure that there should be tears shed over his grave."

When Herod realized that the Magi had outwitted him, he

fell into a violent rage and ordered the murder of all the children in Bethlehem and its environs aged two years and under, "according to the time which he had diligently inquired of the wise men" (Matt. ii, 16). This "Massacre of the Innocents," as it has always been called, certainly accords with what we know of Herod's character; perhaps it seemed less shocking to the people of those times than to us. Suetonius recounts a piece of gossip according to which the Roman Senate, just before the birth of Augustus, hearing a prophecy that a child was about to be born who would rule over Rome, ordered a similar massacre. The number of children slain in Bethlehem could hardly have been very large. The town had then about two thousand inhabitants and if we reckon an annual birthrate of about thirty children per thousand, taking both sexes into account (since only male infants were affected by the decree) and the normal rate of infant mortality, we arrive at a figure of about twenty-five. The Church has always venerated these little victims who purchased the safety of the Messiah with their lives; they are shown with palms and crowns as child martyrs.

For, miraculously, Jesus was saved. An angel of the Lord appeared to Joseph: "Arise and take the young child and his mother and flee into Egypt and be thou there until I send thee word: for Herod will seek the young child to destroy him." (Matt. ii, 13.) Joseph set out that very night for Egypt where, ever since the destruction of Jerusalem by Nebuchadnezzar, there had been a considerable Jewish colony which had continued to expand after Palestine became a Greek province, until it became nearly a million strong. Jewish colonists had even built at Leontopolis a temple said to rival that of Sion. The majority of these Jews remained faithful to Palestine and in constant relations with their compatriots there. It was in Alexandria, where the Jews formed two-fifths of the population, that their savants had made for the library of the Pharaoh Ptolemy II that translation of their sacred books which we call the Septuagint. It was natural that if Joseph had to fly from Palestine he should go to Egypt.

So the family set off with the child. The ass bore all the belongings and all the hopes of these poor people, the good faithful beast plodding along by stages of about thirty miles. They would probably follow the caravan route which hugged the coast as closely as possible, for the interior of the country was frightful, a vast waste of barren sand without the meanest vegetation except on the borders where a thin stony soil supported a scanty growth. All the armies of history which have traversed this hostile land have met ill fortune, from Gabinius and Titus, in 55 B.C. and 70 A.D., down to Lord Allenby in 1918.

The authors of the Apocryphal Gospel of the Holy Childhood, moved by compassion for the hardships of the poor family in flight, tell us two charming stories. The first tells how the Virgin Mary desired to eat some dates which were out of reach, whereupon the child Jesus ordered the branch to bend down. To reward the tree for its obedience, the Holy Child bade an angel take one of its branches and plant it in Paradise where it should give its palms for ever to the blessed to salute the glory of God. This scene is depicted on the choir screen at Notre Dame de Paris and in stained glass at Lyons and Tours. The other story tells how Joseph and Mary were captured by robbers who, taking pity on their poverty, fed them and sent them safely on their way. It was inevitable that one of these charitable bandits should become in due course the penitent thief of Calvary. A plaque of Limoges enamel in the Musée de Cluny depicts this story.

We know nothing about the sojourn of the Holy Family in Egypt. In the old Coptic quarter of Cairo there is a crypt which from antiquity has been venerated as the place where they stayed. At Matariah, some nine miles or so out of Cairo, is a sycamore tree under which Mary is supposed to have loved to sit: it is certainly a very old tree but in spite of the railings which have protected it from the excessive attentions of the pious, it is doubtful whether it could have survived two thousand years. The Apocryphal records, of course, know a great deal more about this period. They tell us that when the child Jesus went into the temple of Heliopolis, the images of the three hundred sixty-five gods which it contained immediately fell to the ground, a sight which on the spot converted to Christianity the governor Aphrodisius, the centurion in charge and all his men. A famous mosaic in the proscenium of Santa Maria Maggiore in Rome shows this marvel, while in the representation in stained glass at Le Mans the statue which has tumbled down is provided, in order to stress the symbolism, with a head made of gold, a body made of silver, a belly of brass, thighs of iron and feet of clay, in accordance with the prophetic description (Daniel ii, 31-35) of the image which symbolized the kingdoms of the earth given over to destruction.

In any case, the sojourn in Egypt could not have been very long for St. Matthew tells us that being told of Herod's death by the angel, Joseph took Mary and Jesus back to Palestine. But hearing that Archelaus had succeeded his father Herod he did not venture in Judea but returned to Galilee. This was a wise precaution, for Archelaus was almost as ferocious as his predecessor and had inaugurated his reign by a massacre of three thousand Jews. Herod died in the March or April of the Roman year 750 and Archelaus succeeded immediately. Jesus, born in the Roman year 749 or 748, would have been somewhere between eight and eighteen months old when his parents returned to their native land.

Childhood in Nazareth

According to St. Matthew and St. Luke, it was to Nazareth in Galilee that the Holy Family returned after the stay in Egypt. St. Matthew adds "that it might be fulfilled which was spoken of the prophets, He shall be called a Nazarene." This statement has provoked infinite discussion, even doubts whether this little Galilean town existed. There are two ideas interwoven in this verse of St. Matthew's: the first that Jesus lived at Nazareth; the second, that there were prophecies which foretold this.

With regard to the second, it may as well be admitted that the words, "he shall be called a Nazarene," cannot be found in any part of the Old Testament text. There could, of course, have been other "prophecies" but we do not know them. The etymology of the word Nazareth, however, is related to a root meaning branch, shoot or seed, and possibly, with an Oriental's love of word play and imagery, St. Matthew was referring to those prophecies where the Messiah is announced as "a rod out of the stem of Jesse" (Isaiah xi, 2); "the branch to grow up unto David" (Jeremiah xxxiii, 15) and "the man whose name is the Branch" (Zachariah vi, 12).

No pre-Christian text, Jewish or pagan, mentions the existence of Nazareth, neither does Josephus nor the Talmud. A single Jewish author, Eleazar Kalir, in a poem written in the seventh century, cites it as one of the localities in Galilee where, after the fall of Jerusalem in the year 70, the Jewish sacerdotal classes sought refuge. The absence of evidence about Nazareth is not, however, as disturbing as it might at first seem. It could not have been anything but a small town in that remote province of Galilee which the Jews of Jerusalem regarded as inaccessible and uncouth. The rabbis would not have shown any interest in a place where their own disciples did not flourish and it is quite possible that it did not even exist when the *Mishna* of the Talmud was put together. Even if it cannot be proved from outside sources that Nazareth existed at the time of Christ, this does not justify the rejection of the precise testimony of St. Luke and St. Matthew, confirmed as it is by St. Mark (i, 9) and St. John (i, 45-46). The often quoted passage from St. John indeed confirms the unimportance and obscurity of the place: "Can there be any good thing come out of Nazareth?" said Nathaniel to Philip.

The non-Christian critic, however, may ask whether, if the location of the childhood of Jesus at Nazareth is mythical, the term "Nazarene" may not have some other significance. The term is certainly applied to the person of Christ throughout the Gospel narrative and it has the character both of a nickname and of a description. But there are other analogous cases; for instance Judas who rebelled against Archelaus is known as the "Gaulonite" without anybody questioning the existence of his native province. It has been advanced that Jesus belonged to that "Nazarene" sect which is mentioned by Epiphanus, one of the Greek Fathers, in the fourth century, and which was probably related to those "Mandaeans" whom we have already discussed in connection with John the Baptist. There is nothing, however, to prove that this sect existed before the time of Christ. It could have been a nickname given to Christ because of some exterior resemblance between these people and Jesus, but it is unlikely that in that case his disciples and he himself would have made use of it. More recent theories, notably Guignebert's, are that "Nazarene" is in fact related to "Nazarite" and that Jesus, who is often called "the Holy One of God," might have been one of those devotees who, like Samson of old, took certain vows. Against this is the fact that it does not seem, from the Gospel narrative, that Jesus was under any such vows and moreover that at the time of Christ the vows of the Nazarites appear to have been limited to temporary observances. None of these ingenious hypotheses solves anything. Renan wrote categorically that Jesus was born in Nazareth, relegating Bethlehem to the fables; Guignebert doubts the existence of both places; and this is what is called the extension of knowledge.

It is just as "scientific" to admit the existence of Nazareth and that Jesus lived there, and even to accept the very old tradition which has always depicted a little green and white town, after the fashion of the Umbrian cities, cut into the sides of the snow crowned heights which seal the plain of Esdraelon on the north. Now, it is a town of some three or four thousand inhabitants, distinguishable from other such towns only by the multiplicity of churches, convents and belfries. It is surrounded by a graceful circlet of hills, sprinkled with primitive farm buildings of wattle and daub, the dark columns of the cypress standing out among the vineyards, the olive groves and the grain fields. The gardens are fragrant with lilies and verbena and the bougainvillea trails its cope of episcopal purple over the white walls.

This is the setting in which we can visualize the child Jesus.

The physical reality was probably less like that charming fourth century statue, now in a museum in Rome, showing a serene, composed child in a long pleated tunic, and more like one of those vivacious nervous Jewish children who can be encountered anywhere along the roads of Palestine and in the Zionist settlements of the plain of Esdraelon, those sparsely clad, barefooted children whose faces display at once a lively intelligence and a sober intensity of passion.

The surroundings of the Holy Family, which so many painters have striven to depict, can have been very little different from those which we can see in any small house in the locality today. Ordinarily there is only one room, pervaded by the sweetish smell of olive oil. Often there is no outlet for the smoke save by the door. At night a lamp made of clay, hung on an iron chandelier or placed on a projecting slab in the stone wall, provides a poor light. A church marks the site which certain archaeological researches have identified as that of the house where Joseph brought up Jesus. Like that where Mary received the Angelic Salutation, the house was largely subterranean, hollowed out of the soft local limestone, with a crude stairway (now richly decorated with mosaics) where the child could climb up and down.

He would have received the same education as all the young Jews of his time. There seems to have been a regular course of studies which the Talmud describes. They revolved around the synagogue and were presided over by the *hassan* who seems to have been a sort of beadle or administrative official of the sacred places where the faithful foregathered. At the *beth-hasepher* or primary school, sitting on the ground around the scrolls of the Law, the children repeated the verses in unison until they knew them by heart. In Hebrew the same word signifies repeat and learn. This education explains the profound knowledge of Old Testament texts which Jesus displayed in later life, for what we learn in childhood is graven on our memories. Every Jewish boy received his preliminary grounding in the Torah; whether Jesus progressed beyond this and attended any of the rabbinical schools which might be found in the neighborhood we do not know and it may be doubted in view of the astonishment expressed later by his fellow townsmen when, at the beginning of his ministry, they discovered that he was wiser and better instructed in religious matters than "the leaders of Israel" (Mark vi, 2).

At this point we come up against the delicate question of whether the child Jesus had any brothers and sisters. The Gospel refers more than once to his brothers and even names them, James, Joseph, Jude and Simon, adding sisters also. But Christian doctrine, and not only among Catholics, has rejected the interpretation that, after the miraculous birth of Jesus, Joseph and Mary had children of the flesh. The Catholic Church insists on the perpetual virginity of Mary—*ante partum, in partu, post partum,* the latter based on a Church tradition which exists from far back.

An objective examination of the Gospel texts does not suggest more than one child in connection with Joseph and Mary and in the account of the loss of Jesus in the Temple we definitely get the impression that he was their only child. Throughout his life, his fellow citizens referred to Jesus as the "son of Mary" and Renan cites this as a proof that Jesus was the only son of Mary, a widow. It is hardly likely that Jesus on the Cross would have confided his mother to the care of John if she had had several other children, and Mary's reply to the angel, "How shall this be, seeing that I know not a man?" seems to imply that she desired to keep her virginity. Nevertheless the expression "brothers of the lord" requires some explanation.

This can easily be found by the most elementary study of Semitic philology. In Aramaic, *aha,* in Hebrew, *ah,* signifies equally brother, half brother, cousin or even a close connection. The Old Testament supplies plenty of examples of this loose usage of the word translated as "brother," as when Abraham says to Lot, who was his nephew, "We are brothers" (Genesis iii, 8), and Laban uses the word also to his nephew Jacob. In the First Book of Chronicles (xxiii, 21-22) the sons of Kish are referred to as the "brethren" of the daughters of

Eleazar, although they are shown in the following verses to have been cousins-german. The word as used in the Gospels would probably refer to the cousins of Jesus, especially if any of his near relations—the children of Mary and Cleophas for instance—lived in the same house as Jesus, as is very common in the Orient. This explanation is accepted by Loisy who states, "This general feeling of the Catholic exegesists should not be dismissed as arbitrary: nothing in the Gospel contradicts it." We can conclude with Fr. Lagrange: "We cannot affirm that it is historically demonstrated that 'the brothers' of Jesus were cousins; we can only say that nothing can be advanced against the tradition of the perpetual virginity of Mary which is implied in several passages in the Gospels."

The familiar picture of Jesus growing up with his father and mother in the humble household at Nazareth has a good deal of historical probability, especially if, after the death of his foster father Joseph, he lived in the company of numerous cousins. Our information about his childhood is scanty. "And the child grew and waxed strong in spirit, filled with wisdom and the grace of God was upon him." (Luke ii, 40.)

A single episode is reported to us, about the time when he was twelve years old, and as Mauriac has said, "A Jewish boy of twelve is already out of his childhood." Legally also, this was the case; at twelve years of age, a son of Israel became a "son of the Law," subject to all its minute provisions and if he violated them, liable to the decreed forfeits and penances. Jesus, as the "son of the Law," was to be the master of the Law which he had come to fulfill and this was probably in the mind of the Evangelist recounting the episode of the Temple (Luke ii, 41-50).

Like all pious Jews, Joseph and Mary would go to Jerusalem for the Passover. Perhaps this would be the first time they had taken their son. The long journey would be lightened by the chants of the pilgrims, reciting those psalms which the Ancients had composed to the rhythm of the march, "I will lift up mine eyes unto the hills, from whence cometh my help. My help cometh from the Lord, which made heaven and earth."

(Psalms, 121.) "Our feet shall stand within thy gates, O Jerusalem. Jerusalem is builded as a city that is compact together: whither the tribes go up." (Psalms, 122.) The pilgrims would eat lamb prepared with bitter herbs and a red sauce, according to ancient custom. So they ate unleavened bread and drank their wine and then, when the last hallelujahs had died down, they started on their way back.

At the first stopping place, Joseph and Mary went to look for their child, whom they had not seen during the march but whom they supposed to be with their friends and relations among the pilgrims. He was not to be found, and, very perturbed, they went back to Jerusalem to look for him. After three days' search he was discovered in the Temple, in the place where the doctors of the Law and other learned men were accustomed to teach their disciples. Groups of children commonly sat around with the students; sometimes they were even permitted to ask questions. Josephus tells us how, as a boy, he used to take part in these debates; modesty not being his characteristic, he adds that many priests and important personages would gather round him for information on many disputed points.

There Jesus was, among the learned men of Israel—"And all that heard him," said St. Luke, "were astonished at his understanding and answers."

His mother, relieved as she was, had to chide him gently and ask him why he had treated them thus. "Behold, thy father and I have sought thee sorrowing." And the Holy Child replied in those strange harsh words which stated, for the first time, the requirement that whoever would follow Christ must forsake all human ties, even the dearest. "How is it that ye sought me? Wist ye not that I must be about my Father's business?"

But this solitary incident, revealing and prophetic as it is, was not enough to satisfy the natural curiosity about the childhood of Christ, and the Apocryphal records, especially those called the Gospel of the Holy Childhood and the so-called Gospel of St. Thomas, have produced a multiplicity of anecdotes about these hidden years. Some of these stories are very charming, as that which tells how Jesus was playing with some other boys making birds out of clay. Then he breathed life into his playthings and when he clapped his hands they flew away. Once he was playing with some other children at the mouth of a cave, when two huge snakes appeared. The other children ran away screaming but Jesus, with unruffled calm, ordered the creatures to lay their heads at Mary's feet. A great many miracles were attributed to the Christ Child, some of them obviously derived from the canonical Gospels: a grain of wheat which he planted in the ground in a time of famine grew up to provide sufficient harvest to feed the people; a young workman was brought back to life. Others are tales of familiar fairytale magic like that of the mule which, when Jesus rode upon it, was released from an evil spell and became once more a handsome young man, or that of the fish pickled in brine which wriggled at the sound of the divine voice. Some of these attributed miracles are unpleasing fables like that of the schoolmaster whose hand withered when he sought to punish the child, or the story of how Jesus, to impress his playmates, changed one of them into a ram while another, who had by accident hurt him, fell down dead. Few of these fantastic stories have any interest or importance except by the fact that they were so often depicted by the artists and craftsmen of the Middle Ages. Apart from that they are valueless and tell us nothing at all about the child Christ.

The Hidden Years

So the years passed by; many years, for it was not until he was about thirty that Christ came out of obscurity and began to teach. We know nothing about these hidden years, save that "he increased in wisdom and stature and in favor with God and man." (Luke ii, 52.) In this small and remote province of the empire, a humble Jew would be as unknown to the great world as one ant out of a hill, and the historical events of the period took place without the slightest connection with those by which the divine soul received his human grounding.

However, in the Palestine of that time they knew little of those events which shook the world outside. They did not know that in distant Rome, after disorder and bloodshed, a man had come forward to seize and hold the supreme power. The glory of Augustus, the disputes about the succession, the heavy reverse which his conquering armies suffered, in the year 9 of our era, at the hands of Arminius's Germans, when Varus lost the famous Legions: all this meant nothing to the Jewish community. Jesus would have been nearly twenty years old when Augustus died in the year 14 in his seventy-sixth year, and was succeeded by Tiberius the son of Livia, whom he had adopted. That the master of the world should be proclaimed divine after his death would be to a faithful Jew nothing but an additional proof that the Romans were idolaters. And when the new emperor gave a free hand to his sinister favorites and began to assassinate his entourage, that would be simply another instance of Roman barbarity. When Germanicus, the hero of the Rhine campaigns, died mysteriously in the year 19 at Antioch, it is doubtful whether the news traveled from Syria to Palestine, least of all to Nazareth.

Only those activities which directly affected the Holy Land held the slightest interest for the Jews. In the year 6, the same year, probably, that witnessed the finding of Jesus in the Temple, Herod's son Archelaus, the tetrarch of Judea, was deposed and exiled by Augustus and a Roman procurator was installed in his stead. First Coponius, who remained three years, was sent; then followed Marcus Ambivius (9–12), Annius Rufus (12–15) and Valerius Gratus (15–26). Jesus was probably thirty-one years old and about to begin his public mission when, in the year 26, a certain Pontius Pilate landed in Judea. Galilee was ruled by Herod Antipas, another son of the great Herod, a pinchbeck kinglet who aped Roman manners and who built at enormous expense his sumptuous and sinful capital, Tiberias, by the side of the lake. He was regarded with hatred and contempt. When in the year 28 he repudiated his legitimate wife and consorted with his sister-in-law Herodias, pious Jews were outraged and echoed among themselves a denunciation of the adulterer in the terms of God on Sinai.

One fact concerning the early life of Jesus may be read between the lines of the Gospel, that is the death of Joseph. He is mentioned in the incident of the Temple but during the whole public life of Jesus he does not appear at all. A very old tradition states that Jesus was nineteen when Joseph died and the legendary History of Joseph the Carpenter even makes Jesus himself tell the circumstances of it. The portrait of Mary given by the Gospels is definitely that of a woman without a husband and we are probably right in imagining her as a grave matron in widow's weeds, presiding at the table in the house at Nazareth in the place of honor which the Talmud allotted to the mother of a family when her husband was dead. Joseph, the good foster father, disappears from the story with the simplicity of one who knew that his task on earth was accomplished and who was content to leave the rest to God. He had protected the child and he had allowed the mother to assume her supernatural vocation; like Simeon he could have said the Nunc Dimittis, and the Apocryphal story which shows the Angel of the Lord waiting at the deathbed of this good man is quite believable.

It was probably Joseph who taught Jesus the craft by which he made his living. In the Jewish community every man had to work with his hands, even those devoted to the study of the Law. Thus the great Rabbi Hillel was a woodcutter and Rabbi Schammai, a carpenter. "Whoever does not teach his son a trade is teaching him to steal," said a rabbinical precept. But Jesus, being a poor man, had to work for his living, to earn his bread by the sweat of his brow according to the obligation God laid on Adam.

The craftsman who was generally known as a "carpenter" was in fact skilled in all kinds of woodwork: he could equally make props for shoring, yokes for oxen or harness poles and goads as well as beds, chests, stools, bins and kneading troughs. The Greek "tekton" and the Aramaic "naygar" which we translate as "carpenter" signified both a joiner and an artisan in wood. "The husbandman, the blacksmith, the mason and the carpenter," says Papini, "are the workmen whose art is most intimately bound up with human life: theirs are the best and most truly religious of occupations."

Jesus led the ordinary life of poor men of his time. He lived in a very humble house, such as has been described, and ate the common food of the Galilean people, barley bread, very little meat, vegetables, and sour milk, and on feast days the "grilled fish which makes man's body fruitful," as a rabbinical writer put it. It is clear from the parables and the teaching of Jesus that he had no acquaintance with riches or the great ones of the earth; his references to luxury have that simplicity commonly to be remarked among those who have little experience of it. The parable of the lost piece of silver was perhaps a memory of his mother, lamp in hand, searching throughout the house for the missing coin and very much relieved when she had found it. It was a life of extraordinary simplicity which we should bear in mind when we contemplate the Messiah in glory drawing the crowds to follow him. Its humility inspired a modern mystic, Charles de Foucauld, when visiting Nazareth to beg for himself the most menial of occupations, that of a sweeper in a convent of Poor Clares.

Among such poor people, fishermen, workmen, laborers in fields and vineyards, Jesus received that grounding in human nature which each of us acquires from those among whom his lot is cast. Galileans were simple people, less preoccupied with formalities than the Jews of Judea, kind hearted if somewhat rough mannered. Jesus used their language, their customs and many sayings and idioms from their common speech. He was to be all his life one of those men of the people whose natural nobility allows them to meet all men as equals.

The face of Galilee itself was also to influence him. As a workman in a small town he would almost certainly have cultivated a small plot of land as well. The tradition is that, as a boy, he took the sheep out grazing and it can be noticed during the Gospel record how often he retired to meditate into some solitary place, perhaps a haunt of his youth, where among the invisible presences which invest the beauty of creation the soul can more easily reunite with its Creator.

It is a beautiful sight from the hills above Nazareth. The plain of Esdraelon, the California of Palestine, stretches below, a checker-board pattern of browns, yellows, ochres, and grays shot with subtle tinges of green, with the blue and silver Mediterranean sparkling in the distance. Toward the north, purple-flanked Hermon lifts its snow-crowned head above the lesser hills, while nearer at hand Tabor stretches those round and swelling contours, once praised by St. Jerome, above a bed of dying foliage, and to the south the mountains of Samaria encircle charming Engannim. At the foot of the heights of the Decapolis range is the deep gorge which conceals within the invisible Lake Tiberias, from which sometimes a light mist drifts up.

The whole Galilean landscape gives an impression of luxuriance and beauty which contrasts with the harshness of Judea. The hills are round and the rich vegetation hides the rocky skeleton. The rainfall is heavy, more so than at Jerusalem and very much more than in the valley of the Jordan. Life is better there and it is fitting that Galilee should have been the scene of the happy part of Jesus's life, his childhood, his peaceful and obscure working days and, later on, the first successes of his ministry. Judea was to be the land of sorrow. It is not without significance that during his formative years the book of nature should have showed its friendliest aspect; throughout the Gospels we can trace references which show that the memory remained.

So we leave him, on a certain day of the winter of the year 27 on the way to that ford of Bethabara where the impressive figure of the Baptist was to reveal his destiny. "Behold, there went out a sower to sow." (Mark iv, 3.) But no man knew where the seed was to fall.

CHAPTER THREE

A PROVINCE OF THE EMPIRE

Rome and Palestine

SOMETHING LESS THAN a century before these events, the Roman Legions, in the process of conquering the East, had added the modest booty of the land of Canaan to the vast spoils of the sons of the she-wolf. In the year 63 B.C., Pompey had breached the walls of Jerusalem with much bloodshed, after a three months' siege. Sword in hand, he had entered the Holy of Holies and had emerged crestfallen and discomfited by these people whose Temple housed no image of any god.

This episode, which marked the final stage in the long history of Israel as a nation, was in no way premeditated; here, as so often, Rome merely accepted the event. But she was not slow in turning it to profit. The severe war maintained by Mithridates, King of Pontus, followed by the marauding raids of his son-in-law, the Armenian Tigranes, had only served to carry the eagles farther and farther still. In the year 64 B.C. the Roman province of Syria was built on the remains of the Seleucid Kingdoms. While those unworthy descendants of the Maccabees, Hyrcanus II and Aristobulus II, used up the remains of Jewish strength in fratricidal strife, it was the simplest thing in the world for the new neighbor to step in and obtain control of the vital passage to Egypt, thus laid open to the greedy designs of Rome.

In Asia as elsewhere Roman policy was marked by that skillful combination of suavity and force which is the most successful tactic for the conqueror. There are more convenient means of gaining control than by plain annexation and a vassal is often more useful than a subject. The Hellenistic cities had been autonomous as were in Palestine the cities of the Decapolis whose territories cut into the various Arab and Jewish principalities. These cities constituted a federation which although loose politically was solidly cemented by common commercial interests. In many of the vassal countries the hereditary dynasties were upheld and charged with the maintenance of order and the collection of taxes. Since the Asmonean dynasty in Judea seemed incapable of playing the Roman political game, the Jews were provided with new masters from a Bedouin family who had shown themselves possessed of a high degree of diplomatic aptitude contrasting with the perpetual disorder which had affronted Pompey and Caesar. In the year 40 B.C. Herod, son of Antipater, the mayor of the palace, prepared to assume the crown of David because Mark Antony and Octavius willed it so, and for thirty-six years the Chosen People suffered the yoke of this Idumean, whose ancestors had been uncircumcised barbarians less than a century before and whose undeniable magnificence was equalled by his despotism and cruelty.

At the time of Christ there was much in Palestine to bear witness to Herod's achievement. Sixty-nine years of civic order, even if founded on cruelty and terror, had produced a solid prosperity, and the monuments of the great builder stood in all their splendor. The marble palace, flanked by three towers, which Herod had called Antonia out of compliment to one of his protectors, lay west of the city. On a mountain close by stood the enormous fortress, the Herodium, which was to be its builder's tomb, and, above all other buildings, rose the particular pride of his reign, the reconstructed Temple, larger than Solomon's and far surpassing it in the number and size of its columns and the richness of its ornament. The governmental methods of Herod had also survived him. It is said that one day the King, incognito, asked an old man what the people thought of him. "Even the birds are in his pay," was the answer. Rome could be satisfied—there was quiet in Israel.

It goes without saying that the only freedom Herod enjoyed was that which his masters allowed him. His foreign policy was entirely directed by Rome. His army of mercenaries, Gauls, Thracians and Germans, was always at the disposition of Augustus. Moreover it was expressly conveyed to him that such power as he had was purely personal and could not be transmitted by him to his successors without the Imperial sanction.

In the year 4 A.D. Herod was called to the tribunal of the Almighty to answer for his crimes. Of the numerous children he had had by his several wives, four only had survived his massacres: Herod Philip I, Herod Antipas, Archelaus and Herod Philip II. His son Aristobulus, whom he had murdered in the year 7, had left a son, the future Herod Agrippa I. Herod had hoped to maintain the unity of his kingdom but hardly had his remains—on a golden litter encrusted with precious stones, escorted by his soldiers and the royal household burning incense—been laid in the Herodium, when trouble broke out among his successors. Archelaus, a young man of eighteen, had seemed likely to gain sole power when, following a Jewish rising which he suppressed after the paternal fashion, he set off for Rome to beg the investiture from Augustus. His brother Antipas, insisting upon his share, also set out for Italy. Meanwhile their half-brother Herod Philip II consolidated himself so impregnably in the northern part of the country that it was impossible to dislodge him. So the Emperor chose the solution most favorable to Roman interest: the division of the Herodian territories into small pocket principalities.

Two of the four sons who survived Herod were living in the time of Christ but neither had anything like their father's power. The older, Herod Philip I, grandson of the High Priest Simon through his mother, had aspired to the sovereign pontificate but the snow white miter and the pectoral cross did not reward his assiduity. Though they were possessed successively by his great uncles, his grandfather and one of his uncles, he was left an ordinary priest and the butt of the sarcasms of his ambitious wife, Herodias.

The royal dignity had evaporated. Augustus had naturally dangled it before Archelaus, the tetrarch of Judea, since he was the ablest; as for the other two, they had to be content with the modest life of tetrarch although their flatterers honored them with the title of King. Herod Philip II and Herod Antipas had adjoining territories around the lake of Gennesaret (Sea of Galilee)—the one as tetrarch of Ituraea and Trachonitis; the other of Galilee and Peraea. They got on very well together, which was something remarkable among the Herodians. Philip was a simple man, living quietly on his estates like any landed proprietor and leaving them only to make the prescribed visits to the Temple. Herod Antipas, whom the Gospel after the death of John the Baptist refers to simply as Herod, had much less frugal tastes. He was richer than his brother and maintained a court and an army and we know that he was a lover of feasting and of women. Both these princelings made an attempt at continuing the work of their father in accordance with their means, which were much less considerable. Each had wanted to have a city in the neighborhood of that beautiful lake which, said the rabbis, "God has reserved for his pleasure." Antipas had built his on the borders of the lake itself, its ripples lapping its courtyards; he had called it Tiberias in honor of the then master of the world and he was inordinately proud of it. But since it was built in part over a graveyard, orthodox Jews regarded it as unclean and turned away from it in disgust. Jesus himself never set foot in it. His brother, meanwhile, seeking to enlarge his capital, the former Panias which he renamed Caesarea Philippi, had chosen a site to the east of the confluence of the river Jordan into the lake. On a pleasant hillside, refreshed by cool breezes from the north, he had built his new "Bethsaida," renamed Juliana in honor of the Julian family which had been privileged to give

Caesar to the world. It was built of the local basalt, a sad-colored stone. The two brothers' cities were within three hours sailing distance. During his childhood, Jesus was a subject of Herod Antipas; he started his mission traveling through the territories of both tetrarchs.

Archelaus was less lucky. Although he had numerous connections at Rome, where he had largely been brought up, he lost the favor of Augustus. Immediately after the death of his father, when he went to ask the Emperor to bestow the throne upon him, he was countered by a delegation of the leading Jews who respectfully besought the emperor to suppress the royal title in Judea and to attach the country to the Roman province of Syria. Archelaus managed to get out of this and obtained the greater part of Palestine, Samaria, Idumea and Judea with Jerusalem as his capital; Augustus further made the princely gesture of refusing the 1,500 talents bequeathed to him by Herod, leaving them to Archelaus. But the son, who had inherited only a part of Herod's ability, had inherited to the full his cruelty and violence. Instead of following the prudent counsel of moderation urged on him by his protector, he began to play the tyrant, deposing priests who did not suit him, punishing the least disorder with fire and sword and increasing taxes without justification. Like Herod, he aimed at being a great builder; he restored magnificently the city of Jericho and built a new one which he called Archelais. But he fell short of the grand manner and when in the tenth year of his reign (the year 6 A.D.), a new delegation went to Rome to complain of his tyranny, Augustus lost his patience and deposed him, exiling him to the town of Vienne in remote Gaul and depriving him of his revenues. A Roman procurator took his place.

So Palestine in the time of Our Lord was divided into three parts, a very minute division of such a small country, for even including the deserts of Transjordania and Idumea it has a territory of about 10,000 square miles, less than Belgium, Sicily or even Brittany. It certainly could not have had a population of more than a million. But the political complexity which is so evident from the Gospel texts deceived nobody; there was no difference between the imperial province or the vassal kingdoms, nothing could be done in either without the consent of Rome. The Governor of Judea, from his palace at Maritime Caesarea, controlled the land unobtrusively from "Dan to Beersheba," in the words of the traditional definition.

The decree of 27 B.C. by which Augustus had divided the administration of the Empire between the Senate and himself provided for four varieties of provincial administration. The regions which might be considered pacified were called "senatorial provinces," and were administered by a proconsul, "spectabilis proconsul S.P.Q.R." (the Senate and the People of Rome), chosen by lot from former consuls and praetors. Those where rebellion might still be apprehended were under the jurisdiction of the Emperor, who sent his personal representative, "clarissimus legatus Augusti." Egypt, on account of the strong monarchical and bureaucratic traditions of the Ptolemies, had a regime of its own; it was administered by a prefect as a sort of steward for the Prince. Various smaller parts of the empire, such as recent military acquisitions or small kingdoms which had been annexed, countries which presented special problems such as being difficult to handle or having unknown or undeveloped resources, were regarded as personal estates whose value the Emperor undertook to improve. Such were the two Mauretanias (in north Africa); Rhaetia (Switzerland); Norica (Austria), Thrace and Judea. Here the representative of the Emperor was known as the procurator and he was almost always chosen from that class of nobility which had provided the Imperial house with so many distinguished servants. The powers of the procurator were considerable, far exceeding those of a fiscal official. He was more like a viceroy, controlling the army, the judiciary, the police and the exchequer, and within his dominions he had sole power over life and death. In theory, the Governor of Syria exercised control over the Procurator of Judea, Idumea and Samaria but in practice he intervened only in the event of actual danger.

When Jesus first began his public career, the Syrian Governor was Pomponius Flaccus, an old boon companion of Tiberius' debauches. The Procurator of Judea, the fifth to hold office, was Pontius Pilate. These high administrative officers who governed the provinces in the Emperor's name were very far removed from the republican proconsuls and praetors whose chief objective had been to enrich themselves during their period of office. The Imperial legates were either senators or aristocrats, ultrasophisticated to the point of skepticism, contemptuously polite to all, but not so far as to be incapable of peremptory action. The Jewish philosopher, Philo of Alexandria, has left us a very black portrait of Pilate, accusing him of cruelty, violence, immorality, injustice and of encouraging corruption. Although Philo is not necessarily to be believed, it is a fact that the procurator was recalled in the year 37 on account of his brutality. The psychology of such a man would be governed by two considerations: his perpetual fear of being denounced to Caesar by some delegation or other and his complete contempt for the people whom he administered.

Protectors and Protected

The presence of the conquerors in Palestine should not be lost sight of when we are considering the story of Jesus. In the background of the Gospel is the Roman soldier with his helmet and his red cloak. During the night in Jerusalem could be heard the rhythmic cries of the procuratorian guard keeping watch from the towers of Antonia. The procedure of the trial of Christ and its tragic issue can be understood only by bearing in mind the immense power wielded by Pilate. Judea was less like an occupied country than a colony where, without mixing in any way with the native population, a white race exercises control over every department involving its own interests of the life of a black people.

In their method of colonial administration the Romans displayed that realism which was one of the bases of their power. Their officials knew how to turn local peculiarities to account in order to keep the conquered people well in hand. They did not govern Sicily or Sardinia, which had been long ago cowed by the exactions of the Carthaginians, in the same way that they governed Palestine, where, as they very well knew, the stubborn national pride, nourished by thousands of years of tradition, was ineradicable. They sought to give the Jews the impression that in all those matters nearest their hearts, and particularly in the domain of faith, they remained absolutely free. But this did not prevent the Romans from deposing High Priests who proved intractable: eight were so dealt with between the years 6 and 41. Their taxes, which were heavy, were collected by local officials, the "publicans" on whom the popular odium devolved. On occasion they encouraged conflicts among local factions, which was easy in Jerusalem. The British held India with some hundred thousand men, of whom the greater portion were native troops. But Rome did not keep stationed as much as a complete Roman legion in Palestine but only auxiliaries—Syrians, Samaritans, Greeks and Arabs, comprising three "cohorts" of infantry and one "wing" of cavalry, about three thousand men in all.

The comparison is startling, especially when the relations between the protecting power and the local kinglets are considered. In theory the sovereignty of the tetrarchs was recognized but we have seen that Augustus deposed Archelaus and it was only the imperial favor which provided a throne for Herod Agrippa I. The diminished armies of the kinglets were controlled by Rome which possibly provided some of the strength. The procurator maintained the utmost courtesy toward them without ever for a moment forgetting that he might have to proceed against them or might even be denounced by them to the Emperor, (Herod Antipas was definitely an informer for Tiberius). It was exactly the same policy as that pursued by the Viceroys of Delhi toward the Maharajahs, vassals whose loyalty was not altogether certain but who were nevertheless received at the court of the King-Emperor.

The truth is that the Roman attitude toward the Jews was complete contempt, a compound of disdain with that total incuriosity, that almost willful lack of comprehension, which echoes in the English use of the word "native" and which is so strikingly shown in E. M. Forster's novel *A Passage to India.* A Pontius Pilate would regard the people he governed as strange animals or as undeveloped children whom it was necessary to chastise occasionally to avert trouble but who could not possibly be considered seriously. This is shown very plainly in his attitude to the crowd during the trial of Christ. He was unwilling to live in Jerusalem among these noisy and malodorous fanatics; the new town of Caesarea, pleasantly situated on the coast, was much more agreeable. It is absolutely certain that the authentic grandeur of the Chosen People, their thousands of years of striving toward the spiritual, the force of their monotheism and their unwearying stubbornness in the face of destiny, made no impression whatever upon the majority of the Roman officials. There was absolutely no trace in their attitude of the modern view of colonization as a means of linking backward peoples with the rest of humanity and raising them to a higher level of civilization.

This more or less obvious contempt was confronted by a pride which was never concealed. For this pride was in large measure the moral bastion of the Jewish community: the thing which had enabled them to resist pagan infiltrations and temptations for five hundred years. It was based on the certitude that the privileges of Israel were beyond human sovereignty and that political contingencies could not affect it in the least. When Jesus said to the Jews, "The truth shall make you free," they replied, "We be Abraham's seed and were never in bondage to any man: how sayest thou, Ye shall be made free?" (John viii, 32-33.) The procurator, the Roman soldiers, the taxes levied by the conqueror did not matter. True freedom was within. In their abasement they felt themselves more than ever to be the people protected by God, the sons of Jacob, of Moses and the Prophets. Rabbi Eleazar, interpreting a passage of Deuteronomy, makes God say, "Since you have recognized me as the sole God I have recognized you as the only people." The Romans despised the Jews, but the Romans themselves had no existence at all in the eyes of those who served Jehovah.

St. Paul, who sprang from this people, has defined their state of mind to perfection (Romans ii, 17-20). "Behold, thou art called a Jew and restest in the law, and makest thy boast of God. And knowest his will, and approvest the things that are more excellent, being instructed out of the law. And art confident that thou thyself art a guide of the blind, a light of them that are in darkness. An instructor of the foolish, a teacher of babes, which hast the form of knowledge and of the truth in the law."

Between these two forces, established on such different planes, relations could not possibly be easy. Every night at sunset when the sound of the trumpet called the faithful to prayer, every Jew heard in it a blast of defiance hurled at the strangers who, because they happened at the moment to occupy the promised land, imagined that they dominated the People of God. It is doubtful whether even today the Jew has revised his opinion of the *goy*.

Sometimes there were actual struggles with the Romans or with their lackeys, the Herodian princes. The bloody opening of the reign of Archelaus has already been mentioned, when the rebels, barricaded in the atrium of the Temple, at first successfully repelled assault. Archelaus had to call on all the force at his disposal to overcome the Jewish resistance, and three thousand men lost their lives. Later, when Archelaus was in Rome, trouble broke out again; the whole country was ravaged by fire and sword. In Judea two thousand of Herod's soldiers deserted and turned against the royal troops. In Peraea, a former slave called Simon burnt the city of Jericho and proclaimed himself King. The same thing occurred in Judea, where the usurper was a shepherd of Herculean physique named Athronges; while in Galilee, Judas, son of that Hezekiah who had given so much trouble to Herod the Great, captured the arsenal and also declared himself King. Varus, the Syrian legate, was forced to bring up two legions and to overawe the people by crucifying two thousand Jews. In the year 6 A.D. there was another explosion of hatred. Another Judas, surnamed the Gaulonite, half brigand and half prophet, seized a great part of the land and was forced to relinquish it only after repeated hammering by armed forces. Five years after the death of Christ, the whole of Samaria was plunged into mourning by a frightful atrocity, the massacre by order of Pontius Pilate of a band of devotees who had gathered on Mt. Gerizim. The struggles were futile; when Rome once put her foot in a country, it was very difficult to make her withdraw.

There were other incidents, less grave but equally significant. Pontius Pilate had barely taken up his appointment when he learned, to his cost, the strength of Jewish pride. During the night he had had placards bearing the effigy of the Emperor to be set up in Jerusalem. The Jews had been horror-struck by these idolatrous symbols and had rushed to Caesarea to implore the procurator to remove them. While he hesitated, a howling mob gathered outside his palace. Pilate threatened death to everyone but the faithful bared their breasts to slaughter rather than surrender. It was Pilate who gave way. On another occasion, when the procurator attempted to divert part of the revenues of the Temple to construct an aqueduct, disturbances broke out again. They were so violent that Pilate ordered his troops to mingle with the crowd in disguise, and then, at the understood signal, to turn on them with cudgels. Many lost their lives. When the procurator caused shields bearing the name of Tiberius to be hung in Herod's palace, the riots broke out again and might have become serious had not the Emperor himself wisely ordered the removal of the offending objects.

Even when it was not in actual eruption, the resistance to the occupying power was none the less persistent and almost universal. The Herodian politicians mentioned by the Gospels (Mark iii, 6 and Matt. xxii, 16) seem to have sought an understanding with the Romans to serve their own interests at the time and to guarantee their security in the future. The majority of the Jews were certainly not disposed to follow the Zelots, those fanatical nationalists and harsh interpreters of the Law, who at the time of Christ started a constant terror campaign against the Romans and against those of their compatriots whom they regarded as too complaisant. Those dagger-thrusting militants whose numbers swelled considerably during the reign of Herod Agrippa, provoked the disaster of the year 70. The inhabitants of Palestine could well indeed have echoed the melancholy words of Josephus: "The people witnessed many things which they regarded with horror but nevertheless they put up with them."

The Closed Community

This interaction of religion and politics made the Jewish state of the time something unique in history. On the one hand, the only political issues which the pious Jew concerned himself with were those which touched his spiritual interests and the safeguarding of his faith. On the other hand the religious question, because it was the backbone of the national existence, was itself a definite political factor. A religious trial in these circumstances immediately became a matter of politics and Jewish astuteness could be relied upon to maneuver the Roman officials to its own advantage.

The little residual state of Israel was in truth a theocracy: everything was done in the name and in the sight of God, a God who was intolerant, querulous and harshly nationalistic. Where their own immediate interests were not at stake, the Romans allowed their protectorates a large measure of liberty. As long as civic order was maintained and taxes collected, it was understood that the Romans would not get themselves mixed up with the innumerable quarrels and the endless complications in which these extraordinary people seemed to delight. This was the ordinary Roman practice. So in a sense the Jews ignored their power, only to have a very rude awakening at the time of the great upheaval in the year 70.

At the head of this theocratic state was the High Priest, the religious head of the people and the master of ceremonies who played an exclusive role in the Temple offices, on such major occasions as the Day of Atonement. By the very fact of this liturgical pre-eminence, he came to be regarded also as the political leader of the Jewish community, a sort of president of the republic combined with pope or archbishop. The Asmoneans, the descendants of the Maccabees, had prepared the way for this union of the temporal and spiritual powers by uniting the offices of King and High Priest. First Herod and then Rome, however, had diminished the High Priest's sphere of action and by reducing him to vassalage had exercised direct pressure upon Jewish policy. In theory a High Priest held office for life; in practice they were frequently deposed. There was much truth in the rabbinical saying, "The more the High Priests compete with their ministers the less will be the number of their days." Invariably ambitious and frequently venal, the Jewish High Priests were far from incarnating that serene authority becoming to the direct representatives of the Most High. Two families disputed the possession of the miter and the breastplate; that of Boètus and that of Annas. Josephus calls one of the latter "fortunate" because five of his sons to say nothing of a son-in-law succeeded to the office, which goes to prove that it had become a family affair. When in the year 29, as the result of a brush with Tiberius, Annas was deposed in favor of Caiaphas, the former was not much concerned, for Caiaphas was a mediocrity who was well content to accept his father-in-law as mentor. The Talmud reveals very forcibly what the ordinary people thought of these distinguished gentlemen: "Woe is me for the house of Boètus, because of its massacres. Woe is me for the house of Annas, and the hissing of the vipers. They are the High Priests, their sons are the treasurers, their sons-in-law the officers of the Temple and their servants belabor the people with staves."

In the exercise of their sacerdotal functions the High Priests were surrounded by an entire world of priests, Levites, sacrificers, treasurers, liturgists, sacristans, musicians and janitors. Twenty-five thousand men were employed in the Temple, maintained by the enormous sums donated not only by the Jews of Palestine but by all those dispersed to the four corners of the world. Only those priests descended from Aaron, the brother of Moses, could actually perform the sacrificial rites on public occasions; the Levites were confined to the less important tasks. Neither had exercised any particular public influence since the coming of the Scribes.

The Scribes were a product of the Babylonian exile. The Jewish people those days, far from the Temple and deprived of any means of fulfilling the obligatory observances of their religion, attached themselves with fervor to the one thing of value that remained to them, a spiritual value as it happens, something that had been transported with them across the desert, perhaps in the actual scrolls but most likely in their memories: the Law. So had the specialists of the Torah come into being; codifying, commentating, teaching and refining with that combination of stubbornness and subtlety in which the Jewish character excels. They would gather around them groups of the faithful, who drew perpetual consolation from these expositions: it was these audiences and disciples that applied to their masters the title "Rab" or "Rabbi." When the Chosen People were again re-established in the land of their fathers, cooped up in a small, closed community, it was natural that the Scribes who knew all the ramifications of the Law should become increasingly influential, since the Law had been the chief agent of their preservation. By the time of Christ they had grown into a definite caste whose members were entered at a very early age and who vied with each other in elaborating ritual minutiae, a caste whose influence was infinitely greater than that of the official Priests of Jehovah who indeed were the prisoners of their ingenuity.

These two chief influences, the Priests and the Scribes, were reflected in the Grand Sanhedrin, the organization designed to assist the High Priest in his work. It was a kind of senate or Council of the Fathers. Tradition dated its origin as far back as Moses but in fact it had taken shape only during the past five hundred years, with the encouragement first of the Seleucid Kings and then of the Romans, who gave it official recognition in the hope of making use of it, discreetly. It was at the outset an aristocratic assembly, recruited from representatives of the lay and clerical nobility. The High Priest presided over it and all the upper priesthood who had discharged their office were members. Little by little, however, other elements were introduced—numerous scribes, "doctors of the law," more popular in tendency, whose unquestionable ability gave them an increasing influence. It also included a quota of simple pious Jews, "the Elders." This assembly of seventy notables combined the functions of a council of state, a supreme tribunal and a theological conclave; it was the supreme directive in the many complex questions where both religion and politics played a part. Jesus was arraigned before the Sanhedrin on the charges of subverting the Law and disturbing public order; both causes were within the competence of the Sanhedrin which in practice tended to identify them.

The same overlapping of religion and politics was manifest in the two schools of thought which divided public opinion: the Pharisees and the Sadducees. The titles denoted both a political party and a religious sect, a certain conception of the spiritual life and of the proper political attitude toward the temporal powers. This division of Israel between two intellectual and spiritual influences was a natural product of the historical conditions attending the establishment of the community on its return from exile. As always in an occupied country, one section of opinion favored a complete rebuttal of alien influence; the other, less uncompromising, sought to extract from the situation whatever it could. The first party clung to an ever-increasing religious austerity: the second stood by the more ancient tradition, basing its spiritual life upon the essential observances and refusing the asperities of the Law, which had already become formidable.

The Pharisees were descended from the Hasidim who had been the soul of the resistance to the decadence which set in when the Maccabean dynasty began to be contaminated by pagan influences. The name by which they were known was originally a nickname (as was "Huguenot" for the French protestants); *peruchim*, "Pharisees," meant "something set apart," "something which was separated." Their own name for themselves was *haberim*, "companions." It is not easy to judge them dispassionately with the terrible attacks which Jesus hurled at them embedded in our consciousness. Perhaps they were not *all* "hypocrites" and "whited sepulchres": perhaps Christ did not engulf them without exception in his condemnation. At any rate his apostle Paul came out from their ranks. They had performed a definite service to Israel; it was their intransigence more than anything else which had safeguarded the integrity of the Jewish spiritual inheritance, but it is certain that they had become fossilized in the exaltation of their pride and the meticulous cult of the letter of ritual observance in which they had sequestered themselves for five hundred years.

They were not very numerous, only about six thousand in the whole of Palestine. They often belonged to the humbler sort of people, butchers, sellers of food, wood cutters, herdsmen, blacksmiths. Although the Gospel associates Scribes and Pharisees together in one condemnation, most of the Pharisees were not professional Scribes and many Scribes and Doctors of Law were not Pharisees. They might be compared with the French Jansenists or the Anglo-Saxon Puritan sects. Their religion was narrow and they were distinguished by their grave demeanor; their austerities, the "phylacteries" which they wore on their temples all day (the average Jew put on these little boxes containing verses of the law only when he prayed) and their long tunics devoid of all ornament. They fled from even the semblance of evil. They forbade, naturally, marriage or even contact with pagans. They would enter the house of a Roman only for a very important reason and were lavish with purification rites afterward. The minutiae of their ritual frequently crossed the border of absurdity.

It is possible to name some of these militant devotees who flourished about the time of Christ. The great Hillel, the pride of the Pharisees during the preceding century, was dead, but his grandson, Rabbi Gamaliel, was certainly teaching, a kindly moderate man whose frail constitution did not affect the ardor of his faith. He was rivaled by the dynamic Rabbi Johanan ben Zaccrai who could whip his hearers into a frenzy of enthusiasm and religious passion. He would be about seventy then and had yet another half century to live. There was also Rabbi Eleazar ben Azarias, a priest descended from Ezra, who, we are told, could improvise three hundred dissertations on one theme of scripture; and Rabbi Joshua ben Hanania who had been taken as an infant in his cradle to the synagogue to listen to the Word of God. On a mountain above Lake Tiberias, Rabbi Yosse the Galilean interpreted the Law. And there were many others. Refined by incessant study of the sacred texts, they all drew from it a multiplicity of commentaries, glosses and problems. Like other casuists they had reached the point where the great doctrinal essentials became lost in the extreme subtlety of their interpretations; and like other devotees they often took more delight in the appearances of virtue than in its practice. It was this, of course, with which Jesus reproached them. Their religious ardor, however, was an essential element in Jewish policy toward Rome.

The Sadducees, who claimed to originate from a certain Sadoc, chief of priests in the time of David and Solomon, were exactly the sort of people described in France today as "bien pensants," people of good position who, like their counterparts in every race and clime, were not inclined to consider spiritual or patriotic principles worth the sacrifice of their dignity and comfort. They did not advocate violent resistance to foreign conquerors of whom it could be said that at least they maintained order in Canaan. Bernanos has said of them, as of their French counterparts, that they were always ready to run after the "lesser evil." It was not that they were bad Jews, but that, in religion, they limited themselves to the terms of the Law—especially when it operated to their advantage—and they regarded with contempt the forest of dogmatic speculation which had sprung up from the old tree of Moses. They did not subscribe to the Pharisaic niceties regarding the keeping of the Sabbath, nor yet to the new doctrine that there was a life beyond the grave. The Book of Ecclesiastes with its disillusioned wisdom, and many of the more practical of the Proverbs, exactly reflect their state of mind. It is not with such as these that the enthusiasm of multitudes is kindled; the comfortable are rarely a political driving force. Thus their influence was singularly small and as time passed the extremists of the other camp came to dominate the scene, which was not to prove to the advantage of Israel.

Such was the division of opinion at the time when Jesus began to preach; Pharisees on the one hand, Sadducees on the other. The Zelots might be called the extreme left-wing of the Pharisees and the Herodians, perhaps, the extreme right of the Sadducees. But it should be remembered that both parties were exclusive and extremely haughty minorities: the one felt itself uplifted by a superior knowledge of God; the others, secure in their possessions, had a contempt for the lower orders, the rabble.

The lower classes were called *am-ha-rez* which in itself means simply "countrymen" but in actual usage the word had a disparaging connotation. The *am-ha-rez* were in fact almost regarded as pagans by the doctors of law among the Pharisees, at any rate as louts sunk in ritual impurity. It was unlikely that the correct tithe had been levied on the fruit they sold or that their meat came from animals killed in accordance with the ritual. It was much better to have nothing to do with them. As for the Sadducees, they had for these clodhoppers the contempt that an exhausted aristocracy often displays when it has lost touch with the land from which it once derived strength. Many of these despised "countrymen" were not in fact poor—the Gospel mentions one who possessed five yokes of oxen—but they all felt themselves equally despised.

This social alignment is important, for there existed an active class hostility in Israel. In St. John's Gospel the Pharisees say: "But this people who knoweth not the law are cursed" (vii, 49). The Rabbi Akiba, one of the most venerated doctors of the Pharisean sect in the second century, left this sect and identified himself with the simple "countrymen." In this position, he relates, he experienced such a hatred for the learned doctors that if he had had one at his mercy he would, like an angry beast, have bitten him to the bone. The Pharisees were no less forthright on the subject of the *am-ha-rez.* Even the gentle Hillel assures us that "a churl has no conscience." Rabbi Jonathan recommended that people who did not know the Law should be "chopped in half like a fish" and Rabbi Eleazar that they should be cleft from head to foot and even burnt because such a "sacrifice" would have religious sanction. It was unanimously agreed that even on the Sabbath it was permissible to use a knife on one of the *am-ha-rez.* In the Jewish Encyclopedia under the heading "Am-ha-rez," the writer, S. Bialoblotzki, concludes: "The division undoubtedly served to strengthen the new Christian sect. The common people found among them a welcome and affection whereas among the learned of the Law they had encountered only the most brutal repulsion. Christianity did not require like the Pharisees the meticulous observance of the Law from those who came into it but it took much more account of the conditions of life among the Galilean people."

Thus, among the Pharisees, the Sadducees and the Am-ha-rez, Jesus began his ministry. It was before the High Priest and the Sanhedrin that he was to be charged because of it.

Dispersal of Jews in the Empire

It is the most astonishing thing that this small, closed community, so set on avoiding relations with others, constituting so unimportant a position in the immense empire of which it found itself a part, should nevertheless have had such powerful ramifications that a religion born in Palestine should have spread rapidly throughout all parts of the Roman world. It was not only on the rocky slopes of Judea and the smiling hills of Galilee that the sower flung his seed. The teaching of Jesus was addressed not only to the inhabitants of Israel but to all those, scattered throughout the empire from Iberia to Asia and from Africa to Byzantium, who were waiting for the great changes which were to come. His doctrine, first proclaimed in the country of the most widely dispersed people in the world, was to become of all religions the most widely diffused. The framework in which it was to expand was the framework of the empire; Jesus had barely died when the Gospel began to push its root as far as the helmets of the most ultimate legions. In less than three centuries history was to make Christianity and Latinity synonymous.

Obviously one of the agents of this rapid diffusion was unwittingly provided by Judaism itself. That Jewish phenomenon, the *Diaspora* or Dispersal, had begun with the Babylonian Captivity when many Jews had remained in Mesopotamia and Persia; Alexander and his successors had favored further emigrations. There were important Jewish business groups in Egypt, Greece and Rome. In the second century B.C. the Jewish Apocryphal Sibylline Books declare "the earth is full of thy race and the sea shall bring them forth." Strabo, writing under Augustus, complains that they have invaded all the cities and that it would be difficult to find a place where they have not been received and have not gradually taken possession. On the whole, however, the Romans had assisted this dispersion. Caesar had been their friend and Rome had witnessed the solemn mourning with which the Jews of the city observed his death. Augustus, Tiberius and Claudius, although they had exacted from them a respect for Roman order and the rights of others, had protected them and there were instances when the Emperors had intervened to punish provincial magistrates who had molested Jews. More than that, the Jews had been allowed to choose their own variant of the obligatory cult of the Divine Emperor: a sacrifice to Jehovah was accepted as a sacrifice to Augustus.

On the whole, the dispersed groups remained solidly united to the Palestinian community; there was very little apostasy and very few intermarriages with pagans. Every year thousands of pilgrims from all parts of the empire went to keep the Passover in Jerusalem, and, from the age of twenty, every Jew paid a religious tax to the Temple. So these Jewish colonies spread the thinking of Israel throughout the Roman world.

The relations between the dispersed Jews and the indigenous population were complex; there were occasional outbursts of anti-Jewish feeling with persecutions and pogroms; and anti-semitic outbursts from the Streichers of antiquity have come down to us. The tone of these throughout the centuries has varied little.

At the same time Jewish philosophy and the religion of the one God exercised a considerable influence. Philo of Alexandria, a Jew contemporary with Christ, deeply religious, developed a philosophy along Platonic lines, postulating the *Logos*, that aspect of the Divine Power in which the Almighty acted upon the world, the contemplation of which should be the object of all who desired union with the Ineffable. His doctrine, although not as brilliant as it was once thought to be, undoubtedly penetrated Egyptian thought and traces of it can be rediscovered in the writings of Clement of Alexandria and Origen.

Throughout the Empire the Jews can be said to have followed the advice given to them of old by Tobias: that God had dispersed them among the heathen nations so that they might spread the word of his glory and reveal his power.

Some groups of proselytes, desiring to participate in such an exalted religion, sought to become in all things Israelites, a decision redounding to their fortitude since they were required to be circumcised. However this may explain why female proselytes preponderated! Others, without subscribing to the full requirements of the Torah, professed to approve the faith and the principal customs of the Jews; these were the Jewish sympathizers, "those who feared God." "There is not a single Greek town or barbarian people," says Josephus, "in which there cannot be found many who observe our laws in regard to food, fasting and the lighting of lamps." This penetration of Judaism into the living fabric of the empire was akin to the similar influence which, as we shall see, many other oriental religions exerted at that time. But, transformed and carried through to its completion in Christianity, which drew in all these various cells of belief, the Jewish doctrine of the One God was to prove the most potent leaven.

The Roman Peace

The ferment set to work in a body which was ripe for it. We can look today on the singular contrast between the display of majesty, order and strength which Rome, fortified by her superb political system, presented then to the world, and the germs of inner decay discernible to the historian. At the moment when a society reaches its apogee, the evil which is to destroy it is already at work. Rome was then more powerful than she had ever been. The lines which Virgil had just written were no more than the truth: "She has lifted her head as high above the other cities as the cypress is above the tendrils of the clematis." The sons of the she-wolf had established that supremacy of spirit which has made their civilization the most potent in history. Their dominion over the races they had conquered was at once firmer and more humane than that of any of the empires which had preceded them. Their institutions, law, arts, language and literature, have had an incalculable effect upon mankind, not for one time but for all time.

The political formula which they had adopted seemed to be the optimum discoverable for the immense variety of problems which their prodigious empire entailed, an empire which then covered something around two million square miles. Some thirty years before the birth of Christ, one man had realized the necessity for a total reform of Roman institutions and methods. Thanks to him, the history of Rome ceased to be that of a city and became that of a vast assembly of countries to which one coherent mind applied conceptions of universal validity. The change certainly operated to his own benefit, but no one grudged him because everyone knew that it was necessary. He was able to abolish the old magistracy and the Senate without opposition, and when in mid-August of the year 29 B.C. his three-day triumph disclosed to the Romans that they had found their master, the sons of those who had assassinated Caesar because they had suspected him of personal ambitions, accepted the fact without a murmur.

Octavius founded the Empire, which was to be the field of action for the Apostles. He was not a sympathetic character, cowardly in warfare, hateful in victory, cruel in reprisals, unreliable even to his friends. His lean face with its long nose and tight-lipped mouth conveys even in official portraits an impression of both harshness and falseness. But he learned little by little to mold his own image and when he became Augustus he reached out to a serene amplitude and a self-mastery which was reflected throughout the empire he controlled. Tiberius, his successor, was certainly far less worthy. He was well-instructed politically, a skillful diplomatist and an excellent general; unfortunately he was also haughty and brutal, suspicious and crafty. It should be remembered, however, that the horrible cruelties to which, as he grew older, his maniacal suspicion drove him, affected only a small number of people in close association with him. The great majority of his subjects enjoyed a peace such as they had never known.

Immensa romanae pacis majestas, the immense majesty of the Roman peace, as the elder Pliny called it, is the most astonishing thing about the Roman empire in its early days. Even an emperor as cruel as Caligula could not disturb its foundations. To assess the importance of this achievement we have only to cast our minds back to the calamitous years preceding the establishment of the new order. During the last century B.C., the Roman civil wars, the revolt of Mithridates and incessant pirate raids had ruined the eastern Mediterranean. The armies of Sulla, Pompey, Caesar, Antony and Octavius had ravaged Italy, Greece and the Orient. There had been appalling massacres; the King of Pontus alone had slain 80,000 Italians in one holocaust and the horrible proscriptions of Sulla have gone down in history. The achievement of Augustus was to put an end to all these miseries, to impose order and peace.

It was he, and he alone, who forbade his officials to exercise their rapacity in the provinces confided to their charge. He fought corruption on the tribunals. He modified taxation, so that it should be less arbitrary and oppressive. He created an efficient police force and brigandage began to decline.

The giant body required a nervous system. Augustus proceeded to construct a network of roads. One of his first charges on the assumption of power was to have the main roads of Italy put in order and all the provincial governments received instructions to repair those in their own territories. From Rome to the Pillars of Hercules, from Armorica to Byzantium or to Athens, from the Rhine to the Danube, it was possible to travel with ease: and from the coast of northern France to the Bosphorus we can still see those magnificent highways with their regular stone slabs, which have been the trade-routes of the continent throughout the centuries. There was even a road across the African littoral from the Nile to the Atlantic, something which we have only just succeeded in rebuilding today.

The sea roads also profited by the peace. The great ports enjoyed a full prosperity. To Rome by way of the ports Ostia and Puteoli (located near the modern Pozzuoli) came corn from Sicily and Egypt, metals from Spain, wool and hides from Gaul, pottery from Greece, spices and perfumes from the Orient. In the center of the Aegean, Delos stored an immense quantity of merchandise; Rhodes, Antioch, Alexandria and Ephesus traded with farther Asia, even with China, along the caravan routes which brought in fine porcelain. Marseilles, Bordeaux, Byzantium and the rebuilt Carthage experienced a great expansion. Shipping Companies handled immense business. There was even a tourist industry: people wintered in Egypt, lingering by the Pyramids, gazing at Apis the Bull-god and feeding the sacred crocodiles.

It is true that a very large part of all this was designed to profit Rome herself—that it was to adorn, to enrich, to feed and to clothe her that all this wheat and all these marbles, all the fine trees and the sturdy slaves were shipped from the distant provinces and protectorates. A great deal of the tax revenue went to the same end. Rome was, at the time of the birth of Christ, in process of becoming one of the greatest urban agglomerations of the world, overstepping even her rival city of Alexandria. Suetonius said of Augustus that he found Rome all bricks and left it all marble. In actual fact Rome lacked the symmetrical plan of the city of Alexandria and there were many indifferently built quarters with narrow streets and houses which lacked both beauty and comfort. But the public monuments were much more numerous and they were everywhere; the groups of temples and official buildings were laid out to form a superb whole. At the top of the Capitol, dominating the Forum on one side and the *Campus Martius* on the other, rose the Temple of Jupiter with its gilded tiles and magnificent chariots. Around it, temples, statues and sanctuaries clustered so thickly that the processions could wend their way through only with difficulty. Opposite was the smaller but equally lovely sanctuary of Juno Moneta. Everywhere Augustus had left his mark upon the town, the Pantheon of Agrippa, Thermes, the Temple of Apollo Palatine, the portica of Octavia, the theater of Marcellus and, above all, his famous Forum with the Temple of Mars. Under Tiberius the magnificent structures of the Forum and the Palatine were completed by a temple dedicated to Augustus himself and by the sumptuous enlargement of the Imperial Palace. All this was the reward of the enormous patience and the methodical tenacity of the Romans. Their desire to commemorate their might was no more than human.

Along their perfect roads and across their guarded seas not only cargoes of merchandise traveled. All civilizations founded on commerce and exchange tend inevitably to become cosmopolitan both in the good and the bad sense of the term. The better elements among the governing class extracted something beyond luxury and pleasure: the advantages of a shared culture, of a quickening of ideas and philosophies and the noble vision of a *societas generis humani,* in the words of Cicero, began to take shape in the minds of many. This conception was to serve the advancement of Christianity, which was to bring to "the society of the whole human race" the Divine Command that men should love one another.

But, as in other times and places, this cosmopolitanism also brought trouble in its wake. It is not good for any society to experience a too rapid growth of unassimilable foreigners in its midst, nor to be swamped by alien notions which accord ill with its native genius. The swarm of aliens and birds of passage in all the principal cities was very much like that in any of the great seaports to-day: the Syrian merchants did not only sell jewels, perfumes, silks and fine leather, the swarm of "grammarians and rhetoricians" from Greece and Asia did not only teach grammar and rhetoric, nor did the Jews, as we have seen, confine themselves to commerce. Through the agency of these foreign bodies something was introduced into the imperial organism, something which carried in it the seeds of death.

A Threatened World

The Roman world had reached the summit of success, but it could not escape the law of nature which loads success with dangers and makes the descent inevitable. Long ago Scipio had wept over the walls of Carthage, which he had just destroyed, seeing a like destiny waiting for his own city. There were certainly many among the intelligent elite of Rome who realized that their society was stricken to the heart and who echoed like Scipio the words of Homer: "Thus fell Troy, the holy city, and Priam and his invincible people." The Parthians and the Germans, still firmly held down beyond the frontiers, were less dangerous to Rome than the doubts and the disharmony within the soul of the people. The day would come when the two would unite and St. Jerome was to say: "What made the barbarians so strong was the aid of our vices."

The latent elements of crisis derived in some measure from the very conditions and necessities of the peace which Augustus had constructed. The policy of pacification expunged liberty, directed thought to the uses of propaganda, tamed art for official purposes, so that nothing was left for those who sought something beyond consumer goods or the satisfactions of discipline or commerce. The mistake made by almost all these authoritarian regimes is to suppose that material prosperity disposes of all other problems. Intellectual liberty becomes more precious than ever, and is driven to question the very foundations of the system. The moment arrives when the importance of preserving the established order does not seem sufficient to condone the injustices, evils and suffering which it entails, the moment when, even at the price of violence, the whole society is willing to purchase a new order.

The crisis preparing for Rome was a spiritual one. Although Rome had provided her empire with an admirable administrative unity, such cultural unity as there was derived not from Rome but from Greece. That conquered Greece had vanquished her fierce master was true above all in the realm of ideas. Further, since the division of the conquests of Alexander and the spread of the Hellenistic culture in the succession states, a Greek came to mean not so much a man belonging to a particular people as a man who had received a certain type of education, who had reached a certain intellectual and spiritual level, and had imposed it as a standard on the Roman world, as defining the highest type of human being. Thus the idea of universalism as it existed in the Roman world was not Latin but foreign. On that essential point by which a form of civilization is measured, that is to say on its conception of life, the Romans were only followers. This, which explains to a great extent the ease with which they adopted another "weltanschauung," the conceptions of the Christian world, rendered their own great successes to some extent sterile.

In the midst of the beckoning of the innumerable ideas and doctrines which the glory of Rome attracted, only a tremendous effort could maintain, or even attempt to maintain, a Latinizing direction. This attempt was made by Augustus, aided by several of his friends, such as Maecenas. Virgil intended the *Aeneid* to be the sum of the ideas, beliefs and traditions of his people. Livy unrolled the glories of the national history from its beginnings down to the age of Augustus. There was a great literary flowering which included Tibullus, Propertius and Ovid. But it could not be called a spontaneous production of the Latin genius. The Greek influence was potent at the base of literature and poetry and the other arts. Outside the realm of law, Rome created very little, and the

Latin classics which we esteem so highly were hardly representative of average opinion under the Empire. The minds of the people were not formed by Virgil and Livy but by the innumerable lecturers and debaters whose schools multiplied everywhere and whose pupils were trained in controversies and analyses of considerable subtlety but little intellectual nourishment. The actual intellectual content began to decline, as witness the poverty of the plays of the period and the multiplication of those extracts, selections and anthologies, of the type compiled by Hyginus under Augustus and by Valerius Maximus under Tiberius, a type toward which even Seneca in his *Quaestiones naturales* and Pliny the Elder in his *Natural History* may be said to gravitate. Perhaps this intellectual crisis was of less importance than the grave social, moral and religious crises which were even more manifest. But it is when the intelligence weakens that a society begins to sag and a new element of creative force is needed to revivify it.

It is usual to instance the moral weaknesses which the pagan society displayed so strikingly but we must be careful not to exaggerate them. In the days of Augustus and Tiberius society as a whole had not reached that state of disintegration which it was to reach later, and Rome of the first century should not be judged by the *Satyricon* of Petronius any more than Paris in the first decade of the present century should be judged by the novels of Marcel Proust.

A wealthy and corrupt governing class can always provide picturesque copy for writers and satirists without being necessarily representative of its time. As soon as we put aside those works of literature which deal only with the rich and the powerful and turn to the less spectacular documents, epitaphs, inscriptions and the like, it can be seen that a good deal of domestic virtue remained. We find charity to the poor and filial and conjugal love frequently recorded in the most moving terms. Even in the imperial circle we find the example of Octavia, the emperor's sister, so loyal to her unfaithful husband Antony that she offers to rear his children by Cleopatra. Public virtue, too, was respected. Piety, dignity and honor, the three words which sum up the antique Latin morality, had not yet lost their meaning for the men of the time of Augustus, and the conception of the virtuous citizen devoted to the public good was a literary subject which was developed in various forms. We find it in Cicero, Virgil, Seneca and many others.

Yet the ethical problem was felt, and particularly among the governing classes. Following the great conquests, money too rapidly acquired and with insufficient effort had promoted demoralization. The booty acquired by Pompey in the East in the year 61 alone represented a large fortune in modern terms, and it was followed by much more. This money had no investment in industrial developments to claim it, as it would today, so it found only one outlet, luxury. Establishments, food, costume and entertainments became extravagantly ostentatious; the numbers of useless slaves swelled enormously. This disastrous tendency was not confined to those who profited immediately from conquest, the generals and the chief functionaries; the humblest legionary also took his cut and by the system of patronage the whole people grew into the habit of preferring idleness and sport to work. There was nothing in whose name men could rally against the works of the Money King.

The other peril which threatened Roman society was that which is always associated with wealth and luxury, the decline of the family. Divorce had become so easy that the powers were moved to action: two decrees, one in the year 19 B.C. and one in 9 A.D., sought to limit it, to punish adultery and to encourage the birth rate. But Augustus himself showed a poor example and his entourage abounded in scandal. It is not enough to declare the family an official institution and to make marriage obligatory; moral rehabilitation is not brought about by the utterance of unimpeachable sentiments. In any case abortion and the exposure of unwanted children seemed not to be regarded as a crime and was generally practiced. It requires more than the will of a sovereign to repair the moral standard.

Livy has summed up for us that position in which a state, however well-intentioned, finds it impossible to remedy evils without recasting the social order. "We have reached the point where we can no longer support either our vices or the remedies which would cure us of them." This confession of complete incapacity, which always appears in societies which have reached a high intellectual level, is perhaps the last and worst symptom of crisis. One can admire the fortitude of the Stoics, whose doctrines increased in influence during the reigns of Augustus and Tiberius; but their fundamental tenet, *ataraxy*, quietude, is a total detachment and a refusal to participate in the affairs of men. "Flee from the crowd," said Seneca, "flee from a small group, shun even a single companion." Nothing can be hoped from a society whose best elements have shrunk away from it. Jesus was to preach the vitalizing doctrine that a man could not exist for himself without existing for all.

The problems of class relations were no less pressing, for social distinctions had become more marked. There was a much greater gulf between the chief citizens and the common people in the days of Augustus than in the days of the Gracchi. The highest class, the *honestiores*, were an aristocracy based on money, for the necessary property qualification for them was very high. They included the *equites*, who lived out of lucrative offices, the senators, the landed proprietors and the highest public servants. All wore a purple band on their tunics, displayed the same prejudices and the same hauteur, and tended to close their ranks more and more against newcomers. This tendency was encouraged by Augustus who conferred senatorial privileges on wives and children down to the third generation, thus creating a *nobilitas* founded on title and not on service.

The mass of *humiliores*, the free or freed men, who no longer filled, under the empire, the role of an electorate, were given over to a humdrum life without opportunity. Memorial inscriptions have preserved for us the memory of their hardships and their cares. Many of them were content in their place-hunting idleness and were resigned to living according to the whims of the great. It is only too plain that these men, softened by the amenities of the cities, condemned to mediocrity, sunk more and more into idleness, could not possibly form the reservoir of a new elite. Society had congealed and it was to become more and more hardened until the day when the passage of the barbarians was to refashion it in blood.

In such a society, slavery constituted an even graver peril. Economic necessity alone does not account for this vast servile element, which certainly amounted to at least a third of the total population. Slaves, in a sense, had their use in days when there were so few mechanical aids, but the taste for luxury was chiefly responsible for the tremendous increase in these hordes of human cattle. The lot of a slave in Rome was often horrible, much worse than in Greece. The slave was a "thing" (*res*) and was reckoned solely as an item of property and nothing more. Domestic slaves were frequently well treated, according to the humor of those with whom they lived, but those who toiled in the fields and the shops, worse still in the mines, were condemned to the most atrocious lives. They included in their ranks not only the sons of slaves, born into servitude, but insolvent debtors and unfortunates who had been kidnapped by pirates at sea.

Slavery was the cancer eating into Roman society and it was also a constant and pressing menace. Tacitus tells us that in the year 24, a little before the public appearance of Jesus, all Rome "trembled" on account of unrest among the rural slaves in southern Italy. Many risings were to follow. These human herds were dangerous because they accustomed men to brutality, a brutality which was to some extent necessary to maintain control. Augustus himself had one of his slaves nailed to a ship's mast, and when, under Nero, a high official was assassinated, his four hundred slaves, men, women and children, all admittedly innocent, were crucified for not having known how to protect their master.

This miserable portion of humanity, recruited from all parts of the empire, had to seek some consolation. The slaves contributed a great deal toward all forms of religious unrest; they were given over to mysticism and superstition. Serving women from Antioch and Alexandria were the proselytizing agents for exotic cults which promised a future less unjust. Later they were to be propagandists of the Gospel. It was at this point that the social crisis and the religious crisis joined forces.

Religious Crisis

The deep-seated disquiet which troubled the mind and soul of Rome at the time has often been the subject of analysis. The old religious cult of Rome, founded on an arid ritualism and an interchange of services between man and god, no longer satisfied anybody. The cult of the city of Rome which had formerly been interwoven into daily life by ceremonial observances had become merged into the new imperial cult and was nothing but a patriotic sentiment or discipline. Although renewed by contact with the Greeks, classical mythology came to be considered either inadequate or absurd and skepticism increased everywhere. Claudius Pulcher, who threw the sacred fowls into the water so that they should not give an adverse sign, and Marcellus, drawing the curtains of his litter so that he might not see the auguries, share the attitude of Juvenal who wrote: "When it comes to the departed, the underground kingdom, the black frogs of the Styx, and a ferryman with a boat-hook who transports on a single vessel so many thousands of the dead, a child could not believe in it."

Yet, as always in decadent societies, this skepticism went with a profound if vague aspiration toward anything—creed, faith or plain superstition—which might fill the void left by the bankruptcy of the official religion. Rome swarmed with sages, soothsayers and charlatans; several attempts at expulsion were made (one by Tiberius in the year 16) but as Tacitus said, "We drive out the Chaldeans with one hand and hold on to them with the other." Agrippa had his horoscope drawn. Horace declared himself fortunate to be born under the same astral conjunction as Maecenas because they were both protected by Jupiter from the menace of Saturn. Tiberius at Capri was surrounded by astrologers and most of the Roman nobles kept soothsayers and magicians in their households.

Oriental cults were brought back by the multitude of men

who had served in the East either as soldiers or civilian officials or who had come thence as slaves; such cults had already taken hold throughout the empire. The black Phrygian goddess who was afterward called Cybele, with her attendant lover, the unfortunate youth Attis; then the Egyptian Isis, guardian of immortality and patroness of courtesans; then the Adonis of Byblos, the slain and the regenerated; then Astarte, Aphrodite, Atargatis and many other cults had made converts in all classes of Roman society. The "mysteries" with their rites of initiation and their esoteric doctrines appealed to the more ardent spirits; in the first two centuries of the Christian era their influence was to extend. Augustus himself was initiated into the Eleusinian mysteries and those of Dionysius had many adherents. Later still came the cult of the Persian Mithra, the young hunter or the sacrificial bull, whose worship was immensely popular among the legions.

It was a welter of speculation and confusion; contradictory elements were united in a synthesis which defied logic and countered the official rationalism with a hydra of irrationalism. The attempts of Augustus to revive the old Latin piety were foredoomed from the start; nobody regarded it as anything but a political move. Men sought in these confused doctrines what the human spirit has always sought from religion. In those cults which enjoined penitence and discipline, also in the more or less reputable practices of the mysteries, even in the frankly sexual character of some of the ceremonies, one principle clearly emerges: the desire to transcend the limitations of mortality and thus to find peace from the all-pervading disquiet.

The more cultivated resorted to philosophy for an answer. The Stoics sought not to console men but to train them to acceptance, to teach them that participation in the divine meant submission to it. The neo-Platonism associated with Philo of Alexandria taught the approach through ecstasy by which the soul could transcend the life of the body and rejoin God. There was another doctrine which, although its sphere of influence was certainly limited, nevertheless played a part which was for a long time underestimated but which has latterly been revalued. This was neo-Pythagoreanism, supposedly derived from the teachings of Pythagoras, the Greek philosopher of the sixth century B.C., whose actual existence is problematical but to whom is attributed the theorem concerning the square of the hypotenuse of a right-angled triangle commonly known by his name. Neo-Pythagoreanism claimed that the human soul was a fragment of the divinity, a focus concentrating the rays of universal consciousness, a *microcosm* mysteriously bound to the *macrocosm*, which, fallen to earth at creation, is perpetually drawn back to heaven as to its own country. Mingled with various Orphic and Egyptian influences, this doctrine began to establish itself in the time of Augustus, not as an arid speculation but as a living faith. Nigidius Figulus, a contemporary of Cicero, drew up a complete exposition, and a subterranean church has been uncovered in Rome wherein met the disciples of this philosophy which was so nearly a religion.

The well known lines in Virgil's Fourth Eclogue which announce the forthcoming transformation of the world in connection with the birth of a child predestined to usher in the age of gold, have been credited perhaps with more "messianic" intention than can be historically justified. But all the same they point to the application of those pythagorean conceptions which foretold a radical upheavel through an imminent event about this time. In the Cathedral of Siena, there is, in the mosaic pavement in the center of the nave, a representation of Hermes Trismegistus with the Sybil of Cumae who unfolds a scroll on which is inscribed the famous Virgilian verse. Whatever its inspiration, the poet has left us a perfect expression of the anxious presentiment which troubled the Roman world, conscious amid all its glory that it was destined to ruin and seeking for a meaning in its foreboding.

"The Fatherland of Christianity from its beginnings," as Mgr. Duchesne has phrased it, the Roman Empire provided the Gospel with a setting in which it could expand, communications which the Apostles were to use, and years of peace which were to permit Christianity to strike roots before the coming of the great disasters. Only the doctrine of Christ could resolve the problems which weighed so heavily upon the men of the time. It was to resolve the intellectual crisis by reconstituting the basis of personality and building upon it a new humanism. It was to solve the moral problem by a reorientation of the moral principles deriving not from collective sanction but from divine ordinance. As for the social problem, the Gospel which proclaimed the dignity of man and the law of love was to rehabilitate the slaves and the depressed classes and set new blood coursing through the veins of society. Finally, the confused religious aspiration toward the ideal of justice in this world and peace beyond the grave was to find fulfillment in a doctrine clearer and purer than any other. The historical fact of the Roman Empire permitted the seed sown in Palestine to take root and spread rapidly and far. But all the evidence is there to show that the seed was necessary and that, in the depths of its consciousness, the Roman world was waiting for it.

CHAPTER FOUR

THE SOWER WENT OUT TO SOW

The Adversary

AT BETHABARA Jesus was made manifest to the sight of men. It would have seemed normal therefore that he should have begun attracting crowds to listen to his teaching as John the Baptist had done. Nevertheless a period of several months elapsed before he began his solemn mission, a period of preparation during which such of his actions as are recorded seem to foreshadow those which he will perform later on. There are certain characteristic episodes in which the man that he is to be are revealed. Perhaps there was a tacit agreement that when the prophetic voice of John was constrained to silence, Jesus in his turn should begin to speak. A strange scene, reported in the three synoptic gospels, suggests that there might have been other motives for this temporary withholding. The scene as reported in the plain words of St. Mark sheds a dim light into that unfathomable region where the human soul of the Messiah strove with the stirrings of divine consciousness.

"The Spirit driveth him into the wilderness, and he was there in the wilderness forty days, tempted of Satan, and was with the wild beasts; and the angels ministered unto him." (Mark i, 12-13.) It is obvious that the experiences of this profound crisis could have been transmitted to the Evangelists only by the one who had lived through them. The Apocryphal Gospel of the Ebionites says definitely, "The Lord told us that the Devil disputed with him and tempted him for forty days." The medieval sculptors who depicted it so often in our cathedrals were profoundly moved by the awe and the mystery of this encounter between total purity and the unclean spirit, by the submission of the man-God to the common lot of humanity, tempering his steel in the fire of the infernal adversary's dialectic. In the Old Testament Jacob, on the eve of his decisive adventure, had wrestled all night with the invisible presence in whom, when the day came, he recognized the Angel of the Lord. Moses also when he went back to Egypt, charged by Jehovah to deliver his people, had passed through similar experiences, although in the case of both Jacob and Moses, the mission was concerned with temporal things.

For such a man as Jesus, it would be natural to go into retreat after the happenings on the bank of the Jordan. There are many instances in the Gospel when he retires from the crowds to place himself once more alone with God. This constant need for meditation is a fundamental trait of his character. "And he withdrew himself into the wilderness and prayed" (Luke v, 16). "He departed thence by ship into a desert place apart" (Matt. xiv, 13). "And it came to pass in those days that he went out into a mountain to pray, and continued all night in prayer to God" (Luke vi, 12). To the mystic, solitary prayer and silence is the necessary means of action.

Ever since God spoke from Sinai, the high mountains have been considered propitious for communication with Him and from ancient times the desert had been regarded as sheltering evil spirits. Therefore the unfortunate scapegoat charged with the sins of Israel was driven into the desert (Leviticus xvi). Forty days was the period which Moses spent on the mountain (Exodus xxxiv, 28), the period spent by Elijah in approaching Horeb (I Kings xix, 8), and it is today the duration of the Christian Lent. The human body subjected to so long and rigorous a fast is prone to the most extreme solicitations of mind and spirit.

Djebel Quarantal, "the Mountain of the Forty Days," the place traditionally associated with Jesus's retreat, stands not far from Jericho. It is composed of chalk and its dull white slopes are riven by the black gorge of a brook, the Kerith. There is a small convent of Orthodox monks, descended from the anchorites of the fifth century, whose cells may still be discerned on the mountain side. The place had figured before in the history of Israel; Simon, the last of the Maccabees, had made his last stand and had perished there. It is one of the most forbidding places in the Judean desert; eagles wheel overhead and the jackals come down to drink. The view from the summit, which is extensive in spite of its precipitance, is magnificent but inimical to mankind. Between two narrow ribbons of verdure the Jordan winds like a silver snake across the yellow sands. To the north the snowy head of Hermon hovers on the horizon above the huddled mountains of Samaria. In a semicircular depression to the west rows of olive trees alone betray the presence of Jerusalem. Toward the south the plain becomes more and more barren, its surface glistening increasingly with particles of salt, until it plunges into the hollow where sleep the motionless waters of the accursed sea.

All this comfortless landscape, this desolate vista devoid of human life, stretched below the eyes of Jesus. He would see the sun rise abruptly behind Mt. Nebo without a heralding dawn and in the evening, in those seconds of delicate luminosity which precede the brusque oriental nightfall, he would experience that poignant sadness which fills the human heart at the silent end of a beautiful day. During that six weeks vigil he would feel, too, rising from the plain to the grotto where he sheltered, the dark breath of the wind from Arabia, the dreaded Khamsin of the desert on whose gusts were borne the challenge of the adversary of mankind.

This is what has been reported to us of this drama played out in solitude. Having fasted forty days and forty nights, Jesus felt hungry. Then the Tempter approached and said, "If thou be the son of God, command this stone that it be made bread." Jesus replied, "It is written that man shall not live by bread alone, but by every word of God." The Devil then transported him to the top of a high mountain and by sorcery displayed to him all the kingdoms of the world, saying: "All this power will I give thee, and the glory of them; for that is delivered unto me, and to whomsoever I will give it. If thou therefore wilt worship me, all shall be thine." But Jesus said to him, "It is written, Thou shalt worship the Lord thy God and him only shalt thou serve." "And he brought him to Jerusalem and set him on a pinnacle of the Temple and said unto him: If thou be the son of God, cast thyself down from hence. For it is written, He shall give his angels charge over thee, to keep thee and in their hands they shall bear thee up, lest at any time thou shalt dash thy foot against a stone." But the invincible one replied: "It is written again, Thou shalt not tempt the Lord thy God." Vanquished at last, the Adversary left him, and angels came and ministered to him. (Luke iv, 1-13; Mark i, 12-13; Matt. iv, 1-11.)

To the "historical critic" the mere presence of the devil in this scene is enough to make it entirely incredible and to relegate it to the realm of myth. Catholic theologians, in affirming that this encounter was certainly a personal struggle between Jesus and the devil, allow that the transportation to the top of a high mountain and a pinnacle of the temple might have occurred in a vision. But the episode has a terrible reality. The Adversary, whose existence was accepted not only by Dante and St. Thomas Aquinas but by Newton and Pascal, is that same "fearful son of chaos" (*Chaos wunderlicher Sohn*) whose menacing, concrete presence Goethe felt around him. Commenting on the episode, Dostoievski's Grand Inquisitor says that three temptations govern the whole of history and display the three images which crystallize all the insoluble contradictions of human nature everywhere throughout the world: sensuality, the will to power, and the desire to transcend the limits of mortality.

The desert is full of blocks of stone, colored a warm brown, almost derisively like bread. Beyond Nebo and the Mountains of Moab the infinite expanse of plain cannot fail to suggest those magnificent dead empires of Mesopotamia and Persia, and the cities of Nineveh and Babylon, whose names are still synonyms for glory and power. The pinnacle of the Temple would be the terrace above the portico of Solomon, dominating the ravine of Cedron, a place open to all, even to the pagans, for it was here that the Roman soldiers stood on guard against disorder during the Jewish feasts. Josephus tells us that the exterior wall rose so abruptly that it was impossible to look down without giddiness. The passage of scripture which the devil, always an excellent theologian, quotes is, of course, our Psalm 91.

The inclusion of this episode at the very beginning of the Gospel conveys an important message. It explains Jesus's own conception of his role as Messiah. The Kingdom of God was not to be established by the means appropriate to earthly powers. The Messiah was not to be the conquering King awaited by almost the whole of Israel. In exposing the wiles of the tempter, in refusing the kingdoms of the world, in denying the facile manifestation of a dramatic sign, Jesus had said "no" to all this. In refusing to change the stones to bread, he displays the characteristic that we shall always notice, that he, who was to work so many miracles for the benefit of mankind, would work none to his own advantage any more than he would deliver himself from the cross.

So far from being incredible, the scene enshrines profound psychological and spiritual truths. The Son of God who was to be assailed by all our human mischance is here at the beginning for us to recognize. "For in that he himself hath suffered being tempted, he is able to succor them that are tempted," says Paul in the Epistle to the Hebrews (ii, 18), and this idea is expressed by the sixteenth century sculptor who places, in the background of his depiction of the Temptation of Christ, the temptation of Adam and Eve in the Garden of Eden. "For we have not an high priest which cannot be touched with the feeling of our infirmities, but was in all points like as we are" (Hebrews iv, 15). When St. Luke finishes his account of the Temptation by saying that the Devil departed from Jesus "for a season" he is reminding us that all his life the Master had to battle with the Adversary, whose presence although unmentioned can be felt continually, particularly in the Garden of Olives, on the eve of Christ's Passion. For it was with him as it is with us, according to his humanity.

So, having proved himself the master of his own soul, Jesus could assume his destiny.

The Eye of God

When he came down from the mountain, it would have been early March. On the banks of the Jordan, and around Jericho, the wheat and the barley would be turning yellow. It would be warm during the day but still cold at night: "In Adar," (March) says a Jewish proverb, "the ox shivers in the morning but in the afternoon he seeks the shade of the fig tree to cool his hide." In the "ghor" near Bethabara, the close heat began to be uncomfortable; John the Baptist himself left the ford to go up into the hills where he continued preaching and baptizing and Jesus himself did not stay long in the neighborhood.

His short stay, however, was marked by one incident of singular importance. It is reported by only St. John (i, 35-50) and a soundly-rooted tradition has always regarded the account as deriving directly from the beloved disciple's memory of the electrifying moment when the eye of God in the form of man fell upon John himself. He has noted the exact time, "about the tenth hour," that is about four in the afternoon. On the crest of the Judean heights the sun had already almost finished its course. St. John, who for once mentions himself here by name, was walking with another who had made the pilgrimage to the ford, a fellow Galilean named Andrew, one of the many who had gone down to the Jordan to hear the word and receive baptism. He had left the fishing boats which he and his brother Simon owned on Lake Gennesaret, in association with Zebedee, John's father. He had heard the prophet call the people to repentance; he had even been there at the time when a responsible delegation had besought John to say whether he was or was not the Messiah.

While they were gathered around him, a man had passed of whom the prophet said, "Behold the Lamb of God," an allusion which they understood as replying both to the questions of the rabbis and to their own expectations. The scene which had taken place six weeks earlier, when the Holy Spirit had descended upon the head of the unknown man at the moment of baptism, could not have been forgotten by the fervent crowds at Bethabara, and when the man passed by, the two disciples of the prophet did not hesitate to follow him. He, seeing them follow, said, "What seek ye?" Like the sturdy peasants they were, they blurted out one of those half embarrassed questions which so often enshrine the most honest sentiments: "Rabbi (which is to say Master) where dwellest thou?" "Come and see," said Jesus. The text adds simply that they went and saw where he lived and stayed with him that day. But the rest of the chapter and the whole Gospel proves that they had immediately penetrated to the secret. It is the first manifestation of that mysterious power which Jesus had of piercing the soul he desires at a glance and taking instant possession. Andrew, John, Simon, Philip, the woman of Samaria, were all seized by him with this supernatural force. "God swoops on the soul like the eagle on the sparrow," said a later Spanish mystic, and if, in the Temptation, the human side of Jesus is paramount, in this brief encounter with his first disciples, we are at once aware of the other side. For this is the face of God.

Andrew's brother Simon was not with him and John when they met Jesus. When they returned saying, "We have found the Messiah," Simon also went to him. "When Jesus beheld him," says the Gospel, "he said, thou art Simon the son of Jona, thou shalt be called Cephas, which is by interpretation, a stone." The phrase must then have seemed very obscure; months were to pass before it was elucidated. But even more startlingly Christ had at once taken the measure of the man before him. At one glance he had gauged his capacity and with sovereign authority he had changed his name. Every Jew knew what that meant. In the Old Testament, the bestowal of a new name is the symbolical expression of divine choice, the promise of an extraordinary mission. Thus Abram became Abraham and Jacob, Israel. All the oriental peoples, the Egyptians and the Chaldeans, have always attached an extreme importance to the name as an occult force influencing the person. To discover the secret name of a God is to lay a claim on him. The name of Jehovah must not be invoked in vain. In modern China there still exists the custom of having a confidential name which only immediate kin have the right to use. Simon, entering into that band of disciples which was later to become the Church, was marked from the beginning by a special sign, by the power of those two syllables, Cephas, Peter, "the Rock."

In Andrew, John and Simon, Jesus the Galilean had chosen, among all the disciples of the Baptist, three of his compatriots and together they returned to their own province. The shortest way to Nazareth follows the Jordan until within six miles of Lake Tiberias, about fifty-six miles in all, then the road turns to the west through the pass across the fair slopes of Mt. Tabor. With his three companions Jesus followed the ancient way through this valley, which so many cohorts of pilgrims had traversed since the earliest times. The pagan cities of Archelais and Scythopolis, with their splendid sinful palaces, where even the idol of Astarte was enthroned, would remind the travelers by their very existence of the dire straits of the people of Israel. When he arrived at the crossroads where they should have parted company, it seems as though Jesus went out of his own way to accompany his friends to the north shore of the lake, where their fishing business was situated, for it was at Bethsaida, in the country of Andrew and Simon Peter, that he annexed two more disciples as summarily as before.

He met Philip and said, "Follow me." The Gospel says nothing more but it is clear that Jesus's hold upon the newcomer must have been complete for he is immediately disclosed as announcing his conversion to his friends and proselytizing with all the neophyte's zeal.

"We have found him of whom Moses in the law and the prophets did write." When they asked him who, he replied, "Jesus of Nazareth, the son of Joseph," doubtless knowing nothing else of the man in whom he had put all his faith. But in Bethsaida they knew all about Nazareth and its inhabitants; the village was only half a day's journey across the mountain, a humble community of simple people with no history or title to consideration. "Can there any good thing come out of Nazareth?" asked Nathaniel, one of his listeners, and he knew what he was talking about since he came from Cana, a village only a few miles away from that which Philip had pointed out as the home of the Messiah. But the neophyte stood firm: "Come and see."

Then ensues another of those scenes where Jesus immediately takes hold of a man, at once and completely. Nathaniel was a character, rugged, forceful, critical but entirely honest. When he came face to face with Jesus, that sudden mysterious illumination in which the soul is revealed descended upon him and left him ardent and trembling. What Pascal has called the "night of fire" must have been full of that supernatural light. "Nathaniel," said Jesus, "before that Philip called thee, when thou wast under the fig tree, I saw thee." It was enough; the man of Nazareth had let in the light on the troubled meditations of Nathaniel. Even although we may not wish it, we are always in a sense delivered to those who see through to the roots of our nature.

The revelation went to the heart of Nathaniel, and filled it with holy enthusiasm. "Rabbi, thou art the son of God, thou art the King of Israel." His soul stretched out in need and Jesus was to fill it to overflowing. "Because I said unto thee, I saw thee under the fig tree, believest thou? Thou shalt see greater things than this." Then, for the first time embarking on the Messianic theme, he alludes to Jacob's famous dream of the ladder reaching down from heaven and promises Nathaniel that he shall see heaven open and through him be joined with the earth.

Between Bethabara and Bethsaida, Jesus had called to himself, by a few simple words, five men of great faith. They were to follow him to death. All of them were to become Apostles. The man who, in the Fourth Gospel, is called Nathaniel is most probably he whom the synoptics call Bartholomew: the first name was probably the given name, the second, "Bar-tholomy, son of Ptolemy," the family name. Four of the five were to be martyred. Those who meet the eye of God are often cast for tragedy on earth.

The Wedding at Cana

Of the five disciples, it would appear that three, Simon, Andrew and John, stayed on the shore of the lake where probably they resumed their work. It might have been that they had not yet realized that the life to which Jesus had called them necessitated a total break and that neither the requirements of family nor calling might hold them back. We shall encounter them later on, these fishermen who were to be called fishers of men.

Philip and Nathaniel, however, accompanied their new master. They went, as we are told by St. John's Gospel, which alone reports the incident (John ii, 1-11), to Cana of Galilee to attend wedding festivities, Mary the mother of Jesus being already there. The site which is associated with the miracle is called today Kefr Kenna; it is a large well-kept village set among gardens and streams on the slopes of a lesser range of hills between Tabor and Djermak. Young Palestinian Christians go there to have their marriages blest. But lower down the hillside there is a place called Kirbet Quana where ancient remains of buildings have been discovered in a field. This has kept archaeologists busy raising and opposing arguments for one place and the other. Both Kefr Kenna and Kirbet Quana are near enough to Nazareth, a little over six and eight miles respectively by road, and less across country. It would be quite natural for Jesus to have friends there without supposing that Nathaniel, who belonged to Cana, had invited him, certainly without going to the lengths of those medieval artists who made St. John the bridegroom and Mary Magdalene the bride.

The road from Bethsaida to Cana rises steeply. The lake is 680 feet below sea level, Cana, about 1640 feet above. It is a long walk, also, eighteen miles at least. As the road rises, leaving the country of the palm trees for the grain fields and the vineyards, the horizon expands, and on the way back, before entering the gorge of Arbela, the traveler has a view of the wide blue estuary of the Jordan as it rushes through the reeds; the snows of Hermon are reflected and, in the spring, a passing flight of flamingos makes a serpentine trail of brilliant rose and black through the clear air. Toward the end of the road over the crest of the hill the golden brown tapestry of the plain of Esdraelon, with its ripening vineyards, stretches below. It is a beautiful country indeed in the spring. "For lo, the winter is past and the rain is over and gone, the flowers appear on the earth; the time of the singing of the birds is come, and the voice of the turtle is heard in our land; the fig tree putteth forth her green figs and the vines with the tender grape give a good smell." Thus says the Song of Solomon and at Cana in this lighthearted springtime, the epithalamium with which the Canticle continues might also be heard: "Arise my love, my fair one and come away. O my dove that art in the clefts of the rock; let me see thy countenance, let me hear thy voice, for sweet is thy voice and thy countenance is comely." (Song of Solomon ii, 11-14.)

The Jewish wedding feasts were celebrated with many rites and rejoicings and lasted from three to eight days according to the circumstances of the couple. That which Jesus attended was in a substantial family to judge from the quantity of water provided for the ritual ablutions and the presence of a "governor of the feast," that is to say a master of ceremonies. Beginning on a Wednesday, the usual day for the marriage of a virgin, it would certainly last at least until the following Sabbath. Once the bride had been carried in the chair borne by grooms to her new dwelling, the ritual vase broken and the oaths exchanged under the shadow of the bridal veil, the festivities would commence. The Jews, ordinarily an abstemious people, eat almost to excess on these occasions; rich foods, meat, game and stuffed fish appear in a succession of heavy dishes, almost all strongly flavored with onion, the basis of Jewish cuisine since the sojourn in Egypt. A great deal of wine was drunk; indeed, in Hebrew, "banquet" and "drinking bout" are denoted by the same word, used without any modification or description. The wines of Palestine are excellent and have a high alcohol content and the vine is so familiar and beloved a plant that Jesus uses it often in parable and metaphor. He even said: "I am the true vine and my Father is the husbandman." (St. John x, 1.) The lore of the rabbis naturally provided many rites for blessing the precious vintage before drinking; if the wine was unadulterated "Blessed be the Creator of the fruit of the trees" was said. But if water had been added the formula was: "Blessed be the author of the fruit of the vine." For wedding feasts, the first benediction would be said for on these days the regulations concerning water would be superfluous, such as that it should not be left uncovered, and should not be drunk from a colored glass. Water, certainly, would only be required for ablutions.

On this occasion, the wine ran out. Jesus, who was taking part in the festivities, reclining among the other guests, saw his mother approaching. "They have no wine," she said. It was a discreet suggestion and Jesus realized it, but he was not going to accede immediately. His reply is given in the gospel as "Woman, what have I to do with thee?" In modern terms, this seems harsh, if not actually unkind, to us, coming from a presumably affectionate son who has not seen his mother for two months. But in Aramaic the tone is quite different. "Woman" is an address of the highest courtesy. It was used by Eleazar to the mother of Rebecca and by Jesus to Mary from the cross. As for the expression which shocks us so much, it can be found often in the Old Testament. (Judges xi, 12; II Samuel xvi, 10, xix, 22; I Kings xvii, 18, II Kings iii, 13.) It means nothing more than: "Why bother me with this?" Jesus indeed makes it quite clear by adding, "Mine hour is not yet come." This willingness to wait before declaring himself has been noted before, but Mary was not put off by it. She knew her son. "Whatsoever he saith unto you, do it," she said to the servants.

Was it solely because he was moved by the chagrin of his host that Jesus decided to accede to his mother's suggestion? We are rather reluctant to accept the harnessing of the divine power to such a very temporal purpose. There is of course a clear symbolic intention in the miracle, but was this the ultimate motive? A clue perhaps is furnished by the Gospel statement that, after the miracle, "his disciples believed on him." Certainly it was one of the surprising things which he had promised Nathaniel that he should see.

At the entrance to the house there would be six stone waterpots provided for the ritual purifications. Each would contain about a firkin so the six together would amount to a very large hogshead. Jesus said to the servants: "Fill the waterpots with water." They did so, to the brim. "Draw out now and bear unto the governor of the feast." When the latter had tasted it he said jokingly to the bridegroom, not knowing whence the new wine had come, "Every man at the beginning doth set forth good wine; and when men have well drunk, then that which is worse. But thou hast kept the good wine until now."

Such was the first of Christ's miracles: "The first, the kind miracle," says Alyosha in *The Brothers Karamazov*, "when Christ joins in human happiness, happiness not sorrow." Saint John, who gives us so few miracles, only seven in all, has deliberately put this one at the opening of his Gospel; clearly therefore he did not regard it as futile. There is a good homely savor about it, such as Christ loved, and those painters are surely wrong who have depicted these rustic revels in sumptuous surroundings. The wine that flowed at the Lord's command was that same rough Galilean vintage that was commonly drunk just as the bread which he transformed into the Eucharist was the bread that everyone ate. The first miracle, which gave such luster to a country wedding feast was not trivial for it marked the consecration of the union between man and woman as Christ was to ordain it.

Tradition has always accorded this first miracle an occult significance, following St. Augustine's definition that it "was not only an actual and extraordinary fact but the symbol of the operation of a higher order." There has always been a special significance attaching to the change of water into wine. It was the miracle of Dionysius and Pliny tells us of the temple on the isle of Andros where the sacred spring turned into wine at the nones of January. The Christian liturgy has fixed the second Sunday after the Epiphany as the date for the miracle of Cana, probably with the intention, as in the case of Christmas, of "baptizing" a pagan feast. For the immediate disciples of the Master, Philip and Andrew, the miracle must have borne a deeper significance. As a symbol of the change wrought by the Messiah on the soul, it was to engage them completely and for all their lives. John, at Bethabara, had baptized with water; the miraculous wine to them was the water of life.

In Jerusalem's Midst

When he left Cana, Jesus went down again to the lakeside to Capernaum (John ii, 12) for a short stay. Possibly this was by Philip's invitation; possibly he wanted to see Simon Peter, John and Andrew again; possibly it was simply that as a Galilean he preferred to make the Passover journey to Jerusalem through the valley rather than through heathen Samaria.

This journey to Jerusalem and the startling episode which accompanied it is one of the first manifestations, still partly obscured, by which Jesus reveals, implicitly rather than explicitly, his divine vocation. It serves to forge that link between the Savior and the holy city of Israel which was to be made irrefragable at Calvary, and it was to establish between the temple of Yahveh on earth and that human body which enclosed the divine spirit the symbolic relationship which was to show forth in the Resurrection.

The Jewish Passover would draw to Jerusalem the sort of crowds that a great pilgrimage to Lourdes draws today. A closer analogy still would be the sort of human gravitation which takes place in India toward Benares or in Moslem countries towards Mecca. From north, south, east and west, from the edge of the desert and the cities of Egypt, from Babylon and from the Jewish settlements in Asia Minor, the faithful would set out, sleeping under canvas for weeks on end and covering every available field and hillside in the precincts of Jerusalem with their heterogeneous encampments during the eight days of the feast. At the ports of Caesarea and Joppa an organized traffic discharged boatloads of pilgrims, just as we can see them today disembarking at Djedda on the Red Sea for Mecca. When they touched the soil of the Promised Land, the pilgrims knelt and kissed it. If Josephus is to be believed, at the Passover feast preceding the destruction of the Temple in A.D. 70, 255,660 lambs were sacrificed. Reckoning one lamb per family of ten pilgrims this gives a total of two and a half million souls, a vast sea of human fervor surging up the sacred hill.

The Temple was that which, fifty years or so earlier, Herod had decided to rebuild, to proclaim his own glory and to propitiate the Jewish people. On the very spot where Solomon had built the first Temple, that holy wonder of the world, and where, after the return from exile, the battered and defeated Jews had raised a modest memorial of it, the tyrant undertook to build his own Temple, which was so rich, vast and glorious that forty-six years after the first stones had been laid it was still uncompleted. Indeed it was not finished until the year 64, six years before its total destruction.

He had visions of grandeur, the Idumean barbarian; his passion for splendid and sumptuous buildings was one of the few admirable traits of his character. He engaged ten thousand workmen and trained a thousand priests as masons so that they might work in those sacred interior quarters of the Temple where the laity were not allowed to penetrate. He sought for stone, wood, rare marbles and precious metals with all the vigor and astuteness with which he was accustomed to enforce his will. The Sanctuary of the new Temple was an exact replica of Solomon's, but the exterior buildings had been multiplied and enlarged enormously and the huge supporting walls built into the surrounding hills enabled the area of the summit to be almost doubled.[1] Upon this artificial plateau were erected four courts, rising higher and higher as they approached the Sanctuary. In the first, the Court of the Gentiles, the heathen were permitted. An inscription, which has been uncovered, marks the limit beyond which they might not proceed on pain of death. "The Court of the Women" was reserved for Jewish women; only the men might enter the "Court of the Israelites" from which opened the exclusive and jealously guarded "Court of the Priests."

The largest of these Courts was that of the Gentiles, a gigantic esplanade, flanked by two porticos, which served as a sort of general meeting place for all sorts of people in Jerusalem. The eastern portico, called the Portico of Solomon, with its sixty-two immense columns disposed in three aisles, served the same purpose as similar porticos in Italy, Greece and Asia Minor where crowds love to foregather. During the Passover, the Court of the Gentiles was filled to overflowing with every sort of picturesquely costumed figure. White, yellow and striped veils jostled black hats, turbans and Phrygian bonnets; every variety of headdress to be found throughout the empire and the Near East could be seen here. The white *taliss*, a ritual veil ornamented with fringes whose knots denoted the thrice holy name of the Lord, indicated the pious Jews, who wore it beneath their tunics, as they attempted to elbow their way through the crowds toward the Court reserved for the faithful.

It would not be an easy progress. The great atrium was not merely an open air meeting place; it was also a bank and a market, for all sorts of merchandise. Doves and sheep were herded there. Money changers stood at their little tables like desks exchanging the pilgrims' "unclean" Roman and Greek

---

[1] The "Wailing Wall" of the Jews is a fragment of the walls of Herod's Temple.

money for the Jewish pieces with which they could pay the obligatory dues for the "sanctification of their souls." Levites and other sacristans had stalls of salt, flour, wine, oil and incense for the Temple offerings. But most conspicuous of all was the cattle which were mixed up with the crowd. On arriving at the Temple, the faithful purchased from an office kept by the priests a "seal" or token which varied according to the means and the piety of the purchaser. It might be a token for a calf or a goat or a ram or for fish. According to its value the owner acquired somewhere in the court a calf or a goat or a ram or even an ox which he would sacrifice immediately the silver trumpets blew three blasts. The sacrificial cattle were sold by the priests, who lived out of this commerce and were naturally keen on advancing it. Discussions about price were naturally accompanied by the arguments and shrill cries such as take place today around the sacred Black Stone at Mecca, and it is more than doubtful whether piety is well served by these doubtless well-intentioned transactions.

Certainly the sensitive and ardent soul blenches at this spectacle, and the base commercialism of many of the shops at Lourdes and Lisieux today offends the same elementary sense of respect due to a holy place. We may feel at the sight of these "washable and unbreakable Virgins" a faint shadow of the holy wrath of Jesus. The Prophet Malachi had foretold that the Messenger of the Lord should come suddenly to the Temple and purify the sons of Levi (Malachi iii, 1-3) and Zechariah that in the days of the Messiah there shall be no more trafficking in the Temple (Zech. xiv, 21).

Finding himself in the middle of all this haggling, Jesus was seized with anger. Knotting the cords of his *taliss* into a whip, he scourged the bargainers, overturned the desks of the money changers and sent the pieces rolling along the court. "For the zeal of thine house hath eaten me up," said the Psalmist. (Ps. 69, 9.) "In the courts of the Lord's house, in the midst of thee, O Jerusalem" (Ps. 116, 19) he had seen scandal. As the Son of his Father he could not tolerate it.

This incident sheds an important light on the character of

Jesus as a living man. He was a man, with a man's indignation; he could argue and belabor. The nervous, excitable Jew who could make his protest in spite of the jeers of the crowd is a much more sympathetic figure to us than the wax and plaster image of dreary pious usage. To those who ask him, "What sign showest thou unto us, seeing that thou dost these things?" —Jesus replied, "Destroy this Temple and in three days I will raise it up." The Jews naturally shrugged their shoulders. "Forty and six years [2] was this Temple in building and wilt thou rear it up in three days?" Probably they turned away then, thinking they had a lunatic to deal with. Yet this statement, which was to be brought up against him later during his trial, was also to be vindicated. The Temple which was to be raised up again in three days was not the Temple of populous courts and proud colonnades but the living Temple in which God was incarnate. Another step was taken toward the fulfillment of the Messianic promises but, says the Gospel, it was only after he had risen from the dead that his disciples remembered that he had said this to them and it strengthened their faith.

Nicodemus

A little while after, another Messianic presage was given, again at Jerusalem. This time it came to one of the leaders of the Jewish community, a senator or member of the Sanhedrin, the incarnation of authority and national tradition. He was a man who would realize to the full the meaning of the encounter but he lacked the strength of purpose to respond and submit his life to the complete transformation required. In this he was only too typical of the fate of Israel.

As John depicts him (iii, 1-15) this Nicodemus seems to have been a good man, one of those whose moral sensitivity enables them to recognize the way to perfection but who are

---

[2] This reply provides a valuable chronological check on the date of 28 A.D. for the beginning of Christ's ministry. Herod began the Temple in the eighteenth year of his reign, according to Josephus that is, in the year 19 B.C. Forty-six years from that date brings us to 27 or 28 A.D.

inhibited from entering upon it with all their heart by intellectual scruples and social responsibilities, and also, to tell the truth, by a fundamental lack of courage. Nicodemus was a rich man—the Talmud says of him that he could have fed the entire population of Israel for ten days—very rich and highly esteemed.

This was why, when he heard about the new prophet and desired to see him, he arranged for a meeting by night. Prudence is a virtue which the comfortably situated respect very highly. He would see Jesus and question him politely; courtesy was another habit of his kind. "We know that thou art a teacher come from God for no man can do those miracles that thou doest except God be with him." But—and this was the decisive question, the one that every pious Jew had in mind—was he really the Long Awaited One, would he restore the Kingdom of God?

Jesus had penetrated this man, like all the others, at a single glance. He saw the deposit of conformity, of second hand opinions, and of suffering in a fundamentally virtuous soul. He replied by removing the question to another plane. "Verily, verily I say unto thee, except a man be born again, he cannot see the Kingdom of God."

Here, for the first time, Jesus expounds his doctrine. To be born *anew* or to be born from *on high* (the Greek of the Gospel permits either interpretation) is to work a complete transformation. It is that integral renewing which crowns the desire for penitence instilled by the Baptist, but it would have a special significance for the strict observer of the Law. Philo of Alexandria might teach that the soul, freed from the trammels of the body, could enter the heart of the Creator and thus achieve a "second birth"; among the mystery cults this was the prime motive of initiation. But Nicodemus would not be concerned with this type of speculation. He said simply, "How can a man be born when he is old? Can he enter a second time into his mother's womb?" Jesus sought to enlighten him. "That which is born of the flesh is flesh and that which is born of the spirit is spirit." *Rouah,* which means spirit, is feminine in both Hebrew and Aramaic; it also means a gust of wind. "The wind bloweth where it listeth and thou hearest the sound thereof, but canst not tell whence it cometh and whither it goeth. So it is with everyone that is born of the spirit." It is the spirit which transforms the soul and gives it new life, breathes into it the force to serve God. A learned man of Israel should know these things.

Suddenly we realize that Jesus was not merely addressing the honest, timid Sanhedrite, but a whole world stretching out beyond him, a world waiting for this revelation. An unexpected horizon opened before Nicodemus; this man in front of him said that he had been sent to preach to men the necessity of being born again. Was he to be believed? To a pious Jew, this was a disconcerting Messiah, conforming not at all to the expected pattern. Nicodemus kept silence; he did not dare to believe and Jesus knew it. He told him that if those to whom the message was first brought hesitated to accept it because they were disconcerted by simple wonders, they would certainly shirk transcendental things. In this the Lord summed up the tragedy of the Chosen People.

But the seed of salvation was not only offered to this solitary witness, entrenched in his self-chosen deafness. Jesus explains his doctrine in a long monologue which is almost an advance summary of his teaching. The Son of Man has descended to earth, God made flesh. He is the only begotten Son of the Most High and he has come to save mankind, to save and not to condemn. Moses in the desert long ago had saved his people from the burning bite of the serpent and so, also, the newcomer brought protection and redemption. He had divided light from darkness and brought light into the world. Those who followed him should have eternal life. "To be born again" was the interior transformation wrought by the spirit.

The Gospel does not tell us the decision of Nicodemus, but as he does not figure among the disciples we conclude that he could not accept. He was a man like most of us, respectable, shackled by conventions and fearful of great decisions. Yet that single night's interview must have remained graven on his memory and he seems always to have cherished a tenderness for the prophet who vainly appealed to his divided heart. When the plot against Jesus was being laid, he dared to speak up in his defence (John vii, 50) and he brought spices to embalm the body after the Crucifixion (John xix, 39). Affected by his good will, an old tradition has him subsequently baptized by Peter and a martyr to Christ. We do not know, but he certainly fulfilled one role of singular importance in providing Jesus with the occasion of the first outline of his mission and his teaching.

"He Must Increase"

The period of preparation and tentative announcement was now over. The dual nature of Jesus, human and divine, had been manifested; the premises of his doctrine had been stated, the power on which he could draw had been displayed; his death and his resurrection had been prophesied. Now the stage was set for events which were to advance his destiny.

While Jesus was in Jerusalem, John, the Forerunner, continued to draw crowds and baptize them. He was, says the Gospel (John iii, 22-30), at "Ænon near to Salim because there was much water there." This place is usually identified as a certain Tell Sarem not far from Scythopolis. *Ainon* in Aramaic means "spring" and *Salim*, peace, so symbolically the place was well chosen. But after leaving Jerusalem Jesus himself baptized or rather (John iv, 2) he allowed his disciples to use this rite in his presence though he did not administer it himself. For the hour of the baptism by the spirit had not yet sounded.

Since the two groups were preaching more or less side by side, some of the Baptist's disciples took offence and that sort of conflict which so often arises among the entourages of great men, both jealous for the honor of their patron, began to develop. Perhaps somebody who had been baptized by the party of Jesus began to boast of the superior efficacy of the rite to some of John's followers who would naturally complain to their master. The Baptist, distinguished always by the greatness of his humility, replied, "A man can receive nothing except it be given him from heaven. Ye yourselves bear me witness that I said, I am not the Christ but that I am sent before him. He that hath the bride is the bridegroom, but the friend of the bridegroom, which standeth and heareth him, rejoiceth greatly because of the bridegroom's voice: this my joy therefore is fulfilled. He must increase but I must decrease." (John iii, 29-30.)

This was sublime language worthy of the great man who was willing to bow himself to the difficult task which God had assigned him. He had said long ago that he was not the Messiah, whose shoe he was not worthy to unloosen. Now he compared himself to the friend and supporter of the bridegroom, the "best man" who bent himself, in Jewish weddings, to the preparations with disinterested devotion. He prophesied that he himself must suffer eclipse so that the newcomer might shine more brightly. He intended to discourage the more zealous of his followers; still we cannot but admire those who, in spite of everything, remained faithful to the Forerunner until the end which he prophesied. Long after his death, St. Paul at Ephesus (Acts xix, 1-7) encountered disciples who adhered to "John's baptism."

"He must increase but I must decrease." The words were to be tragically implemented not very long after. In the spring of the year 28, Antipas, the tetrarch of Galilee, returned from Rome where he had been protesting once more his complete devotion to the neurotic emperor, or perhaps fortifying intrigues and reviving memories of mutual debauches long ago. Or possibly, following the family custom, he was spying on Pilate, the Roman Procurator, for his master. But his stay in Italy had been far from pleasant. With the tyrant installed at Capri, perpetual menace weighed on everybody connected with the court. In those opulent Jewish circles which were also frequented by the Latin aristocracy—even by representatives of the imperial family such as Antonia, wife of Drusus, Tiberius's dead son—everybody was commenting on the sudden disfavor into which Agrippa, grandson of the great Herod, had fallen. He had been suddenly relegated to the fort of Malatha in Asia, a dreary town which was being slowly rebuilt after an incendiary outbreak and was still shrouded in scaffolding. Even if Antipas had gone to see the emperor in his beautiful island, it was doubtful whether he would have got anything, certainly not the recall of the Procurator.

Josephus tells us that when the emperor was implored to replace a cruel or greedy functionary he replied with this caustic anecdote: "A passer-by sought to succor an injured man by chasing away the flies who tormented him. 'O my friend,' said the unfortunate victim, 'leave them alone. For if you drive them off, hungrier ones will arrive and I shall not be able to resist them.'"

Antipas had a potent personal reason also for his speedy return to Palestine. For some time past he had been infatuated with Herodias, the granddaughter of Herod the Great by his adored Asmonean wife Mariamne whom he had nevertheless slain. Herodias was the daughter of that Aristobulus who had perished by the same tyrant and of his wife Berenice, whom Antipas had been visiting in Rome, where she lived. By the command of her grandfather, Herodias had been married at a very early age to her uncle, Herod Philip I, who was very many years her senior. At this time Herodias would be about thirty-four. Like all her race she was ambitious and had long been disgusted with her elderly husband who had no charms and so little astuteness that he had not succeeded in becoming either tetrarch or High Priest. Every day she cast more admiring eyes upon her brother-in-law Herod Antipas, who maintained a court, had built himself a capital on the beautiful Lake Tiberias and royally dispensed the gold pieces which he himself minted.

Although he was infatuated, Antipas might not have lost his head completely had not circumstances favored Herodias in her machinations. The wife of the tetrarch was an Arabian princess, the daughter of the King of Nebaioth. Learning of her husband's infidelity, she arranged to go back to her father in his fantastic city of Petra (Sela), rose-red and solitary among its girdle of rocks. Possibly Antipas was not unaware of the danger which this separation threatened: eight years later it was indeed the cause of a war in which his father-in-law defeated him severely. But at the moment, passion drove him to make the most of the opportunity; he repudiated his wife and Herod Philip, obliging as ever, gave up Herodias without a murmur.

The affair caused grave scandal in Palestine. According to the Jewish Law it was adultery (Leviticus xviii, 16; xx, 21) and John the Baptist, faithful as always to the historic role of the prophet, sought out Antipas and reminded him that it was forbidden to him to take his brother's wife. David did not arrest Nathan when, in the name of God, he came to reproach the king over the wife of Uriah the Hittite. But the paltry kinglet at Tiberias was not sufficiently great to yield himself up to penitence; he flung his accuser into prison so that his voice might not be heard. That, at least, is the Gospel explanation of the arrest of the Baptist. (Luke iii, 19; Matthew xiv, 3-5; Mark vi, 17.) Josephus, however, suggests that there were political implications; the tetrarch, watching the crowds gathered round John and carried away by his teaching, feared that he might use his influence to incite them to rebellion. As the brook at Ænon near to Salim where John taught was in the jurisdiction of Scythopolis, one of the free Hellenistic cities and a member of the league of the Decapolis, it was necessary somehow to inveigle the Prophet into Galilee or Perea to arrest him.

The place where John the Baptist was confined was on the extreme border of the tetrarch's dominions, almost on the frontier of the Nabataeans. Machaerus today is a heap of ruins on the plateau of Moab which stretches out to the east toward the Arabian desert but which, on the west, falls steeply into the vertiginous gorge of the Dead Sea. There was formerly a town here with a considerable caravan traffic but nothing of it remains except a causeway of broken stones, the debris of houses and the foundations of a Temple of the Sun. Yet on the sharp cone of the adjoining hill can still be seen vestiges of the fortress where the Forerunner ended his days.

The citadel at its highest point was over three hundred feet in diameter and dominated all the surrounding buildings by at least five hundred feet. The foundations of the surrounding wall are still visible and in the center there is a very deep well, a cistern and two turrets, in one of which can still be seen the holes in the masonry for the rings of the prisoners' chains.

In this prison the Baptist was to remain ten months. He does not seem to have been badly treated, for Herod Antipas had an uneasy conscience about him. The gospel of St. Mark (vi, 20) tells us that Herod "feared John and observed him," and that he even consulted the Prophet in secret. Doubtless he arrested him only at the insistence of Herodias.

John had instructed some of his disciples to carry on his work. From the great height of the fortress he could look down into the deep cleft, nearly four thousand feet below, where the Dead Sea shone like a scrap of sky fallen into the gulf. To the north where the golden sands faded into a nebulous gray rose like a cloud on the horizon the clear outline of Mt. Nebo from which the dying Moses had looked down, in an ecstasy of hope, upon the Promised Land which he was never to reach. Like that other precursor, the Baptist accepted that another should take his place. "He must increase and I must decrease." Obediently John resigned himself to God.

The Water of Life

John's arrest made Jesus decide to leave Judea and go back to his own province. "The Pharisees had heard that Jesus made and baptized more disciples than John." His ministry was hardly begun yet this small phrase betrays that suspicion and hostility were already aroused. He was not yet ready to risk a clash and police spies appear to have been less zealous in the domains of the tetrarch than in the city of the priests.

He left Jerusalem for Galilee and chose the hill road rather than the Jordan valley, possibly to escape the heat which in May would be oppressive in that enclosed place. Whatever the reason, the choice provided the occasion of one of the most touching and significant scenes in the Gospel. The road runs through Bethel, Sichem, Samaria and Engannim, keeping to the higher ground all the way, and although the hill slopes and fields might be scorched by the sun, at least during the evening there would be that soft wind by which Boaz winnowed his barley on the threshing floor and by which the Bible tells us Jehovah himself was refreshed in the garden. Then, as today, no doubt, the all pervading dust made a carpet for the traveler's feet and inflicted upon him a slowly drying throat. From Jerusalem to the Lake of Galilee by this road is about three days' journey.

All the same, Jesus's choice of this road was surprising for it led through Samaria, which no Jew would cross without hesitation. True, it was long after the Feast of the Passover, so the Samaritans would not be clustered on the roads watching for Jewish pilgrims in order to convey to them the reverse of good wishes, as was their habit during the feast. The differences between the Jews and the Samaritans had long since hardened to solid mutual hate. St. Luke cities evidence of their ill-will (ix, 52-53) when they would not receive Jesus because he was bound for Jerusalem, and Josephus says that they set actual ambushes for pilgrims.

The schism dated from the year 935 when the Kingdom was divided, after the death of Solomon, into the small kingdom of Judah and the larger kingdom of Israel. It was not long before religious and political differences embittered their relations. The northern kingdom became attached to an idolatrous cult of twin golden calves said to represent Jehovah. Omri, one of their abler kings, chose a new site for a capital and built the city of Samaria to rival Sion. When Sargon, king of Assyria, destroyed it in 722 B.C., the men of Judah could find no tears for the city of the impious Ahab and the idolatrous Jezebel. But, from the Jewish point of view, much worse was to follow. The Assyrians deported the Israelites of Samaria but planted there instead colonies of miscellaneous people from all parts of their empire, so that twenty idolatries took the place of one. When the men of Judah returned from exile, more than ever intransigent in their faith, they refused to have any relations with the Samaritans, considering them as heathen or worse. The Samaritans retaliated by intriguing against the Jews and finally, in the time of Ezra, a renegade priest from Jerusalem, having quarreled with the Temple authorities, went to Samaria and set up a rival sanctuary of the Most High on Mt. Gerizim. From that time the Samaritans had stopped at nothing to incense the Jews. About the year 6 B.C. they had thrown human remains into the sanctuary to desecrate the holy place during the Passover. One of the many grievances of the faithful against Herod was that instead of allowing Samaria to remain in the ruins to which it had been reduced by John Hyrcanus in B.C. 128, he had rebuilt it in sumptuous fashion, giving it the name of Augusta or Sebastia. "The water of Samaria is more unclean than the blood of swine," said the rabbis. A Jew would have to be thirsty indeed before he asked for it!

On the second day, having covered about fifty miles, Jesus and his disciples were approaching Shechem, an old historic site famous in the time of the Patriarchs and the Judges, the place where Jacob had given land to Joseph, where Joseph himself had been buried, where Joshua had called the Chosen People together to swear the oath of fidelity to Jehovah. Later it had been the capital of Abimelech. These memories were bitter to pious Jews. Two thousand years after, there remains, of the old historic place, eighteen hundred feet above sea level on the ridge that runs from Mt. Ebal to Mt. Gerizim, a moribund village; for lack of water has gradually caused the inhabitants to desert it. It is now called, not Shechem, but Sychar. The population drifted down toward the valley, where, about the time of Vespasian, they developed the town of Flavia Napolis. Later it became that Nablus which was partly destroyed by an earthquake in 1927. It was rebuilt, more or less, and is today a dreary little town whose only feature of interest is a community of the last surviving descendants of the heretical Samaritans, about a hundred and sixty in all. Pierre Loti and Joseph Kessel, who stayed with them, have recorded their impressions.

The Fourth Gospel, which is so exact in its topography that

Renan declared, "Only a Jew of Palestine who had frequently passed through the entrance to the valley of Shechem could have written this," is not less precise as to time. It was "about the sixth hour" when the party reached the foot of the mountain of Shechem. Leaving Jerusalem early in the morning, anyone on foot would reach this point about noon of the following day. It would be hot; the stubble of the newly harvested plain would rustle with grasshoppers in the sun and beneath the ancient stone bridges the streams would be dried to a trickle among the heaps of pebbles between which, paradoxically, oleanders bloomed. Jesus was wearied by the journey; while his disciples went into the town to buy provisions, he sat down to rest. There was a spring close by, venerated from ancient times as Jacob's Well. (On this site today is the framework of an Orthodox Church begun in 1914 to replace a Byzantine basilica, but it has been almost abandoned for the last thirty years. A crypt shelters the well, and the priest in attendance lowers a lighted candle by means of a windlass to demonstrate the depth—it is about a hundred feet—where lies the water which Jesus once asked to drink.)

The nomad peoples of these dry countries have always centered romantic and poetic associations around wells. It was by a well near the "city of Nahor" that Abraham's serving man met Rebecca, the future bride of his young master Isaac. By a well Jacob first saw Rachel with her father's sheep and instantly fell in love with her. "Spring up, O well," runs a song of the Mosaic period (Numbers xxi, 17). "Sing ye unto it, the princes digged the well, the nobles of the people digged it by the direction of the lawgiver, with their staves." Whoever held possession of the water held power. In the Orient, during the heat of day, men dream of water and sigh for the sight of those porous earthen jars which keep the precious liquid cool. When the "well master" turns the key, the women hurry down, the jars on their heads. And it was to one of these that Jesus said, "Give me to drink."

The request, so natural to us, seemed unusual if not shocking in view of Jewish custom at the time. In the first place, the rabbis had decreed that it was improper to address a woman publicly, even one's own wife on the street or one's sister or daughter in an inn, "because of what might be said about it." Secondly, it aggravated the scandal that a true and pious Jew should address a heathen woman of Samaria. But it was neither the first nor the last time that Jesus calmly broke traditional conventions which, however honored they might be, were really only manifestations of the worst of Jewish exclusiveness.

Marvelously told as it is by St. John, the scene never fails to arrest us. "How is it that thou, being a Jew, askest drink of me, which am a woman of Samaria?" This woman was no frightened hen; she knew how to talk to men; there was a trace of insolence in her tone. But Jesus did not take offence at it. "If thou knewest the gift of God and who it is that saith to thee, Give me to drink; thou wouldst have asked of him and he would have given thee living water." Astonishment lent a shade more deference to her demeanor. "Sir," she said, "thou hast nothing to draw with, and the well is deep. From whence hast thou that living water? Art thou greater than our father Jacob, which gave us the well, and drank thereof himself, and his children and his cattle?" Nicodemus also had replied with a similar question, down-to-earth and rational. Jesus answered: "Whosoever drinketh of this water shall thirst again. But whosoever drinketh of the water that I shall give him shall never thirst." The water of life, a fountain eternally refreshing the heart of man parched by sin and suffering, was a favorite metaphor with the early Christians; it was incised upon their sarcophagi as a promise.

Whether the Samaritan woman understood his meaning, or whether she thought simply to evade an irksome task, at any rate she replied: "Sir, give me this water that I thirst not, neither come hither to draw." But Jesus proceeded to demolish her pretensions; we can imagine his gaze bent upon her as a little while back it had been upon Nathaniel. "Go, call thy husband and come hither." She temporized. "I have no husband." "Thou hast well said, I have no husband. For thou hast had five husbands and he whom thou now hast is not thy husband. In that saidst thou truly." It was enough to convince her. "Sir," she said, "I perceive that thou art a prophet."

This brief dialogue reveals the woman completely and it is absolutely true to life. First she is pert, then uneasy; woman-like, she is touched and finally convinced not by argument but by the revelation of her own story. It was to this woman, in one sense so unworthy, that Jesus chose to reveal one of the most important secrets of his approaching mission. When she suggests, in response to his appeal, that she is ready to return to the Jewish observance, to worship not on Mt. Gerizim but in Jerusalem, his reply was a fundamental proclamation.

Certainly "salvation came through the Jews," for of their race the Messiah was born. But the hour was approaching when their exclusive cult was to give place to a religion which would embrace the entire world, when the God who was a spirit should be adored in the spirit and in truth. It may be that the woman by the well of Sychar did not comprehend this fully but that she understood in some measure is proved by her reply that she knew that when the Messiah came he would tell all things. Then Jesus avowed, to this foreign woman of sinful life, something which he had never before categorically admitted. The Messiah? "I that speak unto thee am he."

This is the climax of the scene. Everything had been said. Just then the disciples came back with bread, olives and cheese, surprised and a little annoyed perhaps, although they did not dare to say anything, to find him talking to this woman. But at this moment we get the impression that Jesus was just beginning to live, to experience the joy of the Good Shepherd in reclaiming the lost sheep. When they offered the food they had brought he said: "I have meat to eat that ye know not of." "My meat is to do the will of Him who sent me and to finish His work." The people of Sychar, assembled by the woman, gathered round him, eager to listen; he drew a lesson from them for his disciples. The fields were already white for harvest, and they, peasants as they were, would recognize the sign. The time had come to reap the harvest of mankind. So after staying two days among the enthusiastic Samaritans, Jesus turned again toward the north.

His Ministry Begins

The return to Galilee definitely marks the opening of the public ministry of Jesus. The three synoptic Gospels date it from this point. Only St. John has told us how, obedient to the laws of his being, the Son of God sought a period of semi-obscurity and preparation as do all men who set themselves a supreme task. (Luke iv, 14; Mark i, 14; Matthew iv, 17; John iv, 45.) Until then, he had spoken only to a few faithful friends, to one solitary Jew in a private interview, to a woman encountered by chance in a strange village. From now on he was to speak to crowds, displaying the powers which his Father had given to him, working miracles and drawing out hearts.

It is convenient to raise here the question of chronology, upon which only the Fourth Gospel throws any light. How long did Christ's public ministry last? Strange as this may seem at first, it is one of the features which history has found most difficult. But if we remember that the object of the Evangelists was not to write history but to record teaching, we shall not be so surprised at their failure to record things which to us would seem essential. St. Mark, for instance, says no more than, "Jesus came into Galilee preaching the Gospel," or:

"He arose and went into the borders of Tyre and Sidon." But how long he stayed or was gone is never mentioned. St. John, who is on the whole more precise, is yet not sufficiently so for his text to serve as anything but an hypothesis. His narrative, moreover, which is obviously inspired by metaphysical and theological conceptions, is suspected by some critics of a desire to agree with certain Old Testament allusions and also to accord with that numerical symbolism so dear to the oriental mind.

To establish a chronology for the life of Jesus, we have to search through the Four Gospels for indications which, by deduction, supply confirmations. When, for instance, one of the annual Jewish feasts is in question, if three of these are mentioned it is safe to reckon a lapse of time of at least two years. Other questions yield to systematic reasoning. When we read in St. Mark (vi, 39) that on the occasion of the multiplication of the loaves of bread, the crowd sat down upon "the green grass," while a little earlier the Gospel had mentioned that the disciples plucked kernels of wheat in the field, we know that the two events are separated by at least ten or eleven months, for the grain in Palestine is harvested at the end of April and the grass then is already burnt yellow by the sun.

Naturally this method leaves a wide field for conjecture and innumerable and ingenious commentators have combed the text to find evidence.

For instance, when, during the episode with the Samaritan woman, Jesus says to his disciples, "Say not ye, there are yet four months and then cometh harvest," some have inferred from this saying, which was probably simply a colloquialism, that the episode can be dated four months before the harvest in Palestine was due. The method has its dangers. In the parable of the vineyard (Luke xiii, 7) Jesus makes the owner say to the dresser of the vines, "Behold, three years I come seeking fruit on this fig tree and find none." But it would be hazardous to conclude from this that the ministry of Jesus had lasted for three years.

Putting aside information pieced together in this way, other difficulties immediately arise. It is not at all easy to correlate the chronologies of the synoptics with the Fourth Gospel, for the former give the impression of covering a much shorter space of time than the latter, or at least of recounting fewer events. For instance, St. Matthew, St. Mark and St. Luke refer to only one Feast of the Passover; the Fourth Gospel refers definitely to two (ii, 13 and xi, 55) and one intervening which modern versions place in vi, 4 but which Ireneus identified with the "feast of the Jews" mentioned in the first verse of Chapter V. It is no part of our task to summarize even a fraction of the innumerable theories which have proliferated during two thousand years' examination of the evidence. The discussion has been going on since the earliest days of the Church. Origen postulated three years, Eusebius favored four, St. Jerome decided for three, and others declared for one year only. Modern estimates vary between forty months (Fillion) and those which would compress all the sayings and actions of Christ into a few weeks on the argument that the Roman police would not have countenanced the agitation for longer (Schweitzer, Guignebert). The most generally agreed period is about two years and a few months; critics supporting this include Grandmaison, Lagrange, C. H. Turner and Ricciotti.

This is a reasonable hypothesis, accommodating the events without undue haste or excessive delays. Basing ourselves upon it, we can reckon something like this: Jesus was baptized by John in January of the year 28 and went to Jerusalem in the March of that year. In the middle of May, he left the Holy City and went through Samaria into Galilee to commence his public teaching. The Sermon on the Mount can be placed in June. The episode of the pacifying of the storm falls naturally in December. He kept the Passover of the year 29 in Galilee, a little after the miracle of the loaves and fishes. The Transfiguration probably took place on a burning day in August. In the autumn of that second year, Jesus once again set out for Judea whence he was never to return to his beloved Galilee: April of the year 30 was the tragic month of the Passion.

The method which Jesus used to reveal his message lends force to the hypothesis that the mission was of some duration. It was definitely a progressive revelation and in that respect the plan of the New Testament corresponds to that of the Old. As the Chosen People continued, through Abraham, Moses, David and the Prophets, to ascend the scale of ineffable knowledge, so, following out the Gospel, we see the mission of Jesus unfolded more and more explicitly. Some have even held that Jesus did not fully reveal his "Messianic secret" until after the Resurrection. We shall see that it is characteristic of him to silence those who called him "the Holy One of God," to restrain the premature and injudicious enthusiasm of his disciples, to minimize his own miracles.

This may have been due to political prudence, a desire not to excite the myrmidons of Antipas and Pilate before the appointed hour. It was more probably a deliberate playing down of that dream of a triumphant and splendid Messiah which buoyed up Jewish pride. To those who would listen, he developed the idea that the Kingdom of God began in the awe of soul and in the will to perfection. He had to reckon with lack of understanding, ill will, hypocrisy and hatred; he had to play his part against increasing opposition. Slowly, as if pursuing the most carefully prepared plan, Jesus came out into the open. In a few weeks he put forward the fundamental doctrines of his teaching; then, when the resistance to it began to show, he had recourse to other methods.

Jesus Teaches

Jesus began his teaching immediately on his return to Galilee. He was to find his largest and most fervent audiences among these good, simple peasants and fishermen, robust morally and physically. Unlike their neighbors the Samaritans the Galileans had remained faithful to the Law since the Maccabean conquest of their country. They were less sophisticated than the people of Judea and capable of greater enthusiasm. They did not refine endlessly on theology and observances; they had a simple love of God.

Jesus at first taught in the synagogues. This fact is worthy of note. We are accustomed to think of him, as so often represented in art, preaching always in the open air, on the slopes of the fair hills above the Lake of Galilee or, in the bow of a boat, addressing crowds assembled by the lakeside. St. Luke, who especially recounts this period in detail (iv, 14-22 and 31-32), shows us clearly the method first adopted; to a Jew of that time wishing to promulgate a religious doctrine, the synagogue was the natural place.

Indeed no better place could be found than this venerated spot, at once a house of prayer and a school of disputation, where faithful Jews from all the country round resorted every

Sabbath. During the past three centuries the Jewish synagogues had been assuming an ever-increasing importance. Tradition dates their foundation from the time of the Exile, when, since the people could no longer go up to the Temple in Jerusalem, it was necessary to have a place where they could fulfill the prescribed rites and assemble to read and comment on the Law. At the time of Christ there was no village in Palestine, however primitive, which could not claim to possess such a building.

The Jewish communities dispersed throughout the Empire had built many of them; Rome had at least thirteen. The synagogue generally comprised one not very large room—eighty by sixty feet at Capernaum—with sober mosaic ornament of stars and palm trees, an atrium bearing the basin for the purifications, a few rooms reserved for public teaching and the use of guests. Archaeological research has uncovered a good many remains of such. They were administered by a "ruler of the synagogue" assisted by a sort of sacristan-cum-treasurer-cum-teacher, the "hassan."

The nature of the services was determined by the Temple of Sion. The Scribes and the doctors of law, who were the kingpins of these institutions, gave instructions there which dealt both with the dogmas (*halaka*) and the history of Israel (*agada*). There was a small raised choir containing the chest or Ark in which the scrolls of the Law were kept and seven members of the community, wearing the prescribed white *taliss*, sat down and proceeded to the Office. There were two opening benedictions, then an extract from the Mosaic books was read in Hebrew, followed by a translation into the local tongue, the Aramaic of Galilee or whatever it might be. After that there was a commentary on the passage read, then the prayer of the eighteen benedictions in which divine goodness was praised minutely. This was read by one of the old men. Next came a reading from the prophets, following the same method as before, and finally came the benediction from Numbers vi, 24-26: "The Lord bless thee and keep thee, the Lord make his face shine upon thee and be gracious unto thee; the Lord lift up his countenance upon thee and give thee peace."

The proceedings were long, very long. They occupied an entire morning. All the sacred texts had to be read, all the benedictions repeated, with the head turned toward Jerusalem.

Probably a good many of those present dozed a little, like that rabbi who thanked God that his head, by nodding, was able to respond of itself.

No special person was charged with the office of taking the lead in the course of the ceremony. The "ruler of the synagogue" could call upon any Jew of good reputation whose discourse he might consider likely to edify, and among people brought up from their earliest infancy upon the sacred writings there could always be found plenty capable of inexhaustible glosses on a few verses from Exodus or Isaiah. In such conditions we can easily understand that Jesus would be called upon to speak.

St. John tells us that he preached at Cana, where the first miracle was performed (John iv, 45-46). St. Luke gives us a vivid sketch of his preaching at Nazareth (Luke iv, 16-21). He rose, mounted the *bema* or dais, unfolded the long role of parchment upon which the text was inscribed, then choosing certain verses as if by chance, handed the scroll back to the *hassan*. Then he began his commentary "and the eyes of all them that were in the synagogue were fastened upon him." The audience were unaware of the immediate relevance of the text that he had chosen. "The spirit of the Lord God is upon me; because the Lord hath anointed me to preach good tidings unto the meek; he hath sent me to bind up the brokenhearted, to proclaim liberty to the captives, and the opening of the prison to them that are bound. To proclaim the acceptable year of the Lord" (Isaiah lxi).

They did not suspect, these rough peasants from the Galilean hills, that he who addressed them was that Emmanuel whom Isaiah had foretold and that he brought a message of peace more profound than that of any Sabbatical Year, when, once in fifty years, the fields were untilled, bondmen received their liberty and lands taken for debt reverted to their original owners. "This day is this scripture fulfilled in your ears," said the Lord, but the behavior of his listeners shortly afterward does not suggest that they understood.

Then he "came down" into Capernaum. The Gospel term is exactly descriptive. We can follow the road today; it is about ten hours' journey from Nazareth to the shore of the lake, traveling along the level plateau till we see framed, in the black basalt of the gorge of Arbela, the perfect lake below, its intense blue set off against the copper-colored shore. Once we have crossed the pass the landscape changes, the road skirts the lake closely and it is dominated by steep heights. But the lapping of the clear water, the gentle motion of the sails and the clusters of lemon trees and flowering oleanders make up a less forbidding picture. As we go down, the heat increases; it is like going into a hothouse. Toward the south, in the time of Christ could be seen the white towers of Tiberias and the shining golden roof of the palace of Antipas. The towns of Bethsaida and Capernaum were then the chief centers of population in the plain of Gennesaret; fishing, agriculture and commerce were all followed.

Capernaum was not a Hellenistic city like Tiberias or Julia, the neighboring towns. It was essentially Jewish although it was open to trade with foreigners from the rich lands of Hauran or from Phoenicia. Its narrow streets exuded a strong odor of fish scales thrown out on the ground, curiously mixed with the smell of roses and orange blossom. The houses were built of dark basalt except the synagogue, which rose up among them in gleaming white limestone. The people of Capernaum were very proud of their synagogue; the centurion in charge of the local garrison and his men had assisted in its building (Luke vii, 5) and Antipas seems to have given financial aid, for his emblem, the palm tree, was found among the ruins, and can still be seen.

Jesus taught there also, although we have only slight reports of his teaching. St. Mark gives a summary of his words: "The time is fulfilled and the kingdom of God is at hand; repent ye and believe the gospel" (i, 15). Repentance and faith were indeed the bases of his message but he must have said many other things, for we read in the same account (i, 22) that "they were astonished at his doctrine for he taught them as one that had authority, and not as the scribes." This single line shows us Jesus in action far more vividly than a long commentary. Unlike the doctors of the law who analyzed the texts, multiplying citations and references, advancing not a single idea without drawing on the Law and the Prophets in acrobatic exegesis, Jesus departed as far as possible from the subtleties and trivialities of the Pharisees, teaching solely the precepts of the Divine Law to which the pure in heart could respond instinctively. He spoke as one with authority because in him resided the supreme authority; he had no need to lean on Rabbi Hillel or Rabbi Schammai or Rabbi Gamaliel or anybody else. He observed the Law faithfully but he transformed and humanized its exigencies and for that the scribes and their fellow casuists could never forgive him.

Jesus Heals

There were other things being done at the same time which displayed the power of the new prophet in a way which was singularly disturbing. The story of the miracle at Cana two months earlier had been bandied around the countryside. One of Antipas's officers, whose son lay mortally ill in Capernaum, appealed to Jesus to cure him, much as today even skeptical persons resort to chiropractic or go to Lourdes, not entirely believing but willing to try anything.

At the time, Jesus was at Cana, perhaps on his way to the lake shore. The officer set out to meet him; he must have started early, risking the heat and he must have been on horseback, since it was about the "seventh hour" that he reached the little hillside town. He besought Jesus "to come down and heal his son" as if it were necessary for him to come down when the divine power could so easily manifest itself over seven leagues. A man of greater faith would have said, "Only say the word," and Jesus realized it. "Except ye see signs and wonders ye will not believe." "Sir," said the father, "come down ere my child die." "Go thy way," said Jesus, "thy son liveth." Something in the tone of the words must have made the officer, who had come to the prophet as a last recourse, suddenly believe, for he remounted his horse and rode away. Night had fallen, the new day had commenced (for among the Jews the day begins at nightfall) when, at some distance along the road, the officer was met by his servants who had come out to bring him the news. The boy lived. He asked them at what time he began to get better. "Yesterday at the seventh hour the fever left him," they said. It was the hour when Jesus had spoken. (John iv, 45-54.)

The *authority* which his hearers had recognized in the teaching of Jesus was thus displayed in acts far exceeding the capacity of ordinary mortals. He had power to cure the physical ills of the human body—power also over those stronger ills which seize and enthrall the mind and soul. In that same Sabbath day at Capernaum, recreated so vividly by the Evangelist, Jesus encountered once more, in a terrifying scene, the Adversary whom he had defeated in the solitude of Djebel Quarantal. He went to the synagogue, to comment on the scriptures, and an expectant silence held the assembled hearers. Suddenly there was an uproar, the meeting was riven by shrieks and cries and a man flung himself forward.

Often the most sacred places are chosen for the manifestations of the powers of darkness as though the very intensity of the spiritual atmosphere favors their designs. There is a rabbinical story of demons accompanying the faithful to the synagogue on the Sabbath and sitting on their knees. Cases of demoniac manifestation in the cloister have been innumerable, while the most extreme temptations recorded were those suffered by the hermit St. Anthony in the solitary cell in the desert where he sought to give himself up to prayer.

The incident as recorded by the evangelists (Luke iv, 33-37 and Mark i, 23-25) has the unmistakable air of veracity. We do not know exactly what the phenomenon was but it was a duel between the force which possessed the wretched man and spoke with his voice and the Messiah, majestically calm, who held his ground and conquered. "Let us alone, what have we to do with thee," howled Satan through the mouth of his victim. "Art thou come to destroy us? I know thee who thou art, the Holy One of God." The last words were designed to cause scandal and confusion; the ineffable name of God might never be pronounced and the pious Jews present would rend their tunics in horror. But Jesus restored order with a few words. "Hold thy peace and come out of him." With a scream and an appalling cry, the possessed man collapsed. It was all over; the unclean spirit had to submit. Those who had been present said among themselves with amazement: "What a word is this, for with authority and power he commandeth the unclean spirits and they come out."

There were still other incidents during that remarkable day at Capernaum (Matt. i, 29-34; Luke iv, 38-41). St. Mark in particular recounts them with such precision that we sense as we read the direct memories of his master, Simon Peter, who is generally supposed to have provided the material of this Gospel. When he reached the lake, Jesus met again the three other disciples whom he had called at Bethabara and it was with one of these—that Simon of whom he had mysteriously predicted that he should be called Peter—that Jesus went to eat after the incident in the synagogue. Before pronouncing the ritual blessing which sanctified all meals, the host hinted to Jesus that his mother-in-law was ill. It was not exactly a request but a discreet suggestion. The illness was most probably a sort of malaria, very common in the Jordan valley; the marshes around Capernaum favor the breeding of mosquitoes. Malta fever with its sudden jumps of temperature is also prevalent throughout the Near East. Jesus bent over the hammock where the sick woman lay; he took her hand and "commanded the fever" to leave her, which it did so promptly that she was able to get up and serve them all at supper.

Tales of these astonishing things must have been rife in Capernaum all that afternoon for the obligatory repose and prolonged meetings of the Sabbath would be extraordinarily propitious for rumor-mongering. By the time the evening came round probably everybody in the town was seized with the desire to set eyes on Jesus. During the Sabbath it was strictly forbidden to make any journey, not even for the benefit of the sick. The rabbis had fixed a limit of two thousand cubits as the utmost distance that might be traversed and only a very small packet might be carried. But, at seven o'clock in the evening, when the sun had gone down behind the ridge of hills, there was a rush. The sick and the demented thronged in all around him and, moving among them all, laying his hands on this one and issuing commands to others, Jesus gave further proofs of his mercy and his power. We can see him, surrounded by the milling crowd, tirelessly giving out the virtue that is in him, as always for the benefit of mankind, and so from the first, displaying the immensity of his compassion.

But when on the following day the crowd began to gather again in front of the house where he was staying, they sought him in vain. Before dawn, while it was still dark, he had risen and gone away into a solitary place. We can gather, from St. Mark's account, the discomfited surprise of Simon Peter and his associates at finding the Master gone. They ran to look for him. In a lonely valley by the lake—calm and a clear, pale gray in the early hours of the morning—Jesus was praying. He was to do this often, after some of the most astonishing incidents of his mission, after the miracle of the loaves for instance, in order to escape excessive displays of enthusiasm and to recover strength in God. In the last days, he was to say to the disciples who had abandoned him, "Yet I am not alone, because the Father is with me" (John xvi, 32).

"All men seek for thee," cried Peter and he would have asked him why he went away. But Jesus would not go back. For the time being, Capernaum had received enough. He had to go further afield, he had to extend the field of his mission, to give to all men the essentials of his truth. The second act of his public life was about to begin.

Jesus Calls

As soon as the task which he had undertaken was due to expand, it was necessary for Jesus to have helpers. Even the events of the first few weeks, rapidly as they had developed, had required a definite appeal to his companions. The men whom he had called on the banks of the Jordan had become his friends; they had to be consecrated as his disciples, by his will and by their own acceptance. Later on (Matt. x) they were to be raised to the apostolate; they would be invested by Jesus with supernatural powers and the Church would be born.

St. Luke places the appeal for disciples at this juncture, which seems logical because, by his teaching in the synagogues and by the miraculous manifestations, Jesus had shown those who were to follow him the nature of the work to which they were to be called. God does not seek to take men by surprise and the Church has always frowned on sudden vocations dictated solely by emotion. It is only to the soul fortified by preparation and knowing its way and its strength that the spirit gives the supreme impulse.

The Gospel shows us this supreme impulse at work when it tells us how Simon, Andrew, John and James were claimed by Jesus with sovereign and imperious authority, how they obeyed and followed him, leaving everything. Three of these four already knew him well, since the days at Bethabara and the return to Jerusalem. The fourth, James, probably met Jesus when he made his first journey to the shores of the lake and he had certainly heard his brother John speak of him. But none of them had so far decided to renounce everything; to set out upon that other-worldly adventure where he who saves his life must lose it. This is shown by the fact that they had left the enthusiastic crowd importuning the Master and had gone back to their work, mindful of their material interests. They would be mending their nets, perhaps, with the mesh pegged out on the ground just as we can see men doing by the shore of the lake today, and at night they would go out fishing. All this had not yet been renounced for God.

Then it was that Jesus called them. St. Mark (i, 14-20) and St. Matthew (iv, 18-23) tell the story in the barest outline yet it conveys most vividly the lightning action of the divine power upon these chosen souls. St. Luke, however, is more explicit; he places the call on the occasion of the miraculous haul of fishes which Jesus bestowed upon his friends. Some critics have disputed the chronological accuracy of this but it has clearly a symbolic rightness for here was plainly announced the destiny of the Apostles, who were to be "fishers of men."

It should not, however, be concluded that the account of St. Luke is therefore only symbolic. It gives the impression of being taken from life; its details are precise and concrete. There are plenty of places today along the Basque coast, around Sicily, even still on the Lake of Galilee, where nets, boats and fishing tackle are shared by a group of associates like Zebedee, his sons and their friends. Even their method, which produced the miracle, is still followed: the *chabakah* or cast-net, the circular net which is rolled round the left arm while the right arm launches it with a deft motion which drops down the weighted end. We can still see the fishing smacks slowly leaving the shore, with the *mehatten,* vertical nets weighted at the bottom and pegged out with floats at the top, to entrap the shoals of fish which will come in during the night. The lake then as now, abounded in fish: Josephus affirms the fact and fishing centers flourished all along its shores such as Capernaum, Bethsaida, and Magdala, whose name in Greek means "the fishing ground."

Many of the species of fish were very like our own, perch, carp and a variety of pike; others were more exotic, like the coracinus which carries its young in its mouth, and which is still called "St. Peter's fish" or "the weeping fish" because it is supposed to bring ill-luck. There is also that curious fish which is supposed to come from the Nile by subterranean and submarine channels. In the bay between Ain-Tabgah and Magdala, the junction of the ice-cold waters brought down by the

Jordan when the snows of Mt. Hermon melt and the hot springs of Capernaum discharged by seven estuaries produces conditions analogous to those in Newfoundland, a great accumulation of plankton and hence an abundance of fish.

We can imagine the scene. It will be early morning, for by the end of May midday is too hot for work. Beneath the white mist, which has barely lifted, the lake is a pale gray and the wash of the fishing boats a silver shimmer. The mountains are a cobalt blue which reflects the oncoming of the sun. Everything is calm; the sleeping pelicans, white and pink, float upon the water but the black cormorants have already begun their patient watch, upright on the stones by the water's edge. The weary fishermen return in bad humor. They have fished all night but since there was no moon and they could not observe the passage of the shoals, they had tapped on wood in order to frighten the fish into the nets. The result, however, had been disappointing.

Simon, who had just brought back his equipment on one of the larger vessels which could carry thirteen people (Luke viii, 22-25; Matt. viii, 23-27; Mark iv, 35-41), sighted Jesus from the shore of the lake. The master, to escape the press of the crowd clamoring for him to speak and to work miracles, had got into a small boat from which he could address those assembled on the shore. Perhaps he noticed the depressed state of his friend, worn out by a night of fruitless labor. He called him. "Launch out into the deep," he said, "and let down your nets for a draught." As an experienced fisherman Simon knew that this was useless: "Master, we have toiled all night," he said, "and have taken nothing." But such was his confidence in the speaker that he added: "Nevertheless at thy word I will let down the net." When the net was let down, such a vast quantity of fish was enclosed in it that the mesh broke, and they had to signal to the other boats to come and help them. The bark of Peter—which was to carry millions of living creatures safely to shore in the name of the Lord—came thus into play for the first time.

The figure of Simon Peter is highlighted throughout this

episode; this is all the more significant when it is remembered that it is taken from the gospel of St. Luke (v, 1-10) which is not considered, as is the Gospel of St. Mark, to recount the direct recollections of St. Peter himself. Peter is the owner of the ship; he receives and carries out the orders of Jesus. From the very beginning, when the Church is symbolized, he is the leader, the one who directs and conducts. Yet for all that, faced with the miracle which was to determine his acceptance or rejection for ever, he was troubled and stammered out: "Depart from me, for I am a sinful man, O Lord." His companions were in the same case. We can sense their awareness of the pressure of great events, of the sounding of the hour of decision. There is no doubt that they knew, by and large, what the Master expected of them; they had had plenty of time to reflect on what they had seen and heard. It was not true, as was subsequently advanced by the pagan philosopher Porphyrius and the Emperor Julian the Apostate, that they were driven blindly to their resolve. But it was a difficult hazard and the stakes were high.

"Fear not," said Jesus to Simon, "from henceforth thou shalt catch men." "And when they had brought their ships to land they forsook all and followed him." Once more the force which Jesus gave out had accomplished something which seems contrary to nature; the sudden transmutation of these humble fishermen was as miraculous as the catch of fish which swarmed at the bottom of the boat. For these men were henceforth to be invested with a colossal task and they were not to be found wanting. Upon them, simple and unlettered as they were, was to rest the newborn Church. These were not men like any others. They were, in a word, the first of the saints.

CHAPTER FIVE

THE SEED OF THE CHURCH

Galilean Days

THE MOST FERTILE PART of Galilee consists of a red alluvial deposit which, when turned over by the plough, leaves a furrow like an open wound. The soil turns to a deeper crimson and when its superb wheat, standing sometimes as high as a man, is in ear, it is like a purple damask richly embroidered in gold. Only the black-earth region of Russia and the yellow loess of China convey a comparable impression of sumptuous fecundity. In the land around Esdraelon and Gennesaret there seems a particular mystic association between the richness of the wheat and the image of flesh and blood.

It was in this bountiful land that the sower went out to sow the seed of his doctrine. He was to remain for many months faithful to this province where his childhood had been passed and where he had begun to explain his mission. More than two thirds of his entire ministry were to be spent on these plains, by these hills and by that lake where he had come to fish for men. Of the other three provinces of Palestine, he was to pass briefly through Perea and Samaria but he was to reserve for Judea his supreme effort; for that harsh land was to provide the bitter herbs, the thirst, the agony and the cross. A softer light illumines the Galilean scenes of the Gospel; on these hillsides, by these gentle rivers, perhaps Jesus had his experience of happiness.

It is only a very small province, less than thirty miles across and fifty or so from north to south, and the population was barely three hundred thousand. We have to remember the very small scale upon which Jesus operated here; it explains to some extent the rapid spread of his notoriety. Although so small, the country is very varied; there is a marked difference between upper Galilee, which is veritably mountainous, the hilly region and the plain around the lake. The long plain which follows the Kidron, that historic torrent running at the foot of the ridge, which terminates in the sea at Mt. Carmel, and the valley cut by the Jordan form the two axes of a surface of very confused contours.

The whole province is fertile and well-wooded. "It invites cultivation," says Josephus, "even by the least industrious; hence it is completely exploited, not a single field lies fallow. Towns and villages are numerous since food is abundant." The fertility of the soil, a relatively moist climate and the precious streams of fresh water coming down from Mt. Hermon all contribute to this richness, which is remarkable in the eastern Mediterranean. "It is easier to feed a legion from the olive trees of Galilee," runs a rabbinical saying, "than to raise a child anywhere else in Israel." Besides the olives there are wheat, barley, grapes, palms, and many other valuable plants in profusion; figs, Josephus assures us, ripen there during ten months of the year.

It is in this countryside, much the same then as we see it today, that we should visualize the Messiah teaching the crowds assembled around him. It is a setting not so very different from portions of France, with its hillsides covered with poppies and daisies, the tiny fields with their complicated hedge patterns, the white villages clustered among the trees just as in France or northern Italy. The Jewish colonists have restored the ancient fertility of the plain of Esdraelon. The lake itself, about six miles wide and about twelve miles long, has not changed in physical character since its surface reflected the passage of Jesus, and its shores, composed of sand and a blackish grit containing quantities of very tiny white shells, were trodden by his feet, but there is nevertheless one very important difference. It was infinitely more populous in those days than it is now; of the flourishing towns which clustered round its waters only one, Tiberias, has any life today. The other sites mentioned in the Gospel have nothing to show but ruins, an occasional nomad encampment and clusters of primitive reed huts. But when Jesus lived we can imagine it as a sort of Palestinian Riviera, with towns, villages and elegant villas reflecting their façades in the clear water.

Jesus remained in Galilee from the end of May in the year 28 until the autumn of 29, a longer period in the Jewish calendar than by our reckoning, because their months were lunar months of 28 days. Thus, during the three years, we must always reckon with the extra month which they had to slip in periodically to catch up with the sun. This intercalary month, veadar, was added between *adar* and *isan,* March and April. The year 29 contained one of the "embolismic" months and thus Jesus would have been nearly five hundred days traveling about the province, mostly on foot, but certainly mounted on occasion; for some of his journeys were too quickly made for anyone walking. Doubtless also he made use of the boats which the fishermen, his disciples, would place at his disposal. During the whole of this time, if we except one very hasty pilgrimage to Jerusalem, he seems to have gone outside the province only twice; once to Tyre and Sidon, the Phoenician cities, and once to the wooded heights where the tetrarch Philip had his capital of Caesarea. The reason for these two short excursions remains obscure; they may have been dictated by elementary caution or simply to escape the heat. In any case they had no effect upon the unfolding of the plan of his mission.

The Galileans to whom he preached were people who made a comfortable living either from fishing, husbandry or by the exercise of various crafts. They were industrious and, as Josephus tells us, and the history of the Maccabees confirms, they were hereditarily courageous and redoubtable defenders of their faith and the Law. The Judeans might despise these provincials and gibe at their accent with its uncouth pronunciation; they might condemn the Galilean's indifference to casuistic subtleties. "If you want to make your fortune, go north," they said in Jerusalem, "but if you want learning, come south," but it was none the less true that the Galilean qualities were those which are conducive to permanence and great enterprises. It was not without deliberate intention that Jesus approached his compatriots first. The seed would not be lost in the rich soil of the province. But all the same there was the danger that these simple, valiant souls, who only a century ago had made such an heroic stand against the pagan invader, might interpret his teaching too literally and conceive the Kingdom of God as temporal and the Messiah as the conquering King. We shall see that Jesus watched out constantly for such a misconstruction of his message, but even at the risk of this, he preferred these simple-hearted people to the subtle clerics of Judea. "In Galilee money counts for less than honor," was another rabbinical saying, and he who was to sell his master for a handful of silver was not a Galilean.

So the soil was chosen for the seed, which was to be the Church. All this Galilean period may be interpreted in these terms. At the same time as he put forward the essentials of his teaching and gathered around him the enthusiastic crowds from whom were to come his followers, he symbolized by means of a miracle not difficult to interpret the first idea of the Eucharist. Then we see him narrow the field, selecting and consecrating the Apostles, and finally, nominating decisively the man upon whom was to devolve the responsibility of carrying on his work after him. In the second period of his life, in Judea, it is the sacrificial aspect which is stressed and although it goes without saying that it was only by the offering on Calvary that the Church definitely came into being, it was in Galilee that the fundamentals of its doctrines and its structure were laid down. Jesus himself said so, about this time, in one of his parables: "So is the Kingdom of God, as if a man should cast seed into the ground; and should sleep and rise night and day, and the seed should spring and grow up, he knoweth not how" (Mark iv, 26-27).

Jesus' Acts

Jesus' method, now that he had fully embarked on his mission, was in no way different from that which he had followed during the period of preparation. He taught and preached, he revealed his power by miracles, but his personality takes on an incomparably greater authority. Already, in the unknown prophet who could see into the hearts of Nicodemus and the Samaritan woman at a glance and in the healer who sent back Antipas's officer in full confidence, the living God is manifest. The mystery of Jesus was unfolded little by little but not until the day when the stone was rolled back from the tomb and the risen Christ showed himself to the holy women, could it be fully grasped. Yet as the days of the Galilean years pass by we can see emerging from the human traits of the prophet the lineaments of the face of God.

To have drawn such crowds to hear him, the words of Jesus must have possessed an extraordinary force. Oriental peoples are highly susceptible to the power of the word and in the Semitic tradition, whether Jewish, Arab or Babylonian, the founder of a new religion must always be gifted with the eloquence that moves hearts. When Jehovah in the burning bush charged Moses to deliver his people, the patriarch replied: "O my Lord, I am not eloquent . . . I am slow of speech and of a slow tongue." And the Lord replied: "Is not Aaron the Levite thy brother? I know that he can speak well . . . he shall be thy spokesman unto the people." (Exodus iv, 10-16.) Jesus certainly possessed this power of moving hearts by his voice. It was to hear him that St. Mark shows us the Galileans flocking and pressing round him so that he was forced to take a boat to escape their attentions, whereupon a number of the more enthusiastic hastily went round the lake to catch him on the other side. Listening to him the crowds forgot the time and even the requirements of their stomachs.

Many of his sayings were of the kind that would cause the Jewish heart to swell with delight. "Ye are the light of the world. . . . Let your light so shine before men that they may see your good works and glorify your Father which is in heaven" (Matt. v, 14-16). "Ye are the salt of the earth" (Mark v, 13). The descendants of the Chosen People, whose pride it had been for two thousand years that they alone were witnesses of the true God, would naturally understand these words. To announce the coming of the Kingdom of God where human sufferings would be recompensed, sins forgiven and salvation and eternal joy would reign, to say to them that "this generation shall not pass till all these things be done" (Mark xiii, 30) would elicit from them the most fervent response and would fill the void of their secular anticipations.

But the message of Jesus was very far from those appeals to Jewish pride which many before him, half-prophet and half rebel leaders, had launched on the Galilean hillside. His message was in truth paradoxical; it came directly into conflict with established conventions of possession and obligation and elementary regard for comfort and respectability. It was a complete reversal of morality to these Galileans when Jesus said: "Ye have heard that it hath been said An eye for an eye and a tooth for a tooth. But I say unto you, Love your enemies, do good to them that hate you." (Matt. v, 38-44; Luke vi, 27.) Even when he did not go so far as this, it would seem curiously extreme to them when he condemned anger as much as murder, looking lustfully after a woman as much as adultery (Matt. v, 21 and 27). Nor did he seek to conceal the tremendous difficulties of the way he pointed out; he prophesied that those who followed him would be insulted and persecuted, falsely accused of many crimes, but they were to accept all these things and bear their cross joyfully. (Matt. v, 11; Luke xiv, 27.)

These stupendous sayings have lost something of their force nowadays. They have become the commonplace of sermons; they have become sweetened as if their pristine bitterness were too much for men to swallow. Certainly they are not easy to understand and it may be that the oriental excessiveness and love of imagery, so perfectly comprehensible to those who heard Jesus, can easily, if taken too literally, exceed the actual intention of the speaker. The Christian paradox certainly lies in the refusal of easy comforts, physical or moral, but it is not necessary to pursue it to absurdity. No disciple of Christ tore out his eye or cut off his hand to escape temptation and even Jesus himself, until he came to his Passion, did not turn the left cheek to him who struck the right. The Church has never lauded Origen for sacrificing his virility in a literal interpretation of these verses of the Gospel (Matt. v, 29-30), for the teaching of Christ must never be pushed to the extremes of scandal and anarchy.

None the less, with certain rare exceptions, the modern tendency is too much the other way. We do not dream of turning the other cheek or giving an overcoat to whoever should take our jacket. With two thousand years of Christianity behind us, we still find these injunctions irritating. How must they have seemed to those who first heard them in their startling novelty, to those Jews as firmly embedded in the exact computations of Mosaic theology as are twentieth century Christians in their bourgeois conformity? Yet these words had the force to liberate the wave of enthusiasm to which the Gospels bear witness, a force which so charged their absolute simplicity that the listeners recognized in them something other than the thoughts of a man like themselves.

This power, which was also demonstrated in Christ's miracles, is the distinguishing mark of the whole Galilean period, as if he sought to give weight to his words and increase the faith of his disciples by manifestations which even the most incredulous would recognize as transcending the natural order. The demonstration of this power was twofold. Firstly, it relieved the physical ills of man, showing the infinite compassion of Jesus whose lot it was to assume all sufferings, in whom the Word was made flesh. Secondly, the manifestation of this power had a direct Messianic intention, it was to reveal, through the mortal flesh, the living God.

Throughout this period of his work Jesus was surrounded by an ever renewed influx of the sick, the crippled, the scrofulous and the paralyzed. As soon as he left a synagogue or got out of a boat, the "court of miracles" in the most literal sense surrounded him. The blind sought him with their sightless eyes, the deaf mutes turned their blank faces, there was no wound too disgusting to be shown to him, and he unwearyingly responded. It was enough for him to feel that their hope was genuine, to discern the smallest embryo of faith; he would put out a little of his power to serve these humblest causes.

Even the leper, in spite of the Mosaic prohibition (Leviticus xiii) ventured in among the crowd, displaying the horrible red crater, sewn with a thick white down, and crying, "Lord, if thou wilt, thou canst make me clean." Here was one who believed in the supernatural power and trusted to receive its benefits. The word "leper" in the East covers a variety of diseases, from skin affections of the psoriasis type which are easily curable, to a purulent tuberculosis of the bone commonly rotting the finger joints which is prevalent in the Orient today, and which it is difficult to treat, and finally, true leprosy, which so far has proved beyond human cure. We do not know which of these this man had but whatever it was, a word and a look sufficed. Jesus put forth his hand: "I will: be thou clean." And immediately the sores disappeared. Transported with joy, the man took the road to Kades, the Levitical center of Galilee, to present himself and make an offering for his cure, as prescribed by the Law (Leviticus xiv; Luke v, 12-16; Mark i, 40-45; Matt. viii, 1-4).

At this time also Jesus restored the use of his limbs to a paralyzed man, cured a man with a withered hand, and, on being appealed to by a centurion, cured one of his slaves who was mortally ill. These beneficiaries of his mercy are unknown and unrecorded; often they were not even of his race. During his journey to Phoenicia, the inhabitants of which country, as Josephus tells us, detested the Jews, we see him nevertheless appealed to by these "heathens" and responding to their solicitations. Among them was the deaf-mute (Mark vii, 31-37), into whose ears he put his fingers and whose tongue he touched with his own spittle, saying: "Ephphatha: be opened, and straightway his ears were opened, and the string of his tongue was loosed." There was also the Canaanite woman who sought his aid for her sick daughter, whom Jesus at first seemed to put aside until she spoke in words of such moving humility. "It is not meet to take the children's bread and cast it to the dogs," he had said and she replied, "Yes, Lord, yet the dogs under the table eat of the children's crumbs." (Mark vii, 24-30; Matt. xv, 21-28.)

The Canaanite woman attributed her daughter's condition to a devil. Devils were thought to be very active in human affairs at the time. The Talmud states that they haunt the sleeping apartments of men, especially the conjugal chamber, and that in the cinders on the hearth the prints of their claw-like feet can often be seen. Most nervous diseases were attributed to them and the Jews frequently resorted to exorcisms, like that of Eleazar who, according to Josephus, claimed in the presence of the Emperor Vespasian to cure a demoniac by placing beneath his nostrils a ring containing "Solomon's root" and pronouncing an incantation over him. Jesus resorted to none of these formulae; by a single phrase the daughter of the Canaanite woman was cured.

But the forces arrayed against Jesus were powerful and the combat was often severe. In the country of the Gadarenes, which is now identified with the region of Kursi south of Bethsaida-Julia on the east side of the lake, he was attacked by a demoniac who lived among the tombs, whose honeycomb hollows can still be seen in the rocks. The maniac was so violent that no one had been able to capture him and the encounter with Jesus gives the impression of a battle between the evil spirit and the divine power. The howling, screaming creature approached, drawn by an irresistible fascination as if he himself desired to exorcise the enemy in possession. "What have I to do with thee," he cried, "Jesus, thou Son of God most high? I beseech thee, torment me not." But Jesus called to the evil spirit and ordered him to tell his name. "My name is Legion, for we are many." "Come out of the man," and the evil spirits obeyed and seized upon the prey nearest to hand, a herd of swine which they drove down the steep rocks into the sea. The man was cured; he sat quietly and peaceably at the feet of the Messiah, quite sound in mind. But the whole affair had been so terrifying that the people of the country became alarmed at the presence of so powerful a prophet. They besought Jesus to depart from them; it would seem that they feared to look on God. (Luke viii, 26-39; Mark v, 1-20; Matt. viii, 28-34.)

The power which Jesus displayed was in truth terrifying although, unlike most magicians, unlike even Moses, he never used it except for the benefit of mankind. Even Death submitted to it. At the little village of Nain, close to Nazareth, Jesus and his disciples were climbing the footpath up the slope, which can still be followed today, when a sad little procession descended toward the tombs hollowed out on the side of the hill, with a dead body on a bier, the young form stiff beneath the shroud. Behind came a woman crying. She said nothing and asked for nothing; she was too distraught for conscious thought. But the divine compassion saw into the heart of this desolate soul, a widow who had lost her only son and sole support. "Young man," said Jesus, "I say unto thee, arise." (Luke vii, 11-16.) Another time he was at Capernaum or close by, just getting off a boat. Among the crowd was a man of some position, a "ruler of the synagogue" named Jairus, whose little daughter was dying. Perhaps he remembered, this pious Jew, how Elijah and Elisha had revived the dead, for when they came to tell him that his little girl had died, he stayed on, having such faith in the power of Jesus. When Jesus went into the house of mourning, the furniture was already overturned, according to the Jewish custom, and the flute players had begun their wailing lament. "Talitha cumi," said Jesus and these two words, which St. Mark repeats in the original Aramaic, had an instant effect. "Damsel, I say unto thee, arise," and she obeyed. Her parents were so awestruck that Jesus himself, with fatherly solicitude, had to tell them to give her something to eat. (Luke viii, 40-42, 49-56; Mark v, 22-24, 35-43; Matt. ix, 18-19, 23-26.)

As we have seen, Jesus never resorted to any exorcism, cabbalistic formulae or paraphernalia of that kind. His will was sufficient to subdue the forces of nature. The evil powers were much more dramatic in their methods, a fact which Goethe doubtless remembered. Jesus performed these supernatural acts with complete naturalness. When he was accused of working miracles in league with the evil powers he replied with perfect serenity: "And if Satan cast out Satan, he is divided against himself: how then shall his Kingdom stand?" (Matt. xii, 22-28.) Everything about the man as we see him in these episodes shows his calm confidence in his mission and proclaims the presence of God.

The extraordinary scenes recounted in this part of the Gospel might almost have been conceived to demonstrate his incomparable majesty to those priviliged spectators from whom Jesus had chosen his collaborators. Miraculous cures, the casting out of evil spirits, even the revivification of the dead, although they might confuse the senses and disconcert logic, are nevertheless given an intelligent application to the problem, susceptible to some kind of explanation. But this man could impose obedience on the elements and alter the fixed laws of nature. One night, tired out with preaching, Jesus lay asleep in a boat belonging to Peter. He lay with his head on the cushions which from Homeric times to our own have always been provided on the back bench. The wind began to rise. It would have been December; through the gorges which, from east to north, cut into the Transjordan plateau, the blast would rush toward the lake setting up, says a Rabbinical description, "a species of terrible whirlwind." These sudden gusts of wind are even today dreaded by the local fishermen. The disciples awakened Jesus. "Master, Master, we perish." He opened his eyes. In a similar pass Caesar had said to the Adriatic boatman, "Why be afraid. You carry Caesar and his fortunes." But Jesus said, "O ye of little faith," and then, with hand outstretched, in the gesture which Rembrandt has for all time illustrated for us, he rebuked the wind and said to the waves, "Peace, be still." (Luke viii, 22-25; Mark iv, 35-41; Matt. viii, 23-27.) Then another and greater fear surged into the hearts of the disciples for, greatly as they trusted and revered him, this display of power was beyond their reckoning.

About this time they witnessed something else hardly less astounding. The disciples were alone in the boat, for Jesus, following his usual custom, was deep in solitary prayer in some secluded place. The disciples were on the easterly side of the lake and were trying to make for Capernaum but the wind suddenly arose and buffeted them to and fro across the lake. They strove until three o'clock in the morning, their arms almost out of their sockets, but they were still some four or five miles from the harbor. Then they saw a form coming toward them, walking on the water. The apparition filled them with terror. They screamed with fright, but a voice said, "It is I. Be not afraid." In the darkness, the face of the apparition was barely visible. Peter, quick and impetuous by nature, replied, "Lord, if it be thou, bid me to come unto thee on the water." And he said, "Come." Peter stepped out, but feeling the water move beneath his feet, he was smitten with doubt and promptly began to sink. But Jesus took him by the hand, guided him to the boat and helped him in. The lesson was plain enough; the first thing the Master asked from those who would follow him was immediate unquestioning obedience, whatever the circumstances.

A somewhat malicious story is told of a very holy man in one of the monasteries on Mt. Athos, who, confronted by a raging stream, had only to recite the Lord's Prayer when he would be miraculously transported to the other side. In due course he became the Superior of his community and in the course of a visitation he resorted to his former method of crossing the river. But his faith had become lukewarm with comfort and the waters soaked him well and proper. God, says the Book of Job (ix, 8), "treadeth upon the waves of the sea." No one, and least of all the immediate disciples of the Messiah, might forget that his power is illimitable. (Mark vi, 45-56; Matt. xiv, 22-36; John vi, 16-21.)

During the eighteen months of his teaching mission in Galilee Jesus constantly displayed his power by miracles. None is more significant than that of the multiplication of the loaves, when to appease the hunger of several thousand people he resumed, in a sense, the power of creation and instituted a repast which in some measure foreshadowed the supernatural food of the soul. He intended that his mission should be unfolded progressively. Just as he frequently spoke in parables, so he always asked those who had benefited by his miracles or had witnessed them not to go round telling everybody. It will be noted that he enjoined silence on the leper and the deaf-mute when he healed them and also on Jairus. But it was not to be wondered at that his injunction was disregarded, for the interest and excitement aroused by his teaching was nothing to the enthusiasm engendered by the miracles.

Our knowledge of the psychology of the orator who can sway crowds by his eloquence can in some measure help us to penetrate the psychology of Jesus as a teacher on the human plane. But we cannot penetrate the mystery of the healer, the caster-out of devils and the raiser of the dead by this means. For here is the mystery of divinity. A brief scene recorded in the synoptic Gospels seems to open this very question, but hardly is it opened than it is closed again, so that these few lines in fact raise more questions than they permit us to answer.

It was on the same day that Jesus brought back the daughter of Jairus to life. Among the crowd was a woman who, according to the Law, should not have been there, since she suffered from internal hemorrhage, which was considered unclean. She had tried everything in search of a cure; doctors, says St. Mark roundly, had ruined her. Probably she had also tried the innumerable strange remedies advised by Jewish sages, echoes of which may be found in the Talmud, such things as applying the ashes of an ostrich egg in a poultice on the chest or carrying a grain of barley embedded in the droppings of a white she-mule. In any case, with little more than hope, she managed to get near to Jesus and to touch the hem of his cloak. "And immediately," says St. Luke, "her issue of blood stanched." Jesus said, "Who touched me, for I perceive that virtue is gone out of me." In the press of the dense crowd that encircled him he had felt the silent appeal to his power. The trembling woman came forward and prostrated herself at his feet. "Daughter, be of good comfort. Thy faith hath made thee whole." We can easily enter into the feelings of the woman but how can we account for Jesus's knowledge that force had gone out from him? Here we touch the unfathomable mystery, the method by which the divine nature of Christ acted through his human nature.[1]

The Sermon on the Mount

We can follow Jesus as he went through Galilee teaching. Reading the synoptic Gospels, we can easily visualize the scene, the open air gatherings where the God made into man sowed the seed of his doctrines. Jehovah the All-Powerful, the Most High, had chosen the magnificent and formidable setting of Mt. Sinai, in the smoke of its storms, to reveal his commandments to Moses. A humbler landscape served the Master who brought the good news; the tranquil bay fringed with oleanders, the soft lapping of the waves on the shore, the gentle plateau framed by hills formed the amphitheater which echoed his voice.

"And he began again to teach by the seaside," says St. Mark (iv, 1), "and there was gathered unto him a great multitude of people, so that he entered into a ship and sat in the sea, and the whole multitude was by the sea on the land." "And he came down with them and stood in the plain," says St. Luke

[1] Apocryphal tradition has identified this woman cured of an issue of blood with that Veronica, the touching but historically doubtful figure, who wiped the sweat from the face of Jesus on his way to Calvary. Eusebius of Caesarea also states that after her cure she had a bronze statue placed outside her house representing her prostrate figure at the feet of a man stretching out his hand toward her.

(vi, 17), "and the company of his disciples and a great multitude of people out of all Judea and Jerusalem and from the sea coast of Tyre and Sidon which came to hear him." For two thousand years since, the Christian world has been striving, badly or well, to put into practice the words which echoed in Galilee and if by some mischance they had not been recorded, how immeasurably poorer humanity would be.

There has been a good deal of controversy about the site of the Sermon on the Mount. Some have held the place to be Tabgha, some eight miles north of Tiberias and a mile or so from Capernaum. It is a graceful hill and an Italian missionary order has built a hospice there. Certainly it would lend itself to a great gathering and a very old tradition has identified it with the scene described in the Gospel and there are several very old trees (not many today) which are called "the trees of the Beatitudes" and are said to have been there at the time. But this pleasant spot, so close to the busy lake, hardly bears out the impression of a solitary and desert place which is so strongly conveyed by the Gospel narrative. Other traditions have advanced a place called *Karn Hattin* (the Horns of Hattin), a high plateau between two sharply conical hills near Tiberias. This, certainly, is a wild prospect, its fields white with the pale asphodel and the yellow heads of fennel, its black basalt rocks splotched with purple anemones like blood. The lake can be seen between the gap of the hills. Here, on July fourth, 1187, Saladin, moving behind a smoke screen of burning brushwood, annihilated the last army of the Crusaders in that final battle in which perished the flower of Christian chivalry and the hopes of the Kingdom of Jerusalem. It must have been in some place like this, some lonely sunlit place of wide horizons, rocks and shrubs and not in the Rembrandtesque setting of classic porticos and ruins that the immortal words were spoken.

The Sermon on the Mount is reported by two of the Evangelists, (Matthew v-vii, Luke vi, 17-49) with considerable differences. The first gives eight Beatitudes, the second only four, but St. Luke follows with four maledictions which St. Matthew omits. There is also a difference of emphasis between the two. St. Matthew seems to interpret the words of Christ more in a spiritual sense than does St. Luke. For instance he says, "Blessed are the poor in spirit" and not simply "the poor," and "they who hunger and thirst after righteousness" instead of "they that hunger now." These differences, which are never contradictory, are easily explained. St. Luke, writing for converted pagans, would emphasize the letter of the law, the doctrine of charity, while St. Matthew felt himself free to bring out the transcendental character of the message. The theory has been advanced that the Sermon on the Mount is in fact a summary of the teaching of Jesus arranged by the Evangelists as a continuous discourse. But in any case, the development of the theme, the general purport and the chief parts are similar in the two accounts and both of them display in the most striking degree that supernatural originality by which we can always recognize the authentic teaching of Christ.

The Sermon opens with those paradoxical sayings which have given it the short title of the "Beatitudes," phrases which state, as it were in the form of a preface, the moral qualities required of those who would enter the Kingdom of Heaven. "Blessed are the poor in spirit," they who know how to give up, "for theirs is the kingdom of heaven." "Blessed are the meek, for they shall inherit the earth." "Blessed are the pure in heart," "Blessed are the merciful," "Blessed are the peace makers."

The listeners could follow all this; Jehovah had enjoined and recompensed virtue. But the strangeness of this doctrine was that those who on earth were underprivileged were those favored of heaven. St. Luke says explicitly: "Blessed be ye poor." "Blessed are ye that hunger now." "Blessed are ye that weep now." "Blessed are ye when men shall hate you," and he goes on to say that the rich are accursed, because they have their consolation here on earth, as have the well-fed, the happy and those of whom the world thinks well. It is not here on earth that the faithful must seek their rewards. The Kingdom, as was said by a Jewish sage about this time, is "the world in reverse," and the only recompense for the virtuous here below will be hatred and persecution as is always meted out to prophets.

At this point Jesus paused to define his own position, he who was more than prophet, with regard to the Law of Israel. "Think not that I am come to destroy the Law or the Prophets: I am come not to destroy but to fulfill." The Law given by God is immutable, and it must be followed through in the spirit of justice, surpassing the justice of the Scribes and the Pharisees. The Law taught that a man might not kill, but he, Jesus, condemned the anger in which violence originated. The Law denounced adultery but Jesus required that man should be pure in heart. The Law permitted divorce but Jesus declared marriage indissoluble. The Law forbade perjury and false witness but the disciples of Jesus were to speak the truth at all times without calling on heaven or earth. The old Law was severe; in practice if not actually in principle it condoned retaliation in kind. But the new dispensation set up an ideal of moral perfection, and commanded men not to resist insult, to renounce the right to vengeance, to accept injustice and to disarm their enemies by their goodness.

The second part of the Sermon explains what is required of the disciples of Jesus. First, that they should strive sincerely and disinterestedly toward the good; that they should not parade their good works, their almsgiving or their fastings. Next, that they should seek to amass true wealth, which resides in virtue rather than the treasures sought on earth. Thirdly, that the light of the divine truth should fill their hearts. Trust in Providence is the first essential of salvation. "Seek ye first the kingdom of God and his righteousness and all the rest shall be added unto you." "For the Lord is merciful, he will respond to those who beseech him, for he it is who gives us, as a father, our daily bread."

The discourse ends with an urgent call to action. "Everyone that heareth these sayings of mine and doeth them not shall be likened unto a foolish man that buildeth his house on sand." It is stamped throughout with the character of the circumstances in which it was uttered. It was probably given about June of the year 28, at the beginning of Christ's ministry and it is unmistakably addressed to those who would follow after him. It is indeed the charter of the future Church. But since it was in the first instance spoken before a miscellaneous crowd, in which popular elements preponderated, it was homely and direct so that the humblest peasant could follow it. And this is precisely the quality by which, two thousand years after, these words can touch the hearts of men of so many different races and countries. "But I say unto you love your enemies." "When thou fastest, anoint thy head." "Ye cannot serve God and Mammon." The naked human heart, with its devouring passions of hatred, pride and covetousness, is most surely reached by simple words like these.

Parables

Yet Jesus abandoned this simple and direct method of teaching. Shortly after the Sermon on the Mount he began to speak in parables. Why? The problem has been often debated and no entirely satisfactory answer has been found in spite of the multiplicity of works on the subject. Some have maintained that there is in fact no change in Jesus's oratorical style, that, in the wider sense, parables are interwoven in the Sermon on the Mount, as for instance in the celebrated passage, "Ye are the salt of the earth, but if the salt have lost his savor, wherewith shall it be salted?" (Matt. v, 13.) Here the faithful are compared with this salt which if long exposed to sun and air is said to lose its efficacy, as we are assured by Pliny the Elder. Other commentators think that there is a deliberate change in Christ's teaching method. Perhaps he was disturbed by the resistance which he was already beginning to encounter at the outset of his ministry and by the intrigues of the Pharisees, so that he decided to cloak his message in veiled terms and to await his time for plain speaking.

St. Matthew (xiii, 10) seems to explain this mystery, yet the explanation itself is so mysterious that it has led to even more discussion. The Apostles themselves asked the Master why he spoke in parables. "Because it is given unto you to know the mysteries of the Kingdom of Heaven but unto them it is not given. For whosoever hath, to him shall be given; but whosoever hath not, from him shall be taken away even that he hath. . . . For this people's heart is waxed gross and their ears are dull of hearing, and their eyes they have closed. . . . But blessed are your eyes for they see and your ears for they hear." These strange words almost shock us, especially when we recall those verses from Isaiah to which doubtless Jesus was alluding: "Go and tell this people: Hear ye indeed, but understand not; and see ye indeed but perceive not. Make the heart of this people fat, and make their ears heavy, and shut their eyes; lest they see with their eyes, and hear with their ears, and understand with their heart, and convert, and be healed." (Isaiah vi, 9-10.) It is the "lest they" which is so terrible and Jesus, quoting the prophet, seems to take it to himself. Was he already weary of the faithlessness of the people around him and abandoning them to their fate? Yet the whole Gospel demonstrates the contrary, that the divine compassion is unwearying.

What we should read into these bitter words, which betray the rejection of love, is a judgment of the entire human condition, of the irremediable weakness of our will and of our devotion. Jesus, who could read all hearts, knew only too well that those who acclaimed him when he worked miracles would abandon him when support was likely to become dangerous. The mystery of the blindness of Israel of which St. John speaks (John xii, 17-40), quoting those very words of Isaiah, is no more mysterious than that of the blindness of Christians whom neither words nor miracles have persuaded during the course of the centuries. And so, the things of God are left to the men of God. "Give not that which is holy unto the dogs, neither cast ye your pearls before swine." (Matt. vii, 6.) Let those who have ears to hear receive the word. In this apparent discrimination and, as it were, deferment of the complete revelation, in making it more esoteric, Christ is passing judgment in advance upon that society of human beings which was later to be called the Church, a society which, though largely engaged with the contingencies and harsh realities of this world, none the less possesses, invisibly in its essence and visibly in some of its members, the supreme gifts which mark the saints.

There is not much point in examining too closely the definition of a "parable" and in classifying it according to the categories so dear to the Greeks. The term, which comes from the Greek *parabalein,* signifies "a comparison" as distinguished from an analogy, an allegory, a riddle or an image; the Hebrew word "maschal" is vaguer and much more complex. St. John in fact uses quite another Greek word, "paroimia," a proverb. A simple saying such as, "Physician, heal thyself," a story with a moral like that of the poor Lazarus, is in Hebrew a "maschal" equally with the celebrated parables of the Sower or the Prodigal Son. This adornment of speech was very much favored by the Jews; it was to them the most telling form of discourse. It may be added that the Semitic mind, unlike our own, which derives its intellectual processes from the Greeks, set less store upon exactitude and logical progression than we should consider necessary.

Whatever else they are, the parables are little masterpieces of literature. Renan found in them something of the quality of Greek sculpture in which the ideal becomes tangible and lovable. We find them throughout the Gospel narrative until the very last days of Jesus on earth and some of them, the Sower, the Grain and the Tares, the Wise and Foolish Virgins, the Prodigal Son and the Good Samaritan for instance, are so embedded in our memories that they are an indissoluble part of the thought of the Western world. They are all characterized by extreme simplicity of expression, by a homely realism and at the same time by an authentic poetry, deriving solely from the genius of the heart.

A certain number of the parables were assembled by the synoptics (St. John does not record a single one) with the evident intention of composing a whole. (Luke viii; Mark iv;

Matt. xiii.) All these relate to the Kingdom of Heaven, which in turn Jesus compares with the seed which fell upon good ground, with the well-tilled field where an enemy comes to sow tares by night, with the grain of mustard seed—"the least of all seeds but when it is grown . . . the birds of the air come and lodge in the branches thereof"; with the leaven which makes the dough rise, with the net thrown into the sea which is drawn up so full of fish that the fisherman takes his choice, picking out some and throwing back others; with the pearl of great price, with the treasure lying hidden in the earth, the possession of which gladdens the heart. Doubtless there was a particular intention in the order of these parables; Jesus first wished to describe the founding of the Kingdom, then the seed thrusting forth. The mustard seed and the leaven exemplify its growth, the pearl and the treasure its supreme importance; the parables of the tares and of the great draught of fish illustrate the necessity and the difficulties of choice. The formula may not satisfy the requirements of strict logic but who can deny that the echoes of these comparisons sound in the most secret places of our hearts?

"The Kingdom of heaven is likened unto a man which sowed good seed in his field. But while men slept his enemy came and sowed tares among the wheat and went his way. But when the blade was sprung up and brought forth fruit, then appeared the tares also. So the servants of the householders came and said unto him, Sir, didst thou not sow good seed in thy field, from whence then hath it tares? He said unto them, An enemy hath done this. The servants said unto him, Wilt thou that we go and gather them up? . . . Nay, lest ye root up the wheat with them. Let both grow together until the harvest. Then I will say to the reapers, Gather ye together first the tares, and bind them in bundles to burn them: but gather the wheat into my barn." (Matt. xiii, 24-30.)

This parable which Matthew retells so admirably is direct and clear cut and the Galilean peasants to whom it was addressed would understand it perfectly out of their own experience. The well-tilled field, the good seed in the ground, the tares, so like the young wheat at first that they can hardly be distinguished until the black and poisonous seeds appear; the harvest, which the farmer surveys sorrowfully, noticing that it is "dirty" and full of weeds; through the simplicity of these homely and familiar scenes can be seen the image of the Last Judgment when Almighty God will come to judge men. We recognize too its revelation of the mysterious origin of evil, we who know from our daily experience that the good grain is never alone and the Adversary is always there, ready to sow the seeds of sin. These parables are far removed from conscious literary artifice but they are nevertheless inimitable. None of the rabbis, who made use of similar methods, and none of the Apostles, who did not venture to imitate the Master in this respect, could ever reach this spontaneous perfection.

The Bread of Life

It may be noted that at least four of the parables relate to grain or to bread. Among the Beatitudes also we find, "Blessed are ye that hunger now, for ye shall be filled." One of the most touching traits of the living personality of the Messiah is its assumption of the level of our daily preoccupations; he, who was God, could range himself with man. He knew and understood our anxieties, our desires and our fears. He knew that "brother body," as St. Francis put it, has its necessities and he was to dignify them and give them spiritual significance. He was not only to draw from bread and wine, our simple basic foods, the illustrations of his teachings; he was to make them the sacramental supports of his own Mystery, as the Church bears witness after two thousand years.

One day when a dense crowd pressed in around Jesus and his disciples, he decided to go a little distance away to find some quiet place for rest and refreshment. It was in springtime, just before the Passover, in early April, that delectable and fleeting period when the young grass is fresh on the hillside, when, under the pale blue sky, the mountain slopes are softened with a patchwork of green fields and scarlet anemones.

Jesus and his followers embarked at Capernaum, heading for the comparatively uninhabited shores south of Bethsaida-Julia. But the fanatical crowd would have none of this; as always where celebrities, which in some sort they were, are concerned, the public has infinite wiles and rejects all restraint. They very quickly guessed the direction which the prophet had taken, and they hastily made off to follow him on foot. From Capernaum to Bethsaida-Julia is less than six miles, allowing for the detour by the bridge which crosses the Jordan above its entry into the lake. So when Jesus got out of the boat, the crowd was already gathered on the shore, shouting and screaming with excitement and joy. Rest and refreshment were clearly for another time.

Jesus showed no ill-humor at seeing his intentions thwarted, but going upon a hill, he allowed himself once more to be surrounded by these unbridled enthusiasts, he preached to them and cured their sick. The time passed by, it grew late. Perhaps it was the disciples, as the synoptics state, who reminded their master that it was time to think of sending these hungry people back home. Or perhaps, as St. John tells it, it was Jesus himself who asked Philip, possibly as a test of faith, where they could buy bread for the people to eat. Anyway, the problem arose. But Jesus himself "knew what he would do." There were about five thousand people there and, "two hundred pennyworth of bread," said Philip, "is not sufficient for them, that everyone may take a little." It was an embarrassing moment for the disciples and they all tried to deal with it. Andrew, Simon Peter's brother, informed them, "There is a lad here which hath five barley loaves and two small fishes," adding derisively, "but what are they among so many?" But Jesus remained, as usual, perfectly calm. "Make the men sit down," he said. The disciples had already acquired the art of dealing with crowds; they divided up the people into fifties and hundreds and seated them in groups on the hillside. Then Jesus took the loaves and raising his eyes to heaven, he blessed them; then, the same with the fish. He then circulated the food among his assistants and as each one received his share without a halt it seemed to grow inexhaustibly so that after all had eaten there was still bread and fish unconsumed. The Jews always carried baskets with them, to serve as knapsacks for provisions. (Martial refers to them as always loaded with baskets.) Twelve of these were filled with the remains of this supernatural feast, to the astonishment, the admiration and the wild enthusiasm of the crowd.

This incident, one of the most famous of the Gospel stories, is also one of the best attested of Christ's miracles. It is recorded by the four texts (Matt. xiv, 13-21; Mark vi, 30-41; Luke ix, 10-17; John vi, 1-15 [2]) in terms which agree in all essentials and nothing is more convincing than the immediate reaction of sympathy and paternal care which here once more we observe in Jesus. It is futile to see in this miracle, as certain rationalists have contended, nothing but a lesson on trusting to Providence, the Messiah having simply given the order to distribute the food because he knew that provisions were concealed among the crowd and would be produced at the opportune moment. And it is quite absurd to talk about an "augmentation of the nutritive power of the five loaves" or of an hypnotic action upon five thousand stomachs. This is one of those incidents which cannot be torn out from the Gospel without denying the whole fabric. The five loaves and the two fishes of the little street peddler from Bethsaida are a defiance to reason and a lesson in humility.

But this miracle had more than a merely human application. St. Augustine asked who should nourish the universe save He who with a few grains of seed provides the rich harvest. Jesus accomplished simply what, as God, he could accomplish. The same power which causes the seed to swell and grow, in his hands caused the loaves to multiply. The five loaves were like seeds which were not put into the earth but were multiplied

[2] Both St. Mark (vii, 1-10) and St. Matthew (xv, 32-39) report a second instance of the multiplication of loaves, which took place after Christ's journey into Phoenicia and the Decapolis, in a place not very far from where the first miracle occurred. The main outlines of the episodes are the same, but on the second occasion there were seven loaves of bread, four thousand people, and seven baskets of fragments taken away.

by the hands of Him who made the earth. It can hardly be doubted that among those Jews who benefited by the miracle many would remember those verses of Genesis, which tell how from the hands of God came all things necessary for the subsistence of life, everything that lives and grows on earth, in the waters and in the air. "The herb yielding seed, the tree yielding fruit." The divinity of Christ bursts forth in this prodigious miracle.

Yet another truth lies hidden in the story. Few of us can read it now without casting our minds forward to that other moment when Christ took bread and blessed it, on the eve of his martyrdom, and offered it as his own body.

Rationalists such as Loisy and Reville, indeed, see in the miracle of the multiplication of the loaves simply an allegory of the Eucharist. The Church itself, while affirming the material reality of the miracle, sees in it a prefiguration of the later sacrament, and its promise.

This interpretation is not open to doubt; the Fourth Gospel indeed plainly says so (John vi, 22-59). After the miracle, Jesus sought to escape from the acclamation of the crowd and went across the lake again, but once more they followed him and found him. Once more, he had to speak to them. In the synagogue of Capernaum he assembled those who had sought him out once more. It could not have been a Sabbath as they had rowed across the water. The synagogue therefore would be empty and at the disposal of the people. Jesus knew quite well that the real significance of the miracle had not been understood; in the words of a commentator, "Instead of seeing in the bread a sign, they saw nothing in the sign except bread." It is human enough to interpret the rarest gifts of God in terms of earthly necessities, but the Messiah was to explain:

"Ye seek me, not because ye saw the miracles, but because ye did eat of the loaves, and were filled. Labor not for the meat which perisheth, but for that meat which endureth unto everlasting life. . . . Moses gave you not that bread from heaven; but my Father giveth you the true bread from heaven.

For the bread of God is he which cometh down from heaven, and giveth life unto the world."

To a similar exhortation, where the symbol had been not bread but the living water, the Samaritan woman had asked him to obtain this water to quench her thirst. The Jews at Capernaum responded in the same fashion, thinking only of bodily needs. "Lord, evermore give us this bread." "I am the bread of life," said Jesus, "he that cometh to me shall never hunger, and he that believeth on me shall never thirst." "This is the will of Him that sent me, that everyone which seeth the Son and believeth him may have everlasting life and I will raise him up at the last day." Astonishment quivered through the assembly, rising to something like indignation. Was this prophet calling himself God? This would be blasphemy. Murmurs ran from one to another. "Is not this Jesus, the son of Joseph, whose father and mother we know? How is it then that he saith, I came down from heaven."

Jesus, who had heard the murmurs, was even more categorical in his response. "Verily, verily, I say unto you, He that believeth on me hath everlasting life. I am that bread of life. Your fathers did eat manna in the wilderness and are dead. I am the living bread which came down from heaven. If any man eat of this bread, he shall live for ever. . . ." Then he made the mysterious announcement, the superhuman tragedy of his message: "The bread that I will give is my flesh, which I will give for the life of the world."

Here St. John, the metaphysical Evangelist, goes beyond the symbolical and plainly affirms the doctrine which on the evening of the Last Supper was to be fully revealed. He is not speaking here allegorically or in riddles. The sacrificial aspect of the fate of the Messiah is plainly indicated. It is doubtful whether the listeners who had applauded the miracle of the loaves understood the real significance of it. It is much more likely that, following their common conception of the glorious Messiah who would re-establish the Kingdom, they reflected that it would be very useful to have a sovereign gifted with such remarkable powers. They hovered and hesitated, missing the true meaning. "My flesh is meat indeed, and my blood is drink indeed." What could the strange words mean? How could you eat a man? Even the disciples quailed for a moment before the forbidding mystery of these words. It did not matter: the words had been spoken and later they would understand—they, the faithful, for whom the generous gift of the multiplied loaves would be as nothing compared with the offering on Calvary—that there is no glory, no radiance and no life save that purchased by blood.

Death of the Baptist

They had been tortured, those of whom the world was not worthy, said St. Paul about the prophets. (Heb. xi, 37-38.) And this applied to the last of the Prophets, whose voice had announced the coming of the Savior, by the ford of Bethabara, who was to bear witness to the law of salvation by blood. News of his death was rumored along the shores of the lake toward the end of March in the year 29, just before the miracle of the loaves and fishes. According to St. Matthew this explains the sudden departure of Jesus into the territory of the more benevolent tetrarch Philip; he would not desire to remain any longer within the power of Antipas, the murderer of the Baptist.

For ten months the Baptist had been in solitary confinement in the fortress of Machaerus. He seemed to have passed already from the world of the living. But however remote the fortress might be and however thick its walls, he still had ways of establishing contact with his disciples and he heard news through them of the progress and the glory of the one upon whom the Holy Ghost had descended. Once during the summer of the year 28 Jesus had even been visited by two emissaries from the Forerunner, in whose name they had asked, "Art thou he that should come, or do we look for another?" By a similar phrase, "he that cometh," the Baptist had described the predestined one who was to baptize with the Holy Ghost. (Matt. iii, 11.) Then he had recognized on the forehead of Jesus the sign by which God had marked out his son. Had the harsh, intransigent prophet changed his opinion? He may have been gnawed by the doubt which is the corroding acid of prison, or impatient, like every other Jew, to see the Redeemer of Israel confirmed by major political action, or perhaps he was simply anxious, out of his humility, to offer the faith and services of his own disciples to the Messiah. We cannot say; the motives behind the enquiry are not at all clear. But Jesus replied: "Go and show John again those things which ye do hear and see. The blind receive their sight and the lame walk, the lepers are cleansed, and the deaf hear, the dead are raised up and the poor have the gospel preached to them." The reply was as pertinent as it was categorical, for Isaiah, in a passage to which the reply clearly alluded, had given as a sign of the coming of Christ these very miracles which Christ had accomplished (Isaiah xxix, 18-19). Even more striking than the miracles was the witness of this new doctrine which was spreading among the people, for Isaiah had also said (lxi, 1) of the Messiah "the Lord hath anointed me to preach good tidings unto the meek." The disciples of John returned reassured, to transmit what they had learnt to their master. (Luke vii, 18-23; Matt. xi, 2-6.)

Herod Antipas, however, continued to watch John with that mixture of disquiet and respect, suspicion and fear, which has already been mentioned. He was a weak man, hesitating in judgment, guided certainly by innate craft but also just as much by his passions and superstitious fears. The man whom Josephus has pictured for us as very much attached to peace and quiet would probably have preferred to maintain his original attitude toward John, to keep him under surveillance, certainly, in order to keep his influence from spreading too much, but all the same, to treat him with respect, for after all, who can be sure of the future and of the judgments of God. But Herodias did not see things that way. Women have little tolerance of anything which threatens their loves and their personal ambitions and the granddaughter of the fiery Asmonean, princess Mariamne, had a very firm character. Between his own secret preference and the agitations of Herodias, Herod did the best he could, he was a good "fox," to use the phrase which Christ himself applied to him, but, as the old proverb says, "Foxes may be cunning but they are caught all the same." Very rarely does a man escape from the will of a tenacious woman.

The purely political explanation offered by Josephus seems to be inadequate. This is that Herod, fearing that John's influence might invite some of his subjects to rebellion, thought it better to execute the man than to incur the responsibility of suppressing a revolt. If the tetrarch's psychology was as simple as all that it is difficult to understand why, having arrested him in May of the year 28, he should have waited till March, 29, before killing him. The prophet could not have initiated any disquieting political action from the depths of his cell in the fortress of Machaerus. The account given in the Gospels (Mark vi, 14-29; Matt. xiv, 3-12) is much more credible. The real cause of the murder of John was the bitter hatred of him borne by Herodias, whom he had denounced as an adulteress and who intended at any cost to silence the voice which had asserted her guilt.

It was possibly during the winter of 28-29 that Herod made that journey into Mesopotamia which Josephus mentions, although he gives no date. The Median king Artabanes had just seized the territory of the Parthians, those old enemies of Rome, and he now slept in the massive gold bed of their princes and wore with a dignity befitting the ancient Persian King of Kings the tiara of Darius and Xerxes. Tiberius, thinking it might be useful to make an alliance with him, had dispatched his legate Vitellius as ambassador and in his elaborate train came the tetrarch of Galilee, who had been entrusted by the emperor with the delicate task of spying on the legate himself. There is every reason to believe that the Jew acquitted himself satisfactorily for Tiberius bore him gratitude and Vitellius an undying hatred, of which Antipas was soon to gather the fruits. On the day when the Median-Roman pact was concluded, the tetrarch gave a sumptuous feast in a pavilion which he had had built on rafts moored in the middle of the river. The festivities were described by Josephus as "prodigiously sumptuous."

The supposition that the journey into Mesopotamia took place during that winter has the merit of explaining two mysteries at least; the first, why the suspicious tetrarch showed no reaction to the popular agitation induced by the preaching of Jesus, the second, why instead of taking up residence in Tiberias, so delightful at that time of year, he should have taken himself to Machaerus, the forbidding hillside battered by the sandladen winds. If, however, he was in fact on his way back from Babylon, the place was one of the usual stopping places on the caravan route through Moab.

However that may be, according to the Gospel he brought an abundant suite to this remote castle, "his lords, high captains and chief estates of Galilee among them," says St. Mark. Herodias was there, proud that she could hold royal court at last and with her her daughter Salome, a young girl in her early teens. Perhaps, too, Agrippa was among the guests, the younger brother of Herodias whom Antipas had persuaded Tiberius to release from his enforced residence at Malatha and whom he had just nominated to the lucrative position of governor of Tiberias, which he was one day to regret. There may also have been Philip—Herod Philip II, brother of Antipas and tetrarch of Gaulonitis and Trachonitis who was shortly afterward to marry Salome. There would be great festivities, for all the Herodians loved luxury. Herod the Great ate from gold plate and the Roman custom of wearing wreaths of flowers had been adopted by these cosmopolitan princes. Stretched out on their litters, perfumed with attar of roses and wearing sleeveless tunics to leave their arms free, the guests would eat through a lavish and protracted banquet of rich and heavy food.

There would be a great deal of drinking. "Sweet music accompanying good wine is like an emerald in a golden setting," says Ecclesiasticus. During these feasts musicians would play on the *kinnar,* a Jewish harp with a deep grave sound, on the zither, which had a higher pitch and on various kinds of flutes and shrill reed pipes. During the pauses for the service of the innumerable courses, dancers would entertain the guests. And among these, at Machaerus, was Salome.

Many artists have been moved to depict this strange girl who materializes from the brief indications in the Gospel story as a disquieting figure. Perhaps Luini has succeeded as well as anybody. His canvas in the Louvre portrays an enigmatic countenance in which vice combines with grace, a red-haired beauty with green eyes, an ambiguous maiden who looks at the head which she bears on a platter, without pity and without a tremor. She would be about thirteen or fourteen, the age when a Jewish girl is most exciting to the carnal passions of men. "She danced and pleased Herod and them that sat with him," says the Gospel. The words and the setting bring suggestive poses to the mind of a modern European. Flaubert, in his *Herodias,* describes a dancer in "black drawers patterned with mandrakes," her shoulders covered with "a square of silk of pigeon's blood red," her feet shod with "little shoes made from humming birds' feathers," her whole person expressing a languor "so that one did not know if she was mourning a god or dying beneath his caress." An austere critic, taking literature rather too seriously, is outraged that Holy Writ should be perverted to turn a proud Herodian princess into a prostitute. But it seems just as accurate to represent Salome's dance as in current music hall versions as to portray her after the fashion of the sculptures in Rouen Cathedral, her head bent and with a long robe chastely covering her body down to her feet!

Bedouin dances, and it should be remembered that the Herodians were of Idumean origin and thus descended from Bedouin tribes, can be seen today in Syria and in the Transjordan. The dances of the Ouled-Naïl in Africa are similar. They employ means which are at once more violent and more subtle than these literary conceptions to stir the senses of the spectator. The dancer in her heavy blue-black draperies, almost as dense as a crinoline, comes slowly forward; her hair unbound, her arms straight by her side, she walks toward a fire which men are tending. She then begins to sway her head to the rhythm of the orchestra and the singers. "By night on my bed I sought him whom my soul loveth: I sought him but I found him not. The watchmen that go about the city found me, to whom I said, Saw ye him whom my soul loveth?" (Song of Songs iii, 1-3.) Then the beat quickens. The girl bends her neck backward, as far as it will go, she twists and turns, her face seems drawn in, her head weighted down by the heavy tresses. The arms now begin to raise themselves and to stretch out imploringly, offering themselves. The upthrust chin defies the unknown partner. For a long time she pivots thus, a top with sweeping raven's wings, endlessly fleeing and returning, the dark mane of hair whips her breasts and her loins, and as the pace slackens the spectators catch sight of her face, the nostrils taut, the mouth set and the eyes blank as in the exhaustion of pleasure. The choristers clap their hands, faster, faster. "Return, return, O Shulamite, that we may look upon thee. What will ye see in the Shulamite? As it were, the company of two armies." By the flames of the brazier she looks like a black and blue torch that flares with the wind. And when the cry of the flutes dies down and the harp sounds no longer, as if her support is suddenly withdrawn, the dancer often collapses, like an extinguished flame.

The story goes on: "The king said unto the damsel, Ask of me whatsoever thou wilt and I will give it thee. And he sware unto her, Whatsoever thou shalt ask of me, I will give it thee, unto the half of my kingdom. And she went forth and said unto her mother: What shall I ask. And she said, The head of John the Baptist. And she came straightway with haste unto the king and asked, saying: I will that thou give me by and by in a charger the head of John the Baptist. And the king was exceeding sorry, yet for his oath's sake and for their sakes which sat with him, he would not reject her." (Mark vi, 22-26.)

Cicero, in his *De senectute,* tells how Cato the Censor, in the course of the debate in which he expelled L. Flaminius from the Senate, recounted how Flaminius, while Proconsul of Gaul, had a prisoner beheaded on the spot because a courtesan whom he was entertaining said that she had never seen a man have his head cut off. This story is also confirmed by Plutarch. Herodotus tells us how the Persian King Xerxes, having drunk too much, made to the queen Amestris a promise similar to that of Herod Antipas to Salome, with the result that he was obliged to execute the Queen's hated rival, her sister-in-law.

"And immediately the king sent an executioner, and commanded his head to be brought, and he went and beheaded him in the prison. And brought his head in a charger and gave it to the damsel and the damsel gave it to her mother." According to St. Jerome, Herodias, transported with joy and triumph, pierced the tongue which had denounced her with a stiletto, as did Fulvia the wife of Marc Antony with the bloodless head of Cicero.

We do not know how the Baptist faced this culminating iniquity. Doubtless he expected it as the accomplishment of his destiny. "I must decrease," he had said. The humble Forerunner sank into the silence of one who knew his work to be well done. The Fathers of the Church, who often commented upon this scene of pathetic grandeur, pointed out its obvious symbolism, evil conquering good, the perpetual conflict of our life on earth. "Nothing can be worse than adulterous women," said St. John Chrysostom, "they are ready to kill whoever opposes their desires." Chrysostom himself was to die at the behest of the guilty empress Eudoxia. "The righteous man slain by the adulterers," said St. Ambrose. "The prophet a dancing girl's fee. O cruel king, it is thy lust more than the mortal blow which hath closed his eyes. Look at that mouth whose warnings you could not hear; it is silenced but you fear it still."

It was true that, although relieved of his embarrassing presence, the tetrarch felt himself more than ever menaced by the preaching of John. For it had become the voice of his own conscience. He believed in ghosts, like his grandfather Herod the Great, who called upon the spirit of Mariamne, the wife he had killed. When Herod heard the talk about Jesus, he believed that he was John risen from the dead. Josephus states that the later misfortunes of Antipas and his wife were held by the people to be a just requital for the murder of the prophet. Herod's erstwhile father-in-law, the king of the Nebaioth, attacked and defeated him. Antipas appealed to Rome for help from his friend Tiberius, who dispatched the former legate Vitellius. But the emperor died in the meantime and Vitellius, who had been enlightened about Antipas's role during the mission to the Euphrates and had not forgotten it, permitted the Arabs to loot and pillage Antipas's territory as they pleased. Then Herod quarreled with his young brother-in-law Agrippa and sent him packing to seek his fortune elsewhere. Unfortunately the clever young man succeeded only too well in this and became the intimate of Caligula. Having obtained from the emperor the succession to the territories of Herod Philip II who had just died, he proceeded to annex those of Antipas, who was ordered by the Roman to leave Tiberias and go into exile in Gaul. Herodias, who seems to have been faithful in misfortune, followed him. As for Salome, a legend very popular in the Middle Ages says that she too went into Gaul where when she was dancing upon a frozen river, the ice split and she was engulfed.

When John died, his disciples received permission to take away his remains. A very old tradition says that he was buried in the country of the Samaritans, and at Sebastia, the old Samaria, there is a church now converted into a mosque which commemorates the Forerunner. Then they told Jesus, says the Gospel, but we are not told how he received the news. He had nothing to learn about Herod, he knew him already, and we too can clearly see in the narrative the tyrant, alternately violent and vacillating, who will one day during the trial have Jesus at his mercy for a brief space. Nor could the news teach him anything about the fate meted out to prophets; he knew better than anyone the path on which he was set. We do not know what he said in praise of him who had made the way for him and who had just shed his blood in a cause like his own. Some months before, when John's disciples had come to him to ask if he were the Messiah, after their departure Jesus had pronounced a solemn eulogy which was intended to remove any vestige of doubt. "What went ye out into the wilderness to see? A reed shaken with the wind? A man clothed in soft raiment? Behold, they which are gorgeously appareled and live delicately, are in Kings' courts. But what went ye out for to see? A Prophet? Yea, I say unto you and much more than a prophet. This is he of whom it is written, Behold I send my messenger before thy face, which shall prepare thy way before thee. For I say unto you, Among those that are born of women there is not a greater prophet than John the Baptist." (Luke vii, 24-28) At the time when the Forerunner was about to disappear, no tribute could be greater than this.

The Catholic Church, in the office commemorating his beheading (August 29), echoes the Psalm (92): "The righteous shall flourish like the palm tree; he shall grow like a cedar in Lebanon." And in calling him a Martyr the Church is surely exact for he was the first of Christ's witnesses to testify with his blood, the first drops of that sanctifying rain which was to nourish, in the centuries of persecution, the seed of the Church.

Hostility and Resistance

The synoptic Gospels relate the story of the death of John to the suspicions which about this time were troubling Herod Antipas on account of Jesus—"for his name was spread abroad," says St. Mark. "It was said of some that John was risen from the dead, And of some that Elias had reappeared. And of others, that one of the old prophets was risen again. And Herod said, John have I beheaded, but who is this of whom I hear such things?" (Luke ix, 7-9.)

Herod's reaction was only one sign out of many that the movement of hostility which had begun almost as soon as Jesus started his public ministry was swelling, growing and organizing into a kind of occult coalition of resistance to him. The heart of this opposition was the sect of the Pharisees, the jealous guardians of tradition and dogma who considered all matters of religion their special province and who would obviously raise their eyebrows at this outsider, not one of themselves or bearing the mark of their teaching, who could nevertheless draw crowds in his train. In Galilee, as in all other Jewish provinces, these fanatical doctors of the law would be bound together in a regular freemasonry of interlocking interests, spiritual and political. We get the impression that in the beginning they watched Jesus, perhaps with some idea that he might be useful to them; then, growing alarmed, the Galileans sent word to their friends and leaders in Jerusalem who sent emissaries to spy on the new prophet. From this time we can observe behind the scenes of the Gospel an organized plan in which these people ask insidious questions, set traps, intrigue and finally conspire to murder him.

St. Mark (ii and iii) and St. Luke (v and vi) have assembled five consecutive instances of the tranquil resistance of Jesus to the Pharisees. St. Matthew (ix and xii) has separated them. The truth in each case is the same; the Master makes it plain that his teaching has nothing in common with the hairsplitting and quibbles of the scribes and he calmly flouts their sterile admonitions.

On one occasion, at the very beginning of his ministry, late May or early June of the year 28, Jesus was speaking in the house of one of his friends at Capernaum. A delegation of scribes and doctors of the law was there too, questioning him and hearing his replies, but reserving their opinion. Outside a crowd had gathered and, just as today at Lourdes, stretcher-bearers brought the paralyzed and helpless in the hope of a miracle. Four of these, realizing that they would never succeed in approaching the healer, had the idea of climbing, with their burden, up the exterior staircase which ran up to the roof, an arrangement which can be seen to this day in many houses in the area. Oriental roofs are mostly composed of a light daub on a foundation of compressed vegetable material and they offer little resistance to anything, even to a heavy rain. It was easy for the stretcher-bearers to make a hole in the roof covering and let down their burden like a package into the very room where Jesus was. Yet this indiscreet solicitation did not annoy him; he saw only the faith of which it was the evidence. "Son, thy sins be forgiven thee," he said. There is no doubt that he directed this phrase specifically to the Pharisees. They leapt to their feet in horror. What was it that this man had said? It was blasphemy. God alone had power to remit sin. But Jesus, who could read their hearts, had used the phrase deliberately to let them know who he was even if they refused to understand. It was no more difficult for the living God to cure the twisted body than to forgive sin. "Arise, and take up thy bed and go thy way into thine house," he said to the palsied man.

Shortly after, Jesus and his followers were on the shore of the lake. Capernaum, being a frontier town, had numerous offices for the collection of tolls and various customs duties with the usual army of excisemen and other money grabbing petty officials. These "publicans" had nothing to do with the big tax-farmers who, in the name of Rome, exploited the resources of the province. They were very minor employees and there is no reason to think that they were all dishonest, but as instruments of the exactions of the tetrarchs and the Romans and the servants of these abhorred masters, they were generally detested. A text in the Talmud bands together "assassins, brigands and publicans." Strict Pharisees held that the slightest contact with them was unclean and their reputation was so bad that St. Mark and St. Luke, in recounting the scene, give its chief figure the name of Levi, a name which does not figure in the list of apostles. At the same time the first of the evangelists humbly informs us that it is he, St. Matthew the publican. (He may have borne both names.) As he passed by the customs office, Jesus directed to one of the men working there the same luminous gaze that he had bent on Nathaniel and Levi-Matthew arose immediately and followed him. This was a pretty scandal for the orthodox, and it was aggravated by the rumor that the prophet even permitted the new disciple to eat at his table, doubtless with others of the same kidney.

The most exasperating thing about Jesus to the Pharisees was his calm disregard of all the rules which they held sacred.

If they reproached him for consorting with people of this kind he replied with calm logic, "They that are whole have no need of the physician, but they that are sick. I came not to call the righteous but sinners to repentance." They asked him why it was that while the Pharisees and even the disciples of John the Baptist fasted stringently his disciples did not. It would have been easy to dispose of this question as having no bearing on anything taught at the rabbinical schools, for the only obligatory Jewish fast was the Day of Atonement, though occasionally the Sanhedrin or the Synagogue would impose a special fast to commemorate some anniversary or national calamity. But these zealous souls could be encountered on all the Mondays and Thursdays throughout the year, clad in sober garments, offering God their hunger pangs, so that the early Christians, after leaving the Jewish communion, specially forbade fasting on these particular days. Jesus could certainly have parried and defeated these arguments by quoting the Law but he did nothing of the kind. His only reply, which was made to his faithful followers, showed that he was already aware of his destiny. "Can the children of the bridechamber fast, while the bridegroom is with them? But the days will come, when the bridegroom shall be taken from them and then shall they fast." Then he added with intentional irony: "No man also seweth a piece of new cloth on an old garment: else the new piece that filled it up, taketh away from the old, and the rent is made worse. And no man putteth new wine into old bottles, else the new wine doth burst the bottles and the wine is spilled." Worn out garments, bottles ready to burst, could these derisory terms be addressed to the Pharisaical practices?

And it was not only these "extralegal" observances which, however time-honored, were not actually enjoined by the Law, which came in for this casual handling. Even the most explicit commandments fared no better. Of all the precepts laid down by Moses none was more honored by the Pharisees than that of Sabbath observance. They had meditated upon it, embroidered it, wrought the most fearful and wonderful glosses so that the relevant section in the Talmud enumerates no fewer than thirty-nine actions which infringe the repose of the Lord's Day. Among these are included the writing of more than two letters of the alphabet, the untying of a knot, and to carry a package more than one thousand yards. There was some difference of opinion as to whether it was permissible to eat an egg laid on the Sabbath, but it was definitely forbidden to wear false teeth or to carry more than three amulets, to wit, a fox's tooth, a locust's egg, a nail from a gibbet. Just the mention of a few of these idiotic prescriptions is enough to show that Jesus was reverting to simple common sense. One might not cut the branches of a tree on the Sabbath nor pluck its fruit. So when the disciples of Jesus, being hungry, picked ears of wheat on the Sabbath day and ate the kernels the Pharisees gaped. "Behold thy disciples do that which it is not lawful to do on the Sabbath." We can almost hear the gentle irony in the voice which replied. "Have ye never read what David did, when he had need and was an hungred . . . how he went into the house of God . . . and did eat the shewbread, which is not lawful to eat but for the priests? . . . The Sabbath was made for man and not man for the Sabbath." But this kind of argument made no appeal to these fanatics of ritual; it only made them more angry. And when, on top of all these provocations, Jesus performed a miracle on the Sabbath, healing a man with a withered hand, the Pharisees hesitated no longer. They went out and held counsel with the Herodian faction as to how they might trap him.

So, at the very beginning of his mission, Christ found himself in opposition to the conformists. He had already become "a sign to be spoken against." The plot which, on the Feast of the Passover in the year 30, was to condemn him to death was already hatching as soon as the Pharisees recognized his aims. The Herodian party, with whom the doctors of the Law consented to ally themselves, could advance political reasons for their opposition to Jesus, that he provoked unrest, but the enmity of the Pharisees was directed to the man who proclaimed that he was God. The episode related in John (v, 1-

47) shows this very clearly. Jesus had gone up to Jerusalem for a feast, probably that of Pentecost. He came to a pool called Bethesda, near that entrance to the Temple to which the animals intended for sacrifice were brought. There has been a lot of discussion about this mysterious pool "having five porches," and many have regarded the reference as symbolic. But the French architect Mauss has discovered what is probably the actual pool, in the precincts of the Church of St. Anne. It is a long rectangle surrounded by a colonnade and divided across the middle by a fifth arcade. It was a popular meeting place and the Jews attributed miraculous qualities to its waters. Periodically the waters bubbled and when this happened the first invalid to be immersed in them would be cured. Consequently a large number of invalids, cripples, paralytics, blind men and others, congregated there waiting for the bubbling of the water. Among them on this occasion was a man who had been paralyzed for thirty-eight years. Jesus asked him if he had come to be cured and the man replied that he had no one to put him down into the water. "Rise, take up thy bed and walk," said Jesus. And it was the Sabbath Day.

The significant thing about this incident, not in itself different from many others previously described, which provoked the same scandalized anger among the Jerusalem Pharisees as its precursors had among their Galilean colleagues, is that for some reason which we can only guess, Jesus elected to explain his attitude. To those who reproached him with violating the Sabbath he replied, "My Father worketh hitherto and I work." To the Pharisees of Galilee he had only said, "The Son of Man is Lord even of the Sabbath Day." Here, in Jerusalem, he is more explicit. He is the witness of the Father, who will show them "greater things than these." Even those who sleep in the grave shall arise at his bidding. He has the authority to execute judgment. The very Law which they, the Pharisees, study so diligently, he tells them they do not understand. He, Jesus, the Messiah, is its true interpreter, Moses himself is their accuser, since in their vanity and pride they have perverted his teaching.

We can see, therefore, that the opposition of the scribes and Pharisees to Jesus was not incidental but vital. If they could not accept him they would have to hound him to death. We today find no difficulty in understanding this; it is the eternal choice which man must always make. Even before it was born, the Church of Christ was shown the field on which it must always accept battle.

The other centers of opposition to Christ's teaching were in the main less serious than the Pharisees who joined issue with it at the cardinal point. St. Luke reports an incident which throws light upon this type of opposition. He places it immediately after the account of Christ's teaching in the Synagogue at Nazareth, but it is probable, as is indicated by the accounts of St. Mark and St. Matthew, that it took place some months later. (Luke iv, 22-30; Mark vi, 1-6; Matt. xiii, 54-8.) When Jesus came to Nazareth he was immediately surrounded by his own countrymen. "Whatsoever we have heard done in Capernaum, do also here in thy country." We can almost hear the jealousy in the voices. But it was not only to his own people that Christ came. And so he reminded them how, long ago, when there was a famine in the land, the prophet Elias was not sent to feed the Jews but to the relief of a widow in Sidon. Nor was it a Jewish leper whom Elias cleansed, but Naaman the Syrian. These words however were hardly likely to placate the people who thought they should have a monopoly of his miracles and their disappointment when he did not perform any turned into hostility. When he declared that other nations would share in the glory of Israel, "They rose up and thrust him out of the city and led him to the brow of the hill whereon their city was built, that they might cast him down headlong. But he, passing through the midst of them, went his way." (Luke iv, 29-30.) The words suggest a sudden, miraculous disappearance.

About a mile southwest of Nazareth, that hill may still be seen. It is not a very high one and close by is a modern church called Notre Dame de l'Effroi. This church stands on the site of an ancient chapel built in the ninth century, and it commemorates a legend that Mary, hearing that the crowd were about to attack her son, rushed up the hill and seeing the milling crowd, but not Jesus, flung herself on the ground in an agony of grief, believing that he had been killed. The earth opened to shelter her, according to the legend, and that is how the chapel got its name.

"A prophet is not without honor, save in his own country, and in his own house," said Jesus, according to St. Matthew. A genius is seldom recognized by his own family, and even more rarely recognized by his fellow citizens. To the rough peasants of Nazareth, Jesus was one of themselves, no different from anyone else. His mother alone carried the mystery of his birth in her heart. It is fascinating to speculate, from these recorded incidents, how far indeed he seemed to be a man like other men. What did his immediate family, his numerous cousins, think of him? Probably that all this fuss would in the long run bring trouble, that it was much better not to talk about him so much, which was, it will be remembered, the opinion of Napoleon's mother regarding her son. Or they would go about saying, as so many others did, that he had taken leave of his senses—*Meschugge,* the word with which so many of the old prophets had been dismissed. It is recorded by St. Mark (iii, 20-21) that some of his friends sought to have him put away.

We know that Jesus was aware of the feeling aroused against him, and of the family opposition, because he took an early opportunity of putting it in its place. He was teaching and someone came to tell him that his mother and his brothers were calling him. "Who is my mother or my brethren?" he said. "And he looked round on them which sat about him and said, Behold my mother and my brethren. For whosoever shall do the will of God, the same is my brother and my sister and my mother." (Mark iii, 32-5.) In those who wish to live the life of the Spirit, the family bond has no part and, in the Church which was to arise from the Gospel teaching, those who accept the same risks, receive the same baptism and live in the bond of mutual love are all brothers.

The "True Family" of Christ

Throughout the Gospel narrative we can perceive the small, fervent band of enthusiasts who stood by to console Jesus for the hostility of the Pharisees and the lack of understanding shown by his own people. These are the first of the faithful; from them will the Church arise. The Gospel often mentions "crowds" but it is not at all easy to arrive at anything like an accurate figure. From the episode of the multiplication of the loaves one would conclude a following of several thousand people, which is very considerable for a country so small as Palestine was then. They came, apparently, from all parts; first from the towns of Galilee, Capernaum, Bethsaida, Beersheba, Magdala, even from towns like Tiberias, where there was a predominating foreign population, Greek and Roman, and from still further off. Throughout the Gospel we hear of men from Idumea, Tyre and Sidon, Syria and Transjordan, along with the Jews from Judea.

Most of them were certainly humble people. St. John says as much when he is telling us about the plot against Jesus (John vii, 48-49). "Have any of the rulers or of the Pharisees believed on him? But this people who knoweth not the law are cursed." There is no doubt that there were few "well placed persons" among the fervent adherents of the Messiah, those who were prepared to give up all to follow him. They were mostly of the common people, the despised by the arrogant doctors of law. To the "righteous" Jesus was to say that publicans and harlots would precede them into the Kingdom of Heaven; there was nothing incongruous in the association of two common criminals in the last agonies of a Messiah who had surrounded himself with men of doubtful repute.

Here and there we can sometimes catch in the Gospel narratives a hint of the psychology of those who believed in him, particularly in the stories of the centurion and of the unnamed harlot. The first incident took place at Capernaum, a little while after the Sermon on the Mount. Jesus came down to the city to meet a delegation of Jews who had been sent to him by the centurion in charge of the local military post. Probably this centurion was an officer belonging to one of the Roman auxiliaries or the mercenaries in the service of Antipas; nevertheless he was imbued by the sacred principles of Legion discipline. Possibly he was an old soldier risen from the ranks to the modest eminence of a company commander. The vine-stock which was the symbol of his authority was probably as near as he would get to a field marshal's baton but all the same, in this little town, he would be a figure of some importance. He was well disposed toward the Jews; he was worthy of help, said the Jewish elders who approached Jesus on his behalf, "for he loveth our nation and hath built us a synagogue." He may have been one of those who "feared God" and who, though not entering into the Jewish communion or accepting circumcision, had become imbued with the Jewish monotheism.

This centurion's servant was ill, and it was requested that Jesus should come and cure him. Jesus consented, and was setting off for the place where the soldier was when a second delegation arrived. The centurion had qualms about asking a great prophet to come to the house of an unworthy person such as himself. "Lord, I am not worthy that thou shouldest enter under my roof. Wherefore neither thought I myself worthy to come unto thee, but say in a word and my servant shall be healed." He did not say "pray that my servant may be healed" but "command that he shall be healed." His faith was complete and he knew also the power of a command; the same disposition which made him believe in military discipline led him to believe in Jesus, whom he recognized as a man having authority. "For I also say unto one, Go, and he goeth, and to another, Come, and he cometh." Jesus turned to the people and said, "I have not found so great faith, no, not in Israel." (Luke vii, 1-10.)

The man whose faith Jesus commended was a pagan, one of those whom the Pharisees rated as "lower than beasts and unworthy of pity." There is no surer road to God than that of faith and humility. There was another, too, who had these same Christian virtues, another of those poor wretches upon whom the scribes and Pharisees poured their scorn. A Pharisee named Simon had asked Jesus to dine with him, doubtless out of curiosity and a desire to observe him at close quarters. The dinner was unexceptionable, but not cordial; the host had not gone out of his way for this man of the people. Contrary to the custom, he had not washed his guest's feet nor anointed his head with the perfumed oil, he had not even offered the kiss of peace. While Jesus was eating, reposing on the low couch and leaning on his elbow, his naked feet toward the wall, a woman came into the room. It is customary in the East to enter freely into any house but the Jewish doctors did not allow women to be present when men were dining and this particular woman was certainly not desirable. She was the local harlot, known by everybody as such. This woman came toward Jesus, bearing an alabaster box of perfumed ointment. Whatever obscure desires and regrets impelled her, she threw herself at his feet, her tears flowing and proceeded to anoint his feet with the rare and costly perfume. The men at the table watched her scornfully but he who could read into their hearts turned to his host. "Simon, I have somewhat to say unto thee." "Master, say on." "There was a certain creditor which had two debtors: the one owed five hundred pence, the other fifty. And when they had nothing to pay, he frankly forgave them both. Tell me, therefore, which of them will love him most?" Simon answered, "I suppose that he to whom he forgave most." "Thou hast rightly judged," said Jesus. "Seest thou this woman?" The lesson goes to the heart of things. The worthy man stood in little need of forgiveness; perhaps that was why he showed so little love. But the wretched sinful woman came with her heart full of love and sorrow and it is this, not the cold consciousness of virtue, which moves the mercy of God. "Thy faith hath saved thee," said Jesus to the harlot. "Go in peace."

This episode, recorded only by St. Luke (vii, 36-50) moved Gregory the Great to say, "When I think of it, I can only fall silent and weep." Papini saw in her tears the symbol of the regenerating waters of baptism, which should recover her virginity. Mauriac, in a magnificent passage, sees in Christ's mercy toward the harlot the recognition of the tragic beauty which the worst of the sensual passions retain if they are entered upon without counting the cost. For his rendering of this story alone St. Luke deserves the tribute paid by Dante, "*Scriba mansuetudinis Christi.*"

The other three Evangelists report a somewhat similar scene as taking place at Bethany (Mark xiv, 3-9; Matt. xxvi, 6-13; John x, 1-2). It has been thought therefore that St. Luke's account is misplaced, but the tradition of the Church is that the episode of the precious ointment occurred twice. As to whether the unnamed woman was Mary Magdalene, "out of whom came seven devils," or Mary of Bethany, sister of Lazarus and Martha, and whether the two anointings were in fact one, this is discussed in detail in a later chapter, where the incident recorded as taking place at Bethany is discussed.

Doubtless there were many similar cases among the crowds who followed him along the roads, across the hills and by the lake, of people whose whole way of living had been changed by the teaching of the Messiah. But all who followed were not his faithful disciples, as many would be drawn by curiosity and thus there would be, as in all popular movements, some irresponsible emptyheads and those who sought to exploit. Jesus knew them all for what they were. He was not one of those tribunes of the people who rely upon the hysteria of the crowd for stimulus. He had no need of their enthusiasm; on the contrary, we read often how he sought to get away from them, to retire into a solitary place and pray. He had no illusions. He knew how very few of those who witnessed his miracles realized their underlying purpose, which was to testify to his divinity. He knew that they had little more than publicity value, for men are always looking for signs in the heavens. Though, when they receive them, they usually ignore them, if the signs are withheld they are sullen and disappointed. No charlatan would have spoken as Jesus did when miracles were asked of him.

When we consider the crowds who followed Jesus as the

forerunners of the congregation of the Church, it must be admitted that it is easy to recognize, coming down through all the centuries, traits only too common among Christians. Side by side with those whose faith is alive and is continually renewed, there are so many who slide into carelessness, indifference and secret infidelity. How many Catholics today hear Mass without ever thinking for one second of the terrible sacrifice there commemorated? How many Christians use the Gospel teaching to bolster up their own selfishness and creature comforts and to evade passing judgment on "the established order of things"? "We have piped unto you, and ye have not danced: we have mourned to you, and ye have not wept." These childish words Christ used to express the attitude of some of them. Doubtless there will be many who have ears that will not hear and eyes that will not see, for to the Kingdom of Heaven "many are called but few are chosen."

There is a tragic quality in the words in which, just before leaving Galilee, Jesus addressed those places where he had given so much of himself. "Woe unto thee, Chorazin; woe unto thee, Bethsaida! for if the mighty works, which were done in you, had been done in Tyre and Sidon, they would have repented long ago in sackcloth and ashes. But I say unto you, it shall be more tolerable for Tyre and Sidon at the day of judgment, than for you. And thou, Capernaum, which art exalted unto heaven, shalt be brought down to hell: for if the mighty works, which have been done in thee, had been done in Sodom, it would have remained until this day." (Matt. xi, 21-23.) The centuries have executed the prophetic vengeance: only ruins remain of Capernaum and Bethsaida while of Chorazin, destined according to legend to be the birthplace of Antichrist, there is today barely a trace. Jehovah himself had experienced, throughout the history of Israel, the ingratitude of the people he sought to lead and Jesus, who was to be abandoned by all in the hour of suffering, would savor the bitter knowledge to the full.

Even among the closest of his disciples there were undercurrents which Jesus had to fight. Why did he not declare himself King in Israel? Why did he not realize the old Jewish dream of a glorious Messiah who should free the land from the pagans? Why would he not let them lead him in triumph upon Jerusalem? We get a distinct impression, immediately after the miraculous multiplication of the loaves, that the Apostles were engaged in trying to promote a political revolution and crown Jesus as King. St. Mark tells us how he made his disciples get on the boat and himself, alone, dismissed the crowd (Mark vi, 45). It was the first but not the last time that particular danger manifested itself. There has always been that secular temptation for a Church, confusing the kingdoms of the world with the Kingdom of Heaven.

The Apostles

It was time for Jesus to designate assistants in the work of directing the crowds of followers who wished to live according to his teaching. He knew, from the growing attacks of his adversaries, that he must prepare for the future so that after he had gone the work could continue. This institution by Christ of a school for the Apostles is of the utmost importance. The philosophers of Greece and the prophets of Israel, including the Baptist, all had their professed disciples, but none of these was invested with the power and authority of the master. The schools of Stoic philosophy, for instance, consisted of individuals animated by the same ideals but working independently. Only the neo-Pythagoreans had anything like a rudimentary hierarchy. But the Church of Christ was hardly born before it found its leaders; a little later we see the founder designating a nucleus of secondary Apostles, the "seventy-two," the beginning of the future organization, whose security was to be assured by giving them a single leader, the keystone of the arch. There cannot be any question that the hierarchical principle preserved throughout the centuries by Catholicism is present historically in the Gospels.

Three accounts in the synoptic Gospels establish the facts beyond dispute. (Matt. x, 1; Mark iii, 13; Luke vi, 12.) "He went into a mountain to pray. . . . And when it was day, he called unto him his disciples and of them he chose twelve, whom also he named Apostles." He gave them power to heal the sick and to cast out devils. It is a wonderful scene which the Gospels describe for us: Christ meditating throughout the night, receiving the inspiration of the Father for the choice he has to make; the men climbing up to the high place and gathering around the Master, who is to choose among them. It should be noted that Christ alone makes the choice, his will alone decides. It is so in all the great vocations. "You have not chosen me, but I have chosen you." (John xv, 16.) Already Andrew and John had been chosen, by Jordan; then Simon Peter, later Philip and Nathaniel.

The word *apostle,* Greek *apostolos,* is an exact translation of the Aramaic word *shaluhah,* which signifies a messenger. The name was given to those who were sent by the Sanhedrin on missions to remote communities. The word "apostle" is rarely employed by St. Mark, St. Matthew or St. John, who generally say "the disciples" or "the twelve." St. Luke, however, both in his Gospel and in the Acts of the Apostles, uses the word continually. There was no doubt a graduation from disciple to apostle and those to whom the latter term was applied were more than ordinary disciples. The number twelve was undoubtedly fixed by Jesus himself; after the treason and death of Judas the eleven survivors immediately elected another, Mathias, to make up the number. It seems incontestable that the number had a symbolic significance. "Ye also shall sit upon twelve thrones, judging the tribes of Israel" (Matt. xix, 28). This was the promise of Jesus to the Apostles, and it is one of the points where the Old Testament and the New confront each other.

The names of the twelve are given three times in the Gospels and once in the Acts of the Apostles (Matt. x, 2-4; Mark iii, 16-19; Luke vi, 14-16; Acts i, 13) but it is not possible to make any two lists tally. Peter is always named first and Judas last; but there are many complications due to the fact only a few personal names were common among the Jews, that homonyms were frequent and surnames therefore a necessity for identification. Jude (which is synonymous with Judas) is often called Thaddeus, "the strong-chested," or Lebbeus, "the great-hearted," while the other, the traitor, is called Iscariot. The traditionally established list is Simon Peter; his brother Andrew; James, afterward called "the great," and his brother John, both sons of Zebedee; Philip; Bartholomew, also called Nathaniel; Thomas; Matthew the publican; James, called "the less," the son of Alpheus; Jude or Thaddeus; Simon the Zealot; and Judas, the traitor.

The Gospels do not throw much light on some of them. Some we only know by name or by some nickname which sheds light on some moral or physical characteristic, as Simon, which is the same name as Peter, and who is called the Zealot for a reason which we do not know. It might have been because of his ardor or because he belonged to the religious sect known as Zelots. Sometimes, too, he is referred to as the Canaanite, but this may be by confusion with "Qanana," the Aramaic term for Zelot. James the Less was presumably of small stature; Hegesippas, writing about the year 70 A.D., mentions a James who was a "Nazir," that is a man who had vowed to God not to drink wine or eat meat; not to cut or anoint his hair or to take baths; and who spent so much time in prayer that "the skin of his knees was tougher than a camel's." Other critics have questioned whether this "brother of the Lord" who became afterward head of the Church in Jerusalem was in fact the same as the Apostle.

But where the Gospel does mention any of the Apostles in detail, the portrait is masterly. There are few more satisfactory internal proofs of the authenticity of the narratives; no one could have invented these human, fallible creatures. There is a miniature of Christ and the Twelve Apostles in a fifteenth century Breviary of King René in the Bibliothèque Nationale and it is astonishing how skillfully the unknown artist has assimilated the various traits accredited to the twelve in the painted faces.

Look at Peter: a stout heart and an enthusiast. St. Mark,

who wrote Peter's version of the story, always tells us, when Peter appears upon the scene, that he did this or that "straightway." He was quick in word and deed. He never hesitated to ask Jesus questions. How many times should he forgive his brother? When his master is arrested, he immediately draws his sword. His reactions are always impetuous and violent. When Christ came to wash his feet at the Last Supper he protested, "Never." "If I wash thee not, thou hast no part in me," said Jesus. "Lord, not my feet only but also my hands and my head." He was very much a Jew and found it hard to understand the real meaning of Christ's coming but he loved, wholeheartedly and loyally, the one he followed. He is always named first of the Apostles and we see him constantly acting as leader and spokesman. When the others are disconcerted by Christ's teaching, Peter remains firm. It was Peter who said, "Thou hast the word of eternal life," and Peter who replied to the question: "Who think ye that I am?" with, "Thou art the Christ, the son of the living God."

John, "the disciple whom Jesus loved," is revealed to us in some of the most moving passages of the Gospel. The young man whose head reposed on the breast of Jesus, who alone followed him to the end, to the trial before Caiaphas and to the Cross, the figure who enshrines the most tender friendship of the life of the God who became man, was yet designated by Jesus, "son of thunder," in prophetic recognition of the Apocalypse. It was he who in the name of the martyrs was to cry, "How long, O Lord holy and true, dost thou not judge and avenge our blood on them that dwell on the earth?" (Rev. vi, 10).

Philip, perhaps richer in faith than in brains, who had no idea how he was going to feed the five thousand gathered together before the miracle of the loaves; Philip who asked Jesus to "show us the Father" at the Last Supper and drew from Christ the sad response: "Have I been so long time with you and yet thou hast not known me, Philip?" He stands before us as an active and friendly soul, one of those simple creatures from whom God has often recruited his saints. Thomas, whose name has become a synonym for doubt, was nevertheless a brave and reliable man who, when the other disciples hesitated to follow their Master into Judea, said heroically if pessimistically, "Let us also go that we may die with him." (John xi, 16.)

Of all the twelve, the least known is Judas the traitor. His dark visage is among those present at the sacrifice by which our salvation was assured; his role was horrible but necessary. Everything about him is dark and obscure. Some have considered that his name, Iscariot, signified the place of his origin and, following a dubious clue in Josephus, have designated a town in southern Judea named Kerioth as his birthplace. Yet others have seen in the combination of the letters S.K.R. of his sobriquet the Hebrew consonants which also signify the "deliverer" or the "betrayer" and think that his name is an anterior reference to the part he finally played. Even his name Judas may be considered to symbolize that it was the Jews, the "men of Judea," who were responsible for the death of Christ. But "all the textual difficulties and other questions of detail fade into insignificance beside the great moral problem posed by the treachery of Judas." (*Catholic Encyclopedia*, New York.) Here was a man who for two years had lived the life of the Apostles; he had addressed crowds, cured the sick and cast out demons. He had even occupied a confidential position among them, he had charge of their communal purse. Yet he became a traitor. Why? None of the innumerable explanations which have been advanced, and which will be discussed more fully later on is conclusive. What is even more mysterious is that Jesus, who knew that he would betray him before it came to pass—"Have I not chosen you twelve, and one of you is a devil?" (John vi, 70)—allowed him to remain among the faithful. In trying to comprehend the feelings of this dark, incomprehensible soul, we should remember the irresistible impulses in ourselves which thrust us toward evil even while we recoil from it. Fallible as we all are in circumstances of infinitely less consequence, we cannot help but feel compassion for the unhappy creature, the instrument of a tragic necessity. Tertullian and Ireneus, among the Fathers of the Church, have rebuked those who have seen in Judas the implement of Redemption. But the enigma remains; without the fall of Adam there could be no Christ: without the betrayal of Judas, no Cross.

All the Apostles seem to have belonged to the same social class; if they were not actually poor, still less were they rich. In the Acts (iv, 13) they are described as "unlearned and ignorant." Of the first six, four were Galilean fishermen, whose whole fortune was tied up in their boats and their nets. They had the advantage of the freedom of their calling. Matthew the publican had probably a little more learning and perhaps a little money, but no higher social standing. Jesus took what he had to hand. He did not require great intelligence or useful connections from his collaborators; he sought only that renunciation of self and singleness of purpose without which nothing great can be accomplished.

Those who followed him were required to give up everything which had hitherto occupied their days—the family occupation, whether it was the nets or the plough or hawking goods in the bazaar; the sociable evenings when, the boats on the shore and the nets stretched out to dry, they sat talking beneath the star-filled sky. Even more serious breaks with their daily life were asked of them. The moral requirements of the Gospel are familiar enough to us but they were revolutionary to the average orthodox Jew accustomed to regard religion as a matter of formal proscriptions, to glory in his national exclusiveness and to look forward to the hour of vengeance. What could these make of a religion of universal brotherhood, forgiveness and love?

The wandering existence imposed upon them in the two years during which they followed their Master would not seem so disconcerting to Orientals as it would to us, but it would be necessary to give up their family life and, with the possible exception of St. John, they would all seem to have been married. The *Acts of the Martyrs* states that Simon Peter had a daughter and Eusebius mentions a granddaughter of Jude.

They journeyed from place to place, sometimes staying at the house of a friend, more often eating and sleeping in the open air. Their food would have been bread and salt, raisins, dates and honey, and fish from the lakes when they had time to catch them. At night they would sleep, wrapped up in their cloaks, beneath the olives and the sycamores. In the presence of their Master they would not preach or expound; for a disciple to do such, the Talmud declared, was a sin so grave as almost to merit death; but when he was not there they had to act as substitutes in transmitting his teaching; and when the eager crowds pressed round him it was their duty to keep order and arrange the people so that all could hear. This task is that of their descendants, the Christian bishops, to this day.

We are apt to think of these men who accepted a new life involving a complete rupture with all familiar things as beings so exceptional that we can see no parallel with ourselves and our own problems. But this was not so. The Gospels themselves refute the conception that these men were miraculously protected from the temptations which beset the human condition. Certainly they had faith, but faith is only won by a profound effort. "But there are some of you that believe not," said Jesus (John vi, 64). St. Peter feared to trust himself to the waves only a moment after the hand of Christ had stilled them and everyone knows that he was to deny his Master three times in the hour when all abandoned him. We can see them flinch at some of the most profound and revolutionary teaching: "I am the bread of life . . . whoso eateth my flesh and drinketh my blood hath eternal life." "This is an hard saying," they said (John vi, 60). Even Peter himself, when Christ revealed the ignominious death which was waiting for him, repudiated it so violently as to draw from Christ the terrible response, "Get thee behind me, Satan." They were men just like us, with the same little meannesses. "There arose a reasoning among them, which of them should be greatest." (Luke vi, 46.) The same ambitions persist today, in the most sanctified places, in cloisters, in religious orders professed to humility.

They were but men like us, the Apostles, but the spirit of life had breathed on them and they were to testify by martyrdom in the end.

The Missions of the Apostles

Jesus seems to have devoted the latter part of his ministry in Galilee to the consolidation of his disciples perhaps because he knew that the sands were running out and that when the blow fell he must be sure that he had men ready to carry on his mission.

Some eight or ten months after the selection of the Twelve, we find them in action, perhaps in preparation for the tasks which were waiting for them when the Master would no longer be with them. (Luke ix, 1-6; Mark vi, 6-13; Matt. x, 5-16 and xi, 1.) They were sent out in twos, and so it was always to be, from the very earliest days of the Church. The missionaries always went in pairs, a wise provision ensuring at one and the same time, support and control and obviating the excessive exaltation of the solitary man who can sway crowds. Christ gave them power to heal the sick, to cast out evil spirits, to raise the dead, even at the risk of a diminution of his own repute. One thing he would not allow them to do—to announce him as the Messiah. In a vague, half-comprehended fashion, they had come to realize this themselves. But Christ bade them only to preach repentance and to announce that the Kingdom of God was at hand. At this stage they were not enjoined to preach to the heathen, the Gentiles or the Samaritans, but only to the lost sheep of the House of Israel.

Above all, Jesus was insistent upon the method which they were to adopt and particularly upon the poverty which they must always accept. The average Jew set out upon a journey with several tunics, girdles, a staff, a satchel, a change of shoes, possibly a cloak and certainly the Books of the Law. But they were to take nothing, no money, no satchel for necessities, no change of tunic or shoes, no staff. How were they to live, then? Providence would look after them, and when they came to a village they would look for a house worthy to receive them because it was an honor to shelter the messengers of God. If they were not welcomed—and they would not always find their path easy, often they would be repulsed, sometimes beaten and thrown into prison—then they were to retire, shaking off the dust of the inhospitable threshold. Once more we see the future pattern of the Church, the poverty and austerity which St. Dominic and St. Francis were to bind on their mendicant friars.

The first mission of the Apostles could not have been very prolonged; it was in fact only a rehearsal. They set out probably in February of the year 29; in April, at the miracle of the loaves and fishes, we find them once more grouped around their Master. From that time on, Jesus concentrated on trying to make them understand the fundamental principles of this doctrine. During this period much of his teaching seems to be specially addressed to the Twelve, to whom he expounds each point minutely, seeking to clarify whatever might be obscure. It was not easy and the Gospels, particularly that of St. Mark, do not conceal the fact that Christ had to strive hard to break the shell of habit and inability to understand which still enclosed the disciples. There is, for instance, the account of how they came in a boat to a place where there was a mixed population, probably mostly pagan. The disciples began to worry whether they would be able to buy bread made according to the legal prescription. "Beware of the leaven of the Pharisees," said Christ. Even then, they could only understand the literal application and Christ had to remind them of the occasions when material bread had been provided for them. At last, it dawned upon them that the leaven of the Pharisees was their hypocrisy and sterile legalism. Many incidents of this kind are recorded, before they could learn to interpret the words of their Master in the real, the spiritual sense. (Mark viii, 14-21; Matt. xvi, 5-12; Luke xii, 1.)

All these anecdotes illustrate how direct, concrete and immediately applicable was the teaching of Jesus. There is no subtle dialectic; it is wonderfully human and grounded in plain common sense. What was the use of ritual washing if the heart was black with sin? A pious Jew, coming in from a market-place who might have been unavoidably contaminated by contact with a heathen, must use about five hundred quarts of water to cleanse himself, an enormous quantity in a dry country like Palestine. Yet what was the use of so much cleansing of cups, pots, brass vessels, household utensils and beds when the soul was impure and the most majestic of the Mosaic commandments broken with impunity and with the tacit consent of all the doctors? The purity of food, upon which the Jews set so much store, could be as nothing against the purity of the heart. "There is nothing from without a man that entering into him can defile him, but the things that come out of him, those are they that defile the man. . . . For from within, out of the heart of man, proceed evil thoughts, adulteries, fornications, murders, thefts, covetousness, wickedness, deceit, blasphemy, pride and foolishness." (Mark vii, 1-23; Matt. xv, 1-20.)

The doctrine which Jesus set up against all these observances was very simple, requiring but few words and no complicated explanations. But it required absolute single-heartedness from those who would follow it. "He that loveth father or mother more than me is not worthy of me." (Matt. x, 37.) God requires us to give ourselves to him without reserve, to consecrate our whole lives to him. Freed of material possessions, with no conflict between God and money, the Apostles could give themselves up entirely to the one Master.

But even more insistently than he preached the love of God, so wholly and utterly a part of him, Jesus enjoined tirelessly the law of universal charity. We must love one another. "This is my commandment, that ye love one another, as I have loved you," he said in one of his last talks with his disciples (John xv, 12). One of the sayings attributed to Christ and quoted by Tertullian is, "You have seen your brother, you have seen God."

The only weapon of the Church is love. It is not by the power of the sword that the Church has won her triumphs;

even the high valor of the Crusades petered out in sterile vanity. But the sacrifice of the humblest missionary, the loving-kindness of the least of the Sisters of Charity, is never in vain. "Where two or three are gathered together in my name, there am I in the midst of them." (Matt. xviii, 20.) There is an echo of this in one of the *logia* found on the Egyptian papyrus: "Wherever there are two, they are not without God." Christians must show untiring forgiveness; they must forgive not seven times but seventy times seven. They must beware of being like that servant, himself freed from his debt by his master, who nevertheless went out and seized his own debtor by the throat. (Matt. xviii, 23-35.) "If thy brother shall trespass against thee, go and tell him his fault between him and thee alone." (Matt. xviii, 15.) Towards those who are not Christians and whose ways may in some respects offend, so long as they have fundamental goodwill, Christians must show forbearance. "For he that is not against us is of our part," said Christ, when John rebuked the man who sought to cast out devils in Christ's name. "No man which shall do a miracle in my name can lightly speak evil of me." (Mark ix, 38-40; Luke ix, 49-50.) The Church must always look not for that which separates but for that which unites.

So, fortified by these teachings, the Apostles were prepared for the task before them, to take up, when the time came, the work which Jesus had begun. It was to them, in a very much more personal sense than to the crowds on the hillside, that Jesus said, "Ye are the salt of the earth." Nothing threatens Christianity so much as a lack of fervor here and there in the Church. Looking down the centuries at the crises which have ensued, we see that they have always had one fundamental and primary cause, the infidelity of Christians to their true law.

Peter and the Glory of God

During the summer of the year 29, Jesus made a series of journeys outside of Galilee. In June, just after revisiting Jerusalem, where he cured a paralytic, he set out for Phoenicia where it is recorded that he cast out a devil from the daughter of a Canaanite woman. Probably he came back by way of Sidon, beautifully set in superb gardens, and crossed the Jordan by the bridge of the Daughters of Jacob, and spent a fortnight or so in one or other of the towns of the Decapolis. The curing of the deaf-mute took place about this time and the second miracle of the loaves, beside the lake. As the heat grew more fierce, he proceeded toward the north among the thickly wooded foothills of Mt. Hermon.

Here was the frontier of Palestine, a country where a Jew from Jerusalem, or even from Nazareth, would look in vain for familiar things. It was the country of Dan, the northernmost limit of the Promised Land, and after the burning plains of Tiberias it was paradise indeed. The air seemed fresh and cool as if it came from the snowy flanks of Mt. Hermon, whence certainly came the innumerable rivulets, threading the undergrowth, falling in cascades, flooding over the footpaths. Almond trees, fig trees, poplars, willows and terebinths grew together in careless profusion. The scent of the oleander was everywhere. No wonder that the Greeks heard among the music of the rivulets and the sighing trees, the eternal call of pagan nature, "Long live Great Pan." Even today, by the sharp break in the escarpment from which arises one of the sources of the Jordan, we can see traces of the grottoes which were used as sanctuaries of the undying nature god. In this region, which from the time of the Ptolemies of the Lagid dynasty had been called Panias, Herod the Great had built, on a jutting ledge of rock above the source of the river, a white marble temple to Caesar Augustus, the ruins of which still remain. It was with the same sycophantic intention that Herod's son Philip, ruler of those parts in Christ's day, had named his chosen dwelling place, the beautiful town he had just built, Caesarea.

Jesus and his disciples went among the villages around Caesarea Philippi (Mark viii, 27). Caesarea itself was too infected with paganism for them to visit it. It must have been on one of these terraces looking out on Hermon or on one of those walks where the Jordan foams over the soft sand, so delightful to bare feet, that a scene decisive in the history of the world took place, the formation of the hierarchy of the future Church.

"Who do men say that I am?" asked Jesus one day of the Apostles. "Some say that thou art John the Baptist, some Elias and others Jeremias or one of the prophets." "But who say ye that I am?" he insisted. Simon Peter, as usual, spoke up. "Thou art the Christ, the son of the living God." Then Jesus said, "Blessed art thou, Simon, for flesh and blood hath not revealed it to thee, but my Father, which is in heaven. And I say also unto thee that thou art Peter and upon this rock I will build my Church and the gates of hell shall not prevail against it. And I will give thee the keys of the kingdom of heaven, and whatsoever thou shalt bind on earth shall be bound in heaven; and whatsoever thou shalt loose on earth shall be loosed in heaven." Then he instructed them to tell no man that he was Christ. (Matt. xvi, 13-20; also, incomplete, Luke ix, 13-21 and Mark viii, 27-30.)

Two fundamental facts are established by the Gospel narrative at this point. The first is the recognition by Peter, in the name of the Twelve, of the divinity of Christ. It was not the first time that the disciples had recognized the nature of their Master. We are told, for instance, that after the miracle of the calming of the tempest (Matt. xiv, 33) they worshipped him as the Son of God. But this formal recognition by Peter had a special significance, coming as it did when the clouds were beginning to gather, when hostility to Jesus was becoming marked and the facile crowds of followers, in spite of the miracles, were falling away. But the Apostles never doubted. They had progressed in faith and the secret of Christ's mission was about to be entrusted to them, though not now and here where the inimical pagan spirit of the place affronted the Jewish ideal. They themselves had more to learn before they could understand fully and that is why Jesus enjoined secrecy upon them and why he was to tell them, a little later, about his coming Passion and Death. They were to become his legatees. The use of the word "Church" immediately afterward has a particular significance. The Christian assembly was to extend the Jewish "community," the *kahal,* in an essential respect. The Church was to participate in the divinity of the Messiah, in his glory as in his suffering.

The other fact established by the text is no less important. The play on words by which Jesus changed the name of Simon is henceforward explicable. We do not know if the name of Peter, *Kephas* in Aramaic, was in use as a nickname before this pronouncement, but the significance of it is clear. Beneath the rock on which Herod had raised a temple to Augustus, this man of unshakable faith, this rock of certitude, was to uphold the Church. Perhaps the play of words was suggested by the situation; because of it the Catholic Church maintains that the authority of the Pope, the heir of St. Peter, is, as he was, the rock upon which the Church of Christ must stand.

"Liberal" critics have suspected this text to be a later interpretation on the ground that it is found only in the Gospel of St. Matthew. It is said to have been put in by a copyist at a later date, when the Church was an historical reality, in order to support the pontifical claims. But every ancient text of St. Matthew which has come down to us includes these verses and they have certainly not been interpolated. Moreover, all the authorities agree with the Rev. Fr. Lagrange that in all the four Gospels there is no passage more distinctively Aramaic in its construction and images. Beyond the word play on Peter, which echoes a passage in Isaiah (xxviii, 16) where the Lord says, "Behold I lay in Zion for a foundation stone, a tried stone, a precious corner stone, a sure foundation," there are many traditional Jewish metaphors. For at least four centuries "the gates" of Sheol in Hebrew, of Hades in Greek, had signified the infernal regions, something analogous to the usage of the "Sublime Porte" for the old Turkish Empire. The allusion to the keys is more typically Semitic; even today Arab notabilities bear large keys on either shoulder as insignia of their importance. In Isaiah also we read (xxii, 22): "And the key of the house of David will I lay upon his shoulder, so he shall open and none shall shut; and he shall shut and none shall open." The expression "to bind and to loose" in the sense which Jesus used it was common among the doctors of the Law: the Rabbi Necmia, some thirty years later, was to implore Jehovah, at the end of one of his sermons, "not to allow what he had loosened to be bound, nor to unloose what he had bound, nor to render pure what had been declared impure."

As for the argument that the text must be spurious because it does not appear in the other two synoptic Gospels, if we are to reject all those sayings which appear only in one of the Gospels unsupported by the others a great many of the most famous and beautiful words of Jesus would have to go. Any critic who will clear his mind of prejudice is bound to admit that there is no more reason for doubting the authenticity of this passage than that of any other in the entire Gospel.

So here we have Peter, set apart from the other Apostles, receiving the confirmation of his belief in the Divinity of Jesus and being told that he is to lead the future community of Christians. We see, too, that small inner circle of the faithful who stay with Jesus after his mysterious words about the bread of life have alienated the more superficial followers (John vi, 66). These are the men who are worthy to receive the divine confidence. They must have asked themselves still how he could give them his flesh to eat and how the flesh and blood of their Master could be given for the life of the world. And even when they proclaim him "the son of the living God" they must have asked what was the dividing line, if such there were, between his nature and God's nature. They were not to remain in ignorance for long.

"From that time forth began Jesus to show unto his disciples how that he must go unto Jerusalem and suffer many things of the elders and chief priests and scribes, and be killed and be raised again the third day." (Matt. xvi, 21; Mark viii, 31; Luke ix, 22.) This is the first revelation of the Passion, the first, but quite categoric, intimation to the Apostles that they were not to believe, as did the rank and file of the Jews, in the establishment of the Messiah's kingdom on earth. The Gospel leaves us in no doubt whatever as to the painful effect of Christ's words upon the simple minds of his followers. Peter, impetuous as ever, even took it upon himself to remonstrate with his Master, "Be it far from thee, Lord; this shall not be unto thee." "Get thee behind me, Satan," said Christ. But no matter how often he predicted his end it was not until it had come to pass that the Apostles, numbed by stupefaction, terror and despair, could be brought to believe in it.

While he was prophesying his death according to the body, Christ also foretold that his death was but a stage in his apotheosis, that he, the Son of Man, would come again in all the glory of the Father, and that he would then reward every man according to his works. (Matt. xvi, 27.) They had even been permitted a glimpse of the supernatural glory.

About eight days after Peter's confession of faith, or six days according to Jewish reckoning, "Jesus taketh Peter, James and John his brother and bringeth them up into an high mountain apart." While he prayed, his aspect changed. "His face did shine as the sun and his raiment was white as the light. And behold there appeared unto them Moses and Elias talking with him." Peter and the others had been asleep but when they awoke and saw Jesus and his two companions Peter, hardly knowing what he said, cried out: "Master, it is good for us to be here. Let us make three tabernacles; one for thee, and one for Moses and one for Elias." But, even while he was speaking, a great cloud passed over them and the disciples huddled awe-struck in its shadow. From out the cloud came a voice saying: "This is my beloved son; hear him." The cloud passed and the disciples, looking fearfully around them, could see only Jesus, alone. As they went down from the mountain, Jesus asked them to tell no one what they had seen and heard till the Son of Man had risen from the dead. They kept silent but among themselves they asked what this could mean, to rise from the dead? (Matt. xvii, 1-8; Mark ix, 2-8; Luke ix, 28-36.)

Throughout the centuries, artists have striven to portray the grandeur and terror of the scene. The various renderings, Fra Angelico's at Florence, the Byzantine miniaturist at Daphnis, the romanesque sculpture at la Charité de la Loire, all concentrate on the awe and terror of those three men, barely awakened from sleep, becoming aware that they are in the presence of God. None of the awe-inspiring scenes from the Old Testament, not even the Presence on Sinai, has the same quality, a shining glory imbued with a still, deep peace. For, over and above the earlier mystic manifestations, this one has a certain human verisimilitude. We see the three men rubbing their eyes, we hear Peter's thoughtless and clumsy outburst, and we realize exactly what he means. For this is the first time that the Apostles, for all that they have followed Jesus and witnessed his miracles, have seen a hint of his glory, seen it face to face, as Moses had looked upon the face of God. "What I seemed I was not: what I am I seem not," says one of the *Logia* in the Apocryphal Acts of John. The glory of Christ had been hidden from men and that legend (in the Pseudo-Matthew) which states that when Jesus slept he was bathed in divine radiance is Apocryphal indeed.

Jesus revealed himself only this once and to his three chosen intimates. At all other times he was a man like other men. The transfiguration on the mountain, or, to use a more exact word—the same word which St. Paul uses in II Corinthians, iii, 18 to describe those who "behold as in a glass the glory of the Lord" —the metamorphosis, was to bestow upon the Apostles, and especially on St. Peter, an irrefutable vision, an overwhelming testimony of the birth of their faith. There have been other historical instances of a similar kind, the voices heard by St. Joan, for instance. The revelation of the Transfiguration, coming as it did immediately after Christ's first reference to his Passion and death, was designed to inspire the apostles with a certitude of their faith which they were later to recall with complete understanding. They had asked among themselves what it could mean, to rise from the dead, but later on they would realize. This is what that great theologian Pope Leo the Great meant when he said, in the fifth century, that the Transfiguration was designed to extirpate in advance, from the hearts of the disciples, "the folly of the Cross." We may wonder if those same three men remembered the glorious vision on that other night, when once again they fell asleep, while Christ wrestled with his agony in the dark garden.

The honor of identification with the place of the Transfiguration has been claimed by those two mountains of which the Psalmist said, "Tabor and Hermon shall rejoice in thy name." (Psalm 89, 12.) A very ancient tradition coming down from the fourth century, designated Mt. Tabor, the round bare hump which rises alone in the middle of the Galilean plain, and which is today crowned by the beautiful Franciscan Church of the Transfiguration. It has been objected that Mt. Tabor, a bare six hundred feet high, does not bear out the Gospel description of "a high mountain." Certainly there is a magnificent view from the top, the undulating fold of the hills, the whole valley of the Jordan, the mountains of Gilead in the east and the Mediterranean sparkling in the distance. Tabor's summit is a narrow ledge of rock, covered with juniper bushes and swept by winds from all quarters; its romantic aspect lends itself to an evocation of the famous, mysterious scene. But in the time of Christ, it carried a Roman fortress and a garrison and even from a photograph we can see that this dome surrounded by cornfields can hardly be considered in the same class as Mt. Sinai as a site fit for awesome revelations. Moreover the Gospel says that after coming down from the mountain, Jesus and his disciples passed through Galilee, which again seems to rule out Mt. Tabor, since it is in the middle of Galilee. Considering these factors, many critics have favored Mt. Hermon as the scene of the Transfiguration. Hermon is close to Caesarea Philippi, where Jesus is known to have been a short time before; it is always referred to as "the foremost mountain of Israel," being over two thousand eight hundred feet high. The view from the summit ranges from the Syrian desert to the Phoenician seaboard, uniting in one sweeping panorama the countries of the Jews and the Gentiles. Even today it takes six hours to climb it, and four hours to get down. Jesus and his disciples did not return until the following day, which suggests a considerable journey. But the evangelists attached little importance to topographical detail when narrating a scene like this; they had seen the Lord in glory and nothing else mattered.

Something of that dazzling radiance lingers over all the episodes occurring just after the return of Jesus and his disciples to the plain. We note that a great crowd assembled to hear him when he came down; that he cured an epileptic when the disciples had failed to do so. (Luke ix, 37-43; Mark ix, 14-29; Matt. xvii, 14-21.) Here it was that he gave that wonderful lesson, holding a child in his arms: "Except ye be converted, and become as little children, ye shall not enter into the kingdom of heaven." Through the accounts we catch a glimpse of the mind of the Apostles, dazzled by what they had seen, puzzled by what they had heard. We find them asking questions of him. What did the presence of Elias signify, for Elias to the Jews was the forerunner of the Messiah. But he told them that Elias had come already, in the form of John the Baptist, who had been put to death, as he, Jesus, would be put to death. The day after they had seen the glorious vision, they are told, not once but several times, of the approaching Passion. Yet once more, before they left Galilee, Jesus spoke plainly of what was to come for the time was drawing near when he must go into Judea, into the town which was to be the scene of the oblation. But only when it was all over did they understand what he had told them, so closed were their minds against the supreme truth, that the Church was to arise from the blood of Christ. He told them: "The Son of man is delivered into the hands of men and they shall kill him; and after that he is killed, he shall rise the third day." But: "They understood not that saying, and were afraid to ask him." (Mark ix, 31, 32; Matt. xvii, 21-22; Luke ix, 44-45.)

CHAPTER SIX

SON OF MAN, SON OF GOD

Portrait of Jesus

PERHAPS WE SHOULD now try to draw a portrait of the man whom, so far, we have tried to discover through the record of what he said and did. There is such complete identity between the acts and the teaching of Jesus that his character rises before us in its uniqueness, in every page of the Gospel. The uneducated men who set down these records have succeeded incomparably in the task which has tried the skill of all the great novelists; the character they describe lives. The personality of Jesus is inescapable in the smallest fragment in which he appears, and when one considers how the Gospels were compiled, from a variety of reminiscences and traditions over scores of years, not only is the force and vitality of the character astounding but also its wholeness and consistency. The personality which could impose itself so unshakeably on these various accounts must have been powerful indeed.

Yet, if we deliberately search the Gospels to build up a portrait of the character and temperament of Jesus, the result is curiously elusive. In the accounts of the lives of all men of genius and sanctity there is always something which evades our grasp and rebuffs our analysis. That something is, precisely, the genius and the sanctity. In Jesus who was something more than a saint and a genius, the secret which eludes us is his divinity. For Jesus was divine and divinity confounds rationalization or psychological explanation.

When Fra Angelico said that to paint Our Lord it is necessary to live with him, the devout artist was not claiming perfection for the work of his own brush; he meant that the ordinary creative methods of the writer and the painter had been revealed to him as inadequate. There is here a mystery beyond analysis: we cannot argue and explain, we can only contemplate and adore.

"Blessed be Jesus Christ, true God and true man." The words of the prayer emphasize the difficulty we encounter when we try to draw a portrait of Jesus. As a man like other men, Jesus is a fit psychological study, but the moment we seek to fix a human trait in his personality we realize that this trait is in communion with the other side of his nature, that it is rooted in it and therefore escapes our definition. The very term "Son of Man" can be taken to mean a mortal being like ourselves, born of woman and dying in the flesh, and also the expression of a supernatural fact, the secret of a living God. The three Apostles, when the veil was put aside at the moment of the Transfiguration, hardly dared to recognize their friend in the supernatural presence revealed to them. In an infinitely more humble degree, anyone who tries to depict Jesus is equally confounded by the effulgence of the godhead woven in with the traits of humanity.

These difficulties are insurmountable, but there are others of a different kind. The Gospels were not composed as historical accounts, much less as psychological documents. The Evangelists were less concerned to tell the story of the life of Jesus than to record his teaching and confirm the faith of their hearers by their testimony. They were not theologians or logicians, still less were they literary artists seeking a conscious effect. They did not bother to set down the characteristics of Jesus; they made no effort to reconcile opposing traits. Yet the result is a portrait astonishingly whole and alive. Haven't they done as well what a master novelist tries to do?

It's a question of what is not said as well as what is said—of leading us to the point where we could feel that the unknowable was suggested. They were not skilled writers, the Evangelists, but somehow they managed to suggest these secrets, these silences that demand respect.

But we must not look for order and precision of detail in the admirable portrait which they have composed. Those who have tried too hard to impose regularity upon the Gospel portrait run the risk of producing a lifeless emasculated plaster figure like so many of those depressing images in our churches. Man himself is a mystery, combining material body and intangible spirit, indissolubly knit together. How much more so was that unique being in whom the play of light and darkness, of spirit and flesh, exemplified, at the supreme level, the relation of the Creator and the created?

His Appearance

How we long to know what he looked like, how we strive to find something about that personality which moves us so deeply which would give us his picture, as of a beloved familiar friend. We scrutinize the Gospels, but they do not help us much on this point. From a certain passage in St. Luke (xix, 1-4), where it is stated that the Jericho publican Zaccheus "sought to see Jesus but could not for the press," it has been concluded that it was Jesus who was "little of stature." This, however, is obviously a misreading; it was Zaccheus who was short since he had to climb up into a sycamore tree. But it is just as misleading to conclude that Jesus was of handsome and majestic presence from the fact that Mary Magdalene picked him out immediately from the other guests at the dinner when she anointed him with the perfume, or from the incident where an unnamed woman lifted up her voice in the crowd to acclaim him. (Luke xi, 27.)

It goes without saying that there is no man-made portrait of Jesus which has the slightest degree of factual authenticity. Yet what a host of them there have been, throughout the centuries. We can trace the influence of an antique cameo from Byzantium brought to Rome at the time of the Renaissance in many of the profile representations of Christ. A panel attributed to Jan van Eyck and a sixteenth century sculpture at Poitiers both show a striking resemblance to this model.

There are a number of legends regarding miraculous portraits of Christ, beginning with the one which tells how, after the Ascension, the Apostles besought St. Luke, traditionally said to have been an artist, to draw a portrait of the Master so that it should not be forgotten how he looked. After three days' prayer and fasting, the Evangelist set down to his work, and a supernatural representation of the Holy Face appeared upon the blank canvas. Another legend says that the woman who was cured of a hemorrhage endeavored to draw the face of the man who had cured her but her rendering was so inadequate that she gave it up in despair. But one day Jesus, after having eaten at her house, took up a cloth and wiped off the face of the picture. Upon the fabric was imprinted a true likeness of the Holy Face. Everybody knows the touching story of Veronica, who might perhaps have been this same woman, and how she offered her handkerchief to wipe away the sweat and blood from his face on that terrible journey to Calvary. At Moscow, in the Cathedral of the Assumption, there was another "Holy Face." Abgar, the King of Edessa, having heard the rumors about Jesus, invited this great prophet to his kingdom. When Jesus declined, the King sent a miniaturist to paint a portrait of him. The artist, awed by the divine effulgence, was unable to produce even the roughest sketch, but Jesus leaned his face against the painter's canvas and there was the miraculous imprint, more lifelike and beautiful than any human hand could make it. Of course they are all legends, but they are none the less touching, and the meaning of them all is clear. It is only in the hearts of those who love him that Jesus implants his image. The stories may not be authentic history; they are none the less authentically Christian.

Little more credence can in truth be given to those accounts of the appearance of Jesus which have come down through the centuries with some pretence of historicity. About the year 550, Antony of Piacenza made a pilgrimage to Jerusalem and reported that he had seen there a footprint left by Jesus, which he describes as "small, delicate and well-proportioned," and also a portrait of Jesus, painted during his lifetime, showing him as of "medium height, with a handsome face and slightly curly hair, fine hands and long, tapering fingers." In the eighth century Andrew of Crete tells of a portrait said to have been painted by St. Luke in which Jesus was represented with "a long face, the eyebrows meeting, the head bent forward, the figure well-proportioned." A little later, a Greek monk named Epiphanus went as far as to say Jesus was six feet high, with a long nose, a "wheat-colored" complexion, black eyebrows, red hair, and even that he greatly resembled his mother! John of Damascus, who lived in the eighth century, and Nicephorus Callistus, who wrote during the fourteenth century but who obtained his information from a tenth century chronicler, are equally unreliable as witnesses.

The most curious of all these alleged descriptions of Jesus is a work entitled *The Letter of Lentulus,* which enjoyed great popularity during the fourteenth century but seems to have been entirely forgotten since. The supposed "Publius Lentulus," who describes himself as "Governor of Jerusalem," addresses himself to the "Senate and the Roman People" according to the time-honored Republican formula (which Tiberius would hardly have regarded as acceptable) and gives certain details of Jesus's appearance, doubtless poetic, yet in some respects psychologically startling, for all that there is not the slightest chance that they could have any historical foundation. "He had a face which called forth veneration, so that those who beheld it felt at the same time awe and love. His hair was nut-brown, falling straight almost to the ears, with bluish highlights in the waves which fell on his shoulders. He had a ruddy complexion; his nose and mouth were perfectly formed. He had a full but not a very long beard, forked at the chin and of the same color as his hair. He was upright and slender; his hands and arms were graceful." The portrait ends with a

Biblical quotation which is doubtless the key to it, for the description must have been composed to fit it. "Thou art fairer than the children of men." (Psalms, 45, 2.)

The truth is that the "face of Jesus in the flesh is unknown to us." This has been repeated by all the Fathers of the Church, this remark of St. Ireneus of Lyons, who lived at the end of the second century but who, through his association with St. Polycarp, could draw upon the memories of a very early Christian community in Ephesus. "We are entirely ignorant as to what his face looked like," said St. Augustine. When we remember that the representation of any form of human likeness was strictly forbidden to orthodox Jews, it is not at all surprising that no authentic portrait of Jesus should have ever been found. It was entirely contrary to the make-up and the intentions of the Evangelists, the only true witnesses of the life of Jesus, to give any thought to his personal appearance; it is not without significance that the only such reference, in all four texts, is to the appearance of Christ transfigured.

This being so, there may seem little point in reviving the discussion which so greatly agitated the early Church, as to whether Jesus was handsome or not. Justin Martyr considered that he had "no presence, no beauty, indeed a pitiful air." The same Ireneus who declared that his face was quite unknown to us considered him to have been "weakly." Origen thought his stature "poor and mean." Commodian saw him "in the guise of a slave." There were even legends that he had been a leper. Gregory of Nissus, John Chrysostom, Ambrose and Jerome, all declared in favor of a handsome appearance. But it is idle to recall these controversies now, for we have less taste than our forefathers for these picturesque details. Clement of Alexandria expressed a profound truth when he said, "For those who seek real beauty, only Our Savior is beautiful." Perhaps the Apocryphal Acts of Peter can be taken to mean the same thing in the paradox, "He was at one and the same time ugly and beautiful."

Both schools of thought serve only to confirm the Old Testament prophecy. The one relies on such passages as the one cited from the so-called Publius Lentulus: "Thou art fairer than the children of men, grace is poured into Thy lips." The other derives from the famous chapter of Isaiah in which the Messiah is described as "despised and rejected of men, a man of sorrows acquainted with grief, and we hid as it were our faces from him; he was despised and we esteemed him not." (Isaiah liii, 3.) There are many other texts of this kind. "They have pierced my hands and my feet: I may tell all my bones"; "I am a worm and no man." The difference between the two conceptions of the Messiah appears in aesthetic discussion, but it sheds no light upon the question of Christ's personal appearance.

The speculation, however, is not altogether as vain as it may seem, apart from the fact that it arises from the love which so many devout Christians have felt. It is not idle curiosity; it symbolizes the profound truth that God, in taking upon himself our human aspect, removed the proscription which Jehovah laid upon Moses and from this release sprang Christian art. The Reverend Fr. Doncoeur, writing on this subject, has said, "In the purest sense, Christ as depicted in art can be no other than the Christ of our Faith. The figure of Christ in art breaks down the mystery of appearance in order that a ray of the interior light may come through."

For fifteen hundred years or more, the Christian world has sought to supplement this deficiency in the Gospel narratives by requiring its supreme artistic genius to give it back the human face of the God made into man. The faithful in the earliest days of the Church were content with the humble symbols we can still see in the Catacombs, the fish, the lamb, the vine stock and the wheat ear. Then appeared certain portraits resembling the figure of Orpheus, often taken as a symbol or precursor of Christ. Later came the figure of the Good Shepherd, which appears so often in the Gospel parables, but with certain Hellenic ornaments and details. The delightful statue in the Lateran Museum, or on that sarcophagus in the Louvre which shows him leading the recovered lamb tenderly, his arm around its neck: these are still pagan in their aesthetic conception, very like the neighboring Hermes Criophore, the "ram carrier."

The pagan influence was slow in disappearing; these early representations of Jesus all show him as young, beardless and vigorous, as the Greeks had depicted the gods. In the Catacombs we find even such venerable figures as Noah, Job, Abraham and Moses represented as young men. It was only in the fifth century that the Byzantine influence grew and established a type which has been, and is even today, most widely accepted. It is the face of a man, with hollow cheeks and salient bones, with a long nose, deep, unfathomable eyes; the hair clear of the forehead and falling to the shoulders, the beard dark brown in color, curly and forked. For a long time the two types appeared together, the beardless image representing Christ in the world, the other Christ in glory. Gradually, the latter came to prevail; it is known today wherever the Cross is known.

Of course there have been infinite variations on this fundamental type and two especial dangers have always threatened the traditional representations of Jesus. The first is an insistence on beauty of face which has too often come to mean insipidity and which has produced for the admiration of the many who fall for this sort of thing countless sugary images by unworthy followers of Raphael, Leonardo, Luini and, most particularly, Guido Reni. The other danger is an over-insistence upon the pathetic and horrific aspect of the Crucified. This tendency dates from the fifteenth century when deliberate emotionalism began to invade art. The grandiose horror of the "Christ of Perpignan," the cadavers of Holbein and Grünewald mark perhaps the reaction against a sickly sentimentality. Other representations have gone much much farther in this direction.

We are all, even today, influenced in some way by the great multitude of artistic masterpieces, whenever we think of Christ in human form. We may see him as the Master, all-powerful and tranquil; as the incorruptible Judge, sculptured on a portal of the cathedral of Amiens. We may think of him as Fra Angelico painted him, with that wondrously serene face and deep all-seeing eyes which remind us of how he looked at Nathaniel. Among so many conceptions the most moving perhaps are those in which the artists have managed to portray the duality of the tragic humanity and the celestial charity, such as the head in the Musée Archéologique at Beauvais, or the other in the Musée de Cluny, which evoke him who said, "I am not come to destroy but to fulfill." But even considering these highest expressions of man's artistic genius, we would not dare to say that any one has evoked the complete personality of Christ.

Every people has the right to recreate the adorable image in their own idiom. "The face of Christ," says the patriarch Photius, writing in the ninth century, "is differently portrayed by the Romans, the Greeks, the Indians, the Ethiopians, for each affirms that Our Lord appears to them in this particular guise." A Christ with a Chinese or Negroid face can outrage only those who fail to understand the Christian testimony. Christ was a Jew by race and it is probable that he had the physical characteristics of the Chosen People, but this birth which derived from the mysterious destiny of Israel, was not thereby limited; the real message of Christ's life was in his death. He died for all men, and it is to the whole family of humanity that he belongs. Every man from that time on has sought to find himself in him.

They are right, those who have said that Jesus "took upon him the form of a servant, and was made in the likeness of men" (Phil. ii, 7) that "he was no different from any other man" (the anti-Christian Celsus), that he had "the same face as all the sons of Adam" (John of Damascus, in the eighth century.) The last word upon the whole question was said many centuries ago. It is attributed to St. Cyprian, bishop of Carthage in the third century. "It is in yourself that you see me," said Jesus, "as a man sees his own face in a mirror." What matters, not only in religion but in history, is not the unknowable physical aspect of Jesus, but the endeavor of millions of

Christians, during two thousand years, to identify their spirits with his spirit, because they know that only in the ultimate hour of judgment shall we see him, not as now, "in a glass darkly but then face to face." But until that day we know that, in the words of the Epistle of St. John, to see him "as he is" we must be "like him."

His Human Life

It is obvious as we read the Gospels that Jesus was a plain man, and that he lived among the humble folk, from whom his disciples were drawn, as one of themselves, eating the same food, wearing the same clothes, apparently no different from others of his race and kind. It is not, however, historically accurate to go to extremes and rank him among the lowest classes, to speak of him, as some have, as "one of the proletariat, the son of a charwoman." Jesus had many traits in common with the crowds who followed him; he had many others, however, which they instinctively recognized as belonging to a higher order. Even as we meditate upon the figure of the lowly born carpenter, there arises before us the figure of the prophet, the miraculous healer and the man whom Peter, James and John saw clothed in light on the summit of the mountain. The two are indivisible.

When we turn from such physical details as what Jesus wore and what he ate to the question of his education and intellectual equipment, what languages he spoke, we come up against the mystery of the Godhead in the flesh, and whether one who possessed within himself all the sources of the spirit could not transcend the limitations inherent in the man as he was.

There was nothing remarkable in his given name. Jesus, *Jeshouah,* is derived from *Yahoshou,* "Jehovah saves," or "Jehovah helps." It is the same as the Hebrew name which in the Old Testament is translated as Joshua. In Greek, the three Semitic variants, *Jehoshua, Joschua, Jeshua,* are all translated as *Jesous* from which we get Jesus. Among the Hebrews, as among ourselves, fashion governed the giving of names, and the name of Jesus, which had fallen out of use for many years, became popular again about the fourth century B.C. We have already discussed at some length his surname of "the Nazarene." Such an addition was extremely common at the time to identify a man precisely. No magical power can be attached to it.[1] Similar examples have already been mentioned.

His clothing can hardly have differed much from that still worn by the Palestinian peasant, the head covered with a piece of cloth, closely drawn in front and hanging loosely to the shoulders behind like the modern *couffieh.* His hair and beard were probably worn long. He would wear a linen tunic in all weathers, adding a woollen cloak in the winter and this, as prescribed by the Law, would have blue tassels, these forming the "hem of his garment" which the woman with a hemorrhage touched, and was cured. When he prayed, he would perhaps put on the ritual white cloak with purple bands and place on his forehead and arm the "phylacteries," little boxes containing verses from the Law. It was customary also to wear three girdles or sashes; one held the garments together, one had pockets and served as a purse; the third, which was some fifteen yards long, served as a traveling rug. His sandals would be the same as those still worn in Palestine, just soles laced with cords, the "latchets" which John the Baptist said he was "unworthy to loosen."

When he went on a journey he would, quite naturally, expect hospitality and shelter wherever he happened to be. This was the traditional custom and, to a large extent, it still exists. A straw mattress, or a sort of string hammock, or even a rug or mat would be laid out in one of the rooms of the house, or on a balcony or terrace, for the climate is favorable to sleeping out of doors. After the heat of the day, the coolness of the

[1] We do not agree on this point with Guignebert's reading of that passage in St. John's Gospel (xviii, 5) where Christ's reply, "I am he," to those who sought "Jesus of Nazareth" caused them to fall to the ground. This is attributed, as is the passage in the Acts where Peter cures the sick in the name of "Jesus of Nazareth" to some magic "power of the name." But we cannot find any indication that either Jesus or the Apostles used the name in that fashion.

night is delightful and it is pleasant to sleep thus, with the head on a fold of the cloak, under the myriad stars, until dawn breaks and peace is shattered by the cries of the herdsmen driving their beasts to feed.

Jesus depended largely on hospitality for food and shelter. The Twelve certainly had a common purse and, according to St. John (xiii, 29) it was kept by Judas. They had rich friends, mostly women, who "ministered unto him of their substance" (Luke viii, 3). But it was not very luxurious living. The Galilean peasant ate bread, milk products, fruit and vegetables and, naturally, fish. Water was the usual drink; wine was reserved for feasts and there was also a sort of beer, called *sicera,* which was brewed from fruit and grain. It is probable that Jesus was sometimes a guest at feasts, like that of Cana, where the Orientals made a great display, and also at funeral celebrations at which only lentils were eaten, because of the rabbinical saying that "as the lentil hath no seed-lobes the afflicted hath no words." The impression we get from the Gospel story is one of great simplicity of life with needs reduced to a minimum not so much for lack of money as for deliberate frugality and renunciation.

There has been a great deal of debate as to what languages Jesus spoke. At the time he lived, as for some two centuries previously, the vernacular of Palestine was Aramaic. The Aramaeans were a branch of the Semitic family, who some time in the second millennium, in the course of various confused migrations, established themselves to the north of the Fertile Crescent at the foot of the Anti-Taurus range. Here Abraham, leaving Ur of the Chaldees, accomplished the first part of his journey, in Haran, and it was to this country, Paddan-Aram, "my father's house," that Isaac and Jacob came to seek their wives. One of the earliest Jewish traditions (Deut. xxvi, 5) says, "A Syrian ready to perish was my father." Throughout Bible history we find these movements of tribes always on the march, these constant invasions of nomads against whom the Hebrew Kings during the ninth and eighth centuries B.C. had always to contend. The Aramaeans penetrated so widely and deeply throughout Palestine, Syria and Mesopotamia that their language had become established throughout the region between Sinai and Taurus and even as far as the Persian Gulf. Jesus unquestionably spoke Aramaic; the Gospel often gives us the actual words of that language as they came from his mouth—such as *Abba* (Father), *Ephphatha* (be opened), *Lama Sabacthani* (Why hast thou forsaken me), *Talitha cumi* (maiden, awake). Word play such as the famous, "Thou art Peter and on this rock . . ." is typical of the Aramaic language and we can often catch echoes of it, as in the precept, "Let the dead bury their dead" (Matt. viii, 22), where Jesus was probably making use of the resemblance between *matha* (the people of the village) and *metha* (the dead). The characteristic rhythms, cadences and alliterations of his speech betray its Aramaic origin.

It is certain, however, that Aramaic was not the only language he knew. St. Luke tells us (iv, 16) how, when he came to Nazareth, "where he was brought up, as his custom was, he went into the synagogue on the Sabbath day and stood up to read." He must therefore have read Hebrew, which, although it had been displaced by Aramaic as the vernacular tongue in Palestine since the fourth century B.C., had survived as the liturgical language, just as Latin survived for the same function after the Romance languages had triumphed for popular use. Every young Jew who studied in the synagogue knew the rudiments of Hebrew since a knowledge of the sacred language was the basis of Jewish culture.

There was, however, a third language in widespread use throughout the country—Greek. Following the march of Alexander and the institution of the Hellenistic kingdoms, the Greek tongue, though hardly by that time the language of Plato, had established itself throughout the Orient and the Mediterranean world as the international language of commerce, as English is today, and as Babylonian was some two thousand years before the Roman era. Though the common people spoke Aramaic, Greek was current throughout the Near East for commercial transactions, politics, diplomacy and cultural matters. All the Roman officials in the oriental countries spoke Greek.

Did Jesus speak it? There is nothing in the Gospel record, no trace of Hellenic style, to suggest that he did. Yet the dialogue between Jesus and Pilate, so forceful and direct, does not give the impression that it was conducted by means of an interpreter. It sounds like a direct exchange between two men who understood each other without the slightest difficulty. But this is only one instance; it is not enough to build upon.

We cannot say that Jesus was, in the usually accepted sense, a "cultivated man." But many of the most esteemed doctors of the Jews were in fact humble people, often working with their hands, though masters of that which the Jews considered the fount of all knowledge, the Law. They were very often self-taught men. Nothing that we read about the boyhood of Jesus suggests that his studies were prolonged. We notice that he makes frequent allusions to Old Testament history, to ancient prophecies and to those ideas which were familiar to the religious mind of the time. He is sufficiently skilled in the dialectic of the Pharisees to counter their attacks, but he never sets himself up as a scribe or a doctor of the Law; when he confounds them it is as a rule by the appeal to common sense and to his "new law" which was in many cases simply a reversion to natural law. The most striking quality of his mind is a tireless curiosity; to complete understanding he brings a natural wisdom which owes nothing to formal study. His utterances are unique and unmistakable. It is in them that we draw nearest to what we can hardly venture to call the secret of his genius, because the word relates to purely mortal things, but to that divine illumination of the human spirit by the Holy Spirit.

Temperament and Character

This illumination shows forth most plainly when we consider the character of Jesus. Considered solely in the natural order, he appeared like other men, yet those "rationalist" critics who have been at pains to consider him simply as a man find that something in his essence eludes them, something which is the decisive element of his being.

There have been those who got out of this difficulty by questioning his mental sanity. Most notorious of these was Binet Sanglé whose *La Folie de Jésus,* Paris, 1908, is as pretentious as it is superficial. There have been similar books by Lousten, W. Hirsch and Rasmussen. The psychiatric critics have been considered, and refuted, in A. Schweitzer's *Die Psychiatrische Beurteilung Jesu* (Tubingen, 1913). The psychoanalysts have made their contribution to the subject also. And over a hundred years ago the German rationalist historian, D. F. Strauss, wrote that he considered Jesus "very close to madness." The formidable array of signs, symptoms and irrefutable proofs which our psychiatrists have catalogued since then is too long to repeat here. To call himself the Son of God and the future judge of mankind is obviously a sign of megalomania. To hold himself up as an example, to begin all his teachings with, "I say," is to display a clinical excess of egoism. Symptoms such as the sign from God at his baptism and the account of the transfiguration reveal the hallucinatory temperament. The perpetual journeys backward and forward across a land as small as Palestine indicate a wandering mania. The psychoanalysts have interpreted many of the Gospel stories, much of the teaching, even those matters on which the Gospels are silent, as expressive of the libido. St. Joseph is never mentioned when Jesus has grown to manhood, therefore Jesus had an Oedipus complex. This is further proved by his harsh speeches to his mother at the Cana wedding feast. Binet Sanglé wrote that "the timidity of Jesus where women were involved" indicated that he was not wholly male, and anybody can guess what the Freudian school makes of the verse (Matt. xix, 12) "and there be eunuchs which have made themselves eunuchs for the Kingdom of Heaven's sake." The doctors also have made their diagnoses: hemophilia, from the reference in St. Luke to "bloody sweat" in his account of the Agony in the Garden; sitophobia, from the fast of forty days and nights; pulmonary tuberculosis, resulting in general weakness and instability, as evidenced by the flow of blood and water when the soldier's lance pierced his side. There is a great deal more of this fantastic stuff, more ridiculous than shocking.

"A mad man is never successful. There is no recorded instance of a lunatic seriously affecting the course of events." The words are Renan's and we should be grateful for their sound common sense. Lombroso's theories about the relation between genius and madness, so much favored by some of the late nineteenth century popularizers of history, science and religion, are pretty generally discredited today but they still have a certain attraction for some of our less weighty minds. If we endeavor to draw a hard and fast line between sanity and madness we are in danger of setting the norm so low that exceptional quality at once becomes suspect and only a John Smith or John Doe can be the archetypes of *homo sapiens.* If Michelangelo, Beethoven, Alexander and Napoleon are all to be classed as "abnormal," this does not mean that they should be ranked below the generality of workaday people. If the average is the normal, the insane is subnormal and the genius certainly super-normal. No one can pretend that Jesus as a man was on the commonplace level; he was immeasurably above it—above and not below.

Anyone who is willing to examine without prejudice the figure of Christ in the Gospels will find not a disassociated or chaotic personality but one which is extremely solid and coherent, built up on unshakeable foundations. There is no self-dramatization in his personality; never once does he play to the gallery. A blasphemous tract current in some circles during the Middle Ages, and attributed to the authorship, or at least the sponsorship, of the Hohenstaufen Emperor Frederick II, grouped, under the title of *Three Impostors,* Moses, Jesus and Mohammed. Nothing could be further from the personality of Jesus than the suspicion of imposture; even that self-deception which we all commit in trying to put forward the best aspect of ourselves was utterly foreign to him. The famous parable of the mote and the beam (Luke vi, 42) is not intended merely as a lesson in humility but as a warning against the danger of trying to make an impression, of failing to see ourselves exactly as we are. This is not only the teaching of Christ; it is the example which he has left us. "The truth shall make you free," he said (John viii, 32); and he never failed to act on this himself.

The personality of Jesus is not only manifestly sincere, it is unshakeable. You cannot doubt that here is a master of the event. He is never deflected from what he wishes to do either by the applause of crowds or by checks and opposition. If he adapts himself to circumstances and submits to affronts without protest, it is biding his own good time. He never capitulates and never hesitates or weakens before the machinations of his enemies. In any ordinary man, this unerring recognition of the time to stand and the time to yield would be considered notable. Not even that mysterious inner certainty of his divine mission could tempt him to an excessive display of his powers; he declined to perform miracles at the devil's behest.

It should be noted that this sureness of himself was not a quality acquired by the hard experience of life, as it is with the majority of people. It is present in Jesus from the very outset, a mastery in which he serves no apprenticeship, and suffers no crises of immaturity. Such human frailty as he displays, like the agony in the Garden, do not affect this spiritual rectitude and never affect his decisions.

Only those who have attained what Charles Morgan so well calls "interior unity," that submission of the will to an accepted pattern of life clearly envisaged and unrelentingly pursued, carry with them that spontaneous authority which has nothing whatever to do with the possession of power and does not derive from any social classification, but is demonstrated in the smallest action or circumstance, a gesture, a word, a look, that famous "look around him" so often mentioned in the Gospels. Jesus, as a man, unquestionably possessed that authority. If we are tempted in some passages of the Gospel to read something supernatural in this quality—for instance in the calling of the Apostles, in the encounter with Nathaniel, in the scene where the soldiers come to arrest Jesus and fall back when he pronounces his name—there are plenty of episodes throughout where the purely human authority of Jesus stands out, the unmistakable accents of a man who has only to speak to be obeyed. In such episodes as the expulsion of the money changers from the Temple, the scene where Jesus, suspecting a plot to make him King of the Jews, tells his disciples to get into the boat and sends the crowds away (Mark vi, 45; Matt. xiv, 22), the note of authority rings out clearly, as it does throughout his teaching. "Behold, I say unto you"; from anyone else the formula would sound arrogant. In the words of Jesus it sounds simply true.

The perfection of the human character of Jesus lies in the union and the balance of these three qualities, sincerity, firmness and authority. Nothing is farther from the truth than the representation of Jesus as a plaster image, unchanging in his attitude, remote from the passions of mankind. There are many scriptural figures—Moses in the Old Testament, John the Baptist in the New—who appear to be wholly of one piece. But Christ can show tenderness—"Suffer the little children to come unto me"—and even malice, as when in the famous "Render to Caesar the things that are Caesar's" he tossed back the ball to the adversaries trying to trap him with a leading question. Even a non-believing historian like Guignebert is struck by "his quickness of wit which could never be confounded." He could be angry, too, a holy and righteous anger which burst forth when the zeal for God which devoured him was baulked by the follies and the willful incomprehension of men. Grandmaison says, "There were times when the virile force within him rose like a river about to burst its banks." It is then that he is seen to belong to that vehement race which gave birth to the prophets and which we can see any day arguing, gesticulating, being carried away to violent excess, in causes often the very reverse of spiritual. When Jesus attacks the money changers in the Temple, when he turns his savage eloquence against the scribes and Pharisees, when he taunts Herod's spies, "Go ye and tell that fox . . ." (Luke xiii, 32), this is a man with blood in his veins, not a pallid conventional seminarian. Like the characters of the great romantic novelists he seems to have contradictory qualities, to admit of "a variety of interpretations." Or rather, he would seem so, if the synthesis of these qualities were not perfected, if the emotions which moved him had ever impaired the purity of the whole. There is no trace of a lie in him or by him; the Redeemer who was to give his life for mankind had the right to be moved to indignation at our wickedness. There is nothing paradoxical, said G. K. Chesterton, in loving and hating humanity at the same time.

Nowhere is the perfect balance of his character more apparent than in his sense of reality. It is one of the traits which does most to humanize him for us and it is continually in evidence. There are visionaries for whom the real world hardly seems to exist; they live on that borderland where the dream and the experience merge, where madness lies in wait to open the door to their soaring ambitions. This is the secret temptation of many who would be great poets—the temptation which Rimbaud and Hölderlin both experienced and from which even the higher mystics are not always immune. But there is no trace of it in the words and the thought of Jesus; his feet are firmly on the ground and the visible world is real.

The Gospel recreates the little world of Palestine with striking veracity; here is the earth, the changing seasons, the wind that blows and the rain so much hoped for; here is the ripening wheat and all the familiar plants of the countryside; the familiar creatures too, the donkey and the scorpion and, above all, the human beings evoked in their characteristic actions. The sower who went forth to sow, the woman who goes down to the well, her pitcher on her head, the fisherman raising his nets. Nothing has ever muffled the directness of the language; in spite of successive translations, it always sounds sharp and clear. In Aramaic doubtless it was even more vital, for a comparison of the texts sometimes reveals a weakening of images. When speaking of the "fowls of the air," according to St. Matthew (vi, 26), who "sow not, neither do they reap yet your heavenly Father feedeth them," Jesus, according to St. Luke, particularized "the ravens" (xii, 24). The "husks which the swine did eat," with which the Prodigal Son sought to ward off hunger, were in fact St. John's bread—the seed pod of the carob tree. Jesus preached to people who lived close to the soil and he used plain peasant language. But this vigorous realism and plain speaking is one more proof of a sane and well-balanced personality, nor can we doubt that Jesus rejoiced in the world which his words so vividly invoke: "Raise the stone and you will find me; cleave the wood and I am there." This saying, which the Apocryphal Ebionite gospel attributes to Jesus, is worthy of the canon, it expresses so well that sense of reality which is love.

We have said enough to show that Renan's picture of the "sweet Galilean dreamer" is false to the point of absurdity. Can we even venture to say that Jesus had the "mystical temperament"? If we do, we must first be careful to strip from the term all that dubious accumulation of confused and equivocal traits which have become involved with it,[2] remembering that the highest mystics have been men and women who were perfectly sane, endowed often with superior common sense and powers of action and not distracted creatures lost in ecstasies. In the hierarchy of true spiritual values, the ecstasy is an inferior phenomenon which serves chiefly to denote the subject's weakness; beyond all this lies that "dark night" where the approach of God may be felt. Certainly Jesus saw visions, the Temptation, the Transfiguration and others, and there is that passage in St. Luke where he says (x, 18), "I beheld Satan as lightning fall from heaven." But he never loses his complete lucidity, he is never seized by a state of exaltation, he is never, in the classic description of mystical ecstasies, "liberated from himself and possessed by the divine."

In truth, he could not be, because in him divinity was ever

---

[2] Jesus was not, properly speaking, an ascetic in the sense that John the Baptist was. John made asceticism a fundamental tenet of his doctrine; Jesus did not. He and his disciples lived very frugally but they did not go out of their way to suffer privation for its own sake nor did they, like the Pharisees, practice extended fasts and mortifications. Most of the great mystics have considered asceticism as an elementary practice which may be disregarded as the spirit progresses to higher stages.

and always present. St. Paul described the supreme mystic communion perfectly when he said: "It is not I who live but Christ in me." But this does not make sense applied to Jesus because he *is* Christ and *is* God. Renan, apostate though he was, understood the truth of this. "God does not speak (to Jesus) as to one outside himself. God is in him, he feels himself to be with God and what he says of his Father comes from the heart. He lived in the breast of God by a continual communication." The greatest saints have trembled in awe at the very thought of God; Jesus did not, for he was equal with the Father. We cannot say of him who is the Alpha and Omega of all mystical endeavor that he is himself a mystic. Once more as in all our attempts to draw a portrait of Jesus we catch a glimpse of the mystery of the Godhead behind the human face.

The Heart of God

No one could be further removed than Jesus from those theologians who, entrenched in the certitude of their rightness, have launched their thunderbolts from on high and have turned the most moving of all teaching into a rigid system of ferocious precepts, an implacable barrier. The Catholic Church in the seventeenth century, seeking to counter the Jansenist heresy, laid emphasis above all things upon the love of Jesus for mankind. Many Protestant thinkers have also found inspiration, in this sense, from the love of Jesus.[3] The medieval contemplatives laid great stress on the loving-kindness of Christ. St. Bonaventure, the Tuscan Franciscan who taught at the University of Paris in the thirteenth century, spoke of "that wounded heart in which we can take shelter from the world," and about the same time the mystic nun of Brabant, Saint Gertrude, had her vision of "the old age of the world in its withering coldness when humanity can only be warmed by the

---

[3] A Dominican writer, Fr. Braun, has justly said: "We are indebted to liberal Protestant thought for its discovery in the Christ of the Gospels of a sum of human perfections and balanced virtues. Through examination of the personality of Jesus they came to love him, even if, in their emphasis on the man, they neglected the God."

mystery of the infinite love of Jesus." The cult of the Sacred Heart dates from 1670, when St. Jean Eudes, that robust and indefatigable Norman missionary, composed an office and a Mass upon this theme. Five years later, St. Margaret Mary Alacoque had her visions at Paray-le-Monial and the shrine which the Church has consecrated there was affirmed with great solemnity by Pius IX and later Pius XI. Although it must be admitted that the aesthetic development of the idea of the Sacred Heart has been of dubious benefit to our churches, since many of the representations are tasteless and unworthy, the instinct behind the devotion is profoundly true to the most essential trait of the personality of Christ.

The Gospel is full of passages which reveal that Jesus could show the most tender affection to people and that he possessed to the full that magnetism which makes us, without knowing why, long to know a certain person and be loved by him. St. John, "the disciple who leant on Jesus's breast," was obviously beloved by him, as was also that family at Bethany for whom he wrought the most startling of his miracles, the raising of Lazarus from the dead. (John xi, 5.) There are few more vivid and realistic scenes in the Gospel than that in which the rich young man, half-inclined to follow Jesus, comes to him and says, "Good Master, what shall I do to inherit eternal life?" "Thou knowest the commandments," said Jesus. "Do not commit adultery, Do not kill, Do not steal, Do not bear false witness, Defraud not, Honor thy father and thy mother." "Master, all these have I observed from my youth." And then this: "*Jesus beholding him, loved him.*" How wonderfully that scene reveals Jesus the man and how well, too, we understand the young man's feelings when Jesus says: "One thing thou lackest; go thy way, sell whatsoever thou hast and give to the poor. . . ." And the result: "And the young man went away grieved, for he had great possessions." (Mark x, 17-22; Matt. xix, 16-22; Luke xviii, 18-23.)

But the love of Christ, whose inexhaustibility is lauded in the hymn by St. Bernard, is something above and beyond the tenderness and affection which Jesus as man displayed toward his privileged intimates. These manifestations of his love move us so profoundly because they bring him close to us. More than that; Jesus shows an unending goodness to all who approach him, to all who beseech him. The firmness and authority which distinguish him is complemented by a welcoming tenderness which is all-embracing and complete. He belongs to, he is indeed the exemplar of, that order of beings which has pity for all the afflicted, mercy for all sinners, love for all the anxious and distressed. The Little Sister of the Poor, busy all day and every day in the relief of human distress, is walking in his footsteps. Whoever calls upon him will surely be heard. How often do we see him, in the Gospels, tired, seeking solitude and rest, called out once more by some importunate, always responding, never showing that his willingness is exhausted, available at all times, to all.

He has his preferences, the poor and the dispossessed most quickly touch his heart. "Blessed are the poor" is a cry which echoes throughout the Gospel, but it does not justify those who would present him as a tribune of the people, preaching a revolt of the have-nots against the haves. His attitude to wealth is made perfectly explicit at the end of the story just related, when the rich young man goes away. "Children, how hard it is for them that trust in riches to enter into the Kingdom of God. It is easier for a camel to go through the eye of a needle. . . ."

Theologians have gone to a great deal of trouble to soften the harshness of this saying; even if it is a typical oriental exaggeration, even if it can be found in the Koran or the Hindu scriptures, the sense is unaltered. To Jesus, the only important thing was that a man should enter into the Kingdom of God and the rich man, impeded by the cares of his material possessions, does not find it easy to enter by "the strait gate." It was not hatred but pity which prompted this reflection, as is evident when he replied to the disciples' question how such a man could be saved: "To God all things are possible."

Jesus did not condemn possessions as such, he condemned our worldly pride in them. Those who incurred his wrath were the self-satisfied, the greedy and those who concealed hypocrisy and meanness behind a screen of respectability. He, who was himself entirely free from the least stain of sin, had infinite mercy for sinners; if they repented in the fullness of their hearts, his own heart went out to them. The scandalized growl of the Pharisees: "This man receiveth sinners and eateth with them" (Luke xv, 2), was perfectly substantiated. It could be said that Jesus showed a marked partiality for sinners. It was natural enough. A mother is more delighted with the recovery of a sick child than with the continued good health of the rest of the family. The shepherd rejoices more at the recovery of the lost sheep than over the ninety-nine others safe in the fold; the woman who finds the coin she thought she had lost, the father who welcomes back the prodigal son, all these familiar parables remind us that Christ came to save "that which was lost." If there is any sense or meaning at all in our human failings, it is that in shattering our pride they incline us to humility and open our hearts to love.

Christ went farther than that. The Sermon on the Mount, in which, at the outset of his mission, he outlined his teaching, lays down an even more difficult precept. "Ye have heard that it hath been said, Thou shalt love thy neighbor and hate thine enemy. But I say unto you, Love your enemies, bless them that curse you, do good to them that hate you and pray for them which despitefully use you and persecute you. . . . For if ye love them which love you, what reward have ye?" (Matt. v, 43-46; Luke vi, 27-28.) This love is a complete reversal of our human tendencies, for it is not the love which we bear to our family and friends; it is not even that love which a generous heart feels for the unhappy and the sinful. Nor does its reference to pardoning offences mean that kind of forgiveness which time and forgetfulness bring us. It means a superhuman turning inside out, a humiliation of our nature and of our legitimate pride, the kissing of the hand which strikes us.

The Gospel narrative does not mince the fact that this doctrine did not work out at all easily in practice. When Jesus was traveling through Samaria, he sent, as was usual, messengers to a certain village to make preparations for his reception. But the old hatred of the Samaritans for the Jews was not allayed, and they refused. "And when his disciples James and John saw this they said, Lord, wilt thou that we command fire to come down from heaven and consume them, even as Elias did. But he turned, and rebuked them, and said: Ye know not what manner of spirit ye are of. For the Son of Man is not come to destroy men's lives but to save them." (Luke ix, 51-56.)

It must be reiterated that the charity of Jesus is associated with virtues which human charity does not always possess. We all know the type of benevolence which rests upon fundamental indifference and the forbearance which is based on ignorance. But we have seen that Jesus was capable of violent anger, and this sets a high value upon his tenderness because we realize that he was never taken in, like so many of those charitable persons who are the prey of any professional beggar. His judgment of men was completely lucid as Peter would remember, Peter to whom his Master predicted that in the hour of danger he would lose his nerve and deny the one for whom he had said he would lay down his life. But with this complete lucidity went an extreme tenderness. We have all known excellent and charitable persons in whom familiarity with misery and the vices it engenders has dried up little by little the wellsprings of the heart so that their benevolence becomes impersonal and stereotyped and a poor man is only a "case" to be given a meal or a pair of shoes. But the attitude of Jesus was totally different. Toward all the sinners who approached him, the Samaritan woman whose secrets he penetrated at a glance, the woman taken in adultery, toward whom he extended the exquisite charity of refraining from comment, to the most degraded of creatures he holds out the possibility of repentance and restoration. He offers them self-respect as well as compassion.

It will be noted that the episodes we have just mentioned concern women, to whom Jesus always displayed a special kindness which is worthy of comment. Jewish tradition had a certain tacit reprobation and contempt for women. Throughout the Mosaic Law we can detect this barely dissimulated distaste for the unclean creature and fierce scorn for those who led the male into temptation. The religion of the Jews was designed for men; upon them alone was laid the obligation of celebrating the Passover. Under the pretext that the Law required a man to see that his son was educated in its precepts, his daughter received no instruction at all. A similar contempt for women existed among the Romans. Not all of them would have associated themselves with the views of that old misogynist Seneca or the cynical Petronius. Yet the exclusion from all participation in official life confined the wife and mother in her private apartments and allowed harlots and divorcees almost complete social freedom. It has taken two thousand years of Christianity to raise women to the place which they hold in our society.

Here again, as in so many other matters, Jesus completely reversed established custom. Saint Luke tells us that he went through every city and village "and certain women which had been healed of evil spirits and infirmities" went with him. "Mary called Magdalene, out of whom went seven devils, and Joanna, the wife of Chusa, Herod's steward and Susanna and many others. . . ." (Luke viii, 1-3.) A prostitute, the wife of a Court official—we get the impression of a very mixed retinue of women. And women of great character and quality have since been associated with many of the saints; Clare with Francis of Assisi, Jeanne de Chantal following Francis de Sales, Louise de Marillac by the side of Vincent de Paul.

The heart of a woman is open to love, she lives on it as the manna of her soul, and throughout the centuries countless women have responded to the mysterious appeal which Jesus made to the Magdalene and the woman of Samaria, finding in the heart of the cloister that burning love and human joy with which all women approach the vital need of their existence, the gift of themselves. There was and is nothing equivocal in these raptures. The tears and the unguents of the penitents excited Jesus to nothing but compassion. A man's interest in a woman can easily become suspect; every priest knows this and is continually on his guard. "Blessed are the pure in heart." The heart of Jesus was a crystal without flaw.

The human personality of Christ, so majestic, so pure, so radiant with its governing power of love, is yet not the sum of what we can extract from the Gospel narrative. Jesus as a man was undoubtedly as he is drawn here, a man who wished to be known and loved. The psychological portrait is so powerful that it can be said to provide one of the most striking proofs of the veracity of the Gospel, for such ordinary men as were Matthew, Mark, Luke and John could not have invented such a portrait without betraying their own deficiences. In the light of Gide's famous saying: "The best intentions make the worst literature," we should consider the work of these poor unlettered men who, inspired by the spirit, have drawn a portrait of perfect virtue without insipidity and perfect charity without sentimentality. And that other thing which comes through in the portrait is that there was something transcending our human nature. The charity of Jesus reached out further, for it is not natural to love your enemies, to turn the other cheek to the hand that strikes you, to feel pity for all suffering, to be able to heal all ills. The Office of the Sacred Heart (John xix, 31-37) recalls to us the lance-thrust with which the soldier pierced the human body of Jesus. "Greater love hath no man than this . . ." (John xv, 13.) The human personality of Jesus is bound up with the twin mysteries of the Incarnation and the Redemption, and this is what he himself tried to explain to his Apostles the night before the blow was to fall.

Messianic Awareness

We are bound to ask whether Jesus was aware of the divinity within him, or, more precisely, whether he ever said that he was God. The great Hebrew prophets knew themselves to be prophets even against the evidence of the flesh. Jeremiah complained that the Lord dealt hardly with him, that his own will must bow to the supreme will, that he must submit to jeers and hard usage. Every religious leader has sought to define his status in regard to the God he preached. Mohammed called himself the messenger and the witness of Allah. Did Jesus, the founder of the religion which declares him God incarnate, so define himself?

Non-Catholic critics have inclined to the view that the historic Jesus did not proclaim himself to be either Messiah or Son of God. This view is based upon such texts as Acts ii, 36: "God hath made that same Jesus, whom ye have crucified, both Lord and Christ," and concludes from them that Jesus had no consciousness of being the Messiah, still less of being God. Some critics hold that the Resurrection revealed to the disciples that their Master was divine; others regard the deification as progressively achieved by the primitive Christian community which regarded him first as the Messiah and later as the Risen Son of God. According to this view Jesus was a prophet who failed in his mission, but who had endeared himself greatly to a handful of faithful followers. "It was their love and their confidence which brought him back to life and thus assured his immortality," says Guignebert. According to this view Jesus was one of those initiators who, in Nietzsche's phrase, only put a match to the fire. He was the small spark which the Apostles, particularly Paul, were to fan into the flames of Christian ardor.

The argument is not good enough. When a critic proceeds by casting doubt upon the veracity of every text which is embarrassing to his theory, the reader begins to cast doubt upon the theory. If Jesus is taken whole and entire as he appears in the Gospel narrative, these partial interpretations cannot be accepted by any unbiased reader. Not only is the charity of Jesus incomparably greater than that achieved by any creature of flesh and blood, but also his dignity, his courage and his holiness, while completely real, are immeasurably greater than that of any man. The prophet Mohammed was allowed by Allah to suspend, in his own interest, the laws which he had himself laid down regarding marriage and to espouse as many as he wished. And, as we know, Mohammed did not refuse the privilege. But the life of Jesus bears the same witness as his teaching; the Gospel is as much the story of what he did as the account of what he said. There was no cleavage, no lapse between what he enjoined and how he lived. Not even the greatest saints have achieved this total identity.

There is one very revealing detail in the general attitude of Jesus. When speaking of God to his disciples he never identified his approach with theirs. His language makes it perfectly clear that he was not a man just like them, that he had a special prerogative. He spoke to them of "Your Father, which is in heaven." He taught them to pray to "Our Father." But when he spoke of himself and God he always said "My Father." This distinction is certainly deliberate and it is maintained throughout the Gospel.

As to whether he spoke of himself as the Messiah, the overall evidence of the Gospel is that he did. He must have done so, for everybody around him proclaimed it. The "messianic consciousness" is clearly apparent from the very beginning of his mission and toward the end when the threads of the drama were being drawn together more tightly, the looming danger did not induce him to dissimulate or retract. Yet, and this is the complicating factor, the messianic revelation appears to remain a mystery, as though Jesus at one and the same time shone forth in glory as coming from God and sought to keep silent about it. The traditional explanation of the theologians seems the most reasonable. Jesus wished to reveal himself and his message progressively; even his closest friends did not understand it until the Resurrection opened their eyes. The explanation has majesty as well as logic. Jesus, as man, bearer of this prodigious secret, had the strength to keep silent, to reveal himself only a little at a time in case his faithful followers mistook the nature of the mystery, knowing all the while the price that must be paid before the final revelation. Among the evidence supporting this view may be instanced the fact that the first to detect the secret of Jesus were the devils whom he cast out (Mark i, 24; iii, 11).

But it still remains to be explained why, even from the beginning of his mission, Jesus sometimes deliberately violated this rule of silence and progressive disclosure of his purpose. Why did he frankly reveal himself to the Samaritan woman? Was it because she was a stranger in a foreign country, not a Jewess? But again, in the Synagogue at Nazareth, he stated clearly who he was. Perhaps he was absolutely sure that no one would understand him, as the ensuing anger of his compatriots proved. Let us admit that, in his human capacity, Jesus could adapt himself to circumstances. It is probably also a fact that the Evangelists were indifferent to chronology and may not always have reported these incidents in their exact place in the life of Christ. One thing is absolutely certain, when the supreme moment came when everything would turn upon his answer, Jesus did not hesitate. "Art thou the Christ, the son of the Blessed?" said the High Priest interrogating him. "I am: and ye shall see the Son of Man sitting on the right hand of power and coming in the clouds of heaven." (Mark xiv, 61.)

The expression, the Son of Man, which Jesus used at this decisive moment, is itself a part of the mystery of the Messianic revelation. It is a strictly Semitic expression, traditionally used both in Hebrew and in Aramaic. In Hebrew *ben-adam,* in Aramaic, *ben-nascha,* signifies nothing more than a man, the son of a man, a man born of men. Did Jesus, who used this term continually of himself, wish to emphasize the human side of his nature, to make his followers feel that he was a man as they were? It is practically certain that he did. But, at the same time, the term had another and weightier significance; it was charged with an esoteric sense because of its use by the prophets of Israel. In Ezekiel it is used no less than ninety-four times and it appears to denote the Prophet as representative of humanity, the human part of him, contrasted with the majesty of God which is using this feeble creature as a mouthpiece. In Daniel (vii, 13-14), the sense is more explicit: "I saw in the night visions and, behold, one like the Son of Man came with the clouds of heaven and came to the Ancient of Days. . . . And there was given him dominion, and glory, and a kingdom, that all people, nations and languages should serve him: his dominion is an everlasting dominion, which shall not pass away." Other Jewish writings, such as the *Book of the Second Vision of Enoch,* speak of the Son of Man as "possessing justice and revealing the secrets of darkness." The image was to survive through the great disaster which overtook Israel in the year 70 A.D., the Apocalyptic Fourth Book of Esdras makes use of it. At the time of Christ, however, it is probable that the Messianic application of the term would be known to only that minority of his audience versed in the Apocalyptic writings. The rest would take it in its usual colloquial sense. This is probably the real reason why Jesus constantly made use of this enigmatic term; only those who had "ears to hear" would understand it. It disappears from the Bible after the Gospels; it is only used once in the Acts of the Apostles (vii, 56) and twice in Revelation (i, 13; xiv, 14). St. Paul never makes use of it at all; it was too charged with Jewish sentiment and would have no meaning for the Greeks and the Romans.

The Son of Man, is, in fact, another way of saying "Messiah," since it covers the double meaning—the glory and the suffering. Christ used it, and was increasingly to use it, in its most authentic interpretation; not that of the Glorious King, the Avenger and the Conqueror to whom the Pharisees addressed their famous prayer *Alennu,* but the suffering Messiah, the sacrificial victim who was to redeem the sins of the world.

The Gospel also refers to Jesus, frequently, as the Son of God. The expression occurs twenty-six times in the synoptic Gospels, nine times in St. John. The Gospel of St. Mark opens with these words: "The beginning of the Gospel of Jesus Christ, the Son of God." What did the term mean? The Jews would interpret it in the most general sense; as the Chosen People they were all Sons of God. Moses had said so (Deut. xiv, 1); so had the prophets. "The Lord hath said unto me, thou art my Son; this day have I begotten thee. Ask of me and I shall give thee the heathen for thine inheritance" (Psalm 2, 7-8). Other texts, such as Psalm 89, use the expression in the same sense.

Son of God is thus, in one sense, another synonym for Messiah, although it is only rarely employed in this sense in the Old Testament and it was not current in Jewish usage at the time of Christ. Another expression, the Son of David, is also used in the Gospel, particularly in St. Matthew (xii, 23; xv, 22). This is a reference to the belief, firmly held by all Jews, that the Messiah would be born of the family of David, and its use in the Gospel signifies no more than that. There is, however, a much greater significance to be attached to the words Son of God.

It was not only because the term had been applied to the Messiah that Jesus bore it. A verse from the Apocryphal Epistle of St. Barnabas says: "This day Jesus is no more the Son of Man but the Son of God." The Church has rejected this text as heretical; it was not after his death that Jesus became more than the Son of Man: he was this throughout his life time. This is clear to anyone who reads the epistles of St. Paul, which were written for the direct instruction of the early Church. Jesus knew that he was the Son of God "who gave himself for our sins, that he might deliver us from this present evil world, according to the will of God" (Galatians i, 4). The whole Pauline doctrine rests upon this assertion: God sent "his own Son in the likeness of sinful flesh" (Romans viii, 3). It should be remembered that Paul, the Apostle to the Gentiles, was a converted Pharisee and that when he deliberately stressed, with all his incomparable power of words, the term Son of God in its precise literal sense, he would realize that, to the Pharisees, this was blasphemy.

Before he saw the light on the road to Damascus, Saul the Pharisee had persecuted the Christians because, in using this term, they blasphemed. Jesus, when he accepted the term at his trial before the Sanhedrin, knew that he was precipitating his death. During the trial of Joan of Arc, when, in reply to a question, she affirmed the divine origin of her voices, the clerk wrote these illuminating words opposite her answer: *Responsio mortifera.* Jesus's reply to the High Priest's question: "Art thou the Son of the Blessed?" was: "I am." And these words also were to write his death sentence. The accusation which the

Jews made against him to Pilate, that he sought to make himself king, was a political pretext. The core of their hatred for him was that he usurped the prerogatives of the One God. The pitiless combination of force and fraud which they turned against him derived from this, that the blasphemer was outside the pale of humanity. Because they felt this, they could gibe at him during his agony: "If thou be the Son of God, come down from the Cross" (Matt. xxvii, 40). The Crucifixion alone proves that Jesus declared himself to be the Son of God, even without the testimony of his words and deeds.

We may be assured, therefore, that the realization of divinity was not a secret so profoundly hidden in his being that the man Jesus was not conscious of it. He did not merely accept that he was fulfilling the final term of the Messianic expectancy; he transformed the Messianic hope by his own assertion of his filiation to God. To use the theological term, he knew himself to be consubstantial to God. When the Law of God was in question, he declared himself the "Master." He did not hesitate to modify its proscriptions, for he knew that he had come to "fulfill" the Law, that while others held to the letter, it was he who commanded the spirit. This serene assumption runs through the whole of his teaching and the exercise of his miraculous power. It is summed up unequivocally in the statement: "I and my Father are one" (John x, 30).

The disciples of Jesus knew, they had learnt it from their Master, the eternal truth which all Christians must forever remember: that the witness of Christ has no power if the individual soul stifles the inmost voice which would persuade and transform it. God can do nothing for the man who refuses him. When Peter wished to proclaim Jesus as "Christ, the son of the living God," he replied, "Blessed art thou, Simon, for flesh and blood hath not revealed it to thee, but my Father which is in heaven." (Matt. xvi, 16-17.) The teaching of Christ can be "the spirit and the life" and "the way leading to the Father" only to those who wish to hear it, and in that sense every man can recreate in himself the divinity of Jesus.

But that divinity existed indisputably and consciously in

the living man Jesus; the famous opening of St. John's Gospel: "In the beginning was the Word. . . . And the Word was made flesh and dwelt among us"—is not, as has been said, the apotheosis of the theological delirium. It is the declaration of something which Jesus knew himself, said himself and himself revealed to his disciples. "No man hath seen God at any time; the only begotten Son, which is in the bosom of the Father, he hath declared him." (John i, 18.)

The Man and the God

One last problem may be touched upon; it cannot by its nature be resolved. It is the most difficult of all questions concerning the nature of Jesus, the relation between the human and the divine elements, between that part of his nature which was made like ours and that part which was so radically different. This matter is not in the domain of either history or psychology. The belief in the simultaneous presence, in one being, of man and God is something which the Church rightly calls a mystery, something not susceptible of discovery by the human intelligence. This is part of what St. Paul called the "folly" of the Cross: "But we preach Christ crucified, to the Jews a stumbling block, to the Greeks foolishness." (I Corinthians i.)

"The Church," wrote Pascal, "has been to as great pains to show that Jesus Christ was man, against those who denied it, as to show that he was God." It is startling to recall that more than three quarters of the heresies which, from the second century to the present day, have divided Christians, have been connected with this matter of the double nature of Christ. It would be impossible to enumerate them all; every conceivable hypothesis which the human brain could devise has been formulated and every imaginable "explanation" of the inexplicable has been advanced. A veritable kaleidoscope of ideas, a theological phantasmagoria in which oriental subtlety has drawn upon syncretic store-houses and the "mystery" religions, has multiplied confusion and elucidated nothing. One curious fact emerges; far more sects have repudiated the theory that

God could become man than have rejected the idea of a man becoming God. It would seem that the old temptation, the words of the serpent to Adam: "Ye shall be as gods," has an abiding echo in the human heart. Pascal remarked that heresy "can never consider the relation of two opposing truths, believing that the affirmation of one involves the exclusion of the other." Hence it will adopt one, and reject the other, but the orthodox teaching of the Church has always sought a synthesis.

Pascal goes on to say, regarding this problem of the two natures present in Jesus, "the Arians could not accept the union of two things which they thought incompatible. In saying that he was man they were Catholic. In denying that he was God, they were heretics. But in pretending that we deny his humanity, they were ignorant." This was the standpoint of those to whom, in the early days of the Church, the formula, "true God and true man," was not acceptable. Among the more prominent of these was a certain Bishop of Antioch, Paul of Samosata, who was under the protection of Zenobia, queen of Palmyra. He declared Jesus to be subordinate to God, and was deposed in 270. The doctrine formulated by Arius of Alexandria (256-336) called Arianism, caused such dissension in the Church that it was formally condemned by the Council of Nicaea in 325. Nevertheless it was entrenched among the barbarians on the marches of the empire and for a long time it was able to disturb the balance of Christendom. Clovis was able to enlist the support of the clergy of Gaul, and with their assistance to vanquish the other chieftains and unite a Frankish kingdom because as the sole Catholic among the Arian chiefs, he appeared as a champion of the true Faith.

This theological argument, then, had tremendous historical consequences. Other heresies were less significant, such as the Adoptionist heresy, brought to Rome from Byzantium about the year 200 by Theodotus, the Byzantine. According to this Jesus on earth had been a man like all other men but surpassing them in holiness. He received, from the time of his baptism by John, the office of the Messiah but even after the descent of the Holy Ghost he did not become God. Another variant held that Jesus did not become God until after his resurrection from the dead. It can easily be seen how certain episodes in the Gospel can be made the pretext for infinite discussions of this kind along very simple lines of reasoning.

Another type of heresy has refused to regard Jesus as a man at all. Among the Hellenized Jews of Alexandria such as Philo, who combined the daring speculative tendencies of the neo-Platonists with the inherited traditions of the Old Testament, it was held that there was an infinite number of immaterial beings between man and God. When, some fifty years after the death of Jesus, Christianity replaced Judaism in their schools, the doctrine known as Gnosticism developed. The word signifies the knowledge of things hidden. The Gnostics claimed that Jesus had no real body, he was not really incarnate and that what men took for his flesh was a false reality, astral or celestial in essence, an *eon,* something analogous to that spiritual double which the ancient Egyptians called *Ka.* Evidence of this doctrine can be traced in the Apocryphal *Acts of John,* which is supposed to be spoken by the beloved disciple himself, where we read that when John leaned on the breast of Jesus he felt "sometimes a material fleshly body and sometimes an insubstantial one without consistence so that the hand could pass through it and encounter only emptiness," and also that when walking behind Jesus "he looked for traces of his footsteps but found none, as though he walked without touching the ground."

The Docetist heresy which, according to St. Jerome, flourished among the Christians almost "before the blood of Christ was yet dry in Judea," was similar. For the Docetists, according to Origen, "the Lord did not clothe himself in flesh but was an apparition, *phantasma.*" A more extreme sect, the Anarodocists, belittling the sufferings of Christ, held that while Jesus had a real body resembling ours, it had been endowed with a miraculous impassiveness.

The Egyptian monks of the fifth century, who launched the Monophysitist heresy, stated that Jesus assumed the totality of human nature, body and spirit, but that it was united to the divinity so as to form one nature, absorbed and, as it were, drowned in the divinity. This theory and others caused so much trouble in the Byzantine Empire that, at the Council of 449, Theodosius II used troops to allay the disturbances, during which many were killed. This assembly of theologians has come down in history as the Robber Synod.

The Nestorians, disciples of Nestorius, patriarch of Constantinople, held the exactly opposite view, that the two natures in Jesus were entirely separate, which led them to the conclusion that it was not God who died on the Cross but simply a man and nothing more than a man. The Monothelites held that in the human nature of Jesus there was only one will, the will of God, and that the body of Jesus during the actions of his life was a kind of puppet in the hands of the Almighty. As we examine the catalogue of these speculations we find ourselves driven to repeat the words of Bossuet: "Is that, then, all? Yes, that is all, for everything has been debated, the body, the soul, the workings of the mind and all the arguments are exhausted."

The Church, as we know, has stood firm and immovable for centuries among this maelstrom of speculation. The Council of Nicaea declared that Jesus was "the only begotten son of the Father, begotten, not made, consubstantial to the Father." This Creed, called the Nicene, which every priest recites daily at Mass, was formulated actually by two Councils, that of Nicaea in 325 and of Constantinople in 381. The text goes on to affirm, no less certainly, the humanity of Jesus who "became incarnate of the Holy Ghost by the Virgin Mary and was made man." God and man, at one and the same time distinct and united, are present in Christ. He who accepts this Creed is orthodox; he who denies it is outside the Church.

Does the Gospel give us any glimpse at all of the mysterious correspondence between the two natures of Jesus Christ? It makes it absolutely clear, at least, that the Monophysitists were quite wrong in supposing that his humanity was swallowed up by his divinity. The wonderful scene of the Temptation shows him very close to the human predicament, obliged to face up to the Adversary. Because he was God he triumphed, but because he was man he had to accept the test. Those words of his which St. Luke reports (xii, 50): "But I have a baptism to be baptized with, and how am I straitened till it be accomplished," are no less moving. They give us a hint of the two wills within him and the grief of the human spirit to whom his divine nature had revealed his frightful doom. The two natures within him are most tragically displayed in the Agony in the Garden, the night before he died: the man Jesus, accepting the will of God, "being in agony prayed more earnestly and his sweat was as it were great drops of blood falling to the ground." (Luke xxii, 44)

We may imagine the divinity in Jesus as a force of which he, the man, was fully aware, which sustained him and lifted him beyond himself in the great undertakings of his mission; a force to which, when the hour of sacrifice came, he would freely submit, at the cost of the total immolation of himself. We can perhaps isolate certain words in the Gospel as indicating this consciousness of divinity by the man. We remember that it is said that when the woman suffering from a hemorrhage touched the hem of his garment he felt that "virtue had gone out of him." Also in St. Luke we read (x, 21) that "Jesus rejoiced in spirit" and in John (xi, 33-38) that when Christ was about to raise Lazarus from the dead he was "troubled" and "groaned."

Farther than this we cannot go. There is an impassable barrier in every direction when we try to press too far the analysis of the physical and spiritual attributes of Jesus. We are up against a mystery and that is all that can be said. No attempt to envisage Christ can make sense if it is limited to our knowledge, and for all our respect we are guilty of blasphemy if in the words of an ancient liturgy we pretend "to see what is veiled as if it were face to face." We must never forget that, in the last resort, these are not matters of knowledge, but of faith.

CHAPTER SEVEN

THE SEED FALLS UPON STONY GROUND

Toward the Last Days

According to the most probable chronology of his life, Jesus left Galilee in the autumn of the year 29. He was never to return. From now on, the scene of his mission was to be Judea, the harsh country with its ancient loyalties, the bastion of the ancestral faith. No prophet could fulfill his destiny except in Jerusalem.

This, certainly, was the fundamental reason why Jesus left his native province. Ever since David, a thousand years before, had chosen for his city that outstanding site, in the center of the hill country, at the meeting place of the principal roads, Jerusalem had been not merely the political capital but the very heart of Israel. Here David had installed the Ark of the Covenant and around it Solomon had raised his sumptuous Temple, to the glory of God and his own temporal power. What Paris is to France and Rome to every Catholic, Jerusalem was to the humblest Jew of the most widely dispersed community. By the waters of Babylon, in the dark days of exile, the People of the Promise had sung this hymn: "If I forget thee, O Jerusalem, let my right hand forget her cunning." Jesus must have known that his message could not assume its full significance until he gave a new meaning to the old Covenant, there in the hills of Zion.

There may have been lesser contributory causes, such as the growing hostility of the scribes and Pharisees. But this would certainly not be lessened by going to the place where they were practically all-powerful. Was he disappointed because all his efforts in Galilee had not succeeded in changing the hearts of men? This is to suppose him to be incredibly naive and unacquainted with the human soul. In any case, if he had received a check in the north, would he be likely to succeed any better in the south? We recall the urgent, perhaps malicious, injunctions of his relations: "Depart hence and go into Judea, that thy disciples also may see the works which thou doest. For there is no man that doeth anything in secret and he himself seeketh to be known openly. If thou do these things, shew thyself to the world." (John vii, 3-4.) But the promptings of ambition, the impatience of his kindred with what they considered to be hesitation or reluctance, did not influence Jesus at all. His reply reveals the real reason: "My time is not yet come, but your time is always ready." At the beginning of the chapters of St. Luke's Gospel describing Christ's mission in Judea, we read these words: "And it came to pass, when his time was come that he should be received up, he steadfastly set his face to go to Jerusalem." (Luke ix, 51.) "When he should be received up." From now on the coming sacrifice is the dominant note; everything that Jesus has said and is to say anew, everything that he has done and is to do again, becomes invested with the aura of tragedy. As the Judean mission unfolds, far off at first, but daily coming closer and clearer, is a figure that we recognize.

There is a deep symbolic harmony between the most tragic episodes of the life of Christ and the land where they took place, a land so different from fertile, fortunate Galilee. The landscape of Judea, barren, rocky and arid, conveys such a forcible impression of disquiet that it is astonishing to remember that it is for ever associated with the memory of the love of God. The configuration of the land is three roughly parallel ridges, with sharp contours through which mountain torrents cut deep gorges, and bare summits from which the earth has been eroded. A pitiless blue sky parches the meager infertile soil and the violent winter rainstorms tend to wrench up the poor vegetation rather than to foster it. In March it is beautiful; the roads are bordered by clumps of iris and by those huge purple anemones which are probably the "lilies of the field" instanced by Jesus as a model of the heedless beauty of nature. But by May, everything is yellowed and withered; only the asphodel, hardly distinguishable from the pebbles among which it grows, displays its pallid foliage and black and white florets. It is a sad landscape, dominated by two colors, ochre and mauve; the perfection of coloring enchants the eye yet its very splendor has a desperate and inhuman quality. Grouped around the well heads, at long distances, the white villages bearing names renowned in history indicate their presence by the green clumps of their fig trees and their sycamores. The more fertile hills had their western slopes covered with olive groves and above them, encircled by its walls and bristling with its towers, was Jerusalem, rose and gold with the patina of the centuries, the rock and the fortress where the Lord would shelter those who trusted in him.

In the parable of the Sower (Matt. xiii, Mark iv, Luke viii) Jesus had spoken of the seed which fell upon stony ground, where it withered away, because there was no earth to sustain it. The land of Judea is chary of giving, and the seed to be sown here, unlike the seed sown in Galilee, would need not water, but blood. From this time on in the gospel narrative we rely less on St. Matthew and St. Mark, who until now have supplied most of the information, and more on St. Luke and St. John. St. John, who is evidently writing from first hand knowledge, reports this period with admirable clarity and in minute detail. St. Luke is vaguer here than in his account of the Galilean days but he shows great power in evoking the scenes and the people. He seems dominated by the tragedy which is to come, absorbed in expectation of the final revelation.

It is not easy to understand why St. Matthew and St. Mark should not have reported a good many events which make plain the final drama. Nor is it easy to reconcile the accounts of St. John and St. Luke, which are absolutely independent of each other. According to the Johannine chronology, Jesus went to Jerusalem for the Feast of Tabernacles, in October; in December he came back for the ceremony of the Dedication, after which we have an account of his movements almost day by day, beyond Jordan, then to Bethany, to Ephraim and then to those early April days when he went up to Jerusalem for the Passover feast of his destiny. There has been much argument as to whether the events narrated by St. Luke took place between October and December and whether the departures for the city indicated in the third Gospel can be related to the departures mentioned in the fourth. But it is futile to enter too deeply into such discussions; what is incontrovertible is that the overall account of the Judean period has an unmistakable and powerful unity.

Jesus is in the center of the picture, always unmistakably himself, and during these six months we have his most moving sayings, the words and the parables which go most profoundly to our hearts. He seems, perhaps, a little more remote from everyday life than when he was in Galilee. We do not see him performing such homely and endearing miracles as the multiplication of the loaves and the miraculous draught of fishes. The God in him is becoming more and more evident. Not for nothing does he say so often during this period: "I am the light of the world." His charity is, as always, inexhaustible; so also is his power, to which even death is subject. But the seed falls on the stony ground of a disunited, disputatious people, ankylosed by rites and ceremonies. He could win over some souls from among them, but he was adding also to the armory of his enemies. The drama of this period lies in the contrast between the magnificent, the supernatural stature of the figure of Jesus and the undercurrent of mean hatreds, jealousies and foul cowardice which the Gospel narratives reveal at every turn. Finally his enemies will triumph, or will believe that they have triumphed, over one who had never used his powers to save himself, and, at the end, the sacrifice will be accomplished. On the bare hill, outside the city walls, we can already see the shadow of the cross.

The Feast of Tabernacles

The Feast of Tabernacles was among the most solemn of the many feasts of the Jewish calendar. "Exceedingly holy and great," Josephus calls it. The crowds which came to Jerusalem in October to celebrate it, although not comparable with the Passover, were none the less considerable. For the agricultural year was completed, the harvests gathered in, and the civil year also began on October first in accordance with the cycle of vegetation. Five days earlier, the people celebrated the solemn feast of the Day of Atonement, *Yom Kippur,* when the symbolical scapegoat, charged with the sins of Israel, was driven out into the desert. But the week of the Feast of Tabernacles was one of rejoicing; it commemorated the days when the people of Israel, delivered by Moses from Pharaoh's yoke, dwelt in the desert awaiting their future glory, the revelation of their tremendous destiny. In memory of their wanderings in the desert and of the tents in which they had lived, the town of Jerusalem was transformed. In accordance with the instructions laid down in Leviticus (xxiii), every Jew had to leave his house and live in a tent, or in a hut made of branches, for eight days. So the balconies of houses and public buildings, the grounds of the Temple and the slopes of the hills around the city were covered with these fragile edifices made of pine, myrtle, olive and palm branches. It was pleasant enough to rest here, with a watchful eye on the produce of the fields and the vineyards, while as for the pilgrims from remote countries, the days in the open air, coming as they did when the weather was mild, were a pleasant relaxation from the hardships of the journey.

Naturally, from the beginning of the day until the end, that is from nine in the morning when the ritual day opened with the morning sacrifice until half-past three in the afternoon, when it closed with the evening sacrifice, the blood of beasts stained the sacred forecourt and the sickening odor of burning fat, supposed to be pleasing to Jehovah, rose continually from the altars. Those who attended the ceremonies had to bear green branches: "Ye shall take the boughs of goodly trees, branches of palm trees and the boughs of thick trees and willows from the brook and ye shall rejoice before the Lord your God seven days." And so, all along the streets, might be seen pilgrims bearing in their right hand the *loulab,* a sheaf of green branches, and in the other, the *ethrog,* or "fruit of Persia," the citron. There are many representations of this in the Jewish catacombs, and apparently the larger the sheaf and the heavier the citron, the greater the devotion. Some of the Pharisees were almost bowed down by the branches they carried. During the rites, the people waved the branches in the direction of the four points of the compass, to the accompaniment of the ritual chant, *Glory to God, Hallelujah.* It was on the occasion of this feast that the kindred of Jesus, and perhaps some of his disciples, implored him to go to Jerusalem. At first he refused, and sent them on alone, ahead of him. Undoubtedly he wished to avoid any attempt at a triumphal entry which would arouse illusory hopes that his mission was that of the "glorious Messiah." But he did come up to the city during the feast, without fuss or proclamation, and he started to preach.

So, in the middle of the happy, excited crowd, excited by religious enthusiasm, he began his mission in Judea. Like all the pilgrims, he slept in the traditional booth of branches. The hut was situated on the Mount of Olives, a little way outside the city. He went to the nightly ceremonies which took place during the Feast of Tabernacles; perhaps he participated in that dignified rite in which a procession of the men of Israel, with the High Priest at the head, followed by the officers of the Temple, all in their magnificent vestments, went to the Holy Well of Siloam to draw the water which was used in the sacred libations. He would see the Temple illuminated by flares stretching out toward heaven from the two giant candelabra, each more than fifty cubits high, while the thousands of torches carried by those taking part in the ceremonies united in a blaze of light which made the sky somber by comparison, even though the moon was full. He would hear, just before daybreak, four blasts on the silver trumpets; the first at cock-crow, the second at the tenth degree of light; the third from the Court of the Women and the fourth swelling as the trumpeter-priests marched toward the threshold of the Holy of Holies. No one certainly would have joined in more fervently than he in the prayer at the dawn: "As our fathers of old turned toward the East to salute the sun rising, so, O Lord, we turn to thee, for we are thy people, O God." To the Jews, there was an obvious symbolism in all this; the ceremony of the waters was a token of the rain which would fall on the parched earth, the seventy oxen ordained for the sacrifice recalled the seventy nations of the earth over which it was prophesied that Israel should reign. But for Jesus these things held another interpretation.

His arrival in Jerusalem was not entirely unnoticed. The miraculous cure of the paralyzed man at the well by the five Courts of the Temple only a few months previously would not have been forgotten and Galilee was, after all, not so far off that rumors of his doings would not have been brought to the city by the provincial pilgrims who swelled the crowds in the Temple. St. John records with great exactitude the reactions which his presence provoked (John vii, 11-12). "Then the Jews sought of him at the feast and said, where is he? And there was much murmuring among the people concerning him; for some said, He is a good man: others said, Nay, but he deceiveth the people." Doubtless as in Galilee, the Pharisees reiterated their complaints about him, that he did not fast, that he was careless about the ritual ablutions, that he frequented the society of pagans, tax gatherers and women of ill-repute; that he took unwarrantable liberties in the observance of the Sabbath. But, as soon as he began to speak, just as in Galilee, people were astonished at his wisdom: "How knoweth this man letters, having never learned?" (John vii, 15.)

Jesus spoke at the gates of the Temple, where the people were gathered around him. "My doctrine is not mine, but his that sent me. If any man will do his will, he shall know of the doctrine, whether it be of God, or whether I speak of myself." (John vii, 16-17.) He had already said, in his sermon on the Bread of Life, that he who would seek God must come to Christ and he alone knew the word, which was given to Jesus. Every incident of the feast must have enlarged his meaning; every detail carried its own particular symbolism for him. The water which the High Priest drew in a golden ewer from the Well of Siloam, with which he would sprinkle the altar of sacrifice, would remind him of those "living waters" of which he had spoken to the Samaritan woman, and which Jeremiah had accused an unfaithful people of abandoning (Jeremiah ii, 13). "If any man thirst, let him come unto me and drink. He that believeth on me, as the Scriptures have said, out of his belly shall flow rivers of living water." (John vii, 37-38.) Perhaps it was the light of a thousand torches blazing up to heaven which gave him the image for those famous words: "I am the light of the world; he that followeth me shall not walk in darkness, but shall have the light of life." (John viii, 12.)

The more he spoke, the more argument he provoked. "Many of the people therefore said, Of a truth, this is the Prophet. Others said, This is the Christ. But some said, Shall Christ come out of Galilee? Hath not the Scripture said, that Christ cometh of the seed of David and out of the town of Bethlehem, where David was? So there was a division among the people, because of him." (John vii, 40-43.) But many believed in him and said: "When Christ cometh, will he do more miracles than those which this man hath done?" (John vii, 31.)

It was at this time that the High Priests, warned by the Pharisees, began to feel uneasy. Jesus had not been three days in Jerusalem before his enemies began to close their ranks against him. In the course of John's vivid and detailed narrative we can almost see them, sending out their spies among the crowds who listened to him to take notes of what he said and what he did, gathering it together to compose what all the police forces of the world call "a dossier." At first they dared not use force either out of regard for public opinion or even perhaps through moral scruples, for there must have been some just men, even among the Pharisees.

But their machinations soon began to do harm. Rumor ran through the streets of Jerusalem: "Is this not he, whom they seek to kill. But, lo, he speaketh boldly, and they say nothing unto him. Do the rulers know indeed that this is the very Christ?" (John vii, 25-26.) They began to consider arresting him, dispatching guards to mingle with the crowds and seize the first opportunity which presented. But they came back empty-handed. "Why have you not brought him?" asked the scribes and Pharisees. "Never man spake like this man," replied the Temple officers. If the very custodians of the Temple were to attach themselves to the rising star of this Galilean . . .

And so, almost as soon as Jesus set foot in Judea, the elements of opposition began to draw together. He was to be "the sign that shall be spoken against," from the first he was to sow discord. It was only six months before the murderous hatred he aroused would bring his tragedy to its dire conclusion.

The Adulteress

The Feast of Tabernacles was inevitably accompanied by a certain amount of licence. Eight days of living in strange conditions had its effect. As we all know, journeys and crusades of all kinds are favorable to casual unions and morality tends to be forgotten. It is probably not accidental, therefore, that immediately after the account of the week of the feast, the fourth Gospel tells the story of the woman taken in adultery, one of the most celebrated and beautiful episodes of the recorded life of Christ. No other incident demonstrates more clearly his complete charity, his delicacy and his profound insight into the character of men. "And the scribes and Pharisees brought unto him a woman taken in adultery; and when they had set her in the midst, they say unto him: Master, this woman was taken in adultery, in the very act. Now Moses in the law commanded us, that such should be stoned, but what sayest thou?" (John viii, 3-5.)

This scene would have taken place by the gate on the east side of the Temple. It was to this place that such guilty ones were dragged, "by the neck of their garment," and this was the direction which Jesus would normally take on the way to his booth on the Mount of Olives. The punishment for adultery, based on the Seventh Commandment of the Decalogue, is not always consistently laid down by the doctors of the law. Leviticus (xx, 10) says that adulterers are to be put to death; but Deuteronomy only specifies the penalty of stoning to death for a betrothed woman who is unfaithful (xxii, 23-4). It seems evident that stoning to death was more customary in the time of Christ than strangulation, which was recommended by the Talmud, but whatever method was selected, the wretched woman, hounded by the crowd, could hardly have had any preference.

John says (viii, 6): "This they said tempting him, that they might have to accuse him." It was indeed a leading question. How could it be answered without revealing his disagreement with the Mosaic Law, or without offending the sentiment of the crowd (which probably inclined to leniency at times like this) or finally, and this was the trap which ultimately was to ensnare Jesus and bring him to death, without contravening the Roman order which had withdrawn from the Jews the power to inflict capital punishment.

"But Jesus stooped down, and with his finger wrote on the ground as though he heard them not. So when they continued asking him, he lifted up himself and said, He that is without sin among you, let him first cast a stone at her. And again he stooped down and wrote upon the ground. And they which heard it, being convicted by their own conscience, went out one by one, beginning with the eldest, even unto the last; and Jesus was left alone, and the woman standing in the midst.

When Jesus had lifted up himself and saw none but the woman, he said unto her, Woman, where are those thine accusers? Hath no man condemned thee? She said, No man, Lord. And Jesus said unto her: Neither do I condemn thee: Go, and sin no more." (John viii, 7-11.)

Nothing could be plainer and more precise than the account of this scene and all elaborations of its simplicity are superfluous. The bare score of lines makes us see everything; Jesus, bending down, quietly, almost indifferently, launching the terrible phrase; the sanctimonious hypocrites crowding around, secretly excited by the torture that they hoped to inflict, yet having a conscience and respect for their Law; these men, feeling themselves pierced to the marrow, going inconspicuously away, while Jesus, disregarding them, went on writing. Everything is in this brief account, even the sly observation "beginning at the eldest." Many have wondered what it was that Jesus wrote in the dust. Vague designs, what we should call "doodling"? Or, as St. Jerome, remembering a text from Jeremiah,[1] thought, the names and the sins of the accusers? Or, as some adherents of the more esoteric sects have maintained, cabalistic calculations? We do not know and it does not matter. The essentials are here.

One of these essentials is that merciful silence which the astonished woman felt around her, after Jesus had spoken. Another is the kindly look he turned upon her, for a moment before he bent down again, in order that she might not feel discomfited by shame. A third is the brief gesture of absolution he would have made, as he told her to sin no more. Every earthly judge should ponder on these things, and accept the lesson.

The episode appears to be interpolated in the fourth Gospel. The early Greek Fathers, Chrysostom and Cyril of Alexandria, do not mention it in their commentaries on St. John's Gospel. Some of the earliest manuscripts do not include it and those which give it do not all put it in the same place. St. Augustine

[1] Jeremiah xvii, 13. "They that depart from me shall be written in the earth." (The Hebrew is much more definite here than the Greek.)

thought that the early Church was reluctant to admit the episode because it might be interpreted as complaisant toward adultery. The idiom is certainly that of the synoptics rather than St. John and perhaps it is a fragment which had been transmitted by the disciples of St. John. Or perhaps, like the Apocryphal Gospel of the Hebrews, it is part of the traditional material thought to have been handed down by St. Peter. We do not know, but the Church subsequently admitted it to the canon, though without affirming that it is by the author of the fourth Gospel. But there is none of the Gospel stories which rings truer, is more moving or more essentially "Christian."

The Parables of Love

Throughout the Judean period we can follow the long debate between hatred and charity, between pitilessness and pity, as the Early Fathers expressed it. Against the background of hostile intrigues and murderous intent unfold those lessons and parables in which Jesus revealed the immensity of his love for mankind. He was not unaware of his enemies' intentions; several times he unmasked and denounced them in terrible words, warning the Jews of the consequences of their willful and criminal blindness. It is not the duped sentimentalist who is the true lover of mankind but he who having sounded the depths of their baseness can yet discover the gleam of gold in the sea of slime.

"Verily, verily, I say unto you," cried Jesus, "he that entereth not by the door into the sheepfold but climbeth up some other way, the same is a thief and a robber. But he that entereth in by the door is the shepherd of the sheep. To him the porter openeth; and the sheep hear his voice; and he calleth his own sheep by name and leadeth them out. And when he putteth forth his own sheep he goeth before them, and the sheep follow him for they know his voice. And a stranger will they not follow, for they know not the voice of strangers." (John x, 1-5.)

The Jews ought to have caught the meaning of these words, for their prophets had so often made a similar comparison.

Jeremiah had said of the Eternal One that he would keep Israel "as a shepherd doth his flock" (Jeremiah xxxi, 10). Ezekiel had launched anathemas against those shepherds of Israel who eat the fat and clothe themselves with the wool of their sheep, caring nothing for them, letting them stray and become the prey of wild beasts (Ezekiel xxxiv). Isaiah and Zechariah had used similar imagery, but nevertheless the Jews affected not to understand. They refused to draw the obvious conclusion and Jesus had to speak more plainly still.

"Verily, verily, I say unto you, I am the door of the sheep. All that ever came before me are thieves and robbers: but the sheep did not hear them. I am the door: by me if any man enter in, he shall be saved, and shall go in and out, and find pasture. The thief cometh not, but for to steal, and to kill, and to destroy: I am come that they might have life, and that they might have it more abundantly. I am the good shepherd; the good shepherd giveth his life for the sheep. But he that is an hireling, and not the shepherd, whose own the sheep are not, seeth the wolf coming, and leaveth the sheep, and fleeth: and the wolf catcheth them, and scattereth the sheep. The hireling fleeth, because he is an hireling, and careth not for the sheep. I am the good shepherd, and know my sheep, and am known of mine. As the Father knoweth me, even so know I the Father: and I lay down my life for the sheep. And other sheep I have, which are not of this fold: them also I must bring, and they shall hear my voice: and there shall be one fold, and one shepherd." (John x, 7-16.)

The realism of this parable and the exactness of its application to the land of Palestine and the customs of its shepherds as they persist today have often been remarked. The village domestic animals are still rounded up at night and fastened up in an enclosure, while an old shepherd, or perhaps one of the sons of the owner if they all belong to one man, watches over them through the night. In the morning, each shepherd comes for his own flock and each has his own particular call which the animals recognize. And it is certainly true that the shepherd often has to risk his life for his sheep. David, it will be remembered, killed a lion and a bear (I Samuel xvii, 3-37), and to this day, jackals, wolves and hyenas are not unknown in the steppes of Palestine and Transjordania. But Jesus dwelt rather upon the shepherd's tenderness for his flock than on his courage in protecting them and here his meaning went far beyond the story, and the phrase which Jesus used and which is repeated three times in the Gospel text would not become clear until long afterward. "I lay down my life for the sheep." As Christians we cherish the image of the Good Shepherd no less because we are of "the other sheep," not of the Jewish fold, but children of the heathen, the Gentiles. The universality of Christ's kingdom is foreshadowed in the last verses of the parable. During the persecutions, an inscription in the Catacombs commemorates one "borne back to the sheepfold on the shoulders of the Good Shepherd." Even so today a bewildered humanity still hears in the depths of the stricken heart the old promise that there shall be one flock and one shepherd.

But, at the time when they were spoken, these words brought nothing but fresh argument and strife among the hearers. "Many of them said, He hath a devil and is mad, why hear ye him? Others said, these are not the words of him that hath a devil. Can a devil open the eyes of the blind?" (John x, 19-21.) Jesus showed no anger to those who opposed him; to the forces of hate he replied by love. Again he reverted, in another form, to his old entreaty, the message he had brought at the very beginning of his ministry: "Verily, I say unto you, All sins shall be forgiven unto the sons of men and blasphemies, wherewith soever they shall blaspheme. But he that shall blaspheme against the Holy Ghost hath never forgiveness, but is in danger of eternal damnation." (Mark iii, 28; Luke xii, 10; Matt. xii, 31.) There is no sin, however vile, which cannot be redeemed by the power of this love. only the sin of refusing that love, ignoring the sin, denying the pardon.

There is forgiveness for all sins. Continuing the image of the Good Shepherd, in a parable reported by St. Luke (xv, 4-7) and St. Matthew (xviii, 12) is the story of the one sheep in a hundred which has strayed from the fold and which the shepherd looks for with such zeal. Ezekiel (xxxiv, 16) had already said that "the shepherd will seek that which was lost and bring again that which was driven away and bind up that which was broken." But in the words of Jesus the true voice of love can be heard in the conclusion: "And when he hath found it, he layeth it on his shoulders rejoicing. And when he cometh home, he calleth his friends and neighbors, saying unto them, Rejoice with me, for I have found my sheep which was lost."

"Either what woman," he went on to say, "having ten pieces of silver, if she lose one piece, doth not light a candle and sweep the house and seek diligently until she find it? And when she hath found it, she calleth her friends and her neighbors together saying, Rejoice with me, for I have found the piece which I had lost. Likewise I say unto you, There is joy in the presence of the angels of God over one sinner that repenteth." (Luke xv, 8-10.)

There is perhaps nothing in the entire Gospel which conveys the immeasurable divine mercy so touchingly as the parable which follows immediately after that of the lost piece of silver, the parable which is told only by St. Luke and which more than anything else has earned him his title of the Apostle of the Compassion of Jesus. Rembrandt's picture of the Prodigal Son, battered, clothed in rags and on the verge of collapse, being welcomed by his father with that wonderful gesture of the outstretched arms is the supreme illustration of those words to which every Christian, in his darkest hours, has turned for consolation. There is no need here to recount the story which everyone knows (Luke xv, 11-32). We can all recognize ourselves in the confident, insolent youth, turning his back on his father's home, wasting his substance in folly and debauchery. We all know those hours of abandonment and self-reproach, we have all eaten the husks with the swine and remembered in bitter longing the peace and calm of our childhood's home. The fortunate ones are those who can throw themselves at the feet of their Father and say: "Forgive me, for I have sinned."

Never perhaps have human words enshrined in such brief phrases such a depth of wisdom and love. Everything in the tale has that accent of truth which pierces the heart. We are moved by the anguish of the exile; we are warmed by the joy of the old father who saw him "when he was yet a great way off, and ran and fell on his neck and kissed him."

Nothing can be added to this story, so perfect in its own words. But perhaps a few historical details may help to place its beauty in an even clearer light. According to Jewish law, the estate of a dead man was divided among his sons, the eldest being given a double portion, so that he might maintain his mother and any unmarried sisters. But, until the death of the father, the sons could claim nothing, hence this younger son who demanded his share before his father's death had no legal claim on it at all. The debasement of the prodigal to the task of swineherd was calculated to shock Jewish hearers, for even the remotest contact with the impure beast was degrading. "Cursed is the man who raises swine," says a Talmudic text and another says: "Israel will repent when reduced to the husks of beans." Once again we see how skillfully Jesus based his imagery upon proverbial and traditional lore. Last of all, we may perhaps quote from a second century Egyptian papyrus, cited by Mgr. Ricciotti in this context, in which a prodigal son writes to his mother: "I send you word that I am naked. I implore you, mother, to be reconciled with me. I have been punished in so many ways. I know I have sinned. But, will you come?"

The episode in the Gospel is rounded off by a paragraph specially addressed to worthy persons, to those who have not left their fathers' home or wasted their substance and are very well aware of this. "The elder son was in the field, and as he came and drew nigh to the house, he heard music and dancing." His sentiments on learning that the fatted calf had been killed in honor of his scapegrace brother are exactly those of a respectable woman asked to welcome a repentant prostitute. The elder brother in the parable is clearly a worthy person and he is in no mind to be defrauded of his legal inheritance, the double portion which is his right. He is hard-working and respectful, but his anger can be read between the lines. He does not even say "My Father," and he accuses his brother of having "devoured thy living with harlots." It takes all his father's tact to reply to him and even so the Gospel does not tell us how it was received.

For the mercy of Jesus does not only reverse the old Mosaic morality; it is also disconcerting to the human conscience of which it asks so much. There are plenty of people who are outraged by this parable, who pretend to regard it as an encouragement to loose conduct, and who are affronted by this violence to the solid law of respectability by which good conduct should be rewarded and bad conduct lead to a bad end. If the father had to forgive the son at least he should have given him a severe reprimanding.

Yet the Gospel goes on from this to the parable of the laborers in the vineyard. How disconcerting, and in the true sense, shocking, to those who have worked all day long, industriously and carefully, in the knowledge that they have fully deserved their salary. How can it be right that those who have only worked a part of the day should receive as much as those who have worked since early morning? The heart of man is so made that it not only demands what it feels to be its just due but demands also that those whom it considers unworthy should receive nothing. Jesus set himself against this morality of the right to have. Every man who finds this hard should search his own conscience for he will find there all too many occasions for which he himself would seek indulgence and count himself happy that he has not received justice, but mercy.

Jewish Hatred

"The last shall be first and the first last." (Matt. xx, 16.) These closing words of the parable of the laborers in the vineyard could only have been heard with bitterness by the pious Jew who, conscious of having fulfilled scrupulously the multiple commandments of the Law and of being a living witness to the eternal covenant between Jehovah and Israel, could not admit that others might find their way into the kingdom where God rewarded his own. It must also have been deeply wounding to his racial pride, which, it must never be forgotten, was the bedrock of his faith, as well as an outrage to his convictions, that Jesus and his disciples should attach so little importance to the venerable rites with which tradition had weighted down the Law.

Just as in Galilee, the question of Sabbath observance proved to be the touchstone in Judea also. More so, in fact, for the hierarchy in Jerusalem, always refining and elaborating the precepts, made themselves felt more than in the northern provinces. It might be an exaggeration to say that a man was judged solely by how he kept the Sabbath but it is certain that he who was lax in this matter would incur severe condemnation.

"And as Jesus passed by, he saw a man which was blind from his birth." Probably this was by the gate of the Temple which, as we are told in the Acts (iii, 2) was a favorite place with beggars. Probably also the blind man was calling upon heaven to relieve him, for Jesus pitied him and "he spat upon the ground, and made clay of the spittle, and he anointed the blind man with the clay. And said unto him: Go, wash in the pool of Siloam (which is, by interpretation, Sent). He went his way therefore and washed and came seeing." (John ix, 1-7.) It was widely believed in the ancient world that spittle, especially upon rising, had curative properties in cases of ophthalmia. Pliny and Suetonius both mention it and it will be remembered that Jesus had already, at Bethsaida, cured a blind man by touching his eyes with spittle. The medical virtues of mud are recommended for cataract in a medical poem attributed to one Serenus Sammonicus in the third century A.D. The waters of the pool of Siloam had always been considered holy since Isaiah (viii, 6) had praised them; every Jew knew that they coursed into the pool through the channel cleft through the solid rock at the time of King Hezekiah. It was from this channel that the pool received its name of Siloam or "sent." It is possible that the well was considered miraculous like that of Bethesda, for in the Middle Ages a Mohammedan writer states that people went to Jerusalem to bathe in the waters of Siloam "which came from Paradise," and to this day we can see the ruins of the church which the Byzantine Empress Eudoxia built on the site. Obviously, however, this was more than a "natural" cure; the Gospel's play on the word "sent" makes this clear. Once again we notice how Jesus in his miracles gave new meaning to the ancient customs; it was from the pool of Siloam that the priests drew the water for the libations.

The blind man returned home and there were scenes of great rejoicing and questioning: "Is not this he that sat and begged? Some said, this is he: others said, He is like him: but he said, I am he."

Then they wanted to know all about the cure and who had cured him. Well, "It was the Sabbath day!" This was the heart of the matter. The Pharisees asked the man a lot of questions; all would have been well had there been no objection to healing on the Sabbath. And then there was the scandalous fact that the mud had been made with spittle upon the holy day; a man who did *that* could not be sent from God. The blind man defended his healer, insisting that he must be a prophet. The Pharisees began an investigation; they visited the man's parents since some of them doubted whether he had in fact been born blind. And then they made the astonishing discovery that the healer was a sinner. "Whether he be sinner or no," said the erstwhile blind man, "I know not; one thing I know, that whereas I was blind, now I see." The Pharisees were by this time beside themselves with rage and they were not mollified when the man asked them whether they were asking all these questions in order to admit themselves as disciples of Jesus. Then Jesus, hearing that the man had been condemned by the Pharisees came to him and the story ends with the significant words: "I am come into this world that they which see not might see; and that they which see might be made blind." Some of the Pharisees present heard the words and asked: "Are we blind also?" Jesus said unto them, "If ye were blind, ye should have no sin: but now ye say, We see; therefore your sin remaineth." (John ix.)[2]

The amplification of this miracle into a warning plainly foreshadows the conflict to come. The irritation and fear of the scribes grew stronger. Another incident bearing upon the same theme is reported by St. Luke (xiii, 10-17): "And he was teaching in one of the synagogues on the Sabbath. And behold, there was a woman which had a spirit of infirmity eighteen years, and was bowed together, and could in no wise lift up herself. And when Jesus saw her, he called her to him, and said unto her, Woman, thou art loosed from thine infirmity. And he laid his hands on her: and immediately she was made straight, and glorified God. But the ruler of the Synagogue answered with indignation, because that Jesus had healed on the Sabbath day." He addressed the people, not Jesus, but it was Jesus who replied. "Thou hypocrite, doth not each one of you on the Sabbath loose his ox or his ass from the stall and lead him away to watering? And ought not this woman, being a daughter of Abraham, whom Satan hath bound, lo, these eighteen years, be loosed from this bond on the Sabbath day?"

It was the eternal conflict between those who clung to the letter of the law and those who interpreted the spirit. There is no common ground between them, because they inhabit different worlds.

More serious even than the dogmatic differences was the hatred which Jesus aroused among the Jews because his message was addressed to all peoples. It was bad enough that he was a Sabbath breaker and that he claimed to be above the letter of the law. But when he said that the Messiah would come for all men and not only for the Chosen People, when he said that the Prodigal Son had the same claim on the Father's love as the virtuous elder brother, and that other

---

[2] A Provençal legend has it that the former blind man afterwards became St. Restitutus, the first bishop of St. Paul Trois Châteaux in Drome, France.

sheep might come into the fold, he struck at the very heart of Israel. All pagans were prodigals to the Jews and swine food was their fitting portion; and there could only be one sheepfold, here in the Holy Land, and one flock, the Twelve Tribes. Jesus knew his people and the challenge was deliberate; explicitly and implicitly he condemned their sterile exclusiveness.

We see this clearly in St. Luke's account of the ten lepers whom Christ cured one day coming back to Jerusalem from Jericho. Only one of them thanked him and he, says the Gospel, "was a Samaritan." Yes, Jesus knew his people. The celebrated parable of the Good Samaritan does not only enjoin charity; it also passes a very definite judgment. A certain doctor of the law asked Jesus what he should do to inherit eternal life. "What is written in the law?" said Jesus. "How readest thou?" "Thou shalt love the Lord thy God with all thy heart and with all thy soul and with all thy strength and with all thy mind and thy neighbor as thyself." The questioner was not a bad man, he had included with the fundamental commandment the precept from Leviticus (xix, 18) about loving our neighbor. But he asked for a definition of his "neighbor" and Jesus replied with the parable. He sketched in a few lines one of those dramas too often to be found along the road from Jerusalem to Jericho which, although it is not long, some twenty miles or so, descends very steeply into a sinister desert of barren hills and tumbled boulders to which a belt of blood-colored manganese ore lends an even more lurid aspect. It was a haunt of jackals and robbers; nobody went along it without trepidation. Once a man lay wounded unto death, lying by the roadside. The passers-by did not care to be mixed up in this affair. A priest passed by, then a Levite, one after another and nobody bothered about the wounded man. At last there came a Samaritan, "and when he saw him, he had compassion on him. And went to him and bound up his wounds, pouring in oil and wine, and set him on his own beast and brought him to an inn and took care of him." And when he went away he left money with the innkeeper, so that the wounded man should be looked after.

Halfway along this road between Jerusalem and Jericho, at a turning point in the gorge, is an old caravansary, now fallen into ruin, which was in its day used as a stronghold by the Crusaders. It has always been known as the Hostel of the Good Samaritan. Oil and wine is still used in Syria to heal wounds.

The lesson was explicitly given in this parable: "Which now of these three, thinkest thou, was neighbor to him that fell among thieves?" But the Jews would say: "An infidel cannot be a neighbor."

We get the impression that whereas while he was in Galilee Jesus did not seek to arouse scandal and provoke a clash before it was due, in Judea he was much less cautious. His words are explicit and categorical; they have the sting of a scourge. "Ye shall die in your sins. . . . I am from above: ye are of this world." (John viii, 21-25.) As the time passes, his judgments become more severe until we come to the terrible prophetic apostrophe of the fall of Jerusalem, which history was to execute with the sword of Rome. It is as though Jesus, knowing what was to come, would do nothing to halt the conflict for even the hatred of the Jews was a providential instrument, a necessity of the divine purpose of the Redemption.

The hatred which he aroused was soon to show itself on almost every occasion. In December, when the people gathered together again in Jerusalem for the Feast of the Dedication, the *Hanouka,* there are questioners among the crowds around him. Jesus does not try to hide, he is there, as always, in the heart of these rites which he respects, the real meaning of which he knows better than anyone, for he has said that salvation comes from the Jews. The people commemorated the purification of the altar by Judas Maccabeus after his victory over the Greeks (I Maccabees iv, 59). Since Jesus accepted their traditions, why did he refuse the logical sequel, when they called upon him—whether out of derision, curiosity or provocation—to tell them plainly if he were the Messiah? "I told ye and ye believed not: the works I do in my Father's name, they bear witness of me. But ye believe not, because ye are not of my sheep" (John x, 24-6). They must have raked up the old calumny which had been circulated in Galilee, that he had a devil from whom he drew his power. It must be Beelzebub, the old false god of the Canaanites, now become the devil of the Jews, who possessed him. But Jesus answered them quite calmly (John viii, 49): "I have not a devil." When he spoke in the Temple, they even picked up stones to cast at him (John viii, 59). His enemies probably hoped to get a legal decision to exclude him from the Temple, a terrible punishment, much worse than the *nezipha,* which was simply a reprimand shutting out the delinquent for a week or two, worse even than the *neddui* "the rejection," which lasted a month during which the offender was ordered to sit upon the ground, wearing mourning garments, to let his beard and hair grow and not to bathe, and forbidden to join in the communal prayers. The *herem* was a major excommunciation, which entailed confiscation of goods and which rendered the excommunicant as completely outcast and untouchable as a leper. It seems probable that they had even approached Herod Antipas, as the deputation of the Pharisees warning Jesus that the tetrarch sought to kill him (Luke xiii, 31-33) seems suspect. It reveals indeed their own secret desires, which Jesus had so often uncovered.

Yet they were not all bent on his destruction. Apart from those who responded to him and those devoted friends who remained faithful there were, even among the Pharisees, some upright spirits who could not condemn him, men such as Nicodemus, who had come to him by night on his former visit to Jerusalem. "Doth our law judge any man before it hear him and know what he doeth?" said Nicodemus in the Sanhedrin on the occasion when the High Priest's guard had returned without arresting Jesus. The plea in that court earned nothing but a sneer: "Art thou also of Galilee?" But it stands forever to his credit in a higher tribunal (John vii, 50-52).

Jesus, knowing all about the intrigues around him, went calmly on his way, still preaching compassion and charity, still performing miracles even for the ungrateful. He was not speaking to those who voluntarily chose darkness but to those who were willing to see the light. If a single soul responded to him, his effort was not in vain. Toward the end of his life, on his way up to Jerusalem for the last time, he was again given the occasion for a miracle.

It was outside the gates of Jericho, that delightful town which Antony had once bestowed on Cleopatra for a holiday retreat and which Herod had extended and adorned. The Jericho region is one of the pleasantest in all Judea, for, situated on a moderate elevation above the bed of the Jordan, it is neither too hot in summer nor too cold in winter, when the temperature is about the same as that of the Algerian oasis. Generous streams water a soil which Josephus described as almost divine in its abundance of rare and beautiful fruits. Its scented balsams and its date palms were famous through Palestine and the Bible refers in many places to the perfume of its roses. Today the town is still surrounded on both sides by a sea of trees—palms, almond, citrons, cherry, and orange, and sugar cane and roses, roses everywhere, yellow, pink, and red in the greatest profusion. From earliest times it has been on a great trade route and in the lifetime of Jesus it was a stopping place for caravans, a center of commerce and a favorite pleasure resort. Excavations have revealed three Jerichos. The present city dates from the time of the Crusades. It is a commonplace town with suburban villas and a golf club. The town which Jesus knew was higher up, on the site now occupied by the wretched hamlet of Er-Riha. But in the days of Cleopatra, of Herod and of Archelaus, it was a luxurious city with a marble palace where the Egyptian queen had once enjoyed the scented airs and the Romans later maintained a garrison. Earlier still was the Canaanitish Jericho, dating from at least 1500 B.C., where archaeologists have uncovered three walls of which one shows traces of the burning by Joshua.

We can picture the setting for this miracle, the blind man, with his companion, turning toward the passers-by that darkened face whose passionate entreaty Poussin has brought to life for us in his famous painting in the Louvre. "Thou son of

David, have mercy on me." Then louder still, because the crowd told him to be quiet. "What will ye that I should do unto you?" asked Jesus. "Lord, that I might receive my sight." "Go thy way, thy faith hath made thee whole." And immediately he received his sight and followed Jesus. St. Mark, who must have known him in the Early Church, says that he was called Bartimaeus.

Friends and Faithful

As, among the blindest, some will see the light; as in the stoniest ground some small seed will take root, so in the gathering forces of hatred there were still those who remained faithful to Jesus. He was not alone as he traveled the roads of Judea; we note the presence of groups of friends, we remember those who acclaimed him on Palm Sunday and the faithful few who followed him even to the foot of the Cross. From these faithful followers two figures stand out, the two women, Martha and Mary, the sisters of Lazarus whom Jesus raised from the dead. The third Gospel does not tell us where it was that they entertained their Master, but St. John in his account of the raising of Lazarus specifies their home as at Bethany, then a flourishing little place on the caravan route to Jericho. Although only an hour's walk from Jerusalem, across the Mount of Olives, its peaceful setting made it seem very remote from the turmoil of the capital. But it is not so today. In the midst of fields of barley is a village of sagging ruins, where the visitor is pursued among tottering arches and collapsing vaults by guides howling for baksheesh and pointing out one tumbledown cottage among the others as the alleged home of Martha and Mary.

It would appear that Jesus stayed in this friendly household during the months of October, November and December of the year 29. It was convenient for him, since he could go to Jerusalem whenever he wished without being obliged to spend the night there. It was off the beaten track and doubtless he felt safe there, but all the same we must admire the courage of this devoted family who were not deterred by any threats of the powerful from welcoming their friend as a guest.

Vermeer has chosen to paint this famous Gospel scene in one of those violent rainstorms which, once the summer has ended, burst over Judea. "The thunder of Marheswhan (November) is like a blast of trumpets." The Jewish people, acclimatized to great heat, shiver in the cold and light their braziers; the flocks of sheep move down to the deep ravine of the Jordan. But between storms, the air is marvelously clear so that the smallest details on the horizon are visible and you can see over to Moab on the south, and to the northeast, through a gap in the hills, glimpse the distant mountains.

In this friendly place, Jesus is at home. Each of the sisters exerts herself for him, in her fashion. Martha, the elder, bustles about the place getting his room ready, laying out milk, dates and figs or frying fish. Mary, her character so finely differentiated by St. Luke, sits at the Master's feet, listening with all her soul. The worthy housewife is annoyed at what seems to her to be laziness. "Lord, dost thou not care that my sister hath left me to serve alone? And Jesus answered: Martha, Martha, thou art careful and troubled about many things. But one thing is needful: and Mary hath chosen that good part, which shall not be taken away from her." (Luke x, 38-42.) This saying has since been taken as ranking the contemplative life above the active live. Certainly the "one thing needful" is the Kingdom of God and it is in the presence of Jesus that we can find it, so that all worldly concerns, necessary and even virtuous as they may be, are little compared to silent adoration.

An incident at Jericho reveals the birth of another of those sudden friendships which Jesus could excite by a word or even a glance. It would be toward the end of March of the year 30, a few days before Passion week. Christ came to the town with his disciples, returning from Perea, where he had been preaching to people who did not yet know him. He had just restored Lazarus to life and he was going up to Jerusalem with the motley crowd making for the Holy City at the time of Passover. The rumor that he was among the pilgrims soon got around and people crowded in to get a sight of him. One man was particularly anxious to see him; perhaps some sayings of Jesus, half caught or comprehended, were working in his mind. But he was a short man, lost in the crowd. Then he had an idea. The road is lined with sycamores, vigorous trees whose exposed roots arch out from their trunks, making them very easy to climb. So up he got into the branches, and Jesus noticed him. He realized the inner drive behind the man's simple desire to see him. "Zaccheus, make haste and come down," he said, "for tonight I must abide at thy house."

Zaccheus, the recipient of this surprising honor, was a publican, one of the collectors of the taxes imposed on perfumes and essential oils; he may even have been one of the chief customs officials who did very well out of their detested office. We know what the Jews thought of the tax collectors and here was Jesus, incorrigible as ever, proposing to stay with one and eat at his table. He lingered there, too, telling the parable of the Talents, which enjoins us to make good use of the gifts which God gives us since one day we shall be asked to account for them. Once again Jesus reminded his listeners that the kingdom of God would not come in the way which they expected. There are many touches in this story which must have caused some malicious amusement, such as the reference to the "nobleman who went into a far country to receive for himself a kingdom," which they would certainly interpret as a dig at their former prince Archelaus. A pleasant, convivial scene is conjured up by this part of the Gospel story and it is clear too that by showing Zaccheus such marked favor Jesus had won his heart for God. For Zaccheus stood up and said: "Behold, Lord, the half of my goods I give to the poor, and if I have taken anything from any man by false accusation I voluntarily restore him fourfold." In his humility Zaccheus thus accepted the legal penalty enforced upon thieves. "This day is salvation come to this house," cried Jesus and once more, as when he called that other publican, Matthew, he reminded his hearers that the Son of Man does not come to save the righteous but to save "that which was lost." (Luke xix, 1-28; Matt. xxv, 14-30.)[3]

So, there was love as well as hatred for Jesus during his Judean ministry. They must have loved him, those men and women who followed him down the roads, the mothers who held up their children to receive his blessing, the unknown woman who cried out: "Blessed be the womb that bare thee." It is true that they did not know how to protect him from his enemies and that in any case they would not have dared, but that is so natural that it should not astonish us. But we should remember that from them was born the Church in Jerusalem, that brave little community which kept alive the memory of the Crucified in the heart of the power of Jewry, and which gave Christianity its first martyr, St. Stephen.

From among this group of friends and faithful disciples, which must have been fairly numerous since after the Resurrection it is revealed as having five hundred "brothers," Jesus chose several secondary Apostles, who were sent to carry his teaching into far countries, as he had previously chosen the Twelve. We know exactly how he chose them and what he asked of them. (Luke ix, 57-62; Matt. xiii, 19-22.) One day a scribe approached him, for even among the doctors of the Law his reputation had spread. "Lord, I will follow thee whithersoever thou goest." The will was there but did the man know what he was undertaking? "Foxes have holes and birds of the air have nests but the Son of Man hath not where to lay his head." Another disciple, whom Jesus had called, asked for a delay; his father had died and he wished to bury him. "Let the dead bury their dead," said Jesus, "but go thou and preach the kingdom of God."[4] Human feelings must be put

[3] The converted publican has always been a favorite in Christian tradition and one legend makes Zaccheus a companion of St. Peter and bishop of Caesarea while another states that he became a hermit living in the remote valley which was to become the Shrine of Rocomadour.

[4] There have been many attempts to explain away this mysterious elliptical saying. "Nineteen centuries of mire have covered the hard, shining steel of this saying," wrote François Mauriac. "Nineteen hundred years of attenuating lax commentaries because we cannot look the truth in the face, the literal truth of

aside in those who are called to follow Christ; they cannot, in the words attributed to Jesus and cited by St. Augustine, "abandon the living to compose fables on the dead." To the disciple who asked for time to make farewells to his household, Jesus said, "No man, having put his hand to the plough and looking back, is fit for the kingdom of God."

These are hard sayings: "If any man come to me and hate not his father and mother and wife and children and brethren and sisters, yea, and his own life also, he cannot be my disciple." "And whosoever doth not bear his cross, and come after me, cannot be my disciple." (Luke xiv, 26-27.) Those whom Christ calls must renounce everything, even the most natural affections, for the law of love which Jesus preached has something terrible in it, and cannot be falsified into sentimental insipidity. The missionary lost in the heart of the jungle, devoting himself to a horde of savages, knows the cost of the divine love. The solitary contemplative in his cell, torn from all human tenderness and consolation, follows out in silence the supernatural task of reversion. Only by the most severe tests of selection can those who would follow Christ be fitted for action.

The team of disciples now formed was extended beyond the original Twelve. There has been a good deal of argument over the probable number. Some have held that it was seventy, a sacred number among the Jews—the number of the Elders selected by Moses (Numbers xi), the number of members of the Sanhedrin. Other authorities, from a scrutiny of ancient texts, have decided on seventy-two. They were sent out because "the harvest truly is great but the laborers are few," and the instructions given them and the powers they received were similar to those originally given to the Apostles, except that the power to raise the dead was not given nor were they forbidden to preach to the Gentiles or the Samaritans.

---

these words which nothing can efface. And in spite of it all, we can judge the truth of them for ourselves, every time we attend a public funeral and see the sick and crafty faces, worn by the double fret of time and sin; the flesh soaked and pickled in vice, the crush of bodies whose corruption is more patent than that of the corpse they are burying."

We do not know who they were, because the Gospel does not give their names. St. Luke who, with St. Paul, stayed a long while in Caesarea, must have known some of them, but he does not specify any. Clement of Alexandria stated that it was to the deacon Philip that Jesus said, "Let the dead bury their dead," and that this Philip made conversions in Samaria and Sharon and had four daughters who were "prophetesses" in the Early Church. Eusebius identifies one of them as Barnabas, St. Paul's coadjutor, another as Sosthenes who is associated with St. Paul in the Epistle to the Corinthians, and another as Matthias, who was chosen to replace Judas in the Twelve. Cleophas, one of the disciples at Emmaus, was possibly another. Whoever they were, their mission must have been successful, for St. Luke tells us that they "returned again with joy." "Lord, even the devils are subject unto us through thy name." But Jesus, reproaching them for their pride, said: "Rejoice not that the spirits are subject unto you but rather rejoice because your names are written in heaven." (Luke x, 17-19.)

Revelations in Judea

The Judean period therefore showed considerable progress in the preaching of the divine word and in the instruction of the future Church. There is not however an equally clear extension of our knowledge of Christ's thought. It is true that the closer we get to the climax of his human existence the more explicitly does Jesus reveal the purpose of his mission and prepare his followers to understand it completely when it shall be sealed by the sacrifice to come. But his actual teaching does not evolve nor is it in any way modified for, as we have said, the philosophy of Jesus, unlike the philosophy of men, does not undergo that almost organic transformation which is wrought by time and experience, by that working of the self upon the self which every one of us undergoes, however little he may be intellectually conscious of it. The ideas of Jesus are a perfect unchanging whole from the beginning of his public life to the end, from the Sermon on the Mount to the Last Supper.

The chief themes of his preaching in Judea are the same as those of the Galilean period: charity first; the parable of the Good Samaritan with its unforgettable lesson, inviting the listeners to ask themselves, "What would I have done in the same position?" and learning in due course that the "neighbor" whom we should help, from whom we may expect help, is anyone who comes our way.

Charity must be accompanied by humility. This is the lesson which Christ drove home when they brought him the woman taken in adultery. How can we be harsh with others when we remember our own faults and the harshness which these merit, for the essence of morality is to recognize our own littleness and not to draw false pictures of ourselves. Hypocrisy was the sin of the Pharisees, those "whited sepulchres" who passed for virtuous among men, "but God knoweth your hearts for that which is highly esteemed among men is abomination in the sight of God." (Luke xvi, 15.) "Two men went up into the Temple to pray," said the Master, "the one a Pharisee, and the other a publican. The Pharisee stood up and prayed thus with himself, O God, I thank thee that I am not as other men are, extortioners, unjust, adulterers, or even as this publican. I fast twice in the week, I give tithes of all I possess. And the publican, standing afar off, would not lift up so much as his eyes to heaven, but smote upon his breast saying, God be merciful to me a sinner. I tell you this man went down to his house justified rather than the other, for everyone that exalteth himself shall be abased; and he that humbleth himself shall be exalted." (Luke xviii, 10-14.)

There is one further precept which, together with the humility to forget oneself and the love which makes us give ourselves to others, constitutes what we may call the "tripod" of the Gospel teaching. This is the command to renounce worldly goods. No one can serve two masters, Christ had said in the Sermon on the Mount. We must choose between God and Mammon. He repeated this injunction many times during his teaching in Judea; for instance, in his instructions to the seventy-two disciples that they should take nothing with them, in the episode of the rich young man debarred by the cares of his wealth from following the road to salvation. We have already discussed the terrible saying that "it is easier for a camel to pass through the eye of a needle than for a rich man to enter into the kingdom of heaven." Then, there is the parable of the rich man who "was clothed in fine linen and fared sumptuously every day" and who, when he died and was engulfed in hell, saw the angels bearing to heaven the body of a beggar who on earth had sat at his gate, covered with sores and begging the crumbs from the rich man's table. The mysterious parable of the unjust steward, which has been so often discussed, seems to say that the faithful, "the children of light," must in this world expect to be subject to the forces of evil, that they must be content to lack the tainted riches of this world in order to acquire merit in heaven.

Charity, humility, renunciation, this is the Christian doctrine. United with it must be, of necessity, a profound trust in God. "Are not five sparrows sold for two farthings and not one of them is forgotten before God." Bidding his listeners consider the flowers in their carefree beauty, the birds whom God feedeth, Christ reminds his followers that they are in the care of the Father; "even the very hairs of your head are all numbered." (Luke xii, 6-7)

We can see from the foregoing that there is no difference between Christ's teaching in Galilee and in Judea; indeed it can hardly be said to have been developed or extended in the later period. But it is rather more particularized. Jesus gives more and more concrete examples; as, for instance, when he was asked by the Pharisees for his views on marriage and divorce. "Is it lawful for a man to put away his wife for every cause?" The Mosaic Law stated: "When a man hath taken a wife and married her, and it come to pass that she find no favor in his eye, because he hath found some uncleanness in her; then let him write her a bill of divorcement and give it in her hand and send her out of his house." (Deut. xxiv, 1.) The woman thus repudiated had the right to remarry. But the rabbinical schools differed as to the grounds upon which divorce might be allowed.[5] The more strict agreed with Rabbi Schammai, that it was permissible only in very grave circumstances, primarily infidelity. The more lax, like Rabbi Hillel, allowed divorce for much less substantial reasons, such as that the wife had gone about unveiled, that she had a wart on the face "even without hairs," and finally, if she burnt the food or spoilt the sauce. Later still, Rabbi Akiba declared that a man might divorce his wife if he did not consider her sufficiently good looking or had met somebody better.

In inviting Jesus to give an opinion on such a controversial matter the questioners undoubtedly hoped to trap him. But Jesus was not to be drawn; he chose instead to lay down his own teaching upon a subject of great importance. "Have ye not read that he which made them at the beginning made them male and female . . . wherefore they are no more twain but one flesh. What therefore God hath joined together, let no man put asunder." The Jews at once reminded him of the Mosaic precept: "He saith unto them, Moses because of the hardness of your hearts suffered you to put away your wives, but from the beginning it was not so." As in the doctrine of retaliation, the old law must be extended. "Whoever putteth away his wife and shall marry another, committeth adultery." When the disciples, in private, protested that his ruling was hard, he replied that there are some "which have made themselves eunuchs for the kingdom of heaven's sake. He that is able to receive it, let him receive it." (Matt. xix, 3-12; Mark x, 2-12; Luke xvi, 18.)

Is this so hard to understand? In the Sermon on the Mount, when he said that a single lustful look was equivalent to adultery, Jesus took the problem of sexual relationship to the plane where it belongs. It is a matter of the purity of the heart.[6]

---

[5] They disagreed also upon the circumstances in which the bill might be legally delivered. If, for instance, the wife was sitting on the terrace when the bill was thrown to her, at what precise moment was she repudiated, when the act was written, when it was thrown, or when she caught it!

[6] Christ's teaching on marriage has aroused a great deal of heated discussion. Comparing the synoptic Gospels, we find that St. Mark and St. Luke condemn divorce absolutely while St. Matthew seems to allow it on one condition by the insertion of "except it be for fornication" after "Whosoever shall put away his wife." The Catholic Church has always interpreted Christ's teaching as affirm-

But if there is no difference in Christ's teaching during his ministry in Judea, as we read those passages of the Gospels of St. Luke and St. John which recount it, we get nevertheless an impression quite different from that given by the earlier chapters. It is a difference not easily definable and its effect is cumulative; we sense a growing undercurrent, a feeling that the hour of destiny is drawing near. There is a sense of secret urgency, of something awaiting revelation, for Christ, who has always, in revealing the secret of his mission, kept something in reserve, even to his closest intimates, will from now on disclose his meaning more and more plainly, preparing the faithful for the ultimate revelation.

He had revealed himself to the crowd gathered in the Temple for the Feast of Tabernacles. "When Christ cometh," they said, "no man knoweth whence he is." This popular belief arose from the misinterpretation of certain obscure passages in the Old Testament. Well, they knew where Jesus came from. He reminded them of it, with that curious irony he frequently displayed. "Ye both know me and ye know me whence I am; and I am not come of myself, but he that sent me is true, whom ye know not." (John vii, 28-9.) The reply would seem blasphemous to some of his hearers. A little later (John viii, 12) he says: "I am the light of the world; he that followeth me shall not walk in darkness, but shall have the light of life." None of those who listened could mistake the meaning of this phrase, for "the light" was one of the terms by which the Messiah was designated in the scriptures. "Arise, shine; for thy light is come, and the glory of the Lord is risen upon thee," cried Isaiah (lx, 1) and more plainly still, the great prophet had said, in the words of Jehovah to his servant: "I will also give thee for a light unto the Gentiles" (xlix, 6), words which the holy old

ing the absolute indissolubility of marriage. St. Paul (I Cor. vii, 10) accepted this, admitting separation, not divorce and forbidding re-marriage. The derivation of this view can be seen clearly if the interpolation peculiar to St. Matthew is put as a clause between dashes when it becomes clear that it refers to the verb "put away," for as St. Augustine says, "It is permissible to put away a wife for fornication, but the previous tie remains, so that whoever marries a woman who has been put away commits adultery." This is the ruling affirmed by the Council of Trent.

man Simeon had used, in a similar prophetic outburst, in blessing the little child Jesus.

Many occasions, in the days which followed, gave Jesus the opportunity of speaking yet more clearly. When the seventy-two disciples returned from their mission, overjoyed at having been able to demonstrate the astonishing powers which their Master had bestowed on them, we are told that Jesus "rejoiced in spirit" and said, "All things are delivered to me of my Father and no man knoweth who the Son is but the Father, and who the Father is, but the Son and he to whom the Son will reveal him." This is a profound and fundamental statement; it excludes all creation from the direct knowledge of God, proclaims Jesus consubstantial with God, united to him by direct and exclusive knowledge. The speaker was not revealing himself as the Messiah, but as God.

Some time before, in Galilee, he had refused to give the people a "sign," some miracle on demand which would cater to the whims of the people without making them any the wiser. (Mark viii, 11-13; Matt. xvi, 1-4.) He had once said that his very presence among them was the true sign. The astonishing miracles were only the consequence of that more astounding fact, that God had sent his Son on earth as the Messiah, the Savior. At the Day of Judgment that generation which had the privilege of seeing God living the life of men will have a special charge to answer in that they could not recognize the sign, not even when (he uses once more a metaphor which he had already employed in Galilee) like Jonah emerging after three days from the belly of the whale, Christ shall arise after three days from another engulfment. (Luke xi, 29-31; Matt. xii, 38-42.)

We can sense a kind of righteous impatience in Jesus as time passes. He knew that he had come to save the world; how long would men continue to refuse him? Could he not arouse the fires of burning love? "I am come to send fire on earth, and what will I, if it be already kindled?" (Luke xii, 49.) "Whoever is near me is at the heart of the fire; he that is far from me is far from the kingdom." Origen cites these as his words. It must be remembered that, as Jesus launched these passionate appeals, growing ever more urgent, he was surrounded by crowds who were predominantly hostile, many of them seeking to turn his words against him in order to encompass his downfall. There are few more dramatic scenes, before the culminating tragedy, than that in which Jesus, at the Feast of the Dedication of the Temple, stood up against the angry Jews and with complete calm and courage made his declaration. There were threatening growls from the crowds—some even began to throw stones—at the man who declared his identity with the Father. "Is it not written in your law, I said, ye are gods?" That every man carries in himself the image of God is the theme of Psalm 82, and even of the first chapter of Genesis.

But Jesus went further than this; he was not merely asserting the dignity of the human creature. If the law has given you the name of God, it follows that he whom God ordained and sent into the world was not blaspheming when he called himself the Son of God. But his words offended and disconcerted the crowd. He did not proclaim himself Messiah, a message which this people would have understood in their own wise, as a kind of political agitator! Jesus knew that he would die but it was necessary that his sacrifice should be recognized for what it was, a testimony to the supernatural truth that the Father was in him, that he was in the Father and that he was the Son of God. "If I do not the works of my Father, believe me not. But if I do, though ye believe not me, believe the works." (John x, 31-38.)

He had said it all before but there are those who have ears and do not hear, and eyes, but not to see.

As the time runs out, we recognize, under the burning ardor of his pleading, a deep sadness that men should be so blind, that they should so willingly call down the judgment that waits on the willful refusal and the hardened heart. The warnings of the pending doom grow stronger. There is the parable of the master returning home after a journey: "Blessed are those servants whom the Lord when he cometh shall find watching." (Luke xii, 37.) "Be ye therefore ready also, for the Son of Man cometh at an hour when ye think not." (Luke xii, 40.) He marvels that men who search the skies for a sign and predict rain or drought from the direction of the clouds and the winds should be blind to the signs of a catastrophe greater than floods or lightning. (Luke xii, 54-56.) "When thou goest with thine adversary to the magistrate, as thou art in the way, give diligence that thou mayest be delivered from him, lest he hail thee to the judge." (Luke xii, 58.) When they came to tell him that Pilate had massacred the Galileans, he asked them whether they thought the eighteen killed by the falling of the tower of Siloam had sinned more than the citizens of Jerusalem (Luke xiii, 1-5). The time was drawing near when the fig tree would be cut down, because for three years it had borne no fruit (Luke xiii, 6-9).

The immortal, terrible words were not addressed solely to the Jews. They were addressed to all those who were to refuse him and every one of us who seeks to justify his faults calls down upon himself the verdict which, in the final account, will decide his destiny through eternity. "The kingdom of God is within you." The material power which the Pharisees expected would never come (Luke xvii, 20-21) but every man knows whether the Kingdom of God is established in his heart, and whether God's peace is in him. For one day the Son of Man will no longer be gentle and merciful, calling the world to respond to his infinite love. In the Day of Judgment he will be swift and terrible and there will be no escape and the Sword of God will strike none knows how or where. (Luke xvii, 22-37; Matt. xxiv, 24-27; 37-41.) Once more, in the last week of his life, Christ foretold his second coming, riding in glory and majesty on the storm clouds and punishing the wicked. Already in Judea we can see, behind the figure of the Good Shepherd, the terrible presence that Michelangelo drew on the ceiling of the Sixtine Chapel, the "Son of Man" at the Last Judgment.

Our Father

One day, when Jesus was praying alone in a certain place, one of his disciples came up when he had finished and said, "Lord, teach us to pray."

If we could keep only one single page of the Gospel, surely it would be the opening of the eleventh chapter of St. Luke that we would choose. For in reply to that perhaps naive request, Jesus gave us, out of his own mouth, the most sublime and complete prayer that the lips of man have ever uttered, the Lord's Prayer of the Christian liturgy, the "Our Father"—our refuge in sorrow and in joy.

It seems strange that Jesus had not already taught his followers to pray and the request, coming after so much counsel and so many commands, is surprising. It may be that the particular disciple who asked was young, new or simple; it may be that he wanted some precise formula to guide and discipline the spiritual aspiration which, in many people, is overwhelmed by the emotions of the heart. The prayer which Christ gave is repeated twice in the Gospel narrative; St. Matthew includes it in the Sermon on the Mount (vi, 9-13), St. Luke relates it in the Judean period, immediately following the episode of Martha and Mary (xi, 2-4). It is impossible to say whether the same words were reported by the two evangelists in different contexts or whether Jesus repeated the prayer, as he well might have done. It seems more likely that St. Matthew, in transcribing the Sermon on the Mount, should have added to that particular occasion. St. Luke, who is always particularly careful to record the prayers of Christ (iii, 21; v, 16; vi, 12; ix, 18; ix, 29; xi, 1; xxii, 32; xxii, 41; xxiii, 34-46), may be taken as a more reliable guide in matters of chronology.

There are also certain differences in the two texts. The Church has adopted that of St. Matthew. St. Luke does not give "Thy will be done" nor the second part of "Deliver us from evil." Authorities on the Semitic languages are inclined to regard the version in the third Gospel as less close to the original. Moreover, the arrangement of the prayer in the first Gospel, an invocation and twice three requests, gives seven verses, which corresponds to Semitic metrical uses.

"Our Father which art in heaven, Hallowed be thy name. Thy kingdom come. Thy will be done on earth as it is in heaven. Give us this day our daily bread. And forgive us our debts as we forgive our debtors. And lead us not into temptation, but deliver us from evil."

Christians have always wondered what was the exact place where this wonderful prayer rose to God for the first time. An ancient tradition, dating from the fourth century, has located a place on the Mount of Olives where a church was built to commemorate both the first pronouncement of the "Our Father" and our Lord's prediction of the end of the world during the last week of his life. The present-day Church of the Pater Noster is that which was restored during the Crusades; it is a little lower down the slope of the hill and since 1876 there has been a Carmelite monastery there. The Italian pilgrim Nicolo da Poggibonsi records in 1345 that he saw a flagstone graven with the words of the prayer, which was said to record the fact that it was first uttered in that place. Other writers have favored a site around Ephraim, where Jesus is known to have spent the last months of his life (John xi, 54), and if this be so, the prayer assumes something of the character of a final message, a supreme spiritual testament. Ephraim, which is known as Taiybeh today, is situated high up on the Judean plateau, on a ledge looking toward the east. It is a pleasant little town, set among vineyards and orchards of apricots. The view over the arid plateau, gashed by deep gorges, extends along the Jordan valley to the Dead Sea and the Mountains of Moab. If we are seeking a place where the physical configuration of the landscape and the sweep of the horizon seems in harmony with divine grandeur, this seems the most fitting spot to have echoed for the first time those magnificently simple phrases in which man talks to God.

"Our Father which art in heaven." Not only our Master, our King. No longer the terrible Jehovah, almighty Elohim, the

Lord of Hosts, but he who, high as is his dwelling, we may address in the name of confident love.

We ask Him to listen to the three wishes which concern him to whom all veneration is due, for our humble obedience must precede our own requests. *"Hallowed be thy name."*

"Thy kingdom come." Because it is the reign of justice, the reign of our Father, better than all earthly dispensations. There is a variant much loved by Gregory of Nyssa which expresses admirably the essential of a world obedient to God. "May the Holy Ghost descend on us and may our lives be pure."

"Thy will be done." May we, in good fortune and ill, learn to recognize God's hand and accept willingly what He may send, and, like Jesus, in the Agony in the Garden, accept the chalice of bitterness and learn to taste in it the savor of God's love.

"On earth as it is in heaven." These words relate to the three preceding wishes and express our desire to venerate God's name, to hope for his kingdom and to submit to his will not only in the supernatural world but here and now in the things of this world so that God may be glorified daily.

The following three requests concern each one of us and our children. God has made us with a fleshly body and an immortal soul and both have need of him.

"Give us this day our daily bread." Both the bread which is made of the earthly grain and that "bread of life" of which it is said that those who eat of it shall hunger no more.[7]

"Forgive us our trespasses" or *"forgive us our debts."* The two versions have the same meaning. If we prefer the second version, St. Matthew's, it is because it reminds us that money is the worst temptation, the one which binds us to this world and hardens our heart. We know that in the last day God will forgive us as we shall forgive others, for God's forgiveness is adjusted to the merit of our own.

"Lead us not into temptation, deliver us from evil." Or as

---

[7] St. Jerome gives another version of this clause, possibly taken from the Apocryphal Gospel of the Ebionites. *Panem nostrum crastinum (id est futurum) da nobis hodie:* "Give us today our bread for tomorrow." There is a good deal of psychological truth in this evidence of human prudence.

the Early Fathers phrased it, "Do not suffer us to be led into temptation" or into "temptation exceeding our strength." Saint Paul has said it in Your name (I Cor. x, 13): Against the evils which threaten us, against the Evil One who lies in wait for us, we must all fight, but in that battle in which everything is staked, Father, lend us your aid.[8]

Such is the prayer which, for two thousand years, millions of Christians have repeated. It is marvelously simple, unlike the long complicated prayers beloved of the Pharisees. It is direct and stripped to the essentials, yet its six requests form a complete spiritual guide to mankind. It is compact, each word counts, and it would be impossible to change it without destroying the sense as well as the rhythm. It is human, for the whole man is considered in it, not only the soul which glorifies God but the mortal flesh which knows hunger. It is a prayer of brotherhood under God; a prayer to be said in unison for everyone can understand it; a prayer to be said aloud together. It is the prayer of Christian unity because it says not "me" but "us." A very old text known as the *Didachus* or "Doctrine of the Apostles," which dates back to the year 150, says that the early Christians recited it three times daily. In the liturgy of the Catholic Church it is said, either aloud or silently, in nearly every divine office. Together with that prayer which the Middle Ages composed from the angelic salutation to Mary, it forms the simplest, the most living and the most complete expression of the Catholic Faith. "Nothing can erase from the books of our people the echoes of the *Pater* and the *Ave*," said the French poet, Charles Péguy.

Its complete originality can be judged by comparing it with other prayers in use at the time or with those of any other time and place. There are some admirable prayers in the Old Testament and the Church uses many of the Hebrew Psalms, but these lack the simplicity and the starkness. There is, too, an

[8] The first of these quotations is from St. Augustine; the second from St. Hilary, a fifth century bishop. It should be noted, as Fr. Lebreton remarks, that the Greek *peirasmos* which we translate as temptation, has a wider sense and can mean trial, tribulation or persecution.

entirely different perspective. Origen, who knew the sacred writings better than any of us can hope to, tells us that he combed the Old Testament without finding a single prayer in which God is addressed as Father and "although we cannot say that God was never called father or those who believed in Him, His children, the text shows clearly that those called the children of God were regarded as *subjects* of God." At the time of Christ, if the name of Father was given to God in contemporary Judaism, the accent was always on obedience and veneration rather than love and trust.

The difference between the "Our Father" and the ordinary Jewish prayer of the time is easily illustrated by a comparison of the Lord's Prayer with the Eighteen Benedictions (*Schemone Esre*) which pious Jews recited daily. This prayer, dating from the return from the Captivity, was, with the "Hear, O Israel," the customary Jewish daily prayer. In its current form, it includes fifteen additional lines (which we do not quote here), added after the great catastrophe of 70 A.D., recording the punishment of the Jews and their dispersal throughout the world: [9]

Blessed art thou, O Lord our God and God of our fathers, God of Abraham, God of Isaac, and God of Jacob, the great, mighty and revered God, the most high God, who bestowest lovingkindnesses, and possessest all things; who rememberest the pious deeds of the patriarchs, and in love wilt bring a redeemer to their children's children for thy name's sake.

O King, Helper, Saviour and Shield. Blessed art thou, O Lord, the Shield of Abraham.

Thou, O Lord, art mighty for ever, thou quickenest the dead, thou art mighty to save.

Thou sustainest the living with lovingkindness, quickenest the dead with great mercy, supportest the falling, healest the sick, loosest the bound, and keepest thy faith to them that sleep in the dust. Who is like unto thee, Lord of mighty acts, and who resembleth

[9] The French text of this Prayer quoted by the author in the original edition is from Edmond Fleg's *Anthologie Juive*. The English translation used here is from Singer's *Authorised Daily Prayer Book* for the Hebrew Congregations of the British Empire. *Tr.*

thee, O King, who killest and quickenest, and causest salvation to spring forth?

Thou art holy, and thy name is holy, Blessed art thou, O Lord, the holy God.

Thou favourest man with knowledge, and teachest mortals understanding. O favour us with knowledge, understanding and discernment from thee. Blessed art thou, O Lord, gracious Giver of knowledge.

Cause us to return, O our Father, unto thy Law; draw us near, O our King, unto thy service, and bring us back in perfect repentance unto thy presence. Blessed art thou, O Lord, who delightest in repentance.

Look upon our affliction and plead our cause, and redeem us speedily for thy name's sake; for thou art a mighty Redeemer. Blessed art thou, O Lord, the Redeemer of Israel.

Heal us, O Lord, and we shall be healed; save us and we shall be saved; for thou art our praise. Grant a perfect healing to all our wounds; for thou, almighty King, art a faithful and merciful Physician.

Blessed art thou, O Lord, who healest the sick of thy people Israel.

Bless this year unto us, O Lord our God, together with every kind of the produce thereof, for our welfare; give a blessing upon the face of the earth.

O satisfy us with thy goodness, and bless our year like other good years. Blessed art thou, O Lord, who blessest the years.

And for slanderers let there be no hope, and let all wickedness perish as in a moment; let all thine enemies be speedily cut off, and the dominion of arrogance do thou uproot and crush, cast down and humble speedily in our days. Blessed art thou, O Lord, who breakest the enemies and humblest the arrogant.

Towards the righteous and the pious, towards the elders of thy people, the house of Israel, towards the remnant of their scribes, towards the proselytes of righteousness, and towards us also may thy tender mercies be stirred, O Lord our God; grant a good reward unto all who faithfully trust in thy name; set our portion with them for ever, so that we may not be put to shame; for we have trusted in thee. Blessed art thou, O Lord, the stay and trust of the righteous.

Hear our voice, O Lord our God; spare us and have mercy upon us, and accept our prayer in mercy and favour; for thou art a God who hearkenest unto prayers and supplications: from thy presence, O our King, turn us not empty away; for thou hearkenest in mercy to the prayer of thy people Israel. Blessed art thou, O Lord, who hearkenest unto prayer.

We will give thanks unto thee and declare thy praise for our lives which are committed unto thy hand, and for our souls which are in thy charge, and for thy miracles, which are daily with us, and for thy wonders and thy benefits, which are wrought at all times, evening, morn and noon.

We cannot deny the beauty of these fervent words. But the God who emerges from them is the God of the Old Testament, the majestic and serene Creator of the earth, the Almighty whose benefits were poured out upon Israel, the just Judge who smote his enemies and rewarded his servants—in short, Jehovah—a conception far above the curious and immoral deities of the pagan hymns of praise. But it is not accidental that the contrast between the conception of Jehovah and the tender confident accents of the "Our Father" should be expressed in these heavy, sonorous phrases, so complicated that one is tempted to wonder whether even believers completely understood them. The *Eighteen Benedictions* are more than ten times as long as the *Our Father,* yet they express much less, and how different are these requests of the punishment of the unworthy and the justification of the righteous from those simple words which go to the heart of all men: "Forgive us our debts, as we forgive our debtors, and lead us not into temptation."

Twice in the Gospel, once on the shores of the lake of Galilee and later in Judea, Christ promised the faithful that the prayer of a sincere heart and unquestioning faith will always be heard. "Ask, and it shall be given unto you; seek and ye shall find; knock and it shall be opened unto you." (Matt. vii, 7.) There is no more complete and efficacious prayer than the seven plain and sober verses which plumb the depths and express the longings of the human heart.

The Resurrection of Lazarus

So the Judean period draws to a close, and with it, soon, the earthly life of Jesus. He went next to Perea, to that region which, only two years before, had echoed to the voice of the Baptist. From certain particulars in the various Gospels (John x, 40-42; Mark x, 1; Luke xiii, 31-33; Matt. xix, 1-2) we can deduce that after his stay at Bethany or elsewhere in the neighborhood of Jerusalem, he traveled through the lowlands, perhaps also into Transjordan, for some twelve weeks before returning to Jerusalem by way of Jericho. But these movements did not interrupt his mission in Judea any more than did similar journeys in Galilee. The famous precept, "Enter ye in by the strait gate," was spoken while he was in Perea as was also the parable of the guests who came too late to the feast and were left in the darkness outside where there was "weeping and gnashing of teeth." Then he came back to Jerusalem, perhaps for the Passover but drawn also perhaps by a secret inner compulsion, for it was not fitting that "a prophet perish out of Jerusalem." (Luke xiii, 33.)

So he returned to Jerusalem and at Bethany, where Martha and Mary lived, there had been tragedy. Lazarus, their brother, had been ill and the sisters had sent word to Jesus, "Lord, he whom thou lovest is sick." It was a delicately formulated message for the two sisters who knew Jesus so well knew that a simple statement would move him more than a heartrending appeal. It may be that Christ was a long way off in the gorge of the Jordan or in the plateau to the east; it may be that the sick man took a rapid turn for the worse soon after the messenger departed. Anyhow, before Jesus returned, Lazarus died. But Jesus knew his own powers when he said, "This sickness is not unto death but for the glory of God."

When the disciples heard that Jesus proposed to return to Judea and even to go to Bethany, which was so close to Jerusalem, they protested. "Master, the Jews of late sought to stone thee; and goest thou thither again?" So obviously the journey into Perea had been for reasons of prudence. Jesus reassured them; the night had not yet fallen, they had nothing to fear, for they walked in the light. But clearly the poor men were only half persuaded. Then Jesus said, "Our friend Lazarus sleepeth, but I go, that I may awake him out of sleep." A

Palestinian proverb says, "Whoever sleeps is half cured," and this was the view of the disciples. So Jesus had to speak plainly: "Lazarus is dead. And I am glad for your sakes that I was not there, to the intent ye may believe; nevertheless, let us go unto him." Seeing that he had made up his mind, Thomas called Didymus, said to the other disciples, "Let us also go that we may die with him."

The worthy Thomas had more generosity than faith, perhaps, for it was he who, before he could believe in the Resurrection, asked to touch the wounds of Christ. We should salute him, however, for being the first of the little band of disciples to volunteer for an expedition which was not without risk. It is the only time we ever see him in the role of leader, for generally Peter steps in with the first word. One wonders whether Peter was absent, whether he did not make the journey into Perea. This conjecture is much strengthened by the fact that the synoptic Gospels do not record the incident at Bethany at all; St. John alone devotes a whole chapter (xi) to it. We know that the earliest Christian teaching was based upon the recollections of St. Peter and his absence in this case would account for the silence of St. Matthew, St. Mark and St. Luke.[10]

When Jesus did reach Bethany, Lazarus had been buried for four days and since the place is so near Jerusalem, a good many Jews came to express their condolences. As soon as Martha heard that Jesus was on the way, she went out to meet him while Mary remained in the house. "Lord, if thou hadst been here, my brother would not have died, but I know that even now, whatsoever thou wilt ask of God, God will give it thee." "Thy brother shall rise again," said Jesus. "I know," said Martha, "that he shall rise again in the resurrection at the last day." Jesus said: "I am the resurrection and the life, he that be-

---

[10] Another explanation which has been advanced is that the synoptics, writing very soon after the death of Jesus, deliberately kept silent about an episode which would have attracted the hostile attention of the Jews to the family at Bethany and perhaps exposed them to the risk of persecution. St. John, who wrote much later, probably after the death of Mary, Martha and Lazarus, would not be under the same obligation to observe discretion.

lieveth in me, though he were dead, yet shall he live. And whosoever liveth and believeth in me shall never die. Believest thou this?" "Yea, Lord: I believe that thou art the Christ, the Son of God, which should come into the world."

Then Martha went in and quietly spoke to her sister: "The Master is come, and calleth for thee." Mary ran quickly to Jesus and fell down at his feet. "Lord, if thou hadst been here, my brother had not died." Jesus was deeply moved by her sorrow and asked where Lazarus had been buried. "Lord, come and see," they said. Then Jesus wept and the Jews said, "Behold, how he loved him." But others criticized: "Could not this man, that opened the eyes of the blind, have caused that even this man should not have died?"

"Jesus, therefore, again groaning in himself cometh to the grave. It was a cave and a stone lay upon it. Jesus said, Take ye away the stone, Martha. The sister of him that was dead saith unto him, Lord by this time he stinketh, for he hath been dead four days. Jesus said to her: Said I not unto thee, that if thou wouldst believe, thou shalt see the glory of God? Then they took away the stone from the place where the dead was laid. And Jesus lifted up his eyes and said, Father I thank thee that thou hast heard me. And I knew that thou hearest me always; but because of the people which stand by I said it, that they may believe that thou hast sent me. And when he had thus spoken, he cried in a loud voice, Lazarus, come forth. And he that was dead came forth, bound head and foot with graveclothes: and his face was bound about with a napkin. Jesus saith unto them: Loose him and let him go."

The precision and force of St. John's narrative cannot fail to strike the reader and it may be noted, too, that his references to Martha and Mary correspond exactly with the psychologically convincing portraits which St. Luke has drawn of these two sisters; the one, an outspoken, determined woman, a believer, certainly, but clearly of the strong-minded sort, never backward in speaking her mind: the other, gentle, submissive and completely trusting. Yet St. Luke does not record the raising of Lazarus and St. John makes no earlier reference to the household at Bethany so that the striking similarity of the persons in the two different accounts must be held as a proof of their truth. The psychology of Jesus is observed with the same true insight; as a man, Jesus is so moved by the death of his friend that he bursts into tears, the only tears of Christ recorded in the entire Gospel save those which he sheds when he prophesies the fall of Jerusalem (Luke xix, 41). We read also that "he groaned" at the moment of performing the miracle as though the God present in him shook the bonds of flesh. How lifelike too is the practical Martha with her reminder that the corpse would stink! (A French primitive painter, Gerard de St. Jean, whose "Raising of Lazarus" is in the Louvre, shows one of the bystanders holding his nose.)

Archaeology has not added much to the concrete detail. At the little village of El-Azarieh, on the side of Bethany, the name of which in itself is a reminder of the miracle, visitors are shown the tomb, but there is nothing to guarantee that it is the one from which Lazarus arose; it is just one of many similar graves in Palestine. These are nothing like the formal tombs depicted by the Old Masters in representing the scene; they are simply small chambers hollowed out of the rock, sometimes with a small vestibule, and they are closed by rolling a heavy stone up to the opening. The bodies are not enclosed in coffins, but are simply swathed in wrapping impregnated more or less with aromatic spices, so that it can well be imagined that after four days they certainly would smell.

The story of the raising of Lazarus has always had a strong hold upon the Christian imagination, far greater than that of similar miracles which Christ performed earlier in Galilee. This may be partly due to the detail and the remarkable literary quality of the Johannine text. Of Lazarus, subsequently, we know nothing, but a long cherished tradition in the south of France represents him, with his sisters Martha and Mary, as bringing the Gospel to Provence. Of the innumerable pictorial representations of his restoration to life, we may mention Nicolas Froment's, with its exquisite detail and sense of the miraculous; the Grotto at Padua, naively drawn perhaps but so touching with its corpse swaddled like a new-born baby as it awaits its second birth; the lovely gold and rose picture by Maurice Denis, with Mary laying her hand on Christ's arm in an instinctively feminine gesture of surprise. But of them all, perhaps the somber magnificent genius of Rembrandt comes nearest the reality. One of his drawings in the Bibliothèque Nationale shows Christ with his arm upraised facing the tomb, bringing forth the dead from the darkness into the light, with a tremendous gesture of absolution and blessing.

The event, recorded with such precision of detail, is not easily explained away. Renan, in the first edition of his *Life of Jesus* (1863), disposes of it by the suggestion that Lazarus had a partial syncope or that it was a trick devised by the two sisters to promote the renown of Jesus. In the third and definite edition, published four years later, he says that the story arises from a misunderstanding of something Jesus said to his disciples when they asked him to perform a miracle which would convince the crowd. "Even if they saw Lazarus raised from the dead they would not believe."—Jesus might have said some such words and from this the story that Lazarus had been raised from the dead might easily have arisen! An historical method resting on this sort of hypothesis seems to us extremely hazardous.

The position of the account of this miracle in St. John's Gospel is one of great significance. Not merely do the recorded facts establish that Jesus deliberately committed himself by the performance of this miracle just outside Jerusalem in the presence of a great many witnesses, that it was meant to provoke the outburst which it did provoke, but there is also a deep supernatural significance. The affirmation, "I am the Resurrection and the Life," uttered only a few days before that last tragic week when Jesus himself was to die, carried tremendous weight. To Lazarus, death was only a passing incident which would not rupture the course of his existence and so, beyond the gathering of the night, the faithful are promised that the light will come. The miracle of Lazarus was not only the final testimony to the divinity of Christ; it foreshadowed another and a greater miracle, Christ's own victory over the tomb.

Predictions of the Passion

Leaving Martha, Mary and the restored Lazarus to their happiness, Jesus left Bethany, went on to Ephraim, the Taiybeh of today, some twenty-five miles off. It may be that he did not want to arrive in Jerusalem until the actual week of the Passover; it may be that he wanted to go to some such solitary place to give his disciples their final instructions, a theory which is strengthened by the fact that he had just taught them the Lord's Prayer. It is unlikely that he took the too-frequented main road which goes by the outskirts of Jerusalem; probably he chose the loop by Jericho and the Jordan valley, as he did on his return. As he came back from Ephraim, after a short stay, accompanied by the disciples who were more and more amazed at his temerity and who "as they followed, were afraid," they must all have felt the menace of Jerusalem, invisible to the eye but pressing upon the spirit, high above them to the right on the topmost of the three ledges of rock by which the plateau descends to the river bed and the Dead Sea.

"Behold, we go up to Jerusalem," said Jesus, "and the Son of Man shall be delivered unto the chief priests and unto the scribes; and they shall condemn him to death and shall deliver him to the Gentiles. And they shall mock him, and shall scourge him, and shall spit upon him and shall kill him: and the third day he shall rise again." (Mark x, 33-34; Matt. xx, 17-19; Luke xviii, 31-34.) It was not the first time that Jesus had referred to his own death. Twice, in Galilee, he had spoken of it. Immediately after St. Peter's confession of faith and his solemn ordination: "Thou art Peter and on this rock . . ." he had told them: "The Son of Man must suffer many things and be rejected by the Elders, the chief priests and scribes, and be slain and be raised the third day." (Luke ix, 22.) He had repeated the sinister and mysterious prophecy just after the Transfiguration, as if he feared the disciples should misinterpret that awe-inspiring scene: "The Son of Man is delivered into the hands of men, and they shall kill him; and after that he is killed, he shall rise the third day." (Mark ix, 31.)

But although a third prediction was more explicit and more detailed, it still remained obscure to the disciples: "And they understood none of these things, and this saying was hid from them, neither knew they the things which were spoken." (Luke xviii, 34.) Men are always reluctant to understand anything which is displeasing and they must have found it difficult to believe that tragedy could enter into their lives here in this place where nature seemed so benign, with the tender green of the corn and the barley in the fields around them, the new moon above them in the night sky, the anemones, the iris and the gladioli flowering along their path, and, above all, the Master here beside them, alive and well, more powerful than any prophet of old, able even to raise the dead.

"If God would not permit the sacrifice of Isaac," the Talmud was to say later on, "would he permit the murder of his Son, without wrecking the universe?" Probably the Apostles thought much the same, and found the thought reassuring, pushing their fears aside. At heart, too, they probably still held to the old belief that the reign of the Messiah meant glory, not suffering, and perhaps even that they, his faithful disciples, would share in it. There is even a certain wry humor in their lack of understanding. "Then came to him the mother of Zebedee's children with her sons"—probably that Salome who had generously supported Jesus—"worshipping him and desiring a certain thing of him. And he said to her, What wilt thou? She saith unto him: Grant that these my two sons may sit, the one on thy right hand, the other on thy left in thy kingdom." (Matt. xx, 20-24; Mark x, 35-41.) Obviously they had understood nothing, neither that the last shall be first nor that whoever wishes to enter into the kingdom must abase himself here below. But Jesus showed no anger at this manifest blindness for the patience of God's love is infinite. He only repeated what he had said already, that the Son of Man came not to be ministered unto, but to minister, and to give his life a ransom for many. (Mark x, 45; Matt. xx,

25-28.) He tried to hold up before them, in contrast to their dream of false glory, the image of the suffering Messiah, the Redeemer, the Sacrificial Victim, whom Isaiah and Daniel had foretold. Very soon he was to say it finally, unmistakably, on the evening of the Last Supper: "This is my body, which is given for you . . . this is my blood, which is shed for you." And even in that hour, they were not to understand.

Yet there was one who, guided less by intelligence than by that intuition through which women so often see clearly the secrets of the heart, was to confirm, by a gesture, the prediction of her Master and to show that she, at least, had understood.

After leaving Jericho, where he restored the sight of two blind men and had dinner with the worthy publican Zaccheus, Jesus took the Jerusalem road and came to Bethany, where a man known as Simon the Leper—possibly one whom Jesus had cured—begged him to dine at his house. According to the fourth Gospel, this was six days before the Feast of the Passover, which in that year fell upon a Friday, so that it would be Saturday, April first of the year 30, when Jesus accepted Simon's hospitality. Entertaining on the Sabbath was not forbidden; indeed, especially in the evening, it was regarded as suitable.

The meal proceeded, Martha serving, assiduous, devoted, a little fussy, just as we have seen her in the two earlier episodes. She would be wearing, most probably, a tunic of fine linen, perhaps embroidered in gold and her hair would be braided. The guests, of course, would be reclining on couches in the oriental fashion and not sitting upright at table, as Western painters have generally shown them. Lazarus, who had been brought back to life, sat with the guests. Then a woman came in with an alabaster jar in her hand; it was Mary, the fervent, meditative Mary, whose portrait has been so admirably drawn in the Gospel. The jar contained "a pound of ointment of spikenard, very costly." She opened the vase and poured the ointment—"on his head," according to St. Mark and St. Matthew and "on his feet" according to St. John, drying them with her hair, and the perfume filled the house.

"Why was not this ointment sold for three hundred pence and given to the poor?" The disagreeable voice was that of Judas Iscariot who kept the communal purse for the Master and his disciples, not too scrupulously, according to St. John. Several of the disciples must have agreed with him for Mary was clearly very much hurt. "Why trouble ye the woman?" said Jesus. "For she hath wrought a good work upon me. For ye have the poor always with you, but me ye have not always. For in that she hath poured this ointment on my body, she did it for my burial. Verily, I say unto you, Wheresoever this gospel shall be preached in the whole world, there shall also this, which this woman hath done, be told for a memorial of her." (Matt. xxvi, 6-13; John xii, 1-10; Mark xiv, 3-9.)

Certainly this prediction has been amply fulfilled for there is no Christian who does not remember and venerate the love and faith of this woman, who dried the feet of Christ with her flowing hair. The grotto of Saint Baume in Provence commemorates the legend that she lived there after Christ's death. Jean Fouquet, in one of his most exquisite miniatures, shows her on her knees in the middle of the group, her eyes closed, completely indifferent to the attitude of those around her, whether curious, surprised or hostile, absorbed in her offering as a mystic in contemplation.

The truth of this episode, which is reported by two of the synoptics and by St. John, is confirmed also by the truth of the particulars given, material and psychological. It was the custom in the Orient, as in ancient Rome, to offer perfumed unguents to honored guests. Vases like those which Mary carried are depicted in Syria, Greece, and Pompeii; it would be a *lecythus* with a long neck, which Mary broke to release the contents. Pliny the Naturalist tells us that alabaster is the best material to retain intact the strength of the perfume. Spikenard was made from a humble little plant like a brown moss and many pounds had to be crushed to obtain a few drops of the essential oil. It was the most costly of the perfumes of the time and the most in demand. There were cheaper imitations, which is why both St. Mark and St. John refer to it as "authentic" in the original Greek; the Vulgate has flattened this out by translating the word as "pure."

When we turn to the psychological details, it is sufficient to consider the portrait of Judas Iscariot, who betrays here his sordid preoccupations and whom Jesus rebukes sharply. According to St. Matthew and St. Mark, he goes immediately after this scene to conspire with his Master's enemies. We look for some trait which may help us to understand his somber determination; was he, solely, the avaricious and dishonest creature whom St. John describes? A year earlier, immediately after his return from Trachonitis, Christ had said to the apostles: "One of you is a devil." The Judas we shall see in the tragic days to come, in the Satanic role he has to play, is recognizable as the man who speaks in the scene of the anointing at Bethany.

There is one insoluble problem connected with this event. Was Mary, the sister of Lazarus, who anointed the feet of Jesus while he was dining with Simon the Leper, the same as that unknown "woman which was a sinner" who figures in a similar episode in Galilee, when Jesus was dining with another Simon? (Luke vii, 36-50.) St. Luke alone reports the earlier instance; the other three Evangelists report the second. Some of the early Christian Fathers, like Clement of Alexandria, held that St. Luke's version is a repetition of the same incident, but the Catholic Church distinguishes between the two episodes, considering that Mary might have heard of the touching gesture of the unknown Galilean woman and have wished to repeat it. If there was only one anointing, then the unknown sinner and Mary of Bethany were one and the same woman, but nothing in the Gospel indicates that the sister of Lazarus had led a disorderly life. Another theory which has been advanced is that the "woman which was a sinner" was that "Mary called Magdalene, out of whom went seven devils," and who St. Luke (viii, 3) mentions with others as contributing to the support of Jesus and his disciples. This seems entirely in keeping with the character of that generous-hearted woman of whom Christ said that she would be forgiven because she loved much (Luke vii, 47). The expression "of Magdala" is capable of more than one interpretation. Magdala, which is called Medjel today, is a little town by the shore of Lake Tiberias, and by a play upon the Aramaic word it might also mean "the perfumer."

There is no doubt, however, that it is Mary Magdalene whom we meet in the shadow of the tomb on the morning of the Resurrection; it was unquestionably she who found the tomb empty, who gave the news to the apostles and who herself received the angels. Yet the striking scene, in which the risen Lord calls her by name: "Mary!" and she responds at once: "Rabboni" (Master), is so reminiscent of that Mary of Bethany whom we have seen sitting at the feet of Christ, wholly given up to love and wonder. The majority of the best qualified exegesists, including Bossuet and Mabillon, distinguish the three women, the unknown sinner, Mary of Bethany and Mary Magdalene. But a persistent legend, perhaps without historical foundation but not without spiritual insight, has always united them. A young Dominican priest, Fr. Lataste (1832–1869), after working among women prisoners in the county jail, founded a congregation where repentant women could be rehabilitated and called it the Order of Bethany in memory of the sinner whom Christ forgave and the mystical sister who chose the better part.

In the Gospel, however, the two scenes are recounted with a very different emphasis. The anointing in Galilee definitely contrasts the love and self-abnegation of the sinner with the stiff self-sufficiency of Simon the host, that typical pillar of respectability. The anointing at Bethany, too, is an expression of veneration and love but it is primarily symbolical of what is about to happen. It was "against the day of my burying that she hath kept this"; this woman alone had some mysterious prescience of the mystery which was about to burst upon the sight of the world. It was perhaps the same faith and the same inner divination which was to lead her to the empty tomb; we do not know. But her gesture in recklessly pouring out the precious unguent never fails to move the heart and to remind us that, only eight days later, other oils and spices would be poured out in a different fashion, upon the body of the Crucified.

CHAPTER EIGHT

A SIGN THAT SHALL BE SPOKEN AGAINST

The Fate of the Man-God

BY THE TIME now reached in our narrative, that is, toward the end of March in the year 30, Jesus had given the world the essentials of his doctrine. What remained to be accomplished was the event which was to give the ultimate meaning to his doctrine, the voluntary sacrifice of the living God. The last stages were to be passed in an atmosphere very different from that of the two years during which we have followed his life. The happiness and the stimulating tasks of the apostolate fade into the darkness of that last tragic week, when we watch the daily growth of the hatred which menaces him and see the figure of the Messiah approaching the supreme revelation in the dark gleam of suffering and death, when the truth of a man always blazes into light.

The relation between the man and his life, the teaching of Christ and the tragedy on Calvary toward which the Gospel narrative is leading us, is not fortuitous. A man's death is rarely simply an accident, a turn of chance unrelated to the life with which it is bound up, casting no gleam of significance upon it. "Grant every man, O Lord, his own death; the death he bears within him," said Rainer Maria Rilke. Above all men, Jesus bore his death within him. His death was at once an explanation and a promise, going back long before his birth, before the prophecy of the Venerable Simeon, back into the long past when Adam and Eve were first tempted, and fell. In terms of history we can say that the death of Jesus stemmed from the position which he had taken up in the world in which he lived, but in the supernatural order it was the fulfillment of the divine intention.

It had been said of Jesus and his teaching that it was to be "a sign which shall be spoken against."[1] Certainly the strong opposition which his teaching aroused is in one sense sufficient to explain the tragedy, but to the Christian, and to Jesus himself, this cause was only secondary and the men who brought it about were only instruments of destiny. When Mary of Bethany, driven by some premonition, poured out the precious spikenard mingled with her tears, over the feet of Christ, the plot which was to bring him to the torture was already woven. Doubtless the scribes and Pharisees considered that they had ample cause to proceed against one whose teaching seemed so scandalous to their ears, but although they did not know it their hatred was less efficacious in bringing about the event than in bringing down their own edifice of formulae and observances.

The Message of Jesus

All the great religions have propounded a version of the universal enigma, the human spirit demands this at least of them. The successive civilizations of the world owe their characteristics to the particular form of the world consciousness of their time. An Egyptian of the Middle Period, a Greek of the Periclean age, a subject of St. Louis, and the nineteenth century reader of Kant differ immensely in their degrees of knowledge, their habits and their technical skills. But, above all things, they differ in their outlook on the world. This essential difference of outlook causes the clash of doctrines and philosophies

[1] Luke ii, 34. The new Catholic version by Mgr. Knox (authorized in England) translates: "a sign which men will refuse to recognise," the Douai version, "a sign of contradiction." *Tr.*

and makes it impossible for these differences to be reconciled. In the wars of religion the apparent cause often seems trivial, a dispute over the form of a dogma, a phrase or even a word, but however small it may seem to us, it carried in it a certain image of man's purpose in the world and his destiny.

By his teaching and his acts Jesus had established himself as one of those daring innovators in religious matters who bring men new forms of thought. He said that from him proceeded a truth which had been unknown until he came. He went beyond and above what had been previously taught and he spoke with an authority which could appear only either supernatural or insolent. It cannot surprise us that he and his doctrine should arouse violent opposition; the only suprising thing is that the opposition took over two years to become effective.

The teaching of Jesus, as understood by Christians of all ages, is a total philosophy which, under very simple forms, explains the mystery of living: all morality is based upon it and all metaphysics. It displays the most profound knowledge of the human heart. A complete polity and sociology can be deduced from it. It would be an intolerable impertinence to attempt to summarize it here. Countless generations have drawn unfailing strength from the four small books in which it is comprised, and of which there is hardly a verse, or even a phrase, which has not given some questioning or tormented soul the answer sought. The Gospel indeed is the "Fountain of Eternal Life" from which men and civilizations draw their strength just as in a charming miniature in the Breviary of Charlemagne the Creation is symbolized by a spouting well-stream to which all the familiar animals come to drink. Nevertheless we should perhaps endeavor to show how the Gospel in setting up "a contradiction" brought about the crisis from which "the Sign" would arise, the sign which was lifted up that April night upon the rock of Calvary, the sign of the Cross.

Firstly, this conception of the world derives from a revelation. God had chosen to teach his truth to the world by progressive revelations to a people chosen for this task. The last words of this revelation, then all but complete, were spoken by Christ, "the only begotten son . . . who hath declared him" (John i, 18). "One is your Master, even Christ" (Matthew xxiii, 10). But since men could not understand the truth of his teaching, it was only after his death that "the Spirit of truth is come that will guide you into all truth" (John xvi, 13). Only divine grace, opening the ears and the heart, can enable men to penetrate the meaning of the revelation.

This God, conceived as one in three persons, the Father, the Son and the Holy Ghost, has created man, but not as the pawn of an implacable destiny, his acts determined for him. The purpose of the Creation, on the contrary, is that man should use the conscience and the freedom with which he has been endowed to discover God and to serve him. For God is infinitely good; he is our Father. The whole visible world proclaims his goodness and man, with his special endowment, is called to participate in the harmony of the divine intention, as he did in his original state of innocence to which he strives to return. He cannot, because he has sinned; he has disobeyed God's laws and brought into the world the germ of mortal disharmony. All the evils which man suffers, beginning with the flagrant disgrace of mortality, are the logical consequences of his error. In this sense, sin and death are synonymous—"the prick of sin is death," St. Paul was to say—just as sin and injustice, sin and disorder, sin and misery are all synonymous.

But God, in his infinite mercy, had pity on the creature who had turned against him, and he sent on earth his own Son, the second person of the Trinity, who was incarnated and made man exactly like any one of us. The role of this "Christ," the "Messiah," the Lord's Anointed, is thus dual. Jesus, in whom God was made man, brought the doctrine of salvation and realized in himself the model of visible perfection. The fundamental doctrine of Christianity is this union of morality and theology; the Christian's one aim is to recover eternal life and to graft himself, through Christ, onto the stem of God: *Esse cum Christo.*

Yet, this is not all. Christ is not only the supreme teacher and the supreme example. In expiation of the faults of mankind he gave his blood as a sacrificial victim. His blood redeemed the fallen creature and opened up the way of Grace. The living God, who died in the most degrading condition, has taught mankind to despise earthly values and to esteem those virtues of humility and sacrifice which the world disdains. Victorious over death in his Resurrection as he had been over sin in his life, he has conferred upon us all the promise of survival; the faithful, in accepting Christ's sorrows and his Cross, have acquired through the promise a share in his resurrection.

How can man identify himself with Christ? Only from within, because to God who knows all things we are only the measure of our secret thoughts. The forms and ceremonies of religion are not without use, because they uphold a man and support his weakness, but they are not the essence. To show ostentation in religious observance is to court condemnation: "When thou fastest, anoint thy head," "when thou doest alms, let not thy left hand know what thy right hand doeth." Do not "cast out the mote in thy brother's eye and ignore the beam in thine own." The realization of his own faults is the first step in the effort demanded of man. Then, following Jesus, he must seek to "be perfect as the Father is perfect," and this requires an interior transformation.

The interior transformation, the necessity of being "born again," is the *alpha* and *omega* of the teaching of Christ. The Greek "*metanoete*" used in the Gospel does not mean "repent ye" but "be ye changed." *Metanoia* is "conversion" in the literal sense, the complete changing of the interior self, the *mutatio mentis*. It is not a mere change of behavior but a seizing of the evil in the place where it is rooted, in the dark zone of the interior consciousness, in the swarming of instincts and passions from which arise our determinations and our acts. We have to make the interior self divine by imitation of the divine nature. Responsibility begins before the act—with the intention: the lustful look and the angry impulse, where the soul does not respond to the divine transformation but is dragged down by the weight of worldly and fleshly things.

The means by which this transformation may be achieved are faith, sacrifice and love. Faith is the first requirement of Christian effort "for therein is the righteousness of God revealed" (Romans i, 17). Faith in God and his providence; faith in the wisdom of his incomprehensible designs; faith in Christ and in his supernatural mission; faith in the Holy Ghost from whom derives the supreme understanding of all things, which is why blasphemy against the Holy Spirit can not be forgiven. Man is free to believe; he can put himself in the state in which he may receive faith, but faith remains a gift for which his free will must prepare acceptance. Faith is powerful, it can "remove mountains," it is the force to which God himself responds.

If he is to put into practice those virtues which faith plants in his soul, man must be prepared to sacrifice all that binds him to earth, the servitude of the human condition. He must escape from the demands of ease, comforts and the agreeable things of life. He must break the domination of wealth, that most tangible sign of materialism, he must escape from the dominion of his vices and his passions, the realm where sin and evil reign.

But more especially must he learn to love, for in a sense love contains the other requirements. The law of love is absolute and universal, the direct command of God, the supreme focus of love from whom love goes out to the humblest and least worthy of his creatures. If the first command is to love God, the second is to love one's neighbor as oneself. Who is my neighbor? Anybody; the man I instinctively dislike on sight; the man who bores me, the enemy I would like to hurt but am exhorted to embrace. "Though I speak with the tongues of men and of angels . . . though I give my body to be burned and have not charity, it profiteth me nothing." (I Cor. xiii.) It is a hard law, going right against the inclinations of our hearts.

At the end of all his efforts, the believer will receive his reward. Or rather, he will have had his reward, because it comes from the efforts themselves, it is that mysterious Kingdom of God, at once within and without, present and to come. It is within, because whoever possesses it has succeeded in establishing Christ's peace within himself. It is visible without in the persons of countless living Christians. In the present because, in these two aspects, the Kingdom of God is manifest. And it will be established in the days to come, when the wheat will be separated from the chaff, good from evil, the just from the unjust, when the Savior will appear in all his glory, attended by his angels, and shall separate men "one from another, as a shepherd divideth his sheep from the goats." (Matthew xxv, 31-2.) "Then shall the righteous shine forth as a sun in the Kingdom of their father," and the unjust shall go to "eternal fire." The Kingdom of God is inaugurated in time and prolonged into eternity.

This is the substance of the revelation of Jesus. A human instrument has been charged with the task of conserving and transmitting it. This is the Church, the first image, however imperfect, of the sublime realization of the Kingdom which is to come. It is open to all men, without exception, without consideration of race or condition, on the sole condition that they all make the doctrine of Jesus their own and that they will strive toward that identification with him which will give them a part in his righteousness. The Church is the guardian of those rites whose origin we have seen in the Gospel: baptism and the Eucharist in particular. She gathers in universal brotherhood all who desire to be one with Christ. The Church is one, unique and eternal, for "Heaven and earth shall pass away but my words shall not pass away," said Jesus (Matthew xxiv, 35.)

This is the pattern of living from which derive the Christian and his conception of the world. This doctrine, this drama of which every man is at once actor and spectator, unites the merits which the heart and the mind may acquire through their own efforts, with those which Christ bought for humanity by his own sacrifice. Its purpose is to transform the heart, to bring about God's Kingdom on earth, which is the union of souls through love. This doctrine was not formulated by a school; it was given by a person whose goodness is so striking, whose wisdom is so impressive, that he is, in the fullest sense, a model. We have the testimony of his disciples—his own, too—as a witness to the truth which he brought, and of the supernatural events which form part of the Christian belief. We know that the forces of nature yielded to him, and the inmost secrets of the soul. Out of all this, so rich, so complex and so exalted, arises that *contradiction* which Jesus indicated.

The Permanent Contradiction

"What is now called the Christian religion," said St. Augustine, "had not ceased to exist since the creation of mankind and up until the time Christ himself came in the flesh." This statement throws a powerful light upon "the sign of contradiction." To the Christian, the teaching of Jesus is not a philosophical system evolved by the brain of a man of genius, but a revelation by God not merely of *one* truth but of *the* eternal truth, that which men have at all times desired, sought and sometimes approached, but which had never been formulated in its entirety. Even more than his message, the figure of Jesus himself outstrips the confines of time and space. The drama of the Redemption is an historical event which happened at a time and in a place precisely known; it is also a permanent element in the eternal drama of mankind which is forever going on in the secret places of our hearts. "Jesus will be in agony until the end of the world," writes Pascal. Every sin committed in every moment of the centuries drives the nails into the hands of the Crucified.

From this derives an essential element of the opposition to Jesus. The historian considering the conflict of paganism and Judaism at the time can isolate this element or that as contributing to the antagonism but it is not there that we must look for the first and most decisive reaction, but in that permanent *contradiction* that is in the teaching of Jesus. The Jews of his time were not the only people to sense it; the forces which inspire modern man to rebel against the teachings of the Gospel are an echo of those which hurled themselves upon Christ while he lived.

Hatred of Christ exists: that hatred of which we see so many manifestations in the account of his trial and death. It is not extinct. It would not be too difficult today to find another crowd which would echo the abominable demand which resounded in the hall of Pilate: "Crucify him." Yet this hate seems so incomprehensible, focused on a man whose whole life, whose whole teaching, was preoccupied with love. But not when we remember the secret promptings of men's hearts.

Jesus, in his acts and in his words, cannot cease to pass judgment on us. He obliges men to do what they least wish, to examine themselves in the nakedness of their wretchedness, to recognize the nothingness of themselves. Is there anyone of us who has not fully earned his rebuke, who of us has never made a false image of himself, sought a high place for himself, passed on a burden to another? We all know too well what is meant by "hardness of heart." Everything which Jesus taught goes against the natural inclination of man to follow his passions. This is probably true also of any moral system worthy the name, but none has gone so far in its insistence upon renunciation, and in the obligation to make life run counter to the natural instincts.

As the judge, the moral reformer with whom no compromise is possible, Christ always arouses antagonism. Even today the majority of those who reject the Christian faith do so not for intellectual or philosophical reasons but because they are incapable of re-making their lives in harmony with the Gospel teaching. The first and most implacable enemies of Christ were the Pharisees, those whom he called "hypocrites" and "whited sepulchres." They must indeed have been shocked, these solemn respectable gentlemen, accustomed to the good opinions of their fellows, stiff with the pride of self-satisfaction, when they found themselves the target of this merciless indictment; they had thought themselves safe in their pious observances, but Jesus unmasked them and stripped them naked. What must have been the feelings of those who brought to him the woman taken in adultery, when they received the lash of his judgment in that quiet terrible phrase: "Let him that is without sin among you." The Jews would find later theological and political grounds on which to attack Jesus but the root of their hatred was in that fury which arises in us when someone discovers something we would wish to keep hidden, a fury which is stronger if a voice within us echoes the accuser's words.

It can be said that in this respect Jesus followed the normal destiny of the Prophets who, throughout the Old Testament, paid for their audacities with their lives. To be "stoned, sawn asunder, slain with the sword . . . destitute, afflicted, tormented" (Hebrews xi, 36) had often been the lot of the Hebrew prophets. Jesus himself called the Jews of his time "the children of them which killed the prophets" (Matt. xxiii, 31). Uriah the prophet had been martyred in the days of King Joachim. Jeremiah was probably put to death by his compatriots enraged by his continual, and just, recriminations. The murder of John the Baptist was the result of the enmity of an adulteress whom he had attacked. Jesus had dared to say more than any man had dared, and in the complex of antagonisms lined up against him, the primordial motive was nothing more nor less than the eternal hatred of Evil for Good, the spirit of darkness warring against the Light.

The Problem of the Miracles

We must, however, take into account one great difference between modern man and Christ's contemporaries when considering the more profound causes of the opposition to him. The doctrine of Christ had not merely been taught by him and exemplified in his life, it had been attested by a number of extraordinary manifestations which, more than anything else, constituted "signs of contradiction."

The fact of the miracles is indissolubly tied up with the

Gospel and it would be foolish to deny it. The passages describing the miracles have passed the textual critics, they are as well established as any others, they are written in the same style, they are indissolubly woven into the drama of the Gospel story. Certain developments—the conversion of the disciples, for instance—are perfectly logical if the miracles are admitted and incomprehensible if they are rejected. Christ's very opponents admitted them—Herod (Matt. xiv, 1-23) and even the Pharisees (John xi, 47-48). And though they sometimes said, "he casteth out devils through the Prince of the devils," they never denied that he did cast them out.

Christ himself instanced his miracles as proof of his divine mission: "The works that I do bear witness of me, that the Father hath sent me" (John v, 36). Forty-one times in his life we read of these "great things," "wonderful things," "strange things," "signs" and "works" (the words vary but the facts remain) by which he proves his supernatural power, to say nothing of many prophetic statements, readings of the heart and other manifestations of superhuman capacities. "A Catholic," writes Fr. Allo, "must believe not merely in the *possibility of miracles* but in the objective and supernatural reality of certain miracles accomplished in history, and most precisely of the miracles of the Gospel."

But it would be useless to deny that one of the chief causes of the resistance to the Gospel today is not so much an objection to its moral content as to the body of strange facts which mark the life of Jesus. It must be admitted that today and for many the miracles are an obstacle to belief rather than an incentive. The modern intelligence, fashioned in the so-called scientific mould, is disconcerted by a miracle. Even among those who are not frightened away by the idea of the supernatural one senses awkwardness, uncertainty and hesitation, a "why?" or a "perhaps."

Skeptics have adopted a variety of attitudes toward the miracles of Jesus, ranging from the flat rejection of the pure rationalist to the hesitant dogmatism of Renan who, while admitting the possibility of miracle in itself, refused to accept those of the Gospel. The problem is not within the scope of this book and indeed the various explanations advanced from time to time are not very important since to deny a miracle is in a sense to explain it by bringing it into the order of natural phenomena, or rather phenomena which science regards as natural. Some of those "explanations" are derisory, such as that which dismisses the miracles as pious fictions. The more subtle ones have recourse to psychology, suggestion or faith healing. It is not inadmissible that the *method* of certain miracles can be so explained but not the force which motivated them. Nothing is really solved by saying that the power of the personality of Jesus was so great that it could persuade a paralyzed man to reconstitute the muscles of his arm. In the perspective of our times the question is: did Jesus, *in his time,* because he wrought miracles, necessarily arouse antagonism to his teaching and to his person?

The answer is, No. The spiritual atmosphere in which Jesus lived and taught was quite different from our own. For at least two centuries we have grown up in an atmosphere of rationalism; science and determinism are in the air that we breathe and for many people today "progress" resides in the elimination of the supernatural under the pretext of conquering superstition. It was not so in the ancient world. The Greek rationalist philosophers did not exclude divine intervention on earth. The pagan world accepted it as a matter of course, with every attendant superstition. Such evidence of skepticism in the ancient world as has come down to us is directed less against divine power than against its absurd parodies in popular tradition.

It can even be said that the antique world was plunged in the miraculous. The Greeks and Romans would undertake no great enterprise without consulting the Gods. Every religious center had its Oracle, Delphi, Delos, Olympus, where the future was revealed to those who consulted them. Beneficent deities also performed miraculous healings, the chief of these being Asclepius, who had shrines at Cos, Pergamum, even in Rome itself, on an island in the Tiber. The center of the cult, however, was at Epidauras in the Peloponnesus, on a splendid site amid pine covered hills. It was usual for the votary to pass the night in a portico of the Temple and the god would come in a dream to cure the suppliant; but sometimes the cures were performed through the media of the animals sacred to Asclepius; his dogs, for instance, were supposed to give sight to the blind by licking their eyelids. Many votive tablets, recording gratitude for these cures, have come down to us. And we all know, of course, that at strange phenomena, such as metamorphoses, miraculous transportation, the unleashing and calming of tempests, and so on, the Olympian gods, especially Zeus, were unrivaled.

It would be absurd, of course, to make any kind of comparison between the miracles of Jesus and those commonly believed in the pagan world. The radical difference between them is immediately apparent and not only because of the puerility of some of the "cures" attributed to Asclepius, such as, for instance, the story of Aristagora, a sufferer from tapeworm, who saw in a dream "the son of god" remove the sufferer's head, plunge his arm into her body to pull out the worm, then, not knowing how to replace the head, call upon the god himself for assistance. This might be hard to believe, if it were not confirmed by an inscription that the worthy woman was relieved of her unwanted guest. The grossest commercialism also flourished in the cult. A magistrate from Athens cured of dyspepsia by Asclepius, records that, in his dream, the priest of the god said to him, "First pay the fee and then you'll be cured." And this in addition to a lot of haggling and question-begging, to say nothing of the fantastic medicines which the supplicant might be asked to swallow. Jesus asked no money for his miracles; he went through no posturings and he did not make use of the powdered horns of white heifers or vipers' heads crushed in wine! But, beyond all this, it is the spirit and intention of his miracles that distinguishes them so sharply from these impure superstitions, that and their superb simplicity.

We have glanced at the pagan attitude; let us now consider

that of the Jews, who, although they had never succumbed to the base credulity of the heathen around them, knew perfectly well what supernatural intervention meant. The *prophetic* aspect of Jesus's acts was not calculated to surprise them; for five hundred years they had suffered from the silence of the great prophetic voices. Any Jew was willing to believe that God might allow a man the privilege of understanding mysterious things and that such a man might be inspired by God to preach on those things hidden in the hearts of men or awaiting mankind in the shadow of things to come. The history of the Jews derived its significance from the prophetic revelations. As for miracles, the Old Testament abounded with them. Moses, Joshua, Elijah and Daniel had all performed miracles. Jesus, in advancing his miracles as a proof of his mission, was reasoning in the same way as Daniel when he called down fire to burn the sacrifice on Mt. Carmel. The Scribes said that "God multiplied miracles that his name might be praised," and one of the prayers in common usage praised Jehovah "for the wonders performed for our fathers."

So it could not have been because he performed miracles that Jesus was bound to arouse antagonism among the people. Even the Talmud was not to deny his miracles; it is content to say that he borrowed the methods of the Egyptian magicians, whose secret signs he bore on his body, or that he had acquired his power through a sacrilegious theft from the Holy of Holies, which had revealed to him the all-powerful secret name of God. And it is obvious from the reactions of the Galilean crowds to such miracles as the miraculous draught of fishes, the changing of the water into wine and the multiplication of loaves that these did assist the propagation of his doctrine.

Yet we may still ask whether his miracles did not contribute to the growing opposition against him, because of their special character. When we compare them with the miracles of the Old Testament, we realize at once that there is a striking difference. The miracles of Moses, Joshua, Elijah and the other prophets, although they were obviously interventions of the Divine Power, worked through the order of nature. We have to distinguish between the *why* and the *how*. The cause of the miracles, certainly, was God's will to manifest his glory and to aid his servants; the method might be through an earthquake, a tremendous storm, an epidemic, a plague of locusts, or a flash of lightning striking the altar. The miracles of Christ are not of this kind. They are not only inexplicable, which is true of all miracles, but they have no parallel in the natural order. Changing water into wine or multiplying seven loaves to feed thousands of people has nothing in common with any natural phenomenon.[2]

The miracles of Jesus thus appeared as direct manifestations of the creative power of God and those who declined to recognize God in him must have been enraged by them. These wonders pushed them into an untenable position, with their backs to the wall. That is why we can say that the miracles themselves constitute another "sign of contradiction."

But, said St. Augustine, "Jesus never performed miracles for the pleasure of so doing." Every one of his miracles has a precise spiritual purpose, to assist his message, to aid his recognition. Each one is a call to faith, a promise of hope or a witness of charity. The moral and spiritual intention is so clear that, in many cases, Jesus attributes his miracle to the faith of those he cures. "Go, thy faith hath made thee whole." We also read (Mark vi, 5; Matthew xiii, 58) that in Nazareth "he could do no mighty work" because of their unbelief, though St. Mark adds, "save that he laid his hands upon a few sick folk and healed them." The sole purpose of Jesus was to make men understand his message; his extraordinary actions were never designed to advance or to help himself. We know that on the

---

[2] Most of the "explanations" offered ignore this aspect altogether. How can "faith healing" or "collective suggestion" apply to a large wedding party or a gathering of several thousand people? Miracles may be accepted or denied but they cannot be understood. Even theologians like St. Thomas have not been altogether happy in their attempts. Speaking of the multiplication of loaves he says that it was done *"non per creationem, sed per additionem extraneae materiae, in panes conversae"* (*Summa*, 111, 94, xliv), that is, that Christ did not multiply the loaves by creating new matter but by the addition to the interior bread of something which was not bread. With the utmost respect to the great Dominican doctor, it cannot be said that his explanation helps much!

Cross he was to refuse to use his almighty power to deliver himself.

A Messiah endowed with such power that he could suspend the laws of nature could have fired with enthusiasm the proud and sorrowful spirit of the Jews and have made himself easily master of the Promised Land. After the multiplication of the loaves the normal reaction of his friends would be a plot to bring him to the throne. How often do we find the Jews imploring him for "a sign." We can sense the bitterness of disappointment in the Jerusalem crowds which turned against the man who, only a few days before, they had acclaimed so loudly. We cannot fail to recognize the significance of the taunt: "If thou be the son of God, come down from the Cross." "Perform a miracle!" It was not because Jesus performed miracles that the Jewish people were to attack Christ; it was because he had not performed the miracle for which they hoped. The true cause of the contradiction was the teaching of Jesus, the position he took up, and his conception of himself, because whoever is not with him is against him.

The Gospel and Paganism

In isolating what it was in Christ's doctrine which was so entirely new to the world in which it was first preached, we must distinguish between the Jewish and the pagan reaction. After the death of Christ his doctrine spread throughout the whole Empire, while the great majority of the Jews continued to deny him. It was among the Gentiles that the Church took root and it was to prove far easier to convert a pagan than a son of Israel, as St. Paul, with his intuitive genius, perceived.

It is not easy to compare the Gospel-teaching with the current paganism of the Roman empire, so infiltrated by Greek philosophers and oriental cults. We must beware of imposing upon this complex and often contradictory ethos a straitjacket of rigorous logic alien to the modes of contemporary thought. We must be particularly careful not to assess it in the light of principles and dogmas which did not exist in the world before

Christ.[3] So far from consigning all pagans to outer darkness, Christians may profitably consider the many who, without the aid of divine revelation, found the right path, groping toward God, as St. Paul says.

But if there is one conception which should be rejected it is that nineteenth century idea which set up, against the lugubrious religion of Christianity, the Dionysiac gaiety of the pagan world. The care-free pagan, vine-leaved staff in hand, drunk with the joy of living, so prominent in the popular poetic tradition, is a purely literary convention. It is true that many in the pagan world sought happiness in pleasure, in beauty, in sensual love and in the exultation of living. But they knew perfectly well that happiness is fragile, that pleasure has inexorable limits and that over all is the encroaching shadow of oblivion. The characteristic mood of the pagan world is not

[3] "There is no direct trace of the influence of pagan philosophy in the teaching of Christ. It would have been surprising if there had been. When we remember how strenuously, since the time of the Maccabees, the Jewish people had resisted every Hellenizing influence, expressly relegating them to the sphere of religion in order to exclude them, it is inconceivable that so religious a man as Jesus should have imbibed anything from the pagan culture. The Jewish and pagan elements in Palestine existed side by side but they never mixed. There were pagan cities in Palestine, the two Caesareas, Philadelphia, Ptolemais, Hippos, Pella, but pious Jews contrived not to visit them, and we notice that Jesus did the same. The only pagan contamination in Israel was among the very rich, inspired by self-interest or snobbery, and there were not many of these. The problem was so insubstantial that we never find Jesus mentioning it although the ancient prophets had so often to rebuke their people's tendency towards idolatry. As for Greek philosophy, no Galilean peasant could possibly know anything about it. Plato and Aristotle were certainly not expounded in the synagogues. The thesis so often put forward during the last hundred years, that Christianity is a synthesis of oriental mysticisms and Greek thought, might possibly be argued in respect of St. Paul (though not even here with any conclusiveness) but it certainly cannot be advanced in connection with Jesus. Those critics who have determined at all costs to "prove" pagan influence have been reduced to finding analogies between certain phrases of the Gospel and classical literature. For instance, a Latin proverb quoted in the *Satyricon* of Petronius says: "You see the fleas on other people but you don't see the lice on yourself." This may perhaps remind somebody, if he is anxious that it should, of the mote and the beam, but everybody knows that there is a reservoir of popular wisdom common to almost all the world. Other "similarities" which those painstaking searchers have found are simply coincidences arising from the fact that religious exaltation has always expressed itself in much the same language and hence it is not all difficult to find such "influences" even in Brahminism.

joy, but a profound sense of the tragedy of the human condition. The great shrines of antiquity, such as Delphi, convey this with a terrifying force. Throughout classical literature we encounter man in despair, in the most fundamental sense of the term, expecting nothing from life and nothing after death. Whether it be Achilles at the water's edge bewailing his sadness as he goes out to his last fight, or Solon crying, "Call no man happy," or Sophocles sighing, "Unhappy race of mortals, your life is the measure of nothing and no man has any happiness save the illusion of it he himself creates." We remember the old fat God Silenus, surprised by Midas in a rose hedge and constrained to yield up the secret of life. "It is better for man never to be born; the sooner he is born the sooner he goes back to the kingdom of darkness." The most admired hero of the ancient world, repeated again and again, is a young man on whom the gods have bestowed all the gifts of beauty and genius, only to break the stalk when the youth is in full flower. Hope, in the myth of Pandora, is loosed upon the world as the ultimate deceit, the permanent temptation; this is the last word, the final judgment of the pagan mind.

This fundamental despondency derives from the pagan conception of the divine and its relations with mankind, which naturally moulded its view of human destiny. This is where paganism and the Gospel are utterly opposed. Certainly not all the pagan world accepted the caricatures of popular mythology as gods. Many Romans did not regard the Immortals as business men to be bribed into granting favors or benevolent neutrality and many Greeks rejected the notion that the absurd and scandalous fables representing the Olympians as adulterous, brutal and double-dealing, sharing the worse passions of men, conveyed the truth about the divine power. Skepticism was a common reaction: Cicero's *De Natura Deorum* gives the most lucid and convincing reasons for it. What is so astonishing is that, in spite of the frustration of the system, certain innately religious spirits succeeded in giving a deep significance to rites and conceptions which in themselves seem to us so deficient in spiritual richness. "I have weighed everything," says Aeschylus, "and no one except Zeus can free me from the burden of sterile anguish." And Hippolytus's plea to the Goddess Artemis, in its mystical phrases, can move us still today. Undoubtedly there was a reaching out to God among the nobler spirits, but how little they received in return!

The breach between man and the gods of antiquity was absolute. The Olympians came to earth to pursue their own selfish designs but they were completely indifferent to the lot of mankind. The ancient world admitted the majesty of the gods but concluded that it was futile to expect any part in it or to receive from their deities any measure of consolation. The official gods, debased as they were by polytheism and anthropomorphism, were yet incredibly far off and completely dehumanized. Vigny's "oppose a cold silence to the eternal silence of heaven" is in the true pagan tradition.

It is true that the gods of the philosophers [4] are much more exalted conceptions but even they brought little satisfaction to the truly religious soul. There are certainly some passages which seem to anticipate Christian sentiments, such as Plato's Socratic Dialogue on Law. "God comprises in himself both the beginning and the end, the means by which all things are done; justice follows in his wake to take vengeance on all who lack the divine Law. If man is to be happy, he must follow humbly and quietly in his ways." But what God does this refer to?

According to Plato, it is the perfect organizer of the *Politics* and *Timaeus*, the abstract idea of Good, the pure state of understanding. According to Aristotle it is the prime mover, the

---

[4] The Greek philosophers sought to understand the problems of existence on an undeniably high level. But, compared with Jesus, it is clear that they *were* philosophers—leaders of thought—and not religious leaders. They gave understanding but not faith. Many of them, too, were very far from expressing their exalted conceptions in their lives. Socrates was not renowned for the rigor of his morals; he had several children by his concubine Myros, and had acted as a professional money-lender. Although his death was magnificent, it should not be overlooked that he offered to forfeit nearly all his property to escape it. But the teaching of Jesus was not only in words; it was in his life and, also, in his death.

necessary agent, immutable and perfect motion. According to Epicurus, it is that cold harmony in which "all is order and beauty, calm and voluptuous." In the Stoic philosophy God is that anonymous Wisdom manifested in nature, that *logos,* the principle of intelligence which is implied in the universal order. But all this is very remote and unlikely to interest the ordinary man. The individual might reach out to the divine through knowledge, through contemplation, through ataraxia, that annihilation of will common to the Epicurean and Buddhist systems. But nothing came down from this remote and abstract God. When, later on, the great Stoics, Epictetus and Marcus Aurelius, sought a personal god whom they could love, they came up against what seemed an impassable obstacle: union with God presupposed that God existed, that he had Being and that he loved mankind.

Here we see the immense difference between the pagan and Christian systems. The Gospel unveils a God who is at once the Creator, the beginning, the Word, the intelligence of the world, perfect harmony and absolute goodness, yet who is a being we can love and who loved us enough to wish to save us.

This revelation at once makes sense of man's destiny for he is in the hands of this almighty and loving God, so that "everything that happens can be adored," as Leon Bloy said, while in the pagan world the enigma of man in the world was insoluble. The ancient poets had tried to find an explanation: Homer postulated in *Ananke* a terrible and fatal power to whom even the gods must submit. The *Dike* of Aeschylus automatically punished sin; the Demi-urge of Plato followed out with impenetrable logic a design which we do not know. But all these high conceptions came down sooner or later to the blind goddess of fortune with a bandage round her eyes, and astrologers and fortune-tellers were consulted in the hope that they might foretell her uncertain ways. Contrasted with these depressing conceptions, the Gospel teaches us that everyone can determine his own future by his acts, that there is no blind fate which can prevail against the conscious choice.

Among the pagans the destiny of man was strictly confined

to this world inasmuch as their religion made no statement regarding the final end. There were vague myths, which might be accepted or rejected; there was no doctrine. We find certain evidence of a belief in the immortality of the soul, such as the inscription, "Gone back to the eternal light," on a burial tablet and representations of the vine and the ivy, symbols of immortality, on many tombs. But other epitaphs display a total nihilism. There were popular myths like that of the Fortunate Isles or the Kingdom of Hades, where men were reported to live a phantom existence in the form which they had on earth. The conceptions of the philosophers are not much more consoling. The Platonic divinization is merely an intellectual operation and neither the Epicurean return to the elements nor the Stoic fusion with the ether can be said to uplift the mind or offer any recompense for effort compared with the Kingdom of God which all men by their virtues may attain.

But it is the moral values of paganism, even more than its mythology or its metaphysics, which contrast so sharply with the Gospel. The essential law of morality, *kalokagathie,* is a respect for the beautiful and the good. That which is correct is moral; virtue was measured exactly in the sense that we conceive of measuring time or distance exactly. In practice this meant a standard of conduct which was not ignoble but which had certain limitations; it enjoined self-knowledge and deplored excess. "Become what you are," said Pindar, do not seek to exceed. The virtues of piety, order and prudence are necessary to the well-being of society; man should therefore live honorably, remain calm in adversity and in face of death, keeping his self-respect. There is certainly a high conception of personal dignity at the basis of the system but there is also a sense of self-interest, because the practice of this morality is recommended to make life harmonious and happy, and if goodness, beauty and wisdom are synonymous, there is a fourth term which may be equated with them, and that is "profit." "Honesty is the best policy."

The message of the Gospel cracked the shell of egotism and pride which had grown up around this lofty conception.

When it came to the relations of man and man, the society of the ancient world was cruel and hard. Compassion, to Seneca, was "a vice of the heart"; to Marcus Aurelius, a weakness. "Why give alms," says a character in a Latin play, "you are only uselessly prolonging the wretched man's misery." It is natural to hate your enemies. "The most delightful mirth," says Athena to Ulysses in the *Ajax* of Sophocles, "is to laugh at one's enemies." The slave, excluded by definition from the sphere of human consideration, was treated with an indifference barely tempered by the recollection that anyone might be taken in slavery. When we encounter a note of authentic pity in classical literature it springs from some cause as far removed as possible from Christian charity, from a kind of inverted egoism and conscious despair. "I plead for him, although mine enemy," replies Ulysses to the goddess, "because I see in him an unfortunate, bound to an evil destiny. And, looking at him, I see myself, for what are we all, all men living, but phantoms and vain shadows?"

A great many in the ancient world recognized the insufficiency of its religious philosophy and that is why, as we have said in Chapter III, there was a considerable infiltration into Greco-Roman paganism of oriental cults which seemed to provide elements of greater spiritual promise. The gulf between man and the divine was reduced in such cults as those of the Mother Goddess, of Isis and Adonis, there was a definite mystical relation not without spiritual beauty. The votary had a status, he was the relation, the servant, perhaps the chattel of the god, but he could give himself and be received. The limits of this type of mysticism, however, are plainly apparent when we remember St. Paul's: "It is not I who live but Christ in me." This fusion with God can be attained only by the imitation of Christ so that the moral effort unites with the spiritual intention. Nothing like this was ever formulated in the mystery cults of the pre-Christian world. The real object of the votaries of the mystery religions was in fact pragmatic; what they sought was not union with God but personal happiness. Initiation promised this result without necessarily requiring any spiritual renewal from within. Here lies the fundamental difference between pagan and Christian mysticism.[5]

So we can see on what plane there was opposition between the pagan and Christian systems. We can say, as Fr. Lagrange has put it, that the pagan soul "felt the need of the light which the Gospel brought but that it was powerless to express it." In many cases, like that of Pontius Pilate, they were totally unable to make sense of Christ's message; in others, like that of the centurion of Capernaum, they were able to grasp it at once. But very few of them, once they were able to get to the root of Christ's doctrine, would say with Julian the Apostate: "I have read it, I understand it and I reject it." The Roman opposition to Christianity was political rather than moral and because such opposition was not fundamental, but only in fact due to ignorance, the pagan system melted away quickly in the light of the Christian revelation.

The Gospel and Judaism

It was quite otherwise with the Jews. Goethe observed with truth that Christianity was more violently opposed by Judaism than by paganism. We can hate thoroughly only something which we understand thoroughly, something to which we have certain fundamental ties. Family quarrels are like wrestling vipers and it is only theologians of the same religion who really know what hatred is. The Jews pursued Jesus with indefatigable viciousness because they recognized him as one of them-

[5] About the time that Christianity was beginning to penetrate throughout the Roman Empire the doctrines of neo-Pythagoreanism had a considerable vogue. These did provide an actual guide to the spiritual life, a method of devotion and a way of reaching God. "Prayer and sacrifice to God" was recommended by Apollonius of Tyana and the neo-Pythagorean doctrine enjoined a rigorous ascetism, celibacy, prolonged abstinences and silence. It taught that the human being could return to its beginning, which was in God, only by moral effort. But it also taught that matter was evil, the body was therefore impure. It involved, in fact, a renunciation of life. It took no account of human weakness and its hero was essentially a preceptor; he was not the consoler, or the friend, still less the Redeemer.

selves and could therefore the better realize how different he was.

What impression did Christ make upon his Jewish listeners? There would be nothing unusual in his style of oratory; the lyrical tone, the complex word play, the alliterations and antitheses would all be familiar enough. These were the recognizable accents of the prophet. When Jesus set up benedictions against maledictions in the Sermon on the Mount, when he attacked the rich and called down woe upon "those who are full" (Luke vi), the Jewish listener would immediately recall other Bible texts where similar antitheses can be found. "Cursed be Canaan," said Noah. (Gen. ix, 25-27.) "A servant of servants shall he be unto his brethren. God shall enlarge Japheth and he shall dwell in the tents of Shem; and Canaan shall be his servant." "Cursed is the man that trusteth in man," cried Jeremiah (xvii, 5), "and maketh flesh his arm and whose heart departeth from the Lord."

Even the parables, the most original feature of Jesus's preaching, would not seem altogether strange to Jewish ears. Their abrupt, elliptic form, with an inconclusive element, would be as congenial to an oriental audience as it is often disconcerting to us. The formula, "To what shall we liken," which opens many of the parables (Luke xiii, 18; Mark iv, 30) was a favorite in certain rabbinical schools, particularly the one which produced the *Mishna.* The *maschal* was an essential element in the Hebrew technique of persuasive oratory and it was sometimes subjected to fantastic and even absurd contortions.[6]

[6] Here, however, is a simple and beautiful example, taken from R. Johanan ben Zakkai, a Jewish doctor who flourished about the time of the fall of Jerusalem. "It is like a king who invited his servants to a feast but did not fix a precise hour. The wise men dressed in their best and presented themselves at the palace gate. But the fools went on with their own business saying, 'There will be plenty of time to prepare for the feast.' Suddenly the king summoned his servants, the wise men came in ready, the fools were untidy and unprepared. The king was pleased with the wise men and angry with the fools. 'Let those who are robed sit down and eat and drink, but let the others stand outside and wait.'" This is very much like the parable of the wise and foolish virgins; it is not, of course, impossible that certain Christian influences may have crept in.

Jesus quoted the Old Testament constantly, drawing arguments and parallels from it, as for instance when he justified himself for having said he was the Son of God, or his disciples for having plucked ripe grain upon the Sabbath.[7] They are perhaps allusions rather than quotations but they indicate a mind which was thoroughly conversant with the Old Testament and they are found continually throughout the Gospel.

The Jewish listener, therefore, would find nothing disconcerting in the form of Jesus's discourses. He would also, on many points, find himself in agreement with their content. Jesus never rejected the principle which the Jews valued most; he never denied that they were the Chosen People. Indeed he emphasized on many occasions their special mission under Providence. He told the Samaritan woman that "salvation is of the Jews"—an idea which St. Paul, later, was to develop in a passage from his epistle to the Romans (ix, 4), that to the Israelites "pertaineth the adoption, and the glory, and the covenants, and the giving of the law, and the service of God, and the promises."

Jesus never denied or spoke contemptuously of any of the great fundamentals of the Jewish religion, quite the reverse. He spoke with respect and admiration of the Law, the *Torah*, which every pious Jew venerated and loved almost as a living being, calling it "the eldest daughter of God," which the universe itself obeyed and God himself followed. "Think not that I am come to destroy the law, or the prophets; I am not come to destroy but to fulfill. For verily I say unto you, till heaven and earth pass, one jot or one tittle shall in no wise pass from the law, till all be fulfilled. Whosoever therefore shall break

[7] Mgr. Battifol, commenting on this point, says, "Many of the Old Testament references woven into the thread of the discourses of Jesus are probably not in fact actual quotations by Jesus but a sort of concordance instituted by very ancient tradition." In other words, we cannot always be sure whether Jesus directly cited certain passages or whether the narrator of the Gospel, anxious to clarify the teaching, instanced them as a kind of reference. This is also probably true of many comments upon the actual events of Christ's life, as when St. Matthew, recording the flight into Egypt, adds "that it might be fulfilled which was spoken of the Lord by the prophet: out of Egypt have I called my son." (Matt. ii, 15.) The prophecy is in Hosea xi, 1.

one of these least commandments, and shall teach men so, he shall be called the least in the Kingdom of Heaven; but whosoever shall do and teach them, the same shall be called great in the Kingdom of Heaven." (Matt. v, 17-19.) These words sounded sweet to Jewish ears, and not only did Jesus proclaim the excellence of the Law by words, he was careful to follow its most fundamental observances. We see that he celebrated the Passover most scrupulously. One of the *logia* cited by Clement of Alexandria even makes him say: "If ye do not fast in the world, ye shall not find the Kingdom of God; and if ye keep not the Sabbath, ye shall not see the Father."

The very commandment which Jesus put first in his teaching was the historic first commandment of Israel, to love God above all. Jesus emphasized many of the characteristics of the God whom, since Abraham, Israel had always venerated. He was the One God, the Almighty, enthroned in the sky with the earth as his footstool. He was the King, the Judge, the Holy One, the pattern. "Ye shall be holy as I am holy," said Jehovah (Lev. xi, 44; xix, 2; xx, 26; xxi, 6) and Christ almost echoes this in Matt. v, 48: "Be ye therefore perfect, even as your Father in heaven is perfect." It is true that Jesus stressed the Fatherhood of God more than the ancient Jewish sages, and that he introduced a more tender and confiding note, but these sentiments were not unknown among the Jews, who indeed, in their proud boast that they were the children of God, and in their confidence in his protection, had more than once shed their blood.

The moral code which Jesus preached was no more disconcerting to the Jews than his theology, for it was in direct accord with the ancient teaching. The prophets, too, had besought them to pay less heed to formal precepts but to practice a true and living morality in their hearts. "To bow down his head as a bulrush and to spread sackcloth and ashes under him, wilt thou call this a fast and an acceptable day to the Lord? Is not this the fast that I have chosen? To loose the bands of wickedness, to undo the heavy burdens . . . to deal thy bread to the hungry . . . bring the poor that are cast out to thy house, when thou seest the naked that thou cover him." (Isaiah lviii, 5-7.) "Rend your heart and not your garments," said the prophet Joel (ii, 13).

The passage just quoted from Isaiah is one of the most beautiful in the Old Testament, an appeal to the purest sentiments of the heart. Many of the more ruthless features of the Hebrew law, the "eye for an eye" and the calm ferocity with which the Chosen People are enabled to rid themselves of any obstacles on their path, are often cited as instances of the difference between the Gospel teaching and Judaism. But it should not be forgotten that a quite different train of thought runs side by side with this throughout the entire Hebrew teaching. The injunction to love one's neighbor as oneself is found in Leviticus (xix, 17-18). The golden rule of all morality, as set down by St. Matthew and St. Luke (Matt. vii, 12; Luke vi, 31), "Whatsoever ye would that men should do to you, do ye even so to them," is a translation into the affirmative of the negative counsel of Tobit. "Do that to no man which thou hatest" (Tobit iv, 16). "That which thou hatest, do to no man," said also Rabbi Hillel. Although there is a great difference between the positive commandment of Christ in the sphere of morality, it is none the less true that the same sentiment inspires both.

If we examine other features of the Gospel doctrine, such as, for instance, the idea of the "Kingdom of God," their Hebraic origin is equally obvious; we are immediately impressed not by their antithesis but by their resemblance.[8]

---

[8] Even in the case of those precepts which seem to us the very incarnation of Jewish exclusiveness and sterile literalism, it may be observed that Jesus although critical is not altogether in opposition. At the beginning of the famous attack on the scribes and Pharisees in St. Matthew (xxiii) he pays explicit tribute to their doctrine: "The scribes and Pharisees sit in Moses' seat —all therefore whatsoever that they bid you observe, that observe and do, but do not ye after their works, for they say and do not."

We should examine a little more carefully the customary judgments upon Jesus's denunciation of the scribes and Pharisees. The earliest Christians naturally dwelt upon the antagonism between the teaching of Christ and the teaching of the Pharisees because their own bitterest enemies were to be found in that sect. The word "Pharisee" has become a term of abuse, but is this altogether deserved? Is it, in fact, even in accordance with the Gospel? It is

For Israel had been given, under providence, the role of preparing the world for the supreme revelation. Stage by stage, during two thousand years, this small people had come closer and closer to the great truths which the Gospel was finally to reveal. More than this even, it had borne and cherished within its consciousness the image of the Messiah, the Savior. Although the Jews could not, at the decisive moment, recognize in Jesus the living embodiment of their hope, it is none the less true that they gave this hope to the world. In the office of Holy

---

worth noting that Jesus never once denounces any of the Pharisees by name; his charity is so much greater than ours.

Pharisaism was a genuinely religious influence in Israel and its fervent faith had been an immense spiritual asset. The fact that it came to share the fate of all exacting and ascetic doctrines, which is to become sterile, ossified, and spiritually stunted, should not prevent us from estimating fairly its historic services to Judaism. Jesus did not condemn all Pharisees, much less all the scribes and doctors of the Law, many of whom were not Pharisees and could not be accused of "raising still higher the hedge of the Law." The criticisms leveled by Jesus against certain of the Pharisees were not unknown to the Jews of his time, who were well acquainted with "whited sepulchres." Among the seven sects of the Pharisees enumerated by the Talmud are the Shechem–Pharisees who adopted the doctrines out of self-interest as Shechem had in earlier times elected to become a Jew (Gen. xxxiv). Also the "bleeding Pharisees" who made their noses bleed by turning abruptly to face the wall whenever they saw a woman; the "tell me my duty so that I can run to do it" Pharisee; the lugubrious Pharisee who always looked as if he were going to his own funeral . . . and so on. It is easy to read between the lines of the Talmud the hatred which a good many lesser people bore this haughty and disdainful sect.

Yet all the same there are many things in the Pharisaic doctrine which seem to anticipate the Gospel teaching. Renan's idea that "Hillel was the true teacher of Jesus" is a tremendous exaggeration for there is absolutely nothing to suggest that this famous doctor had any direct influence upon the young Galilean from Nazareth. But such words as those of Rabbi Johanan ben Zakkai, "It is not the contact with the dead that causes impurity"—"It is not the water which purifies"—"Charity is above the Law," show clearly that there was a good deal which foreshadowed the Gospel in the teaching of the Pharisees.

The later doctors of the Pharisees during the second and third centuries of the Christian era show a marked agreement with the Gospel. "Whoever gives alms in secret is greater than our father Moses," said Rabbi Eleazar about the year 270, and we find in a Talmud text, "Whoever looks at a woman with an adulterous intention, it is the same as if he had had relations with her." It is impossible to say whether such injunctions embody echoes of the Gospel or are logical extensions of Jewish religious and moral thought, but whoever considers the history of the Jews may find it not altogether impossible to believe that the Pharisees, too, received a part of the divine understanding and may have contributed something toward the progress of the world into the light of Christ.

Saturday, after the Fourth Prophecy, the Church asks God to "grant that all the nations of the world may become the children of Abraham and partake of the dignity of the people of Israel" (*in Israeliticam dignitatem*). How better can we acknowledge the link which binds Christianity to the chosen people of God?

But this link does not explain everything, for the tree which is the Church has more than one root. Great as was the Jewish revelation, it was incomplete, for Christians have always, from the beginning, considered that the divine revelation was completed by Jesus. One of the stained glass windows at Chartres shows the four great prophets carrying four young boys; these are the Evangelists and the symbolism is accurate; for the new link rests upon the old but dominates it. "If the New Testament is potentially contained in the Old," said St. Augustine, "it is from the New that the Old derives its significance." "*Quod Moyses velat, Christi doctrina revelat*," wrote the Abbé Suger, the famous minister of King Louis VI and Louis VII. And upon a statue of St. Paul at St. Trophime, in Arles, there is a similar inscription, "The law of Moses conceals what the teaching of Paul reveals; from the seed given from Sinai the Apostle has milled the flour." The Middle Ages often used this symbol of "the mystical mill"; one of the capitals at Vézelay shows Moses, with a sack upon his shoulders, throwing into the mill the wheat grains representing the ancient Law, while from the other end St. Paul gathers up the flour.

"We are the true race of Israel, according to the spirit," said the Early Christian Fathers, and the first Gentile converts did indeed revere Abraham, Isaac, the Prophets and the Kings as their ancestors. Faithful to this great tradition, Paul Claudel has re-affirmed it today, "These are our true forefathers, not some obscure barbarians from nobody knows where. As a tree is grafted upon an old stock, so are we sons of Abraham, inheritors of the promise of the Covenant. It was addressed to us, the Chosen Race; it was we who came out of Egypt and crossed the Red Sea, we who fought with the Maccabees. The words of Isaiah, Hosea, Ezekiel and Jeremiah are as real and alive to us as on the day they were first uttered. The Bible history is our own and the story of the whole world since is bound up with it." [9]

But we must come back to the consideration of the impression made on his hearers by the claims of Jesus and his disciples to be the authentic heirs and upholders of that progressive revelation which God had given to Israel. "Ye have heard it said," cried Jesus, "but I say unto you . . ." What right had he to say this? "For all the prophets and the law prophesied until John" (Matt. xi, 13): did he mean by this that everything that had gone before, including the preaching of the Baptist, was an incomplete revelation? "I am not come to destroy the Law but to fulfill it": the words must have sounded scandalous to pious Jews, for how could the Law which contained the secrets of God require to be extended or fulfilled? The Law could not be that old bottle into which one dared not pour new wine or that fabric worn threadbare which could not be patched. The pious Jews would feel an instinctive and very natural opposition at the very idea of a new *revelation,* for no man likes to be told to give up beliefs he has long cherished, upon which he has based his life. In the literal sense of the term, the message of Jesus demanded a *conversion* of the Jews.

The message, difficult enough in its very inception, became far more so as it was developed. Certainly Jesus respected the Law; also he had far too great a knowledge of human weakness to be one of those innovators who want to sweep away everything. But the least subtle of his listeners could not help realizing that he did not interpret the Law's requirements in the same way as did the rabbis. The Torah, using the term in its widest sense to cover the immense conglomeration of glosses which had become superimposed upon it by centuries of commentaries and refinements, represented the maximum of observances which a man could possibly carry out. A Jew who could manage to fulfill all of them was sure of salvation. Yet, to a Christian was given the minimum of written command-

---

[9] In an unpublished letter to the author.

ment. But the act committed was not the only breach of it; equally culpable was the intention of the heart. Public behavior counted, certainly, for "woe unto him through whom scandal comes," but more important than this were the secret feelings, thoughts and desires, things which men could never know, but which God knew.

Jesus preached the spirit of religion. He did not reproach the Pharisees for their tenets but for the hypocrisy which was an inevitable result of their sterile legalism. They submitted to these tiresome minutiae while living comfortably in other respects. After all, it was easier to wear phylacteries all day and not to put your hand in your pocket on the Sabbath than to help your neighbor in all circumstances. The casuistry of the doctors had reached the stage where it made nonsense of the spiritual problem. They solemnly debated whether a woman who bounced a baby on her knee violated the Sabbath. Or whether a legal impurity of a vessel could contaminate the water which it contained and whether it could be transmitted to the well from which the water had been drawn. "Ye pay tithe of mint and anise and cummin," said Jesus, "and have omitted the weightier matters of the law, judgment, mercy and faith. Ye make clean the outside of a cup and a platter, but within they are full of extortion and excess." (Matt. xxiii, 23-25.)

Whenever there is conflict between a legal observance and the higher principle of humanity and charity, Jesus taught that the law must give way. He performed miracles of healing upon the Sabbath, which in the Jewish view was an almost unpardonable sin. But he never himself violated the Sabbath or authorized his disciples to do so unless a higher principle was at stake. In the Codex of Beza, which Theodore of Beza presented to Cambridge, there is a verse from St. Luke which the majority of our translations omit: "That day, seeing a man working upon the Sabbath, Jesus said to him, 'Man, blessed are ye if you know what it is that you do; but if you know not, ye are accursed for transgressing the law.' " For in the latter case the man was breaking the law for no reason save that it suited him; but if the former, it meant that he realized the truth that the spiritual sense takes precedence of the mere observance.

Even those rabbinical precepts which seem to foreshadow the Gospel attitude, such as Rabbi Eleazar's "Whoever gives alms in secret is greater than our master Moses," assume, in Jesus's words an infinitely higher significance. The rabbinical injunction was founded on Proverbs xxi, 14; "a gift in secret pacifieth anger," and the comment was: "Thus the recipient of the gift is not wounded in his pride." But Jesus said: "Let not thy right hand know what thy left hand doeth," the pride which had to be, not wounded, but obviated, is the giver's pride in his own generosity.

In the parable about the laborers who came last receiving as much as those who had worked all day, Jesus reminded his hearers of God's supreme right to show mercy, to save everyone who, even at the last moment, calls upon him. God, said St. Paul, will have mercy on whom he will have mercy (Rom. ix, 15). In the Talmud, there is a somewhat similar parable about hired laborers protesting against something they consider unfair and the reply is, "He who came last has done more in two hours than you have done all day"—the legalistic, the reasonable reply, as opposed to the call upon the Holy Spirit.

The teaching of Jesus was directed to making religion more spiritual, more a matter of inward observance. But did this necessarily entail conflict with the Jews? It could indeed be said to form a logical extension of a process which had been going on for centuries. The religious thought of Israel, through Jesus, had developed into a personal, out of a collective, religion, and a moral system out of ritual requirements. In that sense the Gospel was the culmination of the Jewish religious development. But, since the return from Exile, devotion to the letter of the law had become, to the Jews, one of the bases of their national existence, for by putting themselves behind the "hedge" of the Torah they had been able to keep out the menace of idolatry. This explained their excessive attachment to their observances, and a Prophet who required them to go above the Law, even on occasions to violate its precepts, could only be suspect.

In so many things this doctrine of extending the Law and enlarging its application hit them in vulnerable places. The law of love which the new Prophet declared to be transcendental had strange connotations. They were used to an all-powerful and terrible God, the avenger, hidden in mystery, whose very name latter-day Jews dared not pronounce. Jesus defined, in an entirely new way, the relations between God and man. "The conception of God as Father," said Renan, "is the entire theology of Jesus."[10] The God whom Jesus defined was above all things loving and merciful; even his justice is tinged with compassion. He is a God to whom we can give ourselves confidently, as do the lilies of the field and the birds of the air, and by this same confidence and trust, he is mysteriously drawn down to us. It is true that there is some similar teaching in the earlier scriptures but the difference of accentuation is such that a pious Jew, accustomed to prostrate himself in awestruck reverence, would find a certain almost sacrilegious familiarity in the new approach.

Worse even than this; the Father-God is the father of all men. The worst sinner has a right to his mercy, and the sun of his righteousness shines on the just and unjust alike. The heathen are not merely under the shadow of his terrible right hand (which the Jews had known for a long time); they are also within the radius of his love. It could even be said that Jesus deliberately stressed the heathen's chance of being saved—all those lost lambs and lost pieces of money and prodigal sons! This attitude toward sinners was a long way from the Jewish tradition. "When thou wilt do good, know to whom thou doest it. Do good to the goodly man and thou shalt find a recompense, if not from him, yet from the Most High. Give

[10] The formula, "Our Father which art in heaven," corresponds to some extent with the Hebrew invocation, *Adonai Schebaschamaim*, but during the latter day of Israel the familiar correspondence between God and man which marked the Patriarchs had given place to a stiff and awestruck reverence.

to the godly man and help not a sinner." (Ecclesiasticus xii, 1-7.)

The new doctrine, it would seem, might lead to all kinds of things which a good Jew could not welcome. It required him to accept as brothers men who did not uphold the law, men "lower than beasts." In Israel of old your neighbor was your brother according to the flesh and according to the Law, he who believed in Jehovah, the God of Sinai, and the Temple. This was the "neighbor" as defined by Leviticus, not the infidel, the renegade and the heathen. Such a parable as that of the Good Samaritan would seem outrageous to a pious Jew, a tale in which none of the servants of the true God were shown in a good light while a heretic of mixed blood was held up as an example.

The Jews had progressed beyond the notion that Jehovah was God only of the Twelve Tribes and many passages of the Old Testament said expressly that God would be revealed to all peoples (Psalm 22, 28; 47, 8; Jer. xxxi, 34). This discovery is one of the glories of Israel. But in practice no Jew could imagine any way of reaching or serving God except by the rites which belonged to Israel. It has been mentioned that there were proselytes from paganism among the Jewish communities of the Dispersion, but these were required to accept all the Jewish ritual observances including circumcision; if they did not they remained "second class believers." Yet Christianity was to declare, in St. Paul's words, that there were no longer Greeks nor Jews—a basic difference.

In breaking the tradition of Jewish exclusiveness, Christianity also broke up the traditional institutions, the *Kahal* for instance, that community of the faithful bound together by a whole network of associations, spiritual and material, moral and social. The community was the basic Jewish institution. It could not see itself as part of the *Church*, a purely spiritual institution, independent of the bonds of race, class or upbringing, following the example of Jesus, and sharing in the divine grace.

More fundamental even than this was the fact that the very

mission of the Chosen People, the favor which God had bestowed upon them throughout the centuries, was menaced by this doctrine which gave strangers and heathen a part in the divine promises and allowed them to aspire to the Kingdom of Heaven.

It is only fair to add that Jewish exclusiveness was not purely selfish. If so often, too often, it was purely vanity which made them cling to this harsh conception, there was also, among the more spiritually-minded, a feeling that certain values more important than life itself had been guarded by the Jewish people, that they were the repository of a unique truth. It would have required superhuman clarity of intelligence and an equally uncommon self abnegation for a people so long anchored to these exalted certitudes to realize that their mission was complete and that the only way in which they could fulfill the revelation which they had guarded so long would be to sacrifice their exclusive claim to it. There were some pure and humble souls among them who could take this difficult step ahead; of such were the Apostles, the first disciples, whose eyes were opened by grace. But the great majority remained blind and in all good faith they considered that the promoter of this blasphemous doctrine merited death and that any means was permissible to bring about his downfall. This tragic blindness of Israel was often represented by the medieval artists in a triptych showing the Church and the Synagogue on either side of Christ, the Synagogue a figure with bandaged eyes.

Only one thing could have torn this bandage from the eyes of the Jews; if they could have recognized in Christ the Messiah, he who was to come from God, for whom they waited with hearts swelling with hope. But, as we have seen, the Messianic idea had taken on certain divergent characteristics which could hardly be reconciled in one person. There was the conception of the glorious king, the conqueror who would give Israel back her independence and permit the Jews the long overdue vengeance upon their enemies. The other, the true image, was the suffering Messiah, the humble victim whose destiny of sacrifice was to form the real victory. But this image, foreshadowed by the prophets, had passed into oblivion and the force of Jewish pride worked to keep it there. Here we begin to see the drama preparing. The greater the suffering and humiliation of Jesus, the more the Jews would hate him because his pretention to be their Messiah was an insult to the all-conquering figure which had fed their hopes for so long. When Pilate cried *Ecce homo,* leading out Jesus, exhausted, disfigured by blows, bleeding and spat upon, he hoped perhaps to arouse pity. But the Jews howled: "Crucify him."

How mysterious is the destiny of Israel. The very qualities which had enabled them to preserve throughout their history the truth which had been revealed to them, drove them to make the supreme refusal. The pride that had kept them for two thousand years the witness to the promise prevented its fulfillment; for them the revelation would remain incomplete. It would indeed have been almost impossible for this people, the people of the Law, living it out to the letter, to capitulate at once to the religion of the heart and to accept the belief that "the letter killeth but the spirit giveth life." It would have been almost as incredible that they should abandon the natural pride which had proved to be their best, if not their only, weapon, for a doctrine which required humility and universal love. We must ask ourselves, however, if there was not a providential element in their refusal, for without it the mission of Jesus could not have been fulfilled, for salvation is only by blood.

The Last "Sign of Contradiction"

Jesus knew, better than anyone, the deep well springs of the Jewish opposition to him and the significance of the drama to come. We see him, as we read the Gospel, undeflected by the intrigues around him and the play of passions and interest, following out the plan which he alone understood.

The progess of the divine plan required a certain precedence. It was not solely to avoid arousing the Jewish and Roman authorities nor even to prevent his followers from misunderstanding his role that the Messiah did not declare himself. It was because his hour "was not yet come," because the opposition to him and his teaching had not yet reached that degree of violence necessary for its culmination in the bloody sacrifice by which alone his aim could be achieved. If there was a Messianic secret[11] during the life of Christ he revealed it only by his death and resurrection, and once again we may see that complete identification between his words and his being. Jesus was not only a man whose acts and whose teaching were in harmony, a man whose whole existence was at once a testimony and a total commitment; he was the Word made flesh who offered himself in expiation. When we enumerate the various causes of opposition which seem to explain the tragedy of Calvary we still do not explain it, for there remains the essential, imponderable cause, the Mystery of the Redemption.

His hour had come and events began to move rapidly to the time when, by breaking off the human life of Jesus, his message would be given its necessary culmination. Has that culmination succeeded in persuading mankind to accept the doctrine for which he shed his blood? Certainly he has found many throughout the ages to see in the suffering Messiah their Eternal hope; many who have been brought to the light by the recollection of his agonies. But to many others his Passion seems the supreme exacerbation of all that is to them intolerable in his teaching and inacceptable in his mission.

St. Paul said of the God who became man and who died on the Cross that he was "unto the Jews a stumbling block and unto the Greeks foolishness." To a Greek, the idea of a man being at the same time a god was inadmissible; it was the sin

[11] It is necessary to point out that the word "secret" in this connection is used only in a very general sense and has nothing in common with that esotericism in which so many religious sects have pretended to enclose their message, and of which some fanciful critics have pretended to discover traces in the Gospel. Christianity is not a religion of *initiates* nor is it a sect. It has never had the character of such communities as the Essenes or the Pythagoreans, nor does it in any way resemble such mystical cults as that of Demeter at Eleusis, or of Isis, Serapis or Adonis in many centers throughout the Roman Empire. Even when Jesus seems to reserve certain portions of his teaching for his most intimate disciples, he makes it quite clear that the reservation is only provisional. "What I tell you in darkness, that speak ye in light; and what ye hear in the ear, that preach ye upon the housetops." (Matt. x, 27.)

of *hybris*, immensurable pride or a delusion of grandeur, while to suppose that a god would elect to die was an absurdity because the essence of divinity was immortality. To a Jew the idea of the incarnation was scandalous; it violated the conception of the One God and savored of pagan anthropomorphism. But the idea of the Redemption went further than that. They recognized the validity of the bloody sacrifice, for beasts were slaughtered daily in the Temple by the priest and long ago human flesh had been offered, as had Isaac or Jephtha's daughter, to appease the terrible Jehovah. But that God should offer himself to God, that God should be a victim, was an outrage upon the conception of the divinity. And to claim that the victim was the Messiah was an intolerable affront to the Holy One of Israel. The King of glory could not accept the death of a slave upon the ignominious cross.

Christianity asks the world to accept the "folly" and the "shame" of the Cross because if we can accept them we may accomplish that reversal of the world's values which Christ enjoined: *metanoette*—to be born again. Then what has seemed foolish will be revealed as wise and what is shameful will become worthy of respect and love. The Cross is the supreme witness to the mission of Jesus. It is also the most decisive of the "signs" that men have refused.

CHAPTER NINE

THE LAST DAYS

Holy Week

In the entire cycle of the liturgy of the Catholic Church, as it is unfurled throughout the year, no period is richer in beauty and more charged with symbolical significance than that which commemorates Christ's last days upon earth. The mention of "Holy Week" at once recalls the contrasted pageantry of those feasts wherein joy and sorrow succeed each other, with soaring hymns and the silence of desolation, in great cathedrals and humble parish churches alike. The week opens with the scent of freshly cut branches, the branches of our own countrysides symbolizing the palm and olive branches of the Holy Land. The *Gloria Laus*, that echo of the *Hosanna* of Israel, falls into silence and the night office of *Tenebrae,* with its alternation of lessons from the Prophets and chants from the Psalms, reminds us of the coming tragedy and the repeated prophecies of which it is the fulfillment. Maundy Thursday, with its Altar of Repose in a mound of sweet-scented flowers, is like a smile on the road to Calvary save that the Host, hidden among the flowers and the candles, is the very flesh of the victim, to whom we bow down in adoration. Then comes the night, when the bells are mute and the candles dead; the sad procession of the crowds making the Stations of the Cross, the veiled statues, the empty tabernacle, monument of a mourning world, until the miraculous dawn when the joyful cry goes up: "Christ is risen."

The alternation of darkness and supernatural light, or rather the simultaneous presence of sorrow and of joy, corresponds exactly with the account given by the four Evangelists of the last days of Jesus. In the background, behind the intrigues and hatred, the knot of the conspiracy which believed itself to be justified is being tied. Jesus knew it and he never considered avoiding it by flight from those who, by killing him, were to seal their own downfall. His hour was come, the hour of darkness when the salvation of man was to be accomplished by the shedding of blood. The serenity which has always characterized him does not desert him now. From the very end of his term we have many of his most profound and beautiful sayings. But the man in him was troubled: his youth, his flesh, protested at the death that the God in him willed. This is the week of those two glorious manifestations, the acclamation by the people and the institution of the sacrament. But it is also the week of the Passion, of the agony, the desolation and the Cross. But "except a corn of wheat fall into the ground and die, it abideth alone."

Jesus did not try to hide. He stayed sometimes at Bethany and sometimes on the Mount of Olives, both near enough to Jerusalem to facilitate his comings and goings into the town. The caravans of pious Jews coming up from the Jordan thought that they were just going to another Passover. An agitator crucified by the ramparts would not astonish them in any way. But the coincidence in time between the feast which commemorated the deliverance of the Chosen People and the sacrifice of the Messiah was obviously no accident. Once before Jesus had gone to Ephraim to escape his enemies; this time he gave himself up to them. It was not chance, but a deliberate intention.

The coincidence between the Jewish festival and the death of Jesus provides some of the most valuable evidence in piecing together the chronology of Christ's life. The four Evangelists report that he died on a Friday (Matt. xxvii, 62; Mark xv,

42; Luke xxiii, 54; John xix, 31). If we follow the fourth Gospel, in which the chronological references are given more precisely, it seems that the death must have taken place on the actual day of the Passover feast, that is, according to the Jewish liturgical calendar, the fourteenth day of Nisan. There are only three dates during the period of Christ's life when the Passover fell upon a Friday. These are April 11, 27; April 7, 30; and April 3, 33. Taking these dates into account with calculations already made regarding the date of Jesus's birth and the duration of his public ministry, the second of these three dates is indicated.[1] Holy Week may therefore be said to have commenced on Sunday, April 2 in the year 30, and it was on Friday, April 7, on a bare hill by the gate of Jerusalem, that Jesus was nailed to the Cross.[2]

---

[1] Allowing for the fact that the Jewish day is reckoned from sunset to sunset, we get the following calendar for Holy Week.

	From sunset	10 Nisan	
Monday	April 3 until sunset	10 Nisan	
	After sunset	11 "	
Tuesday	April 4 until sunset	11 Nisan	
	After sunset	12 "	
Wednesday	April 5 until sunset	12 Nisan	
	After sunset	13 "	
Thursday	April 6 until sunset	13 Nisan	The Last Supper
	After sunset	14 "	
Friday	April 7 until sunset	14 Nisan	The Crucifixion
	After sunset	15 Nisan	The Passover of the Pharisees

[2] Unlike the Jewish Passover, the Christian Easter is, as we know, a movable festival. This comes from the fact that the months of the Jewish calendar were lunar and ours are not. The Jewish Passover was fixed by Moses (Num. xxviii, 16) on the fourteenth day of the first month to coincide with the full moon of the spring equinox, because it was at that time that the Jews went out of Egypt. To show that, in the words of the *Lauda, Sion* (the sequence of Corpus Christi) *Novum Pascha novae legis, Phase velus terminat,* the new Passover puts an end to the old one as the new day ends the night, the Church decided that the new festival must coincide with the full moon of the Passover. But since it was desired to celebrate the Resurrection of Christ upon a Sunday, on which day it in fact took place, it was decided at the Council of Nicaea to choose each year the Sunday following the full moon of the spring equinox which was supposed then to occur always on March twenty-first, as it did in the year 325 when the Council met. If the full moon occurs before the twenty-first of March, Easter falls on the full moon of the month following; thus it can fall between March twenty-second and April twenty-fifth. Various suggestions for a fixed Easter have been advanced but they involve abandoning either the coincidence with the full moon or with a Sunday.

Political Reasons

Toward the end of March, Jesus found himself in a position of increasing danger. His return to Jerusalem alarmed those who, as the jealous guardians of the Law and also of public order, detested him equally as prophet and as disturber of the peace. The resurrection of Lazarus, which caused many people to rally to him, drove his adversaries to take action. The Pharisees warned the Temple authorities, and the chief priests became alarmed. They met to consider the case.

The Gospel reports several of those unofficial meetings, compared by Fr. Lagrange to "meetings of parliamentary groups where whatever decision is taken is sure to be carried out because the majority is behind it." St. John (xi, 45-53) reports one of them in detail. Traditionally it was supposed to have taken place in a villa belonging to Caiaphas the High Priest, situated outside the city on a hill overlooking the sinister vale of Gehenna. This hill is still called the Mountain of Evil Counsel. It could not have been a meeting of the entire Sanhedrin; neither Joseph of Arimathea nor Nicodemus can have attended. We may guess that the two great rival priestly families, that of Annas, his five sons and his son-in-law Caiaphas, and that of Boëtus, represented by his three sons, for once found themselves in agreement. There would also be present doctors of the Law from those Pharisees who were in Jerusalem, but these did not play an important part. From now on they seem to subordinate themselves to the priestly caste, whose business indeed it was, for once the matter passed into the realm of law and politics the Pharisees were no longer concerned in it. The scribes and Pharisees knew perfectly well what they were doing when they denounced Jesus to the authorities, but they did not wish to soil their own hands.

"What are we going to do? This man works miracles. If we let him go on, everybody will come to believe in him, then the Romans will come and destroy our town and our people." We must admit, in justice to the priests, that the danger was not illusory. There had been several cases where mystics had excited the people, telling them that the hour of liberation had come, and there had been sanguinary reprisals. They would remember the revolt of Simon which was repressed by Varus, who crucified two thousand Jews upon the hills. Another attempt forty years later was indeed to provoke the ultimate disaster. Astute politicians, as were most of the members of the Sanhedrin, could hardly have seen the matter in any other light, and even those few who might have been able to distinguish between Jesus and the ordinary agitator had too much at stake to intervene. The Pharisees said nothing; they had set it all in motion.

Fear is a bad counselor. Caiaphas the High Priest arose, supported by the whole priestly tribe of Annas, his father-in-law and his sons. "Ye know nothing at all, nor consider that it is expedient for us, that one man should die for the people, and that the whole nation perish not" (John xi, 49-50). It is no new thing for societies to promote injustice in the interests of the state. The priests and Elders of Israel, sincerely devoted to the welfare of their people, thought they were doing no wrong by supporting this view. There is, indeed, logically something to be said for it, as Goethe implied, when he said: "I would rather have injustice than disorder."

There is, however, the question whether injustice, however unexceptionable may be its reasons, does not introduce a germ of mortal evil into the entire body politic, so that even order is menaced. After two thousand years, the dilemma remains, but from the time of Jesus to our own day there have been far too many against whom reasons of state have been invoked.

The case of Jesus was quite different and St. John calls attention to the fact. The words of Caiaphas were prophetic. Philo, writing about the same time, says that the power of prophecy descended upon the High Priests; he thought it was communicated to them by the possession of the sacred *Ephod.* According to Josephus, John Hyrcanus made several prophetic statements. But Caiaphas, without knowing it, was bringing about something very different from the arrest of a popular agitator. Jesus had to "die for that nation, And not for that nation only but that also he should gather together in one the children of God that were scattered abroad." The astute politicians were only instruments in the hands of the Almighty.

There were several similar meetings, for the matter was fraught with difficulties. If they arrested him when preaching among the crowd, there might be a disturbance, perhaps bloodshed. Then what would Rome do? They had sought vainly for a long time to discredit him. There is a text in the Talmud attributed to Rabbi Akiba: "Kill those who spread pernicious doctrines during a time of pilgrimage," since more people will be intimidated. However, cunning was necessary. Many ruses were debated and it was also suggested that it would be a good thing to put Lazarus out of the way for good and all, since his existence was a living proof of the supernatural powers of Jesus.[3] (John xii, 10-11.) While they were scheming and discussing, the agitator had the effrontery to reappear in Jerusalem, defying the scribes and the doctors, the elders and the priests and the entire Sanhedrin.

Palm Sunday

We can follow day by day, almost hour by hour, the steps of Jesus toward his consummation. Sunday, April 2, we can imagine as one of those lovely spring mornings in Judea when, in the distant clear horizons, in the cool air filled with the scent of growing things, and in the song of a thousand larks, the human soul seems to feel the presence of the divine goodness. Many people had come early along the road from Bethany to Jerusalem in the hope of hearing Jesus, for the rumor of his recent miracles, the restoration of sight to the blind man at Jericho, the raising of Lazarus after he had been dead three days, must have caused great excitement.

[3] The Provençal legend about Lazarus is taken from this passage in the Gospel. After the death of Christ, the Jews put him and his sisters, Martha and Mary, into a boat without oars, sails or rudder. The boat was wafted miraculously to a place near Marseilles and Lazarus became the apostle of that town, where thirty years later he was martyred.

Jesus was already on his way to Jerusalem. The road runs along the eastern slope of the Mount of Olives, leaving the summit on the left, and takes several hairpin bends before coming out upon the flat. Here there is a magnificent view of the city. Here the crowd of disciples and lookers-on had collected. A short distance before this place was a scattered hamlet of a few houses bordering the track. It was known as Bethphage, "The house of the figs," but the site shown today is of doubtful authenticity. There Jesus made a gesture of which the significance was not immediately appreciated, though not one of the Evangelists omits to record it (Matthew xxi; Mark xi; Luke xix, 29; John xii, 14). He sent two disciples into the village and told them "straightway ye shall find an ass tied and a colt with her: loose them and bring them unto me. And if any man say aught unto you, ye shall say, The Lord hath need of them; and straightway he will send them."

Why an ass? Was it simply that he was tired? It hardly seems likely, for Jesus, throughout the Gospel narrative, seems to have been a very vigorous walker. Probably he wished to give some ceremony to his last entry into the city, but there was nothing very dignified in such a mount. Whatever commentators may say about the oriental ass being hardier than our own, and a much more dignified looking animal; and although asses are mentioned in Judges x, 4 and xii, 14 and Absalom is described as mounted upon an ass or a mule; although Homer says that Ajax was "magnificent as an ass," it is certain that a Roman cavalryman, with his mount well in hand, would regard with contempt this rabble-rouser on a donkey.

The significance of the choice becomes evident when we remember that, throughout the Old Testament, the ass is the symbol of peace, humility and a quiet life while the horse is the symbol of war, rapine and luxury. The Prophets reproached the Kings for putting their trust in horsemen. Jesus was King, but the King of Peace. The emphasis laid upon a colt "whereon man never sat" underlines the religious character of the choice; it was widely believed in the ancient world that an animal or an object which had served some profane purpose was not fit for sacred use (Num. xix, 2; Deut. xv, 19 and xxi, 3; Sam. vi, 7). Above all, there is the Messianic prophecy of Zechariah (ix, 9): "Behold thy King cometh unto thee, lowly and riding upon an ass, upon a colt the foal of an ass." By the choice of this humble mount, Jesus gave the Messianic gesture; the triumphal entry he was preparing was that foretold by the prophet and he wished, upon this day when the strands of his destiny were knotting together, to proclaim the fact.

It was not a Roman triumph; there were no marching legions or captives in chains. Of the representations of the scene in art, Fra Angelico's is the most touching in its simplicity and sweetness. Spontaneously, the disciples and the curious onlookers organized themselves into a procession. "And a very great multitude spread their garments in the way, others cut down branches from trees and strewed them in the way. And the multitudes that went before and that followed cried, saying 'Hosanna to the son of David. Blessed is he that cometh in the name of the Lord. Hosanna in the highest.' "

The Church has made the fresh green branches of springtime, the olive for peace and the palm for victory, the common wayside trees of the Holy Land, an emblem of the good deeds with which we may go forth to meet Christ. The custom of strewing garments beneath the feet of those it is desired to honor is common in the Orient; there are many references to it in the *Arabian Nights,* and a hundred years ago an Englishman at Damascus recorded that, as he was passing through Bethlehem, several hundred men and women came out to meet him and, casting their garments upon the ground in front of his horse, implored him to intercede for them with the viceroy of Egypt, whose hostility they had incurred through seditious activities.

The Pharisees, who had spies everywhere, were alarmed. They had expected that Jesus would come to Jerusalem for the Passover but they hoped he would arrive inconspicuously, as he had always done in the past. But, instead, he was being accorded a triumphal entry and ostensibly assuming the Messianic pose. St. Luke (xix, 39) tells us that some of the Pharisees angrily besought Jesus to rebuke the acclaiming crowds. "I tell you that, if these should hold their peace," he said, "the stones would immediately cry out."

At the top of the hill, where the road widens out before it descends rapidly along the western slope, Jesus came to a halt. Before him rose the city, a truly royal prospect. There is no better place to view Jerusalem than from the slopes of the Mount of Olives. The city, on a plateau which drops sharply to the west above the Brook Kidron, has a perfect stage-setting, but it did not look then as it does today, hedged by its crenelated ramparts of rose and gold, a medieval fortress upon which the caprice of history has capped a perfect blue dome, the Mosque of Omar, and sown the white stamens of the minarets among the russet villas of the Western Europeans. In Jesus's day it presented an even more striking spectacle. Then, as now, it was a city built of stone and denuded of vegetation; Chateaubriand said that it was like coming across the confused memorials of a cemetery in the desert. But it must have shone then with a dazzling splendor, for the magnificent tyrant Herod had spent his treasure and his grandiose fantasy in rebuilding the ancient capital of the Jews. The gleaming white walls were formed of cyclopean blocks of stone; gold shone on the façade of the temple in front of Jesus's eyes; and the enormous mass of the sanctuary, with its courtyards, its porticos and its towers, dominated the whole scene in its symbolic superimposition. To the right was the square tower of Antonia, the barracks of the Roman garrison. The priests and the wealthy had built sumptuous palaces and below the town, guarding the approaches to the sea, the Tower of David, rebuilt on those same terraces where once the poet-King had sung his hymns of praise, rose to a height of over one hundred fifty feet, an invincible strongpoint where, forty years later, the defenders of Israel were to make their last stand against Titus's legions.

This was the city as Jesus saw it and in his soul, illuminated by the Holy Spirit, the image of what was to come rose up in shuddering presentiment. This was the city of his most sacred memories; his forefathers had reigned here in this holy place, they slept down in the valley beyond, their white tombs hedged in by the dark cypresses. Here was the Temple, the only place in the world where the true God had always been worshiped: Jesus, more than anyone else, knew the full significance of this. Why must it all end in a tragic dilemma between the providential design and the blind refusal? In the Greek of St. Luke we read that a *sob* rose up from him: "If thou hadst known, even thou, at least in this thy day, the things which belong unto thy peace. . . . For the days shall come upon thee, that thine enemies shall cast a trench about thee and compass thee round and keep thee in on every side. And shall lay thee even with the ground and thy children within thee, and they shall not leave one stone upon another, because thou knewest not the time of thy visitation" (Luke xix, 41-44). They must have seemed strange and mysterious words, and he did not explain them.

He must have entered the city by the Golden Gate, later walled up by the Crusaders who built a chapel there. It is opened every year on Palm Sunday when the Patriarch of Jerusalem makes a solemn entry, mounted upon an ass, while the crowd acclaims him, spreading branches and garments in his path. This gate is the nearest to the Temple to which Jesus immediately went. He saw the same spectacle which had so incensed him two years earlier, commerce making a good thing out of piety, the porticos turned into money-changing offices, the courtyards into cattle markets, the waiting rooms into provision stores, with a hideous din of sharp voices and animals bellowing throughout the holy place. Again his anger rose up and he struck right and left to clear a path for himself. Certainly his arrival was not going to be overlooked.

Since he had brought a considerable crowd in with him, it must have been easy for him to clear the place. Ever since he left Bethphage, more and more people had joined the procession, not all of them converted, to be sure, and mostly activated by curiosity. But there were scenes of genuine enthusiasm. Children acclaimed him (Matt. xxi, 15-16). The Pharisees, growing more and more alarmed, muttered to each other: "Perceive ye how ye prevail nothing? Behold, the world is gone after him" (John xii, 19). The Gentiles too, perhaps some of those God-fearing pagans, "proselytes of the gate," who had been converted to monotheism, asked two of the Apostles, Philip and Andrew, to present them to Jesus.[4] Certainly he was the man of the hour!

But in spite of his triumph and amid all the enthusiasm displayed in this, the very heart of Jerusalem, with his name on everyone's lips, Jesus never lost sight of the purpose for which he had come. When his two disciples asked him to show himself to these Greeks who sought him out with sympathetic curiosity he replied: "The hour is come that the Son of Man should be glorified." And as if he sensed the impatience, the ardent expectation of worldly triumph, he repeated it once, in greater detail: "The hour is come that the Son of Man shall be glorified. Verily, verily I say unto you, Except a corn of wheat fall into the ground and die, it abideth alone: but if it die, it bringeth forth much fruit. He that loveth his life shall lose it and he that hateth his life in this world shall keep it unto life eternal." (John xii, 24-25.)

In that place and time, when the crowds of Jews and Gentiles around him might be said to prefigure the future Christian Church, Jesus tried to explain the price by which this new life must be purchased. The image of the Redemption, the terrible salvation by blood, is clearly in all his thoughts. Still his disciples failed to understand the nature of the triumph he promised them; they could not understand this extraordinary spiritual gamble by which he who loses gains. How could a man hate his life in this world? But Jesus knew. And because he was man, utterly and wholly man, he could not but feel

[4] There is a tradition that these Gentiles were sent to Jesus by Abgar the King of Edessa, offering sanctuary in his small principality. Jesus thanked them but declined and gave them the "miraculous portrait" already referred to. We do not know why these foreigners asked to see him. Perhaps because he had just gone into the Court of the Jews, where they could not follow him, for any uncircumcised heathen who ventured to go into this part of the Temple ran the risk of being killed.

human foreboding and human fear in the face of his destiny, so close now. We recall that he was "troubled" when, in the solitudes of the wilderness, he was tempted by the Evil One. We shall see a few days later the dramatic reversal of fortune in the Garden of Gethsemane. In a few moving lines, St. John records the debate: "Now is my soul troubled; and what shall I say? Father, save me from this hour: but for this cause came I unto this hour." (John xii, 27.) There came a sound like a clap of the sudden spring thunder. "Father, glorify thy name," he said, in total submission and, from the heavens, God replied.

And so this day, which had begun so brilliantly in the light of that triumphal morning, drew to its end in an atmosphere of vague disquiet. The crowd had heard the sudden thunder-clap; some declared that they had heard the voice of an angel. "This voice came not because of me," said Jesus, "but because of you. Now is the judgment of this world: now shall the prince of this world be cast out. And I, if I be lifted up from the earth, will draw all men unto me." The terrible play on words was not understood. The Law had said that the Messiah would abide for ever: he could not be announcing his own death! Lifted up? What did that mean? And who was this Son of Man?

They had been following him all day and they were growing weary. The sun was setting, it would be about half past five, and behind the three towers, Phazael, Mariamne and Hippicus, which commemorated the three beings Herod had loved, the western sky loomed red. There were not so many people around Jesus now, as he lingered on the Temple terrace; daily life goes on and people have work to do. The last rays of the sun touched the distant purple mountains of Moab. The Elder Simeon had spoken of a light to lighten all peoples when a little boy had been presented to him in the Temple. "Yet a little while is the light with you," said Jesus now. "Walk while ye have the light, lest darkness come upon you: for he that walketh in darkness knoweth not whither he goeth. While ye have light, believe in the light, that ye may be the children of light." (John xii, 35-36.)

The Temple was nearly empty now; the believers had gone. The priests returned for the sacrificial banquet, bare feet climbing up the steps to the sacred inner court. A cold air came in with the night. We wonder what the Twelve who remained with their master were thinking. That it would not be today, at any rate, that they would raise the people and force Caiaphas to recognize and consecrate this disconcerting Messiah? So they followed him down to the Golden Gate and back along the road to Bethany.

Monday

Jesus returned to Jerusalem on the following day. "And he taught daily in the temple. But the chief priests and the scribes and the chief of the people sought to destroy him, And could not find what they might do, for all the people were very attentive to hear him." (Luke ix, 47-48.)

When the great Jewish feasts were on, Jerusalem was in a state of great excitement. All the roads were crowded with the caravans of the pious making their way to the Temple of the true God. Every house in the city was crammed full of guests and tents were set up in all the gardens and among the fields and plantations outside the town. Antipas had arrived from Galilee. The Roman Procurator, Pontius Pilate, had come from Caesarea on the coast and had installed himself, as was his custom on such occasions when the Jewish crowds might easily give trouble, in the fortress of Antonia. His wife had come with him, perhaps out of curiosity. The narrow streets of the city, especially around the Temple, were packed by milling, vociferous, strongly-smelling crowds, and above the turmoil of the mob and the bleatings of some hundred thousand sheep, arose the sound of psalm-singing.

We can follow the sequence of events of these last days pretty clearly in the Gospel, particularly in St. Mark. Jesus probably left wherever he was staying at Bethany (the house of Martha and Mary or that of Simon the Leper) quite early. He would go to the Temple where pious Jews would be praying already, reciting the Eighteen Benedictions, their arms stretched above their heads. The crowd would gather round him to hear him speak. Unwearyingly he answered all their questions, taking advantage of any opportunity which offered to expound his teaching.

St. Matthew and St. Mark both report, with a very slight variation, one such incident which probably occurred on Monday morning. Jesus was hungry "and when he saw a fig tree in the way, he came to it and found nothing thereon, but leaves only, and said to it, Let no fruit grow on thee henceforward for ever." (Matt. xxi, 18-19; Mark xi, 12-15.) This curious curse has caused an enormous amount of ink to flow from the pens of the exegesists; for could a fig tree be expected to bear any fruit in springtime? The Talmud, in the *Schabbath,* tells us of two rabbis in Jerusalem who ate fresh figs during the Passover, in Adar, that is March or April. The tree might perhaps have been one of those wild figs which run to leaf and do not fruit. The question seems to be settled by St. Mark, who observes that "the time of figs was not yet." What, therefore, was the significance of this curse, which immediately took effect, for the tree withered—"presently" according to St. Matthew; during the night, according to St. Mark, who says that the disciples found it dead on the following morning.

This is the only example in the entire canon of the Gospel of what may be called "a punishment miracle," though several are mentioned in the Apocrypha, and it was performed on a fig tree, a perfectly good fig tree which had not yet had time to fruit. But there was a lesson to be given from it. "How soon is it withered away!" said the disciples. Jesus answered them: "If ye have faith and doubt not, ye shall not only do this which is done to the fig tree, but also if ye shall say to this mountain, Be thou removed and be thou cast into the sea, it shall be done. And all things, whatsoever ye shall ask in prayer, believing, ye shall receive." There is also a prophetic interpretation: we can see in this miracle one of those symbolic, sometimes curious, dramatic gestures, by which the ancient prophets announced doom; Jeremiah breaking the potter's vessel; Ezekiel shaving his head with a sword. Israel was the accursed fig tree, bowed down with the sterile leaves of the Law, barren of the fruits of love. These parables, spoken on the same day, illustrate this unmistakably.

"A certain man had two sons; and he came to the first and said, Son, go work today in my vineyard. He answered and said, I will not: but afterward he repented and went. And he came to the second and said likewise. And he answered and said, I go, sir; and went not. Whether of them twain did the will of his father?" Bossuet, commenting on this, says that "the worst criminals are often closer to real penitence than is insipid and ineffective politeness." Jesus knows the ill-will and the rebellion concealed in the hearts of so many "worthy Christians" and he loves the honest sinner who repents a thousand times more than the hypocrite who conforms outwardly but denies secretly. Hear, O Israel: "The publicans and the harlots go into the kingdom of heaven before you." (Matt. xxi, 28-32.)

His teaching at this time is obsesssed by his refusal by Israel; he comes back to it again and again, with the limitless sorrow of rejected love. Once again, on the same day, he reverts to the image of the vineyard, which no Jew versed in the scriptures could fail to understand. "The vineyard of the Lord of Hosts is the house of Israel," says one of the most famous passages of Isaiah (v, 7). It was a vineyard from which he expected a good vintage but it gave only a sour and bitter brew. Those laborers to whom the owner entrusted his best stocks, his press and his storerooms but who refused him the wine, assaulted his messengers and killed his eldest son and heir, his hearers could hardly fail to recognize these. That they did is made clear when Jesus concluded the parable by saying that the Lord shall destroy these husbandmen and give the vineyard to others, for some of them cried: "God forbid." Then Jesus looked at them, and said (quoting Psalm 118, 2): "What is this then that is written, The stone which the builders rejected, the same is become the headstone of the corner. . . . Therefore I say unto you: The Kingdom of God shall be taken from you, and given to a nation bringing forth the fruits thereof." (Matthew xxi, 33-46; Mark xii, 1-12; Luke xx, 9-19.)

It would seem as if, having determined not to prolong events, Jesus deliberately sought to arouse Jewish resentment, to make his compatriots face their responsibility. He went on with the parable of the wedding feast, to which the Lord asked his servants, but they declined, preferring to go on with their business. There could be no mistaking his meaning: they were the disloyal servants, some of them were to kill the son of their Lord; they had been the invited guests but they must not be surprised to find others called to fill their place, others from all the highways and byways of the world.

We can see that his words had their effect, for there were violent repercussions among the crowd in the Temple. The Council of the Jews, now more than ever determined to get rid of him but afraid to risk trouble by arresting him in the middle of his following, decided to lay a trap. They sent a delegation to ask him by whose authority he said and did such things as creating an uproar in the Temple, upsetting the stands of the money-changers and the sellers of doves, and publicly insulting the Jewish nation. "By what authority doest thou these things and who gave thee this authority?" The question was cunningly put: if Jesus said he acted under God and through God, he was at once guilty of blasphemy. Would he fall into the trap? Ordinarily Jesus was contemptuous of the Pharisees' method of debate, but he knew how to make use of it on occasion; one may even say that he now displayed a sort of peasant cunning. "I also will ask you one question," said he, "which, if ye tell me, I in likewise will tell you by what authority I do those things. The baptism of John, whence was it? From heaven? Or of men?" Then the doctors reasoned among themselves: "If we say from heaven, he will say, Why did you not believe in him? If we say, of men, the people will stone us for they all regard John as a prophet." So they could only say, "We cannot tell." Then said Jesus: "Neither tell I you by what authority I do these things." (Matt. xxi, 23-27; Mark xi, 27-33; Luke xx, 1-8.) After several encounters of this kind, his enemies were more determined than ever to get rid of him. St. Luke (xx, 19) tells us that when they heard the parable of the servants in the vineyard the chief priests would have arrested him, for they knew "that he had spoken this parable against them." But they were restrained through fear of the people.

Tuesday

The next day was passed in much the same way, with groups of people gathering round Jesus as he preached. On one occasion he was sitting in the Court of the Women facing an alms box—there were thirteen of them, each for a particular purpose—where several wealthy men were ostentatiously making their offerings. He pointed out a woman in widow's clothes, obviously very poor, who came quietly up to the box and put in two small coins. And he said: "Of a truth I say unto you, that this poor widow hath cast in more than they all: For all these have of their abundance cast in unto the offerings of God, but she of her penury hath cast in all the living that she had." (Luke xxi, 1-4.) One of the earliest of Christian art works, a sixth century mosaic in St. Apollonius, at Ravenna, represents this scene, so characteristic of the teaching of Christ.

In the background, his enemies were at work continually, spying, asking questions to entrap him, watching for any false step. The great ones had come together in a united front against him: ordinarily the Pharisees hated the Sadducees and both despised the Herodians, the pro-Roman party of the petty princes, whom they regarded as traitors to the cause of Israel. But they all made common cause against the agitator, for the end justified the means.

The Herodian approach was gentle and apparently respectful. "Master, we know that thou art true and teachest the way of God in truth, neither carest thou for any man. . . . Tell us therefore what thinkest thou? Is it lawful to give tribute to

Caesar or not?" It was a nicely calculated question. Approval of the hated tribute would be very badly received by the crowd around him; condemnation of it would immediately be reported to the Roman authorities, as Jesus very well knew. Once again his shrewd wit got the better of them. "Show me the tribute money." The only coins minted in Palestine were copper coins of low denomination; the silver and gold pieces came from Rome and were comparatively rare, which is why Jesus asked them to bring him one. On the coins was the effigy of the Emperor, in that day, Tiberius Claudius Nero, Caesar Augustus. "Whose is this image and superscription?" asked Jesus. "Caesar's," they said. "Render therefore unto Caesar the things which are Caesar's, and unto God the things that are God's." (Matthew xxii, 15-22; Mark xii, 13-17; Luke xx, 20-26.) Following St. Paul's development of this idea (Rom. xiii, 6-7) many theologians have seen in it a recognition of the rights of temporal powers, but it seems clear that what Christ wished to emphasize once again was that only the pursuit of divine knowledge is important, the primacy of the Kingdom of God.

The Herodians could only retire, secretly admiring the cleverness by which they had been worsted. The Sadducees then came into the attack. They were the orthodox believers of Israel, lording it over the mass of the people. They held to the beliefs of Moses, so much so that for a thousand years or more they had remained at the same stage of development in their ideas about the destiny of man and life beyond the grave. All more liberal or profound extensions of doctrine to them were suspect. The Acts of the Apostles declares that they did not believe in angels or in spirits, nor in the resurrection of the dead, a belief which to them seemed ridiculous, although it was implicit in the teaching of Job, Isaiah and Daniel. The question with which they approached Jesus was in fact designed to make him look ridiculous. The Mosaic Law laid it down that, if a man died without issue, his brother should marry the widow in order to "raise up seed unto his brother." Therefore, asked the Sadducees, if seven brothers successively performed their duty toward the wife of the eldest brother, whose wife would she be after the Resurrection? Foolish as this question may seem, it was the sort of thing with which the Jewish doctors were greatly preoccupied. In the Talmud there is an instance of a man who, having lost twelve brothers and being required to perform his legal obligations toward the twelve widows, decided to take each one for a month and after three years found himself the father of thirty-six children! When we remember Signorelli's terrifying fresco of the dead resuming their garment of flesh, we are appalled that anyone could ask such absurd and obscene questions in relation to one of the most exalted developments of the Jewish revelation. But Jesus answered them: the dead arise in glory, putting off the cares of the flesh "for in the resurrection they neither marry nor are given in marriage." And he reminded them, quoting Moses, "that God is not the God of the dead, but of the living." (Matthew xxii, 23-33; Mark xii, 18-27; Luke xx, 27-40.)

So the Sadducees also retired discomfited. The Pharisees then intervened. They had not been altogether displeased at the way in which Jesus had defeated their rivals, some of them had even applauded his reply, though this conception of the Resurrection seemed very nebulous to them for in their theology the resurrected were not merely "glorious" but very much of the flesh. Still, it was much better to defeat the man on his own ground. So they asked him once more a question which had already been put to him in all sincerity: "Master, which is the greatest commandment of the Law?" The relative importance of the Mosaic precepts was a favorite subject of discussion among the Jewish doctors: what more natural than an enquiry as to which school of thought Jesus favored? Perhaps this prophet would reveal himself less well grounded in the scriptures than they were. Or perhaps he had forgotten the reply he had given to this same question before! But no! They got none of the results for which they had hoped. "Thou shalt love the Lord thy God with all thy heart and with all thy soul and with all thy mind. This is the first and great commandment. And the second is like unto it. Thou shalt love thy neighbor as thyself. On these two commandments hang all the law and the prophets." It was an irreproachable answer according to the most orthodox tradition and the Pharisees could only acknowledge it as such. Then Jesus in his turn took the offensive and put a very embarrassing question regarding the Messiah. Did they regard him as merely human, the son of David? If they did, how could they explain the fact that David addressed him as a superior being? They had no answer to that and took themselves off. (Matt. xxii, 34-46; Mark xii, 28-37; Luke xx, 41-44.)

Although Jesus got the better of all these insidious attacks, he experienced a just and natural anger against the men who fought against a doctrine of charity and simplicity with every trick and shuffle their wits could devise. His wrath was directed to the Pharisees, because he knew that they were the nerve center of the plot. And presently, when he was alone with his disciples, he gave himself up to a prolonged and violent outburst against them, or rather against the qualities which he had always condemned in them, their hypocrisy, their self-satisfaction, the cruelty they hid under the mask of virtue, the spite which they watered down to suavity. These are the most terrible words ever uttered by Christ, the most detailed and ferocious indictment, in which we seem to hear echoes of the imprecations hurled by John the Baptist.

"Woe unto you, scribes and Pharisees, hypocrites! for ye devour widows' houses, and for a pretence make long prayer. . . . Woe unto you, scribes and Pharisees, hypocrites! for ye pay tithe of mint and anise and cummin, and have omitted the weightier matters of the law, judgment, mercy and faith: these ought ye to have done. . . . Woe unto you, scribes and Pharisees, hypocrites! for ye make clean the outside of the cup and the platter, but within they are full of extortion and excess. . . . Woe unto you, scribes and Pharisees, hypocrites! for ye are like whited sepulchres which indeed appear beautiful outward, but are within full of dead men's bones and all uncleanness. . . . Ye serpents, ye generation of vipers, how can ye escape the damnation of hell? Wherefore, behold, I send you prophets . . . and some of them ye shall kill and crucify, and some of them shall ye scourge in your synagogues and persecute them from city to city. That upon you may come all the righteous blood shed upon the earth. . . ." (Matt. xxiii, 1-36; Mark xii, 38-40; Luke xx, 41-47.)

The Revelations of Holy Tuesday

At this moment, beside himself with pain and grief and the certain knowledge that his effort to bring justice and peace would fail, Jesus gave himself up to that prophetic instinct which only two days before, on his triumphal progress to the city, had made him sob with anguish and utter strange sad words. Now, from where he stood on the terrace of the Temple, he could see below the city which had rejected him, its houses huddled together in the narrow, winding streets, crowded with people of his own blood and against whose refusal he could not prevail. For a second time an agonized premonition seized him. "Oh Jerusalem, Jerusalem, thou that killest the prophets and stonest them which are sent to thee, how often would I have gathered thy children together, even as a hen gathereth her chickens under her wings, and ye would not. Behold, your house is left unto you desolate. For I say unto you, Ye shall not see me henceforth, till ye shall say, Blessed is he that cometh in the name of the Lord." (Matt. xxiii, 37-8; Luke xiii, 34-5.)

Once again we feel the mystery of the rejection by Israel, upon which St. Paul in the eleventh chapter of his Epistle to the Romans makes such a magnificent commentary: "God hath not cast away his people, which he foreknew . . . for God hath included them all in unbelief, that he might have mercy upon all. O, the depth of the riches both of the wisdom and the knowledge of God! How unsearchable are his judgments and his ways past finding. . . ." It was the terrible destiny of the Jews to make possible the sacrifice of the Savior, but the design was of God; one day they will realize this and re-enter the realm of grace "for if the casting away of them be the reconciling of the world, what shall the receiving of them be, but life from the dead?"

But the prophecy of Jesus did not relate to that restored and redeemed Israel of whom St. Paul was to write, but to the tangible menace which threatened the living Israel. As they went out of the gate, the little group of men would follow the way down to the sub-structure of the sanctuary, the enormous walls which Herod had built to support it and to enlarge the area. From where Jesus stood in the valley of the Kidron these colossal, irregularly spaced blocks of stone must have given an impression of almost impregnable strength. Rough grass and creepers were matted in the crevices of the stone and innumerable doves had made their nests there, from which they flew out white-winged against the harsh blue sky. Looking at the great piers and the wealth and state of the Temple, his disciples wondered how these things could fail to stand. "Verily I say unto you," said Jesus, "There shall not be left here one stone upon another, that shall not be thrown down." (Matt. xxiv, 1-2; Mark xiii, 1-2; Luke xxi, 5-6.)

The disciples were shaken by the insistence of their master upon these catastrophes to come. They had now come down the slope of the mountain and were alone among themselves. So they began to ask questions about the disquieting things which he had said. Were these catastrophes to be a sign of the end of the world and the coming of the Son of Man in glory? And when would they take place? What signs would there be? There would be no lack of signs, their Master told them. There would be false Messiahs who would deceive the people, there would be wars, revolts and rebellion. Nature would show signs and wonders, earthquakes, pestilences, famines. They themselves, the faithful, would bear witness in their bodies: they would be arrested, persecuted, testifying to Christ by their sufferings. But the Holy Ghost would speak through their lips, with the wisdom which their adversaries could not refute. Then, as the Gospel was beginning to spread through the world, Jerusalem would be destroyed, invested by a foreign army while in the Holy Place would reign that "abomination of desolation" which the prophet Daniel had foretold. In those dreadful days "then let them which be in Judea flee into the mountains. . . . Let him which is on the housetop not come down to take anything out of his house: Neither let him which is in the field return back to take his clothes . . . woe unto them that are with child and to them that give suck in those days. . . . For then shall be great tribulation, such as was not since the beginning of the world to this time: no, nor ever shall be. . . . And when ye shall see Jerusalem compassed with armies, then know that the desolation thereof is nigh." (Matt. xxiv, 15-22; Mark xiii, 14-20; Luke xxi, 20-24.)

Forty years later, at the beginning of the month of Nisan, in the year 70, a Roman army invested the Holy City. Four legions of Syrian and Numidian auxiliaries, sixty thousand men with the finest material equipment, were led by the Emperor Titus, the son of Vespasian, who had been proclaimed only six months earlier by a coup d'état of the legions in Egypt. Titus had need of some military laurels to bolster up his throne. The Jewish people, who had been hounded and humiliated by successive procurators, thought they could repeat the heroic miracle of the Maccabees and they rose against Rome.

The campaign was disorganized but ferocious and certainly the signs foretold by Jesus were not lacking. Josephus catalogues earth tremors and signs in the sky, while as for false prophets, the country seethed with them. Most of them were obviously mad, but no prophet is too mad to gain followers. One mystic from Egypt assembled a crowd on the Mount of Olives assuring them that, on his command, the walls of the city would fall down. A certain Jesus, son of Haran, an illiterate peasant, rushed through the streets howling: "The voice of the Four Winds calling Jerusalem, calling all the people." Some of these agitators were more sinister, such as the Sicarians, an offshoot from the sect known as Zelots, who under the leadership of a strange, satanic creature known as John of Giscala sought to impose a dictatorship of the sword. The rival factions, religious and political, which we have seen in action during the Gospel story, could not compose their differences within the besieged city: Sadducees, Pharisees and Zelots all fought each other, one party holding out in the Tower of David, another closing in on the Temple, occupying Ophel and Bezetha, while a third entrenched themselves within the Holy Place. There was nothing of the Holy War about it: the Sicarians who had risen in the name of God to enforce the keeping of the Law abducted and raped Jewish women, while their executions had no justification save greed and revenge.

Titus, encamped on the Scopus, conducted his attack with care. For, in the beginning, the Jewish position was a strong one; they had some ten thousand soldiers, plus five thousand Idumeans, tough, seasoned mercenaries. The city was ringed by a triple wall and fortified by eighty-two towers; they had also the four hundred ballista and other weapons captured some time before from a Roman legion. Internal unity was more or less achieved and the siege began. But if the Romans needed time for their strength to make itself felt, they had a redoubtable ally who could work more rapidly—hunger, the famine which had been prophesied. Jerusalem was appallingly overcrowded and the Roman advance, as also Jesus had foretold, came so quickly that a large number of pilgrims who had come up for the Passover were trapped there, together with hordes of refugees driven in from the countryside. A completely encircling wall, eight miles long and fortified on every turn means, as Caesar proved when successfully besieging Vercingetorix at Alesia, that no supplies can come in, and the defending soldiers have to loot to eat. Those who tried to escape from the city went straight into the arms of the Romans below who sent them back with their hands cut off, if they were women, or crucified them in full sight of the city if they were men. One of the crucified bodies burst with the weight of the gold pieces which the wretched creature had swallowed rather than give up, and after that the African and Bedouin auxiliaries disembowled all the prisoners in the hope of finding gold. As the famine went on, the most appalling incidents took place. It is recorded that soldiers who went into a house where they smelt burning were received by a madwoman who presented them with the dismembered limbs of her child upon a silver dish.

The agony was endured for a hundred days. Although the third and then the second wall had been breached, the city would not surrender; in many quarters house to house fighting was necessary before capitulation. The frenzied city, peopled by emaciated specters, still seemed to find strength to resist. Even when the Tower of Antonia was invested, the Temple itself still held out. Titus hesitated to use fire; he did not desire that "this marvelous magnificence," as Tacitus calls it, should be destroyed by him. But in the end, he was forced to resort to it; he could break down its resistance in no other way. So lighted braziers were rammed against the doors, the precious cedarwood burned, the gold and silver ran down in molten streams, the portico of Solomon crumbled. Hurtling through the flames came the defenders, with John of Giscala at their head, and tried to cross the bridge of Tyropeon toward their last stronghold in the highest point of the town. But Titus's Nubian cavalry with their lances galloped across the slanting streets, sweeping everything before them as the decapitated heads of the defenders rolled.

Now that he had conquered, Titus and his staff tried to limit the disaster. They went into the sanctuary and ordered the fire to be extinguished. But the soldiers, exasperated by the resistance, paid no heed; they killed, violated and massacred the priests in the courts, while the Bedouins, torches in their hands, spread the fire, now futile in a military sense but felt somehow as inevitable and providential. "It would have been impious," said the victorious Roman, "to hinder the divine judgment: these people were visibly being punished by God." Thus was the pride of Israel abandoned to its fate.

In Pella and in Transjordania there were small communities of Christians, and these, when they heard the appalling news, must have repeated among themselves their Master's prophetic words. Everything that he had foretold had happened. "This generation shall not pass away, till all be fulfilled. Heaven and earth shall pass away but my words shall not pass away."[5] (Luke xxi, 32-33.)

The vision of Israel under the terror of the judgment, which obsessed Jesus during these last days, merged naturally into the wider vision of that other judgment, when the whole world shall be weighed in the balance. It seems as if his knowledge of the tragedy which awaited him, so soon now, forced him into a prophecy of his triumphal return. "The Prophet," said Joseph de Maistre in the *Soirées de St. Petersbourg,* "has the privilege of leaping out of time: his conceptions, not being confined to the present, may run together by virtue of a simple analogy and so entwine as to cause a certain confusion in discourse. In assuming, voluntarily, the prophetic state, the Savior also accepted these conditions; analogous ideas of great disasters separated in time led him to associate the destruction of Jerusalem with the end of the world." There is no real confusion in the words of Christ but unquestionably the sequence of thought was moulded less by logic than by that symbolism which is such a profound but obscure part of the human consciousness. There are other instances recorded where his disciples were clearly not able to follow him and asked him questions about the future of the world.

"For as the lightning cometh out of the east and shineth even unto the west; so shall also the coming of the Son of Man be."

"Lord, where will this be?"

"Wheresoever the carcase is, there shall the eagles be gathered together."

The reply is far from clear, yet it throws a supernatural light

---

[5] Anti-Christian critics have naturally concluded that the words attributed to Jesus were not prophetic but were inserted in the Gospel narrative after the event. Fr. Lagrange, discussing this matter, says: "If it is accepted, as it generally is, that the two narratives, that of Luke and that of the Acts, were composed before the year 70, it can safely be said that the events occurred after that time and that the Christian tradition was based upon the broad interpretation of the discourse."

upon one of the most forcibly charged words of the Gospel. The eagle or vulture, *aelos* in Greek signifies either, knows where to find the body which is its meat, so also shall the righteous know where to find their Savior. Or, again, the body which knows corruption is sin, upon which divine justice will sweep like the avenging eagle.

"Immediately after the tribulations of those days shall the sun be darkened, and the moon shall not give her light, and the stars shall fall from heaven, and the powers of the heavens shall be shaken."

"And then shall appear the sign of the Son of Man in heaven, and then shall all the tribes of the earth mourn, and they shall see the Son of Man coming in the clouds of heaven with power and great glory. And he shall send his angels with a great sound of a trumpet, and they shall gather together his elect from the four winds, from one end of heaven to the other."

We may wonder how these words struck his hearers. The apocalyptic images which he used had been employed also by the prophets. Isaiah had announced the destruction of Edom in similar words (xiii and xxxiv); Jeremiah (v) had spoken of the doom of Jerusalem and Ezekiel (xxxii) of Egypt, while Jole had used almost the exact images which Jesus chose when describing the coming of the Lord (i, 1-10). When he spoke of the coming of the Messiah, any Jew listening would remember Daniel's vision in the night of "one like the Son of Man" who came on the clouds of heaven (vii, 13-14). They must have been moved by fear, so that on their lips is so often found the fearful question: "*When?*"

Jesus replies that the signs of which he has told them will enable them to recognize the hour when it comes, just as they watch the leaves thickening on the trees and the fruit swelling and know that summer is at hand. But only the Father knows the day and hour. Men ate and drank and took wives on the eve of the Deluge; daily life went on in Sodom as the fire and brimstone fell down on the accursed city. So would it be in the day when the Son of Man comes. There shall be two women grinding at the mill, one shall be taken and the other left. And then, what then? "I will come on thee as a thief," says the Messiah in the Revelation of St. John (iii, 3). Watch therefore, for ye know not what hour your lord shall come. Do not be like a careless servant, who goes out drinking while his master is away, and is surprised asleep. Watch and pray unceasingly that you may be found worthy of being saved from disaster.

All the synoptics give the apocalyptic discourse of Holy Tuesday in much the same words. (Matt. xxiv, 23-51; Mark xiii, 21-37; Luke xvii, 22-27 and xxi, 25-36.) St. Matthew appends two parables. One is the charming story of the Wise and Foolish Virgins so often celebrated in medieval art. In sculptured panels at Rheims, Amiens, Sens, Laon, Bourges, Paris and Auxerres we see them, five on the right and five on the left of the divine Master; the wise ones bearing their carefully tended lamps; the foolish ones sadly gazing at their empty, upturned vessels. This parable, based on the Jewish custom of sending a merry procession to look for the bridegroom on the wedding night to bring him to the waiting bride, has the simplicity and force of the greatest parables, and everyone who heard it would know that the cry in the night which awakened the improvident maidens was the terrible last trumpet with which the avenging Archangel would call humanity to the judgment.

The Judgment is clearly the subject of the second parable, the parable of the talents. God gives every man capacities and opportunities; one day we shall be asked to account for them. From those who have received much, much will be required, but not according to the order of the world. In the spiritual order, those who have known how to acquire merit will have yet more given to them; from those that have not, it will be taken away.

Of the Last Judgment, Jesus said:

"When the Son of Man shall come in his glory, and all the holy angels with him, then shall he sit upon the throne of his glory. And before him shall be gathered all nations; and he shall separate them one from another, as a shepherd divideth his sheep from his goats.[6] And he shall set the sheep on his right hand but the goats on his left. Then the King shall say to them on his right hand, Come, ye blessed of my Father, inherit the Kingdom prepared for you from the foundation of the world. . . . Then shall he say also unto them on the left hand, Depart from me, ye cursed, into everlasting fire, prepared for the devil and his angels." (Matt. xxv, 31-46.)

Jesus had several times previously spoken of the Last Judgment and always of the division of the two categories of men, the good and the wicked, those who would see God face to face and those who would burn in everlasting fire: the unjust stewards; the foolish virgins and the wedding guests who would not bother to prepare themselves for the feast; the bad husbandmen; the tares which must be cast out from the good grain. But the great prophecy of the Tuesday of Holy Week took on a terrible immediacy because it followed his prediction of a catastrophe which must have made every Jewish listener tremble. For Christians it has a more dreadful significance; this prophecy of the Last Judgment, given so short a time before the supreme injustice of human history, was the last which Christ uttered.

The portals of many of our Cathedrals bear representations of what men have made of the terrific scene, where on one side of Jesus the elect are ranged, while on the other demons push the damned into the gaping jaws of hell. In the Sistine Chapel, Michelangelo is preoccupied by the majesty rather than the horror of the scene. Its horror is perhaps best caught by the fantastic imagination of Hieronymus Bosch in a picture painted for Philip II of Spain, which shows a Gehenna writhing with damned souls beneath a sky where Christ is entwined among angels blowing curving trumpets, while below, at his feet, a small and shivering group of the elect are huddled on a rainbow, still quaking at the memory of the Judgment.

---

[6] *Ram* would seem to be called for. But the idea perhaps is that the stubborn goat is a symbol of those who rebel against God.

No Catholic can read this page of the Gospel without hearing the solemn chords of the *Dies Irae,* the sequence written by the Franciscan poet Thomas of Celano in the thirteenth century, which is sung for the dead Christian in the Requiem Mass:

Dies irae. Dies illa. Solvet saeculum in favilla. . . . That day of wrath, that dreadful day, shall the whole world in ashes lay, as David and the Sybils say. What horror will invade the mind, the last loud trumpet's wondrous sound, must through the rending tombs rebound, and wake the nations underground. The Judge ascends his awful throne. He makes each secret sin be known, and all with shame confess their own. *Recordare Jesu pie, quod sum causa tua viae. Ne me perdas illa die.*

Forget not what my ransom cost, nor let my dear-bought soul be lost.

Cor contritum quasi cinis, Gere curum mei finis. Lacrymosa dies illa!

Prostrate my contrite heart I rend. Do not forsake me in my end.

With this terrible apotheosis of the Last Judgment, the most dreadful which Christ ever uttered, the day ended. The impression it leaves would be intolerable, almost obscuring the face of the "loving Jesus," were it not for the moving words with which St. Matthew concludes this chapter. In the day of Judgment Christ will say to the blessed: "For I was an hungered and ye gave me meat: I was thirsty and ye gave me drink: I was a stranger and ye took me in. . . . Verily I say unto you, Inasmuch as ye have done it unto one of the least of these my brethren, ye have done it unto me."

And so, behind the terrible warnings, we can hear the voice of the divine love; that love which is the heart of Christ's message and the consolation of all who are willing to hear.

Wednesday, the Day of Judas

On Holy Wednesday, it has been assumed that Jesus stayed in Bethany from the fact that no teaching was given on that day and also that it was then that he had dinner with Simon, since

St. Mark records the incident of Mary's pouring the perfume over the head of Christ. Or it may be that he simply stayed with Simon and that the anointing which St. Mark describes is the same as that which St. Matthew and St. John placed earlier in the record.

The evening before, Jesus left his disciples with a final word. "Ye know that after two days is the feast of the Passover, and the Son of man is betrayed to be crucified." (Matt. xxvi, 1-2.) This is the fourth warning of what was to come, but whether it was on the Tuesday or Wednesday is not clear. Then St. Matthew continues: "Then assembled together the chief priests and the scribes and the elders of the people unto the palace of the high priest, who was called Caiaphas. And consulted that they might take Jesus by subtilty and kill him. But they said, not on the feast day, lest there be an uproar among the people." (Matt. xxvi, 3-5; Mark xiv, 1-2; Luke xxii, 1-2.) It is now perfectly clear that the politicians wished to get rid of Jesus at any cost, save that of provoking a public riot.

Now Judas comes on the scene. He has never been very much in evidence from the beginning; only an allusion here and there has evoked his presence, and these have been slight, obscure and incomprehensible before the event. There is no reason to suppose that he seemed, up to the moment when he committed his infamy, any different from the eleven others. Even on this fatal Wednesday, it would seem that the Evangelists did not wish to record any additional facts which might explain the actions of this man as he goes out to commit the crime which has made his name opprobrious forever.

"Then one of the twelve called Judas Iscariot went unto the chief priests and said unto them: What will ye give me and I will deliver him unto you?" They were delighted at the suggestion and offered him thirty pieces of silver. They could count upon him, Judas promised, and deliberated with the priests and the magistrates how Jesus could best be arrested away from the crowd. "And from that time he sought opportunity to betray him." (Matt. xxvi, 14-16; Mark xiv, 10-11; Luke xxii, 1-6.)

Thirty pieces of silver; thirty pieces of the silver money of the Temple—a clear proof that the priestly caste was really responsible. Enough to buy a suit of clothes perhaps, but only a very modest one. It was little enough for so great a crime. The figure was probably arrived at because thirty pieces of silver was the forfeit for the killing of a slave, in which case it carried a deliberate insult to Jesus. But there is an echo from the words of the prophet Zechariah (xi, 12): "And I said unto them: If ye think good, give me my price; and if not, forbear. So they weighed for my price thirty pieces of silver."

The reason which prompted Judas will always remain obscure. St. Luke and St. John both say: "Satan entered into him," and this of course is true; the spirit of evil—"he who always says No" in Goethe's phrase—dwells in every sinner, however obscure. The statement is probably nothing more than a figure of speech; even today Orientals will excuse themselves by saying "the devil came into me." But if the statement is accepted in its full literal meaning, how was it that Jesus, who cast out so many devils, should abandon one of his own disciples to the Adversary?

If the Gospel is read literally, there would seem to be no other motive than a base desire for gain, so that the devil who came into Judas would simply be Mammon. St. John says definitely that he was a thief and that he stole from the communal purse which was entrusted to him (John xii, 6). But even so, it would seem that he had more to gain by pilfering this way than by selling his master for such a paltry sum. We know, too, that when he realized the full result of his crime, he came to the Sanhedrin and threw the money back at them and rushed off to kill himself to escape from his inexpiable despair. So there must have been something, even in this dark soul, which Mammon did not possess.

If it was not avarice, could it have been anger at what he considered deception? The first reference to the betrayal (John vi, 70) lends some support to this theory. After the miracle of the loaves, Jesus escaped from the crowd who would have proclaimed him King and, by his discourse upon the Bread of Life, he made it clear that in his doctrine there was no place for worldly ambition. Judas, if he had followed Christ only in the hope of temporal power, would at that moment revolt from him. This reading explains Jesus's otherwise incomprehensible judgment: "One of you is a devil." Everything which occurred after that time would serve to convince Judas that there was nothing to be hoped for from Jesus and, in his fury, he might have decided to get rid of a leader who was proving to be an embarrassment.

But this theory also leaves the remorse and the suicide unexplained. We may also see him as a mean creature, proud of his trickiness and not even abashed by the obvious contempt of his paymasters; a coward ready to sink to any depth to preserve his interests or his skin. Yet it is hard to believe that Jesus would have chosen such a man and kept him among his closest disciples for two years. The Gospel is, as we have said, extremely vague about Judas except in the matter of the actual betrayal, but such glimpses as it gives are of a character more disagreeable than cowardly, as witness his criticism of Mary spilling the perfume and later, at the Last Supper, when he "went immediately out."

Perhaps this irritability hid another less ignoble sentiment. Perhaps Judas was even motivated by love, not the pure disinterested love which Peter and the other ten had for their Master, but one of those devouring, exclusive passions which can thrust a man into the worst excesses of jealousy, a love so near to hate that in certain circumstances it indeed becomes hate, only to recover itself when the worst has been committed, in the extremity of pain and despair.

We cannot go any further with these psychological rationalizations of the conduct of Judas, because they do not get to the heart of the matter. The arrest of Jesus by the creatures of the Sanhedrin and his iniquitous execution is not merely a slight episode in Jewish religious history and in the long tale of political injustices. It is the supreme mystery of Christianity, the mystery of the Redemption. It was necessary that Jesus should be delivered to his enemies. Physically, it had to be done by someone close to him to ensure silence and to prevent comment. The prophets had foretold it: "Yea, my own familiar friend, in whom I trusted, which did eat of my bread, hath lifted up his heel against me." (Psalm 41, 9.) "For it was not an enemy that reproached me . . . it was thou, a man mine equal." (Psalm 55, 12-13.) Christ must experience the full weight of the baseness and villainy of man before his sacrifice could be complete. In the first chapter of the Acts of the Apostles, Peter says plainly that the treachery of Judas was a part of the divine plan, that "this scripture must needs have been fulfilled." We must here leave the traitor, remembering those mysterious words in the Gospel which apply to no one so completely as to him: "It must be that offences come; but woe to that man by whom the offence cometh." (Matt. xviii, 7.)

Thursday, the Last Supper

Nothing is said in the Gospel about the events of the daylight hours. There is every reason to think that Jesus passed it in the company of his intimate friends and his family; his mother must have been there for on the day after we find her at the foot of the Cross. The decisive events take place during the evening and all four Evangelists report them with a wealth of detail and in striking similarity. Even St. John, who ordinarily does not dwell upon things which the synoptics have recorded, seems driven by an urge to put down everything he knows, and everything he can remember. Thus we are able to follow Jesus almost hour by hour upon the road which was to be his Passion.

The Passover was the greatest of the Jewish feasts and to understand its meaning and to follow the ritual we must turn to Chapter Twelve of the Exodus in which its institution by Moses is recorded. During the enslavement in Egypt, Jehovah had smitten the oppressors with the "Tenth Plague," in which all the first-born sons of the Egyptians were to be killed. In order that the Angel of Death should spare the Jewish households, the Chosen People were told to mark a sign in the blood of a lamb upon the lintel of their doorways. "And they shall eat the flesh in that night, roast with fire, and unleavened bread and with bitter herbs they shall eat it. . . . And ye shall eat it with your loins girded, your shoes on your feet and your staff in your hand and ye shall eat it in haste for it is the Lord's passover. . . . And ye shall keep it a feast by an ordinance for ever." For seven days the Jews must eat unleavened bread and keep the whole week consecrated to the Lord.

The Jewish tradition observed these rites faithfully and the Talmud had, in a lengthy commentary, the *Pesahim,* amplified the details: the lamb must be whole, with no bone broken, it must be cooked on an open fire on a spit from wood of the pomegranate; the exact number of cups which might be drunk during the sacred repast and the exact proportions, a third of wine and two of water, which each should contain; the bitter herbs were particularized and minute directions were given for the sauce in which they were steeped. Was this the meal which Jesus and his disciples ate on the Thursday night?

"Now the first day of the feast of unleavened bread the disciples came to Jesus saying unto him: Where wilt thou that we prepare for thee to eat the passover?" (Matt. xxvi, 17-19; Mark xiv, 12; Luke xxii, 7-8.)

The exact date of this repast, and its consequent significance, was very much debated in the Early Church. Eusebius wrote a commentary on it and it even gave birth to a heresy. We have seen that the great feast day must have been the fifteenth day of Nisan. The Passover lamb was eaten on the evening of that day. The synoptics, however, suggest that the last supper which Jesus took with his disciples was the Passover feast, but St. John says plainly that the day on which he partook of the feast was the day of his death. According to the synoptics, the Thursday of the Last Supper was the fourteenth day of Nisan and Jesus died on Friday the fifteenth. According to the fourth Gospel, the supper took place on the thirteenth and the crucifixion on the fourteenth. If we conclude, from the reading of St. John, that the Last Supper was *not* the Passover feast, it seems we are going against considerable evidence to the contrary from the synoptics (for example Mark xiv, 12; Matt. xxvi, 17; Luke xxii, 7; Mark xiv, 17; Matt. xxvi, 20; Luke xxii, 14-15.) Should we then conclude that it was? St. John himself states that the Pharisees ate the Passover after the death of Jesus (xviii, 28). From various indications in the synoptics it seems clear that the day when Jesus died was not a holy day when normal activities were proscribed or Simon the Cyrenean would not have been "coming out of the country" nor could a condemned person be crucified and buried.

We cannot go into all the interpretations in order to force the two versions to a mathematical coincidence, though it may be remarked that St. John, writing long afterward in a Greek community, might well have reckoned his days, as we do, from midnight while the Jews would reckon theirs from sunset. Thus the evening of the fourteenth of Nisan, although legally the fifteenth day of the month, might be popularly regarded as the fourteenth. We have still to explain why Jesus and the Pharisees should not have celebrated the feast on the same day, but there is some evidence from rabbinical sources that the Jews differed among themselves in this matter of fixing the date and that the Galileans, in particular, observed the feast on the evening of the thirteenth. When the feast fell upon a Friday, the eve of the Sabbath, it seems to have been the custom, especially among the Sadducees, to transfer the feast to the Saturday in the same way as the Talmud directs in the case of Yom Kippur, the Day of Atonement, should it fall upon the eve of the Sabbath. We cannot go into these interminable discussions so popular with the exegesists; it is enough to say that most modern authorities accept the chronology of St. John, which comes to this, according to the present-day calendar: the Last Supper, when Jesus attended the Passover feast, took place on the evening of Thursday, April 6; the death of Jesus occurred on April 7, the legal day of the Jewish Passover.

In reply to their question, Jesus told two of the disciples,

Peter and John, to make the preparations. He said: "Go into the city to such a man and say unto him, the Master saith: My time is at hand. I will keep the Passover at thy house with my disciples." "And he will show you a large upper room furnished and prepared: there make ready for us." (Matt. xxvi, 18-19; Mark xiv, 13-15; Luke xxii, 7-12.) We do not know who this man was, but doubtless some faithful disciple would put his house at Jesus's disposal. The sign by which Peter and John were to recognize him—"a man bearing a pitcher of water"—Mark xiv, 13; Luke xxii, 10—would not strike them as inadequate, for it should be remembered that in the East the women always drew the water and a man carrying a pitcher would be somewhat conspicuous.

The disciples went into the town, probably by the gate near the Well of Siloam, found the man and carried out their master's instruction. "A large upper room" suggests a formal celebration; certainly Jesus would wish to impart solemnity to this occasion, the inner meaning of which he knew so well. He does not appear to have gone to so much trouble at other Passover celebrations; at least, there is no mention of them.

The Christian, so familiar with innumerable representations of the Last Supper in art, finds it difficult to disassociate this Jewish religious feast from the Sacrament which it was to institute. For this reason, we are inclined to prefer some of the lesser known representations to the more illustrious, not excluding the famous da Vinci, the best known of all. In some of the minor sculpture of the twelfth century, notably in a tympanum of Charlieu and on a mutilated lintel at St. Gilles-de-Gard, we have a more direct and less romanticized presentation, with a far stronger impact of spiritual significance.

Most oriental houses today have a large upper room, sometimes lit by a square lantern hanging from the ceiling, which is reserved for guests, especially those who may be staying for several days. Rugs and divans are provided so that they may settle themselves at their ease. The location of the room where the Last Supper was held has naturally occupied Christian archaeologists. One very old tradition locates it in the upper town, beyond the Tyropeon bridge, near the southeastern corner of the ramparts. The whole quarter was destroyed in the siege of the year 70 and we cannot say how accurate was the recollection which, in the third century, caused a small chapel to be built on the spot. During the following century, it was included in the vast Basilica of Holy Zion. This church was burnt by the Persians in 614 and again by the Mussulmans in 960 and 1011. It was finally rebuilt by Godfrey de Bouillon during the Crusades. In the fourteenth century Sancha, wife of Robert of Anjou, the French King of Naples, obtained the right to maintain this holy place from the Sultan of Egypt and put it in charge of the Franciscans, to whom we owe the present-day monument, a large vaulted chamber supported by heavy columns of porphyry with rather ungainly capitals carved with grapes and wheat-ears.

But it is no longer Christian soil. The place where "the mother of all churches once stood," to quote the chronicler William of Tyre, is now a mosque because the Mohammedans subsequently affirmed, though absolutely without proof, that the same spot was the burial place of David, who as Nebi Daoud is venerated in Islam. And so, at the end of a long quiet garden, its walls covered with trailing vines, where tall red cypresses lift their heads to the sun, an old Arab in a turban admits the Christian pilgrim to the place where perhaps Christ said: "This is my body! This is my blood."

At sunset, on this day about half past five, the feast would have begun. The guests would be reclining around the table. The old custom of eating the Passover with the tunic worn as though ready for a journey seems to have fallen into disuse by the time of Christ. They would thank God for the wine and for the Day, then the Passover dinner began. The chapter of the Talmud called the *Pesahim* was composed about the year 150, and probably the usage in Jesus's day was very much the same as those given in it. The unleavened bread was dipped in a red sauce called *haroseth.* Two cups of wine were solemnly drunk, with sips of salt water in between, in memory of the tears shed in Egypt. Psalm 114, which tells the story of the Exodus and the division of the waters of the Red Sea was then chanted. Then the lamb was eaten with the "bitter herbs," those sharply-flavored aromatics, marjoram, bay, thyme and basil, which are still eaten with mutton in Turkey and Greece. Two more ritual cups of wine were drunk, the last being called "the cup of benediction" because to it was sung the *Hallel*, the famous song of thanksgiving, made up of the four Psalms, 115 through 118: "Not unto us, O Lord, not unto us, but unto thy name give glory, for thy mercy and for thy truth's sake. . . . Our God is in the heavens . . . their idols are silver and gold, the work of men's hands. . . . O praise the Lord, all ye nations, praise him all ye people. For his merciful kindness is great towards us: and the truth of the Lord endureth for ever." The last verses of Psalm 18 contain an allusion to the Messiah which the Apostles must have chanted with special fervor: "Blessed be he that cometh in the name of the Lord."

The Passover was a joyful feast, "as delectable as the olive," says the Talmud and the chant of the *Hallel* lifted the roofs. A Gnostic text of the second century, known as the Acts of John, shows us the disciples joining hands in a circle round Jesus, dancing in solemn rhythm as they sang the psalms to the glory of God. "*Cantarte volo, saltate cuncti*" said St. Augustine. But in the heart of Jesus a deep sorrow pervaded the joy. "With desire I have desired to eat this passover with you before I suffer. For I say unto you, I will not eat any more thereof, until it be fulfilled in the Kingdom of God." (Luke xxii, 15-16.)

This last supper was to be his supreme instruction to the faithful and he began it with a significant gesture.

"He riseth from supper and laid aside his garments; and took a towel and girded himself. After that he poured water into a basin, and began to wash the disciples' feet, and to wipe them with the towel wherewith he was girded. Then cometh he to Simon Peter: and Peter said unto him; Lord, dost thou wash my feet? Jesus answered and said unto him, What I do thou knowest not now; but thou shalt know hereafter. Peter saith unto him, Thou shalt never wash my feet. Jesus answered him,

If I wash thee not, thou hast no part with me. Simon Peter saith unto him, Lord, not my feet only, but also my hands and my head." (John xiii, 4-9.)

Once again Peter's ardent, impetuous character, so very much of a piece through the Gospel record, is sketched in a few brief sentences. "Know ye what I have done to you?" asked Jesus. "Ye call me Master and Lord, and ye say well, for so I am. If I then, your Lord and Master, have washed your feet, ye also ought to wash one another's feet. For I have given you an example, that ye should do as I have done to you." (John xiii, 12-15.) One of the most moving parts of the Catholic Office for Holy Week is when, on Maundy Thursday, the officiating prelate—the Pope himself in the Sistine Chapel—kneels to wash the feet of the twelve poor men who symbolize the Apostles.

Jesus tried, by this dramatic gesture, finally to break the shell of pride and envy, the matrix of the human creature, which stifles even the best of us. When the Passover solemnities were finished, the meal proceeded more informally with the guests reclining upon the litters which the Greeks had brought into general usage. There would naturally be competition for the place next to Jesus and inevitably a dispute arose as to who was most entitled to it, who was the chief of the Twelve. Again Jesus had to call them to order. "The Kings of the Gentiles exercise lordship . . . but ye shall not be so; but he that is greatest among you, let him be as the younger; and he that is chief, as he that doth serve . . . ye are they which have continued with me in my temptations. And I appoint unto you a Kingdom . . . that ye may eat and drink at my table, and sit on thrones judging the twelve tribes of Israel." (Luke xxii, 24-29; Mark x, 42; Matthew xx, 25.)

The night had fallen: they had lit the little clay lamps in the candelabras. It was the night of Judas.

We wonder what he was thinking, there among the others who knew nothing whatever of his doings. He was probably infuriated by those words which he understood only too well—"the last shall be first"—and consumed with anxiety to finish what he had begun. Twice Jesus had made allusions which he alone understood. While he was washing the disciples' feet he said: "Ye are not all clean." A few minutes later he referred to a scripture which should be fulfilled: "He that eateth bread with me hath lifted up his heel against me." (John xiii, 11-18.) Later, during the meal, he spoke even more plainly: "Verily, I say unto you that one of you shall betray me." The disciples were appalled and looked at each other, each asking, "Is it I, Lord?" He did not reply directly, but gave what was perhaps a final warning. "The Son of Man goeth as it is written of him, but woe unto that man by whom the Son of Man is betrayed. It had been good for that man had he not been born." Then Judas, perhaps unconsciously, perhaps in bravado, asked in his turn, "Is it I?" There was perhaps a slight gesture of reply only visible to the questioner, or that murmured familiar response, common among the Jews, the answer Moses gave to Pharaoh (Exodus x, 29): "Thou hast said it!" (Matt. xxvi, 20-25.)

In the triclinium, as we can see at Pompeii, the guests reclined on three divans arranged round the table, leaving the fourth side free for the service. The center place at the bottom was the seat of honor; that to the right of it was called "the bosom of the father" because, since the guests reclined on the left elbow, the slightest move from the person in that place brought him toward the breast of the giver of the feast. This place was occupied by John, the beloved disciple. Peter was probably on Jesus's left. Judas was probably at the head of one of the other groups; as one of the stewards he would need to go in and out without inconveniencing anybody.

With growing alarm, the disciples looked at one another. John—he never names himself in his Gospel, but the identification is unmistakable—was leaning against his Master's breast, and, prompted by Peter, asked: "Lord, who is it?" Jesus answered: "He it is to whom I shall give a sop when I have dipped it." And when he had dipped the sop, he gave it to Judas Iscariot. (John xiii, 23-26.) In St. Matthew's version, Jesus chooses a different method to point out the traitor. "He that dippeth his hand with me in the dish, the same shall betray me." (Matthew xxvi, 23.) Both versions refer to customs still observed at table in the East. Among the Arabs in Syria and Transjordania, to put one's hand in the dish is a sort of rite and if, involuntarily, a guest lays hold of a morsel coveted by somebody else, he casts the evil eye on the other. When two men of equal rank eat dates from the same bowl, it must be covered by a veil. Many a traveler in the East has experienced the somewhat disconcerting honor of having some revolting morsel, such as a greasy kidney, handed across the table to him by the host.

We wonder whether this gesture was a last attempt on the part of Jesus to bring back the wretched Judas to his side. But there are times when the Spirit is so full of violence and resentment that a friendly gesture, instead of soothing, plunges the tortured soul more deeply into its furnace of hate. "And after the sop, Satan entered into him. Then said Jesus, That thou doest, do quickly. Now no man at the table knew for what intent he spake this to him. For some of them thought, because Judas had the bag, that Jesus had said unto him, Buy those things that we have need of against the feast, or that he should give something to the poor. He then having received the sop went immediately out; and it was night." (John xiii, 27-30.)

It was night, the immediate evocation of the eye witness who saw the door open upon the terrace and the traitor hastening in the darkness toward his doom. No conscious artist could have written with greater literary effect; and, beyond its lightning visualization of the scene, the mind calls up a vision of that more impenetrable darkness into which this man, caught up in a monstrous destiny yet impelled by his own choice, is plunged forever, because he confirmed the rejection of Christ.

Toward the end of the supper a new rite, unknown to the Mosaic law, was inaugurated by Jesus in words and gestures by which the tragedy so soon to come was explained. The synoptics report it with only very slight variations. (Luke xxii, 19-20; Mark xiv, 22-24; Matt. xxvi, 26-28.) "And he took bread, and blessed it, and brake it, and gave it to the disciples, and said: Take, eat. This is my body. And he took the cup, and gave thanks, and gave it to them, saying, Drink ye all of it. For this is my blood of the new testament, which is shed for many for the remission of sins."

No Christian can read these words without feeling the presence of Christ living. However they may be interpreted, as the Real Presence according to the Catholic Church or as a solemn commemoration, as is believed by the majority of the Reformed churches, they represent the highest level of the Christian mystery, one we all feel the need to contemplate and adore in silence. In them Christ shows himself plainly, not merely as the perfect exemplar and the incomparable teacher, but as the predestined victim offered for the salvation of mankind.

Rationalist critics have, of course, made great play with comparisons from primitive religions in which eating the flesh of a sacred animal was supposed to confer divine qualities. Certain Asiatic rites, and the Orphic and Dionysiac mysteries, also practiced the "drinking of blood." But comparisons of this kind are in fact very misleading, for they relate solely to the practice and ignore the intention. Union with God has always been man's noblest and highest aim; it is expressed in its most barbarous form by the "god-eating" of primitive people. But the Christian rite is altogether different. The words of Jesus, considered in their deepest sense, mean that in receiving the bread and the wine the faithful absorb the flesh and blood of Christ, however unworthy they may be; the transformation of the substance is in no way connected with the intention of him who receives it. Had Judas "partaken" (which he seems not to have done) he would also, even he, have received the body and blood of Christ. In this sense it is not inadmissible that the mastication is in line with the most ancient traditions of humanity.[7] But it is not a question of in-

[7] In the Greek texts of St. John (vi, 54-58) the verb translated as "to eat" is not *esthiein* or *phagein*, used for eating in the human sense, but *trogein*, to devour or consume.

gesting a substance presumed to be divine which by some magic operation confers virtue on the initiate; unity with God in the sacrament requires more: the intention, the purification and the will to love. The fact of the mastication remains, but the crude act is extended to a spiritual participation in God.

And now we come to a striking instance, that "tacit rather than manifest" accord among the four Gospels, to use Heraclitus's phrase. The actual institution of the rite is related only by the synoptics and we are at first astonished that St. John does not mention it. We conclude that it must have been because he did not wish to repeat his predecessors, but to supplement them. That may be true, yet he does report the Last Supper in detail up to that point, then he stops. But in chapter six, in the relation of events which presumably took place in Galilee, he interpolates a long discourse on the Bread of Life which the others do not give at all. This doubtless explains his silence later on, and it establishes the relation between Christ's words at the Supper and the teaching which he had given before. The discourse reported by John amplifies the brief explanations given by St. Matthew, St. Mark and St. Luke of the mysterious ceremony which Christ instituted at the Last Supper. It may be assumed that when he said, "This is my body," the Apostles must have recalled to mind that strange earlier discourse about the Bread of Life which they had found so difficult at the time.

"If any man eat of this bread he shall live for ever: and the bread that I will give is my flesh, which I will give for the life of the world." There is no question of any magical interpretation of those words; the moral and spiritual sense is strongly emphasized. Those who partake of the Bread of Life are those who listen to the Father and hear his words, those who believe in Jesus. Spiritual renewal is the essential preliminary to union with God, and the Apostles cannot have forgotten this condition, so often reiterated, when Jesus repeated his strange words once again: "My flesh is meat indeed, and my blood is drink indeed. He that eateth my flesh, and drinketh my blood, dwelleth in me, and I in him."

The doctrine of the Catholic Church is that the Sacrament of the Eucharist derives from the actions and the words of Christ at the Last Supper. It affirms that the body of Christ is present —not *in* the blood and *in* the wine, which is the Lutheran position—but under the appearance of the material species, the reality has been miraculously transformed into the substance of God himself. Transubstantiation resides in that. The presence of the body of Christ is not a local presence in the ordinary sense of the word, but it is as incontestable as the presence of the soul in the human body and is perhaps something analogous to it.

This, however, is the realm of theology. Historically, we know that the usage of this rite, as understood in the Catholic sense, is extremely ancient in the Christian Church. The first Epistle to the Corinthians, written in the year 57, refers to it as a rite established in the Early Christian communities, and the passage seems to confirm that it was interpreted in the fullest concrete and spiritual sense. "For as often as ye eat this bread and drink this cup, ye do show the Lord's death till he comes. Wherefore whosoever shall eat this bread, and drink this cup of the Lord, unworthily, shall be guilty of the body and blood of the Lord. But let a man examine himself, and so let him eat of that bread, and drink of that cup. For he that eateth and drinketh unworthily, eateth and drinketh damnation to himself." (I Cor. xi, 26-29.)

In the catacombs of St. Calixtus, we can see a fish, the symbol of Christ, bearing two baskets of small round loaves and in the center of the bread, in transparent effect across the basket, a flask of red wine. This representation of the Eucharist is probably earlier than 150 A.D.

Across the centuries the Church, reproducing in the sacrifice of the Mass the words and actions of Jesus at the Last Supper, has offered the faithful the bread by which they "communicate" with the living God and to every priest at the moment when he raises the Host and the Chalice, pronouncing the liturgical formulae of consecration, descends something of that serene youthful majesty which looks down on us from the arch over the doorway of Rheims, the image of the Messiah, knowing his death to be at hand, as he says to his disciples: "This is my body: this is my blood."

Last Teaching; Last Prayer

When the meal was over, the Jews were accustomed to linger and talk, not, as the Romans did, as an excuse to go on drinking but solely for the pleasure of talking. St. Mark and St. Matthew do not give us anything of this last discourse, considering, no doubt, that it repeated only what Jesus had said before, which they had already recorded. St. Luke gives us only a little, in very few verses (xxii, 31-38). But St. John devotes a whole series of chapters to it (xiii, 3 to xvii, 26) and it is so brilliantly recorded that here, more than anywhere else in his Gospel, do we get the feeling of a direct testimony, a supremely cherished recollection. Just the same it is not improbable, from the lack of continuity and the strange words at the end of chapter fourteen, which seem to indicate some break in the discourse, that the Apostle went over his record more than once to make sure that he had set down everything he could remember about Jesus's last days on earth, and that chapters fifteen and sixteen may be an addition. It is also possible, since this farewell discourse holds the position of prominence in St. John's Gospel which the Sermon on the Mount occupies in the synoptics, that the Apostle may have included in it teaching given by Jesus on other occasions. But, however composed, all the elements combine in a harmony of luminous beauty and sweetness; the words, even if uttered previously, are the more moving because we can hear in them the note of his earthly farewell.

The subject of the discourse is familiar and oft repeated but in this particular hour, speaking to those nearest to him, Jesus found words of the most poignant tenderness. "Little children, yet a little while I am with you. . . ." To those who interrupted him with questions, Thomas, Philip and Jude, he replied patiently. The poor men showed plainly that they had little idea of the real meaning of the tragedy in which they were involved. To Peter, who, with his usual impetuosity and a certain presumption, asked: "Lord, why cannot I follow thee now? I will lay down my life for thy sake," Jesus answered, half sadly, half ironically: "Verily I say unto thee, the cock shall not crow till thou hast denied me thrice."

Little by little, the tension grows. We feel the dramatic conflict between Jesus and these men, asking all too human questions, unable to lift their eyes from the ground, and demanding tangible signs. "Where are you going?" "What is this unknown road?" "Why cannot we go too?"—while another even asked to be shewn "the Father face to face." And Jesus was already so far away from their level, almost drawn up into the region whence he came and whose mysteries he now sought for the last time to explain.

This last discourse is indeed a summary, in the most sublime words, of everything he had been teaching for more than two years. "I am the way, the truth and the life: no man cometh to the Father except by me. . . . I am the true vine and my Father is the husbandman. Every branch in me that beareth not fruit, he taketh away. . . . If a man abide not in me, he is cast forth as a branch and is withered, and men gather them and cast them into the fire." He stresses the vital role of Faith. "Believe me that I am in the Father and the Father in me . . . whatsoever ye shall ask the Father in my name, he will give it you." And, above all, he enjoins them once again to show charity, love is the universal Law. And, though so particularly the Christian virtue, it would become so strong and so beautiful that the pagans themselves would acknowledge it: "This is my commandment, that ye love one another, as I have loved you."

But behind the moving, comforting words is the shadow of a terrifying presentiment, sometimes of triumph and glory, sometimes of unparalleled suffering, and as awe-inspiring in the one guise as in the other. The men who listened to these words, if they failed to understand them could not have failed to respond in fear and disquiet. "Now is the Son of Man glorified, and God is glorified in him." "I go away . . . if ye loved me, ye would rejoice because I go unto the Father." "Let not your heart be troubled." "Yet a little while and the world seeth me no more." "Hereafter I will not talk much with you, for the prince of this world cometh."

He spoke even more plainly than this, he tried to bring home to them the lot that awaited them in the world. "If they have persecuted me, they will also persecute you." "They shall put you out of the synagogues: yea, the time cometh that whosoever killeth you will think that he doeth God service." But the picture he painted was not altogether without consolation; from the darkness of the terrible prophecies burst forth a swelling, conquering light. "I will not leave you comfortless." "Peace I leave with you, my peace I give unto you." "Greater love hath no man than this, that a man lay down his life for his friends." More than consolation was given to the eleven anxious men who sat there listening; the most stupendous of all promises, the promise of the Resurrection: "A little while and ye shall not see me; and again a little while and ye shall see me. . . ." And the promise of the Holy Ghost, the Comforter, who will make all things plain, who will fill their souls with light and will complete, in the order of knowledge, what has been gained through the power of love. "But the Comforter, which is the Holy Ghost, whom the Father will send in my name, he shall teach you all things, and bring all things to your remembrance, whatsoever I have said unto you."

This is the nucleus of the doctrine which St. Paul, with his wisdom and his eloquence, was to develop from the verses which the beloved disciple, out of his treasured memories, had set down: that the Messiah must die for the salvation of mankind, that his death was a revolutionary event which changed the world and inaugurated a new law; and that from that time, through the forgiveness of sin and by the illumination of the Holy Spirit, salvation was made possible and man, through Christ, may re-unite himself to God.

Having said all he could to his followers on earth, Jesus, more and more withdrawn into the supernatural, addressed himself directly to his Father in heaven. This "sacerdotal prayer" is certainly the supreme mystical passage of the entire Gospel, for in it the living God speaks to the unseen God directly and, as it were, face to face.

"Father, the hour is come; glorify thy Son, that thy Son also may glorify thee. As thou hast given him power over all flesh, that he should give eternal life to as many as thou hast given him. And this is life eternal, that they might know thee, the only true God, and Jesus Christ, whom thou hast sent. . . . I have manifested thy name unto the men which thou gavest me out of the world. . . . I pray for them . . . now I am no more in the world but these are in the world and I come to thee. Holy Father, keep through thine own name those whom thou hast given me, that they may be one, as we are . . . that they may have my joy fulfilled in themselves. . . . Neither pray I for these alone, but for them which shall believe on me through their word. That they all may be one; as thou, Father, art in me and I in thee. . . . Father, I will that they also, whom thou hast given me, be with me where I am, that they may behold my glory, which thou hast given me, for thou lovest me before the foundation of the world . . . that the love wherewith thou hast loved me may be in them, and I in them." (John xvii.)

There was no more. The time had come to leave that place and go to the Mount of Olives where they were expected to stay. He had just told them that a struggle was at hand when a sword would be more useful than a garment and as usual, taking his words in their most literal sense, they assured him that they were well armed: "Here are two swords." "It is enough," he said, and, as Cyril of Alexandria suggested, he must have smiled in pity as he said it, the ironical smile of the supernatural being who had plumbed the depths of sorrow and misunderstanding but who could draw from his sad knowledge not the bitterness or the savagery of the misanthrope, but the just comprehension of a greater love.

He went out. From its situation in the highest part of the town the house where the Last Supper was held must have given a complete view of the city. Close by was the High Priest's palace; to the left Herod's, flanked by the gardens of

Gareb; and opposite, beyond the shadow of the Tyropeon, beyond Ophel and Sion at the foot of the Temple, arose the massive tower of Antonia, the symbol of humiliation. Jesus, in a glance around, could count the three "stages" of his "trial." But Golgotha would not be visible; it lay behind the square block of the Tower of David. Over the sleeping town shone the bright moon of the month of Nisan, the full moon of the Passover, "blessed in that it hath delivered us." A burning brazier marked the watchtower of Phazael, and somewhere, in a hidden police trap, Judas also kept watch.

CHAPTER TEN

THE "TRIAL" OF JESUS

Gethsemane

THE DIRECT ROAD from the house of the Cenacle to the Mount of Olives crossed the bridge which led over the Tyropeon to the Temple and through it out of the city by the Golden Gate. Since no one but the priests could go into the Temple after nightfall, Jesus and his disciples would have to descend into the lower part of the town, skirting the southeastern corner of the fortifications. Perhaps they went down by that graduated pathway which has been uncovered by the Assumptionists on their land there, a road with steps wide enough to allow asses and camels to go up and down comfortably. At the bottom of the narrow valley ran the furious waters of the brook Kidron, whose name in Hebrew signifies "dark" or "dirty"; they would not run very long, only during four or five weeks in the springtime, but in this brief period they rush and spume with great force until the heat of summer turns the river into a dry channel full of boulders.

The place for which Jesus was bound this night was a grove planted with olive trees which St. Mark and St. Matthew call Gethsemane, a name signifying "oil press." Probably it was one of those primitive outfits still to be found in Palestine, to which neighboring proprietors bring their olives while a donkey attached to a rotating wheel patiently works a wooden press.

Today, in a rather too tidy little garden planted with formal flower beds, eight huge dessicated trees still manage to produce on their scrawny branches a few meager olives. But there is no possibility that these ancient ruins could ever have given shelter to Jesus in their youth because, although the olive tree is incredibly long-lived and there are trees in Corfu and Mytilene which are said to have weathered more than a thousand years, it is certain that no trees in this particular situation could have survived the assault of Titus. A few yards from the enclosure is a subterranean chapel, with violet stained glass windows in rather poor taste, filled with the odor and the glitter of hundreds of candles. But this is no longer regarded as being the place where Christ prayed in agony, since the Franciscans have uncovered in the actual enclosure of Gethsemane the remains of a fourth century basilica built in commemoration of those dark hours.

"Sit ye here while I go and pray yonder," said Jesus to his disciples, "tarry ye here and watch with me." Only Peter and the two sons of Zebedee, James and John, were with him. Fear and disgust and an overwhelming sadness took possession of him. "My soul is exceeding sorrowful, even unto death." He went a little further off, only a stone's throw, and knelt and prayed: "O my Father, if it be possible, let this cup pass from me; nevertheless not as I will, but as Thou wilt."

The strange tormented hour is reported by the three synoptics (Matt. xxvi, 36-46; Mark xiv, 32-42; Luke xxii, 40-46). It must have been cold there in the shadow. Beyond the Kidron rose the walls of the Temple blue-white under the moon. The rumbling of the torrent made a part of the silence, interrupted at regular intervals by the cry of the Roman sentinels on the tower of Antonia. In that place, only a few yards from his friends, Jesus was more alone than he had been in the wilderness and here, in the hour when destiny took him by the throat, he experienced, in the most agonizing crisis he had ever known, the clash of the two natures within him.

But his disciples, ordinary men, had gone to sleep. "What, could ye not watch with me one hour," he said sadly when he went back to them. "The spirit indeed is willing but the flesh is weak." Again he went away to resume the supplication: "O my Father, if this cup may not pass away from me except I drink it, thy will be done." "And being in an agony he prayed more earnestly, and his sweat was as it were great drops of blood falling to the ground. And there appeared an angel from heaven strengthening him."

The bloody sweat is mentioned only by Luke the doctor, and it is a vivid reminder of the human side of Christ. The physiological phenomenon of sweating blood has been observed in cases of severe stress; it is one of those singular manifestations which nature can wrench from extremity, like the blanching of hair in a single night. Throughout this scene we are deeply conscious of the human nature of Jesus and this is why it moves us so profoundly. He was a young man, only thirty years old, and death was closing in on him; he could breathe it in the cold night air, hear it in the growl of the torrent. He would not have been human had his flesh not quaked and revolted at the thought of the death he must die. No other scene in the entire Gospel narrative, not even that of the Temptation, has such profound psychological truth; how well we recognize the heavy heart, the consciousness so distraught that it implores God for a miracle which would deny everything for which he had striven. If Jesus were an invention and his life story the fabrication of successive hagiographers, would they have produced an episode like this? From the martyrs who were to go joyfully to the torture, like the young Blandine of Lyons, we can learn little—or too much!—because the grace which upheld them seems so exceptional, so far removed from us. "But the example of Jesus shows us that God does not despise the anguish of our nature and that the highest Christian virtue can be content to overcome it without pretending to stifle it," wrote Father Lebreton.

There is, however, something else in this scene besides its moving evocation of human weakness. The troubled flesh was not only man but God; the distraught consciousness was still aware of that to which it aspired. St. Theresa of Avila has written of certain mystic states in which the creature feels the distress of such strivings. "The soul receives no consolation neither from the heaven which it has not reached nor from the earth to which it is no longer bound." *Agony*, the term which St. Luke uses, does not mean in the original Greek the stage before death, as it has come to mean today, but expresses the idea of a mortal combat, a violent drama. This is the sense in which Miguel de Unamuno uses it in his book "The Agony of Christianity." The Agony in the Garden was a conflict of the divine strength against human weakness; a conflict between the most pure and noble of souls and the Prince of Darkness, against the temptation to withdraw and give up. Yet for all its tragic humanity, the supernatural element is so strong that the scene has defeated almost all the great artists; only Rembrandt in an engraving which is little more than a sketch, full of lunar lighting and fathomless shadow, has approached the sense of conflict which the Gospel evokes. "Jesus in his Passion," said Pascal, "suffers the torments men inflict upon him, but in his Agony he suffers the torments he inflicts upon himself—*turbare semetipsum*. It is a wound dealt by a hand which is not mortal but all-powerful, and only the all-powerful could sustain it."

The essential quality of the scene is not its communication of almost unbearable distress but of a decisive acceptance. Distraught as he was, on the edge of death, Jesus can still repeat, in a sort of sublime stammer: "Not my will but thine be done." The union of the Father and the Son, one will, one design, is clearly manifest. When the anti-Christian polemicist Celsus sneered at the God who wept and groaned instead of producing a miracle to confound his enemies, he only revealed his complete misconception of Christianity. The heaviness and disgust which, as the Gospel tells us, rose up in Jesus like nausea is something the sinner knows only too well. "For he hath made him to be sin for us, who knew no sin," says St. Paul (II Cor. v, 21) and a French commentator has remarked on this: "Sin is not transferred from man to Christ but it reaches out from man to Christ . . . the Redemption operated under God in accordance with the principle of solidarity: Jesus Christ had to be man in order to redeem mankind; to be subject to the Law, to deliver men from it; to be a member of the sinful human family in order to save sinners, to assume the flesh that he might conquer it in its own sphere." It was the sin of man that the man-God took upon himself in the hour when his death was to ransom it, and it was the suffering of the world which he assumed, which he dignified and to which he has given meaning.

Then, in the distance, there was a confused burst of sound, voices and the clanking of arms. A red glare of torches became visible through the darkness. Jesus got up and returned to his disciples. "Sleep on now and take your rest," he said. "It is enough, the hour is come: behold the Son of Man is betrayed into the hands of sinners." Some commentators have seen a mordant irony in these words, but the true accent is surely that of an infinite compassion. He was to ensure their salvation very soon now, that was his mission, he who had come to vanquish fear, death and sin.

The Arrest

Judas knew exactly where Jesus would be likely to pass the night for it was not the first time that the band of disciples had accompanied their master there. He might have watched them leave the house of the Cenacle and followed them discreetly. Once sure of his facts, he had to warn the priests and the elders as quickly as possible. If the arrest was to be made quietly without arousing attention before the legal ceremonies of the Passover began, there was no time to be lost. The men who accompanied him would be the Temple servants, bearing lanterns and torches, and a detachment of soldiers armed with swords and staves.

"Now he that betrayed him gave them a sign, saying: Whomsoever I shall kiss, that same is he: hold him fast. And forthwith he came to Jesus and said: Hail, Master! and kissed him. But Jesus said unto him: Judas, betrayest thou the Son of Man with a kiss?" (Matt. xxvi, 48-50; Luke xxii, 47-48.)

The custom of the disciple kissing the hand of his master was very common; the Talmud laid it down as obligatory. But Christian art has always shown Judas as kissing Jesus on the cheek or on the forehead and all who have seen Giotto's fresco at Padua will recall the frightful head of Judas, with its low forehead and gross sneering mouth. There is something symbolical in this horrible kiss, the archetype of all those lying caresses which are the current coin of our human loves, yet perhaps it has a less ignoble significance. It might have been that, at the last moment, shame and remorse prevented Judas from pointing his finger at Jesus and crying, "That is he."

Who was responsible for the arrest of Jesus? It is a vexing question, much in evidence throughout the trial to the end, and history has since debated it incessantly. Is the legal responsibility for the death of Christ to be charged to the Roman or to the Jewish authorities? The records suggest that there was a good deal of confusion and it cannot be said that either authority emerges with much credit. From the four Gospel narratives (Matt. xxvi, 47-56; Mark xiv, 43-52; Luke xxii, 47-53; John xviii, 2-12) there were obviously Roman soldiers among those who arrested Jesus. The Greek *speira,* used in the texts, does not mean a cohort in the sense of a definite military unit but only in the sense of an undefined party of troops. Similarly a *chiliarque* is just an officer, and not, as sometimes it has been translated, a *tribunus,* who was, in the Roman army, a senior officer almost equivalent to a brigadier. It seems most likely that the Roman soldiers took part in the arrest at the request of the Jewish authorities, without knowing whether it had been definitely sanctioned by Pilate or not. In any case, the responsibility of the Jews is established clearly enough. St. Matthew, St. Mark and St. John all state definitely that the arresting party was sent by the priests and the elders and the Pharisees and when reading of the staves carried by the rabble we recall what the Talmud says about the Chief Priests belaboring the people. The Gospel narrative suggests anything but an orderly, judicial arrest and Renan's statement, "A strong sense of public order and protective police action characterized its procedure," seems very wide of the mark. It was obviously inspired by nothing higher than hatred and fear, a sordid get-together of politicians and theologians. The use of a traitor as the instrument of arrest is typical. This, as a matter of fact, was illegal. The Mosaic Law was the only legal code in the ancient world which forbade the use of spies and informers: "Thou shalt not go up and down as a talebearer among thy people; neither shalt thou stand against the blood of thy neighbor." (Lev. xix, 16.)

"Jesus said unto them: Whom seek ye? They answered him: Jesus of Nazareth. Jesus saith unto them: I am he. . . . As soon as he had said to them: I am he, they went backward and fell to the ground." This incident is reported only by St. John (xviii, 4-6). Whether it means that there was a kind of miracle, a last manifestation of the supernatural power of the Son of God; or whether simply that the agents of the Temple were once more disconcerted, as they had been upon a previous occasion by the calm majesty of Christ, we do not know.

At this moment Simon Peter, brave and impetuous as ever, drew his sword for the attack and cut off the ear of one of the Temple servants. "Then said Jesus unto him: Put up again thy sword into his place for all they that take the sword shall perish by the sword." Then he touched the wounded man and healed his ear. St. John, writing a long time after the synoptics, tells us that the name of the wounded man was Malchus, a detail which the earlier Evangelists omit, doubtless because, as we have observed in another context, it would be dangerous to call attention to him if, as tradition says and as we can well believe, he was converted by the miracle. It is a name which occurs often in Josephus and which seems to have been common among the Nebaioth Arabs. Probably he was one of the Bedouin or Idumenean soldiers of whom there were many among the Temple guards as well as in the Roman armies. Jesus had once told his disciples that he came as a lamb among wolves and there was no question of resisting arrest. "Are ye come out as against a thief with swords and staves for to take me?" he asked them. "I sat daily with you teaching in the Temple and ye laid no hold on me."

We wonder how the disciples took this calm acceptance of the fact, whether they succumbed to panic. We know that they all fled. "And there followed him a certain young man, having a linen cloth cast about his naked body; and the young men laid hold on him. And he left the linen cloth and fled from them naked." St. Mark alone records this incident and its few lines are almost a personal signature, for who would have remembered this but the man who experienced it? It has been supposed that the Gethsemane property belonged to his mother, one of those holy women who supported Jesus, and that hearing the noise in the night the young man got up and ran hurriedly to the scene, following Jesus some way behind. Perhaps it was at that moment that he received the gift of faith, which sealed him forever to the one who had set his feet on the way of the Cross.

Before Annas

And so Jesus was taken back, down the stepped pathway and the narrow sloping streets to the place from which he had come. Jerusalem by night is a strange unearthly city and, even today, the visitor has little difficulty in visualizing the nocturnal passage of Jesus surrounded by a hostile crowd. In the darkness one can forget the staring monuments, disproportionate and inharmonious, which the piety of successive generations has built, without the slightest regard for local architectural traditions. We see nothing but the high walls and narrow climbing streets, with their worn, shining stones and the wells of shadow formed by houses massed together above the roadway. Wrapped in their mantles, men lie asleep, on many of the street corners. So it must have looked that night, as the sad procession passed along the road which was to end at Golgotha.

Where was Jesus first taken? St. John alone gives us any information: he says definitely that he was taken to the house of Annas, the former High Priest. Unfortunately, the sequence of events in the fourth Gospel is not at all clear at this point. We read (xviii, 13): "And led him away to Annas first, for he was father-in-law to Caiaphas which was the high priest that same year." Then comes an account of the interrogation followed by the beginning scene of the denial of Peter, which the synoptics place during the interrogation by Caiaphas. Following this we read (xviii, 24) that Annas had sent Jesus bound to Caiaphas, and then the continuation of the denial by Peter. It would seem as though the proper place for verse 24 is after verses 13 and 14 which it, in fact, occupies in an early Syriac manuscript and in Cyril of Alexandria. It is clear that Annas sent Jesus to Caiaphas but we do not know what took place during the first interrogation.

But the mere fact that Jesus was first taken to Annas is of itself significant. Annas was the former high priest; he had received the office under the Legate Quirinius in the year 7 of our era and held it until 14, the year of the accession of Tiberius. This, as Josephus says, was a "considerable time." Although deposed by the Romans, he continued to wield very considerable power in sacerdotal circles, as witness the fact that five of his sons and his son-in-law succeeded him in attaining the miter and the pectoral. He was an able man—"none so astute as he in enriching himself," says Josephus. It is probable that there was a distinctly anti-Roman sentiment among those who supported him; he was unquestionably the leader of the Jewish community. Renan regarded him as "the leading spirit in the drama . . . the real instigator of the judicial murder that was to be carried out."

He may not even have said anything at all to Jesus. He held the strings manipulating those who seemed to be managing the affair, and once it was set in motion he knew perfectly well where it would end. We can picture the encounter face to face between the rigid old man, hidebound in his formalism but consumed by all the passions which hatred and fear can foster in the heart of man, and the young prophet who had flung at him and his kind "the whited sepulchres" of contempt and anathema. Annas considered all this, and sent Jesus on to Caiaphas.

Archaeologists and exegesists are inclined to the view that the two high priests, former and actual, shared the same palace, their quarters being separated only by a courtyard. Between whiles, Jesus was probably put in a cell. On the presumed site of the palace of the high priests, at the end of a small Greek chapel embellished with ivory and mosaics in gold, is a small low-ceilinged room, like a miniature sacristy, which purports to be the actual prison where Jesus spent a few hours during that night. Its walls are covered with faience of a soft blue, it is lit from above by a flush of golden light. Like so many of the holy places in Jerusalem, it appeals only by the memories that it calls up and by the invisible spiritual deposit with which centuries of pious devotion have invested it.

Before Caiaphas

The second stage of the "trial" brought Jesus before Caiaphas. He was the officiating High Priest and, as such, the conduct of the politico-religious proceedings against Jesus devolved upon him. He received the pontificate under the procurator Valerius Gratus in the year 18 and he succeeded in holding his office throughout the term of Pontius Pilate. He was not relieved of his post until the year 36, by the Syrian legate Vitellius, and so long a retention of such a difficult office, which one after another of his predecessors had been obliged to relinquish after a very short time, suggests that he had considerable powers of adaptability. To be quite frank, he was one of those vulgar careerists from whom at all times and in all countries the powerful have chosen their creatures. The chief motivating power of his ignoble soul was fear, that fear of what people may say which haunts such men in office. A man like Caiaphas could not permit an adventurer, a nobody, to upset the established order and perhaps arouse comment in

Rome. He must be got rid of; the religious issue was a mere pretext.

In the meantime, news of the arrest had spread and the priests, scribes and doctors had rushed to the palace to form a council of sorts. Again we are up against a chronological difficulty. The Gospels do not seem to agree upon the time of Jesus's appearance before the court. St. Matthew and St. Mark place it during the night, before cock-crow, and record a continuation of the hearing on the following morning. The fourth Gospel gives one hearing only, during the night, while St. Luke, who also records only one hearing, places it immediately after daybreak. (Matt. xxvi, 57-66; Mark xiv, 53-64; Luke xxii, 54, 66-71; John xviii, 13-14 and 19-23.) There are reasons for preferring the chronology of Matthew and Mark, that is, an unofficial hearing during the night preceding a formal indictment before the Sanhedrin. First, such unofficial meetings had obviously taken place previously, for instance, the meeting which decided to arrest Jesus; secondly it is psychologically more likely that these men who had decided to make the decisive move should get together as quickly as possible, even during the night, to have a look at the man they had laid hold on; finally, had there only been one meeting and that a nocturnal convocation of the Sanhedrin, it would have been so unorthodox that strict Jewish opinion would have disapproved violently, for the *Mishna* states that "all proceedings in which the life of a man is at stake must take place in the full light of day." [1]

The reconstruction of events seems to be that Jesus, after being taken from the palace of Annas, was brought at once before the group of men who had decided upon his death. When day came, the Sanhedrin was convened to pass judgment but

[1] Where passages from the Talmud are cited in criticizing aspects of the proceedings against Jesus in this and the following chapters, it is only fair to remind the reader that the Talmud was not compiled, even the earliest portions of it, until at least two or three centuries after the death of Christ, so that it cannot be affirmed with certainty that usages and customs codified in the Talmud were in fact current in the time of Jesus. But in view of the rigidity of Jewish tradition, many authorities declare that the Talmudic legislation enshrines centuries of unchanging custom and is in direct descent from the Mosaic Law.

the verdict had in fact been decided in advance and the Grand Council could only agree to it. By this means the people, taken by surprise, would have no time to act, while the Roman authorities would be faced with an accomplished fact. All this accords with what we know of Caiaphas, who had said (and St. John reminds us of it) that "it was expedient that one man should die for the people."

The High Priest interrogated Jesus about his disciples and his teaching. "I spake openly to the world," replied Jesus. "I even taught in the synagogue and in the temple, whither the Jews always resort: and in secret have I said nothing. Why askest thou me? Ask them which heard me what I have said unto them: behold, they know what I said." (John xviii, 20-21.) The reply was astute as well as veracious: it was designed to protect the Apostles and to bring the proceedings back to reality, the reality of a trumped-up case in which interrogation was merely a pretence. One of the officers of the Court struck Jesus for these words, saying, "Answerest thou the high priest so?" If any evidence were needed, even at this early stage, that the enemies of Jesus were not going to be embarrassed by regard for the niceties of the law, this incident provides it, for the blow was definitely illegal. The Talmud lays down penalties for judges who strike a prisoner or allow others to do so, and St. Paul, in Acts xxviii, 3, reproves Ananias for ordering him to be struck "contrary to the law."

But it is abundantly clear that the forms of legality were going to be called upon in this case only if they were susceptible of being turned against Jesus. In a capital charge under Jewish law, a single witness was not sufficient; two at least must be found (Deut. xvii, 6 and xix, 15; Num. xxxv, 30). That, however, was no trouble; witnesses could be provided. With that mixture of formality and illegality which characterizes the whole affair, they listened to various witnesses but "their witness agreed not together." Then came two who testified that they had heard him say, "I will destroy this temple that is made with hands, and within three days I will build another made without hands." But their testimony did not agree either.

Jewish law attached great importance to corroboration of details in testimony; it will be remembered that the prophet Daniel, in the affair of Susanna and the Elders, trapped the lecherous old men by discrepancies in their accounts; one said the guilty pair lay under a mastic-tree and the other, beneath an ilex. St. Matthew and St. Mark report these false testimonies differently; in the first as "I am able to destroy"; in the second as "I will destroy." Jesus had in fact said, (John ii, 19) as an hypothesis: "Destroy this temple and in three days I will raise it up," and the words seem to have scandalized nobody at the time. The accusers of the chaste Susanna had, in accordance with the Law, suffered the penalty which would have been meted out to their victim, but we are not told what happened to those creatures of Caiaphas who testified against Jesus.

Then the High Priest put the question: "Art thou the Christ, the son of the Blessed? I adjure thee by the living God that thou tell us." Jesus did not seek to evade the question put to him by the competent authority in the name of God. He replied—*responsio mortifera!*—"I am: and ye shall see the Son of Man sitting on the right hand of power, and coming in the clouds of heaven." "Then the high priest rent his clothes, and saith, What need we any further witnesses. Ye have heard the blasphemy, what think ye? And they all condemned him to be guilty of death."

The scene was well staged and it produced the calculated effect. The cunning priest knew exactly how to manipulate opinion, just as, centuries later, other astute theologians were to secure a verdict by analogous methods against Joan of Arc. If they are examined strictly, the words spoken by Jesus did not justify the verdict of death according to Jewish law, nor need Caiaphas have rent his tunic "the length of the palm of the hand" as was the prescribed usage when blasphemy was heard. For the law as to what constituted blasphemy was very precise and the Talmud gives very lengthy particulars. Blasphemy was to insult the majesty of God and this offense was incurred only if the sacred name of Yahweh, which God revealed to Moses, was uttered, not any of the synonyms which were in general use, such as the Almighty or the Blessed One, not even the abbreviation of the sacred name, Yah, but the name itself. Although Jesus affirmed that he was the Son of God by using the term "the right hand of power," he escaped the charge of blasphemy and if he did utter the sacred name itself—which we do not know since the Gospel texts have come down to us in Greek—it was not only the high priest who should have rent his garments but everyone present. We get the impression that Caiaphas staged the gesture to impress the audience. There was, moreover, a special ceremony necessary for convictions of blasphemy. The two witnesses were installed behind a curtain, the accused was prominently stationed in full view of the court and was questioned very carefully as to why he had used the sacred word and whether he was prepared to retract it, before his conviction could be registered. There is no hint of any of this during these hasty proceedings.

It was not blasphemy for a man to state that he was the Messiah. Caiaphas put forward that Jesus had no right to say so, but there was no legal justification of his case. Everything the accused man said about the return of the Messiah in glory followed logically from his initial affirmation, and was based upon a prophecy of Daniel (vii, 13-14). The accusation of blasphemy in fact was groundless. The appeal of Caiaphas to the court to consider Jesus condemned by his own words was even more flagrantly illegal than the rest of the proceedings, for the Law held that the statement of the accused could not be regarded as valid unless confirmed by witnesses, so that no man who was sick, deranged or ashamed could choose this way of terminating his life. But forms can always be disregarded when it is a question of overthrowing a political adversary: for then the end justifies the means and justice would only serve to cheat equity.

The Denial of Simon-Peter

While the interrogation was proceeding, several of Jesus's disciples, recovering from their first panic, guessed where he had been taken and were loitering about outside the High Priest's house. The courtyards of rich men's houses in the East are always full of gossips, servants, clients and hangers-on. The spring night was chilly, so some of them lit a brazier for warmth and among the circle of men gathered around it the presence of the disciples was noticed and commented upon. One of the Apostles, almost certainly John, since he alone gives the details, had some acquaintance with Caiaphas and so slipped in unnoticed; Peter evidently followed him and also stood in the group of men around the fire.

One of the high priest's maidservants, following the usual Jewish custom, was in charge of the gate. Catching sight of Peter, she came up and scrutinized him. "This is one of them," she said. "Thou also wast with Jesus of Nazareth." But he denied it: "I know not, neither understand I what thou sayest." Then he went out of the courtyard toward the terrace and another maid noticed him and said to the other servants: "This fellow was also with Jesus of Nazareth." At that moment the cock crew. Sick with worry and fear, the Apostle may not have noticed it; he went back around the fire and, it would seem, almost out of bravado, denied Christ again, with oaths.

An hour passed and the incident seemed forgotten. Peter joined in conversation with the others. But the accent of the Galilean peasant was noticeable in Jerusalem, for they confused certain letters of the alphabet and it was said that nobody could tell whether they were saying immar (a lamb), camar (wool), hamar (wine) or hamor (an ass). So it was inevitable that somebody would detect Peter's Galilean accent. "Surely thou art also one of them, for thy speech bewrayeth thee." Then one of the High Priest's servants, a relative of the man whose ear Peter had wounded when Christ was arrested, joined in: "Did I not see thee in the garden with him?" Feeling himself attacked on all sides Peter lost his head, repeating denials and curses, and again, the cock crew.

Peter was no coward, as is shown by his behavior when they laid hands on Christ. But he was one of those men who, although they can cope with danger when it comes, are scared at the thought of it. St. Paul, in his Epistle to the Galileans, reports an incident at Antioch when St. Peter seems to have succumbed to a similar temptation, when he "did eat with the Gentiles," but when certain Jews came he withdrew "and other Jews dissembled likewise with him." "I withstood him to the face," says St. Paul, "because he was to be blamed." Peter inclined perhaps to moral rather than physical cowardice; he was all too human. The passage can at least be taken as guaranteeing the authenticity of the Gospel; no one would deliberately have invented it and it is notable that St. Mark, who is generally regarded as having based his Gospel upon Peter's own reminiscences, gives the fullest account of it.

"And the second time the cock crew." Some witnesses who have made a study of the crowing of the cock in Palestine around the beginning of April have deduced from this that the time must have been about half-past two or three. Other observers say that certain types of birds in the East crow at intervals of an hour or so throughout the night. It may have been the harsh, guttural cry which struck at the disciple's conscience; it may even have been that it was about that time that Jesus, escorted by the guards, was taken out of the council chamber and led across the court. There is no need to suppose that Jesus heard his disciple's denial, for he who could pierce hearts with a single look need only have gazed for a moment at Peter. But it was enough to bring the memory back to him: "That this night, before the cock crow, thou shalt have denied me thrice." The shame and self-contempt we feel when we realize the depths to which we have fallen welled up in Peter; he went out quickly, and he wept. Some three hundred yards from the site of the house of the Cenacle, though a good way from that of the High Priest's palace (which has led to a good deal of argument), can be seen a new church built on the site of a fifth century basilica, the name of which it still bears. St. Peter *in Galicante,* St. Peter at Cockcrow, must be the only church in the world dedicated to the memory of a sin, or rather of its repentance, but if the edifying fashion had caught on the earth would be bristling with them. But perhaps it commemorates not so much the Apostle's lapse, consoling as this may be to all of us, as the look of understanding which Christ gave his unfaithful servant as he passed him in the night. "You see, Peter, how much your fine words about defending me with your life are worth. You are only a man like other men, but it is for you and for all the others, for all the weakness of mankind, that I am offering my agony and my death." (Matt. xxvi, 58, 69-75; Mark xiv, 54, 66-72; Luke xxii, 55-62; John xviii, 17-18; 25-27.)

The First Abuses

The midnight conclave being over, Jesus was left in the hands of the Temple guards and the servants. Such as these need little encouragement to abuse any unfortunate who is at their mercy without any of the safeguards against violence which society normally imposes. Many degrading and disgusting scenes occur in prisons, especially during unsettled times, and there was nobody to protect Jesus. Indeed, the members of the Sanhedrin, in leaving him defenceless, were as guilty as if they had abused him themselves. So the underlings had it all their own way; they spat upon him, jeered at him, bound his eyes and rained blows upon him, saying: "Prophesy . . . who is it that smote thee." This cruel game of blind man's buff [2] went on for some time; blows, oaths and insults were spewed out at him. (Matt. xxvi, 67-68; Mark xiv, 65; Luke xxii, 63-65.)

This was undiluted hatred, showing itself in its most primitive form. Among the dignitaries in the council chamber, hatred had been veiled by the trappings of legality; among the rabble it was unmasked. We can see in the actions of these men all the vilest passions of the human heart, political strife, religious bigotry, the resentment which those who serve the powers that be feel for those who will not submit themselves to the yoke. The prophets had known this too: "They abhor me, they spare not to spit in my face." (Job xxx, 10.) "I gave my back to the smiters and my cheeks to them that plucked

[2] The game is very ancient: it was played by children in Greece under the name of *Kollabixe.*

off the hair." (Isaiah l, 6.) Jesus accepted the full ignominy and, throughout his passion, cruel mockery alternated with cruel suffering to the end. Whoever wishes to walk with Christ must accept his shame, St. Paul was to say, and the silence of Jesus amid his tormentors is a lesson to us all.

Before the Sanhedrin

Jesus was then kept in a cell until the Sanhedrin could be formally summoned, which was as soon as the scribes and the priests could be gathered together, before the first rays of the sun shone on the mountains of Moab, as soon, as the saying went, "as the blue could be distinguished from the white." We notice the same urgency through the whole proceedings; the day pulsates to a feverish rhythm, the haste with which evil deeds are pursued. For the official Passover began when the evening shadows fell upon the hills and no orthodox Jew could forget this.

So, in that shivering dawn, Jesus was brought to the Temple where the Sanhedrin was assembled, down the broad steps of the street of David, across the Xystus, which was a kind of square flanked by the Herodian and Asmonean palaces, and across the bridge which connected the upper town with the Temple esplanade. The British archaeologist Robinson has uncovered the colossal foundations of this bridge, which, in a single giant arc, spanned the valley of the Tyropeon, with the houses huddled together below it.

Already in the courts of the Temple, the faithful, with their faces toward the east, were waiting for the exact moment of the sunrise to begin their psalms: "Blessed be the eternal God, Lord of the Universe, who has created light and darkness."

St. Matthew, St. Mark and St. Luke, reporting the meeting of the Sanhedrin, say that it met "When the morning was come" (Matt. xxvii, 1); "And straightway in the morning" (Mark xv, 1); "As soon as it was day" (Luke xxii, 66). St. Mark emphasizes that it was "the whole council," not a more or less clandestine committee, but the body in which was invested the political and religious authority of Israel. The "trial" of Jesus, if indeed we can use such a term, has now formally begun.

We have already explained the constitution and powers of the Sanhedrin. It was a senate, a permanent council, and the high court of justice by virtue of the principle of the Jewish community which united all the civil and judicial powers under the supreme spiritual authority. The word *Sanhedrin*, which never occurs in the Old Testament but is frequently used in the Talmud, is a corruption of the Greek *sunedrion*, though the rabbis went to great lengths to provide it with a Hebrew origin, deriving it from *san* (order) and *hederin* (applying)—thus, the body which applies the Law and maintains order. The supreme council had, in fact, developed in Israel at the time when the Greek influence, under the Seleucid Kings, was strongest, but with their usual attachment to tradition the Jews related it to the Council of the Elders which God had ordered Moses to institute (Num. xi, 16). The number of its members was also attributed to divine ordinance: "How can we prove," said the Talmud, "that the Grand Sanhedrin should have seventy-one members?" "Because it was said, Gather unto me seventy men of the elders of Israel—and with Moses, this makes seventy-one." It is also recounted, in all gravity, that the venerable founder was greatly embarrassed because he could choose only seventy members. Six from each tribe made seventy-two, so it was necessary to draw lots.

The Sanhedrin was composed of priests, scribes or doctors of the law, and elders of the people, although there was no requirement that the three categories should be equally represented. Members had to be of pure Jewish blood, of a sufficiently impressive personal appearance, and fathers of families. Among those who were explicitly disqualified were blind men, eunuchs, bird sellers, dice players, usurers and those who operated a black market during the Sabbatical year. Recruitment was by co-option and the High Priest laid hands upon the newly elected judge.

Before the Roman occupation the Sanhedrin had definite

political powers. It elected the King and governed in his absence; its consent was necessary before war could be declared. But its powers had been whittled away. Herod received his authority directly from Antony and Augustus, and when Archelaus was deposed, the Sanhedrin was not allowed to elect a new King in his place. But it still retained full juridical authority, at least where violations of the religious Law were concerned. Women suspected of adultery were brought before the Sanhedrin and submitted to the ordeal of being plunged in water up to their heads. False prophets, heretical sects or families came before the Sanhedrin, which was competent to try all the graver cases beyond the scope of the jurisdiction of the provincial Sanhedrins. It was therefore normal that a man charged with blasphemy and sedition, a "false prophet," should come before the Grand Sanhedrin.

It is not possible to give the names of the council of that time, beyond saying that the two great sacerdotal families of Annas and Boètus would certainly be well represented. We may guess that Rabbi Gamaliel, the preceptor of St. Paul, was a member; perhaps also his son Simon, who fell in the defence of Jerusalem in the year 70; Rabbi Jonathan ben Azziel, a disciple of Hillel who, we are assured by the Talmud, lived to be five hundred; Rabbi Onkelos, a circumcised pagan proselyte; Rabbi Helias, the treasurer of the Temple, and Abba Saul, whose amazing powers of dialectic were said to be due to his possession of the shin bone of Og, King of Bashan. A "Life of Jesus," written by one Sepp, and published in Germany in 1814, gives biographical particulars of forty alleged members of the Sanhedrin, but truth compels us to admit that the chronology of the Talmud is so vague that we cannot positively name anyone.

It was usual for Jewish tribunals, as it is in certain Mohammedan countries today, to sit by the gates of the city. The Grand Sanhedrin had an official local meeting place near the gate of the Temple, by the bridge over the Tyropeon. This was the *Liscat Haggazith* or "hall of the polished stones," part of it within the sacred enclosure of the Temple and part on profane ground. The judges entered from the side within the Temple; the accused from the other side, but it is not altogether certain that Jesus was in fact tried here. It was not necessary, save in cases of exceptional gravity, to convene all the seventy members of the Sanhedrin; ordinarily twenty-three members formed a quorum. If a judge wished to retire during a session, he had to make sure that there would be twenty-three without him. There were two presiding dignitaries, the *Nasi* or prince, and the "father of the Assembly" the *Abh-Beth-Din*, the oldest member. The members sat in a circle to the right and the left of these two, so that they could be consulted; at the end of each half circle sat a scribe to record the votes, the one for acquittal, the other for conviction. A third scribe, in the center, kept the register.

The proceedings of this tribunal were in accord with the solemnity of its constitution. A prosecution, which in Jerusalem, as in Greece or Rome, could be brought by any citizen (there was no public prosecutor), was not granted until the High Priest had previously considered the charge and sanctioned its hearing. If the charge related to a capital offence, the complainant was solemnly warned that he bore upon him "the blood of the accused and all his descendants to the end of the world." The witnesses, not less than two, were similarly admonished and the obligation upon them to take part in the execution themselves if their testimony led to condemnation was calculated to make them reflect before giving evidence, though perhaps not so much as the penalties for false witness which were the same as would have been meted out to the accused. The Judges must be "impartial," the Law was very insistent on this, and in the case of capital offences no one under forty was allowed to vote. If a conviction was decided upon, the judges must adjourn for a day spent in prayer, fasting and meditation. Once the verdict was given, it could be reversed only in favor of the accused, and a majority of one was decisive for an acquittal but not for a condemnation. Yet where were these scrupulous, honorable provisions, so creditable to the Jewish law, so just in their regard for the human rights of the accused, in the proceedings against Jesus?

According to St. Mark and St. Matthew, the meeting of the Sanhedrin lasted only a few minutes; they say flatly that "all the chief priests and elders of the people took counsel against Jesus to put him to death." St. Luke gives more particulars but his account conveys the same impression of a hurried session in which the legal forms were barely honored. "The elders of the people and the chief priests and the scribes came together and led him into their council, saying, Art thou the Christ? tell us. And he said unto them: If I tell you, ye will not believe: And if I also ask you, ye will not answer me, nor let me go. Hereafter shall the Son of Man sit on the right hand of the power of God. Then said they all: Art thou the Son of God? And he said unto them: Ye say that I am. And they said, What need we any further witness? For we ourselves have heard of his own mouth." (Luke xxii, 66-71.)

It was merely a repetition of his interrogation by Caiaphas, except that they dropped the accusation of sedition, since it had hardly been established that Jesus had wished to destroy the Temple. The accusation of blasphemy, however, could, through the carefully put question, be based upon Christ's reply to the question: Art thou the Son of God?—which was interpreted as his agreeing that he was. Provided that the accused was given an opportunity of retracting if he wished, the charge of blasphemy might be considered proven, but it is perfectly clear that the decision to condemn Jesus to death had been taken even before the hearing, which was in itself a crime against justice. Even had the forms of the law been respected, the "proceedings" would still have been nothing more than a machination to get rid of a man who was considered embarrassing.

There has been considerable argument as to whether a Jewish tribunal at that time was competent to pronounce the death penalty. Josephus says that the power of condemning to death was taken away from the Jews forty years before the destruction of the Temple. The Romans were unwilling to leave the power of life or death in the hands of a people whose fanaticism they knew only too well, and the Sanhedrin could not even meet to consider a capital charge without the express permission of the procurator. This is proved by the fact that when the Jews went to Pilate about Jesus, he thought that they had come to ask for this authority and he told them to judge Jesus according to their own law. (John xviii, 31.) The Talmud states that, after the Sanhedrin lost the power of condemning to death, they met in the Hall of Polished Stones only in exceptional cases. When the High Priest Ananias, taking advantage of the absence of the procurator of the time, had St. James and other Christians stoned to death, there was considerable outcry, which is reported by Josephus. The assembly which condemned Jesus had, therefore, no legal authority whatever.

Even had the case been sanctioned by Pilate, it does not follow that the condemnation would have been legal. Renan, and many other writers, have held that the Jews could condemn if the procurator implemented the sentence. But such a division of power is inconceivable when we remember the Roman contempt for the Jews. It is hardly likely that they would have consented to be the "secular arm" for the Jewish clergy. In Roman Law there is no division between the *juridicto,* that is, the power to judge the case, and the *imperium,* the power to carry out the sentence. If the Sanhedrin instituted proceedings against Jesus on a capital charge and condemned him to execution, they were usurping the functions of the procurator. They were only competent to lay the charge before Pilate, who could then consider whether he would or would not allow it. It goes without saying that they could not obtain from a Roman official authority to execute a man on some vague religious grounds. That is why, when Jesus was brought before Pilate, the accusation of blasphemy was not even mentioned; three political charges were trumped up instead: he disturbed the people, he condemned the payment of tribute, he proclaimed himself King. The alteration of the charge is in itself an admission.

The Remorse of Judas

It could not be long before the Sanhedrin's decision to put Jesus to death became known in Jerusalem. We know how rumors spread in our own vast cities. In the small towns of the Orient "hearsay flies faster than a bird." More than anyone else, Judas must have been waiting for the outcome of the arrest and we can guess what he, the agent responsible for it, must have felt. St. Matthew (xxvii, 3-10) gives us a last glimpse of the dark soul of the wretched man and the testimony is confirmed later in the Acts of the Apostles (i, 16-20). "Then Judas, which had betrayed him, when he saw that he was condemned, repented himself and brought again the thirty pieces of silver to the chief priests and elders, Saying, I have sinned in that I have betrayed the innocent blood. And they said, What is that to us? see thou to that. And he cast down the pieces of silver in the Temple, and departed, and went and hanged himself." St. Peter in the Acts adds that "falling headlong, he burst asunder in the midst, and all his bowels gushed out."

The scene as reported has a brutal directness. The contempt of the priests for the spy is apparent in their scornful words. His remorse was of no interest. And yet—we seem to see in the abandoned creature some last gleam of the light that had been shed on him, some trace of his attachment to Jesus. Perhaps we can even elucidate from his remorse a possible motive for the betrayal; perhaps he did not desire his master to be condemned but only thought to teach him a lesson. It is not only the riddle of Judas but of so many other men; what if all of us, like him, were made to suffer for our treachery in full! Origen, without venturing to defend the traitor, advances the explanation that Judas hanged himself so that his soul, released from his body, might go before the soul of Jesus and implore mercy. Yet a tear, a word, or a look at the foot of the Cross would have served. The penitent thief was saved.

"And the chief priests took the silver pieces and said, It is not lawful for to put them into the treasury because it is the price of blood. And they took counsel, and bought with them the potter's field, to bury strangers in. Wherefore that field was called, the field of blood, until this day." On the other side of Gehenna, above the frightful ravine where the heathen kings had burnt human sacrifices so that Gehenna is to this day a synonym for hell, there is a piece of that accursed ground, which is still identified as the Potter's Field. Whether it was bought by the Sanhedrin, as the Gospel says, or by Judas himself, as is stated in the Acts (according to the latter account, he hanged himself there), it is for ever associated with the traitor. The name "the Potter's Field" may have been derived from the gate to the city which was close by, called "Sterqueline," or Pottery or Ceramics, just as there was a Ceramic quarter in Athens, and a Jardin des Tuileries in Paris. The word, however, had also a prophetic echo, for the Gospel says: "Then was fulfilled that which was spoken by Jeremy the prophet, saying, And they took the thirty pieces of silver, the price of him that was valued, whom they of the children of Israel did value; and gave them for the potter's field, as the Lord appointed me." It is clear from the prophetic allusions that all these things had to be; it was necessary that the political animosity of the Jews should crush Jesus but it was necessary for reasons that had nothing to do with law and politics. And there could be no question of allowing the victim to profit by the retraction of the man who had betrayed him.

Before Pilate

Meanwhile, Jesus had been brought before the Roman procurator to obtain the executive fiat for the decision to kill him. Thus the second and decisive act of the "trial" opens. It was dawn, says St. John, which on April 7th would be just before six A.M., a strange hour, one would think, to bring an accused man before a high officer. But we know that the Romans customarily rose early, devoting the morning to business, the afternoon to the siesta or to social occasions and amusement.

The moment might have been even more inauspicious had the Jews not already made up their mind in the matter. They treated the Roman magistrate with a mixture of servility and insolence, knowing full well that if they had cause to fear the harshness of the procurators, these also were afraid that the Jews might denounce them to the Emperor. "They themselves went not into the judgment hall, lest they should be defiled, but that they might eat the Passover. Pilate then went out unto them." We can imagine the feelings of a colonial Governor-General, already conscious of the influx of excited people into his capital, when he realized that some obscure and complicated affair was brewing and that he must go out into the street and discuss it with them.

All four Evangelists report the interrogation of Jesus by Pilate and St. John gives us many additional details which, thanks to recent archaeological research, enable us to locate this scene more definitely than any other in the life of Jesus. The fourth Gospel uses the term *praetorium;* the Latin word which had passed into Hebrew and even Aramaic usage, indicated the place where the praetor or magistrate issued his warrants. It was not necessarily the court house. It also was applied to the praetor's camp or tent in times of war and to his residence in his capacity as colonial governor. The *praetorium* would consist simply of a semi-circular dais forming the *tribunal* (*bema* in Greek) on which was installed the *curule,* or traditional magistrate's chair, an uncomfortable stool. To say that Jesus was brought to the praetorium therefore simply meant that he was brought to the place where Pilate lived.

We know, from references in Philo and Josephus, that the procurators when in Jerusalem took up residence in the Antonia Fortress, built by Herod and named by him to curry favor with Mark Antony. This was on the outskirts of the town bordering the Temple, extending along the ramparts but dominating them by a height of over seventy-five feet from the rock upon which it was raised. Normally it was garrisoned by six hundred men who kept watch over Jerusalem from its imposing walls; when the procurator was in residence he brought reinforcements of cavalry from Caesarea. In the year 30 Pilate must have been aware that the people were restless; St. Luke (xiii, 1) mentions incidents involving bloodshed in Galilee, so that it is not improbable that the procurator had actually installed himself in the massive donjon of the fortress.

In his *Jewish War,* Josephus gives us a good deal of information about this. There had been a fortress there since Solomon's time and successive generations had fortified the site, since at this point the crest of Bezetha offers a vantage point for attack. The tower of Hananeel (which the Greeks called *Baris*) had been erected there on the return from Exile and the Asmonean Kings had turned it into a castle which had been further embellished and extended by Herod. As he left it, Antonia was an oblong quadrilateral of about three hundred by one hundred and fifty feet, with square towers rising some ninety feet at each of the four corners. It was, in fact, the key to the Holy City; it blocked the way to the Temple. From it stairs descended to the Temple courts and beneath the esplanade was a honeycomb of secret, mysterious passages. Antonia was destroyed when Jerusalem fell to Titus, but its site seems to have remained in popular memory. As early as the fourth century the traditional site of the "Praetorium of Pilate" was shown and in the sixth century a church dedicated to Santa Sophia was built there, but fell into disuse. In the fifteenth and sixteenth centuries the "Way of the Cross" passed by the site. Today we do not need to rely upon tradition, for archeology has established it almost unquestionably.

More than a hundred years ago, in 1842, two Alsatian Jewish converts to Catholicism, the brothers Theodore and Alphonse Ratisbonne, founded an order of priests and nuns to work for the conversion of the Jews—the order of the Priests and the Nuns of Our Lady of Zion. Thirteen years later, Fr. Marie-Alphonse opened a house of the order in Jerusalem. The building was a shabby house in the quarter where the Temple had formerly stood. Little by little the order extended its premises until its property included the ruins of what had been Antonia, and the imposing Convent of Our Lady of Zion now covers the site. During the building operations, many interesting finds came to light, an underground pool, conduits and the remains of gigantic foundations. The nuns fortunately recognized that these finds were of great significance and enlisted the help of the Dominicans of the Biblical School in the systematic excavation of the site. Between the years 1927–1932 an entire pavement was exposed, covering a surface of about 2,500 square yards. It was formed of huge stone slabs, and it must, from its position, have formed the interior courtyard of the fortress of Antonia. Now we come to the connection: St. John says that Pilate "brought Jesus forth and sat down in the judgment seat in a place that is called Lithostrotos, but in the Hebrew, Gabbatha." (John xix, 13.) The Greek word for pavement is *lithostrotos*.

This, then, may be the Lithostrotos,[3] this pavement that we can now see, these stones that we can touch, their worn and pitted surface marked by the tracks of passing horsemen and the sockets of standards and columns. The circumstances in which the fortress was destroyed favor the supposition, for in their attack on the towers the Romans would have needed to clear the pavement. The Greek word *lithostrotos* which St. John uses means "a paved place" and the Hebrew *Gabbatha* a "raised or elevated place," which suggests exactly the site of Antonia. Perhaps it was in these very subterranean passages that Aristobulus, the son of John Hyrcanus, hid the ruffians who were to murder his brother. The reservoir into which ran the streams from the pavement gutters, through drain holes which we can still see, as well as many underground rivulets, probably formed the water supply of the garrison. The scarp outside the wall of the Convent church probably marks the bank of the hill as it was before Herod's architects set to work on it. All the remains have an unmistakable relationship of period and craftsmanship; they unquestionably date from the

[3] It can be seen today in a crypt and one of the stones has been used to form an altar. On the walls of the crypt are *ex voto* tablets with the names Levy, Bauer, Rabbi D and family. The Convent of Zion is a meeting place for converted Jews.

Roman occupation and the conception and execution of the work corresponds exactly with what we know of Herod's architecture. It can be said with reasonable certitude that this is the site of the praetorium.

It has been suggested that Pilate, in mixing in the affair, was acting contrary to Roman Law. He may, however, have considered that the usual Roman procedure was not applicable to a Jew. This provided that an accusation must be preceded by the *postulatio,* or application to accuse, which the magistrate might allow or refuse. The application was refused, for instance, in cases where a freed slave wished to accuse a former master, or to anyone applying against a citizen absent on national service. After the *postulatio* came the *delatio nominis* in which the accuser stated on oath that he was not activated by personal envy or hatred. The charge itself had to be made in public by a beadle and the accused had the right to call witnesses and address the court. But of all these scrupulous guarantees, none seems to have been accorded to Jesus.

Pilate asked them what accusation they made against him. The Jews did not say to Pilate: "We have condemned him to death and you must execute him," but they did say: "If he were not a malefactor we would not have delivered him up to thee." Whether Pilate saw through the maneuver, or whether perhaps he misunderstood them and thought they had come to ask his permission to try Jesus, is uncertain but he replied: "Take ye him and judge him according to your law." Then they said: "It is not lawful for us to put any man to death." Pilate hesitated; what after all had the man done? "We found this fellow perverting the nation, and forbidding to give tribute to Caesar, saying that he himself is Christ a King." We need not dwell upon the obvious falsity of the accusation; it impressed Pilate sufficiently to make him decide to question Jesus himself.

What sort of man was Pilate, upon whom the fate of Jesus depended? Tacitus mentions him; Josephus and Philo have left us a good deal of information about him. Tiberius made him procurator in the twelfth year of his reign, that is, in

A.D. 26, and he held the office for ten years. We know little of his origins, but he was probably an *equite,* that class of lesser Roman gentlemen whom the Emperors found more reliable than the great aristocratic families. The name Pilate has been derived from *Pileatus,* and from this it has been concluded that he was a descendant of freed slaves, for the *pileum,* or red cap, was the badge of this class. Another derivation cited is from the *pilum,* the javelin-like weapon of the legionaries, and from this it has been concluded that he was the son of some officer who had been decorated. Some writers, indulging in flights of fancy, have reconstructed his entire career. Rosadi makes him a Spaniard by birth, son of that Marcus Pontius who commanded the renegade Asturians, who were the allies of the Romans in Agrippa's Spanish wars. For this service Marcus Pontius is alleged to have received the *pilum* of honor and his son, Lucius Pontius Pilatus, born in Seville, attached himself to the fortunes of Germanicus until the latter's mysterious death. Then, by an astute and calculated marriage, he got in well at Court and received the nomination as procurator of Judea. But all this is guessing; let us turn to the man's psychology which is much more interesting.

It would be unwise to accept without qualification all that the two Jews, Philo and Josephus, say about him, for these fanatical nationalists accuse him of every crime in the calendar. Josephus depicts him as immoral, unjust, dishonest and encouraging violence and corruption. Philo mentions his "rapines, iniquities and outrages" but does not give any concrete examples. We know that the procurator had a heavy hand; reference has already been made to his harsh reprisals in Galilee (Luke xiii, 1). But the man responsible for the order of a province where the population was notoriously hard to manage had small choice of method. The Gospel does not convey the impression that he was a brutal or unjust man. On the contrary, he seems a typical member of the Roman governing class, whom Renan has compared with the English Tories "whose strength derives from their very prejudices," very civilized, in the good and the bad sense of the term, and having nothing but contempt for the rabble among whom they had to keep order. Since the year 19, anti-Semitism had been in the air of Rome; the Jews had been expelled from the city and there is no reason to suppose that Pilate loved them. Moreover, he had had personal experience, over the affairs of the aqueducts and the golden shields, of how tiresome their fanaticism could be. Who was it that they were now bringing to him, as a self-styled King? Some vague prophet, probably mad and perhaps brought with the idea of making him, the procurator, look foolish if he condemned a half wit. In any case, he knew quite well that they had not caught the man in open revolt. It was probably something trumped up by these impossible creatures. Dislike and contempt of the Jews inclined Pilate favorably toward Jesus.

Going back into the courtyard so that he should not be disturbed by the shouting of the crowd, he called Jesus and said: "Art thou the King of the Jews?" There was a mild irony in the question. Jesus replied by going straight to the heart of the matter. "Sayest thou this thing of thyself or did others tell it thee of me?" Insofar as the Roman point of view was concerned, he had never given his adversaries the slightest ground for supposing that he aimed at the throne, but in the Jewish sense, yes, he was a King, the Messiah King, the Lord's Anointed. "Am I a Jew?" said Pilate. "Thine own nation and the chief priests have delivered thee unto me: what hast thou done?" Jesus did not try to dissemble, perhaps because Pilate represented authority. "My Kingdom is not of this world; if my Kingdom were of this world then would my servants fight, that I should not be delivered to the Jews; but now is my Kingdom not from hence." All this, doubtless, meant very little to Pilate; he returned to the concrete point: "Art thou a King then?" Jesus in replying, "Thou sayest that I am a King," gave ground for a charge against him, but he went on: "To this end was I born and for this came I into the world that I should bear witness unto the truth. Every one that is of the truth heareth my voice." The Roman shrugged his shoulders: there was nothing to worry about in this dreamer. "What is truth?" he said, and all the skepticism of the society to which he belonged has come down to us in these words.

He went back to the threshold of the fortress and faced the priests and the crowd outside. "I find no fault in him at all." It is clear that at this moment Pilate had made up his mind that Jesus was a poor, simple, inoffensive creature. But an uproar burst out at his words; the Jews shouted and protested. We can almost see and hear them. "He stirreth up the people," they said, "teaching throughout all Jewry, beginning from Galilee to this place." Pilate seized on the word Galilee. Was the man a Galilean? He was. Excellent idea: send him to Herod.

Before Herod

Herod Antipas, the tetrarch of Galilee, the adulterer who had married Herodias, was also in Jerusalem for the Passover, for the great ones of the earth have always believed in the virtue of appearances. He and Pilate did not get on very well, for the ineffective kinglet had never forgiven the procurator for the highhanded way in which he had settled trouble in Herod's own territory, while the procurator was doubtless well acquainted with the Herodian habit of spying for the Emperor. In affecting to regard Jesus, as a Galilean, subject to the tetrarch's jurisdiction, Pilate killed several birds with one stone. It flattered the tetrarch and, if the affair ended in an execution, he could not go to Rome or Capri and complain to the Emperor that the procurator had been cruel and repressive. There was probably a good deal of irony in this gesture of making the Idumean responsible for a verdict which might be embarrassing and one may also suspect a hidden trap, for if Herod assumed the powers of jurisdiction beyond the borders of his own state, he was probably exceeding his rights.

So once more Jesus, with his escort and the curious and hostile crowd, crossed the bridge of the Tyropean to where, on the Xystus, in the administrative and commercial center of Jerusalem, the Herodian palace stood. Nothing remains today of its elaborate colonnades, nothing is there but a huddle of tumbledown Arab houses in a network of stinking alleyways. Herod, as we have seen when he ordered the death of John the Baptist, was not a brutal tyrant by nature; he was feeble and irresolute, and at once skeptical and superstitious. Like Pilate, he was a typical product of his time and place, of that decadence of civilization in which a confusion of cultures leads to a weakening of moral standards.

"And when Herod saw Jesus he was exceeding glad for he was desirous to see him of a long season, because he had heard many things of him; and he hoped to have seen some miracle done by him." (Luke xxiii, 8.) It will be remembered that Herod had wished to see him a long time before, but Jesus had replied to his messengers, "Go ye, and tell that fox . . ." (Luke xiii, 32.) The attitude of Jesus before Herod was quite different from what it had been before Pilate. He offered a disdainful silence to the petty tyrant's questions, refusing to recognize his authority. Herod understood his attitude only too well so "with his men at arms set him at naught and mocked him and arrayed him in a gorgeous robe and sent him again to Pilate."

There has been a good deal of discussion about the "gorgeous robe." Was it simply a costly and elaborate garment, a truly royal robe for one who had said he was King of the Jews? It might have been this, either in mockery of Jesus or of the Jews, whom the Herodians despised and lost no chance of showing it. Some have thought it a sort of straitjacket such as one might use for a madman, but the majority of commentators think that it was probably a white tunic such as the military tribunes put on before combat and which candidates at the elections were required to wear (the word *candidate* is indeed derived from this *toga candida*). If this were so, the gesture was unmistakably aimed at Pilate. "You tried to pull a fast one on me, here you are, I can play that game." It was a good game for these two sophisticated administrators, but the ball they were tossing backward and forward was a poor, friendless man. The game is still played, from one tribunal to another, by public prosecutors; we have all seen it. Pilate, anyway, seems to have appreciated the joke for he and Herod the same day "were made friends together for before they were at enmity between themselves."

This story is told only by St. Luke (xxiii, 7-12) and there have been doubts as to its authenticity. But it does not break the thread of the narrative and it is not inacceptable in itself, either in matter or style. It may also be observed that St. Luke throughout his Gospel mentions Herod more frequently than the others, as though he had a personal informant in the tetrarch's household. This might have been that Joanna, the wife of Herod's steward Chuza, who is mentioned among those women who helped to support Jesus (Luke viii, 3). It is noticeable in the Acts of the Apostles that St. Luke blames Herod equally with Pilate for lending himself to the Jewish intrigue against Jesus.

A Woman's Dream; a Bandit's Name

So the unhappy man whom the great ones so lightly passed backward and forward came back to the praetorium. The whole procedure probably took about twelve hours, and for the fourth time the angry, shouting crowd followed their victim along the streets of the city and past the Temple colonnades. How long would this Roman hesitate before he gave in to the people? But Pilate was not inclined to abandon justice altogether just because the priests and the Jewish rabble screamed for this man's death. "And Pilate when he called together the chief priests and the rulers and the people said unto them: Ye have brought this man unto me as one that perverteth the people; and behold, I, having examined him before you, have found no fault in this man touching those things whereof ye accuse him. No, nor yet Herod, for I sent you to him, and lo, nothing worthy of death is done unto him. I will therefore chastise him and release him." This is the summing up of a conscientious magistrate; the man must be chastised because he had definitely caused trouble and it was also advisable to pacify the crowd. This is not to say, as Tertullian said, that Pilate "had the soul of a Christian." But it is obvious that he had been impressed by Jesus, and the impression adds another touch to the portrait of the God made into man, so simple and so majestic which we are trying to draw.

Pilate went up to the tribunal and sat in the magistrate's seat to pronounce judgment. At this moment, all four Evangelists (Matt. xxvii, 15-26; Mark xv, 6-15; Luke xxiii, 13-25; John xviii, 39-40) recount an incident which appeared to Pilate to hold out some hope of saving Jesus without exasperating the crowd. There was a custom that on the eve of the Passover the procurator should pardon some condemned criminal. Perhaps some one reminded Pilate of the custom. "And there was one named Barabbas which lay bound with them that had made insurrection with him, who had committed murder in the insurrection. . . ." "Whom will ye that I release unto you," asked Pilate, "Barabbas, or Jesus that is called Christ?" Pilate's intention is plain enough, between a hardened criminal and a man who had obviously done no great harm, the Roman felt that the crowd could scarcely fail to make the choice he desired.

The right to pardon was rare in Israel. The Jewish Kings had not possessed it, although they had had the power to increase a penalty if they thought it insufficiently severe. The Mosaic Law, in fact, did not recognize the principle of pardon, because it regarded crime as an offence against God. In Rome the law allowed an appeal to the *Comitia,* in the case of a man sentenced to death, but it does not appear that the people had any such right to appeal on behalf of the criminal. The custom referred to in the Gospel seems to be confirmed by a papyrus dating from the year 86 or 88, which states that an Egyptian prefect pardoned a guilty man "because of the crowd." The legal point, whether the act of grace took the form of the *abolitio,* or amnesty, which the emperors customarily gave after military victories or on certain feasts, or whether it was an *indulgentia,* the personal pardon which the emperor had it in his right to bestow and could pass on to his representative, is immaterial to us. It would seem anyhow to have been an exceptional occurrence relating to some local custom, the origin of which we are not told.

The crowd do not appear to have replied at once to Pilate's question; we sense a certain hesitation, between the lines of the Gospel account. Pilate must have hoped that his maneuver would succeed. He must have wished it all the more because "when he was set down on the judgment seat, his wife sent unto him, saying, Have thou nothing to do with that just man, for I have suffered many things this day in a dream because of him." Only St. Matthew reports this mysterious detail and we know nothing more than this about Pilate's wife, for no secular text of the period makes any reference to her. The Apocryphal "Gospel of Nicodemus" says that her name was Claudia Procula. Rosadi, whose ingenious reconstruction of Pilate's career we have already referred to, thinks that she was the youngest daughter of Julia, whom Augustus, her father, had been obliged to exile in order to hush up her excesses, after having given her Tiberius for a third husband. The fifth century writer Macrobius, a notorious scandalmonger, says in his *Saturnalia* that Claudia was sent by her mother to Tiberius by whom she was "brought up," a phrase which in that connection might cover a great deal more than academic education. If she were the wife of Pilate, he obviously gained some powerful connections through his marriage.

There is no need to take this gossip too seriously, yet one historical fact lends it a certain amount of support. The old Roman Law forbade proconsuls to take their wives with them to the provinces they governed and, although this law had been mitigated somewhat by the first century A.D., it still remained very difficult to get permission to set it aside, and the applicant had in advance to accept full responsibility for any misdemeanor which his wife might commit. If Pilate had his wife with him in Jerusalem, he and she must have had powerful protectors. It was very common at that time for women of rank to become initiated into one of the secret sects then in vogue, for esoteric and magical doctrines were very much in the fashion. So it was not surprising that she should attach great importance to a dream. We may conclude, also, that she was favorably inclined to Jesus; she may even have been one of those "proselytes of the gate" who had been instructed in the Jewish religion, perhaps even in the teaching of Jesus. In the Greek and Ethiopian churches she is venerated as a saint.

Pilate himself was probably, like all Romans, superstitious and so he would be impressed by his wife's message. He would remember, too, that Julius Caesar was said to have been told by his wife Calpurnia of a dream which she had had, warning him not to go out on the Ides of March. Caesar had refused to heed the prediction and had gone out to meet the assassins' daggers. The Apocryphal Gospel of Nicodemus states that Pilate told his wife's dream to the Jews, who replied, "Did we not say that he was a sorcerer? Behold, he has sent an evil dream to your wife!"

He must have wished more than ever that he could release Jesus but he reckoned without the madness and blindness of the crowd. The priests lost no time in making up their minds, and, with their supporters, started to chant among the crowd, "Barabbas, Barabbas." The crowd took it up. The shouts increased. The astonished Pilate said: "What shall I do then with Jesus which is called Christ?" "Crucify him! crucify him!" "Why, what evil hath he done?" But the murderous cries grew louder and stronger, the burst of hatred from a thousand throats, with which Bach in his *Passion According to St. John* assaults our senses as the choir cries *Crucifigatur, Crucifigatur,* like a howling of savage beasts. St. John, as he wrote afterward, remembered how Jesus had prophesied what death he should die (John xviii, 32) and how extraordinary this had seemed, for the Jewish method of execution was by stoning to death, not crucifixion, which was a Roman practice. But events were to prove the truth of what he had said.

The episode of Barabbas has given rise to all kinds of speculation, as well as to innumerable fictions. Salomon Reinach, whose essays in comparative religion often exceed the bounds of legitimate criticism and sometimes even of common sense, maintained in his *Orpheus* that the episode derives from certain Alexandrian rites in which "we know from Philo that Karabas was the name given to one of those mock Kings who were lauded with derisory honors before they were maltreated." From Karabas to Barabbas is a short step, which the critic can quite easily take in order to conclude that we may suspect from this that the story of the Passion has a certain "ritual and mythical" element and that it resembles those stories of the "sacrificed King" which are common among primitive peoples. Jesus was put to death not *instead* of Barabbas but *because he was* Barabbas. Even if the tradition of Alexandrian carnival did include some such grotesque rite as is suggested, it is difficult to see how this nullifies the reality of the Passion. But, as a matter of fact, if the reference to Philo is examined, it will be found not to refer to any sort of rite in which a *Karabas* or mock-King is immolated but to an actual historical incident when Caligula nominated Herod Antipas II as King. The students of Alexandria demonstrated to show their contempt for him and dressed up a beggar called Karabas, whom they paraded as King. Certainly there are obscurities in the story of Barabbas; Origen, who had access to many ancient manuscripts lost to us, says that his personal name was Jesus, which makes the parallel more striking, and the name Barabbas has been translated to mean "Son of the Father," "Son of the Rabbi" or the holy one, which induces yet further speculation. All we can say definitely about the episode is that it is extraordinarily true to crowd psychology, in which justice is so often swallowed up by hatred.

During all this, Jesus is not recorded as saying anything at all. He was the silent witness in the argument in which his life was at stake but: "Not my will, O God, but thine." He had accepted his lot; it only remained for him to bear it to the end.

The Flagellation and the Crown of Thorns

Now the blood of Christ begins to flow more and more until the end. Pilate said that he would "chastise" Jesus before letting him go, and although he was forced to release the bandit instead, his order to scourge the innocent man stood. St. Matthew, St. Mark and St. John report the horrible episode in one line; St. Luke does not mention it at all. It is as if the Evangelists could not bear to comment on it. In any case, all their contemporaries knew only too well what this punishment was like. There are several descriptions in classical literature which leave us in no doubt of its horror; Suetonius and Livy show us sadistic magistrates exhorting the flagellants to strike harder while, in Cicero and Plutarch, we are told of victims collapsing, streaming with blood, upon the ground and sometimes expiring before the punishment was over.

Scourging had been practiced by the Jews from very ancient times (see Deut. xxv) but only for certain specified offences (for instance, a freeman who cohabited with another man's slave), and the Law also enjoined strict moderation in its use. Only an ordinary whip or rods might be used and no more than forty stripes were to be given. It was in practice customary to give only thirty-nine, thirteen on the chest, and thirteen on each shoulder, to ensure that the legal number was not exceeded. But there was no definition of the punishment in Roman law; it was left to the decision of the judge or the whim of the executioner. There were two instruments of torture in use; the *flagella,* leather thongs often sharpened to a point, forming a sort of knout which if forcibly used could break a rib or a clavicle, and which even more moderately used could flay off the skin of the victim—*horribile flagellum,* says Horace. The other was the *flagra,* iron chains ending in miniature weights. The Greek text of St. Mark suggests that these were used in the scourging of Christ, though St. Matthew mentions "rods," which seems unlikely. The victim was stripped and fastened to a stout, short post, only a little more than two feet high, so that there was no protection at all from the encircling scourges.

Whipping among the Jews carried no special degradation but among the Romans it was an ignominious punishment, meted out to slaves. In his *Verrine Orations,* Cicero reproaches Gaius Verres for inflicting it on free men and it will be remembered that St. Paul, when threatened with it, claimed that as a Roman citizen he was exempted from it. The Romans also used it as a normal preliminary to capital punishment; *virgis caedere* preceded *securi percutere* and Josephus often mentions cases of rebellious Jews being "torn to pieces by the scourge before being crucified." Philo confirms this.

It is impossible for us to describe the horror of the scene and to imagine Jesus bound to the post and receiving the cruel blows. We naturally recoil from the spectacle, and very few of the artists who have chosen to depict it have succeeded. The realistic approach falters; we feel that naturalism is out of place, and the Gothic sculptors, instinctively understanding this, always show Jesus supernaturally calm under the blows. It requires a visionary like Catherine Emmerich to describe the scene, to see the torturers as "little brown men, with upstanding frizzy hair and scanty beard," howling as they batter the sacred victim until at last the bleeding Christ, crumpled at the foot of the column, stands up suddenly and turns his ravaged face to look at a group of harlots who have watched the scene with indecent curiosity.

If we dwell, even a little, on the brutality of the episode, we cannot help but condemn severely the man who gave the order for it. Yet many of the early Christians regarded Pilate not unfavorably; the sensibilities of the ancient world were more hardened to brutality than our own. St. Augustine sees the flagellation as attenuating Pilate's guilt, a view which the Catholic Church seems not far from admitting, for in the *Tenebrae* of Good Friday, the sixth Lesson says: "For he labored what he could to get him out of their hands; and for that reason ordered him to be scourged and shown to them. This he did to Our Lord not by way of persecution, but to satisfy their rage; that the sight of him in that condition might move them to pity and make them desist from desiring his death."

When the scourging was over, "The soldiers of the governor took Jesus into the common hall, and gathered unto him the whole band of soldiers. And they stripped him and put on him a scarlet robe. And when they had plaited a crown of thorns, they put it upon his head, and a reed in his right hand, and they bowed the knee before him and mocked him, saying, Hail, King of the Jews! And they spit upon him and took the reed, and smote him on the head." (Matt. xxvii, 26-30; Mark xv, 15-19; Luke xxiii, 24-5; John xix, 1-3.)

This was gratuitous cruelty, not ordered by Pilate, but the human horde is merciless to the defeated and what could be expected from soldiers let loose? These soldiers would be Syrians or Bedouins, perhaps under a Roman noncommissioned officer, and they would not set much store on a Jew who had just been scourged by the governor's orders. If there is anything in the suggestion that any part of the narrative of the trial of Jesus was inspired by the memory of grotesque carnival customs, it may pertinently be considered here. A good many of the soldiers present would probably have been in the Alexandrian or Mesopotamian garrisons and might have witnessed the Scythian festival which was called the *Sacaea*. During this feast, a carnival King was elected and for two or three days he was allowed to do as he pleased and was entertained by the royal concubines. But at the end of the period of license, the masquerade King was dethroned, whipped and hanged. During the Roman Saturnalia, the legions used to draw lots for the "Saturn King" who, after a period of unbridled revelry, was put to death. The medieval Lord of Misrule was undoubtedly a survival of this curious ancient custom and it is by no means improbable that the soldiers who tormented Jesus got the idea from the Scythian or Saturnalian procedure.

But the archaeological discoveries which revealed the *Lithostrotos* suggest another explanation. In one corner of the pavement which, as we have said, is almost certainly that of the courtyard of Antonia, there are traces of scoring in the stone which were probably the marks of some game played by the soldiers. There is also a mark corresponding with that made by the socket of the lamp standard which would be lit during the night watches. We know that various gambling games were common throughout the Roman empire, including a sort of hopscotch, as still played by children in the streets, also backgammon and checkers. But the commonest of all was knuckle-bones (jackstones) still played throughout the Near East as well as by children in the Western World, which like our dice games had innumerable variants. A terracotta plaque in the Louvre shows four young women kneeling on the ground casting knuckle-bones into a circle with transverse lines marked on the ground. On the corner of the *Lithostrotos* are hopscotch markings which clearly represent "the circle game" mentioned by Plautus. The game was played with four bones marked with letters or figures, and the player had to follow certain figures and observe a complicated set of rules. Certain moves or gambits had names, such as Alexander's Move, the Ephebe, and the Darius; the highest of all was called the Royal, or in Greek, the Basilicus. On the pavement we can trace a perfect circle, a complicated linear pattern cutting across various figures, the "B" for Basilicus repeated and finally a royal crown. It seems quite possible that this was the origin of the baiting of Jesus; if the soldiers were playing the circle game when a Jew who called himself a king was brought in, what more likely than that they should drag him into it, the King's Gambit for the King of the Jews?

The scratchings on the *Lithostrotos* also give a clue to the possible shape of the crown of thorns. It was not a plain circlet, but had radiating points. This spiked crown was commonly in use in the Orient; it can be seen on coins of Antiochus Epiphanus (B.C. 175–164) and was worn by the Arab princes well into the Christian era. The particular plant used for the mock crown has produced an extensive bibliography. Notre Dame de Paris boasts, as we know, the possession of the precious relic, which St. Louis bought in 1239 from a Venetian merchant, and that soaring marvel, the Saint-Chapelle, was built as a shrine to house it. Today the relic in its crystal case appears to be a circlet of rushes (probably the *juncus balticus*) entwined and tied together by some fifteen ligaments. It can only have formed the base of the thorny branches, and these were most probably from the jujube tree (*rhamnus spina christi*). This plant is very common in Judea and is often mentioned in the Bible. The actual thorns from this circlet, which have been distributed through the piety of centuries to something like a hundred and fifty churches, including Pisa, Trèves, Autun and Ragusa, have always been venerated although their authenticity cannot certainly be guaranteed. For the humiliating diadem has appealed to countless generations of Christians as the most striking symbol of that humility and self-abasement which Jesus always placed in the forefront of the virtues. We do not know if he actually wore it on the Cross, as in the beautiful Christ of St. Damien at Assisi, but in the hearts of those who love him he bears this painful crown by which our salvation was gained. *Tua corona spinea tuos coronat aurea* says the thirteenth century Breviary of Sens. This expresses most profoundly the Christian faith.

Ecce Homo

The soldiers' game had gone on long enough; Pilate had just re-appeared. He looked at Jesus, as the soldiers had relinquished him, crowned with thorns, decked out in the scarlet mantle, probably the *chlamys* or mantle of one of the legionnaires, so battered and bemired that an idea came to him. Perhaps a last minute attempt to rouse a glimmer of pity in the mob. Outside the castle, massed in one of the recesses because they would not cross the threshold of Antonia for fear of incurring legal impurity by contact with the pagan, the Jews waited. The Roman came toward them, saying once more: "I bring him forth to you that ye may know that I find no fault in him." Then, waiting on the effect, he led Jesus toward them and said: "Behold, the man!"

Ecce homo, the phrase, with its sorrowful echoes, has reverberated through the centuries of Christian tradition. As he appeared before the Jews who were shouting for his death, he was indeed that "man of sorrows" whom the prophet foretold. Upon him all the sorrows had fallen; he was in the pit of abandonment, the image of all that is tragic in the human condition. Pilate did not wish to say too much, he only led him forward with a brief compassionate gesture. But his words were charged with a meaning weightier than he knew, for it was indeed the man, the whole man, he led before the crowd, and what they hated in him was his very resemblance to them.

Artistic representations of the scene during the Romanesque and Gothic periods concentrated rather on the majesty of Christ, but during the fifteenth and sixteenth centuries, when the subject became extremely popular, there were some paintings and sculptures produced which are truly heartrending. Inevitably there have been attempts to identify in Jerusalem the place where Jesus was shown to the people, and a huge semicircular arch, flanked by two smaller ones, all unquestionably of Roman construction, is included partly in the *Ecce Homo* basilica within the Convent of Zion and partly across the street. The arch is thought to have been built during the reign of Hadrian, when some attempt was made to rebuild Jerusalem under the name of Aelia Capitolina, but it is considered to occupy the place where Pilate handed Jesus over to his implacable pursuers.

For whatever hopes Pilate had of arousing pity were dashed. "When the chief priests therefore and officers saw him, they cried out, saying, Crucify him, crucify him. Pilate saith unto them, Take ye him and crucify him: for I find no fault in him. The Jews answered him: We have a law, and by our law he ought to die, because he made himself the Son of God." The accusation was brought back to the sphere of religion because the Roman authority upheld the Jewish Law and a Roman soldier who had contemptuously burnt some of the Jewish sacred writings had been executed by the governor. So once more the Jews accused Jesus of blasphemy.

"When Pilate therefore heard that saying, he was the more afraid." We can see the supersitious Roman, with the memory of his wife's dream nagging in his mind, pondering the disquieting words, "the Son of God." He went back into the praetorium and asked Jesus: "Whence art thou? But Jesus gave him no answer. Then saith Pilate unto him, Speakest thou not to me? Knowest thou not that I have the power to crucify thee and have power to release thee? Jesus answered, Thou couldst have no power at all against me except it were given thee from above: therefore he that delivered me to thee hath the greater sin."

It certainly seems as if Pilate felt more and more impressed by the serenity of Jesus and the nobility of his words, so that he tried still harder to release the strange prophet who invoked the divine power. But outside he could hear the shouts and cries of the Jews, and what he heard was not at all reassuring to a suspicious and vulnerable imperial functionary. "If thou let this man go, thou art not Caesar's friend: whoever maketh himself a King speaketh against Caesar." (John xix, 1-12.) Pilate was not a weak man and the demonstrations of the crowd did not, in fact, change his attitude, which had from the beginning been strictly in accord with that Roman principle of justice, formulated later by the Emperors Maximilian and Diocletian: "The Judge must not heed the clamor of the crowd which often seeks to release the guilty and condemn the innocent." But the Jews had now found a political argument which carried a good deal of weight with him.

Philo tells us that he feared that a delegation would be sent to Rome to complain of his misgovernment, his extortions, unjust decrees and savage punishment. Doubtless many things had occurred during his term of office about which his conscience was far from clear. But, even had it been perfectly clear, he would none the less have trembled at the thought of denunciation. "The laws," said Tacitus, "were powerless against force, intrigue and bribery," and he adds that, especially under Tiberius, the practice of informing had made them as noxious as the vices they had formerly controlled—the words, "Thou are not Caesar's friend," would be enough to make Pilate's head tremble on his shoulders.

It required courage to show contempt for this maneuver and to risk calumny by releasing an innocent man. Pilate did not have it, and that was his real crime. He mounted the tribunal, doubtless to assert his prestige, and once more said to the Jews: "Behold your King!" But they shouted louder than ever, "Kill him. Away with him. Crucify him." Pilate made one last attempt: "Shall I crucify your King?" But the crowd, taking color from the High Priest, replied: "We have no King but Caesar." Now Pilate was caught and dared say nothing more. "Then delivered he him therefore unto them to be crucified."

What his thoughts were, in that moment when he gave himself over to one of the greatest injustices in history, we may guess from two verses in St. Matthew's account (xxvii, 24-25.) He had given in to the public clamor but wished to make it clear that he did not assume responsibility for the decision. "He took water and washed his hands before the multitude." This was a very old custom and its symbolism is obvious. In Deut. xxi, 6-7, it is cited in the same sense in which Pilate made use of it; it is mentioned also by Virgil and by Ovid. "I am innocent of the blood of this just man. See ye to it," said he. And the Jews shouted back at him: "His blood be on us, and on our children."

Through the long centuries, in all the lands to which the tragic destiny of the Jewish people has dispersed them, their blood has indeed flowed in a constant stream. Their cry of rage which rose up to Pilate's judgment seat echoes in our ears as their own cry of distress, endlessly repeated. The pages of history show us again and again the sorrowing face of the persecuted Jew. Behind that face we see another, also streaming with blood and spittle. But surely these two sorrowful images are an appeal to our pity and mercy rather than an incitation to hate. In the inscrutable mystery of the divine intention, we are not called upon to set ourselves up as judges. Jesus himself on the Cross prayed for his torturers: "Forgive them, Father, for they know not what they do!" And the Church, in the Good Friday Office, prays for the "perfidious Jews, that by acknowledging the light of thy truth, which is Christ, they may be brought out of their darkness." [4]

---

[4] The author has developed this subject elsewhere. Jacques Maritain has written: "Israel is a Church guilty of infidelity—that is the real meaning of the liturgical expression *perfidia judaica,* which does not at all mean that Jews are

As for Pilate, his prudence did not protect him for long. Five years later, when a false prophet gathered the Samaritans on Mt. Gerizim to await a manifestation which would inaugurate the reign of the Messiah, Pilate called out the soldiers to disperse the crowd. Many were killed and in addition the procurator, in an access of severity, executed a number of those taken prisoner. A Samaritan delegation complained to Pilate's immediate superior in the Roman official hierarchy, the Syrian Legate Vitellius, who was probably well acquainted with his subordinate's methods, and ordered the procurator to report to Rome. When Pilate got there, he learned that Tiberius had just died. We do not know the sequel. There is a tradition that he was exiled to the Dauphiné in France. Eusebius and Philo state that he came to a violent end. Medieval legend provided him with a number of curious adventures, almost Dantesque, in which he plays a diabolical role. Cowardice seldom shows a profit.

The Responsibility

Jesus was now abandoned to his enemies and the event which he had foretold was about to take place. He was to be "lifted up" to die upon the cross. Can we allot the responsibility, or pass judgment?

It is certainly quite improper to speak of a legal "trial" in this connection. Both in the Jewish and the Roman Law, the accused had certain substantial rights and guarantees, and it is incontestable that in the case of Jesus the juridical obligations were at times flagrantly violated and at other times perverted by cunning or indifference. Among the Jews involved in the affairs, there was a definite plot to kill a man, possibly for reasons not altogether base but with a total contempt for the justice of the means. The Roman part was played certainly with due ceremonial procedure, but without a trace of that scrupulous gravity which is such an admirable quality in the law which has given birth to our own. Pilate could perfectly

perfidious. The mystical body of Israel is an unfaithful and repudiated Church —but repudiated as a Church and not as a people."

well have charged Jesus with a breach of public order or with inciting to subversive action, but he did nothing of the kind. His interrogation had no bearing on the essential points and no sentence was pronounced. We have previously referred to the fact that Pilate did not find it necessary to report the incident to the Emperor or the Senate; or if he did, it has never been discovered. We can understand his attitude if we transfer the affair to a more familiar setting. Imagine a colonial administrator to whom a tribe of Negroes brings some poor humiliated creature with vague charges of magic or rebellion, and who through levity or cowardice or disregard of justice . . . but we need not go on, the explanation is simple. We have known too many such.

Christians who repeat the words of the creed, "Suffered under Pontius Pilate," place upon this man, and this man only, an everlasting opprobrium. The material and legal responsibility rests upon the Roman magistrate; he is the killer of Christ. But what about the moral responsibility? Writers favorable to the Jews, such as Montefiore and Juster, have produced judicial arguments to show that the Sanhedrin did not really sentence Jesus to death. But the intention and the machination is obvious.

Since they could not, by the laws of the protecting power, execute Jesus themselves, the leading Jews worked with obstinacy and cunning to force the Roman to give effect to their sentence. "Pilate," says St. Augustine, "shares their guilt because of what he did, but compared with them, we must find him less culpable." [5]

It is a complex question, involving as it does the responsibility of a whole people for the acts of their leaders. A Chris-

---

[5] It is interesting to note that there is in modern Jewry a section which does not associate itself with the abusive tradition of the *Toledoth Jeshua* and has tried to shake off the heavy burden of the responsibility. "Contemporary Jews deplore the tragic death of Jesus," writes Enelow. There has even been a movement for the "revision" of the proceedings of the year 30, and it is stated that in 1933 a Jewish court, sitting in Jerusalem, voted for the "rehabilitation of Jesus" by four votes to one. The sentiment is honorable but it is not possible to reverse history.

tian will bear in mind that Jesus came as a witness for and a representative of the whole of humanity. In spite of the profound paradox in this statement, perhaps we can agree with the French poet Charles Péguy, who wrote: "It is not the Jews who crucified Jesus Christ, but the sins of all of us."

CHAPTER ELEVEN

"UNLESS A CORN OF WHEAT DIE . . ."

Parade of Death

SOCIETY HAS ALWAYS found it necessary to surround the most drastic act of human justice with ceremony, as though the death which it is about to inflict had already imposed its own supreme authority. The soldier who is to be shot is given the honor of an "execution parade"; how frightful and derisory these solemnities must seem to the victim.

The Talmud gives full details of the ceremony attaching to Jewish executions and it would seem to have been fully developed in the time of Jesus. The condemned man must be taken to the place of execution in daylight, so that all could see him; a herald went first, calling out the crime for which the condemned was sentenced and carrying a parchment upon which it was inscribed. Two theological students walked with the victim, appealing to him to confess his crime and to offer his death in expiation of it, in order to acquire merit in heaven, and a representative of the Sanhedrin had to witness the execution and confirm that it had been properly carried out.

The Roman execution parade was of a different order. A centurion, detailed as *exactor mortis,* led the column, attended by a minimum of four soldiers. If incidents were to be feared, the number was augmented, it could be as high as a hundred.

We may assume that a fairly heavy guard led the so-styled "King of the Jews" to the cross.

The execution of Jesus had elements both of Jewish and Roman ceremonial. The Gospel narrative mentions the centurion and his men, also the priests and the Sanhedrites, only too eager to follow their victim to the end. The procession must have had a certain formality. Josephus tells us of several executions by the Romans and all of them seem to have been conducted with the maximum of publicity. But in Jerusalem with its hilly, winding streets, many of them only steps, with the crowd milling around the Temple, people shouting and gesticulating, it would be incorrect to imagine a regular and orderly procession befitting the gravity of death. It is not so long ago that it was common in Turkey for the traveler to find himself unwittingly caught up, in the crowded alleys of Stambul, in a ragged procession led by a crier, and a man with bound hands walking between guards, and to discover that this was a criminal on his way to be hanged.

It was obligatory to have an inscription giving the title of the crime; Pilate undertook to do this. Suetonius tells the story of one of Caligula's servants who stole a knife during a banquet, and when he was executed the emperor decided to have, instead of the usual title, the two hands of the robber cut off and placed over his head. It will be seen from this that the great ones did not disdain to play a part in these sordid affairs and Pilate was not the man to lose such an opportunity of getting even with the Jews. So, on the *titulus,* he wrote in Latin, Greek and Hebrew: "Jesus of Nazareth, the King of the Jews." [1] The priests protested: "Write not, The King of the Jews, but that he said, I am the King of the Jews." Now that he no longer feared a denunciation, Pilate recovered his haughtiness. "What I have written I have written." For, even if they did send a copy of the writing to Capri, it could only prove to Tiberius how zealous his prefect had been in dealing with claimants to the throne. "Therefore write, O Pilate," cries Bossuet "the

[1] The title is not given in exactly the same words by the four Evangelists, but the meaning is clearly the same.

words which God dictates to you, the mystery of which you cannot know . . . for soon the Crucified will be crowned with honor and glory."

The centurion in his cuirass and the soldiers in their chain mail surrounded Jesus and among the crowd pressed back against the walls, the red tunics and glittering helmets of the legionaries were mixed with the white, gray and blue garments of the Jews, and a clanking of arms dominated the hubbub as the sinister procession went on its way. We can imagine Jesus in the midst of it, imposing in spite of the abuses he had suffered, the only one who knew the inner meaning of the tragedy about to take place.

At the last minute, the Romans decided to execute at the same time two thieves, armed bandits, if the Greek word used in the Gospel is taken in its strongest sense. We do not know why; it may have been simply because their time was up and the Romans wanted to get them out of the prison. There may have been an intention to insult "the King of the Jews." Isaiah had foretold of the Messiah: "He hath poured out his soul unto death and he was numbered with the transgressors." (liii, 12.) The early Christian martyrs were often put to death with common criminals.

It was between half past eleven and twelve noon (the sixth hour, says St. John, xix, 14) when the procession to the cross left the Antonia fortress.[2]

Stations of the Cross

The Stations of the Cross stimulated by the unforgettable language of the *Imitation of Christ,* has been a favorite Christian devotion since the fifteenth century. The custom was first intro-

[2] St. Mark says, "It was the third hour and they crucified him." But the reckoning of time is somewhat vague in his Gospel. The Jews grouped the hours of the day in four periods: *prime,* from sunrise to nine o'clock; *tierce,* from nine until noon; *sexte* from noon till 3 P.M.; *none,* the night hours. St. Mark's statement simply meant that *tierce* was not over and *sexte* had not begun at the time of the execution. St. Luke is equally imprecise: "It was about the sixth hour."

duced by pilgrims to the Holy Land who followed the stages of Jesus's last journey and, under the auspices of the Franciscans, the devotion spread throughout Christendom. There are famous open-air Stations of the Cross at Locarno, La Verna, Lourdes and La Salette, and the humblest Catholic church has the fourteen stations pictured on its walls. The devotion commemorates the afternoon of Good Friday. In the chill of early spring the slow procession moves round, to murmured invocations and prayers, along the denuded silent aisles, which will not echo to the sound of music until Easter dawns. However feeble the artistic representation of the scene, there is no Christian who can make the Stations without thinking of the man who endured the incidents depicted, that day in Palestine, and without feeling a wrench of the heart.[3]

As early as the fourth century it was the custom for pilgrims to Jerusalem to make the journey by stages, following the steps of Jesus from Antonia to the place of execution. It must be admitted that the route of the journey can hardly be more than hypothetical, having regard to the destruction of the city and the centuries of accumulated ruins and debris. If the centurion who was *exactor mortis* took the direct route along the Temple promenade, then the cortege would have left the city by the Bab-en-Nadir, which was called in medieval times the Sorrowful Gate. But no authority can possibly be claimed for precise identifications, such as that Jesus stumbled and fell on this particular stone, which the guide will point out with disconcerting assurance. In any case, it could not have been a very long journey, not more than five or six hundred yards at most. The place chosen for the execution was the nearest possible place, where there is a sharp recessive angle of the city walls. Jesus must have gone down one of those stepped paths which still lead from the Temple to the

[3] The majority of the fourteen Stations illustrate scenes narrated in the Gospel. One or two of them, such as Jesus meeting his mother and the incident of Veronica, derive from very ancient traditions. A half-ruined Armenian church in Jerusalem commemorates the meeting of Jesus with his mother and there are twelfth century representations of both incidents at Chartres.

Tyropeon river, which was then much more deeply embedded than it is today, and then climbed up the opposite bank toward the northeast. There the streets would be much as we see them now, narrow, lined with tall houses having very few windows, irregularly paved with slippery stones, filled with projections of dark shadow with touches of bright sunlight and doubtless, as today, pervaded by that musky, putrid and penetrating smell which one breathes in every native quarter in the East.

Plutarch tells us that every criminal sentenced to crucifixion had to bear the instrument of execution, thus confirming St. John's brief statement that Jesus bore his cross (xix, 17). Many commentators have thought that this referred only to the cross-beam and that the vertical piece was stationary at the place of execution. In any case, the weight was considerable, some thirty odd pounds if it were only the cross beam, and at least seventy if it were the complete cross. And so, bending more and more beneath the weight, Jesus was led on.

The most moving and truthful of the innumerable representations of the "bearing of the Cross" in art is probably that in Rheims Cathedral where, almost lost in the sculpture depicting the life of Jesus in the bays of one of the great doors, is a simple figure of a wretched man almost collapsing under the weight. In some Christian countries, notably in Spain and in Flanders, processions of penitents, men and women in black hoods, commemorate this, desiring also to bear the cross as their master bore it. "Who does not carry his cross is not my brother," is an old saying echoing the words of the Gospel. "If any man will come after me, let him deny himself and take up his cross and follow me." (Matt. xvi, 24.) When Jesus had said these words announcing his death, at Caesarea Philippi, Peter had been indignant. Only later on was he to understand the full meaning. But to us, who have been instructed by two thousand years of Christian teaching, these words are illuminated by the light of the Passion so that "to bear the cross" is not simply a metaphor. "Is the end of life to live?" says a character in one of Claudel's plays. "It is not to live but to die, not to make a cross but to mount it."

To a man exhausted by a sleepless night of questioning, and by the cruel scourging and the loss of blood it entailed, the weight of the cross would be beyond his human capacity. April can be warm in Judea, especially at that time of the day, and Jesus, as we have seen, would have to go up and down some sharp inclines. Perhaps the centurion feared that his captive was going to escape execution by dying prematurely; for the three synoptic gospels relate that the soldiers requisitioned one of the crowd to carry the cross (Matt. xxvii, 32; Mark xv, 21; Luke xxiii, 26). The legal Passover, when work was forbidden, had not yet set in; the man had just come from the fields, probably from the gardens of Gareb. He was called Simon of Cyrene, and was either a Greek from that famous African city, the capital of Cyrenaica, or a member of the considerable Jewish colony there. St. Mark adds that he was the father of Alexander and Rufus, presumably two persons well known in the Roman community to whom his gospel is addressed. St. Paul, in Rom. xvi, 13, mentions one Rufus who may perhaps be the same. One tradition makes Simon one of the seventy Apostles sent out by Jesus on the second mission and as his sons became Christians it may be admitted that this man who literally "bore the cross" received the grace of conversion from it.

St. Luke tells us that "there followed him a great company of people" all the way (xxiii, 27). Public executions have always attracted unhealthy curiosity and it is not surprising that, exactly five days after the triumphal entry on Palm Sunday, the news of the condemnation should have aroused excitement. They were certainly not all sadistic gapers in the crowd; there must have been many faithful friends and sympathizers. And yet it does not seem that there was any demonstration, not a single cry, in his favor. It was laid down by Jewish law that the intervention of a single bystander, even at the last minute, could suspend the execution of a condemned man. It will be remembered that the protest of the young man Daniel in the affair of Susannah and the elders sufficed to wrest the victim from the tribunal. This provision was considered so imperative that the following arrangements were devised for executions: a herald with a flag was stationed at the door of the Sanhedrin, a horseman followed the cortege which was taking the condemned man to the place of execution and he turned round repeatedly toward the place from which they had come; if anyone came to the Sanhedrin to speak in favor of the condemned man, the flag was waved, the horseman notified the procession and the man was brought back to the judges.

So we must suppose that, if this clause of the Law was in operation, the crowd following Jesus heard the emissary from the Sanhedrin repeating all along the way the formula: "If you wish to prove the innocence of Jesus, hasten, hasten," without one single person raising his voice. Such indifference seems not only monstrous but incredible when we remember the acclamations only five days before. But history gives us plenty of examples of men whom the crowds have lauded to the heights and abandoned precipitately, with similar ingratitude. The human herd is swayed by uncontrollable impulses; prone to enthusiasm, it is even more prone to panic and to rage.

It is only four hundred years since a similar scene took place in one of the most civilized cities in the world. Savonarola, the impassioned prophet, who had tried to reconcile faith and the new learning and to fan the fires of a living Christianity from the decadent travesty which Alexander VI, the Borgia Pope, paraded to cover his debauches, had held the Florentine crowds enthralled, weeping at his words, kissing the ground he had trodden. We are not concerned here to pass judgment on his attempt, or on the pride and excess of zeal which hastened his downfall. But when the rich and the influential had overcome him and on May 23, 1498, he was brought to the stake in the public square with two of his followers, who of the crowd which had acclaimed him yesterday made any attempt to save him? Fallen prophets have few disciples. Some might have wept secretly among themselves but the only voice upraised was in insult and derision. "If thou be the Son of God, come down from the cross."

Some may have felt cheated that Jesus should have not attempted to seize power as they had hoped; some may have hoped for a miracle at the last moment. A hatred and fear of true greatness always slumbers in the miserable heart of mankind. Anyway, they had other things to do than try to save a prophet bent on destroying himself. They had to hurry to buy bread and biscuits, figs, dates, meat and vegetables for the feast before it was too late, as the great Sabbath was fast approaching.

There were however some women, more courageous and less prudent, who had loved Jesus, and who followed him weeping and beating their breasts. He turned and spoke to them for the last time, for a final warning! "Daughters of Jerusalem, weep not for me, but weep for yourselves and your children. For behold, the days are coming in the which they shall say, Blessed are the barren and the wombs that never bare, and the paps which never gave suck. Then shall they begin to say to the mountains, Fall on us, and to the hills, Cover us." (Luke xxiii, 28-31.) The terrible image of the ravaged city rose up again in his mind, when the sins of the people should receive their deserts, for if they, the Jews, could do this to the green tree, the bearer of life, what should be done to them, to the dry wood of their rottenness, if they did not repent?

The sixth Station of the Cross commemorates a very old tradition that one of these women had the courage to come forward and wipe the blood, sweat and dirt from the face of the condemned man. One version says that it was Martha of Bethany and certainly the action would be in accordance with the character of that vigorous, strong-minded woman. But it became the custom to call her Veronica (a variant of the Greek Berenice) and it has been supposed that she was the woman Jesus cured of an internal hemorrhage. She is also said to have been the wife of the publican Zaccheus. Upon the fabric with which she dried the face of Jesus, his portrait is said to have been miraculously imprinted, and this moving story has inspired many of the great painters who represent the faithful "Veronica" gazing in mystical ecstasy at the handkerchief bearing the imprint of the Savior's face, which she holds out in solemn exposition.

Calvary

The place to which Jesus was led to his death is called in the four Gospels the "skull" or "Calvary" and three of them (not Luke) translate this by the Aramaic word Golgotha. *Calvarius* in Latin means a bare hill like a skull. It may be supposed that, conforming to the old Mosaic precept that executions should be as public as possible, that all the people "shall hear and fear" (Deut. xiii, 11), a hill near the gates of the city was chosen, high enough to expose the spectacle and not too high for the cross to be conveniently erected. In the old Arab toponymy of Jerusalem this quarter was called *Ras,* and the word is still used in Abyssinia to denote heights.

The custom, common in many countries but especially in the Orient, of having cemeteries just outside the town, meant that executions commonly took place among the tombs. The sepulcher to which Joseph of Arimathea took the body of Jesus was only some twenty-five yards away from Golgotha. In that chapter of the *Satyricon* in which Petronius tells the story of the inconsolable widow, another crucifixion is described as taking place among the tombs. We can picture Calvary as one of those sinister places given over to death and reeking of corpses over which the "Esquiline birds," so-called by Horace because in Rome executions generally took place in the cemetery by the Esquiline gate, hovered continually, waiting for their prey to breathe its last. Vultures were a familiar feature of the Judean scene.

The place which is today venerated as the spot where Jesus was crucified is to the northwest of Jerusalem, at the foot of the hill of Gareb. Tradition says that the Emperor Hadrian, who about the year 105 rebuilt Jerusalem on the ruins of the city destroyed by Titus, planted the site of Calvary with a grove of trees sacred to Venus. It is doubtful whether the exact place of the execution was remembered by the descendants of those who had carried it out. When, in the fourth century, Constantine and the Empress Helena built basilicas commemorating the sites both of Calvary and the Holy Sepulcher they chose the spot for Calvary which is still venerated today. Much later the Crusaders built the Church of the Holy Sepulchre, commemorating both spots, a building in a composite Arab-Romanesque style, and still bearing on its façade the shields of the French chivalry. There is a considerable body of archaeological authority supporting the authenticity of this site. To the left of the Church, in a corner, is a slightly raised chapel, thick with the odor of burning candles, and this today is Calvary.

The modern visitor to the Holy Places, with innumerable artistic representations of the hill of Golgotha in his mind, is somewhat disappointed by this bump of rock, with a low-vaulted roof, approached by a massive stairway with worn treads, beneath a battery of silver lamps, plated globes and gilt-bronze grapes. The tinsel elaboration beloved of Greek Orthodox Churches is rampant here, for this is the Greek portion of the basilica. Three altars, resplendent with precious marbles, extend along the wall at the end and a great golden retable, glowing with a thousand lights and surmounted by a colossal crucifix, marks the actual place where the Cross stood; Pilate's contemptuous inscription, "The King of the Jews," is picked out in glittering diamonds. Confronted with this disconcerting magnificence, it is difficult to feel any real emotion; here, as almost everywhere else in this city so overcharged with historical memories, the ill-considered extravagancies of Christtion piety make it difficult to recall Christ: they would indeed be an insurmountable obstacle were it not that, among the fervent crowds ascending the marble stairway on their knees, one sometimes catches sight of a face lit by the unquestioning radiance of faith and love.

To give effect to what it calls a just sentence, humanity has invented the most atrocious tortures, in which the desire to show a fearful example and to make the punishment fit the crime play a part subordinate to the sadism of crowds and the unbridled imaginations of legislators. The tale of executions provided by history does little credit to mankind. Men have been broken on the wheel, torn asunder by horses, eviscerated, thrown into pits of serpents, boiled in oil, drowned in slime, buried alive . . . we could go on.

Modern society, largely restricting itself to the rope, the guillotine and the electric chair, believes that it has progressed when it has perhaps only added an inflexible routine and the horrors of mechanization. The method most in use among the Jews was lapidation, in which the condemned was crushed beneath stones thrown or rolled down upon him; the stake was reserved for extreme cases, such as a man convicted of adultery with his stepmother or of seducing a maiden of the priestly caste. Beheading was the punishment of idolators and apostates. There were also such additional tortures as pouring molten lead down the throat which, says the Talmud, "preserved the corpse of the sufferer."

Crucifixion was a Roman, not a Jewish, punishment. It is thought to have originated in the east and it was practiced by the Persians, the Carthaginians and the Phoenicians, though it was introduced into the Greco-Roman world at an early date. Cicero attributes its adoption to Tarquin the Proud. The Asmonean rulers of Judea employed it extensively: Alexander Jannes (103–76 B.C.), a son of John Hyrcanus, repressed a revolt of the Pharisees against him by wholesale crucifixions, and history has left us a picture of this ferocious kinglet, feasting with his concubines in front of six hundred crosses each bearing a victim, raised up on the terrace of his palace. Even women were crucified though, out of modesty, with their faces toward the cross. It was the usual punishment and nobody would be surprised that a man convicted of blasphemy and sedition should suffer it.

It would, however, be recognized as an intentionally degrading death. Renan suggests that the idea behind it was not so much to kill as to expose the guilty slave, fastened by the hands and the feet which he had not known how to use properly. It was, in Rome, a death reserved for slaves, common thieves, provincials and aliens. It was not legal for a magistrate to crucify a Roman citizen.

It was universally held to be a frightful death; *Crudelissimum teterrimumque supplicium,* says Cicero. The body, fastened to the wood, contracted in a rigid tetanization, the wounds swelled, the lungs, heart and head became congested and the agony was atrocious. A devouring thirst attacked the mucous membranes, the whole body suffered torture in every part. What made it worse was that the victim could live for a considerable time, if he were sufficiently robust. Herodotus and Josephus record cases of crucified men being taken down after several hours and then brought back to life, while Petronius states that a man could survive the agony for three days before expiring. It can be well understood that it was regarded with terror; Josephus says that the capitulation of Machaerus during the Jewish wars was prompted by the fact that the Romans, having captured Eleazar, the soul of the resistance, were about to crucify him on the ramparts when his comrades in arms surrendered in order to save him from such a horrible death.

The Latin word *crux* signifies a gibbet, a sort of gallows rather than the two "crossed" beams which our word denotes. It could be a single stake—*crux* also signified the pole of a waggon or chariot—to which the victim was fastened, his hands bound behind the wood. This was the *crux simplex* which many artists use for the two thieves in pictures of the Crucifixion. Usually there was a second stake, a cross bar either placed at the top of the vertical beam like the letter T—this was the *crux summissa* or *commissa*—or else fastened across the upright beam some distance lower—this was the *crux capitata* or *immissa,* the traditional form of the cross as we know it. Finally there was the *crux decussata,* two equal oblique beams crossed in the center like the letter X, which we call the St. Andrew's Cross because the brother of St. Peter was crucified upon it.

The oldest established tradition is that Jesus suffered on the *crux capitata;* St. Ireneus affirmed that it had four extremities.

It was not, however, as high as it is usually depicted in art, only about one and a half times the height of the human body, otherwise the operation would have been difficult to perform.[4] The foot-rest which most artists put in, presumably for aesthetic reasons, is not historical nor even probable. In order that the weight of the body should not break the hands, a wedge or crutch, which Tertullian describes as being like a rhinoceros horn, was placed between the legs of the victim, causing additional agony.

It is futile to try to establish the particular wood which was used for the cross on which Jesus died, for the relics we possess are not of incontrovertible authenticity. Calvin said that if all the wood of all the fragments venerated as of the true cross were assembled, one could build a fleet out of it. The hymn of the medieval French woodworkers guild, which included carpenters, joiners, cabinet-makers and even charcoal burners, had the refrain, probably taken from the words of St. Bernard, "*Ligna crucis: palmes, cedrus, cupressus, oliva,*" but it seems unlikely the executioners would have gone to the trouble of assembling these precious woods to gratify the medieval taste for symbolism. Microscopic examination of the relics in the cathedrals of Pisa, Florence and Notre Dame, and in the Church of the Holy Sepulcher, reveals that these are all of the same wood, pine. The nails, which the Psalmist prophesied should pierce the hands and feet of the Savior (Psalm xx, 16), were almost certainly the long sharply-pointed ones which carpenters use to fasten joists.

This then was the death of the cross, to which was brought one who, throughout his life, had always preached pity and love. No one can contemplate this injustice without a feeling

---

[4] It is most improbable that Jesus was crucified with the arms raised above the head, as depicted by the Jansenist tradition, for the cross beam would be superfluous if the arms were not outstretched along it, in the classic attiude of the crucified. It may also be remarked that the design of many of these so-called Jansenist crucifixes is simply due to the fact that they were made of bone; it was easier and cheaper to make them in one piece with the arms outstretched above the head. If the arms were extended laterally they would have to be joined on, which would have increased the price of an object designed for popular devotion.

of horror; we can well understand why the earliest Christians, who had seen with their own eyes the rigid and contorted bodies transfixed to the beam, refused to allow any artistic representation of Jesus in that posture. The Emperor Constantine, who out of piety abolished crucifixion as a penalty, earns our respect by this touching gesture. As time passed, artists gave way to the urge to depict the most harrowing of subjects in order to move the forgetful hearts of men. A Mantegna, a Rubens or a Grünewald, essaying the realistic approach, calls upon our pity for the agonies of the victim. The "crucifix royaux" of the Middle Ages emphasize the conqueror of death, the man who, even in the depths of agony, preserved the sublime serenity of God. The Monophysisist heresy, which denied that Christ had the two natures simultaneously, averred that he did not suffer agony because his humanity was only apparent and not real. But the doctrine of the Christian Church has always affirmed as an article of faith that he suffered the tortures of the crucifixion to the fullest extent and that by this actual means the redemption of man was secured, and his salvation.

"O crux ave spes unica": the hymn *Vexilla Regis* which the Catholic Church sings on Palm Sunday and on Good Friday, was written in the sixth century by Venantius Fortunatus, Bishop of Poitiers and Chaplain to St. Radegonde. Christianity has made the instrument of ignominious death the emblem of its greatest pride, a symbolic reversal in complete harmony with that reversal of values which Jesus taught. The true victor is he who in earthly life seems condemned to defeat; blessed is he who is wretched and abandoned. It is the humble in spirit and those to whom life is unkind who will realize happiness in heaven so that the most humiliating of deaths becomes the pledge of eternal life. Two crossed sticks drawn on the walls of a cell, two hasty scratches among the *graffiti* in the catacombs are sufficient to make the presence of Christianity felt. The sign of humiliation has become one of the greatest realities in the history of the world.

"Hail, cross, thou only hope of man," says the beautiful

old hymn. "O sacred wood, most royally empurpled, how beauteously thy stem dost shine! How glorious was its lot to touch, those limbs so holy and divine . . . Balance sublime upon whose beam, was weighed the ransom of mankind."

There is in the Musée de Cluny a curious sixteenth century crucifix showing, at the top of an immense cross, a figure of the most horrifying realism, a man in the last spasm of agony, almost a corpse. But the base of the crucifix is not buried in the ground; it forms a kind of triple root or claw holding a shrunken death's head in its grip. This symbol, which can be found elsewhere in late medieval art, notably in Hieronymus Bosch, expresses the reality of the Pauline apostrophe: "O grave, where is thy victory," for ever since the Resurrection the threat of death has been the promise of life. Those men, savage or sorrowful, who led Jesus to his death through the narrow streets of Jerusalem, did not know that, but he knew it, he who had so often foretold it and who had bestowed upon it, long before it came to pass, its supernatural significance.

The Crucifixion

The procession went through the Ephraim gate and soon came to the hill of Calvary. The executioners set to work. The painters of the scene have, in the main, followed two styles of representation. The most usual one shows Jesus being hoisted on to a cross already fixed to the ground: the other shows the cross lying on the ground and Jesus being stretched along it. The historical evidence is that neither was in fact the actual method of crucifixion. The first operation was to nail the hands of the victim to the smaller beam, the one which he had been made to carry, and then by a rope or a pulley to hoist the beam with its burden on to the upright, which, as has been said, was probably stationary at the place of execution; the cross was correctly installed when the wedge or crutch on the upright rested between the thighs of the victim to hold the weight of the body. Mgr. Ricciotti points out that such terms as *ascendere crucem, inequitare crucem* (to mount or to straddle a cross) which are frequently used by Latin authors, are only explicable by such a procedure. When the fourth century theologian, Firmicus Maternus wrote of the *crudeliter in crucem erigitur,* he was expressing the literal truth, for this hoisting of the transverse beam with the victim nailed to it must have been excruciatingly painful.

St. Mark (xv, 23) tells us that before the execution they gave Jesus "wine mingled with myrrh" to drink. This was a very old Jewish custom: "Give strong drink unto him that is ready to perish," says Proverbs, xxxi, 6, and the French still give a glass of rum to the man about to be guillotined. The drink was certainly something supposed to have a stupefying effect and we read in the Talmud of a charitable association of wealthy women who undertook themselves to provide these drugs to the condemned. This interpretation is more likely than St. Matthew's version which seems to confuse *mora,* myrrh, with *merora,* gall, perhaps in allusion to Psalm 69, 21: "They gave me also gall for my meat; and in my thirst they gave me vinegar to drink." In both cases, however, the significant point is that Jesus refused the drink; there must be no alleviation of the death which he had accepted.

Then they took off his clothes. All four Evangelists report this (Matt. xxvii, 35; Mark xv, 24; Luke xxiii, 34; John xix, 23). St. Ambrose, St. Augustine and St. Cyprian, among others, were of the opinion that Jesus was stripped naked, but the Jewish doctors differed on this matter. They agreed that a female victim must retain one garment for decency, but some held that men should be entirely naked while others thought there should be some frontal covering.

The clothes of the condemned man were the perquisites of the executioners, their *pannicularia,* and Hadrian confirmed their right to this, by decree. "They took his garments," says St. John, "and made four parts, to every soldier a part, and also his coat; now the coat was without seam, woven from the top throughout. They said therefore among themselves: Let us not rend it but cast lots for it." And the Gospel goes on to say that thus was the prophecy accomplished: "They part my garments among them and cast lots upon my vesture." (Psalm 22, 18.) The coat without seam had a liturgical significance; the High Priest wore one, and thus it symbolized that Jesus was both priest and victim in the sacrifice. We do not know how he came by it; it may have been a gift from one of the pious women who contributed to his support; it may even have been the "gorgeous robe" in which Herod sent him back to Pilate. But most probably they would have returned to him his ordinary clothes after the flagellation. In Catholic symbolism, the coat without seam is the image of the unity of the Church, which can never be torn by heresies and schisms.

Next, they drove the nails into the living flesh. "And was crucified," Christians repeat daily, in the *Credo*. How often do we think what it must have meant to feel the sharp points tearing their way through nerves and muscles, the welling blood, the irrepressible shudders of the tortured man?

The position of the nails has occasioned much argument. In the earliest traditions the word "hands" is taken in the usual sense and the great majority of artists have shown the wounds of the nails in the palm, where mystics like St. Francis have received the stigmata. But more modern criticism, and particularly medical criticism, has objected that the nails could not have been driven through the palms because the weight of the body would have torn the tissues and that the word "hand" is meant to include the *carpus*, or the wrist, where there is a nexus of small bones and tough tissue. Between these small bones there is a gap into which a nail could be driven and which could support a very considerable pull. This explanation, however, comes up against one difficulty. We have mentioned the custom, in crucifixions, to place a wedge or crutch between the dead man's legs, presumably to stop the hands from breaking and the body from collapsing too soon. If this was done in the case of Jesus, the calculations concerning how much strain the hands would bear are beside the point.

A further commentary in these medical researches is that to drive in the nail through the tissues in the carpus would gravely injure the median nerve, which would not only cause intolerable agony but would draw in the thumb at right angles to the fingers. There is nowhere any ancient representation of the hands of the crucified in this attitude.

The feet were probably crossed over each other avoiding the heels for it would be an exceedingly difficult operation, requiring a nail of exceptional length to pierce these. The nails in the feet were probably inserted between the second and third metatarsal.

The full torture then began. At first the victim, being still in possession of a good deal of strength, would struggle against the crushing cramp in his chest, with horrible convulsive struggles he would try to pull himself up on his feet, in order to breathe. Little by little his strength would give out and his resistance fail, the outstretched arms would sag, and as the body weakened, the knees would bend outward making an obtuse angle with the hips and the feet, so that the human remnant hung in a grotesque zigzag, while the head, after tossing about in agony, would drop finally on the chest, the chin touching the sternum.

Sometimes the executioners, to hasten the end, would light a fire of straw and grass beside the cross, so that the choking fumes would suffocate the victim; sometimes they would give him a thrust with a sword. There was no need to have used either expedient on Jesus, who had said: "I lay down my life that I may take it again. No man taketh it from me, but I lay it down of myself. I have power to lay it down and power to take it up again. This commandment have I received of my Father." (John x, 17-18.) With a single word he could have thrown down the cross, the executioners and the soldiers and dispersed the gaping crowd. "He was oppressed and he was afflicted, yet he opened not his mouth: he is brought as a lamb to the slaughter and as a sheep before the shearers is dumb, so he openeth not his mouth." (Isaiah, liii, 7.) It was around noon when the cross, with its burden, was lifted up and in the Bezetha quarter, not so far away, the sacrificial lambs were being herded into the market to be sold for the Passover feast. The blood of the lamb was about to flow.

Last Moments

The agony of Jesus lasted from the sixth to the ninth hour. Beside him the two robbers, who had been taken along at the same time, were also raised up and the three crosses stood in sinister file along the edge of the road. It was a busy road leading from Jaffa on the coast and, at this particular time, it would certainly be much frequented by pilgrims, so that we must visualize the last agonies of Jesus as taking place among a noisy throng of passers-by, idlers, gapers, travelers with dogs and other animals adding to the confusion, the whole rather like a fair-ground. A guard was stationed but only to see that nobody tried to remove the condemned men, and not to procure a decent quiet for their dying agonies.

The four Gospels all testify to the presence of the crowd while Jesus was dying. He would have friends among them, his disciples and most notably the devoted women who, as we have seen throughout the Passion, were the most faithful and the least intimidated. All these would be utterly cast down, stricken dumb in their grief. There would be passers-by asking who the crucified were and listening to the lies which the Jews of the priests' faction would be only too ready to tell them. Cowardly and light-minded as men are, we cannot be surprised that they should side against the victim. "Ah, thou that destroyest the temple and buildest it in three days, Save thyself and come down from the cross." (Matt. xxvii, 40; Mark xv, 29.) More considerable people, magistrates and scribes, threw in their sneers with the others: "He saved others; himself he cannot save. Let Christ the King of Israel descend now from the cross." The soldiers of the guard joined in; it amused them to see these Jews baiting one of their fellows: "If thou be the King of the Jews, save thyself." (Luke xxiii, 37.) But because they were fundamentally less concerned and therefore less vicious, they offered him their usual drink, *posca*, water sharpened with vinegar. The Chief Priests and the Sanhedrites, who had risked contracting legal impurity to witness the death of their victim, derided him too, saying loudly to each other, so that everyone could hear: "If he be the King of Israel let him now come down from the cross and we will believe in him. He trusted in God; let him deliver him now, if he will have him, for he said: I am the Son of God." (Matt. xxvii, 42-43.) Even in their insults, the words of the scriptures rose to their lips for they echoed a verse of one of the Messianic Psalms: "But I am a worm and no man; a reproach of men and despised of the people. All they that see me laugh me to scorn: they shoot out the lip, they shake the head, saying, He trusted on the Lord that he would deliver him; let him deliver him, seeing that he delighted in him." (Psalm 22, 6-8.)

All this Jesus saw, and heard. His gaze, more and more clouded each minute, may have wandered from the growling swarm at his feet to the great walls of the city and the shining turrets of the Temple. These were the people he had loved, this the humanity he redeemed by his death. Disgust and anger in the face of this barbarous injustice would have been natural enough, but he did not reproach them. During his long agony, Jesus spoke only three times, and the words which broke the silence were words of pity and love.

From the cross on which he who brought salvation hung in agony, a prayer came down to the crowd: "Father, forgive them; for they know not what they do." Only Luke, the "scribe of Christ's compassion," reports these words (xxiii, 34) which are missing from many of the ancient manuscripts, even from the *Codex Vaticanus.* The exegesists, however, regard them as authentic and consider that they were omitted from the earliest texts only because heretics might regard them as too encouraging. Certainly these words are as characteristic of Jesus as any we find throughout the Gospels. It is not merely in theory or when we are not threatened that we should remember to forgive our enemies and love those who hate us, but in the decisive hour of injustice and persecution. Jesus prayed for the Jews, who in their blindness had called down the blood guilt upon themselves; for the soldiers who had scourged him and driven the nails into his flesh; perhaps also for those of his disciples who had deserted him, denied him and betrayed him. His words affirmed once more the meaning of the life that he was offering for them.

In the mystery of the divine intention, this death was required of him. But in the natural order of things it was an outrage. Man in his blindness could ignore the unique importance of the fact that he was witnessing but the deep heart of nature, which also God has made, was convulsed by the sacrilege and "there was a darkness over all the earth until the ninth hour." (Luke xxiii, 44; Mark xv, 33; Matt. xxvii, 45.)

Many early Christian apologists, with the best of intentions, explained this darkness as an eclipse. The so-called Denis the Areopagite states that he himself witnessed the phenomenon at the time at Heliopolis and an eighth century Byzantine chronicler produces other evidence in support of this theory. But Origen, St. Jerome and St. John Chrysostom rejected it. We know that it was the period of the full moon and at this time an eclipse would not be possible during the day. It may have been a sudden uprising of the khamsin, the dark wind from the desert, or a sinister sirocco which plunged Judea into sudden night, as once, at the command of Moses, it had descended on Egypt to punish Pharaoh. Such phenomena are not unknown in April. But if the physical cause of the darkness remains mysterious, its supernatural significance is plain. "And it shall come to pass that in that day, saith the Lord God, that I will cause the sun to go down at noon and I will darken the earth in the clear day." (Amos viii, 9.) The old prophecy was fulfilled on Calvary and it is in this lowering darkness, heavy with disquiet, that we follow the last scene of his agony. Little by little the noisy crowd grew uneasy and silent; many of them went away. The mournful bleating of the lambs waiting for the slaughter became more doleful; even the scoffers and the case-hardened felt constrained and the feeling of distress, linked mysteriously with the oppressiveness of nature, spread through the crowd until the moment when it was to be discharged.

The silence was rent by a savage voice. It came from one of the crosses, from one of the two condemned thieves. Furious and rebellious to the end, this man had to attack somebody, so why not the man on the cross next to him, who was supposed to be able to work miracles? What was he waiting for, why did he not deliver the three of them? "If thou be Christ, save thyself and us." But another spoke from the cross on the further side: "Dost thou not fear God, seeing that thou art in the same condemnation? And we indeed justly: for we receive the just reward for our deeds, but this man hath done nothing amiss." Even in this sinful soul divine goodness was moving. The dying thief turned to Jesus and said: "Lord, remember me when thou comest into thy Kingdom." Did he realize the full meaning of his words or know what Kingdom it was to which he sought admission? But his faith sufficed. "Jesus said unto him, Verily I say unto thee, this day thou shalt be with me in Paradise." (Luke xxiii, 39-41.) Only Luke tells this story. Mark and Matthew state that both thieves reviled Jesus; John says nothing at all.

The story has always appealed greatly to Christian piety; some ancient texts give the thieves the names of Zoathan and Chammatha; the Apocryphal Acts of Pilate calls them Dismas and Geslas; an Arab gospel says Titus and Dumachus, while Medieval legends say Moab and Zandi. Some supposed them to have been Galileans, and others that they were members of Barabbas's band; one legend says that the penitent thief was no other than he who had given food to Mary and Joseph during the flight into Egypt. Tradition also says that the Jews were so furious at his words to Jesus that they prevented the soldiers from shortening his agony by breaking his legs. In some places the penitent thief is venerated as St. Dismas, but all the legends add nothing to the facts. "Who is near to me is at the heart of the fire; who is far from me is far from the Kingdom." The saying is attributed by Origen to Jesus and certainly the generous-hearted thief was "near" to him. Accepting death as a just punishment for his wickedness and offering himself to God, this man, the laborer who came at the eleventh hour, received full wages, for the intention in the heart is enough.

A group of women, perhaps emboldened by the gathering darkness, drew nearer to the cross. With them was a young man, "the disciple whom Jesus loved." This was John, the only one of the Evangelists who records this scene and he gives the names of these brave women who had not deserted Jesus as Mary Magdalene, Mary the wife of Cleophas, and, with one of her sisters, the first of all Mary's, the Virgin Mother. We have lost sight of her since the wedding feast at Cana but she reappears at this supreme moment, by the side of her son. The *Stabat Mater,* the famous sequence written by the Franciscan poet, Jacopo de Todi, recalls the sufferings of the mother watching her son's agony, and unites with them the sufferings of all mothers who grieve for the flesh of their flesh. In prisons, on the battlefield, wherever human cruelty and injustice is unchained, this supreme suffering is offered for all of them. *Stabat Mater dolorosa, juxta crucem lacrimosa, dum pendebat Filius.* "Stood the mother, stood though sighing, Tearful neath the cross where dying, Hung her only Son and Lord. Through and through her soul grief stricken, while the clouds of anguish thicken, Now has pierced the cruel sword." Our Lady of the Seven Dolors, her heart pierced by seven swords, has always been a favorite subject particularly of Spanish artists, but perhaps the most moving of all is the Beaune altarpiece, the lovely sad face upon which even the flowing tears cannot mar the sublime serenity, the confidence looking beyond death.

"When Jesus therefore saw his mother, and the disciple standing by, whom he loved, he saith unto his mother, Woman behold thy son! Then saith he to the disciple, Behold thy mother. And from that hour the disciple took her to his own home." Christian tradition has always seen in this incident St. John as symbolizing the entire human race.

Then came the last words of the Messiah upon earth.

Death had its way, in that terrible face-to-face encounter which we must all experience when our time comes. Jesus is seen only as a man broken by suffering. In a loud voice, which was astonishing, since crucifixion paralyzes the lungs and clamps the throat, he cried: *"Eli, eli, lama sabachthani."* (Matt. xxvii, 46.) The words were in his mother tongue, Aramaic; they are the opening of the Messianic Psalm 22 which the chief priests had quoted, deriding him. Possibly their gibes had struck some chord in his memory. For the Psalm is not only an imploring cry which the suffering flesh sends out in protest, and it is not expressing doubt but supreme confidence, for "thou didst make me hope when I was upon my mother's breasts . . . be not far from me; for trouble is near . . . O Lord, O my strength haste thee to help me . . . My praise shall be of thee in the great congregation; I will pay my vows before them that fear him . . . They shall declare his righteousness unto a people that shall be born, that he hath done this."

The words were heard in the silence and the darkness. "What did he say?" and someone who understood Aramaic replied that he called on Elias. "Let be, let us see whether Elias will deliver him," said one of the scoffers. Still another word drifted down from the poor rag of humanity on the cross, from the tortured flesh came the only complaint recorded throughout the whole story of the Passion. "I thirst." One of the soldiers, pitying him, took a sponge soaked in water tinctured with vinegar, and, according to the synoptics, handed it up to the lips of the dying man on a reed—upon a stalk of hyssop, according to St. John. This has been interpreted as a javelin, a misreading of *hyssopo* for *hysso*, a javelin. "In my thirst they gave me vinegar to drink," says Psalm 69, 21. Nothing was spared and everything was done in accordance with the will which had known from the beginning that all this would be, in accordance with the plan which had been revealed, stage by stage, through the consciousness of the prophets of Israel.

It was now around three in the afternoon and darkness was

everywhere. Everything was over, and, as we turn this page, the most beautiful and the most terrible of the entire Gospel, we may remark upon the simplicity of the words in which the episodes are recorded. Apocryphal texts have embroidered the account, and sometimes in the worst taste, inventing strange incidents presumably to heighten the dramatic effect; such as that the Virgin Mary had to take off her veil to cover her son's nakedness and that demons perched like evil birds on the arms of the cross to swoop down on the soul of Jesus. In contrast with these unworthy fables, St. Matthew, St. Mark, St. Luke and St. John have recorded what they knew without any attempt to heighten the pathos. There is no portion of the entire Gospel which gives more forcibly the impression of plain truth while yet, in its bare sentences, conveying the imprint of divine inspiration.

It was three o'clock, the legal hour of sunset, and in the Temple the opening ceremony of the Passover was about to commence. Three blasts, short, long, short, from the sacred trumpets and the High Priest in a blue cope ascended the steps. The sound of a flute rose up before the altar of sacrifice. On Golgotha, three further words came down from the cross: "It is finished," and then a last prayer: "Father, into thy hands I commend my spirit," a loud cry, the final exhalation of the life that was completed, "and having said thus, he gave up the ghost." (John xix, 30; Luke xxiii, 46.)

It was completed. The message which Jesus had sought to give the world came at that moment to its consummation. Many times he had said that the price of salvation was blood; now that price was paid. An ungrateful Israel was at the very moment absorbed in its rites—at the very moment when these rites were to change in meaning. All that had for centuries uplifted the heart of Israel, all the prophecies, had passed out of the domain of prophecy and had become History. For the last cry of the victim was in itself an echo of the faith of the Psalmist. "Into thy hand I commend my spirit: thou has redeemed me, O Lord God of truth." (Psalm 31, 5.) The son of David echoing the words of his ancestor; everything was mysteriously bound together according to the divine plan; everything was completed.

Probably none of the Jews engaged at that moment in chanting the *Hallel* realized the unique importance of the drama of Calvary. They may not even have regarded the greenish darkness brooding over the city as a warning sign. But nature again reacted dramatically, for the three synoptics report that at the moment Jesus expired "the veil of the Temple was rent." In the Temple, before the "Holy Place" and at the threshold of the "Holy of Holies," hung tall valances, single curtains which were drawn when the doors were opened. But the mystery of the Temple was now revealed and from this time all men could penetrate it. Father Lagrange writes that this phenomenon might have been produced by "one of those violent gusts of wind which can dissipate the black sirocco of springtime in a moment." But St. Matthew says, in addition, that "the earth did quake and the rocks rent."

There were other strange phenomena; dead men came out of their graves and appeared to many; fear swept across the town. There would seem to have been a violent earthquake, which is not infrequent in Palestine. The dome of the Church of the Holy Sepulcher was damaged by an earthquake on July 11, 1927, and in the very rock of Calvary can still be seen a deep perpendicular fissure about two yards long and a foot wide which is almost certainly of seismic origin. Joel the Prophet had foretold that in the hour of judgment "the sun and the moon shall be darkened, and the stars shall withdraw their shining, the Lord also shall roar out of Zion and utter his voice from Jerusalem, and the heavens and the earth shall shake." (Joel iii, 15-16.) For the Jews the hour of judgment had come, but how many of them knew it?

There was one man, however, who felt that there was some connection between the convulsions of the earth and the last cry of the crucified. This was the centurion, *exactor mortis,* whose duty it was to remain with the sufferers until the end. He had heard the Jews say to Pilate that this man "ought to die because he made himself the Son of God." At the time he had paid no attention to the words but the cataclysms of nature, the cramping sense of dread which had spread over the city and the groaning in the very bowels of the earth brought him revelation. In the darkened cemetery, by the three gibbets, light came to him. "Truly this was the Son of God," he said. We know no more of this honest soldier, the first of the countless millions who were to believe in Jesus crucified. Perhaps his military training inclined him to faith by submitting his nature to discipline and his intelligence to the logic of cause and effect; we remember that another centurion had astonished Jesus by his humility and confidence. Tradition has given various names, Petronius and Cornelius, to the first Christian convert, but although these legends have no foundation his avowal has a very real significance.

Jesus hung on the cross, his body sagging from the pierced hands and the arms with their muscles bulging out like cables, stiffening in that attitude of complete abandon. Over the pallid skin blood flowed from the wounds and trickled from the cuts made by the scourges. The blemished flesh, mottled by blows, had already lost the form and substance of the living body, so quickly does a corpse become that curiously inhuman thing, half statue and half anatomical specimen, in which we can only with difficulty recognize the creature we have loved.

The "Descent from the Cross" has been depicted by innumerable sculptors and painters who have tried to portray its full horror. But even the most terrible of these conceptions is inadequate. For as we behold the once beloved body, already threatened with corruption, the heart recognizes an essential truth, that this is the way of all flesh. This is what we all bear within us, this is the unfailing promise of our flesh. As we feel the throbbing arteries we know the inescapable menace within them. Jesus died the death that waits for all of us; but here is consolation as well as mystery. "For I, being lifted up, will draw all men to me," he said. Already we have seen the centurion drawing toward him, and after him the long line of the innumerable millions for whom his death is the only hope of life, the pledge of the resurrection.

The Sepulcher

On the outskirts of the hill lingered some of those who remained faithful to Jesus, watching from some distance, says St. Luke, the death of him they had loved. There would be the group of women, whose presence has already been recorded, and perhaps a few Galileans who had come to Jerusalem for the Passover. Grief and fright had numbed them to silence.

When all was over and the strange manifestations of the wrath of God occurred, many of those who had watched, Jews and pagans both, were already back in the town, shaken with fear and remorse. One of the disciples must have carried back the news of the end. Respect for the dead was very strong in Israel and the disciples would wish to remove Jesus from the cross of shame and perform the last duties.

But it was necessary to obtain Pilate's permission and only a man of some importance could do this, someone of the rank of Nicodemus who in his heart had been converted by the teaching of Jesus but who feared the Jews too much to become his disciple openly. (John xix, 38.) The man who went was Joseph of Arimathea, the ancient Ramathaim, which is called Rentis today. Joseph was a member of the Sanhedrin but he had not, says St. Luke, "consented to the counsel and to the deed of them." (xxiii, 51.) What Jesus living could not do, Jesus dead accomplished: Joseph of Arimathea conquered his prudence.

The Mosaic Law commanded that the body of an executed man "shall not remain all night upon the tree." (Deut. xxi, 23.) It was, therefore, in accordance with the Law to ask for permission to bury him. But, on the evidence of the Talmud, it seems that the bodies of condemned criminals were put in pits belonging to the judicature and remained there until the flesh rotted away and only then could their bones be returned to their families. So it would be asking a favor of Pilate. In Roman custom, to refuse to give the body of an executed man to his family, or to demand money for doing so, was regarded as exceptional severity and Pilate in this case had no reason to be unmerciful. He allowed Joseph's request but expressed surprise that death should have come so quickly.

At the same time he received another request. Some of the more orthodox Jews, fearing that the Passover might commence before the crucified men were dead and removed—which would constitute a legal impurity for the whole town—asked that death might be hastened by breaking the dying men's legs, which was not unusual. Pilate sent a picket for this purpose.

"Then came the soldiers and brake the legs of the first, and of the other which was crucified with him. But when they came to Jesus and saw that he was dead already, they brake not his legs. But one of the soldiers with a spear pierced his side, and forthwith came out there blood and water." St. John, who reports the fact, states that he saw it. (John xix, 31-37.)

The *crurifragium*, or breaking of the legs, was recognized Roman punishment, a cruel supplement to other tortures, but in the case of men already dying on the cross it was normally used to shorten their sufferings. The soldier's lance thrust was probably only a routine gesture to make absolutely sure that the man was dead. From the story of Thomas, doubting the appearance of the risen Lord (John xx, 25-27), we may suppose that the wound was considerable, large enough for a man to put his hand into it. There have been a number of theories advanced to explain the "blood and water." Some have explained it by a rupture of the heart which had occurred before the lance thrust; others, wedded to pathological explanations of the school of Binet-Sanglé, have supposed that there was a pocket of fluid of tuberculous origin. The simplest explanation is that the water was simply pericardial fluid due to the internal transudation brought about by the body's agony.

The lance thrust is sometimes shown in art as being on the right side of Jesus, sometimes on the left. The latter seems more likely, owing to the position of the heart. Yet an artist so scrupulous in his documentation as Rembrandt shows it on the right side, and on the right side of the Shroud of Turin there is the unquestionable trace of a wound. The righthand thrust was the classic maneuver of Roman sword drill since the left side would, in combat, be covered by the shield. But, chiefly, anatomical research reveals that after death the blood collects in the right auricle. If the blow had been struck on the left it would either have penetrated the left auricle, which would be empty or else, since the position of the heart is oblique, the left ventricles, which would also be empty. The thrust must therefore have been on the right side. Physiology also confirms that Jesus must have been dead when the thrust was made; had he been alive the lungs would have retracted and suspended the flow of blood.

The dramatic gesture of the lance thrust and its obvious symbolism have made it one of the most famous incidents of the Passion, and Christian tradition has naturally made much of it. The soldier who used the lance has been given the name of Longin, obviously derived from a corruption of the Greek *Lonche,* a lance. Legend states that he suffered from eye trouble which was miraculously cured when a drop of the sacred blood spurted into his eye, that he became a Christian and died a martyr after having been for twenty-eight years in a monastery at Caesarea. From this incident also arose the body of legend centering round the Holy Grail, the vase or chalice in which the Apostles are supposed to have received the blood of Jesus at the Last Supper. But the legends, however natural, are superfluous: the Gospel narrative itself stresses the symbolism by two texts from the ancient scriptures. The Mosaic Law required of the Passover lamb that "neither shall ye break a bone thereof" (Ex. xii, 46; Num. ix, 12), and in Zechariah (xii, 10) we read that "they shall look upon him whom they have pierced." The Roman soldier was not alone when he looked at that body from which flowed water and blood; all humanity redeemed by Christ stands with him. For water and blood are the emblems of baptism, by faith and by the sacrifice.

The soldiers could go back and reassure Pilate that Jesus

was indeed dead, it was not some conspiracy of his friends to get him down and pretend to bring him back to life so the corpse could be made over to them. Joseph of Arimathea and several others had to take out the nails from the body before taking it away for burial. Innumerable artists have given us their versions of the Descent from the Cross. Let us here consider the scene in its tragic reality. It is a dreadful thing to have to clothe the dead one has loved; the body which has been abandoned is like a huge, disjointed puppet, repulsive to the touch.

In *The Idiot,* Dostoyevsky has Prince Myshkin say of Holbein's masterpiece: "If it was a corpse like this which the disciples saw, and certainly it must have been, how could they have considered that it could ever be resuscitated. We cannot beg the question; if the processes of nature are so frightful, how can they be overcome? When we look at this picture, nature seems a kind of giant beast, dumb and implacable, or rather like some colossal piece of mindless mechanism which clutches, tears to pieces and swallows, without heed or feeling, the greatest, most inestimable of Beings."

The Holbein indeed pictures the moment, when Jesus, taken down from his pedestal, the Cross, seems to be no more than ill-used flesh with muscles knotted by agony. Death would seem to have triumphed. However, artistic tradition prefers, among the innumerable Pietàs—which show, for example, the body stretched out on the knees of his mother, as though he had become a child again for her to bear for the last time—more sweetness and consolation in the conception. The Holbein is closer to the horrible reality.

The Gospel does not tell us what became of the Cross but tradition says that it was thrown in a ditch at the foot of the ramparts, some twenty or thirty yards from Calvary. Here indeed it was found by St. Helena, during the excavations which she had made, and the "Discovery of the Holy Cross" provided the sculptors of Rheims with one of their finest subjects. At the place today is a rather sinister little recess, to the right of the Church of the Holy Sepulcher, much deeper even than the

Armenian Chapel said to be St. Helena's. It consists of a crypt roofed by a dome upheld by four pillars with immense capitals and the visitor goes down by an iron stairway. The place suggests most forcibly a sense of misery and desolation.

The body, removed from the Cross, was prepared for the grave "as the manner of the Jews is to bury," says St. John. They must have made haste since the hour of the Sabbath was near. It is not correct to state, however, as is sometimes done, that the funeral rites were curtailed, for the Law permitted the washing and embalming of the dead even on the Sabbath, according to the Talmud. So, even if the six blasts on the silver trumpet had already announced the holy day, the disciples were at liberty to finish their pious work.

We are told that Joseph of Arimathea had a new grave close by which had never been used. (Matt. xxvii, 60; Mark xv, 42; Luke xxiii, 50; John xix, 38.) This may have been the reason why the disciples got in touch with him. The grave would be of the type usual in Palestine, similar to that from which Lazarus arose. There would be two chambers hollowed out of the rock, the first a kind of vestibule with a door at the end opening into the tomb proper. This would be almost square, just about two yards each way, and against the wall was a kind of shelf for the reception of the corpse. The tomb was closed by a very heavy stone. something like a millstone, which rolled up to the sloping recess of the outer chamber where it was held by a wedge. If this were removed the stone would roll forward blocking the entrance to the tomb itself.

The traditional site of the sepulcher itself is in the chancel of the basilica to which it has given its name. This impressive monument, first built by the Empress Helena, demolished several times and rebuilt again and again, is an imposing building of hybrid style with something barbaric about it. A reddish light glows from the high vaulted roof; a circle of massive black columns, which acquire a bizarre iridescence from hundreds of lamps, surround a circular monument, flanked with lamps, chandeliers and enormous candles. Its surface is completely covered by icons, gilding and ex-voto tablets. It is raised upon three basalt steps. The actual funeral chamber is now a chapel and only priests, duly vested in their sacerdotal robes, may enter. Thousands of candles burn around it and the heat and the smell is almost overpowering.

Nothing could be less like the silence and darkness of the tomb than this flamboyant reliquary. And nothing could be less like the spirit of Jesus than the shocking quarrels of the rival sects over its possession. Latins, Greeks, Melkites, Maronites, Syrian Catholics, Greek Orthodox, Armenians, Copts, Protestants and others have all claimed the right to pray at the Sepulcher. They have not only prayed; sometimes they have savagely fought. O, where is the robe without seam! One part of the basilica is made over to the Greek Orthodox Church; the Catholics have another, in charge of Franciscans. There is a timetable listing the hours for the ceremonies of the various sects. Pierre Loti attacked the spectacle as scandalous; it must be admitted that the Christian can experience only a sad disenchantment.

The tomb was opened. Jesus was wrapped in the grave clothes, which consisted of at least two pieces, as we shall see later in St. John's account of the Resurrection (xx). There was the winding sheet, the *sindon,* and a smaller piece of linen, the *soudarion* or grave cloth, a kind of handkerchief placed over the face. There may indeed have been several wrappings, for the Greek verb which St. John uses, *dèo* (xix, 40) although usually translated as "to wrap" means in fact "to attach" or "to bind," and is translated in the Latin versions of the Gospel as *ligaverunt*. The head was raised on the mound of stones which was provided in all Jewish tombs for this purpose. The devoted women who had followed Jesus from Galilee until the end assisted in the last rites.

"And there came also Nicodemus, which at the first came to Jesus by night, and brought a mixture of myrrh and aloes about an hundred pound weight." (John xix, 39.) It was a pathetic gesture from a pathetic man who had more good will than courage. Nicodemus could not stand up for Christ living but he made a sumptuous offering to his remains. A hundred pound weight would be now about sixty pounds and myrrh and aloes were costly. Myrrh is that scented resin so greatly esteemed in the East; it is mentioned many times in the Old Testament (Ex. xxx, 23; Psalm 45, 8-9; Song of Solomon iii, 6; iv, 6-14; Ecclesiasticus xxiv, 15.) It was brought by the Magi to the child Jesus. Aloes could not have been the medicinal plant we know by that name with its nauseating odor and bitter taste (old-fashioned parents used to put it on children's fingers to keep them from biting their nails), for when it is mentioned in the Old Testament it is always in connection with perfumes. It was probably that sweet-scented wood, rather similar to thuya or sandalwood, which the Syrians call *agaloucoun* and which was also much sought after by the Greeks.

It has been presumed that the sixty pounds of perfumes were used for embalming but it is doubtful whether myrrh or aloes in fact had the requisite properties. In any case, embalming is effective only if the Egyptian method of removing the entrails and impregnating the flesh with preservatives is followed. That certainly was not done. It seems more likely that these spices were offered as a tribute of respect to the dead, rather as we send flowers.

The light was fading; they must make haste to finish, to remove the wedge and let the stone roll up and close the tomb. Then they went away, leaving the body in the silence of the tomb.

"Now the next day that followed the day of the preparation, the chief priests and Pharisees came together unto Pilate, saying, Sir, we remember that that deceiver said, when he was yet alive, After three days I will rise again. Command therefore that the sepulcher be made sure until the third day, lest his disciples come by night and steal him away, and say to the people, He is risen from the dead: so the last error shall be worse than the first." (Matt. xxvii, 63-66.) They were taking no chances, these politicians. But the Roman was annoyed with them; how much longer was this affair to go on. "Ye have a watch (he said). Go your way, make it as sure as ye can.

So they went and made the sepulcher secure, sealing the stone, and setting a watch." Such precautions do men take against the will of God!

In the darkness of the grave, Jesus was now no more than other men, a body of flesh awaiting corruption. So his unhappy disciples must have thought. So also has Holbein painted him and Philippe de Champaigne too, setting before us the anatomy of a man tortured to death: the mouth agape, the eyes upturned, the deathly hue of the flesh now that the blood of the wounds would flow no more. And yet, corruption, which in the natural order must follow inevitably, was not to be. "Except a corn of wheat fall into the ground," said Jesus, "it abideth alone. But if it die it bringeth forth much fruit." The seed lay in the fostering earth; the fruit would spring forth from the seed and the harvest was at hand.

CHAPTER TWELVE

VICTORY OVER DEATH

Descent into Hell

HIS BODY LAY IN EARTH, but where was the soul of Jesus? His disciples must have asked themselves that when, lost without the divine presence and cast down by the dreadful experiences of the past day, they met together and talked of him. Afterward, when the Resurrection brought back their hopes, perhaps on information received from the master himself, they were able to give a reply. There was a very early apostolic tradition, which St. Paul seems to have known and which is reported by St. Peter, that the soul of Jesus, after his expiring cry, did not rise up released to the Father, but continuing its task of salvation, descended into hell where the souls of those who had died in former times lay waiting deliverance. "Being put to death in the flesh but quickened by the spirit, by which also he went and preached unto the spirits in prison, which sometimes were disobedient." (I. Peter iii, 19.) "For this cause was the Gospel preached also to them that are dead." (*Ibid*, iv, 6.)

The Church has retained this tenet of evangelizing in Inferno in a verse of that Apostles' Creed which repeats old traditions.[1] Thus it is part of the faith. We can only regret that

[1] The Credo in the Ordinary of the Mass omits this verse, following the text laid down by the Councils of Nicaea (325) and Constantinople (381).

the Evangelists, especially St. John with his command of mystical beauty, should have kept complete silence on the subject. We have to resort to the Apocryphas, stressing reserves and precautions, to get even a little to satisfy our curiosity. The subject is mentioned in the *Odes of Solomon,* a Christian text dating from the first half of the second century. We read in the *Gospel of Peter:* "Those who witnessed the Resurrection heard a voice from heaven crying: Have ye announced the mission to them that sleep? And from the Cross came the answer, Yes." This is not very enlightening and, as so often in the Apocryphal texts, we notice a bizarre, and indeed absurd, anomaly, for Christ was not on the Cross at the Resurrection.

But the strangest and most detailed account is in the Gospel of Nicodemus. We are giving it in its entirety for it is worth it. The narrator puts the story into the mouth of two of the "shades," Carinus and Leucius, sons of the holy Simeon, who had died before the Crucifixion and who were brought back to life during the supernatural phenomena which attended the Crucifixion and the Resurrection. It must be emphasized that the text has no canonical authority; its value is purely literary, but its strange beauty cannot be denied.

"While we slept with our fathers in the shades of death, we were suddenly enveloped in a golden light as of the sun. Its regal clarity illuminated us. And immediately Adam, the father of the whole human race, trembled with joy as also did the Patriarchs and the Prophets. 'Light,' they cried out. 'It is the light and he who created eternal light promised that light should shine upon us, without diminution or term.' Then all those righteous men under the Old Law rejoiced, awaiting the fulfillment of the promise. But in hell there was great disquiet: the Prince of Darkness quaked at the thought of seeing him who had already demonstrated his power by raising Lazarus. 'As soon as I felt the power of his voice, I trembled,' said he. 'We were not able to hold Lazarus; like the eagle in flight he broke loose from us and escaped.'

"As he spoke thus, a voice burst forth like thunder and like the sound of the hurricane. 'Lift up your heads, O ye gates; and be ye lift up, ye everlasting doors; and the King of Glory shall come in!' [2] Then said the Prince of Darkness to his ministers, 'Shut fast the iron gates, thrust home the iron bolts and let us fight with all our valor.'

"Again sounded the voice like thunder.

" 'Lift up your heads, O ye gates; and be ye lift up, ye everlasting doors and the King of Glory shall come in.' And the Lord of Majesty appeared in the form of a man: he shed light upon the eternal darkness, he broke chains and he came to all of us, to all who were sunk in the dark pit of our transgressions and in the mortal shadow of sin.

"Then the Prince of Tartarus and Death and all the Legions of Hell were seized with terror. 'Who art thou?' they cried to Jesus. 'Whence comest Thou?' But he did not deign to reply.

"Then the King of Glory, crushing Death beneath his feet, seized Satan and robbed Hell of its power. He led Adam toward the fullness of the light, and then he, the Lord, said, 'Come to me, all my holy ones, all ye who bore my stamp and resemblance.' And so, united in the hands of God, they sang, all the Saints, sang his praise. David, Habbakuk and all the Prophets sang the psalms in which they had predicted, in mysterious language, that which was made clear here in this day. Led by the Archangel Michael they came to Paradise where awaited them Enoch and Elias, those two righteous men who had not been subjected to death, and the penitent thief, with the marks of the Cross still on his shoulders."

No one, of course, would propose to take this romantic figment literally. Tradition credits it to the sons of Simeon, who settled in Arimathea after their resurrection, and it is said to have been preserved by the Christian community in Palestine. If we cannot accept it as inspired, in the canonical sense, it is certainly inspired in the literary sense, and its inspiration is that which has prompted the great lyrical visionaries from Isaiah to Dante. It is easy to understand why it was so much

---

[2] A literal quotation from Psalm 24, 7.

valued in the Middle Ages, whose artists took many themes from the Apocryphas. Much of the most beautiful medieval glass, notably in Bruges and Tours, illustrates subjects from these texts.

The liturgy of Holy Saturday, although it makes no direct reference to the Descent into Hell, retains a connection with the theme. The Greek Orthodox church celebrates on this day the Blessing of the Fire; in the Church of the Holy Sepulcher, in the total darkness, a flame springs up in the very place where the dead body of Jesus once lay. From the flaming torch raised by the Patriarch are lit thousands of candles, lamps and tapers so that the vast crowd of the faithful gathered there is transformed immediately into a sea of light, as if in memory of that hour when those who lay "in the shades of death" saw the redeeming light fall upon them. Some forty years ago it was the custom to carry the torch lit at the Holy Sepulcher, stage by stage, on horseback to Athens, Constantinople, Kiev and Moscow.

In the Catholic Church, the ceremonies of Holy Saturday seem to have been devised with the intention of uniting every human soul, those of the past and those yet to be born, in the promise of salvation. The litanies sung in the Blessing of the Font invoke the Christian Saints; the reading of the Twelve Prophecies recalls the Saints of the Old Law, Adam, Noah, Abraham, Moses, and the Prophets. In the early Church it was customary to baptize catechumens on Holy Saturday. In blessing the water to be used for this purpose throughout the year the Church unites all Christians yet to come in the same certainty of salvation. The last day of Holy Week is still vested with mourning but already, in the words of the Collect of the Mass, this "most holy night" is illuminated "by the glory of Our Lord's Resurrection."

Sunday Dawn

Only a poet can find words for the most beautiful and the most shattering of the Gospel episodes, which Bossuet called "the central fact of all history." Once again, as on the eve of Christmas, a tide of memories wells up in us. We remember our childhood, in some small town perhaps, where we were awakened by the sound of the bells on Easter morning and felt suddenly, hardly knowing why, an immense upsurge of joy and reassurance. The heedless and the unbelieving will celebrate too; it is marked on the most secular calendars. The feast of the eternal promise is bound up inextricably with Western civilization and, through it, those who no longer realize its meaning share in its inmost mystery, by which, says St. Paul, we are seated with Christ in heaven.

The Sabbath ended at sundown on Saturday and then, without breaking the Law, men could come and go as they pleased and perhaps, if it were still possible, come to pay their respects to the body which, the evening before, had been so hastily deposited in the tomb.

We wonder what the disciples of Jesus had been doing from the time he was arrested. Except for John, who had dared to go to Calvary, they seem to have given way to panic and gone underground. A tradition says that St. James hid in a tomb in the middle of the Cemetery of Josaphat, a deep hole hollowed out of the rock. This hideout, now furbished with a Doric colonnade, is still shown to visitors. In the Apocryphal *Gospel of Peter*, we read: "I and my companions, pierced to the soul, lay hidden for they were hunting us as malefactors suspected of firing the Temple. We sat in tears and mourning, and fasted." St. Mark (xvi, 10) says that they "mourned and wept" but no more. Yet, what could they do? All human hope must have seemed futile. Some of them probably got ready to return to Galilee: "All ye shall be offended because of me this night: for it is written, I will smite the shepherd and the sheep shall be scattered." (Mark xiv, 27.)

The women, the Mary's, Salome, Joanna the wife of Chusa, behaved as women always do in these crises; they went on with the busines of living. Back in their houses, they prepared aromatic spices, pounding spikenard, aloes and marjoram in the mortars, but during the Sabbath they "rested . . . according to the commandments," St. Luke says (xxiii, 56). They did not go out immediately when the Lord's Day was over, for Golgotha was a sinister place where one would not care to venture out at night. But at daybreak, the Gospel is precise about this, they hurried along the road to the tomb where lay, so they thought, Jesus whom they had loved. We can see them in the clear light of the April morning, the pure unsullied light of the Palestinian spring. To the east, above the rooftops of the city, the horizon was milky with luminous tints of pearl while to the west, night receded slowly, trailing the mauve and gray fringes of her veil on the hills. The "gray-eyed dawn" of which Virgil sings, that "rosy-fingered dawn" beloved of Homer, holds within its brief privilege everything that nature can promise, everything which, even in the most degraded of creatures, stirs the whisper of Divine Grace.

Each of the four Evangelists has recorded in his own style how the holy women found the tomb empty. They all agree that the women were the first to receive the revelation; bolder than the men, responding more readily to love than to prudence, perhaps better equipped by nature to accept facts beyond the power of reason to analyze, but which their unconscious being could perceive with extraordinary certainty. It is not easy to bring the four accounts into line, but this seems to be the order of events.

The women went up to the sepulcher, still overshadowed by the events of the previous two days, uneasy and miserable. They had conquered their fear, but they had need of all their courage for, as they went along the road, at daybreak, there was another earth tremor and a sound like the rolling of thunder, close at hand, almost as if it came from Jerusalem.

Among these heroic women, all the accounts without exception give first place to Mary Magdalene, the woman from Magdala, from whom Jesus cast out seven devils and who had since then devoted her life to him. She seems to have gone ahead faster than the others, driven perhaps by faith and an irrational hope. Behind her came another Mary, the mother of James; Salome and Joanna; five or six in all. "Who shall roll us away the stone from the door of the sepulcher?" they asked, and some old texts add: "Twenty men would be hard put to displace it."

But arriving at the tomb, they found it open. "They found the stone rolled away from the sepulcher," says St. Luke (xxiv, 2) and that the body was not lying in the niche inside. What had happened? St. Matthew tells us that "the angel of the Lord descended from heaven and came and rolled back the stone." The trembling of the earth was the passage of the angel: "His countenance was like lightning, and his raiment white as snow. And for fear of him the keepers did shake and became as dead men." (Matt. xxviii, 3-4.) This is all that the Gospel tells us about this tremendous scene. Jesus, rising from the tomb, above the prostrate soldiers, so often and so triumpantly depicted in art, is made known to us only by these two plain and sober lines.

If we read the Gospel carefully, we see that the actual fact of the Resurrection is not reported in any of the canonical accounts. It would have lent itself easily, in the hands of writers given to the sort of picturesque details which sway the crowd, to all sorts of developments. We may best appreciate the Apostolic restraint if we consult some of the Apocrypha. In the *Gospel of Peter* we have the following: "That night that ended with the dawn on Sunday, as the soldiers went up, two by two, to mount the guard, a loud voice from heaven was heard and they saw the sky open and two men clad in light descended and went toward the tomb. Then the stone which leaned against the doorway rolled away of itself to the side, the tomb was open and the two men went in. When the soldiers saw this, they awakened the centurion and the elders, who were also with the guard. And as the soldiers were telling them what they had seen, they saw again three men coming out of the tomb; two of them supported the third and the cross followed after. The heads of the two supporters reached up to heaven and that of he whom they supported was lost in the clouds." Most of us will prefer the bald account of St. Matthew to this visionary chatter.

The holy women were astounded by the disappearance of the body and, realizing that the guards were no longer there, they were frightened too. Mary Magdalene, who seems to have been the most agile (one thinks of her as the youngest) ran to give the news to the disciples (John xx, 2). The others stayed there, either inside or just outside the tomb, very uneasy, when "two men stood before them in shining garments. And as they were afraid and bowed down their faces to the earth, they said unto them, Why seek ye the living among the dead? He is not here, but is risen: remember how he spake unto you when he was yet in Galilae, Saying, the Son of Man must be delivered into the hands of sinful men and be crucified, and the third day rise again." (Luke xxiv, 4-7.) St. Matthew and St. Mark record only one angel but the meaning of the vision is exactly the same. Jesus is risen.

Meanwhile the Magdalene had found the disciples and told them what had happened. Then the others came back, naturally in a state of intense excitement, with their story. St. Matthew and St. Luke both say roundly that the first reaction of the disciples was to doubt the women's story as an old wives' tale. St. Peter, however, wanted to see for himself and ran to the sepulcher. Another disciple went with him, undoubtedly John, though in his humility he does not say so. The second man ran faster and reached the tomb ahead of Peter (John xx, 4). It was exactly as the women had said; the grave clothes lay on the ground, the stone was rolled away. Peter now came up and saw the same. In a corner of the tomb, the napkin which had covered the face of Jesus lay folded. Then, suddenly, they felt the invasion of faith. Though they could not yet understand that the scriptures had been fulfilled, the promise of the Resurrection of which their master had told them, though they were troubled and distraught, they experienced a secret consolation.

The sepulcher was deserted now. No, not quite, for the Magdalene lingered; that overpowering love which had brought her there the first kept her from going away. Probably she did not realize that Jesus had risen, probably she could not think of anything as she wept. Then she had her vision. Two angels in white garments sat within the inner chamber of the tomb, one where the body had lain, the other where the head had rested. "Woman, why weepest thou?" they asked. "Because they have taken away my Lord and I know not where they have laid him." As she spoke, she heard someone behind her, a man. He also asked, "Woman, why weepest thou?" Thinking that perhaps he was one of the gardeners attached to the cemetery, she replied, "Sir, if thou have borne him hence, tell me where thou hast lain him, and I will take him away." Then the unknown man spoke one word, "Mary," and she looked at him, transfixed. Then, running toward him, she cried out, "Rabboni," which in Hebrew means "Master." Jesus is risen! The realization swept away everything else.

The scene, so moving in its strange realism, has always been a favorite with artists, particularly the Italian school. We see it as they painted it, Giotto, Duccio, Lorenzo de Credi and Raphael: Jesus, tall and upright in a landscape of surpassing beauty, blessing the kneeling Magdalene. We may criticize Correggio for the over-sweetness of his Christ but must praise him for the marvelous light on his garment. This one word sufficed to reawaken in the Magdalene the ardor and certainty of her faith. What Christian has not dreamed of hearing it, the word with which, from all eternity, God calls each one of us, but which the deaf do not hear.[3]

He Rose from the Dead

The second term of the life of Jesus has now begun. He has passed through the frightful valley of the shadow and emerges in the full light of Easter Morning. He will remain forty days

[3] According to St. Matthew, Jesus appeared simultaneously to Mary Magdalene and "the other Mary." An ancient Coptic text, the fragment of an unknown gospel, says he appeared to his mother, to Martha and to Mary Magdalene and that it was Martha who went first to tell the disciples. In the Apocryphal Gospel According to the Hebrews, Jesus gave the napkin which had covered his face to a servant of the High Priest, and then showed himself to James, his cousin. There is also reason to believe that after the episode of Emmaus he appeared to St. Peter. St. Paul (I Cor. xv, 5) refers to this.

on earth, living among his faithful friends, teaching them, making things plain to them, just as of old. This is a basic doctrine of Christianity, solemnly averred by the Apostles' and the Nicene Creeds. It must be admitted that it is a frontal assault on what rationalism considers possible and probable. To those who cannot allow the supernatural a place in the order of things, the dogma of the Resurrection is a scandal and a fable, nothing more nor less. But to those who can understand that the ultimate explanation of the universe does not lie in the realm of how or why, it is the sign of signs, it sums up and justifies the mystery of our being.

The account of the second life of Jesus is based on several New Testament texts, and the details given in the four Gospels are confirmed by various Epistles of St. Paul, the First Epistle of St. Peter and the Acts of the Apostles, to say nothing of the enormous literature of the patristic writings and a number of Apocryphal texts. If we confine ourselves simply to the four Gospels there seems to be no reason to suspect this part of their evidence which is just as well attested as the rest of their writing. There can be no critical justification for accepting the joint evidence of the four Evangelists down to the death of Jesus and refusing to do so after the Resurrection for the reason that the facts reported are disconcerting to our habits of thought.

There is, however, one reservation to be made and it is important. The four Evangelists record very briefly the events following the Resurrection; the synoptics mention them on only two or three pages, St. John on eight or nine. There is an obvious disproportion between the significance of the fact and the brevity with which it is related. Yet we have only to turn to St. Paul to see what an enormous place the doctrine of the Resurrection held in his time, through all the early Church.

If we consider the facts carefully, however, the matter is less surprising. The events of these forty days were, as we shall see, in no way different from those of the daily life of Jesus in the past. Some of them, the miraculous draught of fishes, for instance, seem to be almost repetitions of earlier incidents. This second short life was a prolongation of what had gone before, and considered in relation to other equivalent periods in Jesus's life and teaching, in Galilee and Judea, it will be seen that the events of these forty days are allotted their due space in the Gospels. In fact other periods equal in time, before the Resurrection, received less attention. The restraint of the record in the four canonical Gospels is in fact a strong proof of their authenticity. We realize this as soon as we turn to the Apocryphal texts—such as the Gospel of Bartholomew and the Epistle of the Apostles. Here is all the detail anyone could wish, embroidered according to fancy. But the four Evangelists resisted the devil of the imagination, the most insidious of all which beset the writer.

It must be admitted, nevertheless, that the accounts of the Resurrection in the four Gospels display, if not actual discrepancies, certainly differences of emphasis. In fact, it is not possible to collate them into an orderly account. We must again emphasize, as we did in the introduction to this work, that the Evangelists were not professional historians; the purpose of their writing was didactic. They were instructing converts, not putting together historical documents. Precisely because the Resurrection was, from the point of view of apologetics, the primordial event, each one put down what seemed to him to be the most startling and convincing facts. It is also possible that they drew upon a variety of sources for this period. But even if the divergences of their accounts were ten times more marked than they are, it would not affect their conviction of the fact to which they all testify, that Jesus actually rose from the dead, that he actually lived again on earth for forty days and that many people actually saw him and touched him during this second life.

"Nothing survives like truth," said Renan. "Everything which can serve it is hoarded like a small but solid capital and nothing of its small substance is lost. Falsehood, on the other hand, crumbles away. It cannot establish itself, but the small tower of truth is of steel and it rises continually." It may seem to some that the foundations of the small tower of the doctrine of the Resurrection are not very well founded, but it has lasted two thousand years. Millions of human beings have accepted it, and do accept it, in spite of all the arguments against it, and this also counts for something.

Heaven knows that the attempts to get rid of it have been numerous and ingenious enough. Some have bordered on absurdity. At the time when everyone was dominated by Sir James G. Frazer's ideas of comparative religion, there were critics who proved that Christ was a solar myth and his resurrection a poetical allusion to the rising and setting of the planet on the horizon. The fact that he reappeared upon a Sunday, *dies solis,* is a confirmation of this. This argument would carry more weight if the Gospels had been written in Lapland, where night lasts for six months.

Many critics have simply denied the whole story of the events of that Sunday morning, the empty tomb and the disappearance of the body. According to this theory Jesus had a heart attack on the Cross and was therefore presumed dead although he was not. This hypothesis seems quite untenable for not only is the death of Jesus reported in detail in the four Gospels, but there are numerous references to it in the Acts of the Apostles (ii, 25-32; xiii, 26-30) and in St. Paul's Epistles (I Cor. xv, 3-5; Coloss. ii, 11-12; iii,3). St. Paul was a Jew of the Pharisees who knew the value of evidence. If a man is tortured, scourged, and hanged on a cross for three hours, is it abnormal that he should die? In any case the soldier's lance thrust was enough to kill him. Even if we cede the hypothetical syncope—which seems to us flatly impossible in the circumstances—the sixty pounds of aromatic spices pressed down on him would certainly have asphyxiated him. Renan says the last word on this question: "The historian's best guarantee is the suspicious hatred which his enemies bore Jesus." The Jews were much too involved not to make sure that he was well and truly dead.

If we accept the facts of his death and burial, might not his disciples have succeeded in carrying away the corpse? St.

Matthew tells us that the Jews immediately thought of this story, as soon as the watch which they had set by the tomb came back to report the miraculous events. "And when they were assembled with the elders and had taken counsel, they gave large money unto the soldiers, saying, Say ye, His disciples came by night and stole him away while we slept. And if this come to the governor's ears, we will persuade him and secure you. So they took the money and did as they were taught: and this saying is commonly reported among the Jews to this day." (Matt. xxviii, 11-15.)

Was this fabrication accepted? Some believed it. In 1930 a Greek inscription, apparently of the period of Tiberius, was discovered, it is said, at Nazareth, recording an imperial decree that those who violated tombs, "who roll away stones," shall be punished with death.[4] It seems not impertinent to suppose that the story circulated by the Jews did reach Pilate's ears and that he applied to Rome for instructions in case of a recurrence of such events. But, apart from the evidence of the Gospel, it is difficult to believe that the disciples could have rolled away the immense stone so quietly that some one of the guard would not have been awakened at some stage of the proceedings.[5]

Apart from the question as to whether the body was removed, there have always been those who flatly and totally deny the Resurrection. In the very early years of the Christian era, Celsus, the anti-Christian polemicist, suggested that the whole story emanated from the disordered imagination of an ecstatic, Mary Magdalene. It goes without saying that, if this view be accepted, the concrete details given in the Gospels are immaterial, for if all is in the realm of fantasy the disciples might perfectly well have imagined in all good faith that they found the tomb empty, just as they could have imagined that

---

[4] Franz Cumont. Un rescrit impérial sur la violation de sepulture. *Revue Historique*. March-April 1930.

[5] The theory that the body of Jesus was removed was much favored by the eighteenth century rationalists, such as Samuel Reimarus whose researches were published by Lessing. But the most radical of the nineteenth century critics, such as R. F. Strauss, abandoned it.

they saw Jesus in the flesh. There is a large body of criticism designed to place the whole episode of the Resurrection in the category of those inexplicable manifestations in which the subjective and the objective are so confused that no rational analysis is possible, such as the accounts of autosuggestion among the Camisards of the Cévennes in the late seventeenth century and the metaphysical manifestations studied by F. W. H. Myers and Dr. Richet. Such phenomena as the "voices" heard by Joan of Arc and the visions of Savonarola and Thomas à Becket are often cited in this context.

None of these attempted "explanations" holds. It is not possible to treat the events of the Resurrection as due to the appearance of a phantom. Even if we accept, which is no part of our brief, the appearance of discarnate bodies, as in the Old Testament episode in which the phantom of Samuel appears before Saul in the cavern of the witch of Endor, the texts categorically refute the supposition. It is true that Jesus is not shown as living in exactly the same way as before his death, but it is juggling with words to substitute a phantom for a man who is shown to us eating and drinking and whose actual flesh could be touched.

There remains the theory of collective hallucination; the phenomenon exists and there have been cases where crowds of people, in perfectly good faith, have been convinced that they have actually seen something where there was nothing to be seen. The Church is very careful in its handling of such phenomena and all reports of visions are subjected to the most stringent examination. But the fundamental characteristic of collective hallucination is that all who are connected with it share it; the wave of conviction sweeps everyone along. When we examine the accounts of the Resurrection, however, we find many who hesitated to believe in it. The Apostles were neither visionaries nor ecstatics and their combined faith was not such that it could resurrect Jesus for all of them. We have only to read the story of Thomas to realize this.

It is going beyond the evidence to postulate mystical visions like those of a Catherine Emmerich, or even a St. Catherine of

Siena. On this point Loisy, who certainly does not favor supernatural explanations, writes: "The Apostles and St. Paul are not recording subjective impressions; they speak of the presence of an objective, perceptible and tangible Christ, not an ideal being, still less an imaginary presence." To sum up: either we accept the texts which report the Resurrection or we reject them. In the latter case it is a matter for exegesis, which we have already gone into. But if the texts are accepted as valid then it is impossible to interpret the word *Resurrection* except in its plain etymological sense.[6]

"He rose from the dead": the words of the Creed must be taken literally, not only by the Christian but by the historian. However astounding it may seem to us, Jesus came out of the tomb and lived a second life for forty days. The fact is as well attested as any other in the life of Christ. It can even be dated: Jesus rose from the grave and began his second existence *tertia die,* says the Apostles Creed, the third day after his death.

The Gospel is so precise in this matter that there would seem to be no argument. The Resurrection, say St. Matthew, St. Mark, St. Luke and St. John, occurred on "the first day of the week—the Greeks to this day call Monday, the second day; Tuesday, the third; Wednesday, the fourth; Thursday, the fifth; Friday, the *Parasceve* or day of preparation for the

---

[6] Guignebert's theory combines several attempted explanations, as follows. The disciples, after the death of Jesus, felt and believed that his *spirit* could not die. In the exalted state which this conviction induced, some of them had visions and thus, little by little, the spiritual conviction became materialized into a concrete survival. Diligent examination of the teachings of Christ and of various Old Testament prophesies produced the account of the Resurrection.

The weakness of this hypothesis is this: Guignebert can not propose that this faith created by a myth was founded on nothing. He presupposes visions, but of what kind: metaphysical, mystical or hallucinatory? And if the Apostles transmuted their vision into the real world, providing concrete details, why show the witnesses of the Resurrection, St. Peter among others, as incredulous or doubtful? We notice, in the Gospel story of these forty days, that the life of Jesus is not recounted in exactly the same way as before: his body is in some way spiritualized, removed from some of the trammels of our human condition. If the myth had been concocted by the Apostles, would they have allowed this curious discrimination? It seems more likely that they would have emphasized the material presence of Jesus in the flesh.

Sabbath; Saturday, the Sabbath and Sunday, the Dominical. The Sabbath completes the week, since it is that seventh day upon which Jehovah rested and Sunday is the first. The Resurrection took place on the third day after Jesus's death as he himself had prophesied according St. Matthew and St. Luke. St. Mark says "three days after," following perhaps the Jewish usage of including in a count of days that on which the particular event began or ended. It has been thought that this insistence upon the precise figure is connected with the rabbinical belief that the soul after death hovers around the body in distress for three days before finally abandoning it. It will be remembered that Martha said to Jesus that there could be no hope for Lazarus, her brother, because he had been dead for four days.

Jonah spent three days in the whale's belly; the Son of Man spent the same period entombed. This was the "sign of Jonas" to which Jesus himself had referred. The whale gave up its prey; death yielded its victim, and the news must have spread quickly, that Easter Sunday morning, among the harassed and miserable disciples. It was not long before the Christian Church, wishing to distinguish its own feast from that of the Jews, set aside the day of the Resurrection. From the time of the Acts and the Epistles, *Dies dominica,* the day of the Lord, is the day set apart, and ever since our own Sunday has been kept in memory.

The Second Life of Jesus

It is very difficult to work out any sort of chronology for the events which mark the life of Jesus after the Resurrection. Not only is there no agreement among the four Gospels; they seem, if taken literally, almost to contradict each other. According to St. Matthew (xxviii, 10) and St. Mark (xvi, 7) Christ told the holy women to tell his disciples to make their way to Galilee, where he would show himself to them. St. John, however, states that his first appearance to the disciples was in Jerusalem. There can be no entirely satisfactory reconciliation of the accounts but it is generally accepted that the first appearances of the Risen Christ were in the Holy City but that, since a number of the disciples would already have gone back after the Passover to their native province, there were later manifestations in Galilee.

There is, however, one important fact which should be stressed and it may perhaps have some bearing on the question just discussed. The Gospel makes it quite clear that the circumstances of the life of Jesus after his resurrection were not the same as those of his previous life among men. This is not only evident upon a reading of the Apostolic text; it is also part of the traditional teaching of the Church. His bodily presence was not subject to the ordinary conditions as before; one might say that his appearance was determined by an act of will. When Mary Magdalene in her emotion ran toward him, he said, "Touch me not," but he told doubting Thomas to put his hand in the wound in his side. The Gospel always says that he "showed himself" to his disciples, and the term, which is not used previously, would seem to indicate that they would not have seen him unless he wished.

Several of the details given about his "appearances" intensify the strangeness of this second life. He appears in a room in the midst of them, although all the doors have been closed, and they suppose that they have seen a phantom (Luke xxiv, 36; John xx, 19). After he appeared to the disciples at Emmaus, "he vanished out of their sight." (Luke xxiv, 31.) He assumed different aspects. Mary Magdalene supposed him to be a gardener; the disciples on the road to Emmaus did not recognize him (Luke xxiv, 16). He appeared to them "in another form." (Mark xvi, 12.) Peter himself and the chief Apostles spoke with him on the shore of the Lake of Galilee (John xxi, 4) and they did not know him.

These transformations may have inspired that strange agraph, "I appeared not as I was." But the Evangelists take great pains to make it clear that the Risen Jesus was not a spirit. When his appearance "terrified and affrighted his disciples, he said, Why are ye troubled? And why do thoughts rise in your hearts? Behold my hands and my feet, that it is I myself: handle me and see, for a spirit hath not flesh and bones, as ye see me have." And, seeing that they still hesitated, he asked, "Have ye here any meat? And they gave him a piece of broiled fish and of an honeycomb. And he took it and did eat before them." (Luke xxiv, 36-43.) "I am quite sure," wrote St. Ignatius of Antioch about the end of the first century A.D., "that even after the Resurrection Jesus Christ had a body. He ate and drank with his disciples *although spiritually he was united with the Father*."

These last words explain the nature of the mystery. Various critics have found two distinct conceptions of the Resurrection in the Gospel; one, the more spiritual, stating that the risen Jesus was not subject to the ordinary conditions of human life, the other insisting that he was completely revivified. These two conceptions, say these critics, are irreconcilable. In the natural order of things, perhaps they are, but we are dealing admittedly and explicitly with the supernatural order. It can be conceded that Jesus in his life after death displays qualities which are not human in the limiting sense of the word, as if, while preserving all the characteristics of the flesh, he is able to escape from its bondage as we know it; as if the God in him had, through his death, weakened still further the casing of flesh.

In the famous passage in his Epistle to the Corinthians (I xv, 35-44) St. Paul, preaching on the Resurrection, holds out for every man the hope of this same transformation. "But some man will say, How are the dead raised up? And with what body do they come? Thou fool, that which thou sowest is not quickened, except it die. And that which thou sowest, thou sowest not that body that shall be, but bare grain, it may chance of wheat or of some other grain. But God giveth it a body as it hath pleased him, and to every seed his own body. All flesh is not the same flesh, but there is one kind of flesh of men, another flesh of beasts, another of fishes and another of birds. There are also celestial bodies and bodies terrestrial, but the glory of the celestial is one, and the glory of the terrestrial is another. . . . So also is the resurrection of the dead. It is sown in corruption; it is raised in incorruption. It is sown in dishonor; it is raised in glory: it is sown in weakness; it is raised in power. It is sown a natural body; it is raised a spiritual body." In the sense which St. Paul expounds in this passage, the body of Jesus risen was a *real* human body, but *glorified*.

It may be that the explanation of what seems to us contradictory in the Gospel narratives lies in this very definition. The limitations of time and space are those of our common human existence; we are always conscious of being subject to them. But it may be that "the body raised in glory" is not in bondage to them; it may be here or there at the same time, because for it there is no time or space, today and tomorrow may be co-existent in Eternity. It is noteworthy that in this same chapter of I Corinthians, St. Paul, referring to the various appearances of Christ after the Resurrection, brackets with them his own vision on the road to Damascus, "he was seen of me also," though it took place four years later, long after Christ had ascended into heaven.

Jesus himself, speaking of the Resurrection among the disciples to whom he had just appeared, said, "These are the words which I spake unto you, while I was yet with you, that all things must be fulfilled that were written in the law of Moses, and in the prophets and in the psalms, concerning me." (Luke xxiv, 44.) They were gathered together at nightfall, in the very room where only a few days before, at the Last Supper, Jesus had offered them his body and his blood. They were talking of the astonishing things which had happened, of the empty tomb and of what the women had told them, and because they still feared the wrath of the Jews, all the doors were barred. Two of the disciples, perhaps two of the seventy whom Jesus had appointed to go out and teach, had just come in, excited and out of breath, to say that as they were walking on the road to Emmaus, some little distance off, they had been rejoined by the Master who had talked with them. The others discussed the story, eagerly asking questions. The mystery of the universe hovered over the gathering of men, whose spirits were fired by a hope which their commonsense could still hardly accept. Then Jesus appeared in their midst, and said, "Peace be unto you."

There must have been many such appearances, many more than the Gospels recount, because we have seen that St. Peter is said to have received one, and St. Paul mentions another where there were no less than five hundred witnesses. These men and women, who had for more than two years lived in the orbit of the mystery without entirely understanding it, were now thrown into confusion, and the daily life of artisans and fishermen which they had meant to resume was entirely dislocated.

There were some who still held out. "But Thomas, one of the twelve called Didymus, was not with them when Jesus came. The other disciples therefore said unto him, We have seen the Lord. But he said unto them, Except I shall see in his hands the print of the nails, and put my finger into the print of the nails and thrust my hand into his side, I will not believe. And after eight days, again his disciples were within, and Thomas with them. Then came Jesus, the doors being shut, and said, Peace be unto you. Then saith he to Thomas, Reach hither thy finger and behold my hands; and reach hither thy hand and thrust it into my side, and be not faithless but believing. And Thomas answered and said unto him, My Lord and my God. Jesus saith unto him, Thomas, because thou hast seen me, thou hast believed: blessed are they that have not seen and yet have believed." (John xx, 24-29.) This scene displays the fourth Evangelist at his best, clear, detailed and straightforward, presenting Jesus as we have known him throughout the Gospel record, merciful to doubters and sinners. It has always been popular in Christian art—there is a superb mosaic at St. Mark's—perhaps because it is so reassuring to human weakness, because it brings hope and strength to troubled hearts.

The synoptics only allude to one of Jesus's appearances in Galilee (Matt. xxviii, 16) but St. John devotes an entire chapter to them, obviously as a supplement to his narrative. There is also a passage concerning them in the Apocryphal Gospel of Peter, which unfortunately stops in the middle. "We, the twelve disciples of the Lord sat in sorrow and mourning and each of us sadly returned to his own house. I, Simon Peter and my brother Andrew, having fetched our nets set off for the sea of Galilee and with us was Levi, son of Alpheus, whom the Lord . . ." According to St. John, there were present Peter, Thomas, Nathaniel from Cana, the sons of Zebedee and two others. They had been fishing all night without catching anything. When morning came, they heard an unknown voice calling out from the shore. "Children, have ye any meat?" They answered, "No." "Cast the net to the right side of the ship and ye shall find," said the voice. They did so and immediately the net was filled, so much that they could hardly bring it aboard.

John was the first to understand and said to Peter, "It is the Lord." And, seizing a garment for decency, since when at work he was naked, the leader of the Apostles flung himself into the sea and swam toward Jesus. As once before, on this same lake, the miraculous catch of fish had opened the hearts of these simple men, so now a repetition of the miracle brought them enlightenment. Symbolically, the first miracle marks the first stage of the establishment of the Church; the second foreshadows the great hauls which these fishers of men were soon to make. A delightful picture by Conrad Witz at Geneva transposes the scene to the Lake of Geneva with Mt. Blanc in place of Mt. Hermon in the background. It is an acceptable and touching transposition for it was not only in the Lake of Galilee that these nets were to be cast, and men of all races would be drawn into them.

Jesus's last task upon earth, in those final hours when the second life which had been accorded to him was drawing to a close, was to strengthen the faith of his disciples, to instruct them definitely in their mission, to prepare his Church. "Go ye therefore and teach all nations, baptizing them in the name of the Father and of the Son and of the Holy Ghost." "He that believeth and is baptized shall be saved; but he that believeth not shall be damned. And these signs shall follow them that believe: In my name shall they cast out devils; they shall speak with new tongues, they shall take up serpents; and if they drink any deadly thing it shall not hurt them; they shall lay hands on the sick and they shall recover." "And, Lo, I am with you always, even unto the end of the world." (Matt. xxviii, 18-20; Mark xvi, 15-18.)

The rights and duties of the Church from henceforward are irrefutably established. After the miraculous haul of fish, and after they had cooked and eaten some of the hundred and fifty-three large fish which had come into their nets, Jesus said to Peter: "Simon, son of Jonas, lovest thou me more than these? He saith unto him, Yea, Lord, thou knowest that I love thee. He said unto him, Feed my lambs. He saith unto him again the second time, Simon, son of Jonas, lovest thou me? He saith unto him, Yea, Lord, thou knowest that I love thee. He saith unto him, Feed my sheep. He saith unto him a third time, Simon, son of Jonas, lovest thou me? Peter was grieved because he asked him a third time and said, Lord, thou knowest all things, thou knowest that I love thee. Jesus saith unto him, Feed my sheep." (John xxii, 15-17.) The Good Shepherd, about to go from their sight, confided his flock to the strongest and the most capable. And Peter accepted his mission, although it carried with it a prophesy of the martyr's death. "When thou wast young, thou girdest thyself, and walkest whither thou wouldst: but when thou shalt be old, thou shalt stretch forth thy hands and another shall gird thee and carry thee whither thou wouldest not." (John xxi, 18.) The shadow of the cross on which Simon called Peter was to perish is foreshadowed here, but Peter did not flinch for in his heart he had already accepted it. "Follow me," said Jesus then and along the shores of the Lake of Galilee, gray and black or touched with a delicate rose, dark sands sprinkled with small bright shells, they followed him, for what last council, for what last teaching, we do not know.

For forty days these men lived in the ambience of this supernatural reality, and we know that their faith was forever assured by it. Then one day, not far from the Holy City, by that Mount of Olives where they had once escorted him in triumph, as Jesus talked to them and lifted his hand in blessing, he seemed to be lifted up into the air in the midst of them, but every instant moving further and further from them. He disappeared from their sight, but his peace he left with them.

The Christian Faith

"If Christ be not risen, then is our preaching vain, and your faith is also vain." Thirty years later, St. Paul was to write this in his Epistle to the Corinthians (I, Cor. xv, 14). This prodigious event, this second life of a man after he had died, which agnostics regard as legendary, which Renan tacitly discounted by exclusion, for his story ends with the burial of Jesus, has been made the cornerstone of the Church. In the center of Christian theology, as of Christian morality, is the image of the Risen Savior, the conqueror of death. All Christian hope derives from it, for: "If in this life only we have hope in Christ, we are of all men most miserable." (I, Cor. xv, 19.)

The conception of a god who dies as all men must die but who rises from the dead to teach men that death may be overcome, is one of those ideas which have for thousands of years most persistently haunted human consciousness. The idea, however expressed, is essentially a noble one. We all feel that the thing in us which is unique and irreplaceable has the right to endure beyond the three score and ten years allotted to us. All the great myths proceed from the secret agony of the human condition and witness to the same disquiet so that inevitably, across whatever gulfs of time or place, they resemble each other and are touched with the same sense of awe.

But it does not follow from this that the story of Christ's resurrection belongs to this nexus of myth. "The blow struck at Golgotha," writes Frazer in *The Golden Bough*, that bible of the "comparativists," those concerned with parallels in religions, "sent a million quivering chords of expectation vibrating in unison wherever there existed a memory of the old, old story of the god who dies and rises again." In its wider sense, this statement may be accepted for, like many other elements of the Christian teaching, the dogma of the Resurrection came to fill an expectation which had long stirred the hearts of men, an expectation which the Egyptian and Syrian legends had only been able to express in a base or clumsy form. But the attempt to equate the Resurrection of Jesus with the legends of Osiris, Attis and Adonis is demonstrably erroneous.

There is no trace of the influence of any such pagan myths in Jewish thought at the time of Christ, nothing to suggest the idea of a resurrected deity. Everything that we know about the little community in Israel, during the last centuries of its existence, testifies to its harsh and rigorous exclusion of foreign ideas. It will be remembered that neither the Lagid nor the Seleucid dynasties succeeded in implanting their beliefs in Palestine. The very fact that the idea of a resurrected god was imported from Egypt and Syria would be enough to insure its exclusion from Jerusalem. Can it be said that we are confronted with one of those mysterious waves of human sentience which could spontaneously generate the same idea on the banks of the Nile, in the plateau of Anatolia and in the Holy City of Jerusalem? But the moment the comparison is made the striking difference between the myths and the Gospel story is apparent.

Of the various "dying and rising gods" the oldest and best known is Osiris, whom the Egyptians had, for at least fifteen hundred years before the Christian era, regarded as the divinely appointed guide who could lead the spirits of the departed through the dark valley of the tomb. From the shores of the Euphrates came Tammuz whose legend traveled to the Mediterranean lands where, in the hands of the Greeks, it became the pathetic story of the young hunter Adonis, the beloved of Aphrodite, who was killed by a wild boar and was brought back to life by the goddess. Elsewhere, there was Attis, the spouse of Cybele, whose blood flowed in the Phrygian streams and whose initiates venerated him with orgiastic rites including self mutilations. There were also the Orphic rites of Dionysus Zagreus, "the little horned one," torn to pieces by the savage women in the Thracian forests, whose heart dissolved in wine was drunk by Zeus and germinated in the body of the God to be born again.

We must always remember, however, when we consider these "mystery religions" that we know very little indeed about them. Nothing has come down to us but externals, fragments of hymns or rites, and it is very risky to attempt to reconstruct from these the essentials of the faith within. We must be careful not to seek to explain them in terms of beliefs and modes of thought which are exclusively Christian. When, for instance, M. Moret writes that "the representation of the Passion and death of Osiris was certainly accompanied by the resurrection of the god," we sense a yielding, perhaps unconsciously, to the idea of equating the pagan and the Christian conceptions: the words *Passion* and *Resurrection* have an exclusively Christian connotation and are never found in Egyptian texts. The word *Passion* indeed involves the Christian idea of self renunciation, of suffering voluntarily accepted for redemption, an idea quite foreign to Egyptian modes of thought. As for the adverb, *certainly*, this is in itself an admission, for in the writings of ancient Egypt the resurrection of Osiris is never explicitly affirmed.

When we consider the differences between Jesus risen from the dead and the other "risen Gods" the resemblances, in fact, pall into insignificance. On the one hand we have the indecencies in which the myths abound and from which the Gospel is completely free—the insistence with which Isis, having reassembled her husband Osiris from the pieces into which his body had been cut, mourns the absence of the one part missing and the obligation upon the priests of Attis to sacrifice their virility. These cannot be dismissed as part of that natural grossness of primitive people, which perhaps indicates innocence rather than evil. For these sexual allusions have a definite meaning; they reveal that at the basis of this idea of "resurrection" is nothing more than the desire of the life force, the demanding instinct of the human heart, to extend its ephemeral existence by procreation. An eminent authority, M. Franz Cumont, has seen in all these myths a uniform fundamental, "the cult of the power of generation and of the desire which provokes it." He calls attention to the fact that in all these stories "the principal role is the woman's," for she is the visible agent of the transmission of life and the symbolic agent of the resurrection.

Another common factor of nearly all these "risen god" myths is an even more obvious analogy with natural processes, the connection with the springtime rebirth of vegetation in which, throughout the ages, man has seen a pledge of the endless renewal of life. This theme played a very important part in the religions of Anatolia, Phrygia and Syria: the symbol of Attis was a pine sapling; Adonis was called "the seed within the Great Mother" Cybele, the earth goddess. In Egypt, one of the ceremonies of the cult of Osiris was the planting of a human figure modeled in clay with seeds of wheat and the shoots which thrust forth were a symbol of life reborn. Whatever explanation of these myths may be favored, they are clearly diametrically opposed to the Christian idea.

Even if we take the Osiris legend only in its purest and highest form, the data that we have on it shows its difference from that of the Gospel. Osiris was a benevolent god, the lord of justice, the protector of the family and the city, a moral pattern: but he was not and had never been a man like us. His animist origin is betrayed by his identification with the Nile, the life-giving stream which holds Egypt in its grasp. The drama of his death, his murder by his evil brother Set-Typhon (the arid, burning desert), the dismemberent of his body and the dispersion of the pieces, may be given a symbolic meaning as typifying the struggle between the destructive forces of barbarism and the constructive power of civilization, but there is no suggestion of a conscious willing sacrifice made by a being in order to redeem the sins of men and deliver them from their wretchedness. When Isis, with the help of Horus, succeeds in reassembling the pieces of the body of Osiris she makes it whole by magic but what she makes is a mummy, the first of the Egyptian mummies. He is not brought back to life, but is reconstituted so that life may be possible for him on the other side of death.

When we consider the moral and spiritual significance, an even greater difference is apparent. In the cult of Osiris, as in all the mystery religions, emphasis was laid upon a rigorous imitation of the material circumstances attaching to the god. The Egyptian, in his desire to ensure his survival in the other world, had to embalm his corpse exactly as Isis had done. This essentially materialistic conception, which belongs entirely to the realm of magic, developed through the centuries into the idea of a judgment of souls after death with Osiris as the judge, as he had once been among the living. But the essential was compliance with a ritual, not any moral requirement. An Egyptian funerary inscription says: "Even as Osiris lives, he also will live; even as Osiris was not annihilated, he also will not be annihilated." And M. Cumont notes: "Osiris, the god who died and was reassembled, becomes the prototype to each of those human beings who observe these funereal rites." There is the difference.

To the Christian, the resurrection of Jesus is not an automatic guarantee of eternal life provided that certain rites are performed; to share in the eternal glory of the elect, one must live in Christ and make oneself spiritually like Jesus. This is the factor which, above all others, lifts the Christian idea of Resurrection on to an entirely different plane from any myths or rites associated with "risen gods" in the ancient world.

The Doctrine of Resurrection

The importance of the Resurrection in Christian doctrine thus goes far beyond its historical importance as an episode in the life of Christ. Christianity would indeed be simply a moral system, as certain "liberal" Protestants affirm, if the Resurrection did not transform it into a metaphysic, for to him who believes in the Resurrection a new light is thrown upon the mystery of our being and our human condition. It is not merely a theological conception issuing from the subtle intelligence of St. Paul. Certainly we owe to the Apostle of the Gentiles the most profoundly reasoned explanation of the doctrine in the First Epistle to the Corinthians, but we have only to read St. Peter's discourse in the Acts of the Apostles to realize that all of the first generation of Christians set exactly the same store by it, for when Matthias was chosen to replace Judas he was to become "a witness to the Resurrection." All the Christian Fathers, St. Clement of Rome, St. Ignatius of Antioch, St. Polycarp of Smyrna, St. Justin, St. Augustine and Origen, preached the fundamental importance of the belief in the Resurrection of Jesus.

The Resurrection is the crown of Christian hope. Christ risen from the dead is "the first fruits of them that slept." (I Cor. xv, 20.) Just as he rose from the tomb, so every man in his turn may also hope to rise. "Behold, I show you a mystery," cries St. Paul. "We shall not all sleep, but we shall all be changed. In a moment, in the twinkling of an eye, at the last trump; for the trumpet shall sound, and the dead shall be raised incorruptible and we shall all be changed." (I Cor. xv, 51-52.)

Like so many of the articles of the Christian faith, this exalted hope had germinated, grown and ripened in the inmost heart of Israel. Isaiah had said: "He will swallow up death in victory." (xxv, 8.) "Thy dead men shall live, together with my dead body, shall they rise." (xxvi, 19.) "And many of them that sleep in the dust of the earth shall awake, some to everlasting life, and some to shame and everlasting contempt." (Dan. xii, 2.) And what Christian heart has not risen in response to Job's unforgettable challenge: "Though worms destroy this body, yet in my flesh shall I see God." (xix, 26.)

The resurrection of Christ crowned this hope with certainty. In his lifetime, when Jesus foretold his own end in the allegory of the Temple destroyed and rebuilt in three days, his disciples had not understood; nor had his reference to Jonah in the whale's belly enlightened them. But when the Resurrection tore the scales from their eyes, they understood, they realized, and they taught that this event which involved them personally involved also all mankind. What, in the Old Testament, had been no more than a vague hope or presentiment was to be the fundamental doctrine of the New, for in this matter, as in so many others, the final Revelation had been given.

The hope of the Resurrection does not only offer a supreme hope to man condemned to die; it transforms his whole conception of life itself. The ancient philosophy regarded the body as an affliction, a prison, a fetter, even a tomb. "The soul cannot assert itself until detached from the body," says Plato. "Liberated and purified from the madness of the flesh we may live." But Christianity associates the flesh with the triumph of the spirit, affirming the whole man, a soul and body linked to each other by a mutual responsibility. The body must not be despised for it is called upon to participate in the eternal glory of the whole being. "If the dead rise not, let us eat and drink," but since they will rise, let us respect, in ourselves and in others, this body promised to glorification. As the "first fruits" of the resurrection of man, the Resurrection of Jesus is the affirmation of human dignity. So far from being a legend or a literary symbol, the doctrine of the Resurrection is the evidence of a supreme realism and upon it rests the whole body of Christian morality and sociology.

"O death, where is thy sting. O grave, where is thy victory." The great voice of St. Paul, echoing down the centuries of Christian tradition, has brought us consolation. But he adds: "The sting of death is sin," and in these words lies the whole destiny of man. Jesus, in conquering death, conquered also the powers of evil. It was through sin that death came into the world, but Jesus came to show us that however wretched and debased may be our condition, it can by the promise of God's help be overcome. The Kingdom of the Father, where he will reign in glory, is that Kingdom which is within us, and which, although at first a small seed, will grow, in the souls of the saints, into a tree with myriad branches. If we would share in the glory of Christ risen, we must share in the example of his life. And since death and sin are one, whatever in us yields to sin reaches out to death, but every striving toward good is a step toward eternal life. The Resurrection is not merely an historic fact taking place at a certain point in time. It is the explanation of the drama of human history; we can keep alive in us only that which is worthy of life, and worthy of life eternal.

Centuries before the time of Jesus, in the land where he came to live, to suffer and to conquer death, a small, unimportant people had discovered, by slow stages, that God is not only almighty, the eternal will and the mystery of the universe, he is also and above all things, perfect justice and truth, the absolute good. Slowly this people acquired a deeper consciousness, adjusting their needs in order to relate the tenets of their moral system to the commands of the Almighty and, alone among all the peoples of the world, they proclaimed the truth that there was no morality apart from God. They had to aspire still further to reach a synthesis which no religion had yet dared to formulate, the union of the moral and metaphysical systems so that man might realize his age-old dream of making himself "like the gods."

When Jesus disappeared from the midst of his disciples, he left with them the joy of knowing what the deeper consciousness of Israel had foreseen, that being and well-being are one, not only in God but for every man. The one way by which man can participate in the divine, in eternity, is to practice in this mortal life the lesson which Jesus had taught and lived, the difficult law of love.

The Presence of Christ

Jesus was to rejoin his Father and the eyes of men would see him no more. But, although he had gone, his message remained, the message which he had commanded the disciples to preach. In a very few generations, like the small seed in the Gospel parable, the good grain of his teaching had been sown throughout the countries of the Empire, and it was to yield a miraculous harvest. The teaching of the vanquished was to conquer the world in less than three hundred years.

He left not only his teaching behind him when he ascended into heaven. Most men who leave the world leave no more than a memory, perhaps a few words written down or repeated. Even when we try to evoke the greatest of them from their works or their ideas, they seem somehow fossilized, lacking the breath of life. But what remains of the living God is not only his teaching but his presence. Christianity as a faith is something more than an adherence to a philosophical system; to participate in Jesus requires the identification of our whole being with its model; what Christians call Grace is nothing less than the survival of the God made into man in each of us.

There is one incident in the story of the "second life" of Jesus which, although very simply told, is charged with a mysterious spiritual luminosity. It is told by St. Luke (xxiv, 13-35) and confirmed by St. Mark (xvi, 12)—the appearance of Jesus to the two disciples walking on the road to Emmaus. They were not men of any particular note, just two men like any of us. They were, except for the twelve Apostles and the holy women, the first members of the Church recorded by the New Testament, and they seem to have been favored with a unique revelation precisely because they were like everyone else, foreshadowing the humblest members of the Christian flock. They had loved Jesus devotedly without altogether understanding his message, which they had interpreted in a literal, temporal sense. One of them was called Cleopas, and that is all we know of them.

They went on their way sadly, having witnessed the drama of the Passion. Perhaps Emmaus, the village to which they were going, was their home, and there was nothing left for them but to take up their dull daily life again now that the high adventure which had drawn them out of themselves was over. There has been a good deal of argument over the site of the Emmaus of the Gospel; some have located it at Quobeibeh, which is distant from Jerusalem about the "sixty furlongs" mentioned by St. Luke. Others accept the oldest tradition which identifies Emmaus with the modern Amouas, formerly Nicopolis, which is about a hundred and sixty furlongs (about twenty miles) away from the capital, although it would seem impossible to make a return journey of this length on foot in one day. The traditional Emmaus is a bright little town on the edge of a hill, from which there is a view extending to the fields around Jaffa; it is like a good many others with its square white houses, its cypresses and sycamores and the torrent which in the rainy season runs along the bottom of a dark ravine. Just beside it is the Trappist monastery of El-Athroun, founded by French monks, where the monks, whose silent presence is a lesson in Christian contemplation, have by their labors transformed the arid, infertile soil into luxurant vineyards, olive and orange groves. The speading fields of silver barley on the red earth of the hillside seem like a symbol of divine benediction, a living proof that grace is present in this place.[7]

"While they communed together and reasoned, Jesus himself

---

[7] Most recent works are in favor of the traditional identification. Emmaus must have been close to Lydda in the Sephala plain "at the place where the mountains begin to rise," says St. Jerome. If we take the Gospel text literally it was just a village, and in spite of its brief notoriety as the site of a battle in which Judas Maccabeus annihilated a Greek army, a humble place with nothing to boast of save its "pure waters," which are remembered in Talmudic tradition. In 4 A.D. its inhabitants attacked a Roman convoy and were punished by the destruction of their village which had just been rebuilt by the time of the Gospel incident. In the matter of its distance from Jerusalem it is very hard to arrive at an opinion for some of the early manuscript texts give 60 furlongs and others 160. Two of these MSS. have a marginal scholium which says, "This should be read as 160 according to the correct texts and Origen's confirmation of their truth." It is clear from this that the difficulty of making a journey of more than 20 miles from Jerusalem and back in one day was realized very early in Gospel criticism, but early geographical texts such as Ptolemy's Geography and the *Voyage du pelerin de Bordeaux* confirm the distance as 160 furlongs. It is perhaps possible that the disciples were fired with enthusiasm for the first 20 miles but that the remainder of the journey was made on some sort of mount. A curious additional fact is that Emmaus owed its fame chiefly to Origen who obtained from that half-crazed perverted mystic, the Emperor Heliogabalus, funds to rebuild a new town on the site, which was called Nicopolis. All these questions are dealt with exhaustively in the monumental work of FF. Vincent and Abel, *Emmaus*, Paris 1932, and the smaller work of the same title published by Fr. Duvignau in 1937.

drew near and went with them. But their eyes were holden that they should not know him. And he said unto them: What manner of communications are these that ye have one to another, as ye walk and are sad? And the one of them whose name was Cleopas, answering said unto him: Art thou only a stranger in Jerusalem, and hast not known the things which are come to pass there in these days? And he said unto them, What things? And they said unto him, Concerning Jesus of Nazareth, which was a prophet mighty in word and deed before God and all the people: And how the chief priests and our rulers delivered him to be condemned to death, and have crucified him. But we trusted that it had been he which should have redeemed Israel: and beside all this, today is the third day since these things were done. Yea, and certain women also of our company made us astonished, which were early at the sepulcher: And when they found not his body, they came saying, that they had also seen a vision of angels, which said that he was alive. And certain of them which were with us went to the sepulcher and found it even so as the women had said, but him they saw not.

"Then Jesus said to them: O fools, and slow of heart to believe all that the prophets have spoken. Ought not Christ to have suffered these things, and to enter into his glory? And beginning at Moses and all the prophets, he expounded unto them in all the scriptures the things concerning himself.

"And they drew nigh unto the village, whither they went; and he made as though he would have gone further. But they constrained him saying, Abide with us; for it is toward evening, and the day is far spent. And he went in to tarry with them.

"And it came to pass as he sat at meat with them, he took bread and blessed it and brake and gave to them. And their eyes were opened and they knew him; and he vanished out of their sight. And they said one to another: Did not our heart burn within us, while he talked with us by the way, and while he opened to us the scriptures?

"And they rose up the same hour, and returned to Jerusalem

and found the eleven gathered together, and them that were with them.

"Saying, the Lord is risen indeed, and hath appeared to Simon. And they told what things were done in the way and how he was known of them in breaking of bread." [8]

It is here, with this moving scene, that we must end our attempt to paint a picture of the life of Jesus. Most of us evoke the scene as Rembrandt painted it, in that famous picture of the dark room where all the light seems to come from the figure of Christ. On the table is a linen cloth, bare except for the bread which assumes a supernatural significance. Jesus is praying and the two men are caught at the moment when their eyes are opened, one of them half drawing back, the other bowing in adoration. We know that in a moment the mysterious guest will disappear, but we know too that his presence, although invisible, will still be manifest, that it will remain in that "burning of the heart" which his disciples felt as they listened to his teaching.

For the "burning heart" is the sign of his presence. It has persuaded the martyrs to give up their life in the flesh for another life, more complete. It has fed the heroic fervor of the great mystics in their interior struggles. The most obscure believer feels it within him when he has received the Bread and his soul expands in strength, generosity and ardor. Christians have, throughout the centuries, found many names to express this Presence which Jean de Fecamp called "the invisible hurricane of love" and St. Theresa of Lisieux "the fathomless deep I cannot sound," but they all agree that it exists. "It is not I who live but Christ in me," cried St. Paul, and for two thousand years an incalculable number of men and women have

[8] There has been much discussion as to whether this "breaking of bread" was as at an ordinary meal or whether it was a repetition of the ceremony of the Last Supper. This has been debated inconclusively for nineteen hundred years. St. Augustine held that "we should not hesitate to recognize in the breaking of bread by which the two disciples recognized the Savior, the Sacrament by which we ourselves are empowered to know him." This interpretation held the field until the sixteenth century but later critics have abandoned it or, at most, treat it with reserve.

testified to this Presence as the most certain of realities. Jesus, ascended into heaven, is still the creature of flesh and blood whom many loved in his time and whom so many others, so long after, have also loved. We cannot deny the testimony of a St. Theresa of Avila, a St. Gertrude, a St. Bernard or a St. Francis. When St. Bernard says, "He is closer to me than I myself"; when the poet Claudel says, "the something in me that is more myself than I am," it is this unchallengeable Presence which they invoke.

To those who accuse us of abandoning facts for metaphysics we would say that the affirmation, reiterated a thousand times by perfectly well balanced men and women, "of a superior good sense," as Bergson put it, that Jesus is to them a living being, is itself a fact. The German historian Wellhausen has said: "The career of Jesus leaves the impression not merely of being incompleted but of having been interrupted when it had hardly begun." On the human plane, this may have been so, but this "career" was of those which neither opposition nor death could interrupt: it was to go on for ever in the heart of those who know him.

As he was about to disappear from the sight of his disciples, he said to them those words with which St. Matthew concludes his gospel: "Lo, I am with you alway, even unto the end of the world." In the course of some thirty months, during his mission on earth, he had patiently prepared these men who were to survive him, he had chosen them, taught them, educated them, he had given them the best of himself. It remained for them to bear witness to the Light which they had received; and they did not fail.

And so the history of the living God leads on to that of the "mystical body" animated by his Presence, that tremendous reality engraven upon the heart of the centuries, the Church of Jesus Christ.

APPENDIX ONE

JESUS AND THE CRITICS

JESUS CHRIST, who was "a sign that shall be spoken against" in his lifetime, has so remained for two thousand years. His personality and his teaching have been the subjects of continual inquiry. He is unquestionably the most discussed person in the entire history of the white races. Not a year, hardly even a month, passes without some new book about him appearing. Whether they seek to understand him or to refute him, historians, critics, exegesists are drawn to him by a sort of fascination. There must be something compelling about a figure who can attract, either in love or resentment, so many human intelligences; this fact in itself is a witness which cannot be denied.

The non-Christian attempt to cancel the story of Jesus by proposing "rational explanations" was not born yesterday. The anti-Christian polemicist Celsus, a cultivated Roman of the time of Marcus Aurelius, about 180 A.D., had already mastered the art of combining very subtly exact quotations from the Gospel with calumnious fables of Jewish origin, with the evident design of making Jesus appear absurd. What, a god who wept and wailed and even allowed himself to be crucified; at best he was only an ambitious adventurer, a fanatic whose designs were exposed and whose disciples abandoned him. As for that story of the Resurrection, an absurd fiction that nobody would make head or tail of, it was clearly the fable of some disordered brain.

A century later, the neo-Platonic philosopher Porphyrus, a disciple of Plotinus, hurled his monumental fifteen volumes at the Christians. From what we have left of them—for the Byzantine Emperors, Valentinian III and Thedosius II, had them destroyed in the fifth century—it would seem that his attack was on much the same lines; could a God suffer or a dead man rise again? Certainly not; therefore Jesus could only have been a poor-spirited creature afraid to take up the devil's challenge and leap from the Temple, a man who failed to face death with the requisite philosophic calm. This is a striking demonstration that for two thousand years the mystery of the Incarnation has been the chief stumbling block to the intellectual acceptance of Jesus. Between the classic philosophers who dwelt on the humble human characteristics of Jesus in order to deprive him of divine status and the modern "mythologizers" who deny him any human existence at all and regard him as the legendary embodiment of a spiritual theme, the difference is more apparent than real, for it is always the same "contradiction" which they cannot face, the same mystery which they deny.

The whole body of critical writing about Jesus thus divides automatically into two groups, that which accepts the Incarnation as a fact in history and that which does not. We do not propose to discuss the first group here, not that we have not pursued with pertinacity the task of enlarging our knowledge of Jesus from these sources, so that the adorable personality—so often studied, considered so closely, analyzed so minutely from the smallest details of the existing evidence—has, thanks to so much effort, yielded up its essential qualities without losing anything of its mystery. But what we mean by that great word "orthodoxy" is that all these studies follow the same line and that the attitude of the writer faced with the personality of Jesus has been defined once and for all by the verses of the Apostles Creed. In contrast with the essential unity of orthodox criticism, dissident criticism runs the full gambit of human speculation from the sublime to the ridiculous and the figure of Christ is dislocated according to the taste of the particular hypothesis.

Especially from the eighteenth century onward historians and literary men in large numbers have attacked the problem of Jesus from the unorthodox angle. Many have been fired by a passion which had nothing but impertinence to support it; the works of the eighteenth century "philosophers" are in fact very poor polemic. Voltaire's *The Bible at Last Explained* and the *History of the Establishment of Christianity* are dragged down by spite to a very sorry level, presenting Jesus as an impostor inspired by vanity, Christianity as the fabrication of that demonic rabble-rouser, Paul, and accepting as historical fact that obscene Jewish fable, the *Toledoth Jeshua,* which makes Christ the bastard of a perfume seller and a Roman soldier.

Some years later, Charles Dupuis, a member of the Convention, maintained in his *Origine de tous les cultes* that Jesus was merely a "double of Mithra" and would soon be no more to mankind than Hercules, Osiris and Bacchus, while Volney in *Les Ruines* solemnly advances the theory that the life of Christ is only a symbol of the progress of the sun through the signs of the zodiac. Here we have the obvious ancestors of the comparative religion enthusiasts.

More magisterial, and more solidly grounded, were the German studies which started at the same time and developed into a formidable body of criticism during the nineteenth century. There is little point in detailed discussion of so many conflicting theories, nearly all discredited now, and we propose only to deal here with those which had any influence on French thought. No one now attaches any importance to the *Aufklärung* theory, a word conveying the idea of illumination, and sometimes translated as Illuminism. This theory, advanced first by Hermann Reimarus and taken up by his publisher, Lessing, regarded Jesus as a political agitator of the kind common in Palestine at the time, whose disciples idealized his personality and embellished his story, the supernatural details of which can be regarded therefore as collective delirium or downright fabrications. The theories of Professor Paulus of Heidelberg are now little more than a joke: he had a logical explanation for all the Gospel miracles. When Jesus walked on the water it was an optical illusion; he was really only walking on the edge of the shore and barely got his feet wet! He might have cured deaf mutes and other diseases, for he could have had knowledge of the antique pharmacopoeia and as for the resurrections, both of Lazarus and himself, clearly they were recoveries from trances. David F. Strauss, whose Life of Jesus had such immense popularity in Germany in the middle of the last century, is now remembered only because he demolished the theories of Professor Paulus, and because in some respects he anticipated Loisy and Guignebert. Strauss advanced a "mythical" theory although he held that there had been an historic Jesus, a real man upon whose image the myth had been grafted. By the myth he meant the supernatural incidents which he regarded as borrowed from the prophetic books of the Old Testament, a theory which is refuted by the early date of the writings of the Gospels, for how could so elaborate a process of myth-grafting have been perfected so quickly as to transform the figure of the Messiah during the lifetime of those who had known him?

Seventy-odd years ago all these theories were debated in European intellectual circles. The figure of Jesus became the stake in a war of opposing schools. The materialistic school held on to Paulus, and some of the baser sort of anti-Christian polemicists quoted Leo Taxil. The idealistic school applied the Hegelian method and regarded Christ as the crystallization of a pure idea and his teaching as a *synthesis* between the Messianic Jewish *thesis* and the *antithesis* of a universal conception.

Of all these schools of thought, the most important, since it had a tremendous following which lasted almost to our own times and has directly or indirectly influenced contemporary thought, is the Liberal school. This movement had the most profound influence upon Protestantism, both Lutheran and Calvinist, until the theological and dogmatic reaction associated with Karl Barth set in. It still tacitly influences a good many elements in the Church of England, though it may not be admitted. Such a book as John Middleton Murry's *Christocrary* is a valid testimony to its hold.

Liberal criticism began about 1870 and the chief producers of its literary outputs, noted for their hard labors, were Bernard Weiss, Beyschlag. Wellhausen and Harnack. Seen from our own position in time, these Teutonic thinkers appear like reincarnations of the ancient Arian heretics. Like Arius, the Alexandrian priest of the second century, they would strip from Jesus his divine nature. Very soon he became entirely secularized. He was not God, of course, he was a man, incomparable in his spiritual force and moral grandeur, but only a man all the same. His teaching is only to be taken in its moral and psychological sense; the Kingdom of God is simply that *Euphoria* which results from a consciousness in harmony with itself. The term "Son of Man" should be interpreted as the abstract formula of humanity, the archetypal man.

All the commentators added something of their own conception of the perfect man to the general thesis, which was admirably adaptable to the chief secular ideas of the nineteenth century. When Jesus said, "I am the Way, the Truth and the Life," he meant, they pointed out, the Way of progress, the Truth established by the enlightened intelligence and the harmonious Life of a perfected world, idealized and as little fleshly as possible.

Where the liberal critics went wrong was, oddly enough, in their ignorance of Jesus the man, for all that he is so astonishingly alive in the Gospel presentations. The Liberal Christ was a diagram, a piece of scaffolding. Even Renan, to whom most of these critics owed their conception of Jesus as the supreme teacher of a secular morality, protested against this dehumanizing of the character he had depicted, protesting that their version was "neither Messiah, prophet nor Jew" and that therefore neither his life nor his death made any sense in their perspective.

Renan in fact began to write his famous *Life of Jesus* as a protest against the exegeses of some contemporary critics, but he himself fell a prey to many errors, and not the least of these was to write four hundred pages upon a subject which he said barely provided sufficient authentic material for one page. The avowed intention of Renan was to present Jesus in the proper geographical and technical setting; he assures us that it is impossible to understand the character without having visited the East and he invokes the topography and customs of Palestine as "a fifth Gospel." Without minimizing either the eloquence or the authenticity of his descriptions of the Palestine scene, it is noticeable that his interpretations are always very personal and tend to emphasize the particular traits which he has bestowed upon his character. His work is "literary" in the good and the bad sense of the term and it shows marked influences: the life of Mohammed has obviously affected his conception of Christ and the sorrowful Jesus of the latter part of the book is more or less taken from Lamennais, while the picture of Umbria in Ozanam's *Francis of Assisi* has clearly inspired the delicate coloring of Renan's Palestine. As for Jesus the man, so alive in the Gospel, the illustrious critic loses him in a web of question marks. That he lived, that he taught, that he made disciples and was put to death by a Jewish clerical plot is about all that Renan accepts as historical. The miracles become a Golden Legend. "How do I know?" —this *Life of Jesus* rests on the soft pillow of doubt.

That is why the figure of Jesus which his book portrays, for all its tenderness and its author's affection for the being he creates, arouses more anger than the naive rationalizations of critics like Paulus. The "sweet Galilean dreamer," the "charmer" surrounded by adoring women, the anti-clerical philosopher upon whom his friends gradually impressed the idea that he was the Messiah, this teacher of a vague religiosity, the founder of the great doctrine of worldly disdain, however expertly the writer may dress him up as a Jewish Rabbi we know only too well what he is doing. He is trying, as Saint Beuve puts it, "to get rid of the God," and the man whom he exalts is worth no more than the conceptions of the German liberals. The charm of its style, outmoded though it is, preserves the book from oblivion, but it cannot disguise its cant and its betrayal.

It is, however, thanks chiefly to Renan that students of Jesus have been directed to a whole body of information which has caused a great deal of pother. It is true that a knowledge of the political geography of Palestine under Tiberius helps us to understand a good many things in the Gospel. It is true that archaeology has been of the greatest assistance in helping us to place the events of Christ's life in their proper setting. But it is only since Renan that the so-called historical method has been perfected to such a degree that now everybody who seeks to write about Jesus must advertise his devotion to it. We know that, ideally, this method involves the most scrupulous examination of the documents in conjunction with the latest discoveries of history and archaeology, passing them through the fine sieve of textual criticism and interpreting them as faithfully as possible, without bias, without special pleading. Far be it from us to decry the historical method for it has imposed upon theologians and exegesists a precision of handling which has sometimes been lacking, and the most recent orthodox Christian historians pride themselves upon it as much as their rivals in the opposite camp. Yet the method is not infrequently productive of deceptive and tendentious results.

Deceptive because it can lead to a negation worse than Renan's. "It is impossible to establish the historical Jesus, which is not to say that he did not exist, but only that we cannot positively affirm anything about him." This is the conclusion of such popular practitioners of the "historical method" as Salomon Reinach. It is the more deceptive because in fact it enables anyone to dissect a text and interpret it one way or the other. It is tendentious because, under the pretext of examining documents in the light of purely rational considerations, it simplifies and eliminates the hazards and the contradictions of life. It declares the breaking of the vase of perfume over Jesus at Bethany a "repetition" of the incident involving the woman of Galilee who had been a sinner because it is not "logical" to suppose that this strange episode was enacted twice. By the same reasoning, the story of the end of the Valois dynasty should be considered a "repetition" of that of the Capetian line for each produced three brothers who succeeded each other on the throne and were all childless, which does not seem very "logical." But such criticism is most tendentious because in interpreting the rational in the most literal and limited sense of the term, it is automatically biased against the supernatural. A miraculous fact is therefore too often rejected as inadmissible without further consideration.

The use of the historical method, in conjunction with the remarkable discoveries of archaeological research, of comparative semantics and textual criticism has, for more than half a century now, greatly enlarged the scope of the study of Jesus. There are two rival schools in the field. The more recent, using what is known as the *Formgeschichtliche* method, has developed largely in Germany during the past twenty-five years through the work of Bertram, Bultmann, Dibelius and K. L. Schmidt. It is based upon a close study of the form of the testamentary writings as they have come down to us, and in this respect it has done considerable service. It claims that by examining each phrase closely it is possible to work back to those anonymous popular records of which the Gospels as we have them are presumed to be an assembly. From their observations, this school draws certain conclusions: for instance, if one Evangelist says "Blessed are the poor" and another "Blessed are the poor in spirit," the latter is to be considered of a later date when the Christians included more rich men who had to be placated. Although the technique of the *Formgeschichtliche* method may be accepted, it would be very unwise to accept all its deductions. When it is stated, for instance, that a Gospel, say St. Mark's, was obtained by putting together odds and ends of popular tradition current in various Jewish and Hellenic circles, to which the Evangelist has only supplied a framework lacking any element of historicity, one feels impelled to ask how, in these circumstances, the infrangible unity and solidity not only of the figure of Jesus in all the Gospels but even of such secondary figures as Peter, Thomas, Martha and Mary were achieved, to say nothing of the topographical correspondence of the four accounts. When we are told that the Christian community "created" the oral tradition subsequently enshrined in our Gospels in order to give authority to its usages (for instance, the baptism of Jesus by John was invented to sanction the Christian rite of baptism), one may ask why no single trace of this fabricating process can be found in primitive Christianity. It is noteworthy also that the most recent literary research on Homer or the *Chansons de Geste* has repudiated such hypotheses. There is no mass creation of this order; great creative work springs only from great creative personalities.

French "rationalist" criticism since 1900 displays three main tendencies. The first, the "comparative" theory, is already dated. It was most influential in the early years of the century, following the publication in England of Sir J. G. Frazer's *Golden Bough* and other studies in primitive religions. It was all the vogue to explain spiritual phenomena in terms of the primitive notions of *tabu, totem,* animism and magic. It was very tempting to relate Christ to the various divinities of the Nile, the Euphrates and the Anatolian plateau. From the mass of information, indifferently co-ordinated, presented by Frazer and the anthropological school, haphazard features were selected ranging from the Sumerian Kingdoms to the Maoris of New Zealand in order to compose a figure of Christ which resembles him about as much as a scarecrow resembles a living being. All this is out of date now. The audacious "comparativist" who discovered in the *Agnus Dei* an allusion to the Hindu God *Agni* arouses no more than a smile, as does the Assyriologist Jensen who saw in Jesus a transmutation of the Babylonian epic of Gilgamesh, and added that as Gilgamesh was a solar myth the twelve Apostles are incontestably the signs of the zodiac.

This, as Guignebert says, is "the colossal error of a scholar who believed that he could explain everything in terms of his own subject." But even a short time ago—M. Edouard Dujardin, whose gifts as a novelist greatly surpass his powers of exegesis, wrote that to him "the being known as Jesus is, in fact, the Fish God, or, more accurately, the water serpent, Noun, who inhabited running waters and who was assimiliated by Jehovahism with the accursed land serpent Nahash, condemned to crawl basely in the dust." How delightful is that "more accurately, the water serpent"! We can imagine what critical methods of this kind make of the appearance of the dove at Christ's baptism; or the words "This is my body. This is my blood."

Serious critics today are restrained in their use of the comparative or syncretive methods. Modern criticism divides itself roughly into two groups, each entirely opposed to the other. We have first the "mythological" school, whose chief representative is P. L. Couchoud, author of *Le Mystère de Jésus* and *Jésus le Dieu fait homme*. Couchoud relies on the historical method and regards the Gospel as a doctrinal rather than a biographical work. It can easily be seen that by insistence upon the purely theological character of the Gospels the personality of Jesus disappears. "Jesus certainly belongs to history by virtue of his name and his cult, but he is not an historical personage. . . . He is not a man who once lived and has vanished into death, but the eternal dream of mankind, which lives for ever. . . . He is a Divine being, slowly and progressively evolved by the consciousness of Christians." And, in 1924, Couchoud wrote, "I believe that by 1940 Jesus will have passed entirely from the plane of historical fact to the region of collective moral ideas." What this amounts to is that the early Christian community, being inspired with the idea of a Redeemer god, borrowed a number of prophecies from the Old Testament and "incarnated" him. Couchoud does not tell us why they should have done this. Nothing could be more opposed to the whole tone of Jewish thought at the time.

"Why should the early Christians and Paul not have regarded Jesus simply as a God, if that's what he was? Why should they have chosen to reconcile a parody of humanity with their myth? Why did they leave so many lacunae and obscurities in the God legend which they constructed, if it were not based on any reality? Why encumber him with so many useless traits of common humanity? Why make Jesus' family say 'he is beside himself' (Mark iii, 21)? Why show him as angry, suffering, weeping for himself and for others?"

The arguments we have just quoted are taken, not from any orthodox Catholic apologist, but from one of the great liberal critics, Charles Guignebert, Professor of the History of Christianity at the Sorbonne. Guignebert belongs to the opposing school of rationalist criticism, perhaps the most favored today, which has constructed a beguiling synthesis largely upon the labors of the nineteenth century German critics. Jesus is not a God who was made into a man, but a man who was deified. This conception, which was advanced in the teaching of the ex-priest Loisy, is developed more radically by Guignebert, but has its edges softened a bit in the hands of M. Goguel, who implies rather than affirms it. "Christian propaganda," says Guignebert, "has exploited, elaborated and contracted the mystery of Christ to advance Jesus but it did not invent Jesus who himself, in one way or another, suggested the foundations of the faith which has come to be based upon him." The Jesus whose existence this school is prepared to accept is, however, ringed about with reservations and uncertainties. Many of the recorded facts of his life are questionable and of course anything relating to the supernatural can at once be relegated to the realm of myth. He was, in short, a prophet whose moral teaching was of a very high order; he preached the coming of God's Kingdom, and final things (and because of their attention to this part of his teaching, these critics are sometimes called the *eschatological* school) and although he died physically he left such a dynamic impulsion behind him that his followers after his death proclaimed him God.

Seen from this perspective, what remains of the tremendous figure which is so real and alive in the Gospel narrative? "A few scattered recollections, arranged in the tradition and adjusted to the style of the Old Testament. Several miracles of which the least we can say is that they are in accordance with the sentiment of the time. A number of incidents composed to give drama to the narrative and particularly to conform with Hebrew prophecies or some other apologetic purpose." The quotation is from Loisy and we can only agree emphatically with Couchoud when he says that this doctrine "implies a very shabby view of Christianity. If the great religion of the West is nothing more than the deification of a man, the paltry apotheosis of an individual, then it is, for all its wide diffusion, of a very low type; inferior indeed, in the realm of religion, to Judaism or Islam, which were very careful not to exalt Moses or Mohammed as gods."

Beyond the textual arguments which Christians can advance against such critics—and we have raised a good many of them in the course of this book—there remains one and it is decisive. If the Church invented Christ, how did the Church itself come to be born? How can anyone explain the dynamic fervor which enabled a primitive religious sect to conquer the world, explain the faith which sent countless martyrs to death, account for the enormous success of this great historic fact. "Either Jesus is what Christians have always believed him to be, or else, though visionary, he is a genius of such extraordinary, inexplicable power that we can only call it miraculous." (Fr. Allo.)

We conclude this brief review of the "liberal" critical approach to Jesus by advancing one last consideration: Jesus is a mystery, the mystery of God incarnate. Jesus is God made flesh: if this be accepted, everything else is clear. To those who reject this explanation, it is an incomprehensible puzzle, surrounded with every kind of complication which the human imagination can devise. Loisy himself said, in the *Hibbert Journal,* that outside orthodox Catholicism contemporary theology was "a veritable Tower of Babel in which the confusion of ideas was greater even than the diversity of language."

APPENDIX TWO

CHRONOLOGICAL TABLE

Before the Christian Era

2000	Abraham
1800	Jacob
1630	Joseph in Egypt
1225	Moses, the Exodus
1180	Joshua in Canaan
11th century	The Judges
1012–975	King David
975–935	King Solomon
935	Division of Israel into two kingdoms
753	Legendary foundation of Rome
8th century	Amos, Hosea, Isaiah
722	Fall of Samaria
6th century	Solon at Athens
586	Fall of Jerusalem
539	Fall of Babylon
538	Cyrus allows the Jews to return to Jerusalem
490–480	The wars between Greece and Persia
445	Nehemiah rebuilds Jerusalem
440	Building of the Parthenon
398	The inscribing of the Law under Ezra

332	Alexander crosses Palestine
306	Palestine incorporated in the Greek Lagid kingdoms
264–146	The Punic Wars
200	Palestine in the Greek Seleucid kingdoms
165–160	Judas Maccabeus and the Jewish resistance
134–104	John Hyrcanus
63	Pompey takes Jerusalem for Rome
47	Caesar in Palestine
40–44	Herod the Great, Tetrarch
44	Death of Caesar
30	Augustus emperor and master of the world
20	Herod rebuilds the Temple at Jerusalem
6	Birth of Jesus Christ
4	Death of Herod and division of his kingdoms

Christian Era

6	The Child Jesus in the Temple
6	Archelaus is deposed; Judea a Roman province
12	Tiberius associated with the Imperium
14	Death of Augustus: Tiberius emperor
26–28	Pontius Pilate arrives in Palestine
Dec. 27	Beginning of John the Baptist's Ministry
Jan. 28	John baptizes Jesus
	The Temptation in the Desert
March 28	Jesus returns to the Jordan
	John, Andrew and Simon are called
	The Wedding Feast at Cana
	Jesus goes up to Jerusalem for the Passover
	Jesus expels the money changers from the temple
April 28	The episode of Nicodemus
May 28	John the Baptist is thrown into prison

	Jesus goes back to Nazareth by way of Samaria
	Episode of the Samaritan woman
	Jesus cures the son of a court official
	Jesus begins his public ministry
	He teaches in the synagogues
	First stay at Capernaum
	Cure of the man possessed by devils
	Peter's mother-in-law cured
	The miraculous draught of fishes
	Cure of a paralytic
June 28	Cleansing of the Leper
	The Disciples pick wheat on the Sabbath
	Levi (Matthew) is called
	The man with a withered hand
	The Apostles selected
	The Sermon on the Mount
July 28	The Centurion at Capernaum
	John the Baptist sends a message to Jesus
Sept. 28	Jesus raises the son of the widow
Nov. 28	The parables concerning the Kingdom of God
Dec. 28	The tempest calmed
	The cure of Jairus's daughter
	Cure of the woman with a hemorrhage
	Jesus is asked to leave Nazareth
Feb. 29	Mission of the Twelve Apostles
March 29	Death of John the Baptist
April 29	First miracle of the multiplication of the loaves
	Jesus walks on the water
June 29	Jesus in Jerusalem
	Cure of a paralytic
	Jesus goes through Phoenicia and the Decapolis
	Second miracle of the multiplication of the loaves

July 29	Jesus at Caesarea Philippi
	Peter's declaration of faith and Jesus's promise
Aug. 29	The Transfiguration
	First announcement of the Passion
Sept. 29	Jesus leaves Galilee for Judea
Oct. 29	Feast of Tabernacles
	The woman taken in adultery
	Cure of the man born blind
	The mission of the 72
	Parable of the Good Samaritan
	With Martha and Mary at Bethany
	Jesus gives the "Our Father"
Dec. 29	Feast of the Dedication of the Temple
Jan. 30	Jesus in Perea
	Parables of the Good Shepherd and the Lost Drachma
	Parable of the Prodigal Son
Feb. 30	Cure of Two Lepers
	"Suffer little children to come unto me"
March 30	Raising of Lazarus
	Jesus goes into Ephraim
	Jesus in Jericho: Zaccheus the publican
	Cure of the blind men
	The supper at Bethany: Mary anoints Jesus

Holy Week

April 2	Palm Sunday: entry into Jerusalem
Mon., April 3	The fig tree cursed
	Parable of the servants in the vineyard
Tues., April 4	Jesus prophesies the Fall of Jerusalem and the Last Judgment
Wed., April 5	Judas betrays Jesus
Thurs., April 6	The Last Supper
Fri., April 7	Trial, passion and crucifixion of Jesus
Sun., April 9	The Resurrection

After the Death of Jesus

33 or 34	St. Stephen martyred
35	Conversion of St. Paul on the road to Damascus
42	Beginning of Paul's mission; his Epistles written
50–55	St. Matthew sets down his Gospel in Aramaic
57	First Epistle of Paul to the Corinthians
55–62	St. Mark writes his Gospel in Greek
63	St. Luke writes his Gospel in Greek
64	St. Matthew's Gospel translated into Greek
63–64	St. Luke completes the *Acts of the Apostles*
67	Death of St. Paul
70	Jerusalem taken by Titus
81–96	St. John writes the Book of Revelation
93	Josephus's *Hebrew Antiquities*
96–104	St. John writes his Gospel
112	Letter from Pliny the Younger to Trajan referring to the Christians
116	Tacitus in his *Annals* refers to the Christians in connection with the burning of Rome in 64